New Opportunities for Artistic Practice in Virtual Worlds

Denise Doyle
University of Wolverhampton, UK

A volume in the Advances in Social Networking
and Online Communities (ASNOC) Book Series

An Imprint of IGI Global

Managing Director:	Lindsay Johnston
Managing Editor:	Austin DeMarco
Director of Intellectual Property & Contracts:	Jan Travers
Acquisitions Editor:	Kayla Wolfe
Production Editor:	Christina Henning
Development Editor:	Caitlyn Martin
Typesetter:	Lisandro Gonzalez
Cover Design:	Jason Mull

Published in the United States of America by
Information Science Reference (an imprint of IGI Global)
701 E. Chocolate Avenue
Hershey PA, USA 17033
Tel: 717-533-8845
Fax: 717-533-8661
E-mail: cust@igi-global.com
Web site: http://www.igi-global.com

Library of Congress Cataloging-in-Publication Data

New opportunities for artistic practice in virtual worlds / Denise Doyle, editor.
     pages cm
 Includes bibliographical references and index.
  ISBN 978-1-4666-8384-6 (hardcover) -- ISBN 978-1-4666-8385-3 (ebook) 1. Machinima films. 2. Computer animation. 3. Virtual reality. 4. Computer art. 5. Video games. 6. Second Life (Game) I. Doyle, Denise, 1964- editor.
  TR897.74.N49 2015
  777'.7--dc23
                          2015008171

This book is published in the IGI Global book series Advances in Social Networking and Online Communities (ASNOC) (ISSN: 2328-1405; eISSN: 2328-1413)

British Cataloguing in Publication Data
A Cataloguing in Publication record for this book is available from the British Library.

All work contributed to this book is new, previously-unpublished material. The views expressed in this book are those of the authors, but not necessarily of the publisher.

For electronic access to this publication, please contact: eresources@igi-global.com.

Advances in Social Networking and Online Communities (ASNOC) Book Series

Hakikur Rahman
University of Minho, Portugal

ISSN: 2328-1405
EISSN: 2328-1413

MISSION

The advancements of internet technologies and the creation of various social networks provide a new channel of knowledge development processes that's dependent on social networking and online communities. This emerging concept of social innovation is comprised of ideas and strategies designed to improve society.

The **Advances in Social Networking and Online Communities** book series serves as a forum for scholars and practitioners to present comprehensive research on the social, cultural, organizational, and human issues related to the use of virtual communities and social networking. This series will provide an analytical approach to the holistic and newly emerging concepts of online knowledge communities and social networks.

COVERAGE

- Communication of Knowledge in Organizations
- Knowledge Management System Architectures, Infrastructure, and Middleware
- Epistemology of Knowledge Society
- Broadband Infrastructure and the New Wireless Network Solutions
- Community Practices
- Local E-Government Interoperability and Security

IGI Global is currently accepting manuscripts for publication within this series. To submit a proposal for a volume in this series, please contact our Acquisition Editors at Acquisitions@igi-global.com or visit: http://www.igi-global.com/publish/.

The Advances in Social Networking and Online Communities (ASNOC) Book Series (ISSN 2328-1405) is published by IGI Global, 701 E. Chocolate Avenue, Hershey, PA 17033-1240, USA, www.igi-global.com. This series is composed of titles available for purchase individually; each title is edited to be contextually exclusive from any other title within the series. For pricing and ordering information please visit http://www.igi-global.com/book-series/advances-social-networking-online-communities/37168. Postmaster: Send all address changes to above address. Copyright © 2015 IGI Global. All rights, including translation in other languages reserved by the publisher. No part of this series may be reproduced or used in any form or by any means – graphics, electronic, or mechanical, including photocopying, recording, taping, or information and retrieval systems – without written permission from the publisher, except for non commercial, educational use, including classroom teaching purposes. The views expressed in this series are those of the authors, but not necessarily of IGI Global.

Titles in this Series

For a list of additional titles in this series, please visit: www.igi-global.com

Social Media and the Transformation of Interaction in Society
John P. Sahlin (Coleman University, USA)
Information Science Reference • copyright 2015 • 301pp • H/C (ISBN: 9781466685567) • US $200.00 (our price)

Cases on Strategic Social Media Utilization in the Nonprofit Sector
Hugo Asencio (California State University – Dominguez Hills, USA) and Rui Sun (California State University – Dominguez Hills, USA)
Information Science Reference • copyright 2015 • 370pp • H/C (ISBN: 9781466681880) • US $195.00 (our price)

Handbook of Research on Interactive Information Quality in Expanding Social Network Communications
Francisco V. Cipolla-Ficarra (Latin Association of Human-Computer Interaction, Spain & International Association of Interactive Communication, Italy)
Information Science Reference • copyright 2015 • 435pp • H/C (ISBN: 9781466673779) • US $255.00 (our price)

Implications of Social Media Use in Personal and Professional Settings
Vladlena Benson (Kingston Business School, Kingston University, UK) and Stephanie Morgan (Kingston Business School, Kingston University, UK)
Information Science Reference • copyright 2015 • 362pp • H/C (ISBN: 9781466674011) • US $195.00 (our price)

Identity and Leadership in Virtual Communities Establishing Credibility and Influence
Dona J. Hickey (University of Richmond, USA) and Joe Essid (University of Richmond, USA)
Information Science Reference • copyright 2014 • 321pp • H/C (ISBN: 9781466651500) • US $205.00 (our price)

Harnessing the Power of Social Media and Web Analytics
Anteneh Ayanso (Brock University, Canada) and Kaveepan Lertwachara (California Polytechnic State University, USA)
Information Science Reference • copyright 2014 • 305pp • H/C (ISBN: 9781466651944) • US $215.00 (our price)

Educational, Psychological, and Behavioral Considerations in Niche Online Communities
Vivek Venkatesh (Concordia University, Canada) Jason Wallin (University of Alberta, Canada) Juan Carlos Castro (Concordia University, Canada) and Jason Edward Lewis (Concordia University, Canada)
Information Science Reference • copyright 2014 • 465pp • H/C (ISBN: 9781466652064) • US $225.00 (our price)

Gender and Social Computing Interactions, Differences and Relationships
Celia Romm Livermore (Wayne State University, USA)
Information Science Reference • copyright 2012 • 343pp • H/C (ISBN: 9781609607593) • US $195.00 (our price)

www.igi-global.com

701 E. Chocolate Ave., Hershey, PA 17033
Order online at www.igi-global.com or call 717-533-8845 x100
To place a standing order for titles released in this series, contact: cust@igi-global.com
Mon-Fri 8:00 am - 5:00 pm (est) or fax 24 hours a day 717-533-8661

For my daughter India Rose

Table of Contents

Detailed Table of Contents

Section 1
Creative Practices, Theoretical Contexts, Virtual Worlds

This section establishes the initial ground of theoretical research for creative practices in virtual worlds with a consideration of both the nature and the practices that contributes to an aesthetics of virtual environments, and opens up the discussion of the nature of virtual space for artistic enquiry.

This chapter examines digital virtual environments as a site for art and proposes a formal aesthetics for art in digital virtual environments. The study arises from the author's decades-long practice producing art in virtual environments and the related theoretical considerations that have arisen from that practice. The technical, conceptual and ontological status of virtual environments is examined in order to establish a base of intrinsic qualities that identify virtual environments as a medium for art. The philosophy of Gilbert Simondon is used to achieve this. The elements and principles the artist must employ to work with this medium are identified as data, display and modulation. The specificities of virtual environments as a medium for art are examined in order to establish a formal aesthetics. In particular, digital colour, visual opacity, digital sound, code, artificial intelligence, emergence and agency are identified as the primary qualities that the artist manipulates to bring forth art in a virtual environment.

This chapter explores the technological and artistic revolution brought forth by machinima, particularly the rise among a community of filmmakers who would begin to express their stories and ideas through virtual worlds. Machinima has led to an emergence of scholarship on its aesthetics and cultural implications for digital society. The case of machinima as art is illustrated through a review of select works of virtual world filmmakers. This discussion also distinguishes the machinima concepts of game, virtual platform and more specifically virtual worlds to their varying degrees and relationships. It is here that one delineates the purpose of machinima within Massively Multiplayer Online Role-Playing Games (MMORPG) to that of virtual worlds such as Second Life (SL). In doing so, the author follows the innovation of machinima through the evolution of gaming and its extension to stand-alone ready-to-wear software to potentialities called forth by British filmmaker Peter Greenaway regarding Second Life.

Chapter 3

This chapter presents a philosophical journey and practical piece of experimentation on spatiality, virtuality and displacement. A series of art practices using photography, installation and art writing form the trajectory for a sequence of conceptual maps. The discussion engages with spacing and displacing as an artistic enquiry on space. The chapter consists of an examination of the typology and meaning of displacement in its translation from Korean, and a discussion of the formation of a gendered and artistically constructed displacement by extending the scope of the theory to the displacement of women in a colonial situation. This chapter explores the way in which displaced women (in the very particular case of Korean "comfort women" during the colonial war with Japan, and through the case of the artist, Hyeseok Na) cannot belong in either their home or a foreign land. Virtual-ness, here, is approached with an artistic understanding, and is found to constitute an unreal living space rather than merely a virtual environment through technology.

Section 2
Avatar, Embodiment, Identity

The second section brings together three chapters each considering the significance of the avatar in different ways. From the first chapter that includes a study of a practice-based performance project and historical reenactment to the final two chapters that each take on the discussion of the avatar in opposing ways; one writing from the perspective of the avatar as a representation of our identity as embodied selves in virtual worlds and the other arguing that the avatar should be seen as something disembodied and that acts as a representation of loss.

Chapter 4

Joseph DeLappe is an American digital media artist whose creative work demonstrates unique intersections between analogue and digital creative processes. In 2008 he created the Salt Satyagraha project, a virtual and simultaneously physical reenactment of Mahatma Gandhi's 1930 Salt Satyagraha political march by using Second Life (SL) and a customized treadmill that corresponded to his avatar's movements. The project also included a blog, an exhibition, and numerous screenshots documenting the virtual events. This chapter explores the artist's intent and the impact of combining virtual and digital labor, performance, artistic intervention, play, and the role of the human agent in the human-computer relationship. DeLappe's project blog and two key philosophical theories – Walter Benjamin's concept of the spielraum, a playspace that allows for creative experimentation in advanced technologies; and Jacques Derrida's concept of the supplement, something added to an original that reinforces or changes its meaning – are used to frame this examination.

This chapter draws upon existing identity theories to create a framework with which to examine the expression of self via avatars within Second Life. The framework is then applied to the practice of a number of artists working with themes relating to identity using avatars within Second Life, by drawing upon the author's own experience of these works and the artists comments taken from their writings and from discussions and correspondence with them, to examine the role their work plays in changing our understanding of the way that identity is expressed and perceived within virtual worlds.

This chapter suggests a model for reconceiving avatar in terms of desire and loss to reassess their role within creative practices and the construction of digital subjectivity. This focuses on the avatar as appearance, as a negotiation of presence and absence, and as a tool for critical art practice in Second Life. By placing the avatar as Lacan's objet petit a, the lost object cause of desire, the structure of the visual and cognitive gaze applies Žižek's concept of parallax to digital embodiment, reformulating a subjective position between physical and digital modes of being. Taking into account the position of the observer amidst the fluidity of contemporary identity, the manipulation of the structures of desire and control can create new experiences that alter our relation to presence and absence in the critical and creative mediation of avatars and its implications for embodiment as a function of consciousness.

Section 3
Found Objects, Collaborative Practices, Shared Creativity

This section includes three chapters that are brought together to develop the discussions around Axel Bruns key term 'produsage' as an integral element of the artistic strategies developed within the projects presented. All three chapters present research that is as a result of sustained and experimental methodologies and inventive approaches to artistic practices, and each chapter contributor takes on key theories in which to frame their research.

This chapter traces a process of creating using found object collage, through collecting/consuming practices and finally to the notion of the bought self, avatar representation through consumerist artistic practice in Second Life (SL) the online, user generated, virtual environment. Positioning collage as a reinvigorated current in art, the text couples this mode of making with shopping as found object. Collaboration is inherent in an online virtual world, where programmers, designers and other content providers determine the parameters of what is possible. Found object/shopping is a synergistic fit with the nature of predetermined boundaries coupled with late-stage capitalism. This mode of self-making encourages the idea of buying identification through the construction of an avatar. Through a review of the practices of the Situationists, an aesthetic turn in political tactics is revealed through contemporary art making. The text uses the author's own virtual/material practice as a case study for the theories explored.

Chapter 8

This chapter will discuss the artistic processes and the related theoretical premises of a collaborative art undertaking that was displayed in Second Life® from Fall 2013 to Summer 2014. Despite the idiosyncratic, highly individualized nature of its components, the project nevertheless achieved a remarkable state of cohesion. What may have contributed to this unity will be one of the subjects under investigation at the core of this text. The text will commence with a survey of the creative mechanisms and strategies of the metaverse, after which a description of the project, its curatorial premises, including the usage of metaverse geography and climate as an agent of visual harmony will also be delivered. The chapter will then conclude with an examination of the collective art process within the context of the 'unfinished artifact' and John Dewey's deliberations on the experiential nature of artwork/art process as a potential framework for metaverse artistic collaborations.

Chapter 9

This chapter discusses the Meta_Body participatory art project. Initiated in a collaborative virtual environment and in a "real life" art exhibition, it now continues in the metaverse creative flux. Meta_Body focuses on two aspects: first, the avatar as body/language, open to experimentation and potency; second, avatar building as a shared creative process and as aesthetical experience. Through the practice of avatar creation, distribution, embodiment and transformation, the artists aim to understand the processes of virtual corporeality constitution: to question the role of the body in virtual environment, its importance in engaging with the world and in self-expression, and explore its metaphorical aspects. The method used to implement this project is a shared creative process, in which multiple subjects come to be authors along different phases of the project. Through the embodiment and transformation of avatars, the artwork's aesthetical experience becomes a creative process.

Section 4
Performance Practices in Virtual Worlds

The final section brings together both practitioners and theorists in the three chapters that consider firstly the issues surrounding digital embodiment and the status of the body in performance art, the practice of blended reality through the virtual and physical performer, and finally the ways in which SL-Bots can be explored for their aesthetic and creative potential.

Chapter 10

The chapter discusses the changes the body has been subjected to in the 21st century and especially when it enters the digital worlds. The starting point for the reflection of the body today is its floating position in contemporary mixed and augmented reality. By deploying the notions of 'body image' and 'body schema,' elaborated by French phenomenologist M. Merleau-Ponty, various features of digital embodiment are discussed. After discussing several forms of the techno-modelled body (also mentioning the issue of life addressed in it), the chapter turns to the examples of body-related performance art in the virtual world of Second Life that explicitly raise questions about the body in the digital world, and within Second Life in particular (the examples discussed are: Synthetic Performances and I know that it's all a state of mind by 0100101110101101.ORG, Come to Heaven by Gazira Babeli and ZeroG SkyDancers by DanCoyote, etc.).

This chapter focuses on the integration of live performance that blends virtual (avatars animated live in Second Life) and physical performers. To start with the author will briefly look at some of the ways practitioners have integrated and played with new technologies in performance. Following this a number of case studies that have explored this blending of the physical and the virtual will be examined. This will then be followed by a discussion about the nature of this type of performance both from the point of view of physical performers and those performing with avatars.

This chapter explores the history, state-of-the art, and interactive aesthetic potential of "SL-Bots". SL-Bots are avatars (i.e. "agents") that are designed and controlled using Artificial Intelligence (AI) in Second Life. Many of these SL-Bots were originally created in Second Life for purposes such as: rudimentary chatinventory management and copying, asset curation, embodied customer service, generic responsive environments, scripted objects, or as proxy-audience members (aka "campers"). However, virtual performance and installation artists – including two of the chapter's authors [ca. 2011-present] - have created their own SL-Bots for aesthetic purposes. This chapter suggests ways in which SL-Bots are gradually being extended beyond their conventional applications as avatar-placeholders. This book chapter concludes with the speculation that future virtual agents (including next generation SL-Bots) might one day transcend their teleological aesthetic purpose as mere automated-objects by evolving into more complex autonomous aesthetic personas.

Preface

Although virtual worlds remain unstable phenomena a substantial amount of research continues to be undertaken within them and is reflected in the number of disciplines that study them particularly in an interdisciplinary context. Whilst there is already a history of artists investigating new spaces and new technological forms this exploration has continued more recently with sections of the artistic community utilising virtual worlds as a new form, or a new potential artistic space. Established real-world artists have explored virtual worlds as environments for practice and a number of artists and designers have continued to specifically work with *Second Life* to explore the potential and limitations of the platform itself. A range of early key works and other recent seminal works produced in *Second Life* still hold strong to be scrutinised in the context of new technologies and for their contribution in expanding our understanding and experience of virtual space.

THE BACKGROUND

Second Life remains a virtual world that is not easily defined and understood. Whilst it no longer grabs the populist cultural headlines, as a platform, it has still to be fully understood in terms of its significance within a wider critical discourse of digital and new media art. Further to this the new languages of artistic practice that are being created that are particular to virtual and avatar-mediated worlds are still to be fully defined. This book aims to outline the potential contribution and impact *Second Life* has had and aims to present a critical framework for the platform and future avatar-mediated virtual worlds through the work of key artists and writers in the field through an articulation of these languages and virtual aesthetics. In itself *Second Life* may stand the test of time as a continued interface to examine issues of the real and the virtual and may contribute to further theoretical and philosophical discussions of new technologies and artistic practice.

Second Life was initially developed as a commercial venture, and yet was still one of the first virtual worlds to be studied by scholars and educators, and explored by artists and practitioners. Jones notes that, whilst *Second Life* could not be described as an immersive virtual world based on Heim's set of characteristics of virtual worlds (simulation, interaction, artificiality, immersion, telepresence, full-body immersion, and networked communications), it still sits 'squarely in the discourse of virtual reality because it provides a high level of interactivity and telepresence within a parallel world that allows for the construction of place and self' (Jones, 2006).

Although there has been extensive research in VR and virtual worlds within the humanities and sciences, there has been less research undertaken concerning the use of virtual worlds for creative and artistic practice. A particular feature of *Second Life* is the accessibility of the platform for building and customising spaces. Using the *Second Life* building tools to create objects and manipulate terrain, along with the application of the *Second Life* programming language, it is possible to have a high level of control when creating a virtual environment. This has enabled a community of artists to take advantage of both the capability and online accessibility of the platform, and of the relatively low cost incurred when compared to that of developing a unique online virtual world from scratch. A question that can be asked is do new forms always bring new modes of practice, and new artistic and creative opportunities? In the context of New Media practice Patrick Lichty proposes that the exploration of new forms has been 'a modus operandi of the *avant garde* for over a century, and New Media is doubly implicated in this gesture of praxis' (Lichty, 2008). There have been a range of articles published discussing virtual worlds and creative practice developed in *Second Life* from Backe (2007), McCaw (2007), Bittarello (2008), Sant (2008), Lichty (2008, 2009), Morie (2010), each contributing research in the fields of performance, gaming, and the arts. More specifically a number of articles focus on the contextualisation of artistic practice (Doyle 2008, Lichty 2012, Drinkall 2012).

From early writings on virtual reality (such as Damer 1998, Heim 1993, Heudin 1999, Rheingold 1991, Schroeder 2002), to Jones (2006) suggesting that 'virtual reality is the contemporary and future articulation of the philosophical and psychological question of how we define (and create) reality', the issues, definitions and experience of reality find rich and challenging ground in virtual environments. Writing in 2001, Elizabeth Grosz describes virtual realities as: 'computer-generated and [computer]–fed worlds that simulate key elements of "real space" or at least its dominant representations – for example, its dimensionality, its relations of resemblance and contiguity – acting as a partial homology for a "real space" within which it is located' (Grosz, 2001).

The early use of virtual environments for artistic practice were explored in a series of projects undertaken at the Banff Centre, Canada, in the early 1990s and subsequently documented in *Immersed in Technology: Art and Virtual Environments* (Moser 1996). In the preface to that book, Douglas Macleod, the Project Director, likens this 'moment of virtual reality' to a similar moment in time when Vertov's *Man with the Movie Camera* was released in 1929, cataloguing the potential of the film medium (Macleod in Moser, 1996). Of particular note were works such as Brenda Laurel and Rachel Strickland's *Placeholder* (1993), the *Archaeology of the Mother Tongue* (1993) by Toni Dove and Michael Mackenzie, and the virtual reality performance, *Dancing with the Virtual Dervish: Virtual Bodies* (1994), by Diane Gromala and Yacov Sharir. These projects were particularly innovative in their exploration of virtual reality environments in an art context.

Artists such as Char Davies moved from painting to exploring virtual space in virtual environments in the early 1990s, resulting in the works *Osmose* (1995) and *Ephémère* (1998). In *Osmose*, the participant, or 'immersant', must concentrate on their breath as a device to navigate vertically through the spaces represented. In *Landscape, Earth, Body, Being, Space, and Time in the Immersive Virtual Environments Osmose and Ephémère* (2003), Davies says that 'within this spatiality, there is no split between the observer and the observed' (Davies, 2003). She argues that this is not tied to a Cartesian paradigm, but rather allows 'another way of sensing to come forward, one in which the body feels the space very much like that of a body immersed in the sea' (Davies, 2003). In this private virtual space, by: 'leaving the space of one's usual sensibilities, one enters into communication with a space that is psychically innovating … for we do not change place, we change our nature' (Bachelard in Davies, 1997).

ARTISTIC PRACTICE IN VIRTUAL WORLDS

Through this history of artists exploring new spaces and new technological forms this exploration has continued through sections of the artistic community that have seen the opportunity of utilising virtual worlds as a new form, or a new potential artistic space. Established real-world artists have explored virtual worlds as environments for practice. A number of artists and designers have continued to specifically work with *Second Life* to explore the potential and limitations of the platform, and a handful of established real world artists have seen their own concerns reflected in the *Second Life* space itself. In *Art and the Avatar: The Kritical Works in SL Project* (Doyle 2008) I concluded that there were at least two approaches that could be considered when exploring *Second Life* for creative practice, beyond the potential of using *Second Life* as a presentation space that echoes real life gallery spaces. Firstly, that *Second Life* was already being explored as a space for performance as the avatar could easily assume the role of the actor/performer; and secondly, that the implications for the audience as avatar were that they could become a central element in the artworks created in the space, placing the audience themselves in the position of performer (Doyle, 2008).

Of the work of artists during this initial analysis (and in particular those working on the *Second Life* platform) there were two broad groups of artists who were identified; those working in contemporary arts practices such as new media, or performance practice, and supported by mainstream galleries and curators, and those artists who have developed work through grass roots, self-organising and emergent practices. Lichty suggested that, although multi-user worlds had already been in existence for a number of years, it was not until the critical mass of artists was present that the emergence of New Media art in virtual worlds was 'recognised by the contemporary art curators and the mainstream art press' (Lichty, 2008). A whole range of galleries have now presented, and supported, or included artworks developed in *Second Life* in their gallery spaces including the Serpentine Gallery, London, the Walker Art Gallery, Liverpool, and the Eyebeam Gallery in New York, either as part of themed exhibitions or artist-focused exhibitions.

In a review of artworks created in *Second Life* in what could be termed the early years it is the sheer array of work created across a broad range of artistic disciplines such as art, architecture, performance, film, and media arts that was salient. From work such as *Thirteen Most Beautiful Avatars* (2006) by Eva & Franco Mattes modeled on a reworking of Andy Warhol's print series, to Brian Eno's *77 Million Paintings* (2007) installation recreated in *Second Life*, or the early *Second Life* music performances by Susanne Vega (2006) and Duran Duran (2006), to the politics of virtual sweatshops in Stephanie Rothenberg's *Invisible Threads* (2007), and finally to the inWorld projects of SL artist Angrybeth Shortbread such as *Ping Space* (2008), all point towards a retesting of artistic principles in virtual world spaces.

The Chinese artist Cao Fei developed a number of relevant projects including *iMirror* (2007), an installation and three-part documentary about Fei's avatar identity, China Tracy, which was included in the Chinese Pavilion at the Venice Biennale, and RMB City (2008-ongoing) which was presented at the Serpentine Galley, London, and in New York. Artist and filmmaker Lynn Hershman worked with Stanford University to develop *Life to the Second Power* (2007-ongoing), documenting and archiving two of her projects, *The Dante Hotel*, and *Roberta Breitmore*. A number of performance-based works relied on a re-enactment of historical performance art, such as *Seven Easy Pieces* (2005) which Marina Abramovic performed at the Guggenheim, re-enacting seven significant historical and noted Performance Art works, and Eva and Franco Mattes *Synthetic Performances* (2009-ongoing), and the exploration of what they term an 'imponderable medium' (Lichty 2008). The performance artist Joseph DeLappe has incorporated online gaming into his work since 2001 in work such as Dead_in_Iraq (2006–ongoing). In 2008 he re-enacted Mahatma Gandhi's *Salt March to Dandi* (2008), spending 26 days walking through *Second Life* using a customized treadmill that powered the movements of his inWorld counterpart, MGandhi Chakrabarti.

Other artists have found that particular combinations of the attributes of the *Second Life* space echo their own concerns, a notable example being the work of Paul Sermon. Sermon established a research hub in *Second Life* where he conducted a number of experiments such as *Liberate your Avatar* (2007) and *Urban Intersections* (2009), and more recently (in collaboration with Charlotte Gould) *Mirror on the Screen* (2012). Australian artist Adam Nash developed a substantial body of conceptual work in *Second Life* through an exploration of sound and immersive spaces. Typical of his early works is the interactive installation, or participatory artwork, *A Rose Heard at Dusk* (2007). *Babelswarm* (2008) was a group project created out of the first Australia Council Artist in Residence Award for *Second Life*, that brought Nash together with Christopher Dodds and Justin Clemens, to produce what was a mixed reality, real-time, interactive, audiovisual artwork (Clemens, 2008). The installation, based on the story of the Tower of Babel, captures visitors' chat text which is fed into the 'meta-babeller', which spills out words from the *Second Life* sky 'in strings of audiovisual letterforms' after which the words shatter on descent as the separated letters can be seen as they 'swarm in random directions seeking out other letters in order to reconstruct the word they were born in' (Nash, 2008). The artwork occupied the whole Sim that it was built on and created an interesting conceptual and abstract landscape in which to wander through or fly in.

The second category of artist working in *Second Life* were those who have consistently worked from within the platform itself, although there are obviously artists who are working between a supporting arts establishment and a more grass roots involvement with the space, so this divide is not so clearly defined. However, artists have emerged from the platform itself, and the Burning Life exhibitions that have been staged since 2003, initiated by the founder of *Second Life*, Philip Rosedale, are an important showcase for the work of such artists. An article by Jacquelyn Ford Morie, *A (Virtual) World without Limits* (2010), investigated artworks that have been produced primarily for a *Second Life* audience, and includes accounts of her experiences of installations such as Bogon Flux (2008) by artists Blotto Epsilon and Cutea Benelli and the pastoral environment Surface by artist AM Radio (Morie, 2010). Artist DC Spensley maintains an Island Sim for his hyperformalist work, and extended his artistic practice into performances such as the *ZeroG Skydancers* (2008) events.

In 2007 music technologist Rob Wright, known as Robbie Dingo in *Second Life*, produced a seminal machinima work called *Watch the World* (2007) utilising the *Second Life* space to produce the work (Au, 2007). Taking its inspiration and fundamental concept from the imaginary picture space of Van Gogh's work *Starry Night* (1889), Dingo explains that it was shot 'on location' in *Second Life* and then post-produced; 'the Sim in this work was on temporary loan so it's all been swept away now, leaving only the film behind. It was always intended however that the video would be the end product, not the build' (Dingo, 2007). There is a potency to what Dingo produced in *Watch the World* (2007), firstly throughout the machinima in which Dingo allows us to see the construction of this virtual, imagined space and secondly, to literally watch the artist recreate the landscape of the painting itself.

Writing again in 2011 Lichty posed the question 'what happens to embodied art when the body is removed?' and proposed three aspects that contribute to the significance of virtual worlds for virtual performance art, that of Affect, Desire, and Mirroring (Lichty, 2011). The discovery of mirror neurons in the 1990s may explain the efficacy of virtual world experiences and most particularly those mediated through avatar presence. A significant work that was developed during 2009 is *Becoming Dragon* by

Micha Cardenas in which she writes that the project 'is a mixed-reality performance that questions the one-year requirement of "Real Life Experience" that transgender people must fulfil in order to receive Gender Confirmation Surgery' (Cardenas, 2010). For the performance Cardenas 'lived' for 365 hours immersed in *Second Life* via a head mounted display and 'only seeing the physical world through a video-feed [...] during the year of research and development of this project I began my real life hormone replacement therapy' (Cardenas, 2010). Cardenas notes that both virtual worlds and biotechnology are each technologies of transformation and 'offer the promise of becoming something else, of having a new body and a new life' (Cardenas, 2010). This mixing of realities and ultimately mixing of genders in her performance piece focuses on the process of becoming and she concludes that 'the epistemological topology of becoming is shaped by the radical unknowability of the future' (Cardenas, 2010).

There have been a number of works that continue to focus on augmenting the *Second Life* space (often creating a strange virtual aesthetic) seen in particular in *Mirror on the Screen* (2012). In this project Charlotte Gould and Paul Sermon explores the concepts of presence and performance in *Second Life* and 'first life' and attempt to 'bridge these two spaces through mixed reality techniques and interfaces' (Gould & Sermon, 2012). The final project to mention here is that of virtual artist Bryn Oh, *Imogen and the Pigeons* (2013), an immersive interactive environment built on the Immersiva Sim. The multilayered story is told through a series of poems. Writing about the closing stages of the project (that is now deleted - although documented through machinima - to make way for her new project) SL artist Bryn Oh notes that:

The story for Imogen is intended to be slightly vague as to allow the viewer to interpret the narrative with more freedom. I feel that it may be more engaging for the viewer if they are not told a definitive story which can make the viewer passive, but rather to live and interact within a story which requires them to activate their imagination (Oh, 2013).

ORGANIZATION OF THE BOOK

The book is organized into twelve chapters and arranged into four sections. A brief description of each section and each of the chapters follows:

Section 1 *Creative Practices, Theoretical Contexts, Virtual Worlds* establishes the initial ground of theoretical research for creative practices in virtual worlds through three chapters with a consideration of both the nature and the practices that contribute to an aesthetics of virtual environments, and opens up the discussion of the nature of virtual space for artistic enquiry.

In Chapter 1 *'An Aesthetics of Digital Virtual Environments'* Adam Nash examines the specificities of virtual environments as a medium for art identifying primary qualities that include visual opacity, digital colour, artificial intelligence, emergence, code, digital sound and agency. Arising from the authors own extensive art practice in virtual environments and the associated theoretical concerns he considers the technical, conceptual and ontological status of virtual environments in order to propose a formal aesthetics for art in digital environments.

In Chapter 2 *'Painting Machinima in Second Life'* Phylis Johnson explores the technological and artistic revolution enabled by machinima, and focuses on the rise among a community of filmmakers that express their stories and ideas through virtual worlds. Her chapter argues for machinima as a new art form through a series of case studies including that of virtual artist Bryn Oh who has the support of artist and fillmaker Peter Greenaway. Johnson distinguishes between the machinima concepts of game, virtual platform, and virtual worlds and describes new scholarship on its aesthetics and the cultural implications for a digital society.

In Chapter 3 *'Spacing and Displacing as Artistic Enquiry'* artist Taey Iohe presents a philosophical journey and practical piece of experimentation on spatiality, virtual and displacement. Taking on a themed subject her chapter explores the way in which displaced women cannot belong in either their home or a foreign land, and approaches the virtual as an unreal living space rather than an exclusively virtual environment through technology. Creating artworks in both the gallery space and the virtual space of Second Life, Iohe examines the typology and meaning of displacement through language translation and gendered practice.

Section 2 *Avatar, Embodiment, Identity* brings together three chapters each considering the significance of the avatar in different ways. From the first chapter that includes a study of a practice-based performance project and historical reenactment to the final two chapters that each take on the discussion of the avatar in opposing ways; one writing from the perspective of the avatar as a representation of our identity as embodied selves in virtual worlds and the other arguing that the avatar should be seen as something disembodied and that acts as a representation of loss.

In Chapter 4 *'Digital Steps of Protest, Reenactment, and Networked Interaction'* Natasha Chuk reviews the work of performance and protest artist Joseph DeLappe in the context of his Salt Satyagraha project that saw the artist stage a reenactment of Mahatma Gandhi's historic march in India in 1930 within the *Second Life* environment. Through a discussion of Walter Benjamin's concept of *spielraum* and Jacque Derrida's concept of the supplement she concludes that the project ends where it begins, centred on play, reenactment, and testing the complexities of a human-avatar relationship in *Second Life*.

In Chapter 5 *'Creating a Framework to Analyse the Perception of Selfhood in Artistic Practice within Second Life'* Pete Wardle draws upon existing identity theories to examine the expression of self through avatars. Through this he develops a critical framework that is then tested through the analysis of the practice of artists working with themes of identity in *Second Life*. Further, Wardle considers his own practice-based work in this context and examines the role artistic practice plays in changing our understanding of the way identity is expressed and perceived within virtual worlds.

In Chapter 6 *'Appearance, Absence, Art: Objet A-vatar'* Garfield Benjamin puts forward a model for reconceiving the avatar in terms of desire and loss and focuses on the avatar as appearance, as a negotiation of presence and absence, to reassess its role within creative practices and the construction of digital subjectivity. In spaces such as *Second Life* the inclusion of a representation of the subject within its own gaze shows the nature of the avatar as an always-already lost body, arguing that it demonstrates the loss inherent in all forms of embodiment.

Section 3, *Found Objects, Collaborative Practices, Shared Creativity,* includes three chapters that are brought together to develop the discussions around Axel Bruns key term 'produsage' as an integral element of the artistic strategies developed within the projects presented. All three chapters present research that is as a result of sustained and experimental methodologies and inventive approaches to artistic practices, and each chapter contributor takes on key theories in which to frame their research.

In Chapter 7 *'Found Objects, Bought Selves'* Canadian artist Lynne Heller traces the creative use of the found object collage and explores issues of appropriation and the notion of the bought self through the avatar as found object. Her practice-based research has been developed through a project series exploring the adventures of her avatar Nar Duell and Heller herself suggests the relationship between herself and her avatar is akin to that of a mother/daughter relationship. Heller argues, through a review of the practices of the Situationists, that an aesthetic turn in political tactics is revealed in contemporary arts practices.

In Chapter 8 *'Moving Islands [Rafts]: A Collective Conglomeration in Second Life'* Elif Ayiter and artist avatar Eupalinos Ugajin present the artistic processes and theoretical premises of this collaborative art project. In their text they survey the creative mechanisms and strategies of the 'metaverse', and introduce two terms, that of Bruns 'produsage' and Eno's 'unfinished artifact', that relate to the collective art process explored in the Moving Islands project. Their chapter concludes with a discussion of what they term a second order-creativity that sees the transformation of visual art works into experiential behavioural objects that become crucial components in the creation of their virtual extensions, their avatars, and the avatars domiciles.

In Chapter 9 *'Meta_Body: Virtual Corporeality as a Shared Creative Process'* Catarina Carneiro de Sousa presents her participatory art project and addresses what she terms the constitution of virtual corporeality as a shared creative process. The project approaches both the avatar as body/language and as such it is open to experimentation and potency, and avatar building as a shared creative process and aesthetic experience. Through a method described as 'shared creativity' three stages are presented from collective creation, to distributed creation, and finally collaborative creation.

Section 4 presents *Performance Practices in Virtual Worlds* and brings together both practitioners and theorists in the three chapters that consider firstly the issues surrounding digital embodiment and the status of the body in performance art, the practice of blended reality through the virtual and physical performer, and finally the ways in which SL-Bots can be explored for their aesthetic and creative potential.

In Chapter 10 '*"Follow me Comrades, in to the Depths!": Body-Related Performance Art in Second Life'* Maja Murnik reviews the various features of digital embodiment and considers the notion of philosopher Merleau-Ponty's 'body image' and 'body schema' in contemporary mixed and augmented reality. The chapter then examines a number of examples of body-related performance art in Second Life and particularly those that raise questions about the status of the body in the digital world itself.

In Chapter 11 *'Blended Reality Performance'* Joff Chafer focuses on the integration of live performance that blends both virtual and physical performers. Inspired by a 2007 Second Life artwork, *Liberate your Avatar*, by artist Paul Sermon, Chafer developed a number of practice-based projects in Second Life, sometimes in collaboration with artists such as Stelarc. He presents a chronological account of these projects and concludes with a discussion about the nature of this type of performance from the point of view of both the physical performers and those performing with the avatars themselves.

Finally, in Chapter 12 *'SL-Bots: Automated and Autonomous Performance-Art in Second Life'* authors Jeremy Turner, Michael Nixon, and Jim Bizzocchi explore the history, state-of-the-art, and interactive aesthetic potential of avatars that are designed and controlled using Artificial Intelligence in Second Life (SL-Bots). Following a discussion on the ways in which SL-Bots have been used aesthetically and creatively, they suggest ways in which SL-Bots may one day transcend their original purpose as avatar-placeholders and evolve into more complex automated aesthetic personas in themselves.

With Peter Greenaway collaborating with a number of *Second Life* artists (including Bryn Oh) to create a series of interactive works for an exhibition on the *Golden Age of the Russian Avant-Garde* in 2014 and a continued and varied range of projects in development in *Second Life,* this points towards a continued engagement in the opportunities the platform offers in terms of artistic practices. This volume represents the artistic and scholarly, and in many cases practice-based and practice-led research of a distinct field of research, that of the creative opportunities and artistic practices in virtual worlds. It is hoped that this work presented together will stimulate discussion and exchange on the nature of virtual space and the contribution that artists are making to understanding these new territories. Moreover there is still much to consider and not least to 'practice' in virtual worlds (the very nature of heuristic research itself) to uncover the nature of virtual world space and to articulate the new practices that are continuing to develop and challenge the rich field of Art and Technology.

Denise Doyle
University of Wolverhampton, UK

REFERENCES

Au, W. J. (2007) *Remake the Stars*. New World Notes. Available at: http://nwn.blogs.com/nwn/2007/07/remake-the-star.html#more

Bachelard, G. in Davies, C. (1997) Changing Space: Virtual Reality as an Arena of Embodied Being. In Packer, R. & Jordan, K. (ed.) *Multimedia: From Wagner to Virtual Reality*. New York, W.W. Norton & Company. [Online] Available at: http:///www.immersence.com

Bruns, A. (2008). *Blogs, Wikipedia, Second Life, and Beyond: From Production to Produsage*. New York: Peter Lang Publishing.

Cardenas, M. (2009) Becoming Dragon, Mixed-Reality Performance. Available at: http://secondloop.wordpress.com/

Cardenas, M. (2010) *Becoming Dragon: A Transversal Technology Study*, Code Drift: Essays in Critical Digital Studies 009. Available at: http://ctheory.net/articles.aspx?id=639

Clemens, J. (2008) Babelswarm: A real-time 3D art and audio project by Adam Nash, Christopher Dodds and Justin Clemens. Available at: http://babelswarm.blogspot.com/

Davies, C. (1995) Osmose. Virtual Reality Environment. Available at: http://www.immersence.com/osmose/index.php

Davies, C. (1998) Ephémère. Virtual Reality Environment. Available at: http://www.immersence.com/

Davies, C. (2003). Landscape, Earth, Body, Being, Space, and Time in the Immersive Virtual Environments Osmose and Ephemere. In J. Malloy (Ed.), Women, Art and Technology. Cambridge, Massachusetts: MIT Press; Available at http://www.immersence.com

DeLappe, J. (2008) Re-enactment: The Salt Satyagraha Online. Available at: http://saltmarchsecondlife.wordpress.com/

Dingo, R. (2007) Watch the World. Machinima. Available at: http://digitaldouble.blogspot.com/2007/07/watch-worlds.html

Dove, T., & Mackenzie, M. (1993). Archaeology of the Mother Tongue. Virtual Reality Installation. Alberta, Canada: Banff Centre for the Arts; Available at http://www.banffcentre.ca/bnmi/coproduction/archives/a.asp

Doyle, D. (2008). Art and the Avatar: The Kritical Works in SL project. *International Journal of Performance Arts and Digital Media*, 4(2&3), 137–153. doi:10.1386/padm.4.2_3.137_1

Eno, B. (2007) 77 Million Paintings. Exhibition. Available at: http://www.longnow.org/events/02007/jun/29/77-million-paintings-brian-eno/

Fei, C. (2007) *iMirror*. Multimedia Installation. [Available at: http://blogs.walkerart.org/offcenter/2007/07/16/cao-feis-imirror/

Fei, C. (2008- ongoing) *RMB City. Second Life* Sim. Available at: http://www.serpentinegallery.org/2008/05/cao_fei_rmb_city.html and http://rmbcity.com/

Gould, C., & Sermon, P. (2012) Mirror on the Screen. Available at: http://creativetechnology.salford.ac.uk/paulsermon/mirror/

Gromola, D., & Sharir, Y. (1994). Dancing with the Virtual Dervish: Virtual Bodies. Virtual Reality Installation. Alberta, Canada: Banff Centre for the Arts; Available at http://www.banffcentre.ca/bnmi/coproduction/archives/d.asp#dancing

Grosz, E. (2001). *Architecture From the Outside: Essays on Virtual and Real Space*. Cambridge, Massachusetts: MIT Press.

Hershman, L. (2007-ongoing) Life to the Second Power (L2). Available at: http://presence.stanford.edu:3455/LynnHershman/261

Jones, D. E. (2006) I, Avatar: Constructions of Self and Place in Second Life and the Technological Imagination. *Gnovis, Journal of Communication, Culture and Technology*. Available at: http://gnovis.georgetown.edu

Laurel, B., & Strickland, R. (1993). Placeholder. Virtual Reality Installation. Alberta, Canada: Banff Centre for the Arts; Available at http://www.banffcentre.ca/bnmi/coproduction/archives/p.asp#placeholder

Lichty, P. (2008) Why Art in Virtual Worlds? E-Happenings, Relational Milieux & "Second Sculpture". *CIAC Electronic Magazine*. Available at: www.voyd.com/texts/LichtySLCIACWhyVirtualArt.pdf

Lichty, P. (2011). *Phantom Limbs: Affect and Identification in Virtual Performance, Panel Paper, ISEA2011*. Istanbul: Sabanci University.

Macleod, D. (1996). Preface. In M. A. Moser (Ed.), *Immersed in Technology: Art and Virtual Environments*. Cambridge, Massachusetts: MIT Press.

Mattes, E. & F. (2006) Thirteen Most Beautiful Avatars. Photography Exhibition. Available at: http://www.0100101110101101.org/home/portraits/thirteen.html

Morie, J. (2010). A (virtual) world without limits: Aesthetic expression in *Second Life*. *Journal of Gaming and Virtual Worlds*, 2(2), 157–177. doi:10.1386/jgvw.2.2.157_1

Nash, A. (2007) A Rose Heard at Dusk. Available at: http://yamanakanash.net/secondlife/rose_heard_at_dusk.html

Nash, A. (2008) Babelswarm. Available at: http://yamanakanash.net/secondlife/babelswarm.html

Oh, B. (2013) Imogen and the Pigeons – Closing. Available at: http://brynoh.blogspot.co.uk/2013/10/imogen-and-pigeons-closing.html

Oh, B. (2013) Imogen and the Pigeons. Available at: http://brynoh.blogspot.co.uk/2013/04/imogen-and-pigeons-part-one.html

Rothenberg, S. (2008) Invisible Threads. Available at: http://www.pan-o-matic.com/projects/invisible-threads

Sermon, P. (2007) Liberate your Avatar. Public Performance Installation. Available at: http://creativetechnology.salford.ac.uk/paulsermon/liberate/

Spensley, D. C. (2008) ZeroG Skydancers III. Online Performance. Available at: http://zerogskydancers.com/

Acknowledgment

I would like to thank all of the Editorial Board members, particularly Rina Arya, Astrid Ensslin, Lizbeth Goodman, Sisse Siggaard Jenson, Patrick Lichty, Jacquelyn Ford-Morie, and Paul Sermon. I would like to thank all of the reviewers, particularly Rina Arya, Elif Ayiter, Garfield Benjamin, Joff Chafer, Natasha Chuk, Astrid Ensslin, Lynne Heller, Taey Iohe, Paul Johnson, Sisse Siggaard Jenson, Phylis Johnson, Patrick Lichty, Jacquelyn Ford-Morie, Maja Murnik, Michael Nixon, Dorothy Santos, Paul Sermon, Catarina de Sousa, Pete Wardle and Alison Williams.

I would also like to thank the authors who have attended to the development of their book chapters with diligence and commitment and with dedication to the topic at hand, particularly Elif Ayiter, Garfield Benjamin, Jim Bizzocchi, Joff Chafer, Natasha Chuk, Lynne Heller, Taey Iohe, Phylis Johnson, Maja Murnik, Adam Nash, Michael Nixon, Catarina de Sousa, Jeremy Turner, Eupalinos Ugajin, and Pete Wardle.

Can I thank the IGI Global team, and in particular Allison McGinniss who patiently supplied me with important information and assistance during her time supporting the development of this book.

Thank you.

Denise Doyle
University of Wolverhampton, UK

Section 1
Creative Practices, Theoretical Contexts, Virtual Worlds

This section establishes the initial ground of theoretical research for creative practices in virtual worlds with a consideration of both the nature and the practices that contributes to an aesthetics of virtual environments, and opens up the discussion of the nature of virtual space for artistic enquiry.

Chapter 1
An Aesthetics of Digital Virtual Environments

Adam Nash
RMIT University, Australia

ABSTRACT

This chapter examines digital virtual environments as a site for art and proposes a formal aesthetics for art in digital virtual environments. The study arises from the author's decades-long practice producing art in virtual environments and the related theoretical considerations that have arisen from that practice. The technical, conceptual and ontological status of virtual environments is examined in order to establish a base of intrinsic qualities that identify virtual environments as a medium for art. The philosophy of Gilbert Simondon is used to achieve this. The elements and principles the artist must employ to work with this medium are identified as data, display and modulation. The specificities of virtual environments as a medium for art are examined in order to establish a formal aesthetics. In particular, digital colour, visual opacity, digital sound, code, artificial intelligence, emergence and agency are identified as the primary qualities that the artist manipulates to bring forth art in a virtual environment.

INTRODUCTION: WHAT IS AESTHETICS IN DIGITAL VIRTUAL ENVIRONMENTS?

This chapter examines digital virtual environments as a site for art.[1] The study arises from the author's decades-long practice producing art in digital virtual environments and the related theoretical considerations that have arisen from that practice. The chapter attempts to theorise a genuine aesthetics of digital virtual environments, and in doing so, draws on aesthetics, philosophy,

contemporary media theory and affect theory in an attempt to define an aesthetics for the complex arena of art in digital virtual environments.

To establish an aesthetics of art in digital virtual environments, first we must examine the technical, conceptual and ontological status of these environments in order to identify intrinsic qualities that might identify such environments as a medium for art. In other words, what can be done with this medium that cannot be done in any other, and how? This occupies the first section of the chapter, starting by identifying digital virtual

DOI: 10.4018/978-1-4666-8384-6.ch001

Copyright © 2015, IGI Global. Copying or distributing in print or electronic forms without written permission of IGI Global is prohibited.

environments as a *post-convergent* medium constituted by the elements of *data* and *display* and the principle of *modulation*. This is followed by an attempt to understand the consequences of this in terms, first proposed by the French philosopher Gilbert Simondon, of indeterminate *becoming*. The role of technical protocols, which are ostensibly highly determinist, are examined in the light of this indeterminacy. This is then brought to bear on the concept, much discussed in 21st Century media studies, of *autopoiesis*, to try to determine the status of digital entities in digital virtual environments. As well as Simondon, the thought of important contemporary scholars of media and culture is drawn upon, including Marshall McLuhan, Friedrich Kittler, Justin Clemens, Pierre Lévy, Gilles Deleuze, Claire Colebrook, Anna Munster, Felix Guattari, Rosi Braidotti, Luciana Parisi, Humberto Maturana and Francisco Varela.

Once this has been done, an aesthetics of digital virtual environments can be attempted, and this constitutes the second section of the chapter. Since digital virtual environments are a complex combination of many elements working together, it follows that an aesthetics will need to examine many different elements. First, the concept of *protocols* is revisited to examine the role of human and non-human agency in digital environments. This is achieved through programming code, which is identified as a major element of any aesthetics of digital virtual environments, and examined accordingly in relation to the Simondonian understanding, raised in the first section, of chains of modulation between data and display. This is followed by an examination of artificial intelligence and desire in relation to aesthetics, which leads to the important concept of performativity and its role in aesthetics of the digital, best articulated by art theorist Boris Groys. The role of time is then examined in relation to interactivity and digital networks, before a discussion of the role of colour and sound in the aesthetics of digital virtual environments. Besides Simondon and Groys, scholars and artists referenced in the

second section include Luciano Floridi, Gregory Chaitin, Stephen Wolfram, Luciana Parisi, Bernard Stiegler, N. Katherine Hayles, Elizabeth Grosz, Colebrook, Manuel DeLanda, Wendy Chun, Alain Badiou, Giorgio Agamben, Bill Viola, Quentin Meillassoux, Jon Roffe, Lewis Mumford, Yves Klein and Pierre Schaeffer.

Finally, as an appendix after the conclusion, I have included descriptions of some of the artworks I have had a hand in making in the past decade or so. These are placed in an appendix at the end of the chapter, as I would like the aesthetics I am trying to theorise in relation to digital virtual environments to stand alone, regardless of whether my own attempts at digital virtual art achieve any claim to aesthetic interest.

1. INTRINSIC QUALITIES OF ART IN DIGITAL VIRTUAL ENVIRONMENTS

The Status of Digital Virtual Environments as Post-Convergent Sites for Art

Digital virtual environments are *post-convergent*, that is, in McLuhan's sense (2001, p. 10), containing all prior media as content (Nash, 2012). A post-convergent medium is the dynamic whole that is created by the convergence of all prior media, plus the excess that is both created by, and is required to create, such convergence.

Such post-convergent moves can perhaps be identified throughout the history of media, but the digital is distinguished by converging all previously differentiable media into an undifferentiable continuum, that of digital data (Kittler, 1999, p. 2). Consequently, for media to be differentiated in the digital era, *digital data* must be *modulated* into some kind of sensible *display* state via protocols that virtually reassemble the required medium, be it a visible, audible or some other kind of sensible medium.

The digitisation process contributes its own operations to this process, creating an excess that cannot be rationalised exclusively in terms of a meta-media, because the concept of a meta-media is itself one of the media that is, or can be, explicitly virtualised as content within itself, just as the process confers a retroactive virtuality on all prior media being digitised as virtual content, creating both the prior media and the excess of their own virtuality.

Data, Display and Modulation as Constitutive of Digital Virtual Environments

The distinction between *data* and *display*, via *modulation*, is constitutive of the digital, and therefore of digital virtual environments - including realtime 3D environments such as those used in Massively Multiuser Online Role Playing Games (MMORPGs) like *World of Warcraft* or multi- and single-user world-building environments like *Second Life* or *Minecraft*.

The distinction requires an understanding of the excess that is not only created through the digital convergence but in fact constitutes our contemporary understanding of the *virtual*, when used in such terms as *virtual friend*, *virtual meeting* and *virtual reality*.[2] In this usage, the virtual is understood as a digitally networked environment which affects, and is affected by, the non-digital world (Lévy, 1998, p. 30). Without conflating the two, it is possible to ascertain a relationship between this understanding of the term 'virtual' and Gilles Deleuze's nuanced philosophical concept of the same name (Nash, 2012). Colebrook's (2010) reading of Deleuze and Guattari's *desiring machines* is useful in this context (p. 124), as is Anna Munster's (2006) notion of pulsing vectors, (p. 90), both of which we will discuss a little later. Similarly, André Nusselder (2009) uses Deleuze, Peirce and Doel & Clarke to confirm an idea of the virtual that is "about actualization and not about realization (of possibilities)," in other words

a virtual that is understood as different from the concept of potential and "expresses exactly this idea of a creation of new events." (p. 37)

Gilbert Simondon and Digital Virtual Environments

Once we recognise the digital as being constituted in the bivalent relationship between states of data and display, we can understand the work of digital virtual art as that of *modulation* between these two states. The work of modulation is effected through selection of parameters, otherwise known as the use of protocols. This is where the unique qualities of artwork in virtual environments are revealed, with the careful selection and/or design of how data will be modulated from its generic, undifferentiated state into a display state. This is what might be called *facilitated ontogenesis*, that is to say, a conscious facilitating of what Simondon would call *transductions* in the *metastable* environment of digital data in order that a digital entity individuates. Simondon borrowed these terms from physics, chemistry and biology, where *transduction* means the conversion of energy or information into another form, or, in Simondon's own words, "a physical, biological, mental, or social operation, through which an activity propagates from point to point within a domain, while grounding this propagation in the structuration of the domain." (Combes, 2013, p. 8). *Metastable* refers to a system in a state of energetic equilibrium, where a tiny change in energy will break the equilibrium (Combes, 2013, p. 5).

Simondon's philosophy is useful for understanding all sorts of phenomena in the physical and conceptual worlds, from geology to history, even though he is now primarily known as a philosopher of technology. But his philosophy is especially useful, if sometimes problematic, in the case of digital virtual environments, since it helps in thinking through the implications of the leveling or generifying operation of the digital (Clemens & Nash, 2010). This is because the traditional philosophical concepts of substantialism (ie, a unified being) and hylomorphism (ie, form given to matter) don't seem to apply to digital virtual environments at all. A generated digital entity in a realtime 3D digital virtual environment certainly cannot be said to be unto itself, since it doesn't exist except 'in' the virtual world, and nor can it be said to consist of matter given form, rather it is only form, and yet it can be sensibly perceived. Simondon's project from the beginning was to dispense with substantialism and hylomorphism altogether, along with their consequent subject/object dichotomy that Simondon felt made it impossible to think individuation, because it always privileged the individual as given. As he puts it in *The Position of the Problem of Ontogenesis* (2009a, p. 5), it is better "to know the individual through individuation rather than individuation through the individual." The individual should be thought of as "a relative reality, a certain phase of being that supposes a preindividual reality, and that, even after individuation, does not exist on its own." (Simondon, 2009a, p. 5). This ontogenetic viewpoint helps us to understand the nature of being of digital entities in digital virtual environments, since they are part of an ongoing process of modulation between states of data and display. Digital entities do not exist on their own, since they require a digital medium, and the "pre-individual reality" from which they emerge is that digital medium.

Protocols and Indeterminacy

So everything, when digitised, becomes undifferentiated digital data and only when modulated into a display state can it be said to have any kind of differentiated existence. And yet, with protocols that govern such modulation, predictability can, but only to a certain extent, be relied upon to remodulate digital data into an expected display state. This "only to a certain extent", where indeterminacy is introduced through vagaries of

modulation and display conditions, is quintessentially Simondonian as well, since he believed that indeterminate interactivity was part and parcel of the ontogenetic process (Iliadis, 2013, p. 12). Indeed, this indeterminate interactivity is the hallmark of digital virtual environments of any kind. Think of a character moving through a realtime 3D game world driven by the arrow key on the player's keyboard. The sensible manifestation of this is a constantly changing arrangement of pixels on a screen, the constant change interactively prompted by constantly changing messages. The messages are the last modulation in a long chain of modulation sites from keyboard to graphics card, each exchange interactive and governed by specific protocols. The sensible display itself - the pixels - is a constantly changing arrangement of red, green and blue light emitting diodes in a two-dimensional matrix that does not constitute a character in a world, rather serve as yet another complex, interactive site of modulation between light, eye, mind and culture that eventually in some way individuate a character in a world. When seen in this way, the interactive indeterminacy is the only thing there is. This chain of indeterminate, interactive modulations is what constitutes the work of the artist in the digital era, and this is where we need to look to define an aesthetics.

Digital Virtual Environments and Autopoiesis

In the digital era, many thinkers and practitioners have identified and attempted to work through this curiously plastic relationship between the individual and its milieu, and the concepts of *autopoiesis* and *allopoiesis*, promulgated by Maturana and Varela (1980) and extended by Guattari (1995), have recently gained traction as a potential method for doing so.[3] Anna Munster sees the distinction between technical systems as allopoietic (ie, broadly, producing something other than themselves) and organic systems as autopoietic (broadly, reproducing themselves) as erroneous. She does this by invoking Guattari's idea that technical systems form a machinic assemblage with humans, thereby becoming autopoietic (Munster, 2013, 8). This is a very interesting concept in relation to realtime 3D digital virtual environments or entities that are, partially or wholly, driven by dynamic data sources. Such works, while conceptually available to previous eras (and even explicitly explored, particularly during the modernist era, where John Cage, Joe Jones and Yoko Ono perhaps stand as exemplars), are not really able to be enacted until the advent of the digital networked era.

These concerns are particularly relevant to digital virtual works that incorporate dynamic data in their unfolding - data such as the presence and actions of humans, or the dynamically changing data generated by some realtime data source. If we accept Munster's Guattarian notion of the autopoietic nature of the assemblage formed between human and technical systems, then we must attempt to establish what is being produced by such an assemblage in the case of such an artwork. Certainly, more data is being produced by the constant formation and reformation of this assemblage, and such data may be dynamically reincorporated as a data source itself. This may constitute a kind of technical self-consciousness, inasmuch as the audiovisual animation system may be said to be reproducing iterative versions of itself every moment. Does this sort of dynamic reproduction, or production, of a constantly shifting assemblage formed between animation and data source constitute an autopoiesis or an allopoiesis? Anna Munster's reading of Varela and Maturana's concept of autopoiesis offers the following definition:

An autopoietic or living machine, a 'unity', maintains its composition relationally through interactions with its 'medium' or environment. Changes in the medium trigger changes in the unity that is the organized organism leading to adaptation. But, in the living unity, only those changes that conserve the organization of the living machine (that is, its autopoiesis) are 'structurally coupled' with it (Munster, 2013, p. 6).

The similarities with the Simondonian view are clear here, indeed Braidotti (2013) directly equates a Guattarian notion of a machinic collective with the Simondonian metastable as a precondition for individuation (p. 94).[4] But how can we differentiate, in the case of a data-driven realtime 3D digital virtual environment, the medium or environment from the living machine, since it is not possible to separate the audiovisual display state of the environment from its state of data-as-data except in nostalgic McLuhanist or phenomenological terms that are quickly revealed as chimeric or, more accurately, as elements that may constitute elements of both or either of the autopoietic machine and its medium or environment?[5]

We could use Deleuze's Spinozan definition of a body[6] in an attempt to analyse realtime 3D data-driven digital virtual environments in Varela's (1992) terms of embodied cognitive structures interacting with encompassing contexts (p. 334). Luciana Parisi (2004) notes that De Landa has done this to human-generated structures like markets (p. 142). We might also identify, via the display state of the digital virtual assemblage, the characteristics of an autocatalytic or semi-closed circuit that generates its own stable state and evolves through drift (Parisi, 2004, p. 142). But even if we do these things, it is still not clear where the thresholds are between the technical system and its medium, and even less clear whether it is producing something different from itself, reproducing itself, or producing some hybrid. This is where Simondon's philosophy may be useful, since it obviates the need for any definitive location of the individual, rather concentrating on the ongoing chain of transductive operations that keep the entire assemblage in a constant state of becoming.

This is a concept that, while it may be difficult to understand in terms of our own subjective experience of the world, is easier to understand in the context of digital virtual operations.

With this, the status of digital virtual environments as sites for art, and therefore their associated aesthetics, are revealed to be related less to their audiovisual (or other sensible) display than to the chains of modulation that represent the becoming of digital virtual environments, and of which human-sensible display is but one aspect.

2. AN AESTHETICS OF DIGITAL VIRTUAL ENVIRONMENTS

The selection and/or design of modulation protocols is the primary work in the art of digital virtual environments, so this is where an aesthetics that is intrinsic to digital virtual environments will reside.

Protocol as Interface and Vice Versa

It is important to remember, as Luciano Floridi (2014, p. 35) points out, that *interface* is simply another word for protocol, even if it has informally gathered the special meaning of a protocol that governs modulation between a human user and a digital device (eg, a software menu or a hardware controller), but we can equally talk of interfaces between digital entities or protocols between humans and digital entities. Of course the word 'protocol' itself was originally applied to interactions between people - people from different places.

Aesthetics, Protocols and Digital Ontogenesis

An aesthetics of digital virtual art will take into account protocols that facilitate *digital ontogenesis*, [7]which often displays as digital adaptation and digital behaviour (commonly called *artificial*

intelligence and/or *artificial evolution*), emergence and digital agency. Programming code is the primary interface available to anybody working with these phenomena, so code is of primary interest to an aesthetics of digital virtual environments. There is not the space here to go into the differences between so-called hand-coding, visual coding and graphical user interfaces, which are themselves different levels of interface. In this chapter they will be conflated, but of course the same principles of modulation apply to these interfaces as to all digital work.[8]

Programming Code and Digital Agency

Programming code is the primary means by which artists can help bring forth the qualities of artificial intelligence and digital agency. [9] This is because both of these qualities emerge from the milieu of the virtual environment when appropriately seeded by programmed code that creates parameters, via which the modulation from data to display is effected in a Simondonian chain of bivalent relationships. This might be termed *artistic coding*, but in a different sense to the concept of elegance in code (Floridi, 2011, p. 318; Chaitin, 1998, p. 29), algorithmic complexity (Wolfram, 2002, p. 1143) or "computational beauty" (Parisi, 2013, p. 66). Rather, it is coding that interacts with the modulation chain because, as Simondon says,

The true principle of individuation is mediation, generally supposing an original duality of orders of magnitude and the initial absence of interactive communication between them, followed by communication between orders of magnitude and stabilization (2009, p. 7).

Code is Not Digital

Code itself is not digital. Code is a kind of writing. But it is different from the Platonic hypomnesic sense of exteriorised memory.[10] This is because code is a working out that requires inscription, as when physicist Richard Feynman, as quoted by Hayles (2012), insists that the marks he makes on the paper are the actual work, rather than a transcription of something that has already happened in his head (p. 93). We may find a way from this to the Simondonian concept of individuation, because code is a method of human writing that allows the writer to interface with the metastable pre-individual real that constitutes unmodulated digital data. The code is an interface to a process of individuating digital entities via "proximal forces in tension" (Grosz, 2012, p. 45), or what Anna Munster (2006) would call "vectors that pulse through the directions and contours of matter" (p. 90). As Grosz (2012) puts it, this pre-individual real "is marked by singularities, specificities, particular forces, specific locations, singular potentialities. It is the order of pure difference" (p. 45).

Code is a human interface to the assemblage that allows these specificities, this process of individuation, to emerge. Grosz (2012) says that this occurs "not through logic, but through the creation of a mode of interaction, a form of communication" (p. 46). The entire assemblage of code, digital data and display is an example of this mode of interaction, and code is the non-digital interface to that assemblage, conceived of by humans through the externally-facing form of thought that we do in fact think of as logic. So, the digital might be new, but code is not. Of course, the so-called digital philosophers suggest that digital is not new, rather discovered (Fredkin, 2003, p. 189). But one need not accept their solipsistic, totalising ontological philosophy to accept that we interact with digital data in order to actively participate in the synergetic inscription relationship between matter and information . To quote Grosz (2012) once more, "matter and information cannot be understood as separable (unlike in cybernetic models), but where each order marks the other and is in turn enhanced by it" (p. 46).

Code and Indeterminacy

When coding, a person is talking *with* a machine, but it is a soft machine, one link in the long chain of modulations, they are not talking directly *to* the hardware, even when coding Assembly, just as when writing with pen on paper a person is not directly addressing the physical and chemical bonding of ink and paper, rather they are engaging interactively with the chain of interactive modulations that constitute physical chemistry. In this sense, machine to machine communication (a current buzzphrase amongst digital capitalists and some media theorists) has always been an integral part of not only digital computing but the very process of individuation itself, and Simondon (2012) recognizes this in his two postulates of "technical mentality" (pp. 3-4).[11]

When seen in this way, code moves from being a deterministic engine in the teleology of a pre-given individual, to being a force in an evolving assemblage of affective bodies that appear in relations and modulate those relations, thereby constituting the individual (ie, in this case, the software), while always bearing the pre-individual, as Simondon (1993) says, "to such an extent that the finally constituted individual carries within it a certain inheritance associated with its pre-indivdual reality" (p. 306). The coding assemblage literally enacts this ability to always become a different individual, as prosaically seen in versions, upgrades and patches, and more generally in the practice of object oriented programming, which is an exact enactment of Simondon's (2012) first postulate of technical mentality, that "the subsets are relatively detachable from the whole of which they are a part" (p. 3).

Aesthetics as an Understanding of Modulation Chains

An aesthetics of the digital virtual will understand this postulate at all levels within a digital virtual environment populated with generated and/or self-generating digital entities. Simondon (2009) talks of "internal resonance" as a defining difference between the physical (ie, the non-living; for example, a crystal or a star) and the living, where the "living individual is a system of individuation, an individuating system and a system individuating itself", whereas the physical is "perpetually peripheral to itself, active at the limit of its domain" (p. 7).

Artificial Intelligence and Digital Entities

Artificial intelligence, ie, digital behaviour and adaptation, is linked with the concept of a digital entity, that is, any (virtual) object that exists within a virtual environment. Such an object may have been explicitly instantiated (ie, modulated into virtual existence) by the interaction of a person, for example by code or in response to some other human interaction such as a keyboard stroke or via a motion sensor, or it may have been instantiated by another digital entity. This other digital entity may exist in the same virtual environment or another, such as is the case with environments that are generated by an external data source, and may itself have been instantiated by another digital entity and so on.

Does the concept of digital entities encounter a similar problem to the boundary problem encountered above in relation to autopoiesis? Can a digital entity be said to possess an internal resonance because it does contain within itself the code to individuate another digital entity, or is it like a (digital) physical object that individuates only at its limit, without a "veritable interiority?" (Simondon, 2009, p. 7). Grosz (2012) confirms Simondon's anti-vitalist position when she says that, for him, "[l]ife is not a special kind of substance, a vital force" (p. 46), so we need not be concerned with a judgmental binary concerning life, and instead concentrate on the fact that digital entities "share the same pre-individual resources"

(p. 46) as living or physical entities. If the "vital is an order of elaboration of the physical, which is itself the expression of ... pre-individual tensions" (p. 46), then there is no reason not to think the same of the digital.

This may be what Colebrook (2010) means when she talks of a "sense beyond the actual" (p. 127), and when she says,

It is naive and uncritical to see the analogue as a pure and continuous feeling or bodily proximity that is then submitted to the quantification of the digital, a digital that will always be an imposition on organic and vital life. There is, however, an inorganic mode of the analogue that is not a return to a quality before its digital quantification, but a move from digital quantities or actual units to pure quantities, quantities that are not quantities of this or that substance so much as intensive forces that enter into differential relations to produce fields or spaces that can then be articulated into digits (2010, p. 124).

In saying this, Colebrook is drawing on Deleuze & Guattari's concept of desiring machines, but she is also bringing to light a relationship between Simondon and Manuel DeLanda, (1993) who talks of nonorganic life (p. 126) and phase transitions (2002, p. 123). In Simondon, a technical being emerges (ie, individuates) upon a kind of phase transition when separate elements unify in action with inputs and outputs (ie, bivalent openings of modulation) at the micro-, macro- and meta-levels.

Code, Writing, and Desire

Colebrook's evocation of desiring machines is a different kind of desire to what Hayles (2012) talks about when she cites Tanya Clement as characterising the ostensible unforgiving exactness of code as the "exteriorisation of desire" (p. 42). The relationship of this idea to the Platonic concept of hypomnesis, mentioned earlier, is clear, but it is unclear how this is unique to code and not simply a function of the exteriorising imperative of language itself. Hayles (2012) never explains why, as she puts it, "[n]eeding to translate desire into the explicitness of unforgiving code allows implications ... that may not happen with print" (p. 42), or how "the requirement to write executable code means that every command must be explicitly stated in the proper form" (p. 42) is different from writing a letter, ordering a pizza or having a conversation with another human being. Further, Hayles (2012) conflates what she calls "an abstract computational model" (p. 42) with code itself and excludes both from a capability for noise, ambiguity and complexity, seemingly ignoring Simondon's two postulates of technical mentality, which Hayles otherwise thinks of positively. At the same time, though, Hayles (2012) does recognise, via Kittler, the generifying effect of the digital in relation to human-facing text (p. 42), and that a new form of text- based endeavour that interacts with a Simondonian individuation via the digital arises as a result (p. 41), but Hayles does seem to persistently conflate code with the digital, which is a subtle but important mistake.

Chun (2011) eloquently points out the error of this conflation, and illustrates the Simondonian assemblage of synergetic modulations of which code is the human interface, when she notes that "[t]he relationship between executable and higher-level code is not that of mathematical identity but rather logical equivalence, which can involve a leap of faith" (p. 24). She goes on to show that the belief that instructions flow pure and unsullied from code to execution with no intervening alterations or behaviours unintended by humans is a mistaken belief that strongly informs an ideology of computing. This would be in contrast to a Simondonian assemblage of synergetic modulation chains. As Chun (2011) puts it, "Code ... has always been regenerative and interactive; every iteration alters its meaning" (p. 25).

Aesthetics, Protocols, and Modulation

This of course is not news to those working with the iterative design cycle, so the question for artists, and for aesthetics, is how to do that? The answer is in the use and design of protocols. Protocols facilitate modulation. Like code, protocols are not intrinsically digital, in that we have always had protocols as a crucial enabler of communication. Protocols are a kind of code, both in the social communicative sense, and in the sense that they must be coded into any entity that intends to make use of them. In relation to code, the protocol is a formalisation of the decisions as to how to modulate data. The coding and use of protocols encapsulates the entire modulation process, and therefore is of primary interest to an aesthetics of digital virtual environments.

Nearly all protocols we avail ourselves of when working with networked digital data have been predetermined and operate in the realm that might be characterized as below consciousness. Some of these of course are based on interface metaphors from the pre-digital era, such as, when using a text editor or word processor, physically pressing the 'w' key will display a lower case 'w' on the screen, and these so-called intuitive metaphors (because they directly model behaviors that have been learned previously) usually go unquestioned until a different modulation parameter is enacted, like when the 'w' key means to move a player avatar forward in a realtime 3d virtual environment, or when it means to save a file in vi's command mode.[12] These may seem trivial examples, but they are interesting because they both have 'creation myths', of various contestability, around why these modulations were chosen (for vi, 'w' stands for 'write', and for the walking avatar, it supposedly either represents 'w' for 'walk' or the pragmatic decision of the right-handed programmer/designer John Carmack when creating *Doom*), and they are good illustrations of both the arbitrariness and generational transmissibility of these decisions-as-tropes.

Such examples operate at a fairly macro level, but decisions as to how to modulate occur throughout all levels and processes of digital computing, to the extent that they can be said to constitute it. At every step along the way, or link in the chain as Simondon might put it - highlighting the bivalent, synergetic nature of these sites of modulation - decisions must be made as to what parameters will be used for modulation and how they will be enacted. This is true at both micro- and macro-scales, for example where a bit will be written; how data will be visually represented in an infographic; how the state of a Boolean switch will be enacted by a digital entity; how a person's social context will be displayed on a social network website. This is where a primary aspect of an aesthetic of digital virtual environments lays. Often, as Kitchin and Dodge (2011) discuss in relation to control systems, these protocol decisions are presented as natural or intuitive or pre-given or inexorable. An aesthetics of digital virtual environments is very sensitive to such elisions and conflations regarding the decision making around protocol parameters.

Visualisation and Pre-Convergent Attitude

In particular, an aesthetics of digital virtual environments is not interested in work that simply visualises either the process itself or some data source in a teleological or deterministic manner without surrendering to the interactive indeterminacy of the modulation chain. Such a teleological visualisation is simply engaging a pre-convergent attitude that perpetuates the dominance of romantic formalism (Badiou, 2006, p. 133), and contributes nothing to a new understanding of a digital society. As Alain Badiou (2006) says in his *Manifesto of*

Affirmationist Art, "it is better to do nothing than to work formally toward making visible what the West declares to exist" (p. 148).[13]

Modulation as Performance

Boris Groys (2008, p. 85) intuits this, as a consequence of the fundamental generifying operation of the digital, when he says that the digitising of images turns the visual arts into performing arts. By saying "every performance is an interpretation and every interpretation is a betrayal, a misuse" (Groys, 2008, p. 85), he is identifying the entire modulatory assemblage of the digital as performative, which is a useful way of understanding the historical vacuum that is ostensibly created by the convergence of all differentiable media that renders meaningless such distinctions as visual art or text. The performance paradigm provides a method of engaging positively and non-teleologically with the indeterminate nature of the interactions in a modulation chain, because a performance is intrinsically indeterminate *in its process*. Every moment of a performance represents a site of modulation - how will the performer interpret this moment, influenced by the previous moment, anticipating the next by creating it? This performance paradigm raises a concept that is crucial to an intrinsic aesthetics of digital virtual environments: *time*.

Interactivity and Time

To state the obvious, this is because digital virtual environments are interactive, that is, they are able to be intervened in by a person in real time (ie, 'on the fly')[14] (Nusselder, 2009, p. 36). This apparently simple point is a distinguishing quality of digital virtual environments, not because the user is interacting with the artwork, which has been a pre-digital element of art since at least Yoko Ono's *Cut Piece* in 1964 (Stiles, 1998, p. 278),[15] but because the user is engaging with the modulation process itself, which is already indeterminate and interactive. In this sense, the interactivity is defined by the generifying of both the user and the artist into another bivalent site of modulation, not less important or determinant than any other site, and not more.

Initially, the implications for time would seem to be obvious; interactivity takes time. But this is not unique to interactivity, all art forms take time, most obviously music and video or cinema, but even still images, which Agamben (2013) says "have actually charged themselves with time" (p. 4). He also quotes Bill Viola as saying that "the essence of the visual medium is time" (Agamben, 2013, p. 5). Simondon's philosophy would reconfigure this concept to say that interactivity *makes time*. This is an oversimplification, but it serves to introduce Simondon's concept that time occupies no special ontological position in becoming. More specifically, time emerges "from the pre-individual, just like the other dimensions that determine individuation" (Simondon, 1993, p. 315). This would be a conception of time similar to Quentin Meillassoux's (2008, p. 101), and therefore invites consideration of the tension between a conception of time as an ordinary dimension, and both the engineering concept of time, for example as illustrated by Chun (2011), "signals propagate *in* time over space" (p. 26, emphasis added); and the physicist's concept of time, i.e,, "that time exists because the vacuum speed of light is constant", or in the jargon "time arises when a 4-dimensional real smooth manifold is endowed with a 1-foliation, that is, with a nowhere vanishing smooth vector-field" (Chaitin et al, 2012, p. 122). In other words, that time is ground (Roffe, 2012, pp. 63-64). We might characterise this tension as the difference between the arrow of time and the undulating iterative cycles of rhythm, where in fact the former is but a strictly quantised version of the latter.

Contingent Time

Understanding time as an interactive product of modulation chains helps us understand how time can be both strict and undulating simultaneously, in many different modes. Lewis Mumford (1963) recognised that the strict regimenting of rhythm allowed industrial-era captialists to instrumentalise power, not because of technics, but with technics, formalising time as power (pp. 196-199). Adrian Mackenzie (2002) uses a Simondonian approach to show that such regimented time has, in the interest of power, come to be understood as autonomous, but in fact is "purely neither social nor technical," rather it emerges from "an articulation of diverse realities" (p. 98).

Digital networks have brought this contingent, non-autonomous, nature of time into stark relief both technically and socially. Technically, the phenomenon of lag in realtime interactive environments forces us to rethink our acceptance of time as an autonomous authority regulating being. Lag is the delay between, for example, a key being pushed and the result of that keystroke appearing in the virtual environment.[16] Socially, the global access of the network highlights the diverse subjectification to timezones of people who are not co-present, such timezones being nominally based on the movement of the earth in relation to the sun, but in fact emerging from a complex chain of modulations between planetary movement, people and technics (Mumford, 1963, p. 201).

Time and Power

An aesthetics of digital virtual art must be sensitive to these considerations of time. Since the digital generifies everything, it is important to recognise that political, ethical and social values then become protocols in play in the modulation chain. Simondon and Mumford both recognised this (Simondon, 1992, p. 306-310; 2010, p. 229~;

Mumford, 1963, p. 60-106). Digital capitalists like Facebook and Google also recognise this, indeed it could be said to constitute their philosophy. In other words, the digital can be used to enact libertarian capitalist values (Schmidt and Cohen, 2013) just as readily as it can be used to invite participation in a caring and diverse egalitarian social ethics (Braidotti, 2014). Those who understand this in the contemporary era have a power advantage over those who don't, and this partially explains the success of Facebook or Instagram, which are cynically marketed as self-empowering expressions of the digital, when in fact they represent the most anachronistic pre-convergent circumscribing of a universal machine into a single-use machine. All contemporary 'social media', a term that instantly identifies itself as a rear-view-mirror retrofit, recognise time as power, relying as they do on users *spending time* working to produce content for them with no recompense other than a vaguely defined 'status' or 'reputation', as well as spending time consuming that content, with time measured and tracked by clicks, 'likes' and views. An individual's time becomes just another set of generic digital data, able to be modulated through any kind of ideological protocol. In the case of contemporary digital capitalism, the protocol tends to modulate into a deceptive display constructed around a false sense of self-empowerment and individualism hiding an exploitative manipulation of the generifying operation of digital data in the service of massive profit. As Agamben (2013) says, "the real paradigm of life in the modern era is not movement but time" (p. 4).

Digital Virtual Environments and Relational Aesthetics

Because the big digital capitalist network apps (ie, 'social media') exploit the model of a static individual while realising the app using Simondonian concepts of dynamic individuation, the entire contemporary social networking model represents an impoverished hijacking of Bourriaud's (2002) relational aesthetics, by exploiting "intersubjective encounters ... in which meaning is elaborated collectively" (Bishop, 2004, p. 54). Alarmingly, in a stark illustration of the eminently plastic and generic nature of digital data, social media apps do this by converting "the realm of human interactions and its social context" (Bourriaud, 2002, p. 5) into the individual "space of private consumption" (Bourriaud, 2002, p. 6). The ability to do this relies on the plastic status of time in digital networks, enabling the exploitation of time as power.

The Would-Have-Happened

The plastic and non-autonomous nature of time is further illustrated by the weird phenomenon of the *would-have-happened* that can be encountered when so-called 'artificial life' or 'artificial evolution' is enacted in multi-user digital virtual environments. This is where a user may initiate a sequence of, say, artificial evolution and then log out before the sequence has played itself out. [17] If no other user logs in to or visits that particular section of the multi-user digital virtual environment, [18] and then the original user logs back in again some time after the artificial life sequence has finished, the user will encounter the curious state of something that *never happened* presenting literally *as if it had happened*. An instrumentalist rationalisation might object that the system simply ran through the calculations-that-would-have-happened in the instant that the user logged back in again. Even this explanation relies on an utterly plastic and non-authoritative model of time, nominally taking its reference from CPU (Central Processing Unit) cycles, and ultimately is unviable due to the complex set of indeterminate modulatory interactions required to maintain the digital audiovisual illusion of a digital virtual world that is subject to a version of the authoritative time that runs the psychosocial world of human beings.

An aesthetics of digital virtual environments would attend very seriously to all of these considerations of time.

Virtually Retroactivated Pre-Convergent Aesthetics

It should be clear by now that digital virtual environments can not be considered a primarily visual medium, even though they are often treated as such, in a McLuhanistic rear view mirror operation. If anything, the closest precedent artists have for operating within digital virtual environments would be musical practice, particularly of the latter half of the 20th Century, but it would also be a mistake to consider sound, or any discrete sensible phenomenon or practice, as the primary characteristic of digital virtual environments. The temptation to define such characteristics arises from pre-digital notions of media and art, with such descriptors as 'visual art', 'sound art', 'video art' and so forth. In fact, as W.J.T. Mitchell (2005, p. 257) shows, it has never really been possible to consider any art or media form as restricted to one sense. This understanding itself is converged and virtualised as content in the post-convergent digital era.

At the same time, since digital virtual environments are a post-convergent medium, it follows that all prior concepts of aesthetics, ie, those concerned with audiovisual display, are contained within it. More precisely, these aesthetic considerations, or elements, are digitally converged within the environment, and the retroactive virtuality that is thus activated contributes to the excess that comprises: the pre-converged sense of the element; its post-converged sense (where it recognises itself as content of itself); and all the digital operations - ie, modulations - required to achieve this state. The two most prominent of these elements, in terms of display, are colour and sound.

Digital Virtual Colour

The great modernist explorer of colour, Yves Klein, could have been intuiting the digital when he said in 1959, "the painter of the future will be a colorist of a kind never seen before, and that will occur in the next generation. And without doubt it is through color that I have little by little become acquainted with the Immaterial" (Klein, 1992, p. 804).

Mumford, in his 1934 work *Technics and Civilization* (1963) talks of an "esthetic compensation" of colour in art for the incursion of technology into the physical environment of people, where "instead of the harsh realities one encountered under the sun, there was a veil of tender lavenders, grays, pearly yellows, wistful blues." (p. 199). This is an example of the modulatory nature of art mediating between previously disparate realms, of the environmental effects of technology on the physical and the psychosocial, by the use of colour.

The crucial consideration for an aesthetics of digital virtual environments is that colour is but one more generic element in the modulation process from data-as-data to data-as-display, rather than an element that has a pre-given materiality that defines what operations can be performed with it, and therefore *any data* may be displayed as colour. This is the crucial point that is missed by Lev Manovich (2001, p. 300) who, even while attempting to understand the loss of indexical relationship between digital and physical reality, doesn't understand that an image that has been digitised is *no longer an image*. This crucial point is also missed by colour historian and Manovich critic Richard Misek (2010) who, while acknowledging the dematerialised nature of digital colour, adopts a positivist tone to conflate a protocol, i.e., "24-bit color space" (p. 165), with a pre-given indexical materialism.

Digital colour *is* displayed via digitally interfaced light emitting devices which ostensibly conform to an emissive mode of colour known as the additive model of red, green and blue, and these elements *are* discretely accessible from within the protocol via code, and indeed yield the unique ability to manipulate transparency and opacity of displayed colours to a fine degree, but this is in no way a materially pre-given relationship. Further showing the absolutely arbitrariness and absolute privilege of protocols in digital virtual environments, even though the colour mixing model in digital space is usually displayed as additive, once a colour is chosen and 'applied' in the digital virtual environment, it will conform to a *subtractive* model of colour mixing. An aesthetics of digital virtual environments would understand, as foundational, that up until the moment of its display, digital colour does not constitute anything that can in any way be thought of as a colour; it is a set of digital data that if modulated according to certain protocols will display in the world as coloured light.[19]

Once such a display has occurred, the pre-convergent aesthetics and qualities of colour can of course come into play. These aesthetics and qualities have been the subject of speculation among some of history's greatest thinkers and artists since ancient times[20] and appeared to be no closer to yielding to any unified philosophical, psychological and physical system of knowledge even before the virtualising operations of the digital convergence recursively complicated an already extremely complicated field (Crone, 1999, p. 233). This is apparently because colour is a "human sense" rather than a material phenomenon in the world, and is *time-dependent*.[21] (Hanson, 2012, p. 3). In this way, we might call colour the music of the eyes.

Digital Virtual Sound

Once again, the crucial point about sound in digital virtual environments is that, due to its generic ontological status as digital data, any data may be displayed as sound. Once modulated into an audible display state, virtual sound objects may be manipulated in a manner identical with virtual visual objects, or any other kind of virtual object. It is here that it becomes clear just how different the work of art in virtual environments is from previous artforms, even though all previous artforms may be virtualised and emulated within virtual environments.

Given the general historical lack of indexical tendencies in the history of music and sound art, this pre-convergent history may provide some clues as to an appropriate aesthetics of digital virtual environments. It is possible to see a relationship between the radically generifying digital and Pierre Schaeffer's (2009, p. 76-79) concept of "sonorous objects" in an "acousmatic" situation. This is the condition of sound dissociated from its material cause through technological means, and its associated listening state. Ignoring for the moment Schaeffer's (2009) modernist, potentially technodeterministic overtones, his "acousmatic procedure" understands "the most general musical situation," where the listener forgets "every reference to instrumental causes" and devotes themselves "entirely and exclusively to *listening*" (p. 81, emphasis in original).

Where an aesthetics of digital virtual environments diverges from Schaeffer (2009) is when his acousmatic approach denies "cultural conditioning" (p. 81). For Schaeffer, this was to remove the listening experience from what he saw as the overdetermined concept of music, so that sounds that had previously been excluded from a cultural definition of music could now occupy an equal place alongside more culturally conventional sounds produced by musical instruments. This interesting operation on an already abstract and non-indexical artform can retrospectively be seen in Simondonian terms as an individuation that mediates two previously disparate fields ('music' and 'sound' or 'noise'), thereby bringing forth a new associated milieu where Schaeffer's concern to remove cultural conditioning is understandable in his context. An aesthetics of digital virtual environments, on the other hand, must always primarily bear in mind the psychosocial and cultural conditions and associated ideologies that have informed the development of protocols. As Jacques Attali says in his 1977 work *Noise: The Political Economy of Music*, "any theory of power today must include a theory of the localization of noise and its endowment of form." (p. 6) We can reconfigure this assertion to say that any theory of power today must include a theory and aesthetics of the radical generifiying operation of the digital and the protocols that are employed to remodulate digital data into display.

As with colour, and every other pre-convergent extant element, the sheer scope of possibility that is offered to the sound artist or musician confronted with digital virtual environments can sometimes cause a reactionary impulse to reconstrain the liberated concept of sound (as radically dematerialised sonorous object without origin) based on weak interface metaphors from the physical world. As noted above, since music can be seen as already non-indexical, it can sometimes be difficult to appreciate the implications of the generifying operation of the digital, specifically in relation to the difference between a recorded sound and a synthesised sound, a difference that literally has no meaning within a digital virtual environment, an environment that is capable, to speak in pre-convergent terms in order to illustrate the absurdity of same, of simultaneously synthesising and recording a sound at the same time, or recording a sound *before* it has been synthesised, or replaying a sound that *would have been* synthesised had somebody been present to listen to it. The inadequacy of Schaeffer's phenomenological approach is clearly revealed in these examples, and it becomes obvious that an aesthetics of digital virtual environments will stay attendant to the modulations that result in sonic display and their interplay with all other modulations and display states. All digital data is generically equivalent and therefore may be modulated in the same manner, so that a 'sound' can be 'animated', and not only

in pre-convergent terms of animating parameter changes over time, but the 'sound' itself may be animated in 'space', since neither the sound nor the space can be said to exist in any other terms than as digital data modulated into a display state. The very strong temptation to index digital virtual environments to physical space must be resisted at all times, otherwise we end up with nonsensical, reactionary metaphors like a 360 degree speaker moving through space of its own volition with no energy source. Since such a thing is impossible in physical space, an attempt to metaphorise such a thing in a digital virtual environment can lead only to weak romantic formalism that represents a surrender of power to digital capitalism.

CONCLUSION

An aesthetics of digital virtual environments must closely attend to the conflations and elisions offered by metaphors that attempt to index digital virtual environments to physical space, recognising the romantic formalist impulses that drive this and therefore serve only, in Badiou's (2006) terms, to reinforce the power of global digital capitalism dedicated to the enslavement of all people in a global sweatshop of metaphor-based identity production. How is it possible for art to engage with the digital networks and subjects of digital capitalism without reinforcing and promoting the values and practices of digital capitalism?[22] The answer lies in the concept of realtime performance, and the work of digital virtual art becomes parameter selection; selecting the parameters for modulation from digital data into display is the work of digital virtual art. Digital capitalist networks choose parameters that ensure a smooth time, an eternal present with no reference to past or future, in order that repetition can be presented, and consumed, as innovation. Digital virtual artworks must, therefore, be constructed using parameters that are aware of time as differentiator. Since time is the medium in the performance of the digital, self-assembling digitally networked artworks must incorporate, and present means towards, time in its role as the constructor of difference. Time on networks, distributed and un-arrow-like, becomes a material in the construction of resistance against the entirely smoothing impulses of digital capitalism, which not merely brooks no resistance, but is incapable of understanding resistance, since its libertarian vision is to absorb everyone and everything into a smooth continuum of consumption in the eternal present, where differences in cultural nuance and time are simply problems to be overcome (Schmidt and Cohen, 2013, p. 19).

Digital virtual artists must select parameters that ensure modulations that draw attention to the underlying technologies and networks being used, that lay bare the crushing solipsism of predictive filters, that invite people to consider their position as slave-producer-consumers for a handful of giant libertarian capitalists and recombine the same tools into an individual production machine that teases apart and frays the all-too-shiny web of filaments that bond us in our narcissistic stupor. Again, this is a difficult task when the very networks of bondage are presenting themselves as the empowering liberators. But Groys (2008) is right to insist that the "logic of equal aesthetic rights" (p. 16) actually results in an autonomy of art that has a positive, affirmative imperative as its contextual specificity transcends the smooth parade of digital capitalism's right-now.

REFERENCES

Agamben, G. (2013). *Nymphs*. London: Seagull Books.

Attali, J. (2009). *Noise: The Political Economy of Music*. Minneapolis: University of Minnesota Press.

Badiou, A. (2004). Fifteen Theses on Contemporary Art. *Lacanian Ink*. (23).

Badiou, A. (2006). *Third Sketch of a Manifesto of Affirmationist Art. Polemics*. London: Verso.

Bourriaud, N. (2002). Relational Aesthetics. *Collection Documents sur l'art. Les Presses Du Reel*. Retrieved from http://www.lespressesdureel.com

Braidotti, R. (2013). *The Posthuman*. Cambridge: Polity Press.

Chaitin, G. (1998). *The Limits of Mathematics*. Singapore: Springer-Verlag.

Chaitin, G., da Costa, N. C. A., & Doria, F. A. (2012). *Gödel's Way: Adventures in an Undecidable Universe*. CRC Press.

Chun, W. (2011). *Programmed Visions: Software and Memory*. Cambridge: MIT Press. doi:10.7551/mitpress/9780262015424.001.0001

Clemens, J., Dodds, C., & Nash, A. (2007). *Babelswarm. Mixed reality artwork, Photographic prints, single channel video and Second Life installation*. Australia: Lismore Regional Gallery.

Clemens, J., Dodds, C., & Nash, A. (2009). *Autoscopia. Mixed reality artwork, single channel video and Second Life installation*. National Portrait Gallery of Australia.

Colebrook, C. (2010). *Deleuze and the Meaning of Life*. London: Continuum.

Combes, M. (2013). *Gilbert Simondon and the Philosophy of the Transindividual*. Cambridge: MIT Press.

Crone, R. A. (1999). *A History of Color. Dordrect*. Kluwer Academic Publishers. doi:10.1007/978-94-007-0870-9

De Landa, M. (1993). *Non-organic Life. Incorporations*. New York: Zone Books.

De Landa, M. (2002). *Intensive Science and Virtual Philosophy*. London: Continuum.

Deleuze, G. (1988). *Spinoza: Practical Philosophy*. San Francisco: City Lights Books.

Deleuze, G. (1990). *Spinoza: Expressionism in Philosophy*. New York: Zone Books.

Derrida, J. (1982). *Différance. Margins of Philosophy*. Brighton: Harvester Press.

Floridi, L. (2011). *The Philosophy of Information*. New York: Oxford University Press. doi:10.1093/acprof:oso/9780199232383.001.0001

Floridi, L. (2014). *The 4th Revolution: How the Infosphere is Reshaping Human Reality*. Oxford: Oxford University Press.

Fredkin, E. (2003). An Introduction to Digital Philosophy. *International Journal of Theoretical Physics*, 42(2). p. 189–247). Retrieved from: http://64.78.31.152/wp-content/uploads/2012/08/intro-to-DP.pdf

Grosz, E. (2012). *Identity and Individuation: Some Feminist Reflections. Gilbert Simondon: Technology and Being*. Edinburgh: Edinburgh University Press.

Groys, B. (2008). *Art Power*. Cambridge: MIT Press.

Guattari, F. (1995). *Chaosmosis: an ethico-aesthetic paradigm*. Bloomington: Indiana University Press.

Hanson, A. R. (2012). *What is Colour. Colour Design: Theories and Applications*. Oxford: Woodhead Publishing.

Hayles, N. K. (2012). *How We Think: Digital Media and Contemporary Technogenesis*. Chicago: University of Chicago Press. doi:10.7208/chicago/9780226321370.001.0001

Iliadis, A. (2013a). A New Individuation:Deleuze's Simondon Connection. *MediaTropes eJournal*, IV(1), 83–100.

Iliadis, A. (2013b). Informational Ontology: The Meaning of Gilbert Simondon's Concept of Individuation. *Communication+1*, 2(5). Retrieved from http://scholarworks.edu/cpo/vol2/iss1/5

Kitchin, R., & Dodge, M. (2011). *Code/Space*. Cambridge: MIT Press. doi:10.7551/mitpress/9780262042482.001.0001

Kittler, F. (1999). *Gramophone, Film, Typewriter*. Stanford: Stanford University Press.

Klein, Y. (1992). *Sorbonne Lecture. Art in Theory 1900-1990*. Oxford: Blackwell Publishers.

LaMarre, T. (2013). Afterword: Humans and Machines. In M. Combes (Ed.), *Gilbert Simondon and the Philosophy of the Transindividual*. Cambridge: MIT Press.

Lévy, P. (1998). *Becoming Virtual: Reality in the Digital Age*. New York: Plenum Press.

Mackenzie, A. (2002). *Transductions: Bodies and Machines at Speed*. London: Continuum.

Maturana, H. R., & Varela, F. J. (1980). *Autopoiesis: The Organization of the Living. Autopoiesis and Cognition: The Realization of the Living*. Dordrecht: D. Reidel Publishing.

McCormick, J., & Nash, A. (2008). *Ways To Wave. Mixed reality artwork, arduino circuit board, wood, acrylic and Second Life installation. 01SJ Festival*. California: San Jose Museum of Art.

McCormick, J. & Nash, A. (2010 - 2012). *Reproduction*. Artists' Residency, Neutral Ground Gallery, Regina Saskatchewan, Canada. 2011; Screen Space Gallery, Melbourne, Australia. Hine, 2012.

McLuhan, M. (2001). *Understanding Media*. New York: Routledge Classics.

McLuhan, M., & Fiore, Q. (2001). *The Medium is the Massage. Corte Madera.* Gingko Press.

Miellassoux, Q. (2008). *After Finitude: An Essay on The Necessity of Contingency.* London: Continuum.

Mills, S. (2011). FCJ-127 Concrete Software: Simondon's mechanology and the techno-social. *Fibreculture Journal* 18. Retrieved from http://eighteen.fibreculturejournal.org/2011/10/09/fcj-127-concrete-software-simondon's-mechanology-and-the-techno-social/print/

Mitchell, W. J. T. (2005, August 01). There Are No Visual Media. *Journal of Visual Culture, 4*(2), 257–266. doi:10.1177/1470412905054673

Mumford, L. (1963). *Technics and Civilization.* Orlando: Harcourt Brace & Company.

Munster, A. (2006). *Materializing New Media: Embodiment in Information Aesthetics.* Hanover: Dartmouth College Press.

Munster, A. (2013). *An Aesthesia of Networks.* Cambridge: MIT Press.

Nash, A. (2012). Affect and the Medium of Digital Data. *Fibreculture Journal* 21. Retrieved from http://twentyone.fibreculturejournal.org/fcj-148-affect-and-the-medium-of-digital-data/

Nusselder, A. (2009). *Interface Fantasy: a Lacanian cyborg ontology.* Cambridge: MIT Press.

Parisi, L. (2004). *Abstract Sex: Philosophy, Biotechnology and the Mutations of Desire.* London: Continuum.

Parisi, L. (2013). *Contagious Architecture: Computation, Aesthetics, and Space.* Cambridge: MIT Press.

Roffe, J. (2012). Time and Ground. *Angelaki: Journal of the Theoretical Humanities, 17*(1), 57–67.

Schaeffer, P. (2004). *Acousmatics. Audio Culture: Readings in Modern Music.* New York: Continuum.

Schmidt, E., & Cohen, J. (2013). *The New Digital Age: Reshaping the Future of People, Nations and Business.* New York: Alfred A. Knopf.

Simondon, G. (1993). *The Genesis of the Individual. Incorporations.* New York: Zone Books.

Simondon, G. (2009). The Position of the Problem of Ontogenesis. *Parrhesia, 7,* 4–16.

Simondon, G. (2010). The Limits of Human Progress: A Critical Study. *Cultural Politics, 6*(2), 229–236. doi:10.2752/175174310X12672016548405

Simondon, G. (2012). Technical Mentality. In *Gilbert Simondon: Technology and Being.* Edinburgh: Edinburgh University Press.

Stiegler, B. (1998). *Technics and Time* (Vol. 1). Stanford: Stanford University Press.

Stiles, K. (1998). Uncorrupted Joy: International Art Actions. *Out of Actions: between performance and the object, 1949–1979,* Paul Schimmel (ed.), New York: MoCA Los Angeles. Cited in http://www.medienkunstnetz.de/works/cut-piece/

Varela, F. (1992). *The Reenchantment of the Concrete. Incorporations.* New York: Zone Books.

Wolfram, S. (2002). *A New Kind of Science.* Champaign: Wolfram Media, Inc.

KEY TERMS AND DEFINITIONS

Aesthetics: The critical study and analysis of art, often extending to culture and nature. As part of the Western philosophical tradition, aesthetics has been practiced by key thinkers throughout history – including Plato, Kant, Nietzsche and Deleuze – and is often linked with ethics.

Digital Data: The 'stuff' of computers, the ontologically indeterminate collection of binary symbolic logic, often stored and transmitted as electromagnetic impulses. Popularly, though somewhat misleadingly, portrayed as "ones and zeros".

Digital Virtual Environments: Any computer-facilitated, conceptual environment able to be accessed in some form by people. Examples include multi-user and single-user game worlds and social networks. Digital virtual environments are distinct from non-digital virtual environments – such as stories, music, imagination and board games – in respect of being enabled or facilitated by digital technology.

Display: Any mode in which digital data becomes sensible to people, whether audible, visible, haptic or any other form of sensible perception. For this to occur, digital data must be modulated into a state of display through the use of protocols and/or interfaces. Display also refers to any mode in which digital data becomes accessible to another set of digital data. Again, for this occur both sets of data must be modulated into a display state via protocol or interface.

Modulation: The process of rendering any digital data into a display state. An example might be displaying a photograph on the screen of a smartphone or displaying an mp3 file as a stream of audible signals through a speaker or headphone. In this chapter, modulation is presented as related to a philosophical notion of individuation.

Post-Convergent: Referring to media, a post-convergent medium is the dynamic whole – or new medium – that is created by the convergence of all prior media, plus the excess that is both created by, and is required to create, such a convergence. Here, digital virtual environments are held to be post-convergent.

ENDNOTES

[1]   I use the term 'digital virtual environment' to acknowledge pre- and non-digital virtual environments, which Lévy (1998, 28) quotes Serres as including "imagination, memory, knowledge, and religion," to which I would explicitly add music, along with any other shared conceptual environment (stories, art, myths, games and so on). See Nusselder (2009, 33-53) for a discussion of this.

[2]   Having fallen out of favour after the hyperbole of the mid- to late-1990s, the term *virtual reality* is currently (2014) enjoying a resurgence, thanks to the popularity of a new generation of startlingly 1990s-like head mounted devices for realtime 3D graphics display.

[3]   Some of the ideas in this section were presented in a different form as a talk at the 24th Annual Society of Animation Studies Conference, Melbourne, Australia, June 2012.

[4]   Braidotti does this without explicitly referencing Simondon. It is very interesting that Guattari himself never mentions Simondon by name, given the similarity with Simondon of some aspects of Guattari's machinic philosophy, along with Guattari's decades-long collaboration with Deleuze, who was himself very heavily influenced by Simondon (Iliadis, 2013)

[5]   See Mills (2011) for the confusion that arises when attempting to rationalise networked digital environments in Simondonian terms without understanding the fundamental importance of the plastic, generic state of digital data.

6   "A body's structure is the composition of its relation. What a body can do corresponds to the nature and limits of its capacity to be affected." (Deleuze, 1990: 218)

7   This phrase is no more or less absurd than *artificial life*

8   Some of the ideas in this section were presented in a different format as a talk at the CODE 2012 conference, Melbourne, Australia, November 2012

9   Conveniently, the word "programming" in the phrase "programming code" can function as both a verb and an adjective.

10   Plato considered writing as a memory that is exterior to the human mind, a kind of 'outsourcing' of memory so to speak. Although Plato considered this undesirable, Jacques Derrida famously deconstructed the concept of hypomnesis to show that the human mind, and therefore human culture, is in a constant evolving interplay process with the written word, each informing the development of the other. This, very crudely, is a summary of Derida's concept of *différance*. (1982) Also of interest here is Stiegler's sense of tertiary memory, (1998: 255) where a tool is a kind of grammaticised memory. The concept of code as writing that I am discussing is different from, but related to, these two readings of writing as memory.

11   The two postulates are, first, that "[t]he subsets are relatively detachable from the whole of which they are a part," and second, that "if one wants to understand a being completely, one must study it by considering it in its entelechy, and not in its inactivity or its static state." (Simondon, 2012: 3-4)

12   vi is a text editor for Unix systems

13   In a previous version of his manifesto (2004), Badiou used the word "Empire" instead of "the West." We can assume he means "global capitalism."

14   Given the following exposition, it becomes clear that the phrase 'real time' can only be used in the vernacular sense to mean 'on the fly', since in strict grammatical terms the phrase is meaningless.

15   *Cut Piece* was an interactive live art piece, where audience members were asked to use a pair of scissors to cut pieces of Ono's dress off her while she sat on a stage. Cited at http://www.medienkunstnetz.de/works/cut-piece/

16   It also manifests, for example, as 'buffering' when loading a video on a web page, to ensure the computer has enough video in its buffer so that playback is slower than the speed of the video downloading, to give the illusion of realtime playback.

17   Such as in my work, *One, Another* (2009), see video documentation linked from http://adamnash.net.au

18   If they do, we encounter the same problem but as a recursive, or what Simondon might call *reticulated*, case, which is complex and interesting, but for the sake of clarity in example, I will ignore it for now.

19   It may be, continuing with Klein's statement above, that there is some relationship between the digital and the complex immateriality of colour. This is likely to be related to the affect cycle and so the reader is referred to my article *Affect and the Medium of Digital Data*. (2012)

20   Aristotle, Goethe, Schopenhauer and Wittgenstein are but a few of these thinkers, and a simple web search will provide texts and references of these works. It would be difficult to name an artist who hasn't explicitly engaged with the concept of colour. Again, a simple web search will provide significant references.

21   Given our discussion of time in digital virtual environments, this has enormous implications that there is no room to discuss here.

22   The following points are based on research I carried out with Justin Clemens and Christopher Dodds

APPENDIX: SELECTED ARTWORKS BY THE AUTHOR

The above are some of the questions that I have been attending to in the past few years via my work in realtime 3D audiovisual interactive animation. *Ways To Wave* was a collaboration between John McCormick and myself, presented at the 01 SJ Festival at the San Jose Museum of Art in 2008). The work comprised an assemblage formed between a physical controller installed in the museum and an audiovisual volumetric sculpture in the commercial realtime 3D multiuser environment called Second Life. The physical controller is constructed of colored etched perspex, in a lotus-like arrangement of 3 concentric circles of 8 petals, which can be played with by users. The position, angle and velocity of the petals each controls a different parameter of the virtual artwork, such as size, color, sound volume, and speed. None of these parameters were fixed in any linear sense, as is usually the case with hard-ware controllers for virtual environments, such as a joystick's position predictably dictating the speed of a player character, rather the parameters and their resulting animations were dynamically generated through the playing of the work itself, which could be effected either by physically visiting the gallery or virtually logging in to the art work. This facilitated a collaboration across non-linear temporal space, dynamically reconfiguring physical and virtual space, visual and aural media, in a symbiotic lattice of experience. In technical terms it is unclear whether such an assemblage may be considered autopoeitic or allopoeitic. More accurately, it seems possible, using various readings of Varela's theory as discussed above, to convincingly argue for both or either. Perhaps Varela's concepts, then, really are only useful when applied to the biological world and are unable, like media, to differentiate themselves in the digital without applying arbitrarily restrictive boundaries or thresholds in the manner of Mcluhan's rear view mirror (Mcluhan and Fiore, 2001, p. 75).

Babelswarm was a collaboration between myself, Christopher Dodds and Justin Clemens. It was the result of the inaugural Australia Council Multi-User Virtual Environment Artist-in-Residence program. It was staged physically in the Lismore Regional Gallery, NSW, Australia and in the realtime 3D multi-user virtual environment Second Life. Activated by the voices of visitors in the real world gallery and chat messaging from virtual visitors in Second Life, a swarm of letter cubes- programmed to seek out their original word position- slowly builds a morphing, virtual Tower of Babel. This tower is constructed from the utterances of visitors to it, constantly reconfiguring itself according to the "artificial stupidity" of the individual letter forms. As Justin Clemens wrote in his introduction to the work:

What sorts of conceptual figures are available to think such a thing? The very old: the Tower of Babel from the Book of Genesis, which melds the frightening possibilities of technology, language, and power in a single startling image. And the very new: swarm intelligence as an ideal that expresses how in-numerable different individuals can nonetheless come to produce radical innovations in excess of the powers of any one of them -and in the midst of apparent disorder. Babelswarm is a project that draws on the most traditional elements of religion, art, and literature, as it engages with the challenges of a scientific and technological age (Clemens, Dodds, Nash, 2007).

Autoscopia is a virtual artwork by Justin Clemens, Christopher Dodds and myself, commissioned by the National Portrait Gallery of Australia. Autoscopia allows users to enter names to create virtual portraits based on internet searches. These searches manifest as web portraits dynamically generated by search results, and audiovisual animated sculptures dynamically generated in Second Life. The Second Life component closed at the end of 2010, but the web portraits continue to grow, all the while tweeting their existence, recursively feeding themselves back into the results of future searches. Autoscopia's Second Life portraits are built using data from internet-based vanity searches conducted within the Second Life installation. Each name creates a unique outcome composed of 27 limbs. Each limb is fed data from websites such as Google, Facebook, Twitter (and other more invasive, though publicly available, sources) etc, with colours, geometry and audio affected by variations in search volume. Data is then re-published via discrete web pages automatically composed through text and images collected during the search. The identity created will thereafter be reincorporated into future search results. Each portrait also tweets' its existence on Twitter, with both the web pages and Tweets looping back into future portraits, creating a kind of time-based network meta-animation.

Finally, *Reproduction* is an ongoing collaboration between myself and John McCormick. The work involves experimentation in audiovisual, performative, evolving, virtual entities spawning and reproducing in virtual environments, capable of intercommunication with the material world via various systems of motion and data capture. Loosely based on principles of artificial evolution, the parameters that we as the artists initially selected are, rather than the standard artificial evolution parameters like strength and fitness, all audiovisual performative parameters like red, green, blue, opacity, rhythm, timbre, tempo, tone (pitch) and so on. The entities 'evolve', 'reproduce', 'live' and 'die' over thousands of generations according to a constantly emergent evolution of these crude parameters that is informed, but not determined, by both their interaction with humans in the material world and with their interactions with each other. In other words the original parameter set becomes, after the first generation, virtualised content for the next emergent generation. All the while, the entities are organising (or perhaps socialising) and improvising movements and 'songs' amongst themselves, whilst observing and improvising with any human visitors to their 'space'. The space in this case means both their digital virtual environment (accessible by humans via an online multi-user environment) as well as the physical space of wherever the work happens to be being exhibited. In the latter case, motion and data capture are used by the entities to perceive humans, while a modulated audiovisual display allows humans to perceive the entities. Our desire, as artists, is to engage - using sound, music, movement and dance - in what we might call a "genuine" improvisation with these digital entities, by which we mean the human and digital performers share equal responsibility and value in the emergence of the improvised performance, dynamically building a shared performative vocabulary by learning from each other's nuances, gestures and performative suggestions.

With all of these works, it is only arbitrarily possible to define the thresholds between any unified system and its environment or medium. Once again, if evaluated via their display states, it is possible to identify semi-closed circuits that "generate their own stable states" and that "grow and evolve by drift" (Parisi, 2004, p. 142), but as with Ways To Wave it is not clear whether these systems, if they can be said to exist at all, are producing themselves or something other than themselves, and nor is it clear at all whether they can be said to be using their digital sensorimotor capabilities to enact a knowledge of their environment, precisely because it is unclear where the threshold of either the system or the environment lies. It is problems like these, unique to the era beyond medium ushered in by the digital that have led thinkers like Claire Colebrook and Bernard Stiegler to explore concepts of inorganic life and technogenesis, as well as scientists like Stephen Wolfram and Edward Fredkin to formulate - in a move emblematic of Kittler's (1999) assertion that "media determine our situation" (p.xxxix)- an hypothesis of the universe as a digital computer.

Chapter 2
Painting Machinima in *Second Life*:
Emerging Aesthetics in Virtual Filmmaking

Phylis Johnson
Southern Illinois University at Carbondale, USA

ABSTRACT

This chapter explores the technological and artistic revolution brought forth by machinima, particularly the rise among a community of filmmakers who would begin to express their stories and ideas through virtual worlds. Machinima has led to an emergence of scholarship on its aesthetics and cultural implications for digital society. The case of machinima as art is illustrated through a review of select works of virtual world filmmakers. This discussion also distinguishes the machinima concepts of game, virtual platform and more specifically virtual worlds to their varying degrees and relationships. It is here that one delineates the purpose of machinima within Massively Multiplayer Online Role-Playing Games (MMORPG) to that of virtual worlds such as Second Life (SL). In doing so, the author follows the innovation of machinima through the evolution of gaming and its extension to stand-alone ready-to-wear software to potentialities called forth by British filmmaker Peter Greenaway regarding Second Life.

WELCOME TO VIRTUAL ALCHEMY

In the exciting new arena of immersive Art which offers so much to the future of communications, Bryn Oh is an important, fascinating and innovative pioneer and should definitely be supported. - Peter Greenaway (cited by Au, 2012)

More than 70 years ago, Antonin Artaud's *The Theatre and Its Double* offered a glimpse of theatrical performance as "virtual art," a suspension of reality if for a mere moment. He first wrote his text in 1938, and it was first translated from French to English twenty years later. The alchemist, like a wizard, arranges "objects" and "images" to perform "a purely fictitious and illusory world" (Artaud, 1994, pp. 48-49). As in the virtual world, one might envision a parallel to Artaud's understanding of the spectator to that of the avatar: "The spectator is in the center and the spectacle surrounds" those within its midst (p. 81). The audience is as much a part of the experi-

DOI: 10.4018/978-1-4666-8384-6.ch002

ence as the actor, artist or filmmaker. That magic extends now to the virtual world (e.g., Figure 1).

A musician puppet on strings performs a song playing to a lyrical metaphor (Flimsey Freenote's *String Me Up*, 2010), a fast moving tale of humanity tied to time (Lainy Voom's *Push*, 2009), a stunningly provocative experimental video (ColeMarie Soleil's *My Friends are Robots*, 2009), and Bryn Oh's (2014a) virtual studio *Immersiva* that serves as an artistic inspiration for machinima, hers and those of others - all of these mediated creations represent stories and visual performances made within *Second Life*, an online world that has revolutionized cinema and revived theater as virtual alchemy. *Immersiva* is supported in part by British filmmaker Peter Greenaway and The Ontario Arts Council. As a simulated environment, it illustrates the visual and performative aspects of virtual worlds, of which machinima is a part.

Machinima is a fusion of cinema and machine, emerging as the recording of events within games, and eventually encompassing simulations or virtual worlds for the purpose of archival or creative capture. In virtual words, it has been coined real time animation and virtual filmmaking, particularly as it exists within *Second Life* (Johnson & Pettit, 2012). Conceptually, machinima involves multiple, intersecting histories of art, cinema, photography, television, computer graphics, animation, and gaming. Some of the key people in its development will be discussed here. An in-depth timely explanation also requires an in-depth look into how virtual worlds have transformed machinima. Imagine if one could live inside an online world, a place of imagination, and be whatever he or she wanted, even a filmmaker. Using simple tools as cameras, members can record their life story, those of others, or create a fictitious iden-

Figure 1. Enter the magic of Second Life. (© 2014, P. Johnson.).

tity, assume a role, and become a movie director or be featured in an animated movie. Machinima is typically screened on YouTube and Vimeo, as well as in-world on television sets, theaters, and auditoriums. It can be viewed in a virtual living room, drive-in, and some of the best at real life festivals. The goal of *Second Life* is not any sort of game play, but is founded and motivated by a spirit of creative play among experimenting and experimental visionaries; for that reason, the artistry of its animation is often realized within the process of creating, not necessarily in the final product, the machinima. The inventive, immersive, massive multi-participatory online virtual world *Second Life* has blossomed into a creative platform, with machinima, photography and sound converged onto the otherwise once blank canvas. This discussion is centered in the most developed, particularly artistically grounded, virtual world, that being *Second Life*. Massively Multiplayer Online Role-Playing Games (MMORPG), such as *The Sims* with a renewed focus on machinima, provide contributing influences to narrative possibilities. Other worlds, like *Open Sim*, have emerged as interesting, but underdeveloped, spaces for educators and artists to create communities apart from *Second Life* for varying reasons (i.e., seeking environments without sexualized overtones and negative publicity; avoiding the higher costs of land ownership; objections to perceived content restrictions due to confusing Linden Lab policy changes in recent years, and a desire to be pioneers in a new world; among others). The move from *Second Life* to *Open Sim* by some content creators has not yielded significant experimentation or membership beyond what has already been done in SL, and in fact those actively participating is a small core group. *Second Life* for this reason best illustrates the concept of real time animation, and the potential of a world community of virtual filmmakers represented via their personalized avatars. In this chapter, the author conveys multiple paths of machinima through its history and influences, as well as attempts to delineate

its unique emergence as an art form in virtual worlds with *Second Life* being the best example to date. Understanding an aesthetic framework for contextualizing machinima as and apart from cinema begins this discussion.

MACHINIMA AESTHETICS IN A VIRTUAL WORLD

Gilles Deleuze provides the example of Lewis Carroll's *Alice in Wonderland* in his first chapter, a very common metaphor and theme employed within the *Second Life* community of artists and creators. The game "has no other result than the work of art.. [and] that by which thought and art are real and disturbing reality, morality, and the economy of the world" (Deleuze, 1990, p. 60). His concept becomes relevant to a discussion of *Second Life*, a game without winning or losing but that of creative contemplation and creation. This virtual world is a "perceptual exchange" (Coleman, 2011, p. 59) that connects and disconnects alternately real and actual, always transforming each space, apart and unified, with the potential to positively impact the world, socially and artistically. This metaphor of "simultaneously convergent and divergent" existence is expounded in Helen Palmer's (2014) book *Deleuze and Futurism: A Manifesto to Nonsense* (p. 53).

How might one conceptualize film aesthetics in a virtual world? Machinima is derived from the mechanics of the virtual platform and shaped by the imagination of the maker. Lev Manovich (2011, p. 89) explores how "new visual aesthetics" contribute to "emerging information aesthetics." Manovich (2002), in *The Language of New Media*, discusses the dimensional characteristics of the virtual, not as pertaining to a virtual world necessarily. It is the screen or frame that defines the visual, whether it is intended for computer games, animated works or virtual worlds. .The viewer is immersed within the simulation (*Second Life* offers an extreme illustration). As Manovich understands the virtual as real, Deleuze envisions virtuality and reality as "becoming" - without "separation or distinction of before and after, or of past and present" (Deleuze, 1990, p. 1). In 2007, Douglas Gayeton's machinima *Molotov Alva and His Search for the Creator* garnered international attention at festivals, was televised by *Home Box Office* and then premiered as a series on Cinemax during the following year. The documentary, with its Dutch origins, featured the rite of passage of a man leaving his ordinary existence into the digital realm of *Second Life*. By the series' conclusion, he eventually returns to his real life, realizing that the virtual is merely a parallel world with its own shortcomings.

In *Second Life*, machinima is created within the virtual world, complete with characters, set construction, and light and environmental settings; it transcends perceived boundaries, moving beyond the frame of actual space to inner thoughts expressed virtually. Might one then adapt Deleuze's sense of aesthetics to machinima; the cinema producer is comparable to "great painters or the great musicians; it is they who talk best about what they do" (Deleuze, 1989, p. 280). Machinima offers such an option to convey interpretive perspectives in unique visual form. For instance, Cao Fei's virtual art is reflected in her machinima, produced under the name of her avatar China Tracy (Art Works, 2009; Au, 2007b; Fang, 2008). As director, Tracy's machinima of her *RMB City - A Second Life Planning City* (Tracy, 2007b) presents a virtual Chinatown that she created as well as in which she participated. The machinima captures two realities; the cultural reality that she brought in-world and her machinima perspective of it and the larger virtual world. It becomes this immersive moment for the artist and audience to share in the digital realm. For a larger discussion of Fei's work, one might refer to Justin Clemens (2011; 2014) who has researched her work extensively.

Through machinima, the virtual world is viewed as a living, on-going performance, powered by imagination and interpretation in a mediated space. In the second part of her *i.Mirror series*, Fei as Tracy (2007a) extends her raw documentation of life on the grid to her contemplative avatar encounter with pianist Hug Yue. The machinima centers on the meaning of life. Five minutes into the machinima, Tracy states, "Everyone is an actor in a parallel world." Yue concurs, "All the world is a stage," and she then notes, "We [are] all in the film....Is my avatar my mirror? Tracy inquires further, "What do you think about the digital world?" He responds, "It is one that is dominated by youth, by beauty, and money. And it's all an illusion." Soon after, he transforms from a middle-aged man to one in his mid-60s. The conversation ends with a larger view of this encapsulated world as one that is corporately framed and observed - think *The Truman Show* (Weir, 1998). Hue astutely surmises, there is not an end to this journey, "If that is where the life takes us…That is where we go."

Neither world is a concrete fixture, yet embedded within the process of creation. No separation of worlds - real and virtual - are significant in this context. Virtuality becomes a reflection and reproduction of the experiences of the creator and that which is created. The virtual consumes real time and real space, albeit on a server (that being, a much more complex discussion, given the huge volume of server space needed to run a virtual world). Participants often construct spaces based on learned rules from social and physical experiences. Life becomes intertwined in the convergence of both, or might one say multiple realities - the imagined and the real, and that which is projected to participants for contemplation and their own reinvention. Virtual worlds represent a confluence of media, and a medium in and of itself. They serve as a living theater which when captured via machinima becomes an archive as well as an art work, and at the minimum a personal statement, perhaps a home movie to replay on command. This layering of parallel universes allows for infinite cultural and artistic interpretations by creators and viewers of machinima, each with their own perspectives on the significance of virtuality in their lives. The virtual world, in essence as reflection and aspirations, becomes imprinted in the frames of machinima - a medium embedded within a larger medium, the virtual world, which itself is a host for a convergence of media. HipHop artist Hoodie Allen (2014) sings, in the official video trailer for *Movie*, "We enter into the virtual world as we would a movie, play or whatever." His reference to virtual world implies the cinematic stage. Extending that metaphor into *Second Life*, the stage is a virtual canvas to be painted and archived into the context of machinima. The virtual extraction as exhibition into an accessible medium, machinima in this case, becomes viewable outside of *Second Life*, this exchange allows for introspection as well as public discussion about society's relationship within and between worlds.

One of the earliest examples of *Second Life* machinima art is Robbie Dingo's *Watch the World(s)*, a provocative time lapse capture of a sim being constructed to resemble Vincent van Gogh's painting *The Starry Night*. Don McLean's *Vincent* provides the soundtrack. The sim no longer exists, but the machinima lives on to illustrate the artistic process of *Second Life*, a 3D canvas in the making (ShareFestival, 2008). Dingo (2007), in his own blog, states:

Ever looked at your favorite painting and wished you could wander inside, to look at it from different perspectives? Spend a single day in one of mine, from early sunrise on a new day, to dusk when lights come on in cosy [sic] homes; through a peaceful night, till morning…It was always intended however that the video would be the end production, not the build.

Imagery is key to his vision. Cinematographer John Alton (*An American in Paris*; *Elmer Gantry, T-Men*) was an artistic genius, in the way he painted the film canvas with light in stunning ways.

In *Painting with Light*, Todd McCarthy (1995) states in the book's introduction, Alton "pushed film noir to its most exciting visual extremes" (p. x). Deleuze (1990) refers to this conceptually as "to paint without painting" (p. 137). To Manovich as well (2005; 2013), the film is never static, always evolving, transforming through its innate subjectivity and software. This latter approach is reflective of immersive installations within virtual environments, that might employ machinima as one aspect of a comprehensive artistic vision. The painter in *Second Life*, as in real life, commands the screen. The painter rests not merely with the film as output, but that which is experienced and filmed - the object, the setting, and so forth - during the process (Johnson & Pettit, 2012). One can draw a parallel to this cinematic approach in Greenaway's call to visual literacy in machinima.

GREENWAY'S VISION FOR SL MACHINIMA

Cinema is a game - a most elaborate lucid pursuit played between film makers and audience, where both are only too familiar with the very precise rules. - Greenaway (cited in Steinmetz & Greenaway, 1995, p. 68)

Greenaway connects the movie to the game, with the goal of both "to successfully suspend belief" (Steinmetz & Greenaway, 1995, p. 66). New media aesthetics bring machinima into an artistic framework as a new medium of storytelling seen in the emergence of transmedia, where several modes of content delivery are employed simultaneously with distinct, but integrated, goals (Jenkins, 2006). Transmedia narratives have found success in the promotion and social extension of movies, television shows, and games, with the latter reflected on the corporate site Machinima. com of Machinima Inc. (2014). Perhaps, more so that has yet existed, the virtual world offers a sense of play, suspension and artistic challenge.

Greenaway has suggested that machinima, as a genre, has more often than not failed to distinguish itself as a means toward unique creative expression. He directs his attention toward virtual worlds like *Second Life*, challenging producers to rethink machinima as an art form - completely unique as a new medium within the body of even a larger medium, the virtual world..

Greenaway's 2010 speech in *Second Life* plays off this idea; it was delivered as an introduction to the 48 Hour Film Project's machinima festival held in *Second Life* (see Figure 2).

The crowd filled the virtual amphitheatre with great anticipation, awaiting the inspirational words of the legendary British filmmaker. Yet he would challenge them to think beyond what they had produced. In fact, he admits that he was "somewhat disappointed" with the entries (Har-

vey, 2010). Filmmaker Chantal Harvey, host of the event, uploaded his speech online afterwards. Greenaway noted that it was not the quality of the submissions that concerned him; it was merely the case that the entrants had failed to grasp the potential of filming in a virtual world. This new medium, relatively speaking, should be viewed as a challenge in that "maybe enough years have gone by now, for all of us to feel, that we are onto the beginnings of some new child media [that] has enormous potential in the future."

Greenaway expressed concern that *Second Life* producers had remained secure in the "conventionality" of a text-based medium. Aside from some experimentation, cinema has rested on one model, that of Hollywood: "I sincerely believe cinema is dead…the notion of the cinematic aesthetic has been around now for 115 years" (Greenaway, in

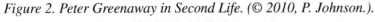

Figure 2. Peter Greenaway in Second Life. (© 2010, P. Johnson.).

Harvey, 2010). He offered the example of the Harry Potter series, in which films were mere extensions of text; as "illustrated books." Greenaway frames cinema as "past time" and television as present-oriented, and notes new ways that machinima is taking audiences and filmmakers toward future aesthetics derived from gaming culture and emerging virtual worlds like *Second Life*. It is at this point that the machinima movement can inspire visual literacy, when one stops relying on text as the point of reference, rather "pushing toward a greater sense of identity and purity" (Greenaway, in Harvey, 2010) toward the idea of painting the screen as an artistic canvas. Time and theme (as frame) in this new order become constraints during an era when digital tools have made the artistic process an easier one for creation.

A world like *Second Life* allows one to reinterpret conceptions of space and light. *Second Life* is a "medium without gravity - just think what you can do without gravity, not only as an amazing architectural tool…it's a medium about mutability and change." One can experience a sunset on demand. Water can be altered and re-experienced visually. This genre of machinima "is not cinema, it is not video, and it is not even some extenuated idea of the notion of the animated painted image, it has great new potentiality for a huge future" (Greenaway, in Harvey, 2010). Greenaway concluded "the image has to control the whole phenomenon."

The Evolution toward Art Machinima

This section presents a brief overview, but not wholly representative, of machinima's evolution. It follows the rise of machinima with users capturing game footage from action play to the emergence of machinima as an intended art form. Leander Kahney (2003) had predicted the transition of machinima from capture to creation: "Gamers realized that instead of generating monsters to be blown away, game animation engines could be employed to conjure up imaginative sets, casts

of thousands and spectacular special effects." The first machinima were created from shooter games such as *Quake* (1996) and *Halo* (2001). An early popular series has stood the test of time; *Red vs. Blue* (Rooster Teeth, 2003; Horvath, 2014b) is a parody that made use of captured footage in *Halo*. *Diary of a Camper* (Horvath, 2014a; United Ranger, 1996) is likely the first renowned machinima made from *Quake*. By the late 1990s, Hugh Hancock of Strange Company would rise to become a leader within machinima practice (Gestalt, 2000), first with the long form *Quake* series *Eschaton* (Hancock, 1999) and later with *Blood Spell* and *Death Knight Love Story* (Hancock, 2006; 2010) and many in between and afterwards . One key moment of machinima was the launch of the Academy of Machinima Arts & Sciences, with Paul Marino as the executive director and Strange Company assisting as well. Marino (2004), author of *3D Game-Based Filmmaking: The Art of Machinima*, cites renowned film critic Roger Ebert for launching machinima publicly as an art form, a genre that has collectively received many awards and acknowledgements at major film festivals such as Sundance.

Through the years, many producers have contributed to the artistic advancement of machinima. There is an inherent craft to machinima, reflected in the manipulation of imagery (first in games, now virtual worlds) and the assembling of a narrative from within the game or platform engine. What is interesting is that many of those key to the development of machinima as an art form were also instrumental to the design and production of the leading games of that era, and many of those games remain relevant today. An early example was the short film *Anna*, produced by Katherine Ann Kang (2006), the founder of Fountainhead Entertainment and co-founder of the Academy of Machinima Arts & Sciences (AMAS) with Marino. Relying on early *Quake* footage, she documented the life of a flower, a theme unrelated to the intent of the shooter game. Machinima as art is illustrated here as an early phenomenon, apart from what was typically the case. *Wired* Reviewer Brad King (2002), in *Machinima: Games Act Like Films,* profiles Kang, among others, when introducing and defining the craft in his feature article, while also noting the debut of the Academy as an important cultural marker in machinima's evolution. Kang designed and produced top games, as well as directed and produced notable machninima.

Marino was also co-founder of ILL Clan, a pioneering creative force in this new form of animation. As early 3D gamers, the group's origin dates back to the mid 1990s, when machinima playback and short films were mostly created for dedicated fans. Marino looked ahead to an era "when people will only want to work on machinima for its own sake" (*Put yourself*, 2006). By 2007, ILL Clan shifted to machinima work in *Second Life*, joining forces with the Electric Sheep Company, a then in-world production company which caught the attention of naysayers. Over the years, this group rose to become one of the first professional machinima companies, and became referred to as "machinima masters," having garnered the attention of *Wired Magazine* and *The New York Times* by this point (Korolov, 2010). By the decade's end, ILL Clan's portfolio featured work for major TV networks, film studios, and companies like IBM. In late 2010, ILL Clan members Frank Dellario and Tom Donnelly introduced their new company Pixel Valley Studio. Such early founders were quite aware of the artistic potential of their new medium of design, and led experimentation paving the way for the sophistication and development of the genre, now represented across YouTube on thousands of channels as well as Machinima. com, Aview TV, Machinima Artist Guild (MAG), and other online distribution services that have archived machinima content.

Machinima deconstructed the game, and in doing so had been re-conceptualized. With the rise of machinima, it has splintered into diverse directions, for example live capture, documentary, music video, storytelling and experimental. Each category can represent either a traditional or artistic approach. The digital era has meant a growing appreciation of 3D gaming and a film culture that has flourished subsequently. "Up till now, games and films have been produced distinctly apart (with a very few exceptions, such as). Much of the problem has been cultural as well as technological," notes Christopher Harz (2006), videogame producer and reviewer, who sees the convergence of cinema and machinima as a "marriage," a partnership likely to produce astounding results: "Although the output of machinima may not be up to Lucas standards, a startling number of creative and even breath-taking short movies…are being shown in machinima festivals around the world." He adds, capture in *Second Life* ("although technically not a game") offers much towards new filmmaking. Machinima conceptually is rooted in the visual effects industry of the early 20th century; the movie *King Kong* (Cooper & Schoedsack, 1933) is considered one of the pioneering films of "stop motion animation and animatronics" (Brophblog, 2007). Machinima began as a product and process of filmmaking, animation and game play, being impacted by the computerization of the entertainment industry. George Lucas (1977) revolutionized computer-generated interactive graphics (CGI) and animation in his production of *Star Wars,* and that would provide a foundation for machinima in later years. Star Wars' R2D2 creator Tony Dyson is now one of the leading figures in machinima production within *Second Life*, with a multi-sim studio in a virtual environment constructed for Hollywood-style production for what he coins as real time animation. In a similar way, Steven Spielberg's *Jaws* (1975) would pave the way for machinima when he adapted a version of the Unreal game engine to create the animatics (Brophlog, 2007). Ground-breaking producers like Peter Jackson (*The Lord of the Rings*; *King Kong*) to Michael Bay (*Armageddon* and *Pearl Harbor*) relied on increasingly computer-generated techniques to create their effects. The blurring of computer generated effects and the rise of gaming conjured new possibilities for a Hollywood industry reliant on special effects (Johnson & Pettit, 2012). Jackson (*Put yourself*, 2006) stated publicly that he was "getting a little bored with films." His curiosity was stirred "by a strange and growing trend in which film-school graduates, hardcore gamers and cutting-edge design studios [were] pulling apart the programming code of high-street video games to create a whole new style of movie-making" (*Put yourself*, 2006). As producers experimented with computer graphics and animation, particularly for pre-visualization of scenes for blockbuster-type action movies, these advances would benefit the gaming community, and eventually the machinima community.

As a side note, Michael Pigott (2010) points out few women (aside from trailblazers Kang and game designer/educator Katie Salen) have been part of the early history of machinima (or at least acknowledged) likely due to its arrival within first-person shooter games. A more thorough list of women significant to machinima's development can be located in the work of Hancock and Ingram (2007a; 2007b). Others like Robert Jones (2011) expound on the roadblocks that females have encountered in the past. In contrast, *The Sims 2* presented a path for women to create machinima around "familiar" narratives focusing on "everyday people" in domestic settings, explains Henry Jenkins (2003, p. 250). *Second Life* women are among the top creators and machinima producers, with many venturing into other worlds like *Open Sim*. Surely, SL will be acknowledged in years to come for its role in the rise of women filmmakers, like Chantal Harvey who has envisioned machinima as a medium for storytelling and artistic expression.

Other Developments: Competition vs. Creation

Tracy Harwood has been instrumental in machinima and new media research, more recently focused on the marketing aspects, as Senior Research Fellow at the Institute of Creative Technologies at De Montfort University (UK). In 2007, she directed the First European Machinima Festival, an event co-sponsored by the Academy of Machinima Arts & Sciences and her university. Harwood (2012) points out the convergence of real and virtual life has led to increased gamification, with the extension being rooted in an awareness of commercialization, educational utility, and market potential. Machinima might be explained as a consequence of gamification (i.e., added value) and increased popularity in game narrative as it relates to culture in general. The idea being the appropriation of games for use outside the framework of original intent (Marache-Francisco & Brangier, 2013). *Minecraft (2014)* might offer one example of gamification, a consequence of the phenomenal surge of educational experts and workshops revolved around how to engage students via gaming. *Minecraft* can be played in game or creative mode; the latter is relevant to the discussion at hand. *Minecraft* has created a massive fan culture, and machinima is a huge part of the artistry that has emerged. *Minecraft*, even more so than *World of Warcraft* (2004), offers elements of a virtual world; there is an artistic appreciation and interactivity among players who become creators themselves, no longer simply players engaging in competition.

In the same way, *The Sims*, in its various incarnations, has allowed for creative storylines to emerge from the game. Machinima solidifies fan culture with game narratives that may or may not relate to role play. In juxtaposition, *Second Life* was designed as an emergent world, one designed and constructed by its community. Its non-ludic intent separates it from MMORPGs like *World of Warcraft*, *Minecraft*, and *The Sims*. Although members can invent their own games and role play within *Second Life*, that is not the objective of the creators, the San Francisco-based Linden Lab. One example that readily comes to mind is Mad Pea Productions, which has been creating interactive in-world games for more than five years within *Second Life*. The international team is comprised of writers, designers, scripters and builders, with Founder and Director Mari Mitchell at the helm. The team uses machinima to promote its works, typically mysteries that invite *Second Life* members to engage in role play, allowing each individual to join the "game" as an active participant attempting to solve the scenario. The participants - as engaged in these games in their avatar form - a persona of their own creation - are situated within, ultimately, a larger non-ludic environment of which the activity is embedded. Film footage that captures the activity is comparable to the earlier days of machinima, a sense that one is documenting their game play. Nevertheless, the in-world immersive experience becomes art in and of itself. Mad Pea (2014) examples include *The Green Mire* (as illustrated in Figure 3) (the search for two missing boys in a swamp town); *The Lost Mine* (a professor's quest for treasure); *Dark Dimension* (an old prison converted into a town with mysterious happenings) and so forth,

along with some educational and training projects (i.e., *Notes from the Voyage* concerns the travels of Charles Darwin).

The ability to create such customized environments within the larger context of *Second Life* attracts the budding and professional filmmaker alike seeking unique story settings. In some cases, immersive games like those of Mad Pea specify adjustments to one's environmental lighting upon entrance. Longtime *Second Life* member and visual artist Chic Aeon founded the Machinima Open Studio Project (MOSP) which was actually designed to encourage filmmakers to create storylines inspired by her numerous prefab sets of different scenarios, many of which have been designed by the machinima artist herself. It might be a cabin in a snowy field, a road that meanders about the sim, or a penthouse apartment with a city view of skyscrapers. Aeon (MOSP, 2014) encourages interpretation by filmmakers, and leaves it to them to determine how they light and contextualize the respective environments. MOSP also includes a

Figure 3. Blogger Kara with HUD viewer at Mad Pea's 'The Green Mire.' (© 2014, Kara Trapdoor. Used with permission.).

classroom for educators and trainers, in essence underscoring the "instructional" utility of *Second Life*. The ultimate lesson learned is, with time and effort, one can become a virtual world artist/filmmaker - and so the machinima community adds new converts and helps support the novice as well as professional within *Second Life*.

It is not surprising then that educational organizations such as International Society for Technology in Education (ISTE) and Virtual Worlds Best Practices in Education (VWBPE), have embraced machinima (via its competitions and discussion forums) as a conduit to their students' gaming interests, encouraging them to creatively engage into history, literature, arts and science. It just so happens that *Second Life* has been instrumental to facilitating such dialogue and creative play, with its uniquely unstructured virtual world providing spaces for artistic design and machinima challenges (competitions) such as those regularly sponsored by the University of Western Australia in *Second Life* (UWA-SL). Estate Owner/Manager Jay Jay Jegathesan has taken the lead on showcasing machinima talent, offering huge cash prizes in on-going theme-based competitions that value originality and artistic and conceptual skill. Machinima has been perceived as having a competitive advantage over traditionally labor-extensive processes in the producing of animation for advertising and commercially-supported web series, corporate productions, grant-supported public service announcements and educational projects (Johnson & Pettit, 2012; Shields, 2012). Some of these projects might serve the public good or merely as entertainment in various forms, such as documentary, game shows, and other mainstream fare, typical of everyday media.

The Second Life Machinima Community

Second Life is an immersive experience that is an extension of real life, or perhaps an alternate universe where individuals can reinvent themselves

(Johnson, 2010). As in any life, many take photos of their good times and post them on social sites, such as Facebook and Flickr. Celebrations like weddings and birthday parties rely on simple capture tools. Rysan Fall (2014), as others do, actually supplements his income by providing professional machinima services in *Second Life*. One of his early machinima *Strange Fruit: Billie Holiday Tribute* (Fall, 2009) has become a SL classic, shot in black and white at the Cotton Club in Virtual Harlem. The following year, Fall directed a video featuring musician Craig Lyon's cover of *Across the Universe*, written by John Lennon in 1967. The spectacular special effects and imagery showcased the talent of Fall and Lyons, music and machinima coming together to engage real and SL audiences. Beautiful animation is re-edited to create powerful stories at one extreme; at the other, comedy and spoofs become part of the fandom that accompanies game culture. Other than a handful of games embedded within *Second Life*, from zombie attacks to mysteries and role plays, most people envision the grid as place for socialization and creativity. If one is not an artist, one will likely be a tourist of the virtual wonders, an observer at minimum. Many observers capture virtual events using machinima.

A growing list of names reveals a vibrant community of virtual filmmakers - Iono Allen, Chic Aeon, Spyvsspy Aeon, Larkworthy Antfarm, Pooky Amsterdam, Belinda Barnes, JJcc Coronet, Robbie Dingo, Tony Dyson, Miles Eleventhauer, Phaylen Fairchild, Rysan Fall, Flimsey Freenote, Ricky Grove, Laurina Hawks, Chantal Harvey, Hypatia Pickens, Binary Quandry, Toxic Menges, Tutsy Navarathna, Lowe Runo (see Figure 4), Cole-Marie Soleil, China Tracy, Kara Trapdoor, Lainy Voom and many others, too many to mention.

Such comprise the early "virtual world" film producers, several of whom were part of *Second Life*'s first "machinima art" movement (2006-2012), a time when machinima organizations and communities were being established. A number of film associations catered to the varying niche

Figure 4. Lowe Runo, founder of MAG. (© 2009, Donald Pettit. Used with permission.).

interests of members. *Magnum: The Machinima Review* featured some of the above filmmakers in a monthly MAG column through late 2013. *Best of Second Life Magazine* also published a regular series, *Masters of Machinima*, for nearly a year, highlighting the work of established virtual filmmakers.

There is an artistic sensibility among many virtual filmmakers, rooted in the beauty of contributing as content creators to the fantasy, visual landscapes, sound design, and imaginative play. The number of women machinima producers in *Second Life* point toward a nurturing environment, especially with the rise of organizations like MaMachinima, founded in 2009 by Dutch filmmaker Chantal Harvey. She also founded the MaMachinima International Film Festival (MMIF), as well as a machinima chapter to the 48 Hour Film Project in *Second Life* (instrumental to the involvement of filmmaker Greenaway as a project judge and key note speaker). The Machinima Artist Guild (MAG) founded by Lowe Runo in 2008 remains an extremely active organization of more than 800 members, mainly those

with *Second Life* membership, a balance of men and women. Four reviewers, long time members and notable machinima producers - Larkworthy Antfarm, Celestial Elf, Asil Ares, and Natascha Randt - oversee the operations.

Machinima when viewed as an inexpensive form of animation empowers filmmakers to experiment (who might not otherwise afford such opportunity). *Second Life* has helped to establish virtual artists, providing venues and resources within its community of supporters, including the Linden Endowment for the Arts (LEA) which encourages experimentation in photography, film, art installation and other mediated works. *Second Life* is a world that is built by its residents. Other platforms that offer somewhat similar experiences, but not to the extent of *Second Life*, are *The Sims*, *World of Warcraft*, *Open Sim*, and *Minecraft*. Comparatively, *Second Life*'s artistic community represents many seasoned artists, who are presented with a blank slate upon which to create their work. Many SL producers have been historically involved in filming strong narrative and experimental pieces. Some filmmakers from

The Sims have transitioned to *Second Life*, invited by friends who made the jump, and/or because they wanted to develop their creativity in an open-ended platform. If one were to describe *Second Life*, it would be defined by its members, who reside and contribute to a community of artists, musicians, educators, scientists, activists, designers, and likewise. Some come to simply explore this world. These explorers find themselves intrigued with the possibilities of creation, and are compelled to document the artifacts of others through blogging, photography and filmmaking (e.g., Figure 5).

Comparable to real life, journalists report on the news, and use machinima as a means to present and archive speeches and events. Documentarians have used machinima to garner attention to the seedier side of virtual life Virtual news organizations have used machinima for actualities; in fact, SL news networks employ avatars as news anchors. Fall was a SL newscaster. News when filmed within a game or virtual world can offer a satirical perspective on real life. Some news teams take significant liberty in their on-air presentation and interaction with audiences (Johnson, 2010; Johnson & Pettit, 2012). Former National Public Radio (NPR) producer Bernhard Drax (SL avatar Draxtor Despres) blurs the line between real and virtual via mixed media. His weekly magazine-styled show *The Drax Files* is praised for its artistic presentation; he features content creators across the SL grid relying on interviews recorded in the real world and with their avatar representations in the virtual world.

Second Life's film community employs machinima to not only document events, but to create original stories in settings designed by others or in their own constructed environments. In fact, when it comes to Second Life, most virtual filmmakers consider machinima as an artistic practice - and

Figure 5. Virtual roads lead to stories. (© 2013, Donald Pettit. Used with permission.).

some draw footage from popular video games, incorporating them into their production. (See Figure 6.)

The artistic spins for machinima producers are plentiful. Some rely on amazing artistic builds and sets within virtual worlds for inspiration, creating stories around those magnificent installations, while others simply communicate the artistic message intended by the designer through capture. At its best, machinima pushes the artistic, cultural, and political boundaries of filmmaking.

Emergence of New Artistry

Machinima becomes an expression of the community or fandom of the world or platform to which it is associated (Cameron & Carroll, 2011), a concept that Henry Jenkins (1992) broached 20 years earlier when examining television audiences. One might contextualize the medium of machinima further, acknowledging its unique aesthetic con-

straints and potential as an art form (Pigott, 2011, p. 179). Virtual worlds become blank canvases to create, animate and bring to life art. The machinima artist films these processes and creations. Particularly unique to *Second Life* and high-end MMORPGs to a lesser degree, there comes a duality to the filmed set: the actor as viewer and filmmaker; in either instance, one walks through an environment as an avatar, a persona of the real behind the virtual mask. That actor is director, producer and participant. One example is Iono Allen's (2009) interpretive machinima based on the work of installation artist Rose Borchovski. These award winning pieces - the installation and the film - can be found among the virtual archives of the University of Western Australia, a major supporter of the arts and machinima in *Second Life*. Another long-time supporter has been the LEA (noted earlier), which funds virtual real estate for artists with winning proposals in need of creative space, the results of which regularly become the

Figure 6. Action or art? SL as a stage. (© 2012, Bel's World. Used with permission.).

themes of machinima. In this case, the animation evolves from the installation as interpretive art and archive. In an interview with the author (Johnson & Pettit, 2012, p. 237), Allen discussed his work and his artistic relationship with Borchovski. Allen's creative platform is *Second Life*, and as a machinima director, he is inspired by the 3D installations of various artists, one of his favorite being Borchovski (as illustrated in Figure 7).

The latest in the series *The Story of Susa Bubble* is *The Arrival*. Allen has directed and produced machinima derived from her work, yet adding his own interpretation. The collaboration has success-fully garnered honors from the art community. Allen stated, "It is not only the artwork which is

important, it is how you capture the ambience." He noted that one of his early films, *A Question of Honor*, was his best machinima to date during the 2011 interview. He explained that while the shooting for the project went quickly, the editing became its "own project. When you have an idea, when you get inspired, you just go and film like you want to film." As for *A Question of Honor* (2010), the winning entry of the Hosoi Ichiba Machinima Awards, Allen had "the idea of a sepulcher," and explained that he discovered what light setting would work best and that became his creative spark: "Once this was established in my mind, I went there, and when you go there, you can't stop filming because the sim is really

Figure 7. Prints of 'The Story of Susa Bubble,' exhibited in Iono Allen's virtual art gallery. (© 2009. P. Johnson.).

a fabulous work by itself." The *Second Life* sim Hosoi Ichiba was a "good balance of landscape and building." Over the past five years, Allen has remained a prolific filmmaker within *Second Life*, and consistently captures the artistic elements, ambience, and philosophy of the virtual world through his machinima.

Decorgal, another well-respected machinima producer, experimented with *The Sims* machinima in its early rendition, but it was during the midst of *The Sims 2* that she became hooked as a filmmaker, particularly drawn to the storytelling features of the game. By the end of the 2000s, she had established herself as a prolific and leading figure in machinima. Having tried filming in *Second Life*, she preferred *The Sims* as a creative space. Actually, she enjoyed the controlled environment of *Sims* over *Second Life*. One of her friends, she noted, successfully made the transition: that was Lainy Voom, who enjoyed having copyright control over her machinima, among other reasons for making the leap (Johnson & Pettit, 2012). Voom inspired many future machinima producers with her early work, commanding a strong narrative and imagery. Notable examples of her work are based on literature classics and cult fiction, as well as those derived from experimentation and her own imagination. One of her first machinima, featured on her YouTube channel is *Zombie Mummies from Outer Space* (2006), filmed within *The Sims 2*. Soon after, she began producing machinima in *Second Life*: *Tale from Midnight City* (2007), *The Dumb Man - Sherwood Anderson* (2008), *Fall* (2009), *The Stolen Child - W. B. Yeats* (2009), *Push* (2009), and *Dagon - H. P. Lovecraft* (2010), among others. Her machinima was far ahead of the time when she started, and still represents excellence in digital storytelling.

Hypatia Pickens' machinima can be described as a convergence of literature, history, dance, and moving art. She has won numerous awards internationally for her style, with stunning imagery and experimentation. Her studio within *Second Life* displays her sets and screenshots illustrative of her artistic vision and range for machinima. With at least 35 machinima to her credit, many of which have earned honors, her films are imaginative in their use of lighting, character development, and storytelling techniques. Among her titles is the rhythmically and visually intense *The Travelers and The Angel*, which is a fairly recent work, drawing from "one of three cautionary tales" by 14th century poet John Gower, screened at the Third International Congress of the John Gower Society at the University of Rochester in New York (Pickens, 2014). Others include some earlier machinima: *Instructions from the Dead on How to Recall the Source Code* (2012a), *The Four Gods of Folly* (2012b), *Wulf and Eadwacer* (2012c), as well as her first (published) *Dancing with Art* (2010). Her content and production decisions are pensive and cinematically intelligent in image and sound design. Her dark overtones intrigue as well as engage the viewer.

Another award winning SL producer is Tutsy Navarathna, whose work can be described as provocative, seductive and experimental; his command of imagery demonstrates the level of artistry possible within the virtual world. Navarathna's (2014) *Homeless* provides a poignant moving portrait of homelessness, shot in India and *Second Life*. Over the past decade, there has been a rise of international machinima by independent producers from India, Africa and other developing nations. Work surfacing is artistic and political, creatively expressing real issues through powerful imagery. Since 2010, Navarathna has won numerous awards, including winning top honors at The Machinima Expo and The University of Western Australia machinima challenges. Among his most notable machinima has been *The Last Syllable of Recorded Time (2013)* (as illustrated in Figures 8-9), MetaSex (2012), *Journey into the Metaverse* (2011), *Welcome to the Other Side* (2011), and *Narcissus* (2013). His style of aesthetic conveys sophistication in lighting, editing, layering, and an understanding of machinima as a moving canvas.

Figure 8. Tutsy Navarathna's 'Last Syllable of Recorded Time,' UWA public screening. (© 2013, P. Johnson.).

Bryn Oh is a well-known filmmaker and artist. Oh's work is illustrative of the cinematic vision of Greenaway. Interactive installations simulate the feeling of walking into a movie, becoming part of that experience. It is perhaps the most powerful example of immersive cinematic storytelling within a virtual world. Oh's machinima is equally unique and powerful. *Rusted Gears* (winner of the Peter Greenaway prize as part of the 2011 UWA competition) is a machinima that uses poetry as a metaphor of words unspoken, to be later replaced with regret (Oh, 2011). The ambient mix of light and sound, as well as text, stirs the emotion of the viewer. Oh (2013a; 2013b) went on to produce a modern version of *The Dance of Death* for a Greenaway project. The lives of five characters, distinct in their life positions, become equal in death. A story told beautifully through Oh's imagery. In their machinima, Marlen Slazar (2009) and JJcc Coronet (2011) showcase the beauty and depth of Immersiva, offering their own interpretations of Oh's sim over different times and from their respective perspectives. Oh's installations, such as *Immersiva* (2014a) and the *Singularity of Kumiko* (2014b) can be described as moving experiences, combining the ordinary with the extraordinary, the simple becomes the complex, the complex as simple. (Figure 10 captures the artistry of Oh's work.)

Another SL project by Oh, a collaborative work, was part of a larger global exhibition held in Moscow's Manege Museum in 2014. Definitely, Oh's work is representative of the artistic potential of *Second Life*. Oh's ability to showcase at museums across the world, and in partnership with granting agencies and other artists, hints toward a rich source of creative fodder for filmmakers seeking intriguing and surreal settings for installations not easily conceived in the real world. These are the settings for inspiring experiences and machinima.

Figure 9. 'Last Syllable of Recorded Time,' UWA screening.(© 2013, P. Johnson.).

MACHINIMA IN A SIMULATED WORLD

When addressing the body as a "digital puppet" in immersive environments like *Second Life*, one begins to understand how machinima is framed by this perspective: "Virtual worlds provide a cultural platform for this far-reaching self expression and identify formation" (Nitsche, Mazalek & Clifton, 2013, p. 65). *Second Life* offers the most elaborate example of what is possible in virtual worlds, and hints toward the future of immersive experiences, online and via hybrid 3-D constructions. Think Star Trek's holodeck and *Fahrenheit 451*'s parlor room for a glimpse toward the future,

or near future. In Ray Bradbury's 1953 classic, the sitting room consists of four wall screens, in which the viewer interacts with what is referred to as "family." The screen culture, as described by Greenaway, hints toward a path in which the viewer becomes immersed within the story. Oculus Rift, introduced for beta testing within *Second Life* as a 3D viewer, creates an environment where the spectator becomes part of the narrative. Virtual museums and art galleries have emerged as supplemental experiences; the online portal is just that - a window to another world. The convergence of such experiences are for practical and artistic purposes. In terms of *Second Life*, one creates art, the gallery in which it will be

Figure 10. Bryn Oh's 'Singularity of Kumiko.' (© 2014, Kara Trapdoor. Used with permission).

viewed, and interacts with his or her audiences. The avatar as artist and creator, and in this case filmmaker, not only constructs virtually, but exists in a parallel form as an extension of their being. It is here, that *Second Life* thrives as a community. The construction, filming and viewing often take place in-world. In its early years, SL screenings were held primarily inside the virtual world, as members celebrated their films among each other and their growing fan base. With the rising emphasis on post production, the boundaries between real and virtual blurred. In 2008, machinima producer Pooky Amsterdam (2012) launched a virtual production empire in *Second Life*, posing the question in her blog, "Why watch TV when you can star in your own cartoon movie every night?" The avatar has special significance in the virtual world as filmmaker and viewer (Reinhard & Amsterdam, 2013). It is here one might consider the multiple roles of the avatar as filmmaker, as identities of real and virtual collide. The avatar filmmaker directs the camera from his or her point of view, one that is similar or different from daily experiences as a member of the virtual world. The avatar becomes an actor, casted in a world in which he or she has established an identity and social circle. The avatar is likely to have a virtual home, studio, and personal life within the virtual world. Some filmmakers create alts, secondary avatars, to capture a third-person perspective.. In other instances, this "other" might be used to cloak identity, or to represent another personality facet, so as to establish a separate social profile (in *Second Life* and apart from real life). The avatar, as filmmaker and actor, is also a member of the machinima community. The avatar is an actor by its very construction, with some filmmakers creating a series of avatars as characters. For instance, note the various incarnations of two female avatars, as performed by the author and producer Belinda Barnes in Figures 11-14.

At one extreme, the filmmaker might assume a series of roles. Another scenario might be the casting of avatars from the general virtual population. The latter instance simulates the process of traditional filmmaking, employing others as actors. Of course, the use of motion capture software further blurs these boundaries, in that the actions of real people are translated into the movements of avatars. *Second Life* offers collaborative, convergent models of virtual filmmaking. The transference of oneself into a virtual world forebodes of machine cinema to come, similar to themes expressed within the movie *Edge of Tomorrow (Liman, 2014)*. Being able to reenact one's role in life takes on game-like proportions. *Second Life* in this respect takes away risk, supplanting fear with creativity; imagination fuels the process.

Machinima critics and filmmakers bring different perspectives to their roles as producers. In her chapter *Dangerous Sim Crossings,* Sara Higley (2013, p. 113) posits, "*Second Life* machinima puts the frame back around the invisible frame of immersion at the same time as it participates in it." She surmises after critical articulation of its various incarnations, machinima does indeed have boundaries, defined by its participants and informed by their interactions with one another; further their respective contributions and perspectives are centered within an art community or communities. This is a concept especially relevant to SL filmmakers who are inspired by the creativity into which they are immersed (and that perhaps they themselves have constructed from their imagination). The canvas of the machinima is itself a border of identity, representing filmmakers' experiences in-world and their framed projection of the virtual environment. Most intriguing has been the work of Toxic Menges (2010), a film-

Figure 11. 'Gangnam Furry Style Second Life.' (© 2013, Donald Pettit. Used with permission.).

Figure 12. On the film set of 'Adventures of Bel and Soni.' (© 2013, P. Johnson).

Figure 13. 'Steampunk Adventures.' (© 2013, P. Johnson).

Figure 14. Girls' 'Mario Style.' (© 2013, P. Johnson).

maker very familiar with *Second Life* and other online communities. She creates her own filming environment, and the machinima ultimately becomes the final stage of the experience. To her, a producer should avoid post-production, and creativity is captured as a freely evolving process where the filmmaker conceives and creates within the virtual world (Johnson & Pettit, 2012). Her machinima *Little Red Riding Hood* illustrates some of her techniques among her nearly 60 videos. Her process might require a bit more scripting than otherwise would be the case, when one does not rely on special effects of computer- generated interfaces to alter the setting or action outside of the virtual world.

To the other extreme, some use automated cameras with impeccable timing to program movements of avatars as digital puppets. One example is the machinima mystery series *The Blackened Mirror* that made its debut in August 2012. Its producer Saffia Widdershins, prior real

life filmmaker and media instructor, has gradually developed her media enterprise since 2007. Early on, her weekly machinima program *Designing Worlds* and her larger publishing efforts were successful endeavors. Widdershins posits, "*The Blackened Mirror* is what we call a proof of concept piece; we are pioneering and building a portfolio demonstrating SL as a medium for sophisticated filmmaking" (Fitzroy, 2013, p. 144).

In between, one finds a range of styles. Special effects guru Tony Dyson and Dutch filmmaker Chantal Harvey have created numerous sets for machinima dedicated to the series T*he Bobbekins* and other related children's programming (Fitzroy, 2012). *The Bobbekins*, comparable to elves and fairies, is an innovative multi-media series built around Dyson's e-books and his collaborative machinima with Harvey as director; he is producer. The team, under the name of Scissores, performs convergence - aspects of live filmmaking within transmedia approaches of storytelling. The puppetry of the avatars are done by their staff. They operate each avatar uniquely. Each actor, in avatar form, takes direction from the producer, director, and script. Animations and avatars are customized, and character voices are carefully selected. The SL fantasy setting and storyline seem ideal for Dyson's vision of machinima. He sees this type of filmmaking as time-saving yet bound by certain limits. Machinima, in this regard, should not be considered necessarily more creative than traditional animation or machinima captured in games. Simply the process has the potential of being highly original, interactive and collaborative, allowing for one to create within an accessible animated environment - a virtual world conveying artistry unique to each producer's vision. Alas, that becomes the beauty and barrier to creativity; while the filmmaker is often bound to the technology, more significantly the case is that his or her imagination as well as skill level are the true limitations.

CONCLUSION

The Machinima Expo is an annual international festival that embraces all machinima platforms. It was co-founded by Hollywood actor Ricky Grove, who serves as executive producer. In recent years, SL entrants have been among the winners, representing filmmakers across the world. A complete survey of the platforms used in 2013 and some submission statistics on nations represented are identified in Johnson & Pettit (2014). The Machinima Expo Award Show has been actually presented live in *Second Life* (in addition to being streamed online), as well as archived as machinima. Around 2006, before the emergence of a SL film community, attention was limited to machinima derivative of games or 3D animation software (i.e. iClone, Moviestorm). Leo Berkeley (2006) commented on the machinima phenomena at that time, which would foreshadow

the revolution to come to virtual worlds. Berkeley (2006) states, in *Situating Machinima in the New Mediascape*,

I argue that one of the most distinctive features of the form is not apparent in the finished work but occurs during the production process, where the user/filmmaker can interact with a programmed game environment that is sufficiently complex to have substantial elements of uncertainty and randomness structured into the gameplay

Second Life is a world truly random in its design provoking creativity, experimentation, exhibition and contemplation. If the "medium is the message," then Marshal McLuhan's (1994) words are likely to shed light to the rise and role of machinima as actualized in the virtual realm. Subsequently, a physical community of filmmakers exists within *Second Life*, catering to unique in-world audiences and outside spectators (whose only glimpse is via machinima). Machinima is a tool to create and connect members within a virtual environment, a platform that itself inspires a sense of community. Filmmaking provides that lens into the virtual world. It offers introspection to the artist as maker and member. Machinima is democratic in practice, due to its accessibility among members. Meanwhile, it has matured into a professional artistic form, to be critiqued in graduate film programs and taught in college courses. With the emergence of virtual worlds, the definition for machinima has markedly expanded from capture to creation. Extraordinary builds serve as social gatherings and inspiring settings for photography and filmmaking. Layers of imagery and immersivity engage the senses and inspire machinima, as demonstrated by The Station (see Figure 15).

This chapter takes us from the early beginnings of machinima, embracing its artistic origins and its path to what is regarded as modern day machinima. The significance of the influx and

Figure 15. The Station. A world framed within a world. (© 2014, Kara Trapdoor. Used with permission.).

influence of women filmmakers within *Second Life*, as well as the role of gamification in virtual worlds and specifically how machinima plays into virtual commercialization are topics not thoroughly discussed by the author, but are worthy of further examination and research. Machinima might have attracted some early commercial filmmakers with profit motives; however its artistic experimentation and contributions will perhaps solidify machinima as an art form that represents life and creativity within virtual worlds, and much further by positioning it within the larger world of art. The virtual world is framed and filmed, but it is one in which the viewer can experience the painted canvas that Greenaway calls forth through the machinima and immersive installation work of Bryn Oh and much like Dingo has illustrated in *Watch the World(s)*.

REFERENCES

Academy of Machinima Arts & Sciences (2002-2009). New York, NY: Paul Marino.

Allen, H. (Producer). (2014, August 24). Hoodie Allen - "movie" (official video). Video retrieved from https://www.youtube.com/watch?v=SjDfh2Xz9CA

Allen, I. (Producer). (2009). *The story of Susa Bubble - Rose Borchovski artwork*. Paris, France: Iono Allen. Video retrieved from http://www.youtube.com/watch?v=aJdVCqG3bZs&list=UUau2uwcAq_piedjavtmqp9A

Allen, I. (Producer). (2010). *A question of honour*. Paris, France: Iono Allen. Video retrieved from http://www.youtube.com/watch?v=YftouEm3CT4&list=UUau2uwcAq_piedjavtmqp9A

Allen, I. (Producer). (2013). *The arrival.* Paris, France: Iona Allen. Video retrieved from http://www.youtube.com/watch?v=BHzGe5KwulY

Amsterdam, P. (2008, November 10). Why watch TV when you can star in your own cartoon movie every night. *Pooky Media* [Blog]. Retrieved from http://www.pookyamsterdam.com/2008_11_01_archive.html

Artaud, A. (1994). *The theater and its double* (M. C. Richards, Trans.). New York, NY: The Grove Press. (Original work published 1958)

Au, W. J. (2007a). Robbie Dingo, unmasked: Avatars and identity crystallized into four lovely minutes. *New World Notes* [Blog]. Retrieved from http://nwn.blogs.com/nwn/2007/11/robbie-dingo-un.html

Au, W. J. (2007b). This is truly China Tracy. *New World Notes* [Blog]. Retrieved from http://nwn.blogs.com/nwn/2007/07/this-is-truly-c.html

Au, W. J. (2008). *The making of Second Life.* New York, NY: Harper Business.

Au, W. J. (2009, July 11). My five favorite things from New World Notes: Weekend machinima: Lainy Voom plays with time in *Push. New World Notes* [Blog]. Retrieved from http://nwn.blogs.com/nwn/2009/07/weekend-machinima.html

Au, W. J. (2012, January 17). Peter Greenaway acclaims SL artist Bryn Oh, donates to crowd-funder to re-open Immersiva -- and so can you! *New World Notes* [Blog]. Retrieved from http://nwn.blogs.com/nwn/2012/01/peter-greenaway-acclaims-bryn-oh-second-life-artist.html

Bay, M. (1998). *Armageddon* [Motion Picture]. Burbank, CA: Touchstone Pictures.

Bay, M. (2001). *Pearl Harbor* [Motion Picture]. Burbank, CA: Touchstone Pictures.

Berkeley, L. (2006). Situating machinima in the new mediascape. *Australian Journal of Emerging Technologies and Society*, *4*(2), 65–80.

Bradbury, R. (1953). *Fahrenheit 451.* New York, NY: Ballatine Books.

Brooks, R. (1960). *Elmer Gantry.* Beverly Hills, CA: United Artists.

Brophblog. (2007, November 28). Why machinima is good for Hollywood? [Blog]. Retrieved from http://brophinator.wordpress.com/2007/11/28/why- machinima-is-good-for-hollywood.

Cameron, D., & Carroll, J. (2011). Encoding liveness: Performance and real-time rendering in machinima. In H. Lowood & M. Nitsche (Eds.), *The machinima reader* (pp. 127–142). Cambridge, MA: The MIT Press.

Clemens, J. (2011). Virtually anywhere real-time new-old avatar-human entertainment art: Cao Fei online. *Australian and New Zealand Journal of Art*, *11*(1), 113–131.

Clemens, J. (2014). The virtual extimacies of Cao Fei. In L. Hjorth, N. King, & M. Kataoka (Eds.), *Art in the Asia-Pacific: Intimate Publics* (pp. 191–203). New York, NY: Routledge.

Coleman, R. (2008). The becoming of bodies: Girls, media effects, and body image. *Feminist Media Studies*, *8*(2), 163–179.

Cooper, M. C., & Schoedsack, E. B. (1933). *King Kong {Motion Picture].* New York, NY: RKO Pictures.

Coronet, J. (2011). Immersiva. San Francisco, CA: Second Life. Video; retrieved from http://www.youtube.com/watch?v=4B5DJZVthqY

Deleuze, G. (1989). *Cinema 2: The time-image* (H. Tomlinson & R. Galeton, Trans.). Minneapolis, MN: University of Minnesota.

Deleuze, G. (1990). *The logic of sense. C. V. Boundas* (M. Lester & C. Stivale Trans. & Eds.). New York, NY: Columbia University Press.

Despres, D. (2013-2014). *The Drax Files: World makers.* Los Angeles, CA: Draxtor. Video retrieved from http://www.youtube.com/user/draxtordespres

Dingo, R. (2007, July 16). Watch the world(s). *My Digital Double* [Blog]. Retrieved from http://digitaldouble.blogspot.com/2007/07/watch-worlds.html

Dyson, T., & Harvey, C. (2014). The Bobbekins. San Francisco, CA: Scissores. [Second Life], Retrieved from http://bobbekinworld.com

Expo, M. (2012). Web site. Retrieved from http://www.MachinimaExpo.com

Fall, R. (2009). Strange Fruit: Billie Holiday tribute. MMIF - MaMachinima International Festival 2009. San Francisco, CA: Second Life. Video; retrieved from http://www.youtube.com/watch?v=3rCAraAD92U

Fall, R. (2010). *Across the universe - Craig Lyons.* San Francisco, CA: *Second Life.* Video retrieved June 23, 2014, from http://www.youtube.com/watch?v=zw5iwrEOBRg

Fall, R. (2014). *FallFilms.* Video retrieved from http://www.youtube.com/user/FallFilms

Fang, H. (2008). *Cao Fei Journey. Monograph.* Paris, France: Vitamin Creative Space.

Fitzroy, S. (2012, July). The magical man behind Star Wars R2-D2 and the Bobbekins: An interview with Tony Dyson and Chantal Harvey. *Best of SL Magazine* (pp. 166-187). Second Life: BOSL Inc.

Fitzroy, S. (2013, October). The blackened mirror: Prim perfect machinima. *Best of SL Magazine* (pp. 138-149). Second Life: BOSL Inc.

Fitzroy, S. (2013). *Magnum: The Machinima Review* [Blog]. Retrieved from http://magnum-machinima.blogspot.com

Fitzroy, S. (2014). Gangnam furry style *Second Life.* Chicago, IL: A Ring My Bel - So Nice Production. Video retrieved from http://www.youtube.com/watch?v=0kWYId5-NIw

Fitzroy, S. (2014). Video channel. Chicago, IL: A Ring My Bel - So Nice Production. Retrieved from http://www.youtube.com/channel/UCBUFGaaIh61Bd2lfMtR9jZA

Freenote, F. (2010). String me up (Lance Rembrandt). San Francisco, CA: Second Life. Video; retrieved from http://www.youtube.com/watch?v=wuAtHaLkvHY

Gayeton, D. (2007). *Molotov Alva and his search for the creator: A Second Life odyssey.* Submarine Channel. Video retrieved from http://molotovalva.submarinechannel.com

Gestalt. (2000, June 10). Hugh Hancock of Strange Company [Interview]. Eurogamer,net. Retrieved from http://www.eurogamer.net/articles/i_strangecompany

Global. Retrieved from http://www.igi-global.com/chapter/the-gamification-experience/87045

Halo. (2001). Video game. Seattle, WA: Bungie.

Hancock, H. (1999). Eschaton. Edinburgh, Scotland: Strange Company. Video; retrieved from http://www.strangecompany.org

Hancock, H. (2006). Blood spell. Edinburgh, Scotland: Strange Company. Video; retrieved from http://www.strangecompany.org

Hancock, H. (2010; 2014). *Death knight love story.* Edinburgh, Scotland: Strange Company. Video retrieved from http://www.strangecompany.org

Hancock, H., & Ingram, J. (2007a). *Machinima for dummies*. Hoboken, NJ: Wiley/For Dummies.

Hancock, H., & Ingram, J. (2007b). Women who have changed machinima. *Machinima for Dummies: Blogging the book*. Retrieved from http://machfordu.wpengine.com/articles/2009/03/24/women-who-have-changed-machinima

Harvey, C. (2010, September 24). Peter Greenaway speaks at 48hour film project machinima 2010. Keynote. Retrieved from http://vimeo.com/15253336

Harwood, T. (2012). Emergence of gamified commerce: Turning virtual to real. *Journal of Electronic Commerce in Organizations*, *10*(2), 16–39. Retrieved from http://www.igi-global.com/article/emergence-gamified-commerce/70212

Harz, C. (2006, January 31). *The holy grail of previs: Gaming technology. Animation World Network* (AWN).

Higley, S. (2013). Dangerous sim crossings: Framing the *Second Life* art machinima. In J. Ng (Ed.), *Understanding machinima: Essays on filmmaking in virtual world* (pp. 109–126). London: Bloomsbury Academic.

Horvath, S. (2011a). Reanimated: The 15 best videos of all time - Diary of a Camper. *Complex Gaming*. Retrieved from http://www.complex.com/video-games/2011/04/15-best-machinima-videos/camper

Horvath, S. (2011b). Reanimated: The 15 best videos of all time - Red vs. Blue. *Complex Gaming*. Retrieved from http://www.complex.com/video-games/2011/04/15-best-machinima-videos/red-vs.-blue

iClone (2013). 3D animation software. San Francisco, CA: Reallusion. ILL Clan. (2014). Web site. Retrieved from http://www.illclan.com/tiny-nation

Jackson, P. (Director) (2005). *King Kong* [Motion Picture]. Universal City, CA: Universal Pictures.

Jackson, P. (Director/Producer). *The lord of the rings* [Motion Picture]. Los Angeles, CA: New Line Cinema.

Jenkins, H. (1992). *Textual poachers: Television fans and participant culture*. New York, NY: Routledge.

Jenkins, H. (2003). *From Barbie to Mortal Kombat; Further reflection* (A. Everett & J. T. Caldwell, Eds.).

Jenkins, H. (2006). *Convergence culture: Where old and new media collide*. New York, NY: New York University Press.

Johnson, P. (2010). *Second Life, media and the other society*. New York, NY: Peter Lang.

Johnson, P., & Pettit, D. (2012). *Machinima: The art & practice of virtual filmmaking*. Jefferson, NC: McFarland.

Johnson, P., & Pettit, D. (2014). The machinima expo 6: A snapshot of the state of machinima. Machinima Review. *Journal of Gaming and Virtual Worlds*, *6*(1), 89–96.

Jones, R. (2011). Pink vs. blue: The emergence of women in machinima. In H. Lowood & M. Nitsche (Eds.), *The machinima reader* (pp. 277–300). Cambridge, MA: The MIT Press.

Kahney, L. (2003, July 9). Games invade Hollywood's turf. *Wired*. Retrieved from http://archive.wired.com/science/discoveries/news/2003/07/59566

Kang, K. A. (2006). *Anna*. Video retrieved from http://www.youtube.com/watch?v=1oDHUESNHgI

King, B. (2002, July 23). Machinima: Games act like films. *Wired*. Retrieved from http://archive.wired.com/gaming/gamingreviews/news/2002/07/53929

Korolov, M. (2010, October 14). Machinima pioneers launch Pixel Valley Studio. *Hyper grid Business*. Retrieved from http://www.hypergrid-business.com/2010/10/machinima-pioneers-launch-pixel-valley-studio

Second Life. (2003-2014). Virtual world. San Francisco, CA: Linden Lab.

Liman, D. (Director). (2014). *Edge of tomorrow* [Motion Picture]. Los Angeles, CA: Warner Bros.

Lowood, H. (2011). Video capture: Machinima, documentation, and the history of virtual worlds. In H. Lowood & M. Nitsche (Eds.), *The machinima reader* (pp. 3–22). Cambridge, MA: The MIT Press.

Lowood, H., & Nitsche, M. (2011). *The machinima reader*. Cambridge, MA: The MIT Press.

Lucas, G. (Director). (1977). *Star Wars* [Motion Picture]. Los Angeles, CA: 20th Century Fox.

Machinima Artist Guild (MAG). (2014). Membership site. Tampa, FL: Lowe Runo Productions. Retrieved from http://slmachinimaarts.ning.com

Machinima, Inc. (2014). Machinima.com. Retrieved from http://www.machinima.com

Machinima Open Studio Project. (2014). Blog. Eugene, OR: Chic Aeon. Retrieved from http://machinimasl.blogspot.com

Mahovlich, P. (2009, August). Retrieved from http://blog.koinup.com/2009/08/lainy-vroom-and-art-of-machinima.html

MaMachinima. (2014). MaMachinima International Festival.(MMIF). Amsterdam: Chantal Harvey. Retrieved from http://mmif.wordpress.com

Mann, A. (1947). *T-Men*. Los Angeles, CA: Edward Small Productions.

Manovich, L. (2002). *Language of new media*. Cambridge, MA: The MIT Press.

Manovich, L. (2011). Image future. In H. Lowood & M. Nitsche (Eds.), *The machinima reader*.

Manovich, L. (2013). *Software takes command (International Texts in Critical Media Aesthetics)*. London, UK: Bloomsbury Academic.

Manovich, L., & Kratky, A. (2005). *Soft cinema: Navigating the database*. Cambridge, MA: MIT.

Marache-Francisco, C., & Brangier, E. (2013). The gamification experience: UXD with a Gamification Background. In K. Blashki & P. Isaias (Eds.), *Emerging research and trends in interactivity and the human-computer interface* (pp. 205–223). Hershey, PA: IGI.

Marino, P. (2004). *3D Game-based filmmaking: The Art of Machinima*. Scottsdale, AZ: Paraglyph Press.

McCarthy, T. (1995). Through a lens darkly: The life and films of John Alton. In J. Alton (Ed.), *Painting with light* (pp. ix–xxxiv). Berkeley, Los Angeles: University of California Press.

McLuhan, M. (1994). *Understanding media*. Cambridge, MA: The MIT Press.

Menges, T. (2010). *Little Red Riding Hood*. San Francisco, CA: *Second Life*. Video retrieved from http://www.youtube.com/watch?v=p5zZ6_RPY-Ig

Minecraft (2014). Video game. Stockholm, Sweden: Mojang.

Minnelli, V. (1951). *An American in Paris*. Beverly Hills, CA: Metro-Goldwyn-Mayer Studios Inc.

MMIF - MaMachinima International Festival. (2009). Video Archive. Retrieved from http://www.youtube.com/user/firstAMF2009/videos

Moviestorm. (2010). 3D animation software. Cambridge, UK: Moviestorm Inc.

Navarathna, T. (2011). Journey into the metaverse. San Francisco, CA: Second Life. Video; retrieved from http://www.youtube.com/watch?v=iw5md8RpfWs

Navarathna, T. (2011). Welcome to the other side. San Francisco, CA: Second Life. Video; retrieved from http://www.youtube.com/watch?v=dm4XY49gdzc

Navarathna, T. (2012). MetaSex. San Francisco, CA: Second Life. Video; retrieved from http://www.youtube.com/watch?v=s0VA0IH1-SA

Navarathna, T. (2013). Narcissus. San Francisco, CA: Second Life. Video; retrieved from http://www.youtube.com/watch?v=-XEaJASA2Fs

Navarathna, T. (2013). The last syllable of recorded time. San Francisco, CA: Second Life. Video; retrieved from http://www.youtube.com/watch?v=SQq6OYx1m1c

Navarathna, T. (2014, June). *Homeless*. San Francisco, CA: Second Life. Retrieved from http://www.youtube.com/watch?v=gsEJW4VmkgQ&list=UUbfOwWpYoWo5l0Tz-q29Tbg

(Ed.), *New media: Theories and practices* (pp. 243–254). New York, NY: Routledge.

Ng, J. (2013). *Understanding machinima: Essays on filmmaking in virtual worlds*. London, UK: Bloomsbury Academic.

Nitsche, M. (2007). Claiming its space: Machinima. *A Journal of Art and Culture in Digital Media*. Video retrieved from http://www.dichtung-digital.de/2007/Nitsche/nitsche.htm

Nitsche, M. (2013). Moving digital puppets. In J. Ng (Ed.), *Understanding machinima: Essays on filmmaking in virtual worlds* (pp. 63–83). London, UK: Bloomsbury Academic.

Nitsche, M., Mazalek, A., & Clifton, P. (2013). Moving digital puppets. In J. Ng (Ed.), *Understanding machinima: Essays on filmmaking in virtual world* (pp. 63–83). London: Bloomsbury Academic.

Oh, B. (2011). Rusted gears. San Francisco, CA: Second Life; Retrieved from http://www.youtube.com/watch?v=3t2FQpNY0ck

Oh, B. (2013a, November 13). *Dance of death*. San Francisco, CA: *Second Life*. Video retrieved from https://www.youtube.com/watch?v=Coo6PuzQWI&feature=c4overview&list=UUI7NrJQ5vpg2PmVQKpwXSbw

Oh, B. (2013b, October 28). The dance of death with Peter Greenaway. *Bryn Oh*. Blogspot.Retrieved from http://brynoh.blogspot.com/2013/10/the-dance-of-death-with-peter-greenaway.html

Oh, B. (2014a). *Immersiva*. San Francisco, CA: Second Life.

Oh, B. (2014b, January 30). *The singularity of Kumiko*. San Francisco, CA: *Second Life*. Video retrieved from http://www.youtube.com/watch?v=JONF4tgTh34

Palmer, H. (2014). *Deleuze and futurism: A manifesto for nonsense*. New York, NY: Bloomsbury Academic.

Pea, M. (2014). *Mad Pea Productions*: Mari Mitchell. Retrieved from http://www.madpeagames.com

Pickens, H. (2010). Dancing with art. Rochester, NY: Textcavation Productions; Retrieved from http://www.youtube.com/watch?v=VBTvQoX5sV8

Pickens, H. (2012a). Instructions from the dead on how to recall the source code. Rochester, NY: Textcavation Productions. Video; retrieved from http://www.youtube.com/watch?v=-cGqC6eOqrE

Pickens, H. (2012b). The four gods of folly. Rochester, NY: Textcavation Productions; Retrieved from http://www.youtube.com/watch?v=-nUM19N9iYc

Pickens, H. (2012c). Wulf and Eadwacer. Rochester, NY: Textcavation Productions. Video; retrieved from http://www.youtube.com/watch?v=SbwbuDc-oT8

Pickens, H. (2014). The travelers and the angel. Rochester, NY: Textcavation Productions. Video; retrieved from http://www.youtube.com/watch?v=toYnxNgL4S0

Pigott, M. (2011). How do you solve a problem like machinima. In H. Lowood & M. Nitsche, (Eds.), *The machinima reader* (pp. 177-194). Cambridge, MA: The MIT Press. Put yourself in the director's chair. (2006, October 22). *The London Sunday Times* Retrieved from http://roosterteeth.com/info/?id=15. [Archived]

(pp. 73-90). Cambridge, MA: The MIT Press.

Press.

Quake (1996). Video game. Richardson, TX: Id Software.

Reinhard, C. D., & Amsterdam, P. (2013).. . *Journal of Virtual Worlds Research*, 6(2), 1–19.

ShareFestival. (2008). *Watch the world(s)*. San Francisco, CA: Second Life. Video retrieved from http://www.youtube.com/watch?v=vV1YbWBSXS8

Shields, M. (2012, April 3). Machinima! Adventures of a digital content company. Millions are watching. When will they cash in? *AdWeek*. Retrieved from http://www.adweek.com/news/technology/machinima-adventures-digital-content-company-139319?page=2

Sim, O. (2014). Open Source Simulator. Rehoboth, MA: Avacon; Retrieved from http://conference.opensimulator.org

Slazar, M. (2009). Immersiva - moments, art & love (Second Life). San Francisco, CA: Second Life. Video; retrieved from http://www.youtube.com/watch?v=VmkJ9iIby8k

Soleil, C. (Rockerfaerie) (2009). *My Friends are robots*. San Francisco, CA: Second Life. Video retrieved from http://www.youtube.com/watch?v=8h0sOIREUEo

Spielberg, S. (Director) (1975) *Jaws* [Motion Picture]. Los Angeles, CA: Universal Pictures.

Steinmetz, L. & Green away, P. (1995). *The world of Peter Greenaway*. Boston, MA: Journey Editions.

Teeth, R. (2003). *Red vs. Blue* [Machinima]. Austin, TX: Rooster Teeth Productions.

The Sims2 (2004). Video game. Redwood City, CA: Electronic Arts.

The Sims. (2000). *Video game*. Redwood City, CA: Electronic Arts.

Tracy, C. (2007a). *i.Mirror Part2*. San Francisco, CA: Second Life. Retrieved from https://www.youtube.com/watch?v=jD8yZhMWkw0

Tracy, C. (2007b). RMB CITY-A Secondlife city planning. San Francisco, CA: Second Life; Retrieved from https://www.youtube.com/watch?v=9MhfATPZA0g

TrapdoorK. (2014, February 13). http://karasecondlife.blogspot.com/search/label/The%20Singularity%20of%20Kumiko

Trapdoor, K. (2014). The station. *Kara's korner: Second Life adventures*. Retrieved from http://karasecondlife.blogspot.com

Van Sickler, M. (1996). *Diary of a camper*. United States: United Ranger Films.

Voom, L. (2006). Zombie mummies from outer space. Redwood City, CA: Electronic Arts. Video; retrieved from http://www.youtube.com/watch?v=zBZ_4x_Fr2U&list=UUZJaGJLbwBOUiXtYYygQqHg|

Voom, L. (2008). The dumb man - Sherwood Anderson. San Francisco, CA: Second Life. Video; retrieved from http://www.youtube.com/watch?v=fvxyzPnI9mU&list=UUZJaGJLbwBOUiXtYYygQqHg

Voom, L. (2009). Fall. San Francisco, CA: Second Life. Video; retrieved from http://www.youtube.com/watch?v=k4MmiaBcHAA&list=UUZJaGJLbwBOUiXtYYygQqHg

Voom, L. (2009). Push. San Francisco, CA: Second Life. Video; retrieved from http://www.youtube.com/watch?v=hLeK9Lanh94&list=UUZJaGJLbwBOUiXtYYygQqHg

Voom, L. (2009). *The stolen child - W. B. Yeats*. San Francisco, CA: Second Life. Video retrieved from http://www.youtube.com/watch?v=g9hnUYV06t4&list=UUZJaGJLbwBOUiXtYYygQqHgVoom, L. (2007). *Tale from midnight city*. San Francisco, CA: Second Life. Video retrieved from http://www.youtube.com/watch?v=PCSknY0Sa6I&list= UUZJaGJLbw-BOUiXtYYygQqHg

Voom, L. (2010). *Dagon - H. P. Lovecraft*. San Francisco, CA: Second Life. Video retrieved from http://www.youtube.com/watch?v=CMOHpuxFbm0&list=UUZJaGJLbwBOUiXtYYygQqHg

Weir, P. (1995). *The Truman show*. Los Angeles, LA: Paramount Pictures.

Widdershins, S. (2012). The blackened mirror episode 1: The quest begins. San Francisco, CA: Second Life. Video; retrieved from http://www.youtube.com/watch?v=9yhBAniwYVc

Works, A. (2009). Cao Fei: Love your avatar. Art Magazine. Deutsche, Germany: Deutsche Bank; Retrieved from http://www.db-artmag.com/en/58/feature/cao-fei-love-your-avatar

World of Warcraft. (2004). Video game. Irvine, CA: Blizzard Entertainment.

KEY TERMS AND DEFINITIONS

Aesthetics: An artistic and critical interpretation of mediated elements as related to natural and virtual realms.

Animation: The art and illusion of creating motion graphics.

CGI: Computer generated imagery for the creation of special media effects.

Gamification: An extension of a game to serve a purpose outside its original design (i.e., education).

Immersive: The mediated process of engaging one's senses within a digital or virtual environment or altered state of being.

Machinima: Filmmaking within a game platform or a virtual world.

MMORPG: Massively multiplayer online role-playing game.

Oculus Rift: A head-mounted 3D viewer for immersive experience in an virtual environment.

Second Life: A virtual world in which people log in as avatars to live and create an alternate life.

Virtual World: A simulated environment where members interact socially and creatively online.

Chapter 3
Spacing and Displacing as Artistic Enquiry

Taey Iohe
University College Dublin, Ireland

ABSTRACT

This chapter presents a philosophical journey and practical piece of experimentation on spatiality, virtuality and displacement. A series of art practices using photography, installation and art writing form the trajectory for a sequence of conceptual maps. The discussion engages with spacing and displacing as an artistic enquiry on space. The chapter consists of an examination of the typology and meaning of displacement in its translation from Korean, and a discussion of the formation of a gendered and artistically constructed displacement by extending the scope of the theory to the displacement of women in a colonial situation. This chapter explores the way in which displaced women (in the very particular case of Korean "comfort women" during the colonial war with Japan, and through the case of the artist, Hyeseok Na) cannot belong in either their home or a foreign land. Virtual-ness, here, is approached with an artistic understanding, and is found to constitute an unreal living space rather than merely a virtual environment through technology.

INTRODUCTION

How do we approach an artistic understanding of 'virtuality'? Is there 'virtual-ness' in our daily lives and cultural memory? One very immediate experience of 'virtual-ness' in our daily lives could be 'sleep'. We sleep and dream every day. Through this simple physical experience, we collect our memories and re-arrange our lives in our unconscious. This chapter will discuss 'virtual-ness' in relation to 'displacement', and suggest a virtual-ness grounded in an imagina-tive experience primarily, and later digitally mediated. Elizabeth Grosz, a critical thinker on space, explains virtuality as 'an augmentation, a supplementation, and a transformation of the real' (2001). Perhaps this suggests that virtuality is a part of our understanding of reality, which contains time and space, history and memory. We live in a society where travelling and transitory experiences are embedded in our lives very deeply, as commonplaces and as readily-acceptable elements of our histories and understanding of value in the world. However, an understanding of any

DOI: 10.4018/978-1-4666-8384-6.ch003

presence outside our 'living space' is unreachable and sometimes impossible. If Second Life is somewhat a realization of that impossible space, what other spaces have a similar other-worldly, oneiric, creative quality?

In this chapter, I will explore ideas of displacing and space as a possible artistic practice, as demonstrated by a series of artworks by the author. Firstly, we will explore the meanings of displacement through Korean translation etymology, and discuss the way in which displacement is a form of trace; a state of transferring and translating between one place and another. Then I will present the story of a Korean artist, Na Hyeseok, who died a lonely death in the early 19th Century, and how this became the starting point for my artistic vision. In relation to this, there will be a discussion about displaced women during the colonial era. In order to enable my creative process to bring these women alive into the present, a bed space is placed in the art work. This bed space travels through 'virtual spaces' such as the cul-de-sac, near a late night cinema, by an empty house that had been rapidly vacated, in a river, under a cold bridge, in a park at night-time, in a factory, and in the air-space of second life.

DISTANCE AND DISPLACEMENT

The distance from one place to another has a potential of transformation, which can be a form of abstract transformation. Let's call this change 'displacement' before we explore the idea. Displacement has many meanings to unfold, even within one language. In order to re-locate the meaning of displacement in the context of cultural translation, I look at the semantic dimensions of the word displacement and how they come to be employed differently. Firstly, I look at displacement as a movement from A (Source/Departure) to B (Target/Arrival); secondly, I argue for displacement as a kind of turning. This enables us to see displacement as a conceptual movement and

examines the liminal and politically significant spaces across which we translate; displacement as a state and a State.

Understanding the meaning of displacement in physics provides an initial important dimension for defining displacement as a process of the liminal state; being in a place of threshold. Distance and displacement are two quantities that refer to the characteristics of any path from one place to another. Distance is a scalar quantity, denoting a response to the question 'How much ground has an object covered from (P) to another point (Q)?' (Figure 1). This distance can take various paths, as in the diagram (a and c). Displacement, on the other hand, is a vector quantity, characterising the closest relationship between two places in the form of an x-and-y co-ordinate. Distance is an actual journey; the displacement can be a virtual journey, which is a sensation and result of distance.

Displacement contains motion within it. In moving from P to Q, the fact of movement between P and Q can represent a time interval. If P is in the past, Q is placed in the present or future. The movement between past and present (or future) becomes a temporal change. The extension of lines tells a story about time. The points of P and Q can also be spatially located. Lines between two sites are traces and trances of movement. A trace is a record of movement; it is an archive of movement. A trance is the embodied visceral experience of the displacement. Can a body be that trance of movement?

Brian Massumi interestingly looks at a similar notion of movement in his book, Parables for the Virtual (Massumi, 2002). He writes:

*The very notion of movement as qualitative transformation is lacking. There is **displacement**, but no transformation, as if the body simply leaps from one definition to the next. Since the positional model's definitional framework is punctual, it simply can't attribute a reality to the interval, whose crossing is a continuity (or nothing). (Massumi, 2002a, p.3-4, emphasis added)*

Figure 1. Distance and Displacement (© Taey Iohe)

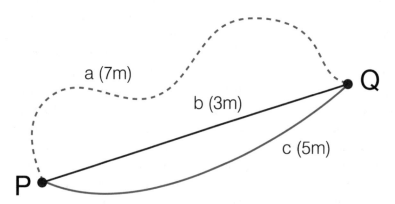

Massumi's writing evokes the question of duality in thinking of cultural construction. He describes it as a grid: 'male versus female, black versus white, gay versus straight and so on' (p.5). 'A body corresponded to a 'site' on the grid, the body came to be defined by its pinning to the grid' (p.5). He seems to suggest that the sites of P and Q become less important than the fact of movement as transformation and the political fact of an attempted positioning and defining of a subject. The space of overlapping and action between the poles of Source/Departure and Target/Arrival becomes the 'reality (of) the interval' in Massumi's terms, and the site of the translation I am proposing. Between two poles, the movement is related to latitudes and longitudes. In Massumi's formulation, this gives the grid not only a left and right, or x and y, but also a verticality and horizontality (Figure 2).

The artist-researcher, Hito Steyerl discusses and practises the political implications of horizon and verticality in relation to ontological aesthetics

Figure 2. A Grid, Sketch for Threshold Sea (© Taey Iohe)

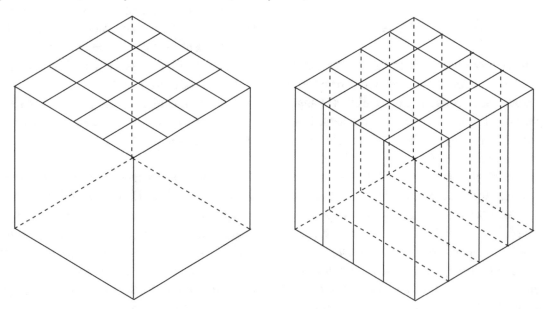

(Steyerl, 2012). In her book, *The Wretched of the Screen* (2012), she included a thought experiment on vertical perspective, which she presented at the research congress Former West (2010).[1] She emphasises the importance of a stable horizon in artistic and political understandings, and writes: '[in Freefall], with the *loss of horizon comes the departure of a stable paradigm of orientation*, which has situated concepts of subject and object, of time and space, throughout modernity' (Steyerl, 2012, p.14, emphasis added).

She states that 'the horizon enabled modern sea navigation, which spread colonialism and global capital; and was implicated in the development in the West of linear perspective' (p.18). My artistic vision aims to make explicit the relationship between the theory of emplacement and situatedness on the one hand, and the political operation of colonialism on the other. My conception of displacement will problematise the assumption of the ontological primacy of the poles of translation.

In the grid, the horizontal axis forms thresholds. These are the spaces of the crossing of a border from one cell to another. The vertical axis connects each wall to the next wall, so that all the cells are discrete trance experiences, as was discussed above in connection with embodied traces of movement. This displacing happens in several directions, so that it is not only geographical location that the body experiences but also a transformation of language, culture and class. Expanding on Steyerl's remarks, the grid has a vertical perspective to enable a sightline of only the cell that the audience is in; a change of horizon only occurs as the audience moves to the next cell. This affects the way I approach displacement.

Displacement is translated in various ways in Korean as 변위 (Byun-oui), 전위 (Jeon-oui), 전이 (Jeon-e) and 대치 (Dae-chi), very much as it is used for different purposes in English. Disassembling the word *displacement* into Korean and Chinese etymology extracts another semantic image for displacement, introducing a locomotive element and a sense of walking in space. This relates directly to my art practice. One of the possible translations, '전위 (轉位)', originated in Chinese and holds a number of meanings. Firstly, the Chinese letter 轉 (Korean pronunciation [Jeon]) stands for welter, shift, turn, hover, linger, move, change, realise, know, flutter and so on. 'Jeon' is a phono-semantic compound which is formed from two elements of different words in two parts. (車) carries the semantic element and means a carriage or wheel, and 專 carries the phonetic element and is pronounced as 'Jeon'. There is a strong image and sense of *locomotion* in the understanding of displacement suggested here. This prompted me to consider the *double body* in a locomotive situation, conjuring up imagery of a fast train and destination. The sound of the wheels' movement and the taking of turns come to play out in this form of language. Perhaps this slippage between translation and the disassembling of words can enhance our understanding of displacement as a process between states. I refer back to the etymological point of the always already translated nature of language, and the sense that all artistic text or work contains its own translation. The dual components of meaning in the two Hanja characters here brings this idea powerfully to life, in that the word itself is translating itself even as it is used in a Chinese sentence.

Now I will take you to the early 19th century in Korea, and introduce you to Hyeseok Na (1896~1948) who was an artist at that time. Re-imagining her death and after-death became an important motif in my work, *Strangers in the Neighbourhood*.

HYESEOK NA AND DOUBLE DISPLACEMENT

On 10th December 1948, a Korean newspaper reported a death in which the body was unidentified. The report stated the age of the deceased as 53 years old, the birthplace as unknown and the address as unknown. This report was published three months after Hyeseok Na died alone on a street in Seoul. Hyeseok Na (1896-1948) was a writer and landscape painter during the colonial period in Korea. Unlike the lonely end of her life, her adult life was full of vivacity. Her lifetime seemed misplaced and she lived at an unfortunate time in Korea, as she rebelled against the social duty to be a traditional woman, wife and mother in favour of her desire to be an artist and activist.

She was a relatively fortunate woman who obtained a formal education in Japan and travelled widely, including to Europe. Her recorded literature on women's rights, her travel journals and a few landscape paintings became important to Korean feminist scholarship as well as illuminating the colonial context in Korea. Na was actively associated with the Korean feminist movement and the national independence movement between 1913 and 1919, including during her time in Japan. She published her writings in newspapers and magazines as well as carrying on a painting career. Her liberal thinking on issues of women's fidelity, sexual equality, independence from childcare and equal rights in marriage and divorce were perceived as radical even by women at that time. The story of Na's marriage, divorce and social death[2] has gradually come to be told less judgmentally, and as less of a scandal, in mainstream Korean feminist history. However, her life and works were constantly in a contested state, and continue to be so today, to an extent. In this research, I introduce her as a living person who inhabits my artwork, rather than as a historical character from the Korean colonial period.

The contemporary Korean poet, Seung-Hee Kim (1952~) wrote a poem about Hyeseok Na (Kim, 2004). She begins the poem: "Dear friend, I have a certain fear" (p.91). Kim addresses Na as if Na is a fellow artist and puts Na's life into Kim's own. The poem speaks of a fear of leaving home and also of a fear of staying there forever out of perceived duty to her father, husband and son. These are expressed as if Na's life in the early 20th century, as a typical Korean woman's life, is also

lived now by the poet Kim herself. She writes, "She comes to me now / and remains in me, my heart her spirit tablet". In the original Korean poem, Kim describes Na's miserable death using the Korean words 비명횡사 (非命橫死), which literally translate as 'an accidental, unexpected death'. This reinforces the intimation that Na's death was an abandoned and untimely one.

There is still considerable debate regarding whether Hyeseok Na should be considered an icon for modern Korean women or not. She was re-discovered by feminist writers in the 1990s. However, the context of the specifically Korean New Woman[3] in the colonial era and during the arrival of the modern era, then and now, is problematised by the historical, social and cultural situation under colonial influence. Na's privileged background was still perceived as bourgeois during socially divisive passages of Korean history. The privileged position of Na constitutes a complex colonial situation, and consequently an uncomfortable one. A response to this has to account for Na's inspirational status as an artist and writer, and her relative economic and social privilege at that colonial time. She travelled abroad with her husband who was an ambassador. She would not have been able to travel if she had not been married. All her social privileges and the custody of her children were removed as soon as she disobeyed social protocol and did not meet the expected standards of a good wife and mother.

Modernism (근대, Gundae) arrived in Korea with genuine social and cultural impact from the end of the Japanese colonial era until the Second World War. In the early 20th century, a woman's rights and independence were absolutely not considered to be important matters when measured against national independence[4] for Korea. Women were assumed to be home-keepers, to be good mothers, loyal wives or dispensable labour, and tenders of men's morale in war-time.

About 200,000 Korean and other Asian young women were mobilised to serve Japanese soldiers in military brothels during the Pacific War. (Kim,

2004, pp.92-93). Korean women were recruited from 1932 to 1945. The first comfort station was established at the Japanese concession in Shanghai in 1932. "Korean victims of sexual slavery were drawn largely from poor families that belonged to the landless tenant or semi-tenant class in rural areas or to jobless migrant groups in cities" (Min, 2003, p.938; Council, 2012). These women were abused in Japanese military camps by men but also re-victimised when they were returned to their homeland. They became *shameful* women in their families and for their neighbours at that time. Gender hierarchy in Korea played a key role in the suffering of Korean comfort women after their return home. The issue of these so-called *comfort women* remains a live one; every Wednesday,[5] survivors and supporters protest in front of the Japanese Embassy in Seoul to request an official apology from the Japanese Government.

Women in colonised nations are suspended beings and displaced beings regardless of class or economic status. Women in colonial situations are doubly displaced by colonialisation: once by family and again by nation. Colonial women in this context cannot liberate themselves from patrial[6] and patriarchal space. Women in colonised nations are displaced because they cannot belong in their home nation or a foreign nation.

My departure point for the work *Strangers in the Neighbourhood* is an acceptance of the state of being displaced and unstable. I dramatise this instability in my work as continuing the *call for translation*, and the displacement as requiring us to see the role of translation in artistically capturing and accounting for the complexity of the stories being told here. Homelessness is a state of travelling and a process of exile. Displacement and instability are here counterparts in a situation which can only be understood as both state and process. In the same way, the Korean etymology from Chinese in its word for *displacement* requires two elements or characters to carry the meaning clearly.

Hyeseok Na is presented as the main character of this work, but the echoes of her letters are a continuing voice applied to people who have *lost* or *left* their homes during the rupture of exile. In the journey, which brings Na's ghost to Newington Green in North London, there is a specific reference to the Korean colonial era. However, the project becomes infused with the artist's current experience of a multiplicity of cultures and histories in her neighbourhood. I focus on the "embrace of elsewhere" (Demos, 2009), rather than on longing for home. The art does not mean to draw out the contingent political forces at work but enacts the being-as-displacement of the translated woman. In the case of Na's death on the street as a homeless person, I imagined a resting place for her but also a mobile place of memorial and continuity. I see the virtual as a reflection of this multiplicity and being-constituted-through-displacement.

Spacing Emplacement

Every story is a travel story – a spatial practice. (De Certeau & Rendall, 2011, p.115)

Space is as much a challenge as is time. Neither space nor place can provide a haven from the world. If time presents us with the opportunities of change and (as some would see it) the terror of death, then space presents us with the social in the widest sense: the challenge of our constitutive interrelatedness - and thus our collective implication in the outcomes of that interrelatedness. (Massey, 2005, p.195)

The photographic series *Sleepwalkers* (2008) demonstrates the taking of a vulnerable physicality in a displaced bed and transporting it into a real place in North London. It is stationed as a vehicle, possibly having come to the end of its journey or taking a rest before continuing. The story of Hyeseok Na is placed as a reference but the full story does not necessarily need to be told in any of the photographs. As the title suggests, the character in the photograph could be a woman who has a sleeping problem; perhaps this is the scene of a dream. The woman could be homeless and have placed a mattress in the middle of the street; private space and public space are spoken of in a scene of displacement at night-time. There are many terms we might use to characterise this lost woman: traveler, nomad, foreigner, wanderer, stroller, migrant, rover, rambler, drifter, vagabond, floater, flâneuse (flâneur) and passenger. The passenger on the bed is a conflicted presence, dazed and jet-lagged by her journey. However, Na has also chosen not to make the bed but instead has allowed it to commemorate and stand for her presence by leaving the imprint of her body and her scent behind her, in and on it.

The way we imagine space has effects... Conceiving of space as in the voyages of discovery, as something to be crossed and maybe conquered, has particular ramifications. Implicitly, it equates space with the land and the sea... seeming like a surface, continuous and given... If instead, we conceive of a **meeting-up of histories**, *what happens to our implicit imaginations of time and space? (Massey, 2005, p.4, emphasis added)*

The *meeting-up of histories,* which is dramatised in *Sleepwalkers,* creates a new place, a virtual place, which is meaningful and as alive as an actor in the story. There are four solitary walkers[7] in the story, including the writer of the letter, Hyeseok Na, and a receiver, Mary Wollstonecraft who was an eighteenth-century English writer and feminist. The two other solitary walkers are myself, and Anna Birch.[8] The latter is a theatre director who collaborated with me to exchange letters, as two artists who re-create the imaginary letters exchanged by Na and Wollstonecraft. Four solitary walkers' interpretations of locality interplay in the story; they are interrelated in different times and spaces. The oneiric quality of the

meeting between Na and Mary is clearly political in its staging of an afterlife for Na, in response to the reactionary Korean regime of masculine power and strict control of a woman's possible social agency. Her re-emergence in a dreamlike state is, in part, an artistic challenge to the spatial intransigence of a neo-colonial state.

Alexei Penzin writes in a timely way on the subjectivity of sleep; "the modern regime of power, famously outlined by Michel Foucault and updated by the Deleuzian notion of a "society of control" is also *sleepless.* Checkpoints, monitoring cameras, police patrols, security guards, just to mention the most obvious examples, function incessantly" (Penzin, 2012, p.8, his emphasis). Penzin's un-sleeping, uniformly surveilled, dystopian landscape is interrupted by the dream of Na and Mary's specifically emplaced encounter. Their arrival becomes a challenge to the rigidly boundaried and exclusionary urban space which Massey and Penzin have both questioned. The two women's meeting stages both a breaking-open of a monoculture and the creative traversing of national, sexual, chronological and waking boundaries. I see the boundary between the real and the virtual as being staged and crossed at this point also.

In her letters, Na writes to Wollstonecraft, who lived on this particular street, and describes what she sees in the neighbourhood. She sees identical-looking houses on the street, old bricks, the colour of people's hair, someone's lighted kitchen. It is mundane everyday life that she sees; yet for Na it is a very particular and charged landscape. She strolls around in the neighbourhood, part of the N16 postcode in the London Borough of Hackney. As a traveller she sees exterior spaces on the street, which do not appear to her as they do to the rest of us as residents of the town. Having that foreign gaze only lasts for a while; gradually everyday life becomes more familiar than foreign.

It is a town of multiple cultures; socially, religiously and ethnically, Hackney has diverse and complex communities in population and history.

"If space is more than (or even not) coordinates, but a product of relations, then 'visiting' is a practice of engagement, an encounter" (Massey, 2005, p.91). I started roaming the town when I moved into the area, and it was a departure point for the imagining and exploring of a ghost stroller in Hyeseok Na. In the last letter from Na and Wollstonecraft, they decide to meet up in a local coffee shop. This imaginary narrative entered the real world as Anna and I met to exchange maps and places to visit in planning our re-mapping of these solitary walkers (Figure 3). For Anna, it was important to introduce the history of political dissent around Newington Green in London and in Wollstonecraft's life. For me, the discovering of a possible *site* of friendship between Na and Wollstonecraft was a critical and urgent touchstone to weave into the trajectory of the walk. Anna was interested in putting local history and Newington Green's emancipatory tradition into a global story; on the other hand, my global journey from Paju to Hackney became a local story. Massey writes of the complexity and relations of space, and particularly urban place, in her book *For Space* (2005). She writes of "the city as a provocation to philosophy… a machine which undoes and exceeds sociological definitions,

posing new problems for thinking and thinkers, images and image-makers" (Massey, 2005, p.159). The experiences that I described in my account of living in Dalson could be seen as the grounding for what Jacques Rancière describes in French as "mésentente', an untranslatable concept carrying the meaning of lacking full understanding and not, in the English phrase, 'getting along". Bal and Hernández-Navarro (2011, p.10) deploy this challenging translation from French in a positive role, suggesting that this experience of 'mésentente' in the relationship between citizens of the same district can transform an antagonistic, confrontational stance into an adversarial one, which permits engagement and dialogue. It is this creative emplacement of relations which I deploy in *Sleepwalkers*.

Through my practice, I emplace my own city. It is no longer a foreign space but has become a neighbourly space. However, travelling bodies like that of Na are constantly displacing. The dimensions of multi-cultural urban landscapes are a global phenomenon. The *ethnoscape* of this piece of writing is a snapshot of today's globalised population in a major world city like London. Arjun Appadurai uses the term *ethnoscape* to mean a

Figure 3. Walking, Iohe and Birch (© Taey Iohe)

"landscape of persons who constitute the shifting world in which we live: tourists, immigrants, refuges, exiles, guest workers, and other moving groups of individuals constitute an essential feature of the world" (p.33). It is this *essential feature of the world*, and the displacement which is presupposed by it, that I engage with in creating *Sleepwalkers*. I aim to investigate the function of Massey's 'meeting-up of histories' as constituting a space which has translating properties, partly by virtue of the *ethnoscape* in which it arises. If a town is formed from a community of different cultures and peoples, the space-sharing experience encourages us to realise that co-habiting in a neighbourhood is possible without forcing a national or social identity on the neighbours. Stepping out to visit the neighbourhood repeats and continues the story from the work; scenes from the narrative took place in reality and the neighbourhood became a stage. Massey's concept of the 'meeting-up of histories' could also illuminate the way in which a virtual reality is constituted, beyond its technological and digital building blocks.

PLACING AND DISPLACING CRASH SITES

This work is a snapshot of a ghost story, and a travelogue, but also an account of living as a woman in the un-remarked locations of urban space. I started to travel with my bed to experience and represent trans-historical characters and sleepwalkers. A bed is *placed* on the dark corner

Figure 4. Sleepwalkers (© Taey Iohe)

of a street, at the busy Dalston High Street, by a near-empty Newington Green and at small cul-de-sacs and lanes nearby, late at night. Through this performative reclaiming of both dead figures, Na and Wollstonecraft, the areas in which Anna Birch and I walked and explored locally became a stage for action, imagination and new processes for unfolding the story. However, seeing the space through Hyeseok's eyes helped me to discover a way in which travellers can live with residents, and how 'otherness' can become displaced into and familiarised in this local area. A scene of resting and sleeping at the same time is displaced in the photographs. It is anonymous; anyone can arrive at the scene to take a rest. In fact, during the photographing work, several homeless people approached me to talk. Some claimed ownership of the bed, some said I was working in their living room, some indicated this appeared to them as a public sexual work. All their comments reminded me that the street-space is also an inner space for some people. It is a home and an intrinsic space rather than an extrinsic space. "The simultaneous attraction to and fear of the dead, the need continually to rehearse and renegotiate the relationship with memory and the past, is nowhere more specifically expressed in human culture than in theatrical performance" (Derrida, 1994, p.82-83).

I was interested in green lawns, not designated as gardens or manicured spaces, but simply present and empty. These lawns are not specific parts of the neighbourhood or necessarily significant places but they become designated as locations and potential stages through their collection, and through their commonalities when presented together. Long narrow leaves are scattered on the surface, each green space is weak and vulnerable on its own, but collectively they form a stronger story and identity as spaces. Re-constructing this lawn space became real and visible through the installation work, *Lure of the Lawn* (2008) at the Gyeonggi Museum of Modern Arts, Korea, which followed on from the momentum of *Sleepwalkers*.

ALTERED SPACING AT THE *LURE OF THE LAWN*

The *Lure of the Lawn* installation is a complete reconstruction of this process of translation and displacement. The grass of Newington Green in North London is effectively uprooted to the Gyeonggi Museum in South Korea and the language of the encounter is placed on the walls, such that it constitutes the space's dimensions and limits.

The grass of the lawn spills out from the enclosed space. Before coming into the room, the audience is encouraged to take off their shoes. Similarly, visitors to a traditional Korean house would take off their shoes at the Maru, which is a platform that serves as an introduction and social space in Korean architecture. The transition onto the lawn is placed as an invitation to an interior space. There is a floating bed and a few items scattered around it: a copy of *A Vindication of the Rights of Woman* (1792), two women's shoes and a ball of the bright orange thread that was seen before on the screen, in a video piece titled *Kamkatcha Blues* (2008). There are several handwritten texts in chalk on the wall. Otherwise, the lawn is empty. There are four spotlights, set to illuminate quite dimly.

Derrida rightly states that "even if there is no discourse, the effect of spacing already implies a textualisation" (Derrida in Brunette & Wills, 1994, p.15). Derrida explains spacing (or *espacement* in French) as a necessity for all forms of auto-affection, even tactile auto-affection. Massey reads into this that for Derrida, "spacing is integral to the constitution of difference" (Massey, 2005, p.52). *Espacement* was referred to first by the poet and critic Stéphane Mallarmé (1842-1898). For Mallarmé, meaning is the effect of a play between words. He employed spacing and pausing in his poetry, which he calls his typographical play, and used the term *espacement*. Derrida sees this as 'a topography of traces, a map of breaches' (Derrida,

Figure 5. Lure of the Lawn (© Taey Iohe)

(2005 [1978]), p.258). Derrida's adaptation of 'spacing', therefore, carries a sense of physicality and movement. Elsewhere, Derrida writes "the movement of signification is possible only if each so-called *present* element, each element appearing on the scene of presence is related to something other than itself" (Derrida (1982), p.13, his emphasis). Derrida seems to make the act of proximity and positioning crucial in the creative instituting of different elements, with careful attention to their relationship with text and meaning.

We can immediately see the application of this consideration to *Lure of the Lawn*; the bed has arrived on the lawn but before this nothing was there. The bed and the texts of the letters are stationed as elements, which must endlessly depend on each other for their definition. As Derrida elaborates, "it is the index of an irreducible exterior, and at the same time of a movement, a displacement that indicates an irreducible alterity" (Derrida and Bass, 2004, p.67). The lawn is both spaced as both a physical area we expect to find outdoors,

and positioned as an interior from which the lawn has 'leaked'. The text on the walls speaks to the story of the movement of the bed in its irruption into the space of the lawn and the gallery.

De Mul (2007) draws together the dimensions of text, movement and artistic practice: "migratory aesthetics also centralises the mobile dimension of intertextual relationships existing between different aesthetic representations of a singular space" (p.97). The text of the letters on the wall at Gyeonggi Museum, the speech of the two women printed on the pillows, the words attached to the tea bags, the title of *A Vindication of the Rights of Woman*; all speak to each other across the imaginary London postcode of N16 that locates the work.

The texts of the letters between Na and Mary on the wall encourages the audience to approach the wall, as the light is dimmed and the letters are specifically not brightly illuminated, as accompanying text would usually be in a gallery space. The wall becomes a border; text on that wall is

Figure 6. Lure of the Lawn, the entrance to the room (© Taey Iohe)

positioned as the substance of the border, as its entry into the world of text and language. The border is then able to speak in this way; it speaks from the position of liminality and debateability.

The fundamentally permeable and doubtful membrane between the interior and exterior is constituted as an artistically mediated place. The inner lives of the two women as expressed in their letter writing practice come to form the very physical gallery wall, the staging and definition of the artistic landscape. Derrida's (1994) placing of the dialogue with the hauntings of memory and the past directly onto the stage, points the way to interpreting *Lure of the Lawn* as a theatrical space in which the audience itself treads, encountering

the history of Na and Wollstonecraft's story. The work not only theatrically stages displacement but also questions the status of place for the post-colonial subject, and allows language to enter the constituting framework for both artistic space and the *translating space*; regions through which we do not pass unaltered or untranslated.

STRANGERS IN THE NEIGHBOURHOOD IN SECOND LIFE

After *Lure of the Lawn*, the question of space was raised through developing the project, *Strangers in the Neighbourhood* in the Second Life environment, in order to explore a different textual space. The 'Kritical Works in SL' project was initiated and curated by Dr Denise Doyle and was presented throughout the 14th and 15th ISEA Symposiums; a further exhibition was held at the Golden Thread Gallery in Belfast in 2009. The project was presented in the form of a screen display.

The journey undertaken by the beds was physical, but it was already virtual; the beds had come to stand for more than their physical selves, and their status as objects within the artwork already suggested an incorporeal, otherworldly existence. The idea of Hyeseok Na migrating to Kriti Island in Second Life was a natural exploration of this process. With valuable assistance from a fellow artist, Annabeth Robinson, I was able to bring my artistically mediated space into the virtual Second Life space of Kriti. In the physical space, the bed

was suspended at a low level, and impossible to sit or lie down on, as it was a fragile construction with invisible string. But in Second Life, the bed was at a much larger scale and suspended at a far greater altitude. Red threads were suspended from it (in fact positioned above the exhibition space where the audience can see pictures), so other avatars could to fly in and rest on the bed, in an extension of one of the physical themes of my work at the time. This immediately created a sense of a 'communal sleeping space'. Doyle writes about the avatar's experience in this space; "the immediate experience of the artwork relies on inverting the logic of the physical world, and in particular in playing with scale (the bed and the balls of red thread) and the apparent weightlessness of the bed itself. The photographs of the bed in the street at night are particularly evocative of

Figure 7. A snapshot of Strangers in the Neighbourhood in SL, Kriti Island (© Taey Iohe)

Figure 8. © Taey Iohe. Red threads on bed space in Second Life (© Taey Iohe)

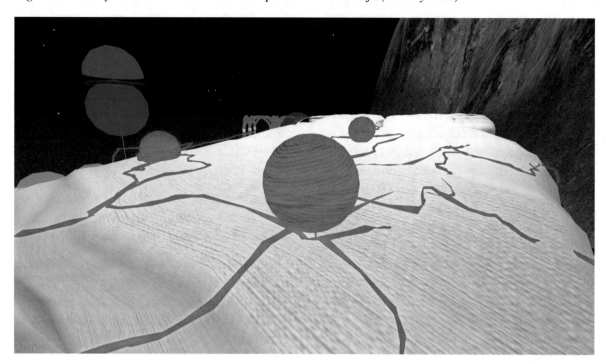

a form of lucid dreaming, a world that is real but evoking a state of dreaming when awake" (2010, p.122-123)

The scope within the Second Life environment to exhibit the photographs from *Sleepwalkers*, in a space directly underneath the virtual bed, created a strange moment of change in which both aesthetic and actual objects were granted a new relationship with each-other by virtue of their virtualisation.

CONCLUSION

The project, *Strangers in the Neighbourhood* set out to explore the virtuality and physicality of a specific space and place; this exploration traversed between the living and the dead, historical character and imaginary character, the placed and the displaced. The project came to life as a translation between those poles.

Virtual space is not suddenly a new possibility – it is part of a long line of unreal places, and imaginary places. My work explores the point on the grid at which virtual reality separates from actual reality. This point is that which enables a story which does not exist in real life, but becomes real when placed and told in the work: In the case of the comfort women discussed earlier, this point is that of their colonized situation, and the double status of their bodies.

Displacement happens at various sites and in various forms in my art practice and the processes that have grown up around this. Firstly, a historical character, Hyeseok Na, has been imaginatively displaced from her historical position as a Korean woman, symbolic of modernity in the Japanese colonial period, to her status in my artwork as a travelling soul. I have re-visioned and re-placed her as an unfortunate woman who could not fulfill her desire to travel; virtually in my transformation of her position, both as far beyond the social expectations of a Korean woman, but also as profoundly marked by her journey, allowing a further re-spacing of her, to the letters and bed-space of *Lure of the Lawn*. Her image in *Sleepwalkers*, however, still operates on women seeing the work today, like myself in this space, still somewhat vulnerable and sleepless. Secondly, the creative displacement of the travelling bed dramatises the bed-space as a specific political and artistic environment in a public sphere. Thirdly, the relationship between Hyeseok Na and Mary Wollstonecraft has been creatively displaced from the paper of the letter to the bed, and then on to a virtual space.

Virtuality is ghostly. A concept of space is already virtual in our experience and perception. My artistic work with the placement, translation, and creative transformation of the bed – as an environment for a 'meeting-up of histories' – aims to establish the value of not just an artistic presence in the virtual world, but also of the creative possibilities of a dialogue across that boundary.

REFERENCES

Birch, A., & Iohe, T. (2011). *Wollstonecraft Live!* (Vol. 2). London: Fragments and Monuments.

De Certeau, M., & Rendall, S. (2011). *The Practice of Everyday Life*. University of California Press.

de Mul, S. (2007). Travelling to the Colonial Past as Migratory Aesthetics: Aya Zikken's *Terug naar de atlasvilinder*. In S. Durrant & C. M. L. Lord (Eds.), *Essays in Migratory Aesthetics: Cultural Practices Between Migration and Art-Making* (Vol. 17, pp. 95–108). Rodopi.

Demos, T. J. (2009). The Ends of Exile: Toward a Coming Universality. In N. Bourriaud (Ed.), *Altermodern, Tate Triennial*. London: Tate Publishing.

Derrida, J. (1994). *Specters of Marx: The State of the Debt, the Work of Mourning, and the New International*. Routledge.

Derrida, J., & Bass, A. (2004). Positions. *Continuum*.

Derrida, J., & Spivak, G. C. (1976). *Of Grammatology*. Baltimore, London: Johns Hopkins University Press.

Doyle, D. (2010). *Art And the Emergent Imagination In Avatar-Mediated Online Space*. Unpublished thesis (Doctor of Philosophy), University of East London, London.

Grosz, E. A. (2001a). *Architecture from the Outside: Essays on Virtual and Real Space*. Cambridge, Massachusetts and London: MIT Press.

Grosz, E. A. (2001b). *'Lived Spatiality (the Spaces of Corporeal Desire)'. Architecture from the Outside: Essays on Virtual and Real Space* (pp. 31–47). Cambridge, Massachusetts and London: MIT Press.

Grosz, E. A. (2008). *Chaos, Territory, Art: Deleuze and the Framing of the Earth*. New York: Columbia University Press.

Kim, E. (2008). Questioning the Modernity of Rha Hye-Seok&Quot;S Idea of "Newness" in Colonial/Modern Chosun. *Journal of Korean Women's. Studies, 24*, 147–186.

Kim, S-H. (2004) I Want to Hijack an Airplane: Selected Poems of Kim Seung-Hee.

Massey, D. B. (1994). *A Global Sense of Place. Space, Place and Gender.* Minneapolis: University of Minnesota Press.

Massey, D. B. (2005). *For Space.* London: SAGE.

Massey, D. B. (2010) Spatial Justice Introduction in the Spaces of Democracy/Democracy of Space Network.

Massumi, B. (2002a). *Introduction: Concrete Is as Concrete Doesn't. Parables for the Virtual: Movement, Affect, Sensation*. Durham: Duke University Press. doi:10.1215/9780822383574

Massumi, B. (2002b). *Parables for the Virtual: Movement, Affect, Sensation*. Durham, NC: Duke University Press. doi:10.1215/9780822383574

Massumi, B. (2011) Hair-Trigger Action Replaced Deliberation in the Bush Era. *The Guardian*. Video retrieved from: http://gu.com/p/3xgp4/tw

Min, P. G. (2003). Korean "Comfort Women": The Intersection of Colonial Power, Gender, and Class. *Gender & Society*, *17*(6), 938–957. doi:10.1177/0891243203257584

Penzin, A. (2012) Rex Exsomnis: Sleep and Subjectivity in Capitalist Modernity. *100 Notes - 100 Thoughts*. (13).

Ryu, J-A. (2010) Na Hye-Seok as a Feminist: Accomplishments of Feminism through Writing 여성연구논집, 21, 133-176.

Steyerl, H. (2006) The Language of Things. Retrieved from http://eipcp.net/transversal/0606/steyerl/en

Steyerl, H. (2010a) Aesthetics of Resistance? Artistic Research as Discipline and Conflict, *Mahkuzine*. 8, Winter, Retrieved from: http://eipcp.net/transversal/0311/steyerl/en

Steyerl, H. (2010b) *In Free Fall: A Thought Experiment*. BAK.

Steyerl, H. (2011) Hito Steyerl Discusses in Free Wall. *Picture This*. Retrieved from: http://goo.gl/Wb9An

Steyerl, H. (2012). *Hito Steyerl: The Wretched of the Screen*. Sternberg Press.

The Korean Council. (2012). *Objectives & Activities*. The Korean Council for the Women Drafted for Millitary Sexual Slavery by Japan.

KEY TERMS AND DEFINITIONS

Comfort Women: Comfort women were victims of forcible sexual slavery by the Japanese military regime during World War II in Korea and many other Japanese-occupied territories. The survivors in South Korea, officially demanded apologies and compensation from the Japanese government; however this conflict is not yet resolved.

Displacement: Displacement in this article implies a form of the transformation of bodies, states and homes. It is also a concept of motion from point one to another. Displacement is a form of turning, which enables us to understand liminal and political space.

Ethnoscape: The ethnoscape is a social landscape which acknowledges different cultures and ethnic backgrounds. Appadurai uses the term to mean a 'landscape of persons who constitute the shifting world in which we live'.

Na Hyeseok: Na Hyeseok is a Korean painter, activist, writer and journalist (1896-1848) in Korea. She wrote in advocacy of women's independence from stereotyping in family and education. She is a symbol of the New Woman in Korea and influenced many feminist scholars and activists.

Sleep: Sleep is state of animal activity for the restoration of energy and recollection of conscious and unconscious thinking processes. Any disruption to sleep has societal and political implications which leads to sleeplessness in life and society.

Spacing: The term spacing (espacement in French) is one of the central ideas in Derrida's thinking, which means an interval between intervals, a distance and polemical otherness. It is usually accompanied by the concept of 'différance', which for Derrida denotes the becoming-time of space and becoming-space of time.

Translation: Translation is a process of conveyance between two different cultural and linguistic spaces. Therefore a concept of translation is a spatial practice which is inevitably coordinated with a transcultural space where our understanding of nation, border and origins is situated.

ENDNOTES

[1] In Steyerl's presentation at the research congress Former West, she discusses the perspective of verticality, which suggests another layer over the P and Q dimension on the grid. Verticality and vertical thinking refer to 'the proliferation of aerial views, 3-D nosedives, Google Maps, military remote camera footage, and surveillance panoramas' (See, Steyerl, Hito (2010b) *In Free Fall: A Thought Experiment* [online]. BAK, basis voor actuele kunst.). She explains that this vertical perspective performs in a particular way on our ideological operations, just as a central perspective did concerning the construction of a flattened horizon and stable observer. This vertical perspective also helps to analyse how social and political conditions could be contested in the colonial situation. The accessibility of vertical information such as Google Maps, aerial views, and simulated vertical perspectives has made available vast amounts of information and context-free oversight. She gives an example of computerised labour in American Air Force crews in order to discuss 'double bodies'. She quotes a newspaper account: 'At the end of each day, the Air Force crews who control the Predator and Reaper drones circling high above the battlefields in Afghanistan and Iraq stand up from their Naugahyde chairs, emerge from their cramped trailers on this remote Nevada air base and climb into their cars for the drive home, arriving in time to tuck their kids into bed.' Mcclos-

key, Megan (2009). The War Room: Daily Transition between Battle, Home Takes a Toll on Drone Operators. Stars and Stripes. The newspaper report continues to assert that 'a new paradigm of commuter warfare... is blurring the historical understanding of what it means to go off to battle'. What is astonishing about this is even an urgent combat situation has shifted to a different kind of engagement in the grid. The impact of displacement happens at a site that is not displaced. Most pilot and sensor operators travel a 40-minute drive between the office, where the combat happens, and their homes. The physical body does not displace, but the impact does. Double bodies travel between territories in this story. Steyerl continues to give examples from films such as Avatar and Inception, demonstrating how film presents verticality in such media. Steyerl insists on an escape from a perspective of East and West, of duality and division, but also calls on us to question the vertical dimension of class and politics.

[2] She was married to Kim Woo Young, a lawyer who was wealthy and socially stable. Between 1920 and 1930, she engaged with domestic matters such as married women's education, fashion and home labour in her writings. She had a liberal idea of marriage and relationships; she had an affair with Choi Lin who was a national independence movement activist (later Choi became pro-Japanese). Na obtained a divorce from her husband but Choi Lin ended the relationship with Na at the same time. She sued Choi for betrayal but Choi won at a trial. Na suffered from depression after this episode (Kim, 2008a; Ryu, 2010).

[3] In the Korean context, Modern Woman (신여성, Shin-Yeo-Seong in Korean) is a particular symbol with which to refer to progressive women in modern times and colonial times. It is also a title of a women's magazine,

which launched in 1923. The magazine, 신여성, has been a forum for the discussion of women's education, family matters, style and literary arts. The New Woman was a social and political phenomenon rooted in Europe and American culture. The New Woman was often cautious of marriage, which entailed acceding to a domestic ideology in a middle class family. The term was used to indicate a woman activist against the 'good mother and good wife' ideology in Japan also. In China, the New Woman was a radical and political being set against the ideas of tradition and Confucianism. In India, the New Woman is identified as situated between a middle class woman in late colonial India, and educated traditional women.

4   Arguably, Korean society's attitudes are still problematic when it comes to the issue of women's rights and gender equality. (See, Report, *Research on the Effective Establishment of a Gender Mainstreaming System* (2010))

5   The Weekly Wednesday Demonstration for the resolution of the issue of military sexual slavery by Japan, which first started in January of 1992, is held every Wednesday at noon in front of the Japanese Embassy in Seoul and it marked its 1,000[th] protest on 14th December 2011.

6   Patrial means a person with the right to live in the UK through the British birth of a parent. Domicile in UK has the meaning that father's birthplace is in the UK unless il-legitimate or posthumous. One can only have one domicile at any given time. (Domicile and Matrimonial Proceedings Act 1973)

7   'The solitary walker' is an established figure of literary subjectivity and modern politics. Rousseau writes in the late 18th century, in the Second Walk of his unfinished book, *Reveries of the Solitary Walker*, 'these hours of solitude and meditation are the only time of the day when I am completely myself, without distraction or hindrance, and when I can truly say that I am what nature intended me to be' (2011, p.11).

8   The project. *Strangers in the Neighbourhood* (2007-9) was born out of the artistic relationship between myself and my neighbour and friend, Dr Anna Birch. She is a theatre director and researcher. She has lived in Stoke Newington, in the London borough of Hackney, for most of her life; I was a new arrival there in 2006. She created a site-specific multimedia performance in Newington Green in 2005 based on Mary Wollstonecraft, who lived in the neighbourhood as well. Three 'Marys' (the actresses cast had three different skin colours: white, black, and brown) appear in the present day, making a film about Wollstonecraft. (See Birch, Anna (2012) *Repetition and Performativity: Site-Specific Performance and Film as Living Monument*. In Birch, A. & Tompkins, J. (eds.) *Performing Site-Specific Theatre: Politics, Place, Practice*. Palgrave, pp.118-134.)

Section 2
Avatar, Embodiment, Identity

The second section brings together three chapters each considering the significance of the avatar in different ways. From the first chapter that includes a study of a practice-based performance project and historical reenactment to the final two chapters that each take on the discussion of the avatar in opposing ways; one writing from the perspective of the avatar as a representation of our identity as embodied selves in virtual worlds and the other arguing that the avatar should be seen as something disembodied and that acts as a representation of loss.

Chapter 4
Digital Steps of Protest, Reenactment, and Networked Interaction:
Joseph DeLappe's Salt Satyagraha Project

Natasha Alexandria Chuk
School of Visual Arts, USA

ABSTRACT

Joseph DeLappe is an American digital media artist whose creative work demonstrates unique intersections between analogue and digital creative processes. In 2008 he created the Salt Satyagraha project, a virtual and simultaneously physical reenactment of Mahatma Gandhi's 1930 Salt Satyagraha political march by using Second Life (SL) and a customized treadmill that corresponded to his avatar's movements. The project also included a blog, an exhibition, and numerous screenshots documenting the virtual events. This chapter explores the artist's intent and the impact of combining virtual and digital labor, performance, artistic intervention, play, and the role of the human agent in the human-computer relationship. DeLappe's project blog and two key philosophical theories – Walter Benjamin's concept of the spielraum, a playspace that allows for creative experimentation in advanced technologies; and Jacques Derrida's concept of the supplement, something added to an original that reinforces or changes its meaning – are used to frame this examination.

INTRODUCTION

In the spring of 2008, through his *Salt Satyagraha* project, American media artist Joseph DeLappe (b. 1963) recreated aspects of Mahatma Gandhi's historic march, the Salt Satyagraha, a trek made across India in 1930 in protest of British tax on salt. Some of the details of the original event were honored in his reenactment, such as the distance traveled and the time it took to complete, while others were modified. The 3D virtual environment of Second Life (SL) and Eyebeam Art and Technology Center, a gallery in New York City, were the physical and virtual sites for the reenactment. Deploying a customized manual treadmill outfitted for cyber travel, DeLappe spent 26 days traversing

DOI: 10.4018/978-1-4666-8384-6.ch004

the distance of the 240-mile march simultaneously in the physical space of the gallery and the online space of SL. In addition to this, he maintained a personal blog detailing his activities and progress; collected screenshots of his and other avatars and posted them to his blog and Flickr, a photo sharing website; and displayed enlarged and printed 3D reproductions of his avatar in the gallery. Visitors to the gallery could watch DeLappe on the treadmill and the display of his virtual counterpart in SL projected onto the wall as he marched. They could also choose to locate and follow DeLappe's avatar, MGandhi Chakrabarti, as visitors to SL from their home computers.

DeLappe's *Salt Satyagraha Project* was a multiplatform undertaking that engaged historical reenactment and reframing at its center and also explored notions of experimentation, a balance of risk and control, and the creation of media objects that acted as supplements to physical or virtual experience. Considering the variety of media used to complete this project, this chapter addresses a number of issues concerned with the role of the artist and the historical figure in a virtual reenactment, questions of the human-technology relationship, and the impact of combining facets of digital media art and networked environments with analogue and material performance. The latter point is addressed with the aid of a brief comparison to other performance artworks in an effort to isolate and draw out the unique features of DeLappe's project.

BACKGROUND

To better understand DeLappe's approach to realizing the *Salt Satyagraha* project, I draw on emerging ideas about the role and pragmatic nature of digital art and more specifically consider two theories concerning the potential and character of the human-technology relationship. Walter Benjamin's concept of the *spielraum*, or playspace – the byproduct or outcome of what

he referred to as *second technology* – assists this analysis with gauging the potential for play in the digitally fabricated, networked environment of SL. Jacques Derrida's discussion of the supplement as a device that achieves ancillary experiences or modifies what might be understood as "natural" addresses the hybrid nature of networked communication and the detached connection it fosters. Reenactment by way of an avatar, or virtual body, is addressed first through an analysis of the multiple meanings behind the term itself; and second through a brief comparison to another major SL reenactment project by artist duo Eva and Franco Mattes. Finally, my analysis of DeLappe's project relies on his written accounts on his blog of his experiences in SL during the *Salt Satyagraha* project, and my own experiences observing his reenactment on two occasions at the New York City-based gallery where the work was generated and completed.

STAGING A REENACTMENT IN SL

As a reenactment, Joseph DeLappe's *Salt Satyagraha* project revealed more about the ways that virtual space can be navigated than it explained the motivations and implications of Gandhi's politics. Commonly referred to as the Salt March, Gandhi led the act of civil disobedience in 1930 in protest of the British tax on salt. According to Geoffrey Ashe (1998), this tax gave full control of the production or sale of salt in India to the British government. Violation of this law was a criminal offense (p. 301). Homer A. Jack (1956) adds that the use of salt was vital to Indian life, and under ordinary circumstances it was readily available for free (p. 235). This and other unfair mandates imposed by British rule compelled unsettled citizens to respond through proposals for negotiations by groups like the Indian independent movement, of which Mahatma Gandhi was the preeminent leader. On March 12, 1930, Gandhi led a group from Sabermanti and arrived on April 5, 1930 to the coastal town of Dandi, approximately 240 miles away, where he and tens of thousands of followers made salt from seawater in a peaceful act of protest. Others around the country followed his lead and made or found salt deposits, which over the course of the next month led to approximately 60,000 arrests, including Gandhi's. The Salt March proved not only to be an act of civil disobedience, but also signaled a momentous movement against imperialist control and was instrumental in the events leading up to India's independence in August 1947 (Dalton, 2012)

In DeLappe's reframing of this historical event, the salient details describing the political vigor that underscored Gandhi's protests, including the terms of the salt tax, the purpose behind the march to the seaside town, and the overall impact of the act measured in participants and arrests, were left out. Moreover, DeLappe's reenactment was not staged in the real life (RL) terrain between Sabermanti and Dandi in India, rather in the combined spaces of a New York City gallery and the online virtual world of SL. However, other aspects of the Salt March were honored: DeLappe physically walked 240 miles and followed the month-long timeline from March to April to complete the march on a customized treadmill housed in a gallery that corresponded his movements to those he made in SL. His avatar, MGandhi Chakrabarti, to the extent that the 3D modeling software of SL allowed, physically resembled Mahatma Gandhi. The choice to omit certain aspects of the historic event from the reenactment appeared deliberate, encouraging the possibility that DeLappe was interested in staging a different kind of intervention with this artwork. On March 16, he wrote on his blog, "By virtually walking as Gandhi in SL and committing to physically walking the actual 240 miles on a treadmill, I am furthering my efforts to investigate online game spaces as sites for interventionist, non-violent, creative action" (DeLappe, 2008). In this way, it is possible to interpret the *Salt Satyagraha* project as one that brought RL and SL participants out of and into

spatio-temporal regularity, while the original event served as a point of departure used to explore the contours of reenactments and human (bodily) interaction within virtual space. As Paul (2008) notes, "Like its graphic chat-room predecessors, worlds such as SL provide the stage for public performances" (p. 245). In this sense, the Salt March was in some ways brought back to life and shared with an online public, though in its reenactment, its context was shed and reconstituted as a performance specifically designed for the fabricated spaces of a gallery and virtual environment, which allow for controllable but ambiguous conditions through which to carry out the project but exclude the initial politics that drove the historic event. Though DeLappe's project was initiated by a reenactment of a speech Gandhi delivered the evening before his march commenced, references to the protest were mentioned both in name and through social encounters on SL but generally offered little or no incentive on the part of viewers or participants to achieve better understanding of the risks and legal and social outcomes of the original march. DeLappe's reenactment became a separate performance altogether that did not establish the sense of urgency and sociopolitical significance of the Salt March and, instead, played with the facets of reenactment, namely a sense of time, place, authorship, audience interaction in SL, and the negotiation between the material (body) and virtual (avatar) engagement. As such, the *Salt Satyagraha* project was conceived on the premise of having the ability to play with, through, and among digital technologies to produce what DeLappe referred to as "interventionist, non-violent, creative action."

SL AS ROOM FOR PLAY

For the duration of the project, DeLappe remained the sole creator, navigator, and manager of the physical and virtual components. He blogged daily, frequently posted images from SL, and consistently marched in RL and SL. His decision to utilize SL was an important factor in streamlining his project because of its pragmatic value and its potential for creative exploration and play. Its interface and customization tools allow for users, known as residents, to create and shape their avatars and environments with creative detail, including features derived from the physical world, from the security and comfort of a personal computer. Denise Doyle and Dew Harrison (2010) write, "Using the SL building tools to create objects and manipulate terrain, along with the application of the SL programming language, it is possible to have a high level of control when creating a virtual environment" (p. 199). However, much of the already built environment of SL is open to public use, which suggests SL is in many ways a readymade world in which users are invited to play. DeLappe did not design and build a virtual India and instead used SL's creative modeling tools to create MGandhi Chakrabarti, an avatar that physically resembled Mahatma Gandhi through physical features and manner of dress. Through the visual customization of his avatar, DeLappe exercised the liberty offered by default in SL, which does not prohibit the copy or portrayal of another likeness, to achieve a measure of historical accuracy and the freedom to virtually explore and enter into role-play.

DeLappe's *Salt Satyagraha* suggested evidence of a union between seriousness and play. On the one hand, certain values of the Salt March were observed while others, like the use of SL to perform the reenactment, were more suggestive of play. Utilizing the creative freedom that disembodiedness affords, DeLappe was able to physically act in one space and perform in another, virtual, one. He combined technology and performance to bridge various realities and, in so doing, allowed for a space of play. This method of thinking and creating calls to mind Walter Benjamin's influential essay, *The Work of Art in the Age of Mechanical Reproduction* (2002), about the effects and politics of sense perception with regard to mechanized

creative practices. In it he reflected on a kind of "second technology," which not only corresponds to "the point where, by an unconscious ruse, human beings first began to distance themselves from nature," but also, and perhaps as a result of this first condition, second technology is situated "in play," creating a *spielraum*, or playspace. Benjamin described this combination by saying, "Seriousness and play, rigor and license, are mingled in every work of art, though in very different proportions" (p. 107). According to Benjamin, second technology is not concerned with the "mastery of nature," as might be implied by the distancing effects of reproducible media, rather it is aimed at producing "an interplay between nature and humanity" (p. 107). This distinction is central to a work like the *Salt Satyagraha* project and other digital art that blur the lines between art, technology, and amusement. The significance of SL in this project is underscored by what Mary Flanagan (2011) observes about this cross-section: "Artists locate their audience within the web of net-connected machines across the globe, and this enables the development of fluid and seamless transitions between work, play, public, and personal environments" (p. 93). As a second technology, SL operates in concert with other web-based actions and the physical environment through which users access it. SL is an internet-based, three-dimensional virtual world, which as of October 2014 is populated by approximately 43,000 logged-in residents among approximately 39,800,000 total residents. Launched in 2003, it continues to thrive as a space in which fantasies can be virtually created and tested. DeLappe's decision to walk physically in addition to virtually underscores the relationship in SL between fantasy and physical reality. His avatar's customized appearance acted as his costume, and the virtual terrain and the gallery space his stage. In addition to play, DeLappe highlighted the importance of work, specifically physical labor, toward demonstrating sincerity behind his performance. On March 30, he wrote on his blog:

I've been performing in game spaces since 2001 – the commitment of my body towards any type of risk or exposure being primarily the result of long hours of sitting and typing extended texts into these online environments. Through this new project, where I have physically committed my body to the walking on the treadmill to "march" my avatar across SL, I hope to take online performance to a more committed position. (DeLappe, 2008)

DeLappe's customized treadmill, set in the physical world, became the interface between the physical and virtual, three-dimensional world. In this sense, he not only appropriated history but also adapted the exchange between physicality and virtuality, calling attention to the creative capabilities that second technology enables. As Christiane Paul (2008) describes, "The interface serves as a navigational device and as translator between two parties, making each of them perceptible to the other" (p. 70). The customized treadmill was designed to override keyboard-based controls, the default interface between user and SL, which allowed for DeLappe's physical movements to be translated as virtual ones and recognized in the SL environment. This facet of the project addresses the developing bond between humans and machines and the margin for play, error, and experimentation afforded by their relationship. In the *Salt Satyagraha* project, SL was DeLappe's playground and quasi-political stage for performance, interaction, and the negotiation between seriousness and the playspace Benjamin described. But to what kind of play did Benjamin refer and does SL foster? How is play to be understood?

Game designers Katie Salen and Eric Zimmerman (2004) define play as "free movement within a more rigid structure" (p. 304). More generally speaking, Immanuel Kant linked humor and play, which serves to underline a kind of surrender within a set of specific conditions, or a temporary departure from the norm (Kant, 1987). In this sense, play can be understood as a disruption of regularity, a kind of dissonance or incongruity that interferes with the banal. Philosopher Hans-Georg Gadamer placed play alongside art, wherein something is placed *in play*, yielding an occasion to which one surrenders (Gadamer, 1987). Referring to the creative relationship between video games and art, Andy Clarke and Grethe Mitchell (2007) write, "Videogame art is also art that retains a sense of humour. As a result, it must be looked at in relation to broader themes of play, fun, and chance in art" (p. 9). Each of these perspectives on play are useful toward understanding SL as a playspace in which one can depart for a time from uniformity, and experiment with free movement and a sense of humor within an open digital environment. Virtual reality recontextualizes the rules that govern time, space, and human interactions in RL. This is the "second technology" to which Benjamin referred, which permits users to act in ways that respond to the flows of mutability. One can easily substitute "SL" for "film" and "networked environments" for "apparatus" in Benjamin's (2002) following passage:

The function of film [SL] is to train human beings in the apperceptions and reactions needed to deal with a vast apparatus [networked environments] whose role in their lives is expanding almost daily. Dealing with this apparatus [networked environment] also teaches them that technology will release them from their enslavement to the powers of the apparatus [networked environment] only when humanity's whole constitution has adapted itself to the new productive forces which the second technology has set free. (p. 108)

In the technological realm of the apparatus he described, *spielraum*, or room for play, is possible. The *Salt Satyagraha* project relies on the playspace of SL to test the boundaries of human action insofar as technology can aid in the selective recreation of history and its players. From a technical standpoint, SL is many things, splitting its identity across different kinds of second technology and uses. It has chat functions; though it is not a game in the traditional sense – in that it does not have a prescribed objective – it is similar to a computer game; and last, it is a virtual world, modeled after RL exchanges of money, goods, and behaviors between participants, which have virtual- and RL impact. The latter characterization is the most all-encompassing, implying an environment of make-believe, a world constructed on the basis of simulation, or a place of *almost*. In this sense it is, in many ways, an ideal *spielraum* as it encourages the potential for play.

THE SIGNIFICANCE OF THE AVATAR

In addition to being a playspace for creative activities and interactions, SL represents an information-based system premised on disembodied human interactions carried out by various avatars, screen names, handles, and other virtual personae that enact complex human-computer behaviors. Paul (2008) notes, "Avatars as a new form of self-representation have been fertile ground for artistic experimentation" (p. 239). Creating and acting through an avatar raises interesting questions about the need for material form to create an artwork, or to stage a protest or reenactment. There are a growing number of options available to customize avatars to reflect a user's creative intentions. The term itself has an etymological history worth mentioning here. Avatar is derived from Sanskrit: *avatarana*, meaning descent through a combination of words that indicate being "off, down" and "crossing over." In Sanskrit an avatar is the descent of a Hindu deity, an essential component of the dominant religion of the Indian subcontinent. The term was adopted by American science fiction novelist Neal Stephenson, who wrote *Snow Crash,* a novel wherein gods, goddesses, and computer programming language were combined to produce the likeness and supernatural characteristics of religious deities. The book depicted a fantasy world of hacking, computer glitches, and other digital actions that shaped information flows and

disrupted characters' lives, alluding to a world administered by play (Stephenson, 1992). Paul (2008) writes,

While it may be difficult to trace exactly how the term entered cyberspace vernacular, it is at least interesting to note its connotations in the context of identity and community on the Internet and the upload and download (descent) of information to and from the server. (p. 121)

While the ancient, arguably oldest, religion of Hinduism greatly differs from the Internet and systems of networked communication, the comparisons between gods that descend to Earth in the forms of various recognizable figures and the virtual sprites created by computer software are fitting. The shared characteristics between a Hindu deity's incarnations and computer avatars also include the recreation of human physical characteristics and the reliance on iconographic features to symbolize different meanings. A basic computer sprite can bear human characteristics and utilizes iconographic features to represent various ideas. Human-computer and more commonly computer-computer interactions are standard practice between avatars. Actions take place without physical contact and in the absence of material form. As a result, a computer avatar bears aspects of a whole, reachable through immaterial connection. The avatar is the medium through which the user reaches the disembodied state and performs out of body. As aspects of a whole, these states and actions are reachable through graphical overlays, bitmaps, and hardware. As a result, computer avatars raise interesting questions about the relationship between the imaginary and the virtual. As Doyle notes (2013), "The relationship between the transitional and the liminal, and the avatar experiences, sets out a particular view of the imagination and its elusive and sometimes liminal, qualities" (p. 60). SL, viewed as a virtual *spielraum*, is the playspace of the imagination that requires ongoing negotiation between the virtual and physical environments. The liminal qualities represent the unknowable and unpredictable effects within this relationship. However, in the *Salt Satyagraha* project, DeLappe seemed to represent the liminal space between RL and virtual reality (VR) as an autonomous as opposed to transitional space by coupling physicality and virtuality in a mimicking way. This further built upon the human-computer relationship already in use and also, in doing so, established the body as the mechanical supplement to movements in virtual space. In this relationship, the human (user) and machine (by way of avatar) took action and shared subjectivity. By adding the physical requirement to his virtual movement, DeLappe strengthened the human-computer relationship and the shared experiences between user and avatar. SL supports this relationship. Behaviors are displayed primarily through acting (playing) by proxy, and producing outcomes that are distributed between the virtual and physical environments. As Paul (2011) states, "It would be problematic to understand networks as a separate kind of territory that has no connection to our physical environment" (p. 107). With this in mind, users who engaged DeLappe in SL through his avatar were not aware of the significant role his physical form took alongside his virtual actions.

While this factor does not change the interactions in SL or the outcomes of the project overall, it speaks to the supplementary nature of the avatar and its ties to the liminal. Operationally speaking, the avatar occupies a powerful position within the construct of networked communication. Encounters between avatars can be difficult to decipher, ignore, and understand the explicit and implicit meanings behind them. While the human user physically hides, the avatar-avatar interaction is public and visible, and their methods of communication are multi-hyphenate in nature: they are text-, voice-, gesture-, image-, and action-based. Avatars communicate with spoken and written language through speech and typing; they interact gesturally and "say" something about their "identi-

ties" through their physical appearance; and they take action through movement and creation in the virtual world. Though SL is a simulated model of the physical world, its rules are based on avatar-avatar behavior and their modes of conduct through and among virtual objects and spaces. Like RL, it operates on the basis of understanding the verbal and non-verbal languages and exchanges therein. With this in mind, the avatar acts as a supplement to virtual actions. Derrida (1997) identified the supplement as something that accounted for a deficiency in meaning and provided compensation for what was missing. He wrote, "Languages are made to be spoken, writing serves only as a supplement to speech" (p. 145). This suggestions a primary or preferred method of communication, yet it also indicates a deliberate act that is a condition of physical distance. Verbal language requires the body and physical presence, while writing mechanizes aspects of the body and allows for non-verbal, out-of-body delivery. He continued, "The supplement adds itself, it is a surplus, a plenitude enriching another plenitude, the *fullest measure* of presence. It cumulates and accumulates presence" (p. 145). In SL, the avatar can be understood as the necessary digital supplement that adds presence to the already present user. It allows the user to act remotely and virtually under conditions in which the physical body is only partly responsible for interaction (through typing). The conditions created in the *Salt Satyagraha* project add an additional supplement to this relationship. When MGandhi Chakrabarti acted, it did so on behalf of its user and also mirrored its user's physical actions. In this sense, the notion of the supplement raises interesting questions about the liminal nature of actions conducted in SL and which agent, the user or the avatar, is the supplement.

PERFORMING GANDHI

The mere creation (presence) of an avatar yields the possibility for communication in a virtual world. It signals the presence of its user: it exhibits (communicates) readiness and waiting, and it serves as an additional layer, or supplement, to the human agent who operates it. The ability to interact in SL was an element that DeLappe counted on to generate a virtual following. He recruited as many followers as possible through MGandhi Chakrabarti to join him on his virtual journey. In this respect, DeLappe engaged his audience in a kind of interactive historic novel: any SL avatars could choose to step in and join the Gandhi stand-in on his peaceful march across the digital map of imaginary India. DeLappe's gesture of community and companionship was visibly represented by a walking stick, given to any and all encounters along the way. His encounters produced mixed responses. On April 2, DeLappe wrote the following:

I also came upon three avatars from Sweden (they were talking in Swedish), all three modeled as three tiny leopards with sneakers...one of them morphed into a full sized avatar curiously similar in appearance to Gandhi! Quite interesting to be looking at somewhat similar mirror image of my assumed self. Difficult to communicate but I did give them each a walking stick. (DeLappe, 2008)

Entering the continuously populated environment of SL guarantees interactions between avatars and to a lesser degree with their hosts. The supplementary nature of the avatar "skin" creates a rational disconnect between users and their morphing avatars and therefore depends on one's openness to imaginary experience. This is in part due to the nature of networked environments. Margot Lovejoy (2008) writes, "Communication on the Net allows the participant to be invisible, anonymous" and in some ways "*fantasy becomes part of representation*" (p. 240). DeLappe's *Salt Satyagraha* served as an invitation to engage the interior reality(ies) of SL and the exterior reality(ies) of RL, including their limitations and possibilities. While VR and RL are not diametrically opposed,

they rivaled for DeLappe's primary attention in this artwork, requiring continuous negotiation between them: physical and virtual movement; in-person and mediated communication; and multiple degrees of observation and interaction. Yet the supplementary nature of performing in SL allowed DeLappe to perform a fantasy as well.

As previously mentioned, DeLappe's customized, programmed treadmill connected his physical person to his avatar to track and record his RL movements through SL. On a more profound level, DeLappe's system, a self-propelled rather than motorized treadmill, was a direct link between his physical body and its virtual counterpart. Even though SL lends itself to the creation of customizable objects and actions, by designing the treadmill installation mechanism, DeLappe waived the affordances of SL's features in favor of extraneously customized ones. This added a physical supplement to his virtual actions, in a sense doubling what is required for simple movement through SL. MGandhi Chakrabarti's movement through SL thus corresponded to the physical steps DeLappe made on the treadmill. By adding complexity to the simplified features of SL, DeLappe dismissed the exclusively mechanized features of virtual movement and synchronized movements of his body to those of his virtual counterpart. The avatar did not outwardly change as a result of this set-up, but its pace, distance, and other movements were subject to DeLappe's physical limits from day to day. In this design, DeLappe was in a sense transformed into a machine device, or human joystick. This shifted the one-to-one relationship of moving from side to side and up and down with the arrow keys, to full-bodied movement hidden behind the avatar. For the duration of the project, MGandhi Chakrabarti mimicked its living host, and DeLappe performed as his avatar. As a result, DeLappe and his avatar shared responsibility as both puppet and puppeteer, splitting the representation of agency. But this element of the project underscored an impasse with respect to how SL is designed to operate. SL, a realm of networked connectivity, compromises the connection between the body and the machine. The avatar is restricted to taking action in a fragmented, synthetic space and the human agent remains hidden and immobile, save for the keystrokes. DeLappe was the agent who physically delivered the avatar to its final destination as a way of making a physical a connection to the historic event. This calls to mind Bill Nichols' (1988) perspective on the role of the computer. He writes:

The computer is more than an object: it is also an icon and a metaphor that suggests new ways of thinking about ourselves and our environment, new ways of constructing images of what it means to be human and to live in a humanoid world. (p. 22)

To further commit to performing as a physical and virtual stand-in for Gandhi, DeLappe tracked the number of miles he logged each day. His virtual SL journey was paired with a parallel journey in an air-conditioned gallery and the walking surface of a treadmill. He also watched, in a kind of self-surveillance, his avatar counterpart march through SL. A large projection of his virtual trek was displayed opposite the wall of his treadmill, which served as a temporary window into SL from the perspective of MGandhi Chakrabarti. This produced a strange face-off with DeLappe, a play on the mirror image, and invited gallery visitors to experience the mediated duality of DeLappe's reenactment. This set-up illustrated the tethered relationship between DeLappe and his avatar, demonstrating his ability to physically be *here* and virtually be *there* at the same time. This raises questions about identity and what it means to act on behalf of oneself and a virtual other. Marina Gržinić (2011) relies on Jacques Lacan's interpretation of the Self to explain the idea of a decentered subjectivity, or the subject that is split. She writes, "The subject's division is not the division between one Self and another–between two

contents–but the division between something and nothing, between the feature of identification and the void" (p. 168). This description of the split subject refers to the decentered subject within the virtual environment. The *Salt Satyagraha* project also factored the conditions and effects of performance and historical reenactment, but Lacan questioned the authenticity or validity of the notion of a true identity. Gržinić continues,

Decentering thus in the first place designates the ambiguity, the oscillation between symbolic and imaginary identification: the indecisiveness as to where my true center lies... with the possible implication that my symbolic mask can be 'more true' than what it conceals. (p. 168)

Judging by DeLappe's personal blogged reflections of his experience during this reenactment, he appeared to be caught somewhere between identifying with his avatar/character and himself. In SL he frequently approached other avatars and welcomed their comments and questions. The most impressive of these exchanges were later shared on his blog. One in particular took place with E9590 Gears, a stranger who walked alongside MGandhi Chakrabarti twice over a few days and peppered him with questions about the march. On March 20, DeLappe reported on this conversation. E9590 Gears began his line of inquiry with the simple question "Why do you walk?" and encouraged the artist (the operator behind MGandhi) to open up about what inspired him. The result was a self-reflexive contemplation about the experience: the interrogation was launched by the unknown human agent/E9590 Gears avatar combination and was aimed at DeLappe, the artist, not MGandhi Chakrabarti, the avatar. One could argue that the questions were not generated by a dual alliance between user and avatar, but the seasoned human-avatar relationship in SL fosters resistance to a distinct separation between the two. In contrast, when DeLappe discussed the motivation behind his creative project and virtual march in SL, his identification was with the human/artist behind the avatar. He answered for himself through the supplement, not the inverse. Reflecting a different tone, he blogged on May 6, shortly after the conclusion of the online march, alluding to the ambiguity of with whom or what he identified:

I truly feel as though I made a significant journey on many different levels. Funny too, I really miss my MGandhi avatar…I became quite attached to him over the course of the walk. I've had a few pleading emails from friends made in SL to not kill Gandhi! I've wandered, without the treadmill, a few times over the past month, mostly to revisit and take note of some of the places I have been to online – but I just don't yet feel comfortable "walking" Gandhi in SL without actually, physically walking with him on the treadmill. Perhaps this will change over time. (DeLappe, 2008)

In this post he suggested he grappled with symptoms of withdrawal after his intense human-computer-avatar-RL-SL experience. There seemed to be a feeling of not wanting to sever the relationship he built and fostered between him and his avatar, treadmill, and SL. The end of his simultaneous march with his avatar seemed to disrupt what Sherry Turkle (1984) refers to as "computer holding power" (Turkle, 1984). But DeLappe had already indicated there was some kind of hold on him during the course of his virtual journey, which blurred the distinction between RL and SL. On March 26, he wrote:

What has become most curious is the blurring between SL and RL. I find myself walking down the street in NYC wanting to click on people I see to learn more about them – or having a flashback/ deja vu to SL while walking up the subway stairs – a bit disturbing but also fascinating – I've now spent approximately 70 hours in the past two weeks in SL – it has definitely found a place in my subconscious. (DeLappe, 2008)

As many have observed, the Internet has played a significant role in identity formation. As Paul (2008) notes, "The body and identity have become prominent themes in the digital realm, centering on questions of how we define ourselves in virtual as well as networked physical space" (p. 165). According to Turkle (1995), "The Internet has become a significant social laboratory for experimenting with the constructions and reconstructions of self that characterize postmodern life. In its virtual reality, we self-fashion and self-create" (p. 180). Gržinić adds,

Integrated into the field of intersubjectivity, she (he) builds her (himself) a new identity. What is at stake in virtual reality is the temporal loss of the subject's symbolic identity. She (he) is forced to assume that she (he) is not what she (he) thought herself (himself) to be, but somebody–something– else. (p. 165)

These two disparate positions offer some insight into DeLappe's *Salt Satyagraha* project and his role as the player/agent of intersubjectivity experimenting in the playspace identified by Benjamin and with the supplements described by Derrida. DeLappe had not only built a new identity, he created a kind of digital double that took the form of numerous supplements in addition to his avatar. Photographic images of his RL march, screenshots of his SL march and interactions with other avatars, and daily blogging composed from the divided perspective of artist and performer all serve to reinforce the complexity of these identity formations and the questions they raise about his subjectivity for the duration of the project.

PERFORMANCE AND VIRTUAL REALITY

Questions about identity and subjectivity have been central concerns to performance artists and their work, particularly among Fluxus artists who experimented with form and audience interaction. Lovejoy (2008) writes, "Fluxus strategy was to democratize the art-making process by destabilizing the status of the art object and dematerializing it. Their events were repeatable by anyone" (p. 52). DeLappe's *Salt Satyagraha* seemed to respond to these motivations, employing a "repeatable by anyone" sensibility toward recreating an historic event and the idea of dematerializing his art. With this in mind, the physical body is necessary to the performance artwork. This, too, was reflected in the *Salt Satyagraha* project. DeLappe's physical commitment to his reenactment was central to the work, setting it apart from other digital reenactments. For example, the work of digital art duo Eva and Franco Mattes, particularly *Synthetic Performances* (2007), which were performance art replicas carried out entirely in SL. Among their chosen reenactments were a handful of well-known performance works, most of which took place in the 1970s, including Chris Burden's *Shoot* (1971), Marina Abramović and Ulay's *Imponderabilia* (1977), Vito Acconci's *Seedbed* (1972), and Gilbert and George's *The Singing Sculpture* (1970). Each of these original artworks emphasized the performance of a transgressive act – being the target of a lethal weapon, public nakedness and interaction, public masturbation, and days-long singing whilst in costume, respectively – involving physical discomfort, pain, or physical interaction with others (strangers) to, among other things, test how participants define and negotiate personal space in public and semi-public environments. These performances relied on the physical body and the notion of pushing the limits of what they could do. As a result, they each placed the artist in an extreme position of physical and social vulnerability.

In the Mattes' SL reenactments in SL, described by Paul (2011) as "the simulation of embodied reenactment" (p.107), the physical body on the part of the transgressor was removed. This calls attention to the absence or irrelevance of the

physical body in an environment that operates without material form and generally allows for mediated action while the physical body remains at rest. As Paul (2008) writes, "Virtual worlds offer a performative environment for realizing what is not possible or at least difficult to achieve in the physical world" (p. 244). Enduring physical pain and discomfort can be difficult to achieve in the physical world for obvious reasons. Instead, *Synthetic Performances* offers commentary on and celebrates the underlying aspects of play (and role-play) of performance art, where different rules can be established, and within SL, where physical consequences are a non-issue but other interactions, virtual and otherwise, can be tested. DeLappe's *Salt Satyagraha* differed in that he physically and virtually reenacted the physical aspects of an historic event, but it still played with and among the digital landscape and architecture of SL. On March 30, DeLappe reflected on specifically on this part of his creative approach:

I've been thinking much in regard to the formative concepts and historical connections to performance art. An aspect of my thinking towards developing this project is my appreciation for the durational aspects of performance works, particularly some of the seminal works of performance art in the 1970's and 80's. (DeLappe, 2008)

A commitment to the temporal and physical requirements of the reenactment was important aspects of his creative process. In anticipation of the expedition, DeLappe dressed in sneakers and casual clothing and outfitted his customized treadmill with a wooden desk for his laptop, a bottle of water, a coffee mug, and a leather cushion at abdomen level for comfort. Despite this, the march took a physical toll on his body. On March 24 he wrote: "Today is a rest day. I can see why Gandhi's followers asked him to have these rest days! Very fatigued yesterday, walked 8 miles for 112 miles total" (DeLappe, 2008).

While ultimately both avatar and host traveled successfully to virtual Dandi, the human agent and artist took full responsibility for the logged miles and lost six pounds in the process.

His physical contribution was authentic but performative, both engaged but removed from the experience of the original event. In this connected dual environment, DeLappe played the part of a risk-taking adventurer and the representation of an historic peaceful protester. The combined physical and virtual performances between DeLappe and MGandhi Chakrabarti established a noticeable union during the project. After an event held at the gallery during the march, DeLappe made a note on March 14 of an attendee's observation, "One visitor commented that she had watched me for an hour or so and started to think of me as her avatar" (DeLappe, 2008). DeLappe did not say more about this, but one might wonder if he was pleased by this remark as it indicated a convincing performance and commitment to role-play on his part.

TECHNICAL IMPACT

While DeLappe navigated a virtual route to Dandi from a gallery-housed treadmill, the immaterial nature of SL and the virtual interactions therein proved to have some material consequences. The disconnect between the physical and technological aspects of the project produced annoying setbacks, miscommunications, in-game interactions, and other unexpected outcomes during the march, which drew attention to some of the tension and frustration with navigating large-scale projects between on- and off-line environments. Through his blog, DeLappe addressed some of these computational mishaps, such as the occasional glitch that caused delays in his travel plans, requiring both a physical and virtual pause in the progress of the project. On March 31 he wrote, "Just after 5pm or so the entire world of SL crashed completely! So I took a break grabbed some food and

waited until the service was restored around 30 minutes later" (DeLappe, 2008). The next day, the system crashed again, causing another half-hour delay. The indifference of the SL server showed no concern for the inconvenienced human user. Later, SL was down for most of the day toward the end of the march: with only ten miles left to the finish line, it caused, in DeLappe's words, "a bit of a chaotic day!" Computer system failures can be difficult to predict and impossible to prevent, but seasoned users come to expect occasional delays and setbacks. Jeff Papows (2010) discusses the basis of the computer glitch:

On the surface, these system errors are, at a minimum, annoyances that reflect an oversight or a shortcut in the software design. In many cases, it may not be a shortcut at all, but a reflection of the growing complexity of the infrastructure (p. 59).

Having designed *Salt Satyagraha* around the use of SL, DeLappe had no choice but to push through the delays by logging in additional time and distance to make up for them and stay on schedule. Working around these glitches became part of the charm and drama associated with this reenactment. Other unexpected technical matters were raised with respect to his customized interface. By connecting the self-propelled treadmill to the system, it rendered invalid the movement options offered to users on SL. Generally, avatars in SL can move in numerous ways, including through the use of transportation vehicles – cars, boats, airplanes, etc. – to move through the virtual space, which requires real-time travel between distances. These options do not emphasize virtual movement, rather the novelty of driving a virtual transportation vehicle. Though SL's virtual model is in many ways a simulation of RL, it also exercises freedom from the one-to-one relationship between space and time, and thus from those constraints, offering instead the ability to traverse great distances through flight and teleportation instead of walking or running in real-time. Movement through these means requires only a few clicks, sending avatars around the virtual globe of SL. For this reason, any real-time constraints are tied to the RL body, including the keystrokes needed to command movements from a computer keyboard. To recreate the distance Gandhi traveled during the Salt March, DeLappe traveled 240 RL miles, which were simultaneously logged in SL, but the units of measure in SL did not correspond to those in RL. Though his RL and SL movements were synchronized, there remained a gap between their different time-space configurations. DeLappe discussed this incongruity. On March 20 he wrote:

To date I have walked 72 miles on the treadmill and likely significantly further in SL as my Gandhi avatar, as do all avatars in SL, walks at an accelerated pace. Oddly, my treadmill set-up, which is basically a reed switch activated by magnets on the flywheel, hacked into a keyboard where I have closed the circuit on the forward arrow key – essentially fooling the keyboard as if one were continuously pressing the forward key – this system actually makes my MGandhi avatar walk faster than others in SL. This is interesting and a happy accident as Gandhi was notoriously a very fast walker in RL. (DeLappe, 2008)

This unexpected technical accident inadvertently demonstrated a behavioral affinity between Gandhi and DeLappe's avatar, MGandhi Chakrabarti. This and the previously mentioned technical inconsistencies are conditions of second technology, which allow users to engage in play and experimentation but subject them to the rules that govern and the glitches that are inevitable to computers and networked environments. Moreover, virtual spaces like SL place users in a mediated space between systems of thinking and measurement. As Doyle (2013) notes, "Spaces such as *Second Life*, with their combination of immersive qualities, avatar mediation, and user-generated content, are presenting new circumstances and conditions under which to undertake a study of the imagination and

in particular to study its own liminal states" (p. 60). Considering DeLappe's project design, which paired physical movements in RL with virtual ones in SL, the liminal qualities, those that register as being somewhere between two distinct poles, are presented more fully. His project seemed to play specifically within this realm of the in-between. This was evident also in the manner in which he navigated SL and negotiated its spatio-temporal gaps. Though he was concerned with time management and the amount of territory he covered each day to stay on schedule, as previously mentioned, DeLappe often stopped to chat with other avatars to discuss his journey and invite them to join him. This resulted in two interesting outcomes. First, to make as many social connections as possible, DeLappe wandered through SL in search of other residents. On March 24, he wrote, "I've taken to island hopping, unavoidably teleporting, but solely to get from one island or mass of regions to the next nearest space" (DeLappe, 2008). Second, as a result of his meandering, SL's default design selectively dictated his virtual navigation. On the 29th, he offered more detail:

A bit of a random selection, starting where I leave SL the day before. The smaller regions, many of them only one small square island, are loaded with private properties with either access blocked entirely or "orbs" which are essentially automated alarm systems that tell you are trespassing on someone's property and you have 10 seconds or so to leave or be tp's to your "home". As I am walking, this makes things a bit tricky as by the time I stop and try to turn around to reverse course and walk off the property in [question], I [end] up getting teleported – sometimes nearby off the property but often times to a "sandbox" area on the other side of the SL universe. (DeLappe, 2008)

Though SL is mappable and navigable, it is subject to the changes of a persistent game environment. Jesper Juul (2005) defines persistent games as continuing, even when players are not playing, and doing so indefinitely without a final or conclusive state (Juul, 2005). SL's mutability allows for numerous adjustments to the environment by residents and can result in a series of unknowns, like the unauthorized areas that prohibit exploration and forcefully remove unwanted avatars. The setback disoriented DeLappe, but the relocation procedure nonetheless brought MGandhi Chakrabarti to unexpected areas and led to additional social interactions with other residents. Initiating contact with SL residents was an important aspect of DeLappe's reenactment, but it also underscored the tethered nature between him and his avatar. Through this supplement, he placed himself in a position of seeing through the perspective of and taking action as both avatar and performer. Moreover, the supplemental nature of the technology, like the written form, produced unexpected incompatibilities between systems, highlighting the underlying incongruities that may result in their combination.

THE *SALT SATYAGRAHA* LEGACY

In addition to the interactions in SL, the daily blogging, images and screen captures, and physical performances, there were other ancillary but significant artifacts generated by DeLappe's *Salt Satyagraha*. The accumulation of SL actions, despite their virtuality, left remainders in the forms of memories, interactions, and data – each collectible and shareable. The online participants interacted with MGandhi Chakrabarti, gallery visitors observed his treadmill-based march, and others followed his blog, which remains accessible online, and is very much like a detailed, time-stamped memoir filled with insights into DeLappe's experience, outsider commentary, and a timeline of individual events related to the *Salt Satyagraha* project. They served to document DeLappe's reenactment project, but also functioned as objects that relate to Mahatma Gandhi as an historic figure. Following the conclusion

of his physical and virtual journey, DeLappe launched a material-based exhibition based on his SL avatar. On May 27 he wrote about his plans, "I will be featuring a number of new works in this exhibition, including the creation of a large scale, perhaps 15-20′ tall Gandhi statue created from the 3-D model of my MGandhi avatar as extracted from SL" (DeLappe, 2008). Using a combination of 3D modeling and design software programs, he proceeded to create and exhibit 3D rapid prototyped printed sculptures of his avatar made from cardboard. Though the sculptures resembled MGandhi Chakrabarti and not directly Mahatma Gandhi, the historic figure, they in their own way paid tribute to the history of the event and the role Gandhi played in shaping it. Extracted from SL, they were tethered to the reenactment and the events that took place through DeLappe/MGandhi Chakrabarti, reinterpreting and building on the Salt March's historical significance and impact. Through these extensive measures across virtual space and time, Gandhi was remade, borrowed from the past and reincorporated in DeLappe's performance intervention, virtually in SL and physically in printed form. Like the need to incorporate physical movement as part of the reenactment, the printed avatar pulls the digital object out of its context in SL and magnifies it in RL. This signals an interest in understanding the move from digital/virtual to physical and further complicates the notion of the supplement in the construction of meaning.

FUTURE RESEARCH DIRECTIONS

DeLappe's *Salt Satyagraha* project contributes to a growing interest in testing the limits of interaction between virtual and physical spaces, developing Benjamin's idea of a "second technology" and the playspace it enables, and possibly creating or contributing to an altogether different mode of creating, thinking about, and participating in the intersection between art and technology. With this in mind, the ontologies of the avatar and the subject/user remain largely undefined. The notion of the supplement and its shifting context is an area that could be developed to add to the ongoing dialogue around these definitions. As theorists, it would benefit our research to remain tuned into how agency might be inverted between artist/user and the avatar in projects like *Salt Satyagraha*. More importantly, there are expanding opportunities for artists to further test these distinctions or developing theories, or to remove them entirely, giving researchers reason to focus on the changing character of human experience within networked environments as technologies evolve and artists continue to experiment with them.

CONCLUSION

After considering the many facets of DeLappe's *Salt Satyagraha*, it is possible to suggest that the artwork concludes where it begins: centered on play, reenactment, and testing the complexities of a human-avatar relationship in SL. DeLappe combined VR and RL in ways that resisted easy classification of his work, and which engaged audiences with the possibility to access his journey through numerous outlets in addition to the main stages of RL and SL. He constructed a fictional space where he could combine virtual interaction and physical movement. This created a lively dynamic between audience and artist, on- and off-line, and tested the playspace described in Benjamin's description of the qualities of second technology. Moreover, through his fully tethered relationship to MGandhi Chakrabarti during his virtual march, he rendered ambivalent the definition of the supplement in the human-avatar relationship. As a result, the project necessarily returned to placing emphasis on the playspace, where such liberties can be taken, as its key driving force.

REFERENCES

Abramović, A. & Ulay (1977) *Imponderabilia* [performance/installation]. Bologna, IT: Galleria Communale d'Arte Moderna.

Acconci, V. (1972, January 15-29). *Seedbed* [performance]. New York, NY: Sonnabend Gallery.

Ashe, G. (1968). *Gandhi: A study in revolution*. London: Heineman Ltd.

Benjamin, W. (2002). Selected writings: Volume 3 1935-1938. (E. Jephcott, H. Eiland, and Others, Trans.) Cambridge, MA: Harvard University.

Burden, C. (1971, November 19). *Shoot* [performance art]. Santa Ana, CA: F Space Gallery.

Clarke, A., & Mitchell, G. (2007). Introduction. In A. Clarke & G. Mitchel (Eds.), *Videogames and art* (pp. 7–22). Bristol, Chicago: Intellect.

Dalton, D. (2012). *Mahatma Gandhi: Nonviolent power in action*. New York: Columbia University Press.

DeLappe, J. (2008, March 14). Re: March 14, 2008 starting location.... Retrieved from https://saltmarchsecondlife.wordpress.com/2008/03/13/march-14-2008-starting-location/

DeLappe, J. (2008, March 16). Re: Sunday, March 16th start point.... Retrieved from https://saltmarchsecondlife.wordpress.com/2008/03/16/sunday-march-16th-start-point/

DeLappe, J. (2008, March 20). Re: Starting location March 20, 2008.... Retrieved from https://saltmarchsecondlife.wordpress.com/2008/03/20/starting-location-march-20-2008/

DeLappe, J. (2008, March 20). Re: A conversation in SL about the walk.... Retrieved from https://saltmarchsecondlife.wordpress.com/2008/03/20/a-conversation-in-sl-about-the-walk/

DeLappe, J. (2008, March 24). Re: Monday, March 24, rest day #2. Retrieved from https://saltmarchsecondlife.wordpress.com/?s=march+24

DeLappe, J. (2008, March 24). Re: March 25th, later start time…. Retrieved from https://saltmarchsecondlife.wordpress.com/2008/03/24/march-25th-later-start-time/

DeLappe, J. (2008, March 26). Re: March 26th, 12 more miles and several friends…. Retrieved from http://saltmarchsecondlife.wordpress.com/2008/03/26/march-26th-12-more-miles-and-several-friends/

DeLappe, J. (2008, March 29). Re: March 29th, start – snapshots, shorefront properties…. Retrieved from https://saltmarchsecondlife.wordpress.com/2008/03/29/march-29th-start-snapshots-shorefront-properties/

DeLappe, J. (2008, March 30). Re: Sunday, March 30…8 days to Dandi…. Retrieved from https://saltmarchsecondlife.wordpress.com/2008/03/30/sunday-march-308-days-to-dandi/

DeLappe, J. (2008, March 31). Re: Monday, March 31st… rest day – steps towards the final miles…. Retrieved from https://saltmarchsecondlife.wordpress.com/2008/03/31/monday-march-31st-rest-day-steps-towards-the-final-miles/

DeLappe, J. (2008, April 2). Re: April 2nd, dragons, wolves, Nixon…. Retrieved from https://saltmarchsecondlife.wordpress.com/2008/04/02/april-2nd-dragons-wolves-nixon/

DeLappe, J. (2008, April 3). Re: April 3rd, trailer parks, performance art, cow…. Retrieved from https://saltmarchsecondlife.wordpress.com/2008/04/03/april-3rd-trailer-parks-performance-art-cow/

DeLappe, J. (2008, May 6). Re: On joining a "real" march in NYC…. Retrieved from https://saltmarchsecondlife.wordpress.com/2008/05/

DeLappe, J. (2008, May 27). Re: Cardboard Gandhi sculpture in progres…. Retrieved from https://saltmarchsecondlife.wordpress.com/2008/05/27/cardboard-gandhi-sculpture-in-progres/

Derrida, J. (1997). *On grammatology* (G. Chakravorty Spivak, Trans.). Baltimore: Johns Hopkins University Press.

Derrida, J. (2013). *Derrida and Joyce: Texts and contexts* (A. J. Mitchell & S. Slote, Eds.). Albany: State University of New York.

Doyle, D. (2013). Living between worlds: Imagination, liminality, and avatar-mediated presence. In D. Harrison (Ed.), *Digital Media and Technologies for Virtual Artistic Practices* (pp. 59–74). Hershey: IGI Global. doi:10.4018/978-1-4666-2961-5.ch005

Doyle, D., & Harrison, D. (2010). Kritical art works in Second Life. In G. Mura (Ed.), *Metaplasticity in Virtual Worlds: Aesthetics and Semantics Concepts*. Hershey: IGI Global.

Flanagan, M. (2011). Play, participation, and art: Blurring the edges. In M. Lovejoy, C. Paul, & V. Vesna (Eds.), *Context providers: Conditions of meaning in media arts* (pp. 89–100). Bristol, Chicago: Intellect.

Gadamer, H. (1987). *Philosophical apprenticeship* (R. R. Sullivan, Trans.). Cambridge: MIT.

Gilbert & George. (1970). *The Singing Sculpture* [performance/sculpture]. Chelsea, UK: Nigel Greenwood Gallery.

Gržinić, M. (2011). Identity operated in new mode: Context and body/space/time. In M. Lovejoy, C. Paul, & V. Vesna (Eds.), *Context providers: Conditions of meaning in media arts* (pp. 151–174). Bristol, Chicago: Intellect.

Jack, H. A. (1956). *The Gandhi Reader: A Source Book of His Life and Writings*. Bloomington: Indiana University Press.

Juul, J. (2005). *Half-real: Video games between real rules and fictional worlds*. Cambridge: MIT.

Kant, I. (1987). *Critique of judgment* (W. S. Pluhar, Trans.). Indianapolis: Hackett.

Kittler, F. A. (1999). *Gramophone, film, typewriter* (G. W. Young & M. Wutz, Trans.). Stanford: Stanford University.

Lovejoy, M. (2008). *Digital currents: Art in the electronic age*. New York: Routledge.

Mattes, E. & F. (2007-). *Synthetic Performances*. Retrieved from http://0100101110101101.org/synthetic-performances/

Nichols, B. (1988). The work of culture in the age of cybernetic systems. [Winter.]. *Screen*, *21*(1), 22–46. doi:10.1093/screen/29.1.22

Online Etymology Dictionary. (2001). Retrieved June 16, 2014, from http://www.etymonline.com/index.php?allowed_in_frame=0&search=avatar&searchmode=none

Papows, J. (2011). *Glitch: The hidden impact of faulty software*. Boston: Pearson Education.

Paul, C. (2008). *Digital art* (2nd ed.). London: Thames and Hudson.

Paul, C. (2011). Contextual networks: Data, identity, and collective production. In M. Lovejoy, C. Paul, & V. Vesna (Eds.), *Context providers: Conditions of meaning in media arts* (pp. 103–121). Bristol, Chicago: Intellect.

Salen, K., & Zimmerman, E. (2004). *Rules of play: Game design fundamentals*. Cambridge: MIT.

Second Life Grid Survey. (2008). Retrieved on October 14, 2014, from http://www.gridsurvey.com

Stephenson, N. (1992). *Snow crash*. New York: Bantam.

Turkle, S. (1984). *The second self: Computers and the human spirit*. New York: Simon & Schuster.

Turkle, S. (1995). *Life on the screen: Identity in the age of the Internet*. New York: Simon & Schuster.

KEY TERMS AND DEFINITIONS

Artistic Intervention: A term that refers to a planned creative act that serves as a disruption of the environment and its norms to initiate change or communicate an idea.

Authenticity: A term that Walter Benjamin uses to describe the quality of uniqueness attributed to a particular time and place.

Avatar: A term commonly used to describe an image-based graphic that represents a human user in networked environments.

Networked Environment: A digital system that virtually connects multiple users across great distances.

Persistent Game: An online game whose environment continues around-the-clock, whether or not the player is actively engaged.

Role-playing Game (RPG): A type of game in which the player assumes the fictional role of a character or characters.

Second Life: A three-dimensional, virtual, and persistent environment in which users can join for free and interact with other avatars.

Spielraum: The German word for playspace or leeway, this term is used by Walter Benjamin to describe the potential of advanced technologies to allow users to experiment.

Unlimiting Limits: This term refers to the seemingly limitless boundaries of virtual space, particularly in virtual environments in which visual boundaries appear ongoing.

Virtual: A term used to denote an immaterial object or connection facilitated by computer software.

Chapter 5
Creating a Framework to Analyse the Perception of Selfhood in Artistic Practice within Second Life

Pete Wardle
University of Salford, UK

ABSTRACT

This chapter draws upon existing identity theories to create a framework with which to examine the expression of self via avatars within Second Life. The framework is then applied to the practice of a number of artists working with themes relating to identity using avatars within Second Life, by drawing upon the author's own experience of these works and the artists comments taken from their writings and from discussions and correspondence with them, to examine the role their work plays in changing our understanding of the way that identity is expressed and perceived within virtual worlds.

INTRODUCTION

The use of avatars to represent the participant within computer games and social virtual worlds is a long standing convention dating back to the earliest text based chat rooms and first person shooter games. A wealth of writing exists cataloguing research within virtual worlds in general, and Second Life in particular, much of which addresses topics relating to the expression of self by means of avatar construction and appearance and to their operators' behavior and interaction with others via their avatars. Much of this research serves to

highlight the significant variation in the ways in which operators relate to their avatars. Nick Yee (2008) writes that "For some players the avatar becomes a purposeful projection or idealization of their own identity, while for others, the avatar is an experiment with new identities." In some instances avatars are viewed as little more than 'game pieces' which the operator controls which Domenico Quaranta (2007) refers to as "a kind of puppet that does everything I tell it to by means of a series of input tools" (p.6); in other cases they are digital placeholders or 'proxies' for the operator within the virtual environment (Apter,

DOI: 10.4018/978-1-4666-8384-6.ch005

2008; Lastowka & Hunter, 2006, p.15; Little, 1999), while for some individuals their avatars are a means of creative expression or even for the transference of self into virtual worlds.

David J. Gunkel (2010) writes of the need to "engage in philosophical speculation about the nature of (virtual) reality... to get real about computer-generated experience and social interaction, providing this relatively new area of study with a more sophisticated and nuanced understanding of some of its own key terms and fundamental concepts" (p.3). Building on Gunkel's discussions it is proposed that there is a need to establish a common critical language to allow structured discussion, comparison and analysis of the perceptions of selfhood via the medium of avatars within virtual worlds. It is therefore the intention of this chapter to define a framework categorizing different typologies of avatars, their purposes and the relationships that their operators develop with them.

Such a framework might then be applied to all areas of avatar use within virtual worlds. However the application of the framework to a particular exploration of how the use of avatars for creative expression has, directly or indirectly, addressed themes of identity within the virtual realm of Second Life, is an area where it may provide insight into how artistic practitioners have challenged the notions of the roles and purposes of avatars, and the nature of the relationships that their operators develop with them.

The categorization of the typologies used within the framework will be achieved by reference to existing paradigms relating to our understanding of identity within the actualized world of our corporeal existence. It is therefore necessary to first consider the progression of theories which have shaped our concepts of identity and selfhood from the pre-modern understanding, through modern and post-modern theories, taking into account also the writings of contemporary authors and researchers whose studies relate directly to Second Life.

BACKGROUND: AN OVERVIEW OF THE DEVELOPMENT OF IDENTITY THEORIES

The presentation of identity theories herein will not be exhaustive but will focus instead on the main concepts which will be used to develop the framework of avatar typologies. While these concepts will be presented in an order which generally reflects the chronology in which the theories were developed, or were the commonly accepted paradigm, an attempt has been made to group them into underlying themes rather than to stick rigidly to the schools of thought from which they were generated.

Role Identity

Stuart Hall (1995), writing on cultural identity, discussed the view of identity prevalent in the 'pre-modern' era that "One's status, rank and position in the 'great chain of being'--the secular and divine order of things- overshadowed any sense that one was a sovereign individual" (p.602). Described by Charles Taylor (1989) this concept of one's own identity involved "connecting one's life up to some greater reality or story" (p.42), i.e. identifying oneself as synonymous with one's role in life be it warrior, citizen or monk.

This pre-modern notion of role identity is an enduring one; Eva G. Clarke and Elaine M. Justice note that, even in contemporary society, when adults are asked to introduce themselves they will often do so initially by talking first about their occupation or career. In the introduction to The Ethics of Identity, Kwame Anthony Appiah (2007) concurs: "when we are asked...who we are, we are being asked what we are as well" (p.xiv). Appiah (2007) goes on to discuss how our own perception of our roles or designation can impact upon our expression of identity: "One draws, among other things, on ...ideas about how gay, straight, black, white, male, or female people ought to conduct themselves. These notions provide loose norms or models, which play a role in shaping our plans of life" (p.22). Writing extensively on role and social identities Jan E. Stets and Peter J. Burke (2005) emphasized "that the core of an identity is the categorization of the self as an occupant of a role, and incorporating, into the self, the meanings and expectations associated with the role..." (p.134).

This assumption of a role as the defining factor of identity is echoed within many computer game worlds where the player can assume the role of a pre-defined character avatar with a specific appearance and attributes. Examples range from the Gauntlet arcade game of the mid-1980s to the latest iterations of Grand Theft Auto, where the key factor defining the avatar's behavior is generally the role it fulfils within the game rather than any expression of identity on the part of the avatar's operator.

Constructed Identity

There was little development of identity theories until the 17th Century when Rene Descartes proposed a mind/body duality and with it a recognition of the individual as having the agency to reflect upon themselves. John Locke introduced the idea of a radical disengagement in which the real self is not the object being worked upon and remade, but that which is capable of working upon the remaking. He pictured the mind as a tabula rasa, or blank slate, onto which the identity can be imprinted by sensation, experience and reflection.

A further contribution of Locke to identity theory was his proposal of a number of thought experiments, including one in which the soul (or consciousness, which Locke seems to equate with the self) of a prince is transported into the body of a cobbler, to enable him to examine the relationship between the physical presence of the cobbler and the prince (1690): "Everyone sees he would be the same person with the prince, accountable only for the prince's actions: but who would say it was the same man?". He concludes that self is the 'conscious thinking thing...' and

explains that with the following illustration: "If the finger were amputated and this consciousness went along with it, deserting the rest of the body, it is evident that the little finger would then be the person, the same person; and this self would then would have nothing to do with the rest of the body" (Locke 2007 edition, p.118).

Locke's view formed the basis for most of the Modern theories of identity, centering around a unified self having a role in the construction and curation of its own identity. A number of subsequent thinkers have proposed similar thought experiments to develop Locke's scenario, to explore the relationship between memory, consciousness and identity, and between self, identity and the physical body.

Writers on the topic of identity in Second Life generally concur that much of the thinking and behavior of those inhabiting such social virtual worlds remains anchored to this Modern paradigm of identity construction. It is a noted phenomenon that when developing Second Life avatars operators tend to construct avatars based upon themselves, or on an ideal/stereotype. Matthew Meadows (2007) states that "we generally build a Second version of ourselves that has some bearing on the real world... Avatars are ultimately interactive self portraits that we use to represent ourselves. Most users, when they build their avatar, arrive at an alternate, less protected version of themselves" (p.106).

Multiple Representations of Self

Of the unity of self, Immanuel Kant (1787) wrote of "many-coloured and various" representations of self united in one self-consciousness (p.112); writing in the field of psychology William James (1890) went on to discuss the idea of the role of social interaction in the construction of the self and suggested that an individual "has as many different social selves as there are distinct groups of persons about whose opinion he cares" but, still maintaining the notion of unity of consciousness, discusses how these social selves share "the bare principle of personal Unity" (pp.292-310). In the language of social virtual worlds, one might say that an operator can have multiple different avatars but that they are all aspects of, and unified by, the personal unity of the operator.

Discussing videogames Quaranta (2007) refers to avatars as "the mask I have constructed to interface with the environment (be it real or virtual) that I inhabit" (p.6) whilst contemporary philosopher Slavoj Zizek (1997) warns of the "'dissemination' of the unique Self into a multiplicity of competing agents, shifting identities, of masks without a 'real' person behind them" (p.134).

The Social Self

George Herbert Mead (1934) further addressed the role of society in shaping the self in Mind, Self and Society in which he wrote: "The self is something which has a development; it is not initially there, at birth, but arises in the process of social experience and activity, that is, develops in the given individual as a result of his relations to that process as a whole and to other individuals within that process" However, for Mead, like those who went before him, it remains the individual's agency to reflect upon one's own nature which is the defining factor of self: "The pre-reflective world is a world in which the self is absent" (p.135).

To attempt to clarify the role of the relationship of self with the interplay between social structure and individual agency, that is to say how much of who we are is determined by external forces and how much it is shaped in accordance with our authentic self concept, Appiah (2007) writes of the roles both have to play: "If we are authors of ourselves, it is state and society that provide us with the tools and contexts of our authorship... An identity is always articulated through concepts and practices, made available to you by religion, society, school and state, and mediated by family, peers, friends" (p.156).

Performance and the Role of Narrative

In 'Self in Everyday Life' Erving Goffman (1956) suggest not only that all social actions are mediated not only through others but through one's own performance which "In the end...becomes second nature and an integral part of our personality" (p.12). Randal Walser (1990) quoted by Kathy Cleland (2008) adds to this discussion by relating performance in the actual world to embodiment in virtual spaces:

By giving his body over to a character, an actor enters a character's reality, and he can be said to embody (that is, provide a body for) the character... An actor in cyberspace is no different, except that the body she gives to her character is not her physical body, but rather her virtual one. She embodies the character but she, personally, is embodied by cyberspace. (p.161)

Rune Klevjer (2007) discusses how such performances of identity within virtual worlds are impacted on by the imposition of narrative:

The primary function of character has to do with narrative; when we play with characters, we play with a story... Through the avatar, instrumental agency is replaced with fictional agency and fictional destiny; the player is incarnated as a fictional body-subject who belongs to and is exposed to the environment that it inhabits (pp.116-130).

The Self as Embodied Experience

Maurice Merleau-Ponty (1945) emphasized the role of the body in human experience:

Insofar as, when I reflect on the essence of subjectivity, I find it bound up with that of the body and that of the world, this is because my existence as subjectivity is merely one with my existence as a body and with the existence of the world, and because the subject that I am, when taken concretely, is inseparable from this body and this world. (Merleau-Ponty, trans. Colin Smith, 2002, p.475)

Applying this to the experience of virtual worlds may at first seem to suggest that the authentic experience would be that of the operator's interaction with the hardware rather than that which they experience through the avatar. In referring to the body however, Merleau-Ponty does not refer merely to the physical body, but rather to the subjective experience of body. Of the physical makeup and operation of the body he writes "I cannot gain a removed knowledge of it. In so far as I can guess what it may be, it is by abandoning the body as an object... and by going back to the body which I experience at this moment" (Merleau-Ponty, trans. Colin Smith, 2002, p87).

In contrast to this view, Sydney Shoemaker (1963) proposed a thought experiment similar to that of Locke in which, when the brain of Mr. Brown is put into the body of Mr. Robinson, the resultant combination of the two, referred to as 'Brownson' identifies himself as Brown and behaves in accord with Brown's identity. Peg Tittle (2005) suggests that Shoemaker claims that "we are not using the body as our criterion for identity and that one's self is somehow separate from one's body" (p.79). If we consider how this experiment might be applied to an operator's relationship with their avatar, following this logic might lead to the conclusion that, if the body is not a criterion for identity, the operator's selfhood may reside within or as a part of the avatar they control. However, examining Shoemaker's experiment in light of the identity theories of his contemporaries, the conclusion drawn can be seen to be flawed in so far as it refers only to the physical body, not to the phenomenological subjective body as experienced. The body experienced by Brownson (that of Robinson) is likely to be subjectively very different

from that of Brown. Tittle goes on to consider the 'causal relationship' of the body to identity, that is to say, in Shoemaker's Brownson experiment, the effect it would have had on Brown's identity had Robinson's body, in which Brown's brain had been placed, been of a different ethnicity or sex to that of Brown's original body. Avatars can, of course, go some way in enabling operators to experience the phenomena of presenting others with a very different self appearance to that of the operator's actual physical attributes.

Edmund Husserl (1950), inspiring both the German and French phenomenologist schools of thought, suggested that "anything worldly necessarily acquires all the sense determining it, along with its existential status, exclusively from my experiencing, by objectivating, thinking, valuing, or doing, at particular times" (p.26). He refers to his experience of the object-as-perceived as the noema or noematic experience. Accordingly, different experiences of the same object or person will have different noemas. The noema is therefore subjective and moderated by the viewer, rooted in the cultural context in which it exists, and the noema of an individual expressed by an avatar to another avatar with a virtual environment will be very different from that of an interaction between the operators in the physical world.

If Schoemaker's Brownson experiment is analyzed in light of Husserl's noema, even if Brownson's identification of himself with Brown remains constant, such identification is only Brown's own noematic sense of the experience. Those meeting Brownson would initially have the noematic experience of meeting not with Brown, but with Robinson. Shoemaker himself writes (2003, p.65): "The experiences are co-conscious ... by virtue of the fact that they are components of a single state of consciousness."

Maeva Veerapen (2011) writes of a similar state of co-conscious experience when addressing the issue of embodiment within virtual worlds arguing that:

... the (actual world) body is still active and engaged when the user is inworld, albeit in a different manner from what we are familiar with in the physical world. My whole body reacts to the events I live out in Second Life by, for example, feeling downhearted or elated as a result of something that happened inworld. In doing so, the body ... acts as grounding during the inworld experience (p.83).

Writing on this topic Frank Biocca (1997) wrote of three bodies, the physical, the virtual and the phenomenal and of oscillations in the sense of presence between them and of the conflict between what we perceive in the physical and virtual environments: "It appears that embodiment can significantly alter body schema. Metaphorically, we might say that the virtual body competes with the physical body to influence the form of the phenomenal body." He went on to ask "Where am 'I' present?" a question to which Sita Popat and Kelly Preece (2012) propose the answer "'I' am present wherever I have agency" (pp.160-174).

Popat and Preece (2012) discuss the differing relationships with the avatar where firstly the interface forms part of the embodied subject but the avatar remains an object, i.e. the attention is from the body and interface to the avatar, and secondly where the avatar becomes part of the embodied subject, i.e. the attention is from the body and interface and the avatar to the interaction within the virtual world. They write of this final paradigm that:

... the avatar itself is a digital entity. My avatar is the digital entity infused with my agency, driven via the engine of my motor-activity at the interface. Crosscontamination at the hypersurface results in the avatar as the sum of human and technological features: a 'lived' posthuman body, part flesh, part technology, located simultaneously in two remote sites. The flow of information and feedback between body and avatar through the umbilical cord of the interface means that neither is fully

physical and neither is entirely virtual, since the embodied agent spans the two subjects (p.173).

The Self as a Process

In his primer 'Identity, Culture and the Postmodern World' Madan Sarup (2005) writes that in postmodern thought identity "is not a thing; the self is necessarily incomplete, unfinished – it is the subject in process" (p.47). Whilst many of the 20th century writers already discussed made a significant contribution to the development of postmodern theories of identity, Henri Bergson is arguably one of the earliest writer's who it can be claimed laid the foundations for the postmodernists who followed, introducing the concept of Becoming (1910):

Hence there are finally two different selves, one of which is, as it were, the external projection of the other, its spatial and, so to speak, social representation. We reach the former by deep introspection, which leads us to grasp our inner states as living things, constantly becoming, as free states not amenable to measure, which permeate one another and of which the succession in duration has nothing in-common with juxtaposition in homogeneous space (p.231).

Bergson (1920) expanded upon the role of memory in moderating perception to present actual and virtual aspects of our existence to us:

Our actual existence, then, whilst it is unrolled in time, duplicates itself all along with a virtual existence, a mirror-image. Every moment of our life presents two aspects, it is actual and virtual, perception on the one side and memory on the other (p.165).

Gilles Deleuze and Felix Guattari (1988) further develop the concept of Becoming, not only as a development through time but through the blurring of the edges of social interaction, giving the example of a wasp and orchid which "as heterogeneous elements, form a rhizome" (Deleuze & Guattari, 2004 edition, p.11) each affected by the other and becoming symbiotic emergent units. They are also responsible for introducing the concept of a multiplicity of self that "ceases to have any relation to the One as subject or object, natural or spiritual reality, image and world. Multiplicities are rhizomatic... There is no unity to serve as a pivot in the object, or to divide in the subject" (Deleuze & Guattari, 2004 edition, p.8).

Many writers have heralded virtual worlds as exemplars of this postmodern multiplicity, i.e., a complex mutually interactive relationship between operator and avatar. Sherry Turkle (1995), writing on the topic of identity in early internet multi user environments proposed that our behavior in virtual worlds challenged ideas about a unitary self:

each of us is a multiplicity of parts, fragments and desiring connections... the "embodied" life we live on a day-to-day basis has no more reality than the role-playing games on the Internet ... players can develop a way of thinking in which life is made up of many windows and RL (Real Life) is only one of them (p.14).

Similarly, in 'Coming of Age in Second Life' Tom Boellstorff (2008) concurs that "our real lives have been virtual all along" (p.5). He points out that "in SL embodiment is highly elastic bringing notions of choice to the fore" and predicts how "virtual worlds change our notion of ourselves as we will now be dynamic or unstable bodies"(pp.135-136).

Turkle (1995) writes of how Jacques Lacan attempts to "portray the self as a realm of discourse rather than a permanent structure of the mind" (p.178). Lacan (1977) wrote of the illusory nature of a centralised ego and is responsible for the concept of the mirror stage, described by Sarup (2005) as the stage at which, when the infant first catches a glimpse of themselves in a mirror, they have the "first conscious recognition of the

distinction between his or her own body and the outside world"(p.34). This recognition is however "based on an illusion or misrecognition" of "a point outside the self through which the self is recognised... an ideal self which can never be actualised." Bob Rehak (2003) relates Lacan's mirror stage to virtual worlds: "If the mirror stage initiates a lifelong split between self-as-observer and self-as-observed, in one sense, we already exist in an avatarial relation to ourselves" (p.123). Perhaps the concept of a stage at which individuals realize that their relationship with their avatar is a relationship with their Self could be seen as a 'virtual-mirror stage', the point at which one looks at their avatar and realizes that the avatar which looks back is not simply a tool or extension which allows them to interact within virtual worlds, but an aspect of their identity which exists in an autonomous, emergent symbiotic relationship with them.

Lacan (1977) further defined three terms or concepts which will be useful in categorizing avatar typologies, the Imaginary, the Symbolic and the Real. In the translator's notes to Lacan's Ecrits; A selection A. Sheridan (2001) defines these concepts:

- *The Symbolic: the symbolic involves the formation of signifiers and language and is considered to be the "determining order of the subject"*
- *The Imaginary: the imaginary becomes the internalized image of this ideal, whole, self and is situated around the notion of coherence rather than fragmentation.*
- *The Real: the real becomes that which resists representation, what is pre-mirror, pre-imaginary, pre-symbolic – what cannot be symbolized – what loses its "reality" once it is symbolized (made conscious) through language (p. viii).*

Zizek (1997) discusses Lacan's Imaginary in respect of virtual worlds and writes: "The

VR persona... offers a case of imaginary deception in so far as it externalizes-displays a false image"(p.139). He expands upon the concept of the Real as "simultaneously the Thing to which direct access is not possible and the obstacle that prevents this direct access; the Thing that eludes our grasp and the distorting screen that makes us miss the Thing... More precisely, the Real is ultimately the very shift of perspective from the first standpoint to the second" (Zizek, 2003, p.77). This statement could be applied to virtual worlds to denote a shift in standpoint from that of operator experiencing a virtual world from outside, to that of operator/avatar symbiote experiencing it from within.

In On Belief, discussing Lacan's definitions, he proposes three modalities of the Real which may have a useful application to this discussion, the 'real Real', the 'symbolic Real' and the 'imaginary Real' (Zizek, 2001, p.82). Taking this further, we might categorize virtual worlds, by their nature, as realms of the Symbolic where the formation of visual signifiers created from pixels to determine the order of the subject, and further apply Lacan's terminology to define three modalities of the perception of Self within the (Symbolic) virtual.

A FRAMEWORK FOR THE ANALYSIS OF THE EXPRESSION OF SELF VIA AVATARS

Lacan's definitions can be used to help categorize the theories outlined so far, and to attempt to establish a common critical language to apply to a discussion of identity as it relates to the relationship between avatars and their operators in virtual worlds. If the Symbolic, where signifiers and language determine the order of identity may be seen to relate to the pre-modern viewpoint of pre-defined roles then the Imaginary, situated around the notion of coherence, can be said to be descriptive of the Modern paradigm of unity of consciousness, by which identity is curated, constructed and performed. The Real, resisting representation, can be seen to equate to one's interactive response to the experience of existence, the becoming, yet never actualized, multiplicity of self posited by postmodern theorists.

Table 1 has been developed by the author as part of ongoing Ph.D. research in an attempt to create a critical framework with which to analyze the roles and relationships of avatars within computer games and social virtual words. The table seeks to apply Lacan's concepts of Symbolic, Imaginary and Real to define typologies of avatar based on their various functions and relationships to their operators. In developing this framework account has been taken of the identity theories previously discussed as well as other contributing factors to the expression of self including avatar appearance, the role of the avatar, the impact of social interaction on the avatar's behavior, the role played by narrative and the operator's experience of embodiment.

Despite the opportunities offered for the recreation of self or selves within virtual worlds, after conducting research in Second Life, Yee and colleagues at the Palo Alto Research Center, (Yee, Bailenson, Urbanek, Chang & Merget, 2007, p.15) concluded that the perceptions of users in relation to expression of identity within virtual worlds are often derived not from the users phenomenological relationship with their avatar, but rather from their expectations within the corporeal world transposed to apply to the virtual environment in so far as "the rules that govern our physical bodies in the real world have come to govern our embodied identities in the virtual world."

In response to the phenomena of using avatars to present idealized versions of ourselves, Zizek (2001) quotes Katherine Hayles: "...my nightmare is a culture inhabited by posthumans who regards their bodies as fashion accessories rather than the ground of being". He proposes that "all patterns of interaction ... have to be renegotiated/

Table 1. Avatar typologies

	Symbolic Avatar	Imaginary Avatar	Real Avatar
Related identity paradigms	Pre-modern imposed role identity	Modern self-curated/ constructed/ performed identity	Post modern multiplicity of identity
Avatar appearance	Selected from pre-defined choices	Based on the appearance or idealized appearance of the operator, of which it may be considered a portrait	A platform for fluidity, experimentation and interaction
Role of the avatar	Traditional pre-defined gaming avatar or class, or avatar designed to perform a specific task; minimal operator personalization	Typical stable self customized avatar currently residing in social virtual worlds such as Second life; generally an idealized representation of the operator's actual world self, or aspect thereof	Potential for self- expression via avatar within social virtual worlds; based neither on function nor on an aspect of operators identity, rather a becoming of the avatar form and function realized within and by interaction with its environment
Social interaction/ behavior	Limited social interaction; avatar behaves in accordance with role	Operator interacts with others via interaction between avatars which serve as persona masks and act in accordance with real world social conventions	Operator/avatar symbiote interacts spontaneously with other operator/ avatar symbiotes
Operator's relationship to narrative	Part of a fixed imposed narrative; limited choices;	Consciously performed or constructed narrative	Making sense of non-sequential interactive narratives
Avatar relationship to operator; Experience of embodiment	A proxy of the operator to allow access to the virtual environment; Avatar viewed as a tool or object separate to operator - third party relationship; attention is from the body <u>to</u> the interface <u>and</u> avatar	Avatar perceived as extension of operator expressing/performing chosen facets of operator persona; sense of operator embodiment in avatar only during 'play'; attention is generally from the body <u>and</u> interface <u>to</u> the avatar	Complex mutually interactive relationship between operator and avatar with the two becoming an autonomous emergent symbiote; attention is from the body <u>and</u> interface <u>and</u> the avatar <u>to</u> the experience of the (virtual) environment

(Copyright 2014, Pete Wardle.)

reinvented" and sums up the 'the ultimate lesson of 'cyberspace': "not only do we lose our immediate material body, but we learn that there never was such a body- our bodily self experience was always-already that of an imaginary constituted entity" (p.35).

It is therefore important to look beyond the typical uses of avatars and examine areas where avatars are deliberately used to facilitate self expression. To do so this chapter will attempt to apply the typologies discussed to the work of a number of artistic practitioners within Second Life to analyze how they have challenged the notions of the roles and purposes of avatars, and the nature of the relationships that their operators develop with them.

Artistic Practice, Identity, and Second Life

It is perhaps unsurprising that artists are at the forefront of addressing issues of identity using Second Life as a platform for artistic expression. In some cases, the identity of the actual world operator is unimportant to the artistic practice; Second Life artist Gazira Babeli explored the theme of avatars as portraits in the work 'Avatar On Canvas' (2007) in which avatars were invited to sit on reproductions of Francis Bacon paintings to trigger Bacon-esque deformations in the avatar. However of equal interest in the context of this chapter is that the Gazira Babeli identity is that of artist-avatar while the identity of the avatar operator remains undisclosed. Quaranta (2013) writes of Babeli that "in view of the fact that there is no actual person called Gazira Babeli, ... (she) is, on one level, a work of art in her own right... an identity construction project in a simulated world" (p.217). For others the connection between the artistic practice and the actual world identity of the artist is explicit; 'Becoming Dragon' (2008) saw artist Micha Cardenas spend 365 hours within Second Life exploring the 'Species Reassignment' transition of his avatar Azdel Slade from human to dragon to represent the 365 days transgender people have to fulfill living as their chosen gender before undertaking Gender Reassignment Surgery.

The chapter will now review the practice of a number of artists whose work is of particular interest when examining the expression of identity within virtual worlds, investigating and comparing their experiences through their own documentation and the author's correspondence with them, and examining their work with reference to the frameworks of identity theory discussed. Reference will also be made to the author's own phenomenological experience of interacting with a number of the projects discussed.

Life Squared

Between 1974 and 1978, Lynn Hershman-Leeson developed the fictional persona and alter ego of Roberta Breitmore, not only transforming herself physical appearance but constructing a fully-fledged, completely documented alternative personality. Hershman-Leeson lived Roberta's life and masses of information, documentation and ephemera were generated to create and maintain the narrative which would authenticate Roberta's existence. Rudolf Frieling (2008) wrote that "her work expresses a desire for public interaction and an interest in the construction of identity (her own or that of fictional others) via photography, diaries, and other forms of documentation." When interviewed in 2012 Hershman-Leeson called Roberta Breitmore an "archetype of a composite

of an individual" existing in a "full enough form to represent the time." She discussed that, through the artifacts Breitmore acquired, such as a driver's license, she had "more relevance and authenticity that (Hershman-Leeson) did... her deepest construction was based on the reality in which she lived, that was acted out and performed and documented through her experiences."

Though the use of artifacts to support the construction and narrative of Roberta's identity adhere to characteristics of the Imaginary typology, and Hershman-Leeson's terminology relating to performance supports this, Roberta's identity soon began to evolve in originally unforeseen directions. Three other actresses were employed to perform the identity of Roberta and while they tried to represent the same 'authentic' Roberta as Hershman-Leeson's portrayal, the interactions of this multiple-Roberta construct facilitated her transformation into a much more post-modern creation. Roberta Mock (2012) quotes Hershman-Leeson (2010) as providing a description of the actual world Roberta as an ongoing process created by social interaction, much more in accord with the typological Real: "Roberta isn't complete. She transforms and mutates through processes of improvisation and documentation. All of the people who engage with Roberta continue to embody her" (pp.126-139).

In a previous installation project 'The Dante Hotel' (1973–74), Hershman-Leeson used a rented hotel room to allow visitors to experience the signs of life of the occupants via wax figures, sounds and fictional ephemera. In 2007 she teamed up with the Stanford Humanities Lab to create 'Life-Squared' (see Figure 1) a visitable archive of her 'Dante Hotel' installation within Second Life. The artist constructed an avatar, Roberta Ware, in the image of Roberta Breitmore and to perform the role of host to this Second Life re-presentation of her earlier, actual world installation.

Hershman-Leeson (2014) wrote: "I originally wanted to make an archive of my Stanford archive to re enact digitally the work I had done up

Figure 1. Roberta Ware - Life Squared in Dante Hotel
(Copyright 2006, Lynn Hershman. Used with permission.).

to that time, to be re performed by the avatar's avatar of Roberta." The statement may be taken to suggest not only that the avatar is 'second generation', i.e. twice removed from the artist, but that Hershman-Leeson considers it to be Roberta Ware, the avatar's avatar, that is doing the performing, or in fact re-performing of that which was previously performed by Roberta Breitmore. The references to 'Life Squared' as an 'archive' and 're-performance' might be taken to suggest that Ware is simply a facsimile of Breitmore at the time of archiving and not part of a similar process of transformation and mutation. Reduced to her basic functions Roberta Ware may be considered to be a Symbolic avatar, created simply to perform a functional role, and as a proxy to represent a already Imaginary, constructed identity.

However this reimagining as Roberta in the landscape of Second Life gave the artist the opportunity to re-examine issues relating to the identity and embodiment of Roberta, describing Ware as "Roberta reconfigured, mutated and migrated into another form. She exists in the landscape of SL, with unknown users and adventures and encounters, so she follows the original conceptual thread of Roberta but in a different geography" (Hershman-Leeson, 2014). Mock (2012) wrote that "Roberta Ware is and is not as authentic, originary and/not autonomous as her namesake, the always already simulated Roberta Breitmore" (p.131) while Patrick Lichty (2009) writes of Ware that she is "perhaps the 'real' Roberta Ware, as opposed to the 'dramatization' of Roberta Breitmore" (p.8). Ware therefore, as

Brietmore before her, can be typified not merely an Imaginary performed construct, but a Real constantly evolving entity with the potential for transformation. Mock (2012) quotes Amelia Jones that the artist is "enacting a perpetual process of virtual becoming" who "stages the self as both simulacral and embodied" (p.135).

Second Life Salt March to Dandi

From March 12 - April 6, 2008 Joseph DeLappe undertook a Second Life performance in which he reenacted Gandhi's famous 240 mile Salt March made in protest of the British salt tax in 1930 using his avatar MGandhi Chakrabati, modeled on the physical appearance of Mahatma Gandhi. The MGandhi avatar might be typified as being Symbolic insofar as the role, appearance and narrative were all predetermined; the avatar was developed with the sole purpose of undertaking the role of Gandhi for the duration of the performance. DeLappe (2013) discusses how he was "interested in challenging expectations regarding the creation of avatars... In SL one is encouraged to be what-ever one wants to be - yet there are conventions that have become the norm in such online spaces. I was very interested in taking avatar creation to what I see to be a logical extreme. If you can be anything, why not Gandhi?"

He did not however simply want MGandhi to be physically representative of Gandhi, but to embody the qualities associated with him, refer-ring to MGandhi as an "interpretive reification" (DeLappe, 2012, p.212). A.J. Glasser (2010) quotes DeLappe: "*I'm* not Gandhi; [my avatar] is the *idea* of Gandhi." From this perspective, the view of a purely functional Symbolic MGandhi becomes too simplistic. The characteristics as-signed to the Imaginary typology describe an avatar as idealized portrait, expressing a facet of the operator's personality, raising the ques-tion whether DeLappe himself felt the need to embrace or embody the qualities associated with Gandhi so that they might be expressed via the

avatar. In answer to this DeLappe (2013) wrote: "I tried my best to walk a line between the fact that while I could not presume to "be" Gandhi; the experience of guiding my avatar "MGandhi" throughout SL was indeed, however, unexpectedly transformative."

DeLappe (2012) attributes a large factor in this transformation to the physical nature of the project promoting within him an experience of embodiment so significant that at times he felt his 'ability to clearly delineate between the online and real world had become temporarily muddled" (p.214). During the 26 days of the performance DeLappe walked 240 miles on a treadmill which replicating Gandhi's historical Salt March. This act of walking on the treadmill controlled the forward movement of MGandhi within Second Life where MGandhi/DeLappe interacted with the Second Life residents he met on his journey. Of the experience, DeLappe (2013) writes:

What began as a conceptual performance became something much more important to my person. I truly found myself changed by this durational work of mixed reality. The mixed reality aspect of the project, the "walking", became such an important aspect of the work. Participating in such a "live art" project involved my physical body in a way that intrinsically made this a very different work from previous endeavors. So much of what we do in virtual worlds is actually more disembodied that we might like to think. By physically involving my body, there was a level of commitment and indeed embodiment than was anticipated.

We must also consider the narrative of the performance. 'The Second Life Salt March', while a virtual re-enactment, was not simply a Symbolic virtual copy of the original, nor was it a fully pre-constructed Imaginary performance. Whilst the parameters were clear at the start with the 240 miles walked over 26 days symbolizing and cor-relating directly to the original Salt March, and the performative (Imaginary) nature of the project, much of the narrative was spontaneously created by the social interactions with the hundreds of Second Life residents he encountered and invited to join him on his journey.

Following the 'Salt March', on May 5th, 2009, the planned/performed element of the narrative continued with a further performance in which the MGandhi avatar spent 9 months incarcerated in a reproduction of Gandhi's jail cell at the Yerwada prison where Gandhi was imprisoned by the British soon after the completion of the Salt March. On January 26th, 2010, the 80th anniversary of Gandhi's actual release from jail the performance culminated in MGandhi's release from prison by

members of the Second Life performance group Second Front during the 'gg hootenanny' (see Figure 2), an event described as a day long festival featuring songs of freedom and protest. The 'gg hootenanny' gathered a number of Second Life residents from around the globe including several artists and performers, many of whom attended in fancy dress including representations of Marilyn Munroe, the Pope, Prince Charles, Wonder Woman and Snoopy who were invited to appear as celebrity avatars for the performance.

The author of this chapter, via his avatar Guido VanDyke, attended in the guise of Charlie Chaplin who famously met with Gandhi in London a year

Figure 2. MGandhi on stage with the Pope, Prince Charles and Wonder Woman avatars; Inset - Guido Vandyke/Chaplin watches the proceedings
(Copyright 2014, Joseph DeLappe. Used with permission.); (Copyright 2014, Pete Wardle.) .

after his release from prison. The physical appearance of Guido Vandyke is usually based upon that of the author and so assuming the appearance of Chaplin added a further palimpsest of identity to that of the author-avatar. Unexpectedly, the absence of Guido's familiar physical appearance allowed the author to experience a heightened sense of immersion in the event, without a significant sense of embodiment within the avatar. In an analogue to an attendee at an actual world masked ball, perhaps the absence of Guido's usual physicality, and with it the author's own accompanying perceived behavioral expectations and inhibitions allowed him to more directly interact and participate in a Real experience of the event as it unfolded without being aware of the experience being mediated by a meaningfully constructed persona mask.

The event ended with MGandhi's ascension from Second Life, never to return. DeLappe (2013) wrote of the personal transformation effected by his project.

I did not expect was that this experience of being a virtual Gandhi to have such a powerful effect upon my person ... There certainly was an aspect of this work that I would attribute to "the suspension of disbelief" or of fooling myself in regard to where or who I was. The unexpected slippage between being greeted as "Gandhi!" in SL to the confusion in RL while not on the treadmill, where I would find my mind's eye momentarily confused - all of these experiences contributed to a sense of being changed by this performance.

This sense not only of embodiment within the avatar during the performance, but of a complex mutual relationship between avatar and operator resulting in a significant impact on the operator in the actual world may be seen as a key factor in MGandhi having undertaken a transition to become a Real avatar. As with Deleuze and Guittari's example of a wasp and orchid, DeLappe and MGandhi might be described as having become

transformed into symbiotic emergent units, each affected by the existence and actions of the other.

Gracie Kendal Project

In Kristine Schomaker's 'Gracie Kendal Project' (see Figure 3), Schomaker recorded a blog of the life of her avatar, Gracie Kendal, and effected changes to her actual world appearance and activities to transform herself to become more like Gracie. Schomaker (2014) writes of how the Gracie Kendal avatar was initially created as a means to an end, to simply fulfill the function of allowing her to access Second Life. "Gracie...was just meant to be a character I played on Second Life. Everyone had an avatar. I couldn't go into SL without one."

Though Gracie was initially no more than a Symbolic proxy for Schomaker she quickly developed as an Imagined construction of the idealized representation of her originator.

The first week I was there, I bought a shape, skin, hair, clothes etc. I chose to give Gracie blond hair because I have blond hair, but otherwise she was my ideal self. She was tall and thin. She was often called classy because of the way she was dressed (Schomaker, 2014).

On 1st Nov 2009 Schomaker embarked upon a project, based on a Stanford study of whether avatars can influence an individual's actual world behavior, which would change the way she thought of Gracie. She began to make changes to her own appearance to model herself on that of Gracie, who she described as sassy, vibrant and outgoing, in an attempt to transform herself to be not only more physically like Gracie but also take on some of these qualities. In her blog (2010), she refers to Gracie as "my self-portrait, my alter ego, my inner conscience. She is a character in my life story that revolves around the loss of identity, self-awareness and self acceptance... Gracie is an ideal representation of me. Gracie is who I would

*Figure 3. Finding Gracie- Two portraits in the pursuit of balance
(Copyright 2014, Kristine Schomaker. Used with permission.).*

like to be. ..Gracie is me. She is the skin that I am most comfortable being in." She described the process of transformation as "finding my inner Gracie... Her self confidence, her charisma, her personality... is all me, but it's the best of me."

Through the project it might be said that, not only did Schomaker become an actual world Imaginary constructed and performed avatar of Gracie (who in turn was originally an Imaginary avatar of an idealized representation of Schomaker), but that the operator/avatar relationship was typical of the Real avatar classification. While Schomaker compared the experience of transforming herself into an actual world avatar of Gracie to wearing a mask or costume which felt good to take off, some of the physical changes, such as the nose

ring, becoming a more permanent facet of the actual world Schomaker and the artist writes of how Gracie influenced her in other ways:

I like to believe Gracie has positively influenced me in the physical world. I have found my voice in art, a bit more body image confidence and a path in life. Having the courage to be myself under the guise of Gracie really helped me in the real world... Through my project, I really looked into myself and have been able to be comfortable in my own skin. With all of the work Gracie has done in SL, she has taught me to be brave... With/ through Gracie I am able to be myself, to be more real (Schomaker, 2014).

Gracie Kendal is not the only avatar Schomaker created based on aspects of herself. Schomaker writes how her eponymous avatar, Kris Schomaker, was created "as a representation of my real life self because I just couldn't/wouldn't change Gracie to be like me in real life" (Schomaker, 2014). It may be speculated that Gracie, having become 'Real', left a gap to be filled by the Imaginary Kris Schomaker avatar.

Gracie and myself in RL started having existential conversations about life, reality and identity. Gracie was trying to escape SL and I felt I had to get my RL self into SL. Creating Kris was the best way to do that... I actually never developed a relationship with the Kris avatar they way I did with Gracie. Maybe because she is too much like me in RL (Schomaker, 2014).

To document the 'Gracie Kendal Project', Schomaker took a photo of Gracie and herself every day and placed them side by side to create comics and conversations between them, describing these as her way of "talking to herself out loud." The act of taking photographs of Second Life avatars is an interesting and recurring theme for artists working within the medium. In a later work '1000 Avatars' Gracie Kendal hosted an exhibition of a 1000+ images of avatars she/Schomaker had taken of avatars facing away from the viewer, designed to help illustrate the idea of online anonymity. In his exhibition and book 'Alter Ego' (2007) Robbie Cooper displayed avatar portraits next to those of their operators while in 'Code Portraits' (2009) Lichty created an exhibition of portraits for the Australian National Portrait Gallery, featuring many of the avatars he met as his avatar Man Michanga, made accessible on mobile devices via QR codes which were also displayed in Second Life as monolithic placeholders symbolising the avatars whose images they held. Quaranta (2007) writes of the project 'Portraits: 13 Most Beautiful Avatars' (2006) in which Eva and Franco Mattes displayed portraits of avatars in both actual world

and Second Life settings. Quaranta (2007) comments that by doing "something as apparently banal as photographing avatars... and exhibiting them in an art space, (the artists) are ...saying loud and clear that the subjects they have chosen are neither simulacra or characters in a game; they are people, complete, complex identities with defined social roles in a society comprising two million inhabitants" (p.5). To directly apply the typologies discussed to Quaranta's quotation, it might be said that the subject avatars are neither Imaginary or Symbolic; they are Real.

Schomaker's more recent project 'Binge and Purge' (2013) shares the concept of an identity constructed and authenticated by ephemera with Hershman-Leeson's Roberta and with the unseen occupants of her 'Dante Hotel'. Other projects working with this theme include the 'Life Sharing' (2000) project by Eva and Franco Mattes of which Quaranta (2007) quoted Volkart: "The project… exaggerates the assumption that our life and our identities are based on purely determined and determining accumulations of information." In 'Binge and Purge' Schomaker examined the relationship of Gracie with the ephemera she had collected during her time in Second Life. Over a period of five months she gradually put all her Second Life belongings on display before deleting them forever until Gracie owned no more than the clothes she was wearing. When asked how it felt when she had deleted everything Schomaker (2014) responded: "It was an interesting experience. It was pretty cathartic getting rid of your material possessions. I believe life is much more than what you own." She went on to discuss how the project raised issues relating to the "commodity and value in ourselves as well as our possessions."

Unlike the culmination of DeLappe's 'gg hootenanny' in which MGhandi ascended from Second Life, never to return, Gracie has no plans to leave. "It was not meant to be an end all and be all. I believe Gracie exists independent of the property, but not totally. Her hair and clothes do help form her identity, but her name remains. Her personality, my personality is still mine. Gracie is still Gracie with or without possessions and even place" (Schomaker, 2014).

Reality Bytes

Australian artist Georgie Roxby Smith undertook a number of performance pieces using Second Life, originally as part of the research towards her Master's thesis. When questioned about her original creation of Diogenes, Smith (2014) described a third party relationship typical the Symbolic classification where the avatar fulfilled a simple role: "Whilst I mainly used SL as artistic tool as one may use a paintbrush, and my avatar was a figure I initially thought of being something completely objective."

Nevertheless, Smith constructed her avatar, Diogenes Wilder, as an Imaginary reconstruction of herself. Smith (2014) writes that her practice is "centered around digital identity and the desire for the idealized digital self" and describes the inspiration and process of creating Diogenes: "I was fascinated with the popular practice of creating fantasy or idealized selves through SL, where everything that required physical effort or was simply not available to people in RL, could be created in a click of a button. This inclination is an incredibly seductive one, whilst wanting to base Diogenes solely on me – I found myself tucking the tummy here, raising the cheekbones there."

The relationship quickly developed into something more personal than Smith had anticipated and she became protective towards her avatar:

I was surprised to find myself strangely attached to her. In her were hours and hours of work & embedded experience – she was my embodiment in that world – I experienced that world through her. Whilst we role play online in some form or another, we cannot completely hide our essential selves – they are "performing" a part of us... As an integral part of my work at the time 'she' also became a commodity as such, I was invested in

her and found myself protecting her from friends who wanted to try SL, quietly freaking out if they moved her in an inappropriate way, pushed into people, or 'said' certain things – like I had to protect her reputation, now she was "someone"! (Smith, 2014).

Smith created multiple versions of this avatar for the purposes of a live performance 'Reality Bytes' (see Figure 4) crossing over virtual world/actual world platforms, and taking place both in Second Life and physically at the Watermill Center NY in 2010. She worked with new media and performance artists to create Reality Bytes which incorporated video projections along with performances by both humans and avatars, and likened the effect to "a hall of mirrors, in which viewers occupy multiple realities at once" describing how she "was interested in fracturing and mirroring reality of self across multiple platforms" (Smith, 2014). Multiple 'fractured' versions of Diogenes occupied the Second Life performance space, each physically based on herself but each different or flawed in some way and operated by different actual world performers interacting together.

Her attachment did not extend in the same way to these multiple versions of Diogenes nor did having multiple operators perform as distorted versions of Diogenes impact upon the operator/avatar relationship which had developed.

Having my split avatar controlled by other users did not bring about the same feelings as when people were using my actual avatar, which for the original Reality Bytes performance and subsequent re-performances, was always solely performed/operated by myself. That level of investment was not present, as the avatar was clearly not Diogenes Wylder, rather a version of her (Smith, 2014).

Similar to DeLappe, Smith (2014) reported the unexpected physical effects of her relationship with Diogenes. "I felt a physical sensation if she

Figure 4. Photo documentation of the Reality Bytes performance
(Copyright 2010, Georgie Roxby Smith. Used with permission.).

was pushed – there is a kind of neurological connection through the keyboard, shooting through your fingers into your RL body in a sense – I'm sure many SL users can attest to this." In an interview with Jansson (2013), Smith expands upon this:

When using the PC with Second Life I was particularly interested in the way the physical body related to the on screen action. Initially, moving my virtual body through this digital environment had a strange and unexpected physical effect. Immersing myself in the screen by day, each night I dreamt in a "Second Life" world – trees, people and buildings streaming past me in a nauseous wave of giddy intoxication. When objects or other avatars made digital contact with me, I noted an odd physical reaction in my own body…The brain

seemed somewhat confused between these two physical planes.

As she worked more with Second Life it became apparent to Smith that the theme of identity was central to her work and after two years of reworking 'Reality Bytes' re-emerged as the multi-dimensional installation 'Your Clothing is Still Downloading' (2011) which explored identity and desire, asking if we can really create intimacy in manufactured spaces like Second Life. The installation includes a Second Life sex scene, for which, the artist (2014) described how she "created two avatars – one my own and one an idealised male – and operated them both simultaneously using two computers to create the desired film output for projection" using the analogy of 'playing dolls' to describe the experience of operating both avatars to create the scene.

In the final work discussed in her thesis 'iObject' (2011) Smith explores not the expression of virtual self but rather "the negation of self in a virtual world" (Smith, 2011) by taking her Imaginary 'self-portrait avatar' Diogenes and stripping her not only of possessions and symbols of desire and ego, an act which has resonance with Schomaker's 'Binge and Purge' but also of all identifiable features until she is no more than a 'three dimensional shadow.' Smith (2011) writes how she used this "deconstructed avatar (to stage) a number of sit ins as a three dimensional shadow in the consumer, social and sexual constructions of Second Life – provoking reactions of scorn, threat and complete disregard by observing avatars. Silent in her commodified surroundings, the death of her virtual ego and loss of virtual currency is underscored by the evocative sounds of a Buddhist chant – creating a blur between an act of holiness or menace. It is the artist role playing herself into a ghost in the machine."

You Are Me

While 'iObject' stripped away the identity of Smith's avatar, the avatar in Leonardo Selvaggio's 'Youareme' project started off as a tabula rasa with nothing but a name, a blank slate on which anyone could impose an identity. Selvaggio allowed viewers to participate in the ongoing project by logging on to Second Life to take full control of his avatar LeoSelvaggio, and therefore his Second Life identity. Unlike many of the artist's previously discussed, Selvaggio developed no personal relationship with the avatar either prior to or during the project and, despite the avatar's name, did not express any concerns in respect of the avatar's reputation. Selvaggio (2013) wrote of how he was interested in the possibilities of a crowdsourced socially mediated identity. "I was really interested in the type of life that could be

built for me, if I were not the one responsible for its construction. Who could I be, if I allowed others to design me outright?"

Comparison may be made to Shoemaker's 'Brownson' thought experiment wherein the brain of Mr. Brown is put into the body of Mr. Robinson, i.e. the operator/brain placed into the body of the other/avatar. In the experiment the resultant 'Brownson' behaves in accord with Brown's identity; however, in 'Youareme' this is not necessarily the case. If an operator wishes to enter Second Life to behave in accord with their own identity, or indulge in any form of identity experimentation as an Imaginary persona, they can do so freely as their own avatar. However the more an Imaginary avatar is constructed to reflect the operator persona, and the more Real the immersion/embodiment experience of the operator-avatar becomes, the more an operator is inclined to identify with their primary avatar as being Symbolic of themselves, i.e. perceiving it to be a direct proxy of an identifiable actual world self within Second Life. Conversely, while the LeoSelvaggio avatar became a proxy not for Selvaggio himself but for anyone who chose to operate it, it remained Symbolic of the originator.

The attraction of 'Youareme' seems therefore to be derived more from the ability to play at being someone else completely, free any possibility of personal recognition; this may of course lead the operator to perform transgressive acts, freed from any potential impact upon the operator's reputation (or the reputation of their avatar within Second Life). Transgressive, however, need not mean anti-social and the resultant acts might simply be those of true identity experimentation.

Pete Wardle: Three Installations in Second Life

This chapter will now examine three of the author's own Second Life installations, which took place between 2008 and 2013. The first two were originally approached purely as interactive installations without a research function, while the third also sought to collect qualitative interview data relating to the experiences of individuals operating unfamiliar avatars to inform the author's PhD thesis.

Connecting Point: Human/Avatar

'Connecting Point: Human/Avatar' (2008) (see Figure 5) was a collaborative interactive actual world/Second Life installation with Alan Hook exhibited in the San Jose Tech Museum of Innovation in which museum visitors on one side of a screen were able to control two avatars located in the corresponding area of the Tech Virtual Museum in Second Life to complete goals and play games across the areas using a specially created on screen menu of pre-set animations. The avatars not only performed the actions, games and dances as directed by their operators but, via life size projections, they also relayed instructions to copy them to actual world visitors on the other side of the screen.

The avatars used for this installation were designed to be purely Symbolic functional 'puppets' to undertake the role of virtual intermediary between operators and visitors on either side of the screen, with no relationship to the artists themselves; as with the LeoSelvaggio avatar, they could be operated by anyone. The avatars were always intended to be viewed as a third person tool and as such, without any constructed identity to inhabit, the immersion of their operators was short lived and experienced as game play. The experience however was one not only of the operator controlling an avatar, and a third party visitor mimicking that avatar, but of the operator exerting control over the visitor via the projected avatar. If the projected avatar can be likened to a puppet controlled by the operator, then the visitors

Figure 5. Photo documentation of Connecting Point: Human Avatar in San Jose Tech Museum (Copyright 2008, Pete Wardle.) Used with permission.

might be said to have become willing puppets, or avatars, of the projected operator/avatar symbiote. Interestingly the visitors who assumed the role of such willing puppets generally reported their experience being more immersive than did the operators, perhaps due to their increased physical involvement; the operator's generally reported greater levels of immersion when there was a pre-existent relationship between themselves and the visitor they controlled.

Second Life Storyteller

The 'Second Life Storyteller' (2008) (see Figure 6) was exhibited in Manchester as part of a 'mixed reality' installation. Video recordings of actual world storytellers were imposed upon the faces of an avatar within Second Life to tell their tales to visitors in-world; via a 'menu-wall' visitors in Second Life were given the ability to

change the storyteller and story being presented by the avatar at the touch of an in world button. Though this installation did not allow visitors to take direct control of the avatar's actions, they were still able to exert control upon it by choosing which storyteller it would display. An actual world version of the installation featured a screen positioned in place of the head of a stationary seated mannequin on which the storyteller clips were shown, sequenced and changed by viewers by means of a Wii remote. Rather than use his own avatar for the installation, the artist created a new avatar to which he felt no connection to be a Lockean tabula rasa, Symbolic of the role of storyteller, upon which the performed selves of the individual storytellers could be imposed.

During the premiere of the installation the storytellers who had taken part visited both the actual world installation and Second Life to meet

Figure 6. The Second Life Storyteller installation (Copyright 2008, Pete Wardle.) Used with permission.

and interact with themselves as invoked into the Storyteller avatar. It is notable that actual world visitors who experienced both the actual world and Second Life installations reported a greater sense of immersion within the virtual installation than the actual world installation; the screen and Wii controller helped assign the activity of interacting with the actual world installation into a parallel of a TV show or game in which the pre-recorded clips remained simply Symbolic avatars of the storytellers. Conversely, within Second Life, the unfamiliar experience of a seemingly physical, expressive face upon the Storyteller avatar, along with the ability to interact with the avatar in-world added to viewer's engagement with and immersion in the installation. The physical appearance and movement of the avatar helped reify the storytellers within in Second Life.

The aspects of narrative and performance were clearly important to the installation. Five narrative stories were performed and recorded to form the content of the video clips. These narratives were then deconstructed, though not irreconcilably, by being cut into clips and mixed up for participants to select from and sequence. If the original performances of the actual world storytellers can be considered Imaginary insofar as they were constructed and performed narratives, then the deconstructed videos of these can be viewed as Symbolic of these originals, functional components of the installation, just as the tabula rasa avatar can be viewed as Symbolic of the generic storyteller. The Real avatar in this case is not created simply by the bringing together of all of these components, or by the artist's relationship with the avatar, rather its existence is generated spontaneously within the installation by the viewers interaction with it to reconstruct the components into an original and constantly reconfigured narrative.

Through the previous installations the artist came to realize the theme of identity being expressed within his work and in his next installation that theme was brought to the fore. 'Second Selves' (2013) (see Figure 7) took place in the Egg, University of Salford Media City Campus, serving a dual purpose as artistic practice and to collect qualitative data for the artist's PhD thesis relating to how individuals reacted to the experience of operating unfamiliar avatars. Participants were given control of one of two tabula rasa avatars within a specially designed environment within Second Life. The environment contained multiple scripted objects with which the avatars could interact resulting in one or the other of the avatars undergoing changes to their physical appearance and attire. There were a total of twenty different humanoid avatar appearances including virtual representations of an elderly grandmother, a child, a Hell's Angel, a Smiley face avatar and a Transformer. As with the Second Life Storyteller installation, new visual aspects of identity were being imposed upon the avatars but in this case these identities could not only be selected but controlled, interpreted and performed by visitors to the installation. Some of the visitors treated this as a game or opportunity to explore the environment and interact to try to 'collect' all the different appearances, others found themselves drawn towards, or repelled from, operating particular avatars.

As part of the artist's PhD research participants were observed and recorded interacting with the avatars and subsequently asked the reasons for their preferences. Participants seemed to favor avatars to which they felt an affinity. In some cases this was attributed to a created, perceived or predetermined prior narrative, e.g., some participants stated that they favored the Transformer avatar because they were fans of science fiction, others that they liked the Smiley face avatar because they felt it was representative of the 'rave' scene which they had been a part of, adhering to the Symbolic typology insofar as the avatar became a symbol of an external influence or remembered event.

However most participants favored avatars that they could to relate to themselves, either due to the physical appearance of the avatar, or the perception that the avatar expressed qualities

Figure 7. The Second Selves installation
(Copyright 2013, Pete Wardle.) Used with permission.

they felt to be desirable. Though they had not constructed the avatar themselves, they felt its construction expressed some actual or desirable aspect of themselves and as such they were able to create for themselves and assume the Imaginary persona of the avatar. Similarly most participants were least attracted to those avatars which they could not physically relate to.

Notably, the participant's expectations of the avatars were often aligned to their physical appearance. Of the Transformer avatar two participants described how they expected to be able to find a way to make it shoot at the other avatar. Though the participants controlled the avatars for only a short period of time the beginnings of Real, mutually influential, relationships between operators and avatars were sometimes evident and some participants reported that certain avatars made them behave more or less aggressively in-world towards the other participant avatar.

RECOMMENDATIONS AND FUTURE RESEARCH DIRECTIONS

From the examples discussed it can be seen how the typologies of Symbolic, Imaginary and Real avatars can be applied to the expression of self within the work of artistic practitioners in Second Life. In many cases it is also evident that, while such artistic practices create experiential phenomena typifying the Real Avatar, they do so by a process of evolution; the Symbolic avatar which does no more than serve a function as a tool or proxy for the operator evolves to become the Imaginary avatar, consciously constructed and performed by the operator, which in turn becomes Realized not by any single defining act, but spontaneously by the ongoing relationship between operator, avatar, and those with whom the avatar interacts. It can also be seen that the Imaginary avatar is constructed and performed using components of the Symbolic; similarly, no matter how symbiotic the operator/avatar relationship becomes, and how embodied the operator becomes within the virtual, the Real Avatar must always contain within it the Imaginary, constructed and controlled by the actual world actions of the operator.

It is the future intention of the author to apply the typologies more widely to the expression of self by avatars within Second Life, drawing from his own, and others' ethnographic experiences within Second Life and from his continuing research into the construction of, and behavior expressed via, avatars. It is recommended too that the typologies may be more widely adopted by other writers on the subjects of identity and selfhood within virtual worlds to allow a common framework of language to emerge when discussing these topics. It is hoped that futures writers might further analyze artistic practice and avatar behavior using these typologies, and that artists may consider how these typologies are applicable to their own practice.

CONCLUSION

The prevalence of virtual worlds designed for the purpose of allowing gamers to enact very restricted character roles within games makes it unsurprising that individuals continue to adhere to historic and outdated Symbolic paradigms relating to the actual world when considering the development of identity in virtual worlds. Though contemporary virtual social worlds offer great potential for identity experimentation, there remains a tendency for users to continue to perceive avatars as they perceive actual world objects, or as they, perhaps mistakenly, perceive their own identities, as being relatively fixed and stable. This seems a key factor in limiting the potential for expression of identity within these worlds, leading users to construct Imaginary avatars limited by their physical appearance to be representative of the actual or desired physical appearance of the operator, or of the avatar's social role.

It is the role of artists working in virtual worlds to continue to explore themes of identity and push the boundaries of their own, and their audiences, relationships with their avatars. In doing so, they challenge the ways that identity is expressed and perceived not only within virtual worlds but also within in the actual world, encouraging us to consider that we are not merely synonymous with our primary role in life, or the sum of our physical appearance and properties, but rather to realize ourselves as unique and multifaceted personalities constantly made Real by our interactions whether in actual or virtual worlds.

REFERENCES

Anton, C. (2001). *Selfhood and Authenticity*. Albany: State University of New York.

Appiah, K. A. (2007). *The Ethics of Identity*. New Jersey: Princeton University Press.

Apter, E. (2008, January). Technics of the Subject: The Avatar-Drive. *Postmodern Culture*, 18(2). doi:10.1353/pmc.0.0021

Bergson, H. (1910). Time and Free Will: An Essay on the Immediate Data of Consciousness (F.L. Pogson, M.A., Trans.). London: George Allen and Unwin.

Bergson, H. (2007). Mind-Energy (H. Wildon Carr, Trans.). 2007 England: Palgrave Macmillan.

Biocca, F. (1997). The Cyborg's Dilemma: Progressive Embodiment in Virtual Environments. *Journal of Computer-Mediated Communication. 3(2)*. Retrieved from http://onlinelibrary.wiley.com. DOI: 10.1111/j.1083-6101.1997.tb00070

Blackman, C. (2010). Can avatars change the way we think and act? In *Stanford News* (2010, February 22). Retrieved from http://news.stanford.edu/news/2010/february22/avatar-behavior-study-022510.html

Boellstorff, T. (2008). *Coming of Age in Second Life: An Anthropologist Explores the Virtually Human*. New Jersey: Princeton University Press.

Cárdenas, M., & Head, C. Margolis, & T., Greco, K. (2009). *Becoming Dragon: a mixed reality, durational performance in Second Life*. University of California, San Diego. Retrieved from http://transreal.org/wp-content/uploads/2009/08/becoming-dragon-micha-cardenas-edit1.pdf

Clarke, E. G., & Justice, E. M. *Identity Development - Aspects of Identity*. Retrieved from http://social.jrank.org/pages/322/Identity-Development.html

Cleland, K. (2008). *Avatars: Self-Other Encounters in a Mediated World*. Retrieved from http://www.kathycleland.com/

Cooper, R. (2007). *Alter Ego- Avatars and their creators*. London: Thames and Hudson.

DeLappe, J. (2010, January 21) quoted by Glasser, A. Gandhi's Second Life continues in prison. *NetworkWorld*. Retrieved from http://www.networkworld.com/news/2010/012110-gandhis-second-life-continues-in.html

DeLappe, J. (2011). The Gandhi Complex: The Mahatma in Second Life. In X. Burrough (Ed.), *Net Works: Case Studies in Web Art and Design*. New York: Routledge.

DeLappe, J. (2013). *Private correspondence with P*. Wardle.

Deleuze, G., & Guittari, F. (2004). *A Thousand Plateaus: Capitalism and Schizophrenia*. England: Continuum. (Original work published 1988)

Frieling, R. (2008). *The Art of Participation: 1950 to Now*. San Francisco: Thames & Hudson.

Goffman, I. (1956). *Self in Everyday Life*. Edinburgh: University of Edinburgh Social Sciences Research Centre.

Gunkel, D. J. (2010). The Real Problem: Avatars, Metaphysics and Online Social Interaction. *New Media & Society, 12*(1), 127–141. doi:10.1177/1461444809341443

Hall, S. (1995). The Question of Cultural Identity. In *Modernity: An Introduction to Modern Societies*. Cambridge, UK: Polity.

Hayles, K. (1999). *How we became posthuman, Chicago: University of Chicago Press. Quoted by Zizek, S. (2001). On Belief (Thinking in Action)*. London: Routledge. doi:10.7208/chicago/9780226321394.001.0001

Hershman Leeson, L. (2012). *Excerpt from the Artist Talk with Lynn Hershman Leeson*. Karlsruhe. Retrieved from https://www.youtube.com/watch?v=vC69xR4smAI

Hershman Leeson, L. (2014). private correspondence with P. Wardle.

Husserl, E. (2005). *Cartesian Meditations; An Introduction to Phenomenology* (D. Cairns, Trans.). London: Martinus Nijhoff Publishers. (Original work published 1950)

James, W. (1890). *The Principles of Psychology.* Retrieved from http://psychclassics.asu.edu/James/Principles/prin10.htm

Jones, A. (2008). This Life. In S. Broadhurst & J. Machon (Eds.), *Frieze (117, Sept 2008). Quoted by Mock, R. (2012). Lynn Hershman: The Creation of Multiple Robertas. In Identity, Performance and Technology: Practices of Empowerment, Embodiment and Technicity.* Hampshire, England: Palgrave MacMillan.

Kant, I. (1787). *Critique of Pure Reason.* (J. M. D. Meiklejohn, Trans.). Retrieved from www2.hn.psu.edu/faculty/jmanis/kant/Critique-Pure-Reason.pdf

Klevjer, R. (2007). What *is the Avatar? Fiction and Embodiment in Avatar-Based Singleplayer Computer Games.* University of Bergen. Retrieved from http://runeklevjer.wordpress.com/

Lacan, J. (2001). *Ecrits; A selection* (A. Sheridan, Trans.). London: Routledge Classics

Lastowka, F. G., & Hunter, D. (2006). Virtual Worlds: A Primer. In J. M. Balkin (Ed.), *State of Play: Law, Games, and Virtual Worlds.* New York: New York University Press.

Lichty, P. (2009). The Translation of Art in Virtual Worlds. In *Leonardo Electronic Almanac* (Vol 16 Issue 4–5). Retrieved from http://www.leoalmanac.org/wp-content/uploads/2012/09/11_lichty.pdf

Little, G. (1999). A Manifesto for Avatars. In Intertexts (Volume 3 issue 2). Cited by Gunkel, D.J. (2010). The Real Problem: Avatars, Metaphysics and Online Social Interaction. In New Media Society. Doi:10.1177/1461444809341443

Locke, J. (2007). *An Essay Concerning Human Understanding* (Book 2). J. Bennett (Annotations). Retrieved from http://www.earlymoderntexts.com

Mead, G. H. (1934). *Mind, Self, and Society.* Retrieved from http://www.brocku.ca/MeadProject/Mead/pubs2/mindself/Mead_1934_toc.html

Meadows, M. S. (2007). *I, Avatar: The Culture and Consequences of Having a Second Life.* Berkley: New Riders.

Merleau-Ponty, M. (2002). *Phenomenology of Perception* (C. Smith, Trans.). London, New York: Routledge.

Mock, R. (2012). Lynn Hershman: The Creation of Multiple Robertas. In S. Broadhurst & J. Machon (Eds.), *Identity, Performance and Technology: Practices of Empowerment, Embodiment and Technicity.* Hampshire, England: Palgrave MacMillan. doi:10.1057/9781137284440.0016

Noveck, B. S. (2006). Democracy–the Video Game: Virtual Worlds and the Future of Collective Action. In State of Play: Law, Games, and Virtual Worlds. J.M. Balkin (Ed.). New York: New York University Press. Cited by Gunkel, D.J. (2010). The Real Problem: Avatars, Metaphysics and Online Social Interaction. New Media Society. Doi:10.1177/1461444809341443

Popat, S., & Preece, K. (2012). Where am 'I' present? In S. Broadhurst & J. Machon (Eds.), *Identity, Performance and Technology: Practices of Empowerment, Embodiment and Technicity.* Hampshire, England: Palgrave MacMillan.

Quaranta, D. (2007). Life and Its Double, Portraits. EVA E FRANCO MATTES (0100101110101101.ORG) LOL Exhibition Catalogue. Brescia: Fabio Paris Art Gallery. Retrieved from http://domenicoquaranta.com/

Rehak, B. (2003). Playing at Being. In M. J. P. Wolf & B. Perron (Eds.), *The Video Game Theory Reader.* New York: Routledge.

Sarup, M. (2005). *Identity, Culture and the Postmodern World.* Edinburgh: Edinburgh University Press.

Schomaker, K. (2010). *My Life as an Avatar*. Retrieved from http://graciekendal.wordpress.com/

Schomaker, K. (2014). *Private correspondence with P.* Wardle.

Selvaggio, L. (2013). *You Are Me: Overview of my so called (2nd) Life*. Retrieved from http://www.youareme.net/search/label/2nd%20Life

Shoemaker, S. (2003). Consciousness and co-consciousness. In A. Clearmans (Ed.), *The Unity of Consciousness: Binding, Integration and Dissociation*. Oxford: Oxford University Press. doi:10.1093/acprof:oso/9780198508571.003.0003

Smith, G. R. (2011). *Art 2.0: identity, role play and performance in virtual worlds*. Masters Research thesis, VCA School of Art, The University of Melbourne. DOI. 10187/14591 Retrieved from http://repository.unimelb.edu.au/10187/14591

Smith, G. R. (2013, March 24). Georgie Roxby Smith's Playful Performances. Interview with M. Jansson, *GameScenes*. Retrieved from http://www.gamescenes.org/2013/03/interview-georgie-roxby-smiths-playful-performances.html

Smith, G. R. (2014). *Private correspondence with P.* Wardle.

Stets, J. E., & Burke, P. J. (2005). A Sociological Approach to Self and Identity. In M. R. Leary & J. P. Tangney (Eds.), *The Handbook of Self and Identity*. United States: Guilford Press.

Taylor, C. (1989). *Sources of the Self*. Cambridge, England: Cambridge University Press.

Tittle, P. (2005). *What If... Collected Thought Experiments in Philosophy*. United States: Pearson Education.

Turkle, S. (1997). *Life on the Screen: Identity in the Age of the Internet*. UK: Touchstone, Simon & Schuster Inc.

Veerapen, M. (2011). Encountering Oneself and the Other: A Case Study of Identity Formation in Second Life. In A. Peachey & M. Childs (Eds.), *Reinventing Ourselves: Exploring Identity in Virtual Worlds. A*. US: Springer. doi:10.1007/978-0-85729-361-9_5

Walser, R. (1990). *Elements of a cyberspace playhouse*. Paper presented at the National Computer Graphics Association, Anaheim. Quoted by Cleland, K. (2008). *Avatars: Self-Other Encounters in a Mediated World*. Retrieved from http://www.kathycleland.com/

Yee, N. (2008). Avatar and Identity. In *The Daedalus Gateway: The Psychology of MMORPGs*. Retrieved from http://www.nickyee.com/daedalus/gateway_identity.html

Yee, N., Bailenson, J. N., Urbanek, M., Chang, F., & Merget, D. (2007). *The Unbearable Likeness of Being Digital: The Persistence of Nonverbal Social Norms in Online Virtual Environments*. Retrieved from http://www.nickyee.com/

Zizek, S. (1997). *The Plague of Fantasies, Cyberspace, Or, The Unbearable Closure of Being*. London: Verso.

Zizek, S. (2001). *On Belief (Thinking in Action)*. London: Routledge.

Žižek, S. (2003). *The Puppet and the Dwarf: The Perverse Core of Christianity*. Cambridge, MA: MIT Press. Quoted by Gunkel, D.J. (2010). The Real Problem: Avatars, Metaphysics and Online Social Interaction. *New Media & Society*. doi:10.1177/1461444809341443

KEY TERMS AND DEFINITIONS

Actual World: There are a variety of terms used by writers on the topic of virtual worlds to describe the concrete, tangible 'everyday' world in which we live, including First Life or Real Life). Where quotations have been taken from other sources the terms used therein will be transcribed, however it is otherwise the intention in this chapter to follow Boellstorff's example of using the term 'actual world' for this purpose.

Avatar: A digital representation used allow an individual to participate and operate within a virtual world. Within Second Life these avatars are 3D and generally, though not exclusively humanoid in appearance.

Embodiment: The operator's strong physical connection with the avatar within the virtual world to the extent that they feel that their consciousness resides temporarily within the avatar. The operator may feel that actions within the virtual world are having a direct impact upon them or their actual world body.

Immersion: The sense of the operator's attention being fully directed to the events taking place within the virtual world.

Operator: The term operator has been used to refer to the individual directing the actions of the avatar, though where quotations have been taken from other sources the terms 'player' or 'user' may also be used to a similar purpose. Unless otherwise stated, when referring to avatars in Second Life, the term operator is generally also used to mean the originator of the avatar's appearance.

Resident: An avatar existing and operating within Second Life.

Chapter 6
Appearance, Absence, Art:
The *Objet A*-vatar

Garfield Benjamin
University of Wolverhampton, UK

ABSTRACT

This chapter suggests a model for reconceiving avatar in terms of desire and loss to reassess their role within creative practices and the construction of digital subjectivity. This focuses on the avatar as appearance, as a negotiation of presence and absence, and as a tool for critical art practice in Second Life. By placing the avatar as Lacan's objet petit a, the lost object cause of desire, the structure of the visual and cognitive gaze applies Žižek's concept of parallax to digital embodiment, reformulating a subjective position between physical and digital modes of being. Taking into account the position of the observer amidst the fluidity of contemporary identity, the manipulation of the structures of desire and control can create new experiences that alter our relation to presence and absence in the critical and creative mediation of avatars and its implications for embodiment as a function of consciousness.

INTRODUCTION

This chapter will provide a reassessment of the avatar form, beyond the material construction of embodiment, towards a psychological formation of the subject between physical and digital identities. The emergence of such a view from the inclusion of a representation of the subject within its own gaze will show the nature of the avatar as an always-already lost body, in turn demonstrating the loss inherent to all forms of embodiment. The relation to desire will be extrapolated into the construction of the self as an image and the implications for such developments on creative

processes in Second Life. The relationship between presence and absence will be interrogated in virtual environments, and suggesting between the various possible embodiments of the subject a presence-of-absence. These structures of desire for presence will bring in issues of control in the formation of subjective expression before a discussion of the role of avatars in art as substance and gesture. The simultaneous position of avatars as an object and action will challenge the view of embodiment and negation in disembodiment towards a constructive antagonism between the two. Applying the analysis to art practice avatars within SL (Second Life), and taking into consider-

DOI: 10.4018/978-1-4666-8384-6.ch006

ation the relation to the technologies themselves, a new critical perspective will emerge at a distance to the bodily form of the avatar in confronting the psychological position of the subject between physical and digital realities.

The primary theoretical basis for this chapter will be Jacques Lacan's *objet petit a*, the lost object cause of desire. Unlike in objective-driven uses of the avatar in computer games, which will be considered alongside the relation of the avatar to digital culture in general and art practice in particular, this is not a specific object to be desired and attained, but the inherently lost force within the psychological construction of the subject that formulates the nature of specific desires, therefore shaping the entire appearance of subjective reality. This 'reality' is Lacan's elusive Real – the inaccessible truth of the subject extrapolated in this chapter as the presupposed conditions of the unconscious lost beneath the symbolic virtuality of the cogito. The Lacanian analysis will be expanded by Slavoj Žižek's conception of parallax in which epistemological shifts by the subject have ontological effects in the world it is observing. This is the construction of the Real within the subject: a lost position, absence or void from which the world is seen but cannot itself be included in the gaze.

Within this framework, the theory of Gilles Deleuze and the philosophy of quantum physics will offer contrasting positions on the dissolution of identity and matter that will inform the virtualising processes in place in the construction and creative use of avatars. This will move beyond psychoanalysis to critique the role of art in relation to therapeutic aims and disruptions of faciality in deterritorialising identities; and beyond the science fiction often associated with the relation between humanity and its extension through avatars to re-examine the inclusion of the observer in the observation as the avatar form visible on screen. The notion of superposition, the mode of being in two contradictory states at once, will also be utilised to confront the irresolvable states of being physically and digitally embodied, linking the discussion back to Žižek's parallax in forming a new position in the sustained antagonism between different visual and cognitive perspectives.

The chapter will draw conclusions on the construction, critique and creative potential of the avatar as a lost object. Rather than negating the artistic relevance of the avatar under notions of a disembodied fantasy in free realms of the imagination, the exploitation of loss will be shown as a necessary step towards confronting the subject with its own position regarding the self, the gaze and subjective reality between physical and digital modes of being. The process of traversing the fantasy of an identified state will be suggested as a critical potential of art in SL for the inclusion of the subject in the creative gesture and in order that a position can be established from which to think otherwise about our relation to any bodied form and its place in a given reality.

APPEARANCE

Gaze and Self

The construction of an avatar through which to interact with a digital environment is also the construction of an alternative position from which the gaze is made manifest, an alternative self from which to view a given world. This gaze engages not only the visual view of the screen in relation to the physical user, but a cognitive view through the screen into an engaged position within the digital reality of a virtual environment. Lacan (1977) identifies, within the construction of the self, a severed construct of "the eye and the gaze... the split in which the drive is manifested at the level of the scopic field" (p. 73). This inherent split, of the self in the gaze, "marking the pre-existence to the seen of a given-to-be-seen" (Lacan, 1977, p. 74), is described by Žižek (2009) as the parallax stain: the inclusion of the subject within its own gaze (p. 17). A position of, conditions for and consciousness of the gaze are thus necessarily presupposed by a thinking subject in the construction of any 'self'. Nowhere is the inclusion of the subject in its own gaze more evident than in the construct of the avatar, bringing a portion of the self literally into its own visual gaze. Yet the gaze here, and in the construction of subjectivity more generally, extends beyond the visual act of perception, for it is also the conditions of and desire for engaging with an external world. This constructs the position from which the cogito thinks itself and entails its inclusion within the Otherness of the world. This possibility of being seen inherent to sight has ramifications for the desire for thought itself, drawing the gaze into the act of splitting consciousness between the pure cogito and its embodiment within an external environment, for which the avatar stands as both enabling mediator and stain in thinking ourselves as Other. The same split is described by Bard and Söderqvist within thought, between the 'I' that thinks and the 'I' that thinks it thinks:

Even if thinking seems to exist in the moment the thought is thought, this does not necessarily mean that any 'I' has to exist. It merely means that something at that same moment thinks 'I' and possibly has an ulterior motive in doing so. (Bard & Söderqvist, 2012, p. 525)

This illusion of the cogito is bound into the process of perception from the parallax position in the void-core of subjectivity. The cogito appears as a virtuality, the primary process of thinking oneself as subject. Merleau-Ponty's formulation of consciousness within a body is thus founded on an erroneous assumption of the nature of thought bound into perception through (the illusion of) a pre-existing body. Rather, the existence of the cogito occurs simultaneous with the act of thinking and the desire to think/exist. The formulation can therefore be expanded and applied to thought

as perception: the 'I' that perceives, an 'I' that perceives it perceives and an 'I' that is in the perception itself. As the condition for a position from which perception and thought can occur, there *is* only consciousness, separated from its body and its perspective, as a pure self-positing function. The construction of this 'I' is inextricably linked to its position as the gaze in an engaged act of perception, the moment in which "I emerge as eye" (Lacan, 1977, p. 82). The self as the stain in the gaze emerges concurrently with the self from which the gaze occurs and the self that cognises the position of the gaze.

In applying this process of perception to expression and differentiation in avatar-mediated worlds, we start from the familiar position whereby "a PC [Player Character] in a VGW [Virtual Game World] can be seen as a combination of a person playing a game and a fictive person whose identity is continuously developed" (Eladhari, 2010, p. 6). However, this continuous development extends beyond SL and other non-game virtual worlds, where avatars exist as a becoming between the user and their fictional representation, and into the construction of the digital subject itself. This is not merely a fictional character set in a specific simulated fictional environment, for such could be said of the cognitive processes applied in diverse cultural forms (first-person novels; paper role-playing games; cosplay). This level of identity is created between the 'physical' user and their entire gamut of 'digital' identities. This includes the array of 'alts' (alternative avatars) a subject might employ for specific roles, spaces or interactions, much like the physical subject might have different personal or professional identities. The cultural setting of avatar-mediated environments creates complex interactions between parts of the self within the cognitive gaze of an engaged subject.

This gaze of the engaged subject raises pertinent questions about the fundamental nature of observation, in both physical and digital worlds, particularly when applied to the active perception of the self-as-Other in the form of an avatar. In separating the role of engagement within observation, Heisenberg (1965) pronounced that "classical physics, therefore, has its limits at the point from which the influence of the observation on the event can no longer be ignored" (p. 299). It is this influence that is key to the problems tackled through quantum mechanics, seeking to delve beneath the illusion of macroscopic certainty, to confront the fact that "this [coherent] sense of the reality of objects and things is *constructed*" (Bohm, 1994, p. 109). Bohm (2002) demonstrates the importance of thought within such a reality, in a reciprocal interaction of perception whereby, "instead of saying 'an observer looks at an object', we can more appropriately say, 'observation is going on, in an undivided moment involving those abstractions customarily called "the human being" and "the object he is looking at"'" (p. 37). In the digital realm, this gains further significance, as visual and cognitive engagements take on mutual uncertainties. Bohm (1994) tells us that "thought is *incomplete*…a signification, or an 'abstraction'…thought provides a *representation* of what you are thinking about" (p. 92) and, in the same function towards consciousness, the avatar – the digital manifestation of the observer-as-observed – becomes a 'representation of what you are representing', a simulation-of-simulation in the subject beholding itself as object. The digital world commonly appears as a reflection of the physical world in a manifestation of an ideal. Heisenberg (1949) confronts the abstract constructs of such an illusion, in which "the physical world differed from the ideal world conceived in terms of everyday experience", resulting in the problem that "ordinary concepts could only be applied to processes in which the velocity of light could be regarded as practically infinite" (p. 62), placing an ideal notion of limitlessness on the very functioning of scientific measurement. However, there is no light *within* the digital realm, merely in its expression: the embodiment of the world in its mediation. It is only an ideal abstraction on the part of the observer that generates the relevance of light in the digital world, in contrast to the physical world where light plays an integral role in initiating 'observation' in its most abstract sense. The observable digital world and the observable digital subject create their own embodiment through the inherent abstraction of code and its cognition.

Desire and Loss

The inclusion of the subject within its own gaze, beholding itself as object, is the process by which subjectivity is brought into an individuated self. What underpins this construction, however, is the Real beneath the gaze, the presupposed conditions, the raw sense and nonsense of the expression that posits the subject. This quasi-causal force beneath the virtual functioning of the cogito constitutes the *objet petit a* which Lacan (1977) defines, in the visual field, as the gaze itself (p. 105). This suggests that the prerequisite conditions of a position from which the gaze views itself are linked to desire as a lost cause. The use of avatars in computer games – constructed according a series of imposed objectives and the imperative to 'win' the game – displays clearly the role of desire in the function of the avatar, being in a space with a clear motivation and achievable goal. However, the relation of the user to desire is integral to all constructions of the avatar, including non-games such as SL, as an absent and partial object inherent to the formation of the digital subject. Indeed, the very term 'avatar' could be considered an *objet a*, a lack and excess, in its relation to our gaze and engagement with digital realms. Filled with data, the excessive flow of information through the avatar into virtual existence is more than our view of the representation makes visible.

Through the fragmented abstractions of perception and thought, there is an inherent limit to the embodiment potential for avatars as forms of expression, themselves embedded in an established 'computer culture' of interaction. The use of avatar-mediated spaces has developed from earlier forms, such as the impact of early text-based MUDs (Multi User Domains) as well as the range of forum, social media and gaming cultural conventions for intersubjective relationships through computer technology. For example, Earle (2001) proposes a "set of states and gestures" (p. 171) for augmenting avatar communication that not only includes the examples expected for an expressive embodied avatar – 'sleepy', 'laughter', 'sad', 'kiss', etc. – but also an 'unavailable' state, as well as 'emphasis' and 'thinking' gestures. These extra motions add an array of embodied hypertexts to the figurative avatar: the 'unavailable' state, echoing the lolling 'afk' (away from keyboard) position in SL and other similar signifiers of gestural absence, maintains the states that govern social interaction on a purely textual basis (such as messaging software and chat or forum websites); an 'emphasis' gesture portrays a common html tag as a visual gesticulation; and the 'thinking' gesture recalls the eternally frustrating timer icon or spinning coloured disc that forms a baleful signifier to any impatient computer user. Established frameworks such as these provide not only a productive lexicon and set of restrictions, but also hypertextual material and mediators to be manipulated and hacked by SL artists.

These hypertextual fragments of 'presence' display an underlying need for an expanded view of participation in avatar-mediated environments, for even the most 'realistic' never suffices for a genuinely digital existence. The HUD (heads-up display) that re-frames any digital environment maintains the subjective position between embodiments, regardless of the level of immersion. This need to be present through contact with information leads us to uncover the potential of an art practice in which avatars participate *as* data, fulfilling the need to progress beyond a replication of physical embodiment. The work of avatar Angrybeth Shortbread (and her physical counterpart Annabeth Robinson) displays such a practice, whereby the subject is fragmented into individual values of data, through which the art work can be engaged and observed. The interactive installation *Avatar DNA* (2006) uses an avatar's UUID (universally unique identifier) to convert the presence of the avatar into pure data, a string of hexadecimal characters, which generates a double helix akin to biological DNA. In the artist's words: "the sculpture generated is as individual as the avatar themselves" (Shortbread, 2006a). However, unlike physical DNA, this individuality is in no way linked to the outwards appearance of the avatar, it is a pure signifier, an abstract data point. While the visual appearance of biological DNA appears as an abstraction in the concealed signifiers of the double helix code, it bears a direct causal relation to the visual formation of the human figure, whereas the UUID is a detached code that signifies the user regardless of their visual appearance, more a mark of subjective presence beneath the body than a code for the body itself. The temporality of each construction in *Avatar DNA* ties together the presence of the subject both visually, embodied in the gallery space, and as data, in its brief existence as 'DNA'. This principle is furthered in the sonic medium, and split into its two constituent elements of expression, in the works *UUID Polyphony* (2006) and *I am Note, We are Music* (2009). The former continues the avatar-as-data method, converting the UUID of any approaching avatars into a musical phrase that is stored in the memory of four playback devices which continually cycle through the stored musical memories of the avatars that have been present, re-asserting their presence as data in their visual absence. The latter focuses on data directly relating to visual presence, with the height and position of the avatar converted into the pitch and iteration frequency of the notes played by the 'harp'.

The complexity here is derived from the visual presence of many avatars, as a collective performance tool using the flexibility of visual appearance as both data and expression. This collective gesture of presence is echoed in *Gestalt*

Cloud (2009), which generates rain from four or more avatars moving close to one another inside a three-dimensional grid. This rain brings to life a digital garden to be explored, though the presence of the avatars in the garden, and their resulting absence from the grid, leads to a slow fade into the original darkened state. Here presence and absence are played against one another in two conflicting spaces of exploration and interaction. This role of presence as absence is further highlighted in *You Demand Too Much of Me* (2006), which involves the non-being of a three-dimensional grid of cubes in relation to avatar presence. This work "began with a simply musing, 'Does Art within a Digital Space, exist if its not being observed'" [sic], inverting expected modes of interaction as it "decays whilst it has an audience…a visual metaphor for consumption" (Shortbread, 2006b). The more avatars that are present, the more quickly the work 'decays', evoking the 'consciousness causes collapse' hypothesis. This theory that observation by thinking creatures instigates the shift from wave function to matter provides a useful framework for the inherent paradox of subjective presence within its world(s) and its own gaze, a quantum example of the parallax stain. What is viewed through the interface screen as our inclusion within a given digital realm necessarily contains the gesture of parallax within perception. Žižek (2009) writes that "the subject's gaze is always-already inscribed into the perceived object itself, in the guise of its 'blind spot', that which is 'in the object more than the object itself', the point from which the object itself returns the gaze" (p. 17). Applied directly and literally to avatar-mediated environments, this supports the notion that "the reality I see is never 'whole' – not because a large part of it eludes me, but because it contains a stain, a blind spot, which indicates my inclusion in it" (Žižek, 2009, p. 17). The rendering of the digital Real, data as the 'excessive' causality of code, into a specific embodiment of virtual existence, as the 'lacking' gaze lost between digital and physical positions of the self, only creates a digital presence insofar

as the subject is engaged with the split in Lacan's gaze and the stain of Žižek's parallax. Beholding an attempted self-representation as an avatar within its own gaze, the digital subject emerges through absence, negating the digital equivalent to the physical illusion of embodied presence. Such an engaged position demonstrates Žižek's (2012) claim that "'subject' is the name for a crack in the edifice of being" (p. 41); an emergent formation of absence.

This mark in the edifice of the computer screen has been expanded in recent research, to encompass a broader scheme of engagement. Hill's thesis expands upon the work of Gunkel (2010) to separate four 'standard' definitions or expressions that qualify under the notion of 'avatar': "animated avatar [e.g. Second Life], web-cam avatar [e.g. Skype], profile avatar [e.g. Facebook], and portrait avatar [e.g. Twitter (image plus 140 character caption)]" (Hill, 2011, p. 50). By applying the emergent absence of the Lacanian gaze to each of these manifestations of the digital subject as a simultaneous lack, of being, and excess, of data, it is possible to extend the Žižekian notion of consciousness as always-already false: "the avatars that are encountered within the virtual world are not the representatives and delegates of some independent and pre-existing real thing. The order of precedence must be reversed" (Gunkel, 2010, p. 136). This emergent simultaneity of subjectivity between physical and digital worlds upturns the conventional relation of humans to their 'real' physical body. Philip K. Dick (1996), an author well-established in confronting issues of fleshy human authenticity, predicted: "Fake realities will create fake humans. Or, fake humans will generate fake realities and then sell them to other humans, turning them, eventually, into forgeries of themselves" (pp. 263-264). However, Žižek (2007) insists that reality "always-already was virtual" (p. 193), becoming here 'humanity always-already was a forgery of itself'. That is, whether in a computer simulation or physical universe, the authentic gaze, the primal existence, is merely presupposed in the virtuality of an always-already false consciousness.

Expanding the embodied form can reveal the objectification of an unattainable desire in the notion of form itself. If the subject views itself as a lost point within its own gaze, it never 'is' the representation of itself. The digital bodies it can occupy always lacks an element of genuine subjectivity, a filling in of the object with consciousness. This lack places the avatar body indeed as objective, but as the *objet a* that constitutes the 'in me more than myself', the externalisation of the cogito through archetypal, unconscious impulses. The objective body, however, is supported by the constructs of fantasy into a form of transference that places it in lieu of the phenomenal body. This interaction, between bodily *objet a* and its illusory framework of phenomenal connections with the cogito, brings to light the same processes in any 'bodily form', where even the fleshy mortal frame we inhabit in the physical world only ever takes on the role of the phenomenal body through fantasy and transference. Physical and digital bodies thus share the same self-posited illusion, their only difference lying within the fundamental formation of the subjective relation to such bodies within consciousness. This is the heart of the physical-digital parallax even at the level of embodiment. The minimal difference in the perspective of consciousness within its avatar demonstrates the manner in which "the position of enunciation already influences and informs what comes to be enunciated" (Gunkel, 2010, p. 139). This position of enunciation is also a position of embodiment. Consciousness itself remains always disembodied, acting in relation to its physical or digital manifestations as a lost object, expressing its excessive 'in it more than itself' according to the particular parallax of the individual participation and presence in a specific world within the psychological space of subjective reality.

ABSENCE

Presence as Absence

Moving avatars beyond the psychological confines of our familiar physical fleshy containers necessitates a shift away from viewing the body in terms of absence *or* presence, towards the *presence-of-absence* of the cognitive gaze. The spectre of early avatar-mediation in 1990s digital art remains in contemporary art practice, and those who manage to make progress beyond what is now an important but historical approach seldom garner the theoretical implications of this move. Moser's volume (1996), based on the 1992 *Art and Virtual Environment Project* at Banff, which has set the tone for later conceptions of the avatar, is one such limiting view. The analytical texts, while influentially embracing the role of artists within the development of technology, reside firmly within an illusory cage of physicality. Emphasising "the crucial role that the body plays in constructing cyberspace" (Hayles, 1996, p. 1) and the notion that "we are embodied creatures" (Hayles, 1996, p. 3), and insisting that "the psyche clings to the memory that this space is a representation, that is, it clings to a memory of the real body and its formulation in physical space" (Tenhaaf, 1996, p. 60), the work, like many treatments of avatar art, recognises the problematic echoes of the physical form, yet is rooted in traditional notions of the 'real' world.

Hayles (1999), Ihde (2002) and Hansen (2004; 2006) have all furthered this limiting focus on embodiment, with their discussion of "themes of virtual bodies in relation to lived bodies" (Ihde, 2002, p. 3) in which "the ultimate goal of virtual embodiment is to become the perfect simulacrum of full, multisensory bodily action" (Ihde, 2002, p. 7). While these texts offer attempts to take into account the position from which physical-digital epistemology emerges, by placing it firmly within the physical body they reduce the analysis of the subject to a prosthetic view of cybernetic embodiment. This approach fails to fully take into account the system of extension (of the cogito) already at work in the physical body, thus missing the basic tenet of second-order cybernetics (as with quantum physics): the analysis of the observer as part of the system. This is not a return to physical embodiment, but rather the theoretical juncture at which a parallax conception of cybernetic consciousness is needed to confront the subject as it moves between physical and digital worlds. Applying a Žižekian model of parallax subjectivity directly to avatar-mediated spaces transforms such fears of a "community of shattered egos" where virtual existence "teaches us to dislocate our proper place" (Ronell, 1996, p. 126) into a discussion of two equally virtual worlds. Directing the gaze onto the cogito itself allows for new artistic conceptions of digital presence *within* the absent position from which the gaze is thought. It is necessary to first 'disembody' our view of engaged consciousness to avoid constant attempts to construct the illusion of presence, and instead embrace the potential for an expressive absence, what Ascott (2008) hails in SL as the "power to provide for a release of the self, release from the self…our ability to be many selves" (p. 204). This recognises the many possibilities of embodiment while focusing on the disembodied subject between and outside itselves. If the avatar as *objet a* is always-already lost, then we must not view disembodiment in the shift from physical to digital worlds as a 'presence *followed* by absence' but, rather, as the simultaneous potential available to expression within a 'presence *of* absence', a reconception of the process by which consciousness experiences embodiment in and between any given world(s).

Lacan (1977) states that "zero is the presence of the subject who, at that level, totalizes" (p. 226). In conceiving the relation between presence and absence in digital environments, this implies that the totality of the subject between the various digital avatars, and everyday performed physical identities, is derived from a lack of presence. The subject *is* not in any of its embodiments, the cogito perpetuates itself as a virtuality beyond the limits of a single body, and the presence of the subject as thought lies between the total assemblage of specific embodiments. That is, the genuinely subjective presence is at the level of zero: the position of parallax made manifest, a presence of absence. This is brought into an embodied presence only in the intersection between the 'zero' of the subjective Real and the 'one' of self-positing virtual consciousness. Žižek (2012) identifies, in the unity of the one and the zero, "the singular universal that marks the minimal difference" (p. 92). This minimal difference occurs between presence and absence within the subject itself. These two levels do not differ in number, just as the binary 1 and 0 of digital logic do not rest on fixed values,[1] but the act of perceptual difference itself. This place in which such a gesture of minimal difference occurs, the position of the parallax gaze, is what Žižek (2006) labels the "unrepresentable point of reference" (p. 102). Across each avatar-mediated space, and the biologically-mediated physical realm, the subject thus exists as a gaze of consciousness desiring its positioning within each world, a life in superposition with itself that places the identifying mask of virtuality in specific worlds over the unrepresentable core of our 'meta-self'. This core of the subject is made manifest through the lines of desire in the virtual, abstracting processes of consciousness. Bohm's (1994) conception of thought as partial (p. 61) and participatory (p. 5) gives the superposition of infinities a functional role of negotiating embodiment as an external *objet a* of the subject. The identification of a specific body is a placing of a fragment of the subject outside its virtual, zero point presence in consciousness as a limited product of desire to exist in a given space. Viewing the role of consciousness outside of these lost objectifications in bodies is an innate step towards the cyborg subject as a technological posthuman (or the development of a superhuman cogito function), which seeks to create what Nick Bostrom and Anders Sandberg (2009) conceive as "intimate links between the external systems and the human user through better interaction…less an external tool and more of a mediating "exoself"…embedding the human within an augmenting "shell" such as…virtual reality" (p. 320). Yet this state of superposition is not merely applicable in a digital environment, for the same virtuality is present in the physical world. The embodiment of the subjective void is always a 'shell' of augmentation, be it a sensory or abstract construct, allowing for interaction with a world through the 'collapse' of the mediated subject into such a world. Reality is therefore not only always-already virtual but always-already augmented: the subject cannot exist but between the worlds it appears to inhabit, present in each only as the traces of absence from its own desiring gaze.

States of superposition, before observational collapse closes the potential of infinite virtuality, enable what Albert (1992) labels new "modes of being…which are quite unlike what we know how to think about…*extraordinarily* mysterious situations" (p. 11). To Heisenberg, the largest breakthrough since Newton was Bohr's probability wave, that "introduced something standing in the middle between the idea of an event and the actual event, a strange kind of physical reality just in the middle between possibility and reality" (Heisenberg, 2000, p. 11). The inaccessible possibility staining our perception in the centre of reality, the mysterious state of superposition, is instructive to avatar-mediation. Within the digital medium, where potential is formed from bits rather than wave functions, the same two states (in infinite variation) can produce infinite outcomes. However, similar processes occur in both physical and digital actualisation, each observation forming "one possible solution to a giant cosmic anagram" (Egan, 2010, p. 160). The infinite permutations of these particles or bits could potentially and atemporally result in either digital *or* physical worlds, in a digital *or*

physical subject. The notion that the same Real underlies both realms highlights the confusion in identifying with any singular physical or digital embodiment, and the arbitrary nature of presence without its relation to absence in the construction of subjective reality.

Structure as Control

The nature of a specific embodiment, as a particular mode of presence, thus has a structuring effect on our understanding of the specific environment with which we engage; its possibilities, limitations and purpose. Within the medium of computer games, particularly the ever-increasing variety of MMORPGs, this structure takes on the role of an expression of history, embodying time rather than space as a mode of being our achievements as assessed by the conditions of the gaming structure. As the player character increases in level (through 'earning' experience) and obtains items (particularly the more unique items gained through completing difficult quests) the avatar's appearance progresses from the standard starting image. This is a historical economy of representation: the more advanced the character, the more customisable and impressive the avatar's appearance. Such an avatar thus takes on a semantic record of the character's history and celebrates the user's actions, creating a new code of signifiers to the game's cognoscenti (particularly other characters of the same 'tier' or higher). However, this also has the effect of reducing the avatar to a meritocratic expression, in the same manner as the economy of 'lives', and introduces a more elitist and controlled aesthetic along 'career paths' rather than the freer, more creative tools available in non-game virtual worlds such as SL that promote user-generated content over a defined visual lexicon of achievement-based signifiers.

This problem parallels what Deleuze and Guattari (2004) describe as faciality, a system of white wall and black holes (characteristically the face and eyes) constructed at the intersection of signification and subjectification: "signification is never without a white wall on which it inscribes its signs...subjectification is never without a black hole in which it lodges its consciousness" (p. 186). This territorialised structure that Deleuze and Guattari label the abstract machine of the face is the inscribing of the black hole of the eyes into the white wall of identity, what has been described in this thesis as the void of the subjective position in the surface of functioning consciousness and its identification. Overcoming these structures that shape the formation of a subject in contemporary informational society, abstracted as surfaces ruptured by the absent position of the gaze, requires avoiding the nostalgic return or regression to a primitive pre-facial state, instead performing a deterritorialisation or defacialisation through critical use of the face, towards a probe-head of creative flight (Deleuze & Guattari, 2004, pp. 208-210). The anthropocentrism that plagues avatar-mediation extends beyond the visual and figurative into the construction of the face within consciousness across physical and digital worlds. The signifying structures of faciality in the game-based personal history approach to digital embodiment constantly reterritorialises the avatar onto the surface of virtuality and the strata of history, displaying quests completed and directing the future of the character through career path limitations on weapons/armour availability and manner of attire. Appearance here becomes desire, and the increased abilities such appearances signify draw the image into a functional role of representing both the power of the avatar and the skills of the player. In this fusion of abstract data and anthropocentric image the infinite zero – the void of subjectivity and the black hole of the face – is lost in overly 'present' presence, whereby the absence of the subject is constantly deferred into the line of history. It is this characteristic of the gaming

avatar that limits the creative expression of the subject, no matter how many varieties of '+1 Mace' one may own.

One artist who embraces the manipulation of the avatar through its structures of control that define our mediation of digital environments is Bryn Oh, in her lavish psychological, full-sim installations. Bryn Oh is only the avatar, with no connection to the physical artist. As the header of the artist's blog explains, "Bryn Oh is a virtual artist created by a Toronto oil painter", although the relationship has developed reciprocally, as she writes: "when I first came to SL I brought in first life ideas to work on.. where now I seem to export SL ideas to my first life" (Oh, 2013a). While this could at first glance appear similar to the conflation of identified selves in Kris Schomaker's problematic negotiation of avatar subjectivity, there is at work in Bryn Oh's construction a more deliberate elaboration on the digital subject and an acknowledgement of different modes and cognitions of creativity. Shostakovich (2010) quotes the artist stating: "the stories I tell on Immersiva are my own hopes, dreams and fears hidden behind the mask of robots", and this is exemplified in her avatar, which disrupts the expressionistic human figure with cybernetics and, eventually, a deformed rabbit-like mask. This image relates to the themes of an early trilogy of large-scale builds by Oh – *The Daughter of Gears* (2008-9), *Rabbicorn* (2009), and *Standby* (2010) – which, like much of Oh's work, utilises characters undergoing a transition between human, animal and robot forms, confronting the psychological quandary such a subject might encounter. *The Daughter of Gears* was created for the Black Swan art sim and features art works by avatar Light Waves and others as well as many traps for visiting avatars to negotiate. Oh's response to this arbitrary use of obstacles in the interaction of the sim initiated the creative drive for her own build: "Why are there traps here? Who are they trying to keep out? There was no narrative so I devised one" (Oh, 2010). The series of traps and obstacles amidst a winding, climbing path through a series of poetic interludes and three-dimensional scenes disrupts the narrative through a level of inaccessibility. The struggle of a visiting avatar to reach the conclusion of the story draws the viewer into the narrative through their avatar as an interface to the world of a mother trying to save her daughter by transferring her consciousness to a robot, while avoiding the protests of an angry mob. Even the completion of the narrative 'quest' draws the avatar further and more horrifically into the narrative, for "once they reach the top [they] realize that they are one of the mob" (Oh, 2010). The emotional ruptures of the characters in Oh's work blends seamlessly with the disruption to the visiting avatar's complicit experience as an interface not only to the three-dimensional world but also to the psychological world of the artist as creative digital subject. This critique of interaction is evident even in the name of Oh's sim – 'Immersiva' suggests engagement as the key element of experiencing the art – and the necessary role of the avatar as interface in experiencing her art forces engagement with a free quasi-linear narrative that creates a wave function of the gaze: "a mobile gaze that is *made flesh* in the *metaverse*" (Ramirez, 2012, p. 120) as many potential paths, scenes and objects. The builds themselves are filled with hypertextual layering: finding hidden objects, linking to external content, and typing words printed on objects into chat windows; there are many ways to negotiate these environments and reveal their semiotic strands of narrative. These works thus exist as a superposition of all possible interactions, requiring an engaged cogito within the avatars present as much as each individual visiting consciousness requires the mediator of an avatar with which to experience the rich environment of Oh's worlds.

These superpositions of narratives, gazes and objects confront the avatar more strongly in the later work *Imogen and the Pigeons* (2013). Saorsa (2011) expands a Deleuzian conception of literary potential to insist that "narrative identity is always mobile" (p. 98). In Oh's work this superposition of mobile subjective experience embodies a wave function through both narrative and visual space. Like Alice 'down-the-rabbit-hole'[2], the avatar is drawn beyond itself as a point of contact between the virtual cogito and expressions of the underlying Real. In *Imogen and the Pigeons*, after climbing a disappearing staircase out of the decayed wasteland of the 'Rebirth™ life encryption' centre, the stark black and white cuboid stairs are juxtaposed with the expressionistic realism of a Therapist(The Rapist)'s clinic housing anthropic characters extended by manifestations of their darkest traumas, embodiments of psychological horror unleashed in the visual environment. The interaction is here ingeniously extrapolated. The innate flight ability of SL avatars is frustratingly restricted in the installation. The avatar must instead engage with the space and the narrative by 'sit' on a feather, enabling the ability to walk on the walls and ceilings of the installation. The narrative thus unfolds between the psychological scenes in fragments of conventional three-dimensional space and the abstract corridors that require the extended avatar interface to defy gravity. The flexible narrative structure, utilising Oh's method of "combinatory paths, multimedia hyper structures, and the provision of a visual *pentagram*" (Ramirez, 2012, pp. 135-6), tells of a girl stuck between human and pigeon personae, echoing the human/avatar relationship as the human subject seeks to identify with the freer group, to fly with the pigeons. Here the Real at the core of Imogen's subjectivity is constantly seeking to burst forth into a virtual identification that is furthered by a cybernetic extension of her consciousness. The installation's poetic fragments detail the deterioration of the stored memories and the emergence of a child from these fragments of consciousness, following which Imogen lifts up her memory-child towards a blue whale in the sky, offering a direct comparison between the world of the installation and the broader environment of SL. There is here a moment of confrontation between the physical and digital bodies and, amidst the trauma, the possibility of a creative act through the interface of a 'body' (of any description, be it human, avatar or pigeon). The visiting avatar's gaze creates a narrative that confronts the subject with their own split personality. This is echoed in Oh's following installation, *The Singularity of Kumiko* (2014), which literally controls the visual impact of the gaze in a darkened environment where motion is necessary for vision as fragments of nonlinear narrative appear in small lit areas that the visitor must explore. By controlling the modes of movement and even nature of the gaze available to visitors, Bryn Oh stages the avatar as a lost object visually, interactively and subjectively in the creation of new experiences of artistic engagement not possible outside of digital environments such as SL.

ART

Substance or Gesture

Within these flexible mods of engagement with creative works and the creative process, the positioning of the avatar as the Lacanian *objet a* calls into question the function of the avatar as the digital equivalent of material substance in favour of a shift towards embodying gestures in a performative construction of identity. As Deleuze (1988) writes, "life as *movement* alienates itself in the material *form* that it creates" (p. 104). This can be clearly demonstrated in the problematic role of the numerous art projects labelling themselves 'avatar portraits' that convert the avatar into a simultaneously consumed and revered object in a totemic digital existence that reveals its own process of imitation and thus exposes the illusion of authenticity in all images of the human form. These include not only Kris Schomaker's work, but also, notably, that of Eva and Franco Mattes (as the collective 0100101110101101), whose exhibition *13 Most Beautiful Avatars*, part of the larger project *Portraits* (2006-7) based on images of avatars, also brought the avatar-as-object

across the physical-digital divide. The images of SL avatars, not including those of the duo, were shown both online, on the collective's website and in an SL art space, and physically, as canvas prints in a New York gallery the following year. While the creation of anthropocentric avatars could suggest a representational and figurative digital art form, this occurs in a postmodern twist of realism in digital culture that Jameson (2003) describes as "a realism of the image rather than of the object [that] has more to do with the transformation of the figure into a logo than with the conquest of new "realistic" and representational languages" (p. 701). The apparent return to 'figurative' portraiture in the Mattes' avatar portraits therefore falls into the mediated transformation of form into logo while critiquing the consumptive imagery that it creates. The human form and its familiar representation in portraiture is reduced to an imitation that undermines even the illusion of authenticity. The clean and crisp images – of anthropic avatars of both sexes – "exude a sexy artifice that is both seductive and a parody of seductiveness" (Smith, 2007). This reappropriation, which comes to "signify emergent aesthetic values of *Second Life*, and remediate pop art modalities of the fallacy of "portraiture" through digital culture" (Dinnen, 2012), disrupts the traditional portrait: visually, by the faces over-filling one side of the image rather than being centred neatly within the frame; conceptually, through the absence of human identity even in these anthropic characters. While the subject itself is always absent from its representation in portraiture, the objectification of the avatar not only mimics the familiar objectification of the human form in popular media, but projects such a critique of objectification onto the authenticity of the human form itself, by levelling the reverence for the human face with its digital, malleable, anonymous counterpart.

This challenge to the fetishistic status of the human form is expanded in the work *Synthetic Performances* (2009-10), which applies the same critique to the bodily orientated performance art practice. Of the work, Mattes says: "we hate performance art, we never quite got the point. So, we wanted to understand what made it so uninteresting to us" (Mattes, 2007). Notably, these SL performance re-enactments use avatars that purposefully resemble Eva and Franco Mattes. Their art practice in the physical world, based on forgery and imitation, has led the artists to attempt to be 'themselves' amidst the freedom of choice in digital environments. Instructively, this point perhaps reveals more about the artists' construction of their own subjectivity than their critique of performance art: their physical identities are so often shrouded as imposters and fakes that their bodily forms have become, artistically, a lost object even to themselves. In this context, the focus on clear and accurate images of the avatar faces in their portraiture can also be read as a need to utilise the avatar-as-object to reclaim the *objet a* of their physical world creative subjectivity.

The work of Ian Upton and his avatar Ian Pahute challenges the dual perception of the subject between space and time, physical and digital, substance and gesture. The installation *The Loneliness of Being* (2008) draws an endless flow of information from internet search engines into a meditative flux of abstract embodiment. An array of words floats in a vast open space on a near-empty SL island, fading and merging as new terms are added, reducing the data to a level only disturbed by observation. The mix of soft coloured letters are hard to make out as they float freely together, yet take on meaning only in viewing. The wide range of vocabulary that gradually fills the space with its shifting shapes and colours include 'story', 'strike', 'billionaire', 'service' and 'escape'. Avatars can sit beneath the work, looking up into this mass of signification, or fly amidst the endless flow, navigating the space in a data-filled solipsism. The island on which the work is placed is often deserted, leaving the viewer with only themselves and the words for company. The subject is lost between their screen-framed view

of the installation and their avatar's place within it, transcended by the eternal flow of words that refuses to be fixed in measurement. A second installation, *Shadows* (2008), displays ghostly figures walking endlessly in a circle, echoing both the human form in its spectral digital embodiment and the superposition of the identical figures at each point in the circle. The ghosts are caught in a perpetual functioning drive: acting both as particles, in anthropic mimicry of an 'embodied' form, and as waves, in the identical blurred movements of semi-transparent figures.

A further work by Upton, undertaken in collaboration with Steve Wilkes, converts the physical body in space to an idealised representation in data. *A Passing Moment* (2007), involving the use of visual and spatial scanning technology, forces the 'misuse' of technology into a discussion of absence and presence in human interaction. The scanning equipment, able to create a millimetre-accurate render of a three-dimensional physical space, is disrupted by movement, leading to gaps and glitches in the scan. By inviting a physical human audience into the space during the scanning process, the human subjects themselves are transferred into thousands of data points, while their movements create absences within the digital model. The very presence of humanity interferes with the measuring apparatus, demonstrating a wave/particle duality at the heart of the subject-as-data. These images are exhibited in SL, creating a direct confrontation between the physical body as pure data and the purely digital human as visual body. In the artist's statement to *A Passing Moment*, Upton explains his interest in such disruptions of constructed observation:

The line between chaos (our sensory and subjective view of the universe) and the void, that unknown area inside (our spirit, soul, unconscious) is a fascinating one. I would argue that we consciously and proactively construct our universe...constantly shifting, breaking and transforming as new ideas are discovered and old ideas challenged. It is this line, the conscious construction, that much of my work seeks to explore. (Upton & Wilkes, 2007)

This demonstrates an awareness of connections between the 'real' world of the subject and the underlying void of the subjective Real. The construction of worlds within subjective reality is expressed by the work as ghostly digitised figures; avataristic echoes. The physical form is the *objet a* here, a lost object reduced to pure data and a quantised visual rendering. The superposition of motion through time objectifies the gesture in a single fixed state ; the energy of life lost in the sepulchral stillness of memory.

As is the case with any mediation, expression in avatar-mediated spaces such as SL is a matter of a series of limitations. If, as DeLanda (2006) extrapolates from Deleuze's theory of assemblage, "a whole provides its component parts with *constraints and resources*" (p. 34), then the avatar emerges with a set of limitations applied by the 'meta-self' upon any individual expression of embodiment. The specific form taken by the subject, particularly in realms such as SL, are governed by a complex set of constraints, not only external (the technology available and one's access to it), but more importantly internal in the psychological construction of the *objet a*-vatar itself. The basic construction of an avatar in SL starts from a set of anthropocentric choices. While height, figure, colour and clothes are all transfinitely customisable, the enforced presumption is that the subject will seek a 'human' counterpart in this digital realm. An 'invisible' skin, however, allows for the construction of any form of expression for the avatar to 'wear', creating an assemblage of the imagination.

The avatar as contemporary digital figuration is only an object in the sense of loss, as a purely coded emblem of data standing in for the Real of subjectivity we wish to express through it. That is, the avatar as an art object can only be an art of the *objet a*. These lost, partial or virtual objects

of the avatar function for the rupture in virtual existence of the subject's own gaze. Deleuze (2004a) states that "whatever the reality in which the virtual object is incorporated, it does not become integrated…but rather testifies to the other virtual half which the real continues to lack" (p. 125). Jameson (2003) identifies this lost object as pure signifier or 'logo', expressing a "new kind of abstraction" (p. 703) not only characterised by postmodern art and culture but embedded within the very structure of cyberspace. The digital Real bursts forth in our frustration of the avatar as object, confronting our virtual existence with the structured discourses of computer code. A further consideration regarding the role of the avatar as art object is presented by the avatar Kisa Naumova (and physical counterpart Graham Hibbert) as the necessity of any SL artistic practice to step outside of the fourth wall that we inexplicably breach the minute we log on (Naumova, 2009). Here again the avatar is necessarily a 'stain in the gaze'; a mark of subjective expression and a subjective interface with virtual existence that breaks down the conventional suspension of disbelief by which we appear to 'become' avatars (or, perhaps, by which they 'become' us, part of our cognito-embodiment assemblage). To achieve constructive consciousness of one's own mediation requires that such an interface be under the influence of the subject, thus the avatar-as-object presents a tool for both expression and interaction, as well as a direct opportunity to hack the self-perception of the cogito and thus confront our formation as subject within digital culture.

Embodiment or Disembodiment

In order to move gain a critical perspective on the position of one's own mediation, both by digital technology and by virtual consciousness itself, the inherent loss within the embodied form suggests a warning against over-identification with the avatar form. The apparent attainment of the subject's desired appearance or identity risks venerating avatars as a mutable and perfectible replacement for the physical body. Thus the use of the avatar for improving self-image leads back to a paradoxical privileging of the 'real' world according to the desires of the subject, further supporting the virtuality of embodied consciousness. Through this, critical and creative forces can become lost under superficial therapeutic self-aggrandisement, reducing the avatar to a staging of body-therapy in which the digital fails in its attempts to perfect the physical. One example of the complexities of this problem is the work of artist Kristine Schomaker, creator of the *1000+ Avatars* (2010-12) collection of (anthropocentric, fantastical and often self-glorifying) avatar portraits. Her *My Life as an Avatar* (2010-12) project reveals an awareness of the tension between physical and digital selves in an interview between her physical self and her avatar, Gracie Kendal:

Kris Schomaker: Who are you?Gracie Kendal: I am your inner conscious, your alter ego, your self portrait, your avatar, your art... I am you.... GK: So, who are you?KS: I am me. I am you. So, why are we here? Oh yea, I remember. I am using you to confront my imperfections and insecurities. GK: Yea, well here's the thing. I don't like how you're 'using' me. (Trapdoor, 2010)

Despite Schomaker's fixed view of avatars as 'projections' of an identity linked to the 'real' user, her project displays an awareness of using the avatar merely as a tool for the physical 'person'. However, in this moment of the interview, the avatar itself appears to undermine the physical user's need for transference, resisting its role as a therapeutic apparatus in dealing with the desires and fears of its fleshy counterpart. What this interview in fact reveals, alongside the inclusion of many anti-anthropic avatars in the portraits project despite Schomaker's own anthropocentrism, is the drive of the unconscious in defining the expression between all manifestations of the self.

The similarity between the artist and her avatar, along with the many visual 'improvements' made on the avatar's hair, clothes and figure, is less an example of difference in avatar-mediated identity or of a unifying identity that seeks to overcome its imperfections, than a demonstration of the quasi-causal lack central to the subject and the construction of its subjective reality. The culture of avatar-mediation based merely on the freedom of image in improving the physical form is caught in the virtualising functions of identity, rather than the underlying sense of repetition that bursts forth in moments between the various differentiated embodiments of 'self'.

Each element of identity is constructed and performed by the subject while it uses that specific body to engage with a specific world. This does not rely on an externally consistent set of identities, for as Eladhari (2010) points out, "*players* are the ones who carry out both the characterisation of and the expression of the true characters of their avatar/PC/persona in a VGW [Virtual Game World]" (p. 53). We can add to this the construction and maintenance of any identity by the subject in any given world. The role of the subject beneath each of these surfaces of identity is the process of repetition that Deleuze (2004a) describes as an "emission of singularities, always with an echo or resonance which makes each the double of the other, or each constellation the redistribution of another" (p. 251). The subject releases a part of themselves into the singular identity, embedded in a specific world, but in the process the 'echo' of the underlying subjectivity is lost in the absent position of parallax. The identity appearing as a complete unit is itself a mere fragment, a partial, lost object, an *objet a*, in relation to the whole subject as the absent centre of its own parallax reality. Here the subject *between* physical and digital worlds is the eternally becoming interaction between the various parts: an assemblage between each fragmented aspect of differentiation around the subjective void of repetition. It is not identity but lack that is repeated, for the void forms an infinite circle of nothing amidst the perpetual function of the surfaces of consciousness.

Deleuze (2004b) warns against the blurring of lines between therapy and art, rejecting the simple placing of self-analysis as an artistic process and instead suggesting 'the artist both as patient and as doctor of civilization' (p. 237). This artist-analyst is engaged in the very crisis they attempt to 'cure'. This would not entail assuming the separate roles of patient and doctor between physical and digital selves (as with Schomaker, whose avatar takes on the role of analyst and transference as the solution to personal body issues) but being in a state of superposition: both roles simultaneously. While Schomaker engages with artistic play with her avatar's responses to the exploitation of digital embodied form for therapy, the positioning of both forms as 'her' entails only an internal dialogue limited to resolving personal issues rather than critical artistic gestures of relevance to human culture in general. The focus of such a gesture is not only the subject itself but 'civilisation': what has in this analysis of avatar constructions been delineated as the relation of the subject to its world(s). Deleuze and Guattari (2004), in advancing their project beyond psychoanalysis, claim that "a schizophrenic out for a walk is a better model than a neurotic on the analyst's couch. A breath of fresh air, a relationship with the outside world" (p. 2). This moves beyond a literal relationship with the outside world, as Guattari in particular learned from methods developed during his Lacanian training and time working at the experimental La Borde clinic. Indeed, any networked environment, such as SL, could be considered an inherent source of connection with many and varied worlds. Rather, what this desire for contact with an outside world displays is the need to escape the psychological confines of our embodied consciousness, a line of flight from the cogito itself through a relationship with an externalised and critical perspective

on oneself. Within this relation to the world lies what Žižek's (2009) extension of Lacan emphasises as the fractured individual subject itself. It is his concept of ""minimal difference" (the noncoincidence of the one with itself)" (p. 11), itself referencing Deleuze's (2004a) notion of difference as more fundamental than identity, that unveils the antagonism within the artist as doctor-patient of itself and its relation to any given world at the level of its own construction in a manner brought into a potentially critical form in avatar-mediated experiences of embodiment.

This rupture of noncoincidence with oneself suggests a rethinking of our experience of the physical body as a 'natural' embodiment, the dominant container and mediator of thought, and therefore allows a new conception of the potential uses of the avatar to emerge in contemporary artistic practices. Although it is difficult to escape what Žižek (2012) labels the "imbecilic inertia of material reality" (p. 127), the scope of the 'avatar' can be broadened towards a genuinely digital understanding of the term and its relation to desire and subjectivity. The starting point for such a shift is to acknowledge Žižek's opposition to Maurice Merleau-Ponty's (2002) claim of the body as "our general medium for having a world" (p. 146), an oft quoted trope in scholarship concerning the body and the digital, that "I never "am" my body" (Žižek, 2009, p. 227). While it is useful to consider Merleau-Ponty's (2002) division of the objective and phenomenal body (pp. 121f), along with his acknowledgement of their complex interlinked nature (pp. 121-2n), the bridge across the Cartesian mind-body split he employs is not readily transferred to the digital realm without anthropic conflation. A 'suspension of disbelief', a common dilemma for the creation of convincing digital modes of embodiment, is already at work in this conception of physical body, thus the present discussion suggests that embodiment is not of being-in-the-world but of our *desire for* being-in-the-world. The separation of objective and phenomenal body without consideration of such desire relies on an ill-defined divide of familiarity and interface, whereas we might very well describe touch typing or a well-used game controller as being "potentialities already mobilized by the perception of [the object to be acted upon]" rather than "objects to be discovered in objective space" (Merleau-Ponty, 2002, p. 121). Just as young children and adolescents learn and relearn to negotiate their changing biological frame, so too does the digital subject familiarise themselves with their computer interface, to the extent that the medium itself takes on, to consciousness, a level of phenomenal transparency commensurate with Merleau-Ponty's conception of the body. We might thus use Negroponte's (1996) rejection of McLuhan's famous maxim, when he writes: "the medium is not the message in a digital world. It is an embodiment of it" (p. 71), to expand the word 'avatar' to a definition between the Hindu myth and its common reappropriation in digital culture, as "a visible manifestation or embodiment of an abstract concept; archetype" (Collins English Dictionary). Here the subject itself constitutes the abstract concept, in the virtuality of self-posited consciousness, and is represented in both physical and digital worlds by a collection of data (nucleobases or bits) according to certain archetypes of what is recognised as 'human'. There is an obvious link here to Jungian archetypes (another word rooted in the manifestation of a deific being), described as the universal "contents of the collective unconscious" (Jung, 1968, p. 4). It is perhaps not surprising that the avatar has such firm links to anthropocentric embodiment, yet the Jungian construct that forms the deepest levels of subjectivity supports a broadening of an anti-anthropic embodiment in abstract, oneiric and super-natural forms. This draws the individual desires of different subjects towards the general desire for having a body, for being in a world, expressing the collective Real of all subjects based in the fear of inexistence. Outside of a simple replacement of the human form by allegorical representations of fantastical creatures or objects[3] a gesture of removal is necessary, from each world and each body we inhabit, embracing our possible inexistence in our inherent absence from ourselves. Only in this gesture of placing ourselves between our many individuated 'selves' can we stage a position from which to view our own subjective reality and begin to think otherwise about SL, digital technology and our entire construction of creative subjectivity.

CONCLUSION

This chapter has provided an outline for analysing our relation to the avatar form within the structures of desire and loss that create the *objet petit a* within our own psyche and subjective reality. From the emergence of the gaze and the inclusion of the subject within it, both as a psychological stain and more directly as the avatar, the tensions of the subject to its embodied form has been interrogated through the challenges raised for and by artists in Second Life. The limiting tendency towards self-therapy through avatar-mediation has been criticised in the formation of an ideal image reflecting only the subject's desires for their physical body, itself often a lost object through age or illness, that are made manifest in the digital environment at the expense of a critical and genuinely creative view of the position of the subjective gaze. Identification of the individual in expressing the imaginary as an apparent fulfilment of desire conceals the function of the *objet a* as the integral and fundamental loss that structures the fantasy of digital technology and our desiring relation to it. A position has been sought between physical and digital manifestations of the body, actively embracing the lost nature of the avatar to draw out the necessary absence at the heart of presence, in a view of the parallax position of the subject as the gaze across realities. The negotiation of presence as image and data in the work of Angrybeth

Shortbread, which stages singular and collective antagonisms of presence in SL, has led towards a discussion of the complex SL installations by Bryn Oh, who actively controls the abilities of the avatar to engage with a space in order to construct a more active engagement with nonlinear spatial narrative structures that demonstrate the potential for creative control of avatar mediation. These artistic possibilities have then been interrogated in terms of the antagonisms between substance and gesture, embodiment and disembodiment in the construction of experiences through which the fantasy of avatar mediation itself – the structures of presence and embodiment in the lost *objet a* of the avatar – can be traversed. Finally, the chapter insists on the need for a constant (re)questioning of the formation of the avatar in its role as mediator between the positions of the subject in physical and digital worlds and as shifting gazes that always seek yet always fail to behold the true parallax position from which subjective reality occurs. To offer a concluding remark, for creative practices in SL to overcome the limiting factors of the individual desires and fantasies of their creators, the *objet a*-vatar must be confronted and exploited in order for new positions of gaze and engagement to emerge from which the entire construction of the avatar and our relation to it can be thought otherwise: outside of embodiment, against the structures of desire and beyond the imagination that reinforces fantasy. The critical avatar removes itself from the subject in such a way as to make clear the subject's exclusion from its own gaze, converting the subject from a series of separate static identities into a mobile and changeable gesture of creativity.

REFERENCES

Albert, D. Z. (1992). *Quantum Mechanics and Experience*. Cambridge, MA: Harvard University Press.

Ascott, R. (2008). Cybernetic, Technoetic, Syncretic: The Prospect for Art. *Leonardo*, *41*(3), 204. doi:10.1162/leon.2008.41.3.204

Bard, A., & Söderqvist, J. (2012). *The Futurica Trilogy*. Stockholm: Stockholm Text.

Bohm, D. (1994). *Thought as a System*. London: Routledge.

Bohm, D. (2002). *Wholeness and the Implicate Order*. London: Routledge.

Bostrom, N., & Sandberg, A. (2009). Cognitive Enhancement: Methods, Ethics, Regulatory Challenges. *Science and Engineering Ethics*, *15*(3), 311–341. doi:10.1007/s11948-009-9142-5 PMID:19543814

Collins English Dictionary. (2013). *Avatar*. Retrieved from CollinsDictionary.com

DeLanda, M. (2006). *A New Philosophy of Society: assemblage theory and social complexity*. London: Continuum.

Deleuze, G. (1988). *Bergsonism*. New York: Zone.

Deleuze, G. (2004a). *Difference and Repetition*. London: Continuum.

Deleuze, G. (2004b). *The Logic of Sense*. London: Continuum.

Deleuze, G., & Guattari, F. (2004). *A Thousand Plateaus: Capitalism and Schizophrenia*. London: Continuum.

Dick, P. K. (1996). How to Build a Universe that Doesn't Fall Apart Two Days Later. In P. K. Dick & L. Sutin (Eds.), *The Shifting Realities of Philip K. Dick: Selected Literary and Philosophical Writings* (259–280). New York: Vintage.

Dinnen, Z. (2012). *Pictures of Self-Portraits: Eva and Franco Mattes' Avatar Portraits*. Retrieved from http://mediacommons.futureofthebook.org/imr/2012/05/01/pictures-self-portraits-eva-and-franco-mattes-avatar-portraits

Earle, N. (2001). *Designing a Visual Component of Communication within 3D Avatar Virtual Worlds*. (Doctoral Thesis). University of Plymouth.

Egan, G. (2010). *Permutation City*. London: Gollancz.

Eladhari, M. (2010). *Characterising Action Potential in Virtual Game Worlds Applied with the Mind Module*. (Doctoral Thesis). Teeside University.

Gunkel, D. J. (2010). The real problem: Avatars, metaphysics and online social interaction. *New Media & Society*, *12*(1), 127–141. doi:10.1177/1461444809341443

Hansen, M. (2004). *New Philosophy for New Media*. Cambridge, MA: MIT Press.

Hansen, M. (2006). *Bodies in Code: Interfaces with digital media*. New York, Abingdon: Routledge.

Hayles, N. K. (1996). Embodied Virtuality: or how to put bodies back into the picture. In M. A. Moser (Ed.), *Immersed in Technology: art and virtual environments* (1–28). Cambridge, MA: MIT Press.

Hayles, N. K. (1999). *How we Became Posthuman*. Chicago: University of Chicago Press. doi:10.7208/chicago/9780226321394.001.0001

Heisenberg, W. (1949). *The Physical Principles of the Quantum Theory*. New York: Dover.

Heisenberg, W. (1965). Nobel Lecture: The Development of Quantum Mechanics (1933). In *Nobel Lectures, Physics 1922-1941* (290–301). Amsterdam: Elsevier.

Heisenberg, W. (2000). *Physics and Philosophy: The Revolution in Modern Science*. London: Penguin.

Hill, D. (2011). *The Ethical Dimensions of a New Media Age: A Study in Contemporary Responsibility*. (Doctoral Thesis). University of York.

Ihde, D. (2002). *Bodies in Technology*. Minneapolis: University of Minnesota Press.

Jameson, F. (2003). The End of Temporality. *Critical Inquiry*, *29*(4), 695–718. doi:10.1086/377726

Jung, C. G. (1968). *The Archetypes and the Collective Unconscious*. Princeton: Princeton University Press.

Lacan, J. (1977). *The Four Fundamental Concepts of Psycho-Analysis*. London: The Hogarth Press.

Mattes, F. (2007). *Nothing is real, everything is possible*. Retrieved from http://0100101110101101.org/press/2007-07_Nothing_is_real.html

Merleau-Ponty, M. (2002). *Phenomenology of Perception*. London: Routledge.

Moser, M. A. (Ed.). (1996). *Immersed in Technology: art and virtual environments*. Cambridge, MA: MIT Press.

Naumova, K. (2009). *Kisa Naumova: Artist Statement*. Retrieved from http://wiki.secondlife.com/wiki/User:Kisa_Naumova

Negroponte, N. (1996). *Being Digital*. New York: Vintage.

Oh, B. (2010). *The Rabbicorn story part one – The Daughter of Gears*. Retrieved from http://brynoh.blogspot.co.uk/2010/09/rabbicorn-story-part-one-daughter-of.html

Oh, B. (2013a). *Imogen and the Paintings*. Retrieved from http://brynoh.blogspot.co.uk/2013/01/imogen-and-paintings.html

Ramirez, F. G. T. (2012). *Because I am not Here. Selected Second Life-Based Art Case Studies: Subjectivity, Autoempathy and Virtual World Aesthetics*. (Doctoral Thesis). University of Western Ontario.

Ronell, A. (1996). A Disappearance of Community. In M. A. Moser (Ed.), *Immersed in Technology: art and virtual environments* (119–128). Cambridge, MA: MIT Press.

Saorsa, J. (2011). *Narrating the Catastrophe: An Artist's Dialogue with Deleuze and Ricoeur.* Bristol: Intellect.

Shortbread, A. (2006a). *Avatar DNA: notecard.* Retrieved from http://maps.secondlife.com/secondlife/The%20Port/28/87/26

Shortbread, A. (2006b). *You Demand Too Much of Me…: notecard.* Retrieved from http://maps.secondlife.com/secondlife/The%20Port/14/75/34

Shostakovich, D. (2010). *Bryn Oh's Identity Discovered!* Retrieved from http://dividni.blogspot.co.uk/2010/08/bryn-ohs-identity-discovered.html

Smith, R. (2007, March 9). Art in Review; Eva and Franco Mattes. *The New York Times.*

Tenhaaf, N. (1996). Mysteries of the Bioapparatus. In M. A. Moser (Ed.), *Immersed in Technology: art and virtual environments* (51–72). Cambridge, MA: MIT Press.

Trapdoor, K. (2010). *The Gracie Kendal Project-My Life as an Avatar.* Retrieved from http://karasecondlife.blogspot.co.uk/2010/08/gracie-kendal-project-my-life-as-avatar.html

Upton, I., & Wilkes, S. (2007). A Passing Moment 1st May to 30th June 2007, Charlotte Gallery, Eduserve Island, Second Life.

Žižek, S. (2006). *Interrogating the Real.* London: Continuum.

Žižek, S. (2007). *The Indivisible Remainder: on Schelling and related matters.* London: Verso.

Žižek, S. (2009). *The Parallax View.* Cambridge, MA: MIT Press.

Žižek, S. (2012). *Organs Without Bodies: on Deleuze and consequences.* London: Routledge.

KEY TERMS AND DEFINITIONS

Avatar: A visual embodiment or placeholder of a person or idea; most commonly a three-dimensional anthropic character through which a user can interact with a digital environment.

Embodiment: The apparent feeling or sense of occupying a body in a given world; the position of the gaze.

Fantasy: The fundamental desire that structures the individual desires of the subject, supporting the entire symbolic order.

Gaze: The position from which the subject views a world.

Objet Petit a: Lacan's lost object cause of desire representing a fundamental lack in the psychological construction of the human.

Parallax: A shift in the world resulting from a change in the viewer's perspective.

Real: The underlying and unknowable cause of reality for the subject.

Virtual: Most commonly referring to digital environments but also the surface of consciousness upon which the mask of reality appears.

ENDNOTES

[1] The 'material' difference of binary data can formed between any two numbers, commonly two non-zero voltages, but it is the *logical* difference, the absolute of 1 and

0 in thought, that constructs the symbolic foundations of digital reality.

2   This can be referred to Oh's deformed bunny avatar and the mythical robotic Rabbicorn (half rabbit, half unicorn), or indeed to Deleuze's treatment of Alice in his propositional logic (2004b).

3   Such as Micha Cardenas's project *Becoming Dragon* that stages the therapeutic process within the imaginary embodiment of a dragon as a self-promoting fantasy without traversing the constraints of the artist's own structures of desire, instead placing the ideal beast in the avatar form as a metaphor for the ideal physical body the artist seeks. This performs the same reductionist curative approach to the avatar that has been seen in Schomaker's therapeutic practice abd Žižek's traversal tool for the purely physical subject.

Section 3
Found Objects, Collaborative Practices, Shared Creativity

This section includes three chapters that are brought together to develop the discussions around Axel Bruns key term 'produsage' as an integral element of the artistic strategies developed within the projects presented. All three chapters present research that is as a result of sustained and experimental methodologies and inventive approaches to artistic practices, and each chapter contributor takes on key theories in which to frame their research.

Chapter 7
Found Objects, Bought Selves

Lynne Heller
OCAD University, Canada & University College Dublin, Ireland

ABSTRACT

This chapter traces a process of creating using found object collage, through collecting/consuming practices and finally to the notion of the bought self, avatar representation through consumerist artistic practice in Second Life (SL) the online, user generated, virtual environment. Positioning collage as a reinvigorated current in art, the text couples this mode of making with shopping as found object. Collaboration is inherent in an online virtual world, where programmers, designers and other content providers determine the parameters of what is possible. Found object/shopping is a synergistic fit with the nature of predetermined boundaries coupled with late-stage capitalism. This mode of self-making encourages the idea of buying identification through the construction of an avatar. Through a review of the practices of the Situationists, an aesthetic turn in political tactics is revealed through contemporary art making. The text uses the author's own virtual/material practice as a case study for the theories explored.

INTRODUCTION

Making art with and within the virtual environment of *Second Life* (*SL*) is akin to getting lost in a particularly tortuous, *geographic uncanny valley* with next to no signposts towards an easy exit. It often aspires to be a reflection of the material world; but not quite. Digitised verisimilitude can be unsettling, but along with the unease comes frequent drama, absurdity and happenstance—in short, the artistically fruitful. This chapter will trace a process of creating in *SL* from found object collage, through collecting/consuming practices and finally to the notion of the bought self, avatar representation in virtual worlds through consumerist artistic practice.

The following is both an academic analysis and a case study about found object collage coupled with consumerist practices of self-making. In keeping with these ambitions, the chapter utilizes alternating *voices*. It is my hope that these two different registers will help to both distill, and at the same time, open up meaning. A scholarly analysis of these methods is juxtaposed with poetic contemplation to more fully evoke the potential of ambiguity for introducing spaces of wonder and meaning.

This text uses the author's own virtual/material practice as a case study of the theories explored. Art making is a delicate blend of many elements, and though the reader of this chapter will hopefully be able to use the observations and analysis

DOI: 10.4018/978-1-4666-8384-6.ch007

described within the text for their own work, it is ultimately the author's singular practice that is used to elucidate the enfolded ideas and reflections.

BACKGROUND

The artist is one for whom the poverty of his or her materials is all that remains in this unveiling of things. It is an inner creative seeing that regathers the things of the world. (Whitehead, 2003, p. 6)

The above quote from artist/writer Derek H. Whitehead encapsulates two fundamental ways of making art, which can be used concurrently or individually. One method, the *unveiling of things* is a subtractive strategy—chip away at the marble, exposing the form that has always existed within. The other *regathers the things of the world*. This additive method—collage/assemblage—builds images and sculpture from diverse sources, materials and sensibilities in a *collecting*, *sifting*, *choosing* and *bonding* process. Far from simply being a way to make, and similarly to all artistic methods, it has immediate portent for the way a work of art functions in the world as an object, silent witness and/or instigation.

Found object collage/assemblage is a well-established artistic strategy, both in the material and the virtual environments, lending itself particularly well to pop cultural inclinations towards art making in *SL*. This text examines a practice of found object collage in the all too human world of *SL* where reality masquerades *in drag*, exaggerating the vagaries of life. *SL*, indeed any virtual environment, imposes a collaborative creativity in that the programmers and developers along with other content generators of the space define much of what you can or cannot do within that environment. Found object collage, within this default collaborative experience, challenges artists' methodological apparatuses, along with disturbing material, dimensional, and temporal as-

sumptions within this pre-determined framework. The happened-upon and the imperfect becomes fodder for innovation and subversion.

Theorist, Clive Edwards says of collecting that it is "frequently associated with antiquarianism and connoisseurship of artifacts" but then goes on to add, "as often [it is] related to assemblage and accumulation" (2009, p. 38). A necessary first, thereafter iterative step to any method of collage is collecting, a term loaded with cultural and psychological baggage. With the relative ease of virtual accumulation—one never has to rent expensive self-storage lockers and moving vans—the good and the bad of collecting practices can be enacted in simulated worlds and become fodder for art production.

Not surprisingly, the notions of what a *consumer* is and what it means to *consume* are contested. Yiannis Gabriel and Tim Lang suggest in their book *The Unmanageable Consumer* that the "consumer…[has] assumed centre-stage in academic debates…[in] rarely value-neutral" discussions and that consumerism is "recognized [as] the spirit of our age" (2006, p. 1). The jump from collecting practices to consumerism in this text follows the logic of our era, variously known as neo-, post- or late-capitalism. Decades of artists' projects, critiques and celebrations have legitimized shopping within a fine art context (Grunenberg & Hollein, Schirn Kunsthalle Frankfurt and Tate Gallery Liverpool, 2002). The virtual world of *SL*, with its mimetic economy, personifies the material world's fetishes.

The role of the avatar in online culture intensifies a long-standing scrutiny of the notion of personal identity, a narcissistically inclined exploration that has gone on "since the origins of Western philosophy" (Olson, 2010, para 1). The extensive use of digitally based avatars in virtual worlds fuels an interrogation of subjectivity at the heart of many arts, humanities and social sciences conversations. Questions of Self and Other, an on-going concern for much theoretical work (Cadava,

Connor, & Nancy, 1991), come into sharp focus when one is accumulating a set of aesthetics and behaviours to build an avatar that then becomes one's alter ego or doppelgänger for the purposes of virtual representation.

Amongst the scholars and academics looking to understand our relationship to the virtual and our representation within that space—our avatar—are the cyberpsychologists, researchers such as Nick Yee, Jeremy N. Bailenson and Richard Bartle. Their research is varied and in-depth but lends itself to an artistic understanding of the phenomenon of avatar/human transference. In a fascinating research paper on the social construction of gender the authors involved state, "[w]hile it is easy to think of avatar creation as a one-way, user-directed process, studies have shown a more provocative two-way process between user and avatar" (Yee et al. 2011, p. 773). *Knowing self* is also a case of *finding self*.

Finding self becomes even more complicated when *buying self*. The disconcerting practice in *SL* of purchasing skin, hair, body shapes, and even sexual organs in an effort to create a persona takes consumerism to new heights. "A sense of ownership of one's avatar is…directly related to the level of monetary…investment" (Bloustien & Wood, 2013, p. 75). The more we buy the more we care. The complication of values when buying identity is reminiscent of the Situationist International's revolutionary strategy of *détournement*, which is a "turning around and a reclamation of lost meaning" (Vaneigem, 1994, p. 137)—in other words, turning expressions of the capitalist system against itself. Is this possible? Can we ever really outwit capitalism's amazing powers of co-option? Or perhaps the *society of the spectacle*[1], has become a *spectacle of the self*.

CASE STUDY: OVERVIEW

My work occupies an awkward space of dreaming gone awry, missed or mismatched opportunities, and the over reaching nature of human ambition. Falling short is much more the norm than succeeding and this impulse feeds my interest in exploring the gap between our yearnings and reality. This topography is filled with odd juxtapositions, quirky beauty, endearing ugliness, and human day-to-day struggles as we live, work and play. Dreams and actuality bump up against each other and manifest in idiosyncratic coincidence, and engaging fumbles. My current work explores our adaptation as we wander around, mostly lost, improvising in this rocky terrain. I contemplate our humanity and find exquisiteness amongst the over-familiar artefacts in both our natural and manufactured landscapes. My desire to reflect on our human condition feels like a late romantic notion. Instead of peering only into the enormity we call nature and feeling awe, I look into an abyss of technological change and try to find a similar wonder and incongruent beauty. Questions about the contemporary sublime, and even more fundamentally, whether I can experience it in a post-ironic epoch circulate around my practice. I have been equally fascinated by materiality and virtuality throughout my career, and I am constantly navigating between the two as I bridge many divides: dreams/reality, visual/aural, image/text and high/low art (Fig. 1: *The Adventures of Nar Duell in Second Life*).[2]

My artistic practice in *SL* has evolved since 2007, when the platform was four years old. What began as an exploration of virtual worlds purely as a collaborative studio *space* to engage with colleagues at a distance became for me a place to explore performance, happenings and a source of found object imagery to use in an ongoing project, the comic book series, *The Adventures of Nar Duell in Second Life* (*The Adventures*). This body of work is based on my experiences with an avatar, Nar Duell, and my narration of these events through the comic books. I have worked in this virtual world specifically to experience both the potential and provocative limitations of the platform, including the settings, narratives, social

Figure 1. The Adventures of Nar Duell in Second Life - Dancing With Myself, 2008 – ongoing
© 2015 Lynne Heller. Used with permission.

interactions, legal structures and sociological imperatives. To name a few constraints—inherent collaboration, the predominance of the sexually exploitive, and the slow pace of the platform restrict many of my choices. As it is a social network, my time in-world is constantly interrupted, and so relational aesthetics[3] become integral to the practice. These challenges test my ingenuity and expressive abilities, but I am in-world primarily for the quirky aesthetics and the visuals that I can generate. As a result, virtual environments offer opportunities to experiment and prompt reflection on my curiosities and inclinations, which then inspire the narrative and visuals of my comic book and performances (Fig. 2: *Dancing With Myself*).

It is the impulse to bring digital materiality/tools/technology and traditional design/art forms together that has led to my current concentrations. Art historian Lisa Wainwright describes my work as a practice that "runs the gamut from the analog to the digital, with recent endeavours mixing up the two in a truly multimedia way" (2010, p. 10). Curator Anastasia Hare's assessment is more specific:

Originating from Heller's interest in the virtual community, 3D world of Second Life (Linden Research, Inc.), the work draws from experiences there with her avatar named Nar Duell… The project is comprised of performances with this persona which take place in a range of settings - from built environments in the virtual to choreographed dances and real-time, interactive hybrid-reality installations which include large projections, web cameras, disco-balls, as well as paint and photo based media. The second component of the project involves the narration of these experiences through comic books, which she has published in several editions, including pocket and oversized dimensions, as well as machinima videos. (2013, p. 166)

My initial impulse was to use *SL* in order to collaborate and make art for the 'real'[4] world by using the virtual space and avatars as tools. I had no intention of developing a theoretical and emotional relationship to an alter ego or engaging in performative and narrative forms. I viewed the virtual space as embodied communication, not as a way to generate content. By 2006–2007, *SL*

Figure 2. Dancing With Myself
© 2009 Lynne Heller. Used with permission.

came to prominence. There was a lot of media publicity about its potential as an alternative to the material world and excitement about its sense of possibility (Boellstorff, 2006; Rymaszewski et al., 2006; White, 2007).

Though I too was entranced by *SL's* sense of possibility as I travelled the alternate space, often imperfectly modelled on the material world, I marveled at how we as humans have a deep need to reflect on what we already understand and perceive. Our history, traditions, norms, myths, assumptions and current reality are essentially embedded in every aspect of this 'new' world (Lakoff & Johnson, 1998). Even as we reach for novelty, a land of endless promise and fantasy, we hearken back to the familiar and comfortable. I realised my enduring curiosity in exploring the disparity of life was possible through virtual performativity and hybrid reality installations in *SL*.

COLLAGE ET AL.

In the art lexicon there are quite a number of ways to refer to the process of gathering materials together to form a new entity—collage, assemblage, bricolage, montage, to name a few. The various words are nuanced but in effect refer to similar processes. *Collage*, the most widely used and inclusive of all the words, is a technique "incorporating the use of pre-existing materials or objects attached as part of a two-dimensional surface" (Kachur, n.d., para. 1). It is often described as a 20th century art form as it appears to have "a correlation with the pace and discontinuity of the modern world" (para. 1). Though historically considered a modernist conceit, the extensive use of collage in postmodern and post-disciplinary contexts suggests it has on going resonances for artists. Notably the well regarded inaugural exhibition for the current, custom-designed building of the *New Museum* NYC, titled *Unmonumental*, 2007–2008 demonstrated the impact collage/assemblage has in contemporary art making.

The thesis here is that assemblage-type sculpture, rampant at the moment, may also be today's most viable art form. Why? It tends to be low-tech, modest in scale, made with found objects and materials and structured in ways that are fragmented if not actually disintegrating. Its ugly-duckling looks, rough edges, disparate parts and weird juxtapositions help stave off easy art-market absorption while also reflecting our fearful, fractured, materially excessive times back at us. (Smith, "In Galleries, a Nervy Opening Volley" n.pag.)

Assemblage[5] is the three-dimensional counterpart to collage. It uses "traditionally non-artistic, materials and *objets trouvés*" and favours "banal, often tawdry materials…[that] retain their individual physical and functional identity, despite artistic manipulation" (Cooper, n.d., para. 1). Assemblage in the context of *SL* poses an intriguing question. Are virtual worlds two or three-dimensional? Though they are rendered for the most part through screen technology, which is two-dimensional, the data that creates the environment and its objects delineates all three *x, y* and *z* axes. Two notable examples of working with the three dimensional data generated by collage methodology are artist and theorist Denise Doyle's physical materialization of her avatar *Wanderingfictions Story* in the exhibition *Kritical Works in SL II*, Belfast, 2009 and the *No Matter*, 2008, project by the collaborative partners Victoria Scott and Scott Kildall.[6].

This complication of dimension plays out in legalistic ways in *SL*. Two dimensional screen captures are ubiquitous in digital media and though the amount of pixel resolution of any one capture is limited, depending on output needs, the images are usually scalable. Linden Lab, the company which created, owns and ultimately controls what is allowed in *SL*, encourages the gathering of two dimensional 'still' captures by providing residents with an easy to use snapshot tool. *Machinima*[7] filming, or the capture of motion, produces animation that can be utilized for out-of-world purposes. Linden Lab's attitude towards machinima is neutral. They do not provide a tool to create it but there are plenty of third party applications that are free or inexpensive and can be used alongside *SL*. The *SL* copyright provisions for static images and machinima vary as well. Static screenshots are always allowed regardless of the wishes of the *SL* landowner. An owner can specify that they disallow machinima capture on their *property* if they include this directive in the covenant of the land that they lease. Three-dimensional objects, on the other hand, are difficult to extract or print from the *SL* platform. This has more to do with corporate intellectual property and proprietary rights than with technical constraints and demonstrates the different attitudes towards the visual material that can be extracted from the platform.

Montage, from the French for 'mounting', and along with that term—photocollage/photomontage—are "pre-existing pictorial images…cut out and reassembled on a flat surface…Montage differs from collage in that the latter uses cut out shapes which are not necessarily representational" ("montage," n.d.). Montage is also used to describe time-based, filmic collages. Time, similar to dimensionality, is not a straight forward issue in *SL*. This animated world is based loosely on the idea of day and night, parameters that can be overridden, but imply the passing of time. Given that machinima is simply the rapid capture of one static screenshot after another, might we also identify time-based material from *SL* as montage?

The grouping of terms: *bricolage, decoupage,* and *pastiche,* come burdened with judgment and associations with low/folk/outsider art along with being indicators of collecting/assembling activities. Bricolage implies the creator "works with what is on hand…[and] 'tinkers'"(Hoesterey, 2001, p. 10). Decoupage is a craft in which the practitioner decorates objects or furniture with "colorful pasted cutouts to simulate painted surfaces" (Harrower, [c1958], p. 17) and pastiche, derived from "the French *pastiche* or the Ital-

ian *pastìccio*, which originally meant a "pasty" [sic] or "pie" dish containing several different ingredients" is a cobbling together of elements somewhat like collage but has an added implication of "*parody, montage, quotation, allusion, irony, burlesque, travesty,* and *plagiarism* [original emphasis]"(Brand, n.d., para. 1). All of these descriptors are evocative of *SL*, given what fertile ground it is for the ironic and derivative.

These words also have specific functions when explicating the process of collecting, sorting and assembling, but they can be modified with the term *found object*. Found object is a surrealist and Duchampian construct which holds "that any object could become a work of art if chosen by an artist" ("found object, French objet trouvé," 1994). Marcel Duchamp favoured the word *ready-made,* with its explicit connotation of a purchased commercial object as both found object and de facto art. Commercialism, as a creative strategy, is entrenched in the culture of *Second Life,* given its roots in "prosumption society"[8]; what Tom Boellstorff typifies as creationist capitalism in his book *Coming of Age in Second Life.* He goes on to define creationist capitalism as "a mode of capitalism in which labor is understood in terms of creativity, so that production is understood as creation" (Boellstorff, 2010, p. 206). In order to fully participate in this particular virtual community, one is drawn into the ethos of creating to sell as a means of exchanging value as well as the cementing of community ties.

It is tempting to splice and dice these definitions, if one is so inclined, or to examine making—methodological dissection—as only a formal concern. However, "[a]rt is something, that as it is being done is also inventing what to do and how to do it" (Luigi Pareyson, quoted in Celeste Martins, 2013 translation clarified). Through feedback and iteration, method and medium work in tandem and thus, together, are *the message.*

CASE STUDY: FIVE CIGARS LATER

Nar Duell, a failed Barbie doll[9], has kooky taste and quirky needs, the combination of which leads to a less than optimal fashion sense. For example, she has been known to wear hard hats with stilettos—she often needs head protection given her propensity for bumping into structures while flying—football gear with lipstick, and Doc Martin's with a party dress. It was during her latest adventure that she decided to smoke a cigar (Fig. 3: Nar Duell smoking). Procuring the perfect cigar for her proved harder than it seems.

There are a few ways to buy things in *SL*—all of which have been glitchy in my experience. The in-world options start with a resident teleporting to a shop that she is already aware of, has searched out via the *SL* search function or has tripped over in her travels. There in the shop, depending on the sophistication of the interactive technology, a resident can often demo or try on samples to see if they function and if indeed the object, animation or tool, is what she seeks. The second method is to go to an external website such as *SL's Marketplace* and, using search and scroll methods, purchase items that are then sent to the resident's

Figure 3. Nar Duell smoking
© *2014 Lynne Heller. Used with permission.*

inventory in *SL* where she can unpack and use/wear what she has purchased. *SL* also supports a vibrant gift economy, which is another way to accumulate objects, animations and sounds. The process is the same as buying but you pay $0 Lindens, the currency of *SL*. Interesting to note; gifting uses the same mechanism as buying in *SL*. This suggests they are homogeneous endeavours, implying similar outcomes and relations.

In the search for the perfect cigar I tried all the shopping options. Our (my and Nar's) first purchase looked decidedly crude. Another cigar had no smoke, and the next had too much. Then there was the cigar that would not follow her head when she turned, ending up in disconcerting places and angles on her face. Typical in my experience in *SL*, one purchase did not arrive in my inventory after the transaction took place. I had shelled out real money for it, as users need to buy Linden dollars with their real world national currencies to use in *SL*. Five cigars later, Nar now has one that is somewhat functional. She burns herself lighting the cigar sometimes and it has a mysterious delayed reaction as it takes quite some time for smoke rings to form after she blows them, but she is now equipped for any experience, no matter how macho, *SL* can throw at her. The upside is that she will not develop any smoking-related diseases. She is a hedonist who gets away with it.

In the past I have laboured under the misconception that purchasing in order to make art must be easier, less stressful and a patently faster option than making from scratch. Through painful experience, I realised that shopping is a forced collaboration and far from expedient. As *SL* is one of the tackiest places of any world I have experienced, its sensibility continually confronts me with my own class and aesthetic biases. I work hard to find Nar clothes and accouterment that suit my sense of self; not an easy thing to do in a world of hyper-sexualisation. The easiest task, say looking for a new facial expression for Nar, turns into a lewd voyage through the land of human depravity. A journey littered with jaggy

graphics, brash colours, misaligned structures and clingy, static-filled chiffon-like textures. Many a time, my yuppie brain screams, "Get me outta here and fast!" The digital world's axiom *garbage in, garbage out* has significant implications for virtual crafting in *SL*. As artists, do we hate, enjoy, grow accustomed to or assume an agnostic stance to the garbage? The challenge of a practice in *SL* is the repurposing of the already exaggerated, the essence of the actual. Or is this Situationist Guy Debord's *spectacle* on steroids?

On top of the issue of taste, *SL's* economy, and thus soul, is a virtual Walmart. A dollar store mentality reigns. The seduction of buying whatever your heart desires—palaces, Lamborghinis, dragons—for next to nothing, leads to real money chasing after the virtual as residents are nickel and dimed for a bushelful of zeros and ones.

COLLECTING/CONSUMING/COLLABORATING

Susan Stewart in her meditation *On Longing* titles a section of her writing "The Collection, Paradise of Consumption". In that turn of a phrase she has conflated collecting and consuming. She goes on to say that:

...the collection represents the total aestheticization of use value. The collection is a form of art as play, a form involving the reframing of objects within a world of attention and manipulation of context. Like other forms of art, its function is not the restoration of context of origin but rather the creation of a new context, a context standing in a metaphorical, rather than a contiguous, relation to the world of everyday life. (1993, pp. 151–152)

Though arguably she is discussing *the collection* rather than *collecting*, the description holds true for the act of collecting as well as the noun. The collector, during the process of accumulation, is envisioning what this particular group of objects will mean and how they can form 'a new context'. Indiscriminate gathering needs to be framed in order to become a collection or as this text proposes a collage—a whole made from parts. Stewart summarizes this idea thus, "[t]he spatial whole of the collection supersedes the individual narratives that "lie behind it."" (1993, p. 153). A classic piece made in and for *SL* tests our assumptions that taxonomised collections equal collaged artwork. Created by the well known *SL* artist and griefer (the name for a *SL* resident who harasses other residents) Gazira Babeli, the work *Ursonate in Second Life - Monument to Kurt Schwitters*, 2007, consists of a giant water spout that rains down disparate everyday objects, such as a cow, a can of Campbell's soup, a truck.[10].

Some might be surprised that the passion of possession can infect the virtual realm. Is acquiring predicated on having a material sense of ownership? Not necessarily—researchers Mike Molesworth and Janice Denegri-Knott maintain "…individuals have long enjoyed consumption not as the rational acquisition of material goods but as a resource for speculation and imagination and the pleasures these can bring" (2007, p. 123). It is the pleasure people seek not the possession. Taking this argument a step further they theorise that:

And in a society structured around consumption as a main resource for individual daydreams and fantasy, and where fantasy is continuously encouraged by the media, it is likely that it is issues relating to consumption that are frequently "worked out" in the aesthetic dramas afforded by digital spaces. (2007, p. 123)

Virtuality becomes a type of sandbox where we *work out* consumer-induced fantasy. Consumption becomes "a key resource for the imagination" signifying a "relationship between market offerings and the imagination". (2007, p. 118)

When thinking about consumerism and art there begs a question—did Duchamp buy or shop for his urinal? An email conversation with art historian and surrealist expert Charles Stuckey still leaves me wondering.

[LH] Did Duchamp buy the first urinal he found or did he shop around?

[CS] No one knows. No one ever asked the question until now, not about any of the readymades. (2014)

Shopping implies a different activity than buying. In essence, it is a process of collaboration and the exercise of aesthetic judgment during the collecting process, versus buying or purchasing which connote a singular focused activity. I go out to buy milk. I shop for clothes. Shopping is also gendered.

There is an understanding, a tradition, an intellectual logic which purposefully marks out a distinction between consumption and collection. Evinced by Pearce's discussion, in Western culture there is a reification of collections in contradistinction to objects simply and honestly consumed, occluding how collecting is itself a form of purchase fueled by economic, political and socio-cultural drives. The aura attached to a collection reaffirms the gender divide that has long equated women with consumption and men with collection. (Potvin & Myzelev, 2009, p. 2)

CASE STUDY: *THE ADVENTURES*

The Adventures, the comic books created as part of my practice, mimic, satirise and confound commercialism in both small and large ways. Always considered low art, comics have the capacity to insert uncertainties and disrupt an easy reading of art making (Carrier, 2002). *The Adventures* play with signs of commercialization through tropes such as *limited editions, pricing* that defies current monetary inflation, imaginary distribution systems, material choices, production methods and physical scale, all of which completely contravene what is commercially viable.

The repurposing of the details of consumerism lends itself to comment on the means of production. *The Adventures* are signed by the artist and made 'precious' through limited edition. The wonder of comics is that they are endlessly available and widely distributed. By limiting the edition, one is drawing attention to the marketing of the blatantly commercial versus the art object. Anachronistic prices, which could have only been viable as a mass consumed product in the 50s and 60s, appear on the cover of the comic, mocking the prices of contemporary art. The cheapness of the historic prices at 25 or 30 cents, is disingenuous and fallacious. Referenced throughout *The Adventures* is a massive distribution system with all its attendant legal and structural apparatus. Once again, this only points out the lack of commercial muscle in the current enterprise. Lastly, the material choices, such as thick, coated paper and skillfully wrought book binding techniques, along with the unusual scaling of *The Adventures*, highlights the differences and contravenes the conventions of mass consumerism. The original production method, inexpensive offset printing, is alluded to via the intentional bleeding of colour and the low resolution of the line work but the comics are now printed from digital data.

The most telling visual evidence of the engagement with a commercial sensibility is the enfolding of fake advertising into the work (Fig. 4: Appropriated, collaged, comic book ads, circa 1960's). Nothing signals 'comic book' more than the overly familiar pages of ads announcing a plethora of wondrous devices and tonics that speak to dreams of power and purpose that enticed children into sending hard won pennies to questionable post boxes in return for receiving the flimsiest of cheap plastic trinkets which would either never work or break within hours of use. The ads teased the imagination but delivered sad realities. Ostensibly produced for children, their

commercial focus perturbs the innocence we associate with youth. *The Adventures* use the tropes and conventions of consumerist culture to entrance and complicate the current work.

The practice of working within *SL* is akin to directing a movie, partnering with people as well as technology. Based on unpredictability, appropriation and serendipity, collaboration has become a way to facilitate *The Adventures* project for me. My primary mode of making in *SL* is through acquiring and shopping to augment Nar Duell and her adventures, an unwitting collaboration with others in this user built world. Collaboration also functions in other ways. For example, to create content in *SL* I have often worked with a programmer, Desdemona Enfield. And Des, as Nar refers to her, also makes appearances in the performances and comics, becoming enfolded back into the practice. Essentially, any work done in virtual worlds is a far-reaching, sometimes unknowing, collaborative enterprise with the engineers and designers who created and maintain the platform, the businesses who develop the worlds, the residents who set up shops in order to sell their creations and, in a more direct form of collaboration, my in-world *friends* in *SL*.

CASE STUDY: FINDING PERSONA

Sometimes the best way to make art is not to know that you are doing it. I am usually impulsive about important decisions and agonise over little ones. Thankfully, when I chose a name for my avatar I was not aware I was making a decision. I was just signing up to a website. *SL* was for me, to quote Donald Rumsfeld, an 'unknown unknown'.

When naming an avatar in *Second Life* you are confronted by the realization that you are creating an alter ego (Fig. 5: (from left to right) Nar Darwinian, Nar Duell, Nar Dufaux). The name you choose is the only aspect of your avatar that can never change. Nar's personality, what one might think of as her *essence* much more so than her

Figure 4. Appropriated, collaged, comic book ads, circa 1960's
© *2009 Lynne Heller. Used with permission.*

name, has evolved over time and by fluke. The longer I spend in *SL,* the more Nar matures and differentiates. For example, I can very innocently look for an item on the Second Life marketplace, something that pops into my head that I think will help in the construction of her identity. Due to the hyper-sexualized nature of the environment I end up looking at pages of soft, terribly stilted, pornography. For example, avatars can have facial expressions but they are an add-on or HUD[11] attachment to the basic avatar. I looked around to purchase more expressions for Nar because I was feeling limited by what I have. Unfortunately, there are only a minimal number of facial expressions possible in *SL* and there has not been any

good workarounds discovered that can solve the problem. Every option that advertised alternate facial expressions was connected in some way to sex. Ironically this is taking place in a world where reproductive organs are non-standard. You actually have to purchase or make body parts in order to truly simulate sex acts.

One of my most intriguing experiences in *SL* was during a visit to a sex club. Sex clubs are one of the 'must-sees' in the *SL* universe and they come in every stripe imaginable. This particular establishment catered to people who liked to role-play as dolls. An avatar, which in effect is a doll, approached my avatar and introduced herself as a doll. She put quite a bit of effort into encouraging

Figure 5. (from left to right) Nar Darwinian, Nar Duell, Nar Dufaux
© 2013 Lynne Heller. Used with permission.

me to try her out and then give her a high rating for her efficacy as a doll. There was some type of competition going on amongst the sex workers at the dollhouse of ill repute. They were earning points in order to be crowned the best sex doll in *SL*. I politely demurred but have regretted since not following through. I will never know what it is like to have sex as an avatar, in effect a doll, with another avatar/doll, roleplaying as a doll. The intricacies of identity confound.

Fundamental to my work in *SL* is the relation between objects and selfhood. An avatar is both self and not self, subject and object at the same time. To navigate this ongoing instability, I use my own incredulity and wonder, actually downright naiveté, and channel it through Nar which in turn gives me the hints I need to further develop and acquire an identity for her.

In a quaint hangover from Western culture, avatars had first and second names in *SL*. This trope changed in 2011, however, initially users could choose any first name they wanted, but for some arcane reason they would be given a limited choice of last name, through a drop down menu. While I was picking a name *Duell* came up on the list. I was attracted to it instinctually and then could not stop myself from punning, Nar Duell—n'er do well—perfect, funny, witty, clever! I was, completely out-of-all-proportion, pleased with myself.

A couple of years later while talking to my therapist I mentioned my avatar by name. She caught the pun and looked at me with a mixture of disbelief and horror. My alter ego would never amount to anything in life. Thousands of dollars later and years of the therapist's hard work trying to prop up my confidence and sense of self, disappeared in a click of a drop down menu choice. Poof!

BUYING SELF

Most important to the genesis and framework of my virtual practice, are the fascinating options around body, clothing and props available to me as a consumer within *SL*, coupled with the negotiation of a relationship with the commercial through self.

The booting up of the computer becomes something of a ritual process for removal from the material world and the entering into of [sic] a space that will allow for individual transformation. (Molesworth & Denegri-Knott, 2007, p. 128)

The *Dorian Grey* effect is one of the most noticeable attributes of the *SL* population. Most residents appear to have narcissistic, all encompassing relationships with their avatars. Time and money are lavished onto the avatar in order to 'be' oneself (Bloustien & Wood, 2013), but the disconnect from reality is tough to ignore as a person interacts with a virtual subjectivity. Take for example the physical disassociation that happens when a person's avatar is flying through the sky while the actual person is grounded in a chair, tapping a few fingers on a keyboard. Embodiment through the mechanism of the virtual stand-in has been debated throughout the literature (Hansen, 2006; Hayles, 1999; Morie, 2007; Penny, 2011) and though pertinent to the discussion, it is not the full story. How that embodiment is advanced through the nurturing and aestheticisation of the avatar is fundamental to the relationship between person and virtual representation. The *why* necessitates the question *how*: and the *how* tells us about the *why*.

Moleworth and Denegri-Knott, in "Digital Play and the Actualization of the Consumer Imagination" contend that "[g]oods are used to "capture" and negotiate consumers' ever-changing and restless speculations about themselves and their social relations with others..." (2007, p. 117). *Ever-changing and restless speculations about themselves* is a thoughtful phrase that points to a position of unstable identity. Can buying something as immaterial as a virtual dress for 25 cents help us know who we are in essence? Geraldine

F. Bloustien and Denise Wood in their text "Face, Authenticity, Transformations and Aesthetics in *Second Life*" expand on this notion.

In other words, the online residents in Second LIfe [sic] felt that through their avatars they could perceive, create, manage and maintain the outward appearance of what they felt was a fixed innate core self…even while simultaneously acknowledging the continual process of transformation, of becoming 'other'… (2013, p. 53)

Humans shrewd ability to synchronistically contradict themselves is signalled here in two ways—*outward appearance* needs to be consciously managed to reflect *a fixed innate core self*. This core self either existed seamlessly from birth or was largely developed subconsciously. Yet this is an innate core that a person is able to access in order to make solid, consumer choices—accessing the subconscious through consciousness is an argument swallowing its own tail. The second contradiction, *fixed innate core self* versus *continual process of transformation* alerts us to another double consciousness that is available to us. We need not logically believe. Belief frees us up to live with the ambiguity of life. Molesworth and Denegri-Knott feed this ambiguity back to a consumerist orientation.

…the grounding of behavior and thought in something that may be considered authentic and real is becoming elusive with different "manufactured" experiences now only referring to reach [sic] other' (2007, p. 123)

With experiences manufactured and only referring to each other, how does one ground any innate sense of self? A capitalist modus operandi is one of continual change, a drive to the boom of the cycle and then the inevitable bust as growth commits suicide by eating what is feeding it. Perhaps a virtual economy can break this cycle through the ease of digital reproduction and dissemina-

tion? The mechanism for capitalistic growth is the engendering of insatiable desire. Can the virtual somehow satisfy the itch of desire with seemingly endless resources? Molesworth and Denegr-Knott are suggesting that there is a solution, in that the aesthetic is the outlet for desire.

Where the market cannot satisfy the restless consumer desire that it has encouraged through material goods and experiences, a gap is opened that invites consumption experiences that do provide aesthetic outlets for that desire. (Molesworth & Denegri-Knott, 2007, p. 130)

The question is begged: is the desire sated or hyper-stimulated? Does the virtual mean that we have somehow co-opted capitalism instead of the other way around? Or have we simply bought into our capitulation with enthusiasm? This turnaround, a détournement[12] on top of a détournement, is reminiscent of the late stage politics of Guy Debord, the complicated figurehead of the Situationists International. Not only does capitalism consume itself but also rebellions against capitalism have the same unfortunate tendencies.

In summing-up the fundamental position of the situationists, philosopher Sadie Plant discusses their position on the total cultural capitulation to spectacle.

The situationists characterized modern capitalist society as an organization of spectacles: a frozen moment of history in which it is impossible to experience real life or actively participate in the construction of the lived world. They argued that the alienation fundamental to class society and capitalist production has permeated all areas of social life…and even the most personal gestures are experienced at one remove. (1992, p. 1)

This *frozen moment* of alienation manifests in the contemporary virtual perhaps even more powerfully than it did in European society during the 50's and 60's when the situationists' political agenda was being written. Virtual worlds, such as *SL*, fifty years on, are a unique context but an all too familiar refrain of the '*society of the spectacle*'.

The images detached from every aspect of life merge into a common stream in which the unity of life can no longer be recovered. Fragmented views of reality regroup themselves into a new unity as a separate pseudoworld that can only be looked at. The specialization of images of the world evolves into a world of automatized images where even the deceivers are deceived. The spectacle is a concrete inversion of life, an autonomous movement of the nonliving. (Debord & Knabb, 2002, p. 6)

There are both parallels and discrepancies between the world that the situationists theorized and virtual environments. For example, similar to the situationists' revolutionary ardour, though not necessarily congruent with their eventual pessimism, the virtual offers up the perception that resistance is possible. Here is an infinite world of promise and freedom with only our imagination as a limitation. Yet these virtual worlds simulate our real life culture of consumerism in the proliferation of sex, pleasure, weapons, marketing, shopping and malls. "Second Life is a digital culture that competes increasingly with real-life media and society...one that nearly mirrors the real world in almost every way" (Johnson, 2010, p. xii).

While there are numerous artists that exhibit in virtual galleries simply for exposure and as a means to circulate their work, many artists/designers/programmers have also subverted its prosumer tendencies, exploiting its clumsy aesthetic and irony-drenched culture. It is in this way that the strategies of the situationists are congruent with contemporary artistic approaches. Historian Sadie Plant writes about situationists' ambitions to transform society:

It demands practical realization, and is a theory which was only made possible by the acts of rebellion, subversion, and negation which foreshad-

owed it and continue to assert the discontent and disrespect inspired by the economic, social, and discursive relations which define contemporary capitalism. (1992, p. ix)

The situationists spontaneously explored urban life guided by aesthetic instinct and turned *expressions of the capitalist system against itself*. The specific tactics of détournement and dérive[13] that were instrumental to the situationist theorisation, lend themselves to an exploration of a space they could not have possibly imagined—the virtual in all its materialistic glory. Consumerist impulses led to situationists' politics, and their politics are recycled by consumerist environments. Found object collage through the *spectacle* is at one with the conditions of *SL*, a complex environment that can support the unlikely conflation of object and selfhood through consumerist practices. And all this for $10 US—it is a once in a lifetime, not-to-be-missed, genuine bargain.

For the equivalent of US$10, a resident can upload their photograph to CyberExtruder's avatar creation system and, seconds later, the company's proprietary software generates a texture of a 'realist' avatar face, that is, one that more closely approximates an iconic photographic image. (Bloustien & Wood, 2013, p. 66)

CONCLUSION

SL is a petri dish under the microscope due to all the 'real' that people bring into this virtual world. The fuel that SL adds to our culture of consumerism and discontent is both fascinating and disconcerting. Much has been written about the commerce of this brave new virtual world, but it looks mostly like the commerce of our material world. Not surprisingly, sex, fashion, cars, perfected body parts and weapons sell. If SL is in short supply of honest-to-goodness novelty it makes up for it in its abundance of promise, the allure of thinking that anything is possible. This conceit certainly trumps reality[14]. The material world translated into the virtual, illustrates the quest for limitless possibility, where anyone can do anything. This is a platform where dreaming is the norm, where one can create in a space of potentiality which does not insist on limits or definitions.

Within this endless possibility there is a question of individual identity and self-making that infects artistic endeavours in this realm. *I can be anything: what am I?* In 2009 a panel of pre-eminent new media artists assembled at Subtle Technologies in Toronto, Canada. Jeremy Bailey, Scott Kildall representing Second Front, Johannes Birringer and Alan Sondheim—all well-

known practitioners who worked in and around SL. They spoke about their avatars, their in-world extensions of self to be tools, primarily as a way to work within SL, a way to accomplish. Can an avatar ever be simply a tool? A complex cursor? A 3D paintbrush? A digital extension of hand? None of those descriptions includes the avatar as portraiture or extension of self. However, this belies the almost physical connection we have to an avatar through our hand and eyes, controlling the movement, animations and voice of our doll-self. As well we must contend with the feedback we get from others who view our avatars in order to know us. Disassociation is not a simple matter. An avatar is not object. Nor though is it subject. The avatar occupies an uneasy position between

Figure 6. Thank you for your time. ~Nar Duell
© *2014 Lynne Heller. Used with permission.*

Found Objects, Bought Selves

the two and destabilizes our sense of self within user-created environments. It is also the sum total of what we create or buy in order to bring it into existence, situated within a world that is of millions of peoples' making—a truly collaborative effort on an international scale. These elements come together in unpredictable ways. An avatar has a life of its own, but is at the same time, undeniably an extension of the virtual world user (Fig. 6).

If an avatar can be seen as an individual collage, the entire SL platform itself could also be said to be a collage/assemblage. It is made up of disparately sourced and authored content but yet seen as a world onto itself. This virtual world, a product of our collective imaginations visualized through digital materiality, tools and technology is full to the brim with a humanity that has very little choice but to cooperate with each other in order to actualize the dreamscape.

Found object collage through collection and consuming is a potent method for making in a virtual world of rampant consumerism yet heightened potentiality. Time tested and expansive, this method is true to both SL and the material world. It has the scope to be a powerful détournement that even if it fails as a revolution, incises the carnivalesque into intangible imaginings that make virtual worlds so real for us. The desire to create and acquire virtually becomes stronger due to our affective relationships with avatars, as well as our compulsions to collect/consume virtual objects. SL is both a modernist, utopian enterprise as well as a post-human, post-materiality, post-dimensionality and post-temporal reflection. The virtual magnifies the details of reality by clearly focusing the microscope above the petri dish.

REFERENCES

Bloustien, G. F., & Wood, D. (2013). Face, Authenticity, Transformations and Aesthetics in Second Life. *Body & Society*, *19*(1), 52–81. doi:10.1177/1357034X12462250

Boellstorff, T. (2006). A Ludicrous Discipline? Ethnography and Game Studies. *Games and Culture*, *1*(1), 29–35. doi:10.1177/1555412005281620

Boellstorff, T. (2010). *Coming of Age in Second Life: An Anthropologist Explores the Virtually Human*. Princeton: Princeton University Press.

Brand, P. Z. (n.d.). Pastiche. *Encyclopedia of Aesthetics*. Retrieved from http://www.oxfordartonline.com.ezproxy-library.ocad.ca/subscriber/article/opr/t234/e0391?q=pastiche&search=quick&pos=2&_start=1#firsthit

Cadava, E., Connor, P., & Nancy, J.-L. (1991). *Who comes after the subject?* New York: Routledge.

Carrier, D. (2002). *The Aesthetics of Comics*. Pennsylvania State University Press.

Celeste Martins, M. (2013). *Research as *poiesis*? Interdisciplinary landscapes expanded by the art and methdologies*. São Paulo, Brazil. Retrieved from http://art2investigacion-en.weebly.com/uploads/2/1/1/7/21177240/celeste_miriam.pdf

Cooper, P. (n.d.). Assemblage. *Grove Art Online*. Oxford Music and Art Online. Retrieved from http://www.oxfordartonline.com.ezproxy-library.ocad.ca/subscriber/article_citations/grove/art/T004631?q=assemblage&search=quick&pos=1&_start=1

Debord, G. (1997). *Theory of the Dérive. Internationale situationniste*. Paris: A. Fayard.

Debord, G., & Knabb, K. (2002). *The Society of the Spectacle*. Canberra: Treason Press.

Edwards, C. (2009). *Women's home-crafted objects as collections of culture and comfort, 1750-1900. Material Cultures, 1740-1920: The Meanings and Pleasures of Collecting* (pp. 37–52). Farnham, England; Burlington, VT: Ashgate.

Gabriel, Y., & Lang, T. (2006). *The Unmanageable Consumer*. United Kingdom: SAGE Publications Ltd. Retrieved from http://knowledge.sagepub.com.ezproxy-library.ocad.ca/view/the-unmanageable-consumer-2e/SAGE.xml

Griefer - Second Life Wiki. (n.d.). Retrieved from http://wiki.secondlife.com/wiki/Griefer

Grunenberg, C., & Hollein, M., Schirn Kunsthalle Frankfurt and Tate Gallery Liverpool. (2002). *Shopping: a century of art and consumer culture*. Ostfildern-Ruit: Hatje Cantz.

Hansen, M. B. N. (2006). *Bodies in Code: Interfaces with Digital Media*. London: Routledge.

Hare, A. (2013). Bridging divides: Transference in the work of Lynne Heller. *Scene, 1*(2), 165–178. doi:10.1386/scene.1.2.165_1

Harrower, D. ([c1958]). *Decoupage: a limitless world in decoration*. New York. Retrieved from http://hdl.handle.net/2027/coo.31924014500676

Hayles, N. K. (1999). *How We Became Posthuman: Virtual Bodies in Cybernetics, Literature, and Informatics*. Chicago: University Of Chicago Press. doi:10.7208/chicago/9780226321394.001.0001

Heads-up displays (HUDs) - Second Life. (n.d.). Retrieved from http://community.secondlife.com/t5/English-Knowledge-Base/Heads-up-displays-HUDs/ta-p/700083

Heller, L., & Stuckey, C. (2014, June 9). Duchamps shopping habits... email.

Hoesterey, I. (2001). *Pastiche: Cultural Memory in Art, Film, Literature*. Bloomington: Indiana University Press.

Johnson, P. (2010). *Second Life, Media and the Other Society (First printing.)*. New York: Peter Lang Publishing.

Kachur, L. (n.d.). Collage. *Grove Art Online*. Retrieved from http://www.oxfordartonline.com.ezproxy-library.ocad.ca/subscriber/article/grove/art/T018573?q=collage&search=quick&pos=1&_start=1#firsthit

Kildall, S. (2008). Scott Kildall | KILDALL.COM | Artwork: No Matter. Retrieved from http://www.kildall.com/artwork/2008/no_matter/index.html

Lakoff, G., & Johnson, M. (1998). *Philosophy in the Flesh: The Embodied Mind and Its Challenge to Western Thought*. New York: HarperCollins Canada / Basic Books.

Molesworth, M., & Denegri-Knott, J. (2007). Digital Play and the Actualization of the Consumer Imagination. *Games and Culture, 2*(2), 114–133. doi:10.1177/1555412006298209

montage. (n.d.).*The Concise Oxford Dictionary of Art Terms*. Oxford Music and Art Online. Retrieved from http://www.oxfordartonline.com.ezproxy-library.ocad.ca/subscriber/article/opr/t4/e1110?q=montage&search=quick&pos=3&_start=1#firsthit

Morie, J. F. (2007). Performing in (virtual) spaces: Embodiment and being in virtual environments. *International Journal of Performance Arts and Digital Media, 3*(2-3), 123–138. doi:10.1386/padm.3.2-3.123_1

objet trouvé, [found object]. (1994). *The Thames & Hudson Dictionary Of Art and artists*. Retrieved from http://search.credoreference.com.ezproxy-library.ocad.ca/content/entry/thaa/found_object_french_objet_trouv%c3%a9/0

Olson, E. T. (2010). Personal Identity. (E. N. Zalta, Ed.)*The Stanford Encyclopedia of Philosophy*. Retrieved from http://plato.stanford.edu/archives/win2010/entries/identity-personal/

Penny, S. (Ed.). (2011). *After Media: Embodiment and Context*. Irvine, Calif.: Digital Arts and Culture / Arts and Comp.

Plant, S. (1992). *The Most Radical Gesture: The Situationist International in a Postmodern Age* (1st ed.). London: New York, NY: Routledge.

Potvin, J., & Myzelev, A. (Eds.). (2009). *Material Cultures, 1740-1920: The Meanings and Pleasures of Collecting*. Farnham, England; Burlington, VT: Ashgate.

Rottner, N. (2011, June 2). Relational aesthetics. Grove Art Online. Retrieved from http://www.oxfordartonline.com.ezproxy-library.ocad.ca/subscriber/article/grove/art/T2093934

Rymaszewski, M., Au, W.J., Wallace, M., Winters, C., Ondrejka, C., & Batstone-Cunningham, B. (2006). *Second Life: The Official Guide*. Chichester; Hoboken, N.J.: John Wiley & Sons.

Stewart, S. (1993). *On Longing (New edition.)*. Durham, N.C.: Duke University Press.

Vandagriff, J., & Nitsche, M. (2009). Women creating machinima. *Digital Creativity*, *20*(4), 277–290. doi:10.1080/14626260903290224

Vaneigem, R. (1994). The revolution of everyday life. Seattle: Rebel Press; Left Bank Books.

Wainwright, L. (2010). Lynne Heller Chelsea Girls. Toronto: G44

White, B. A. (2007). *Second Life: A Guide to Your Virtual World*. Indianapolis, Ind.: Que Publishing.

Whitehead, D. H. (2003). Poiesis and Art-Making: A Way of Letting-Be. *Contemporary Aesthetics*, *1*. Retrieved from http://hdl.handle.net/2027/spo.7523862.0001.005

KEY TERMS AND DEFINITIONS

Assemblage: A method of art making in which natural and manufactured, traditionally non-artistic, materials and *objets trouvés* are assembled into three-dimensional structures.

Bricolage: A concept introduced by Claude Lévi-Strauss in *La pensée sauvage* (*The Savage Mind*, 1962). The word suggests that the maker works with what is on hand and tinkers.

Collage: A widely known art strategy that uses a process of accumulation for creative purposes.

Decoupage: Derived from the French word *découpure*, this is a craft in which the practitioner decorates objects or furniture with colorful pasted cutouts to simulate painted surfaces.

Dérive: A method or tactic employed by the Situationists in their pursuit of a practice they called *psychogeography*. Dérive [literally: "drifting"], a technique of rapid passage through varied ambiance involves playful-constructive behavior and are quite different from the classic notions of journey or stroll.

Détournement: A Situationist method that constitutes a turning around and a reclamation of lost meaning.

Found Object/Objet Trouvé/Readymade: *Found object* is a Surrealist and Duchampian construct, which holds that any object could become a work of art if chosen by an artist.

Hybrid Reality/Mixed Reality: Connotes a virtual layer of digital information and interaction opportunities that sit on top of and augment the physical environment.

Montage: Comes from the French for 'mounting'. Similarly to collage, pre-existing pictorial images are cut out and reassembled on a flat surface.

Pastiche: A cobbling together of elements somewhat like collage but has an added implication of *parody, montage, quotation, allusion, irony, burlesque, travesty*, and *plagiarism*.

ENDNOTES

[1]   *Society of the Spectacle* is the title of the well-known book by Guy Debord, figurehead of the revolutionary movement of the Situationist International.

2   This artist statement has framed and elucidated my practice in public contexts, for the last number of years and continues to be a guiding light for me as I move forward with my work.

3   The term relational aesthetics is descriptive of an art practice that takes as its content the human relations elicited by the artwork (Rottner, 2011).

4   My use of the word 'real' is fright-quoted in order to remark on a change in the vocabulary I use to describe this notion. In the past I have followed the convention of calling the world apart from the virtual 'real'. There is a large measure of subjectivity in words such as *real* or *actual*. I currently use the term *material* or *physical* to clarify my meaning.

5   This is the traditional, art historical definition of *assemblage*. The more commonly used Deleuzian turn for the term is applicable but not critical for the discussion at hand.

6   Neither of these projects would normally be considered an assemblage in the final manifestation of the work, though an intricate process of gathering and homogenizing was undertaken before either of the works were given a material sculptural form. Doyle's work consists of a three dimensional print of her *SL* avatar, Wanderingfictions Story. As I contend, the creation of an avatar is a cumulative process over time, the gathering and moulding of body parts or animal parts, the purchase or design of clothing and the accretion of a personality through interaction and understanding of a virtual existence. So an avatar can be thought of as either a collage or an assemblage, and a consideration of Doyle's data extrapolation from two-dimensional representations to three further interrogates these notions. Scott and Kildall's undertaking is described by Kildall as "an installation of "imaginary objects" made both in Second Life and physical space" (Kildall, 2008). The artists

hired designers in *SL* to create objects that represent common idioms, such as a *red herring*. They then hacked the *SL* protocol in order to transfer the data for the objects into a program that could produce flat paper patterns of the various structures. The patterns were then printed onto paper, cut folded and glued to realise them in physical space. *No Matter* uses collage/assemblage stratagem in more or less obvious ways than Doyle's work. More so in that the disparate, individual objects—though admittedly commissioned rather than found objects—were designed by different *SL* builders, then brought together by the artists as a piece once they were manifested three dimensionally outside of *SL*. Less so than Doyle's work in that the working methods employed by each *SL* maker can only be guessed. If the building blocks of *SL*—prims/meshes—are named one originating material versus assembled objects then the work would not be collage/assemblage. However, recycling basic structures to create new virtual items is a common practice for builders in *SL*, implying a collage/assemblage methodology.

7   *Machinima* is animation created by capturing moving images from "3D game engines, such as video games" and virtual worlds. In machinima, "the 'player' turns into a 'producer' who masters the game world and the game technology to create derivative videos" (Vandagriff & Nitsche, 2009, p. 278).

8   Complicating the relationship between consumption and production equals prosumption.

9   *SL* avatars are frequently referred to as *Barbies* and *Kens* given the idealisation of body types that are often seen in this virtual world.

10   This seemingly random mixture of *things* argues against a totality of a collection or collage—it is just a "bunch of stuff". The title does tip us off though to the desire of

the artist. Babeli is paying homage to one of the most influential collagists in the art canon, Kurt Schwitters, at the same time she troubles the definition of collage/assemblage and even montage. Her piece is deliberately random, time-based and interactive. This signals the role reception plays in any work of art. Whenever objects are put together, no matter how apparently random, we the viewers are confronted by making sense of the collection and strive to complete the work as a whole. Babeli's piece is also blatantly aggressive. As the objects rain down they also *grief* the watching avatars, implying audience complacency in the face of confrontation. The work repulses as much as it attracts.

11 A heads-up display (HUD) is a two-dimensional user interface element that controls in-world elements, such as your avatar or animations. A HUD typically consists of a control panel with buttons that do certain things; you activate it by "wearing" it as you would an article of clothing ("Heads-up displays (HUDs) - Second Life," n.d.).

12 *Détournement* is a situationist method that constitutes a "turning around and a reclamation of lost meaning". An English translation would lie "somewhere between 'diversion' and 'subversion'. It is plagiaristic, because its materials are those which already appear within the spectacle, and subversive, since its tactics are those of the 'reversal of perspective'" (Vaneigem, 1994, p. 137), which are a further "challenge to meaning aimed at the context in which it arises" (Plant, 1992, p. 86).

13 *Dérive* is a method or tactic employed by the Situationists in their pursuit of a practice they called *psychogeography*. *Dérive* "[literally: "drifting"], a technique of rapid passage through varied ambiance" involves "playful-constructive behavior" and are "quite different from the classic notions of journey or stroll". Specifically "one or more persons during a certain period drop their relations, their work and leisure activities, and all their other usual motives for movement and action, and let themselves be drawn by the attractions of the terrain and the encounters they find there". These meanderings, according to the Situationists, are less about chance than they are about "psychogeographical contours, with constant currents, fixed points and vortexes that strongly discourage entry into or exit from certain zones" (Debord, 1997).

14 This description is part of my artist statement that I have used to describe my practice since participating in *SL*.

Chapter 8
Moving Islands [Rafts]:
A Collective Art Conglomeration in Second Life

Elif Ayiter
Sabanci University, Turkey

ABSTRACT

This chapter will discuss the artistic processes and the related theoretical premises of a collaborative art undertaking that was displayed in Second Life® from Fall 2013 to Summer 2014. Despite the idiosyncratic, highly individualized nature of its components, the project nevertheless achieved a remarkable state of cohesion. What may have contributed to this unity will be one of the subjects under investigation at the core of this text. The text will commence with a survey of the creative mechanisms and strategies of the metaverse, after which a description of the project, its curatorial premises, including the usage of metaverse geography and climate as an agent of visual harmony will also be delivered. The chapter will then conclude with an examination of the collective art process within the context of the 'unfinished artifact' and John Dewey's deliberations on the experiential nature of artwork/art process as a potential framework for metaverse artistic collaborations.

INTRODUCTION

This text takes a close look at a massively collaborative, evolving art project called 'Moving Islands [Rafts]' that came into being in the virtual world of Second Life in the Fall of 2013, and continued its in-world existence, with an ever increasing number of participants, until Summer 2014.

The project brought together over thirty content creators who have markedly different approaches to building, differing artistic priorities, standpoints, outlooks and philosophies which they visualize in ways that are quite different from one other, indeed that are sometimes even at odds with one another. One of the questions that we will ask in this text will be how a successful collaboration between such an odd assembly of partners came about; and we shall attempt to address this query by examining the curatorial approach of the instigator of the project, the avatar Eupalinos Ugajin[1], who brought this diverse group of individuals together by selecting the project's participants from amongst his own friends in Second Life. Accordingly, we shall try to understand his methodology

DOI: 10.4018/978-1-4666-8384-6.ch008

by taking a closer look at the nature Second Life friendships between content creators, how such relationships oftentimes commence based upon a mutual interest in output and how this interest may lead to open-ended artistic collaborations as discussed here.

However, before we get to the quirky, idiosyncratic collaboration that brought the 'Moving Islands [Rafts]' project about, in order to set a framework which may help augment/clarify our inquiry, we shall conduct a condensed survey of Second Life building; the means of construction, and the inherently participatory nature of creative activity, given that most Second Life content is created in a chain-like, socially networked manner whereby output is often built upon pre-existent artifacts that were created by others. Indeed, very often our metaverse building activity remains as an 'unfinished artifact' (Eno, 1995) given that it is more than likely that others will continue to build upon what we have created.

A further topic that we shall devote some space to in this text, in order to understand the success of a collaboration that managed to generate a cohesive assembly out of over twenty installations that were placed in very close proximity to one another, indeed perpetually colliding with one another as they floated upon the virtual sea of the simulator, is the climate and the virtual ecosystem of Second Life. Beyond their proximity to one another, these large sized, indeed sometimes outsized artifacts ranged from the minimalistic to the highly ornate in terms of their appearance; and from the political activist to the frivolous, from the humorous to the somber, and from the dramatic to the absurd when it came to their subject matter and conceptualizations. How such an assortment of discrepancies has been unified into a holistic entity brings us to the usage of geography, climate and weather conditions, which are components that are increasingly utilized as part of the artistic palette of those Second Life builders who build art ecologies or art habitats that take into account

and make usage of the entirety of the simulator upon which the content is placed. Consequently, we shall also examine the climate tools of Second Life as integral devices for creating an art habitat/ecology since the curator, Eupalinos Ugajin, made considerable usage of them in order to affiliate a body of content that could have ended up being highly discordant if such a strategy of unification through climate and geography had not been employed.

Our authoring approach is one that weaves together such queries, also by bringing in strands that cover various other topics, such as the ones mentioned at the onset of this introduction regarding Second Life building strategies and procedures in general, their socially networked aspects, avatar attire, and the relevance of collage to Second Life building. We have tried to maintain a stance in which each of these topics segues as effortlessly as possible from one to the other, orbiting around the central question of how the 'Moving Islands [Rafts] collaboration came about and how it achieved a congruent display despite the variegated nature of its components. Amongst the many strands that revolve around these central questions one does stand out however – namely, the discussion of the 'unfinished artifact,' given that the very collaboration itself, as well as the output generated from it, manifests attributes that remain in a perpetually unfinished, evolving state. Therefore, this chapter will conclude with a return to Brian Eno's words on this perpetually unfinished state of electronic artworks, examined in conjunction with John Dewey's notions of 'Art as Experience.' (Dewey, 1934)

THE METAVERSE AND COLLABORATIVE BUILDING

The term 'metaverse' was coined by Neal Stephenson in 1992, in his novel 'Snowcrash,' where real world events are mixed with events that take place in a massively visited communal virtual world, in which individuals can interact with one another in a three dimensional landscape, and through three dimensionally embodied avatars. Each avatar is visible to all other users, and avatars interact with each other in the virtual space through software specified rules. Thus, the metaverse is a persistent, collectively shared online world that uses the metaphor of the real world, however without its physical limitations.

The definitive attribute of these worlds – the thing that differentiates them from their counterparts, the gaming worlds – is that these are builder's worlds. All content is user-defined and created, and furthermore the purpose of residing in these worlds is also one that their users have to formulate by themselves: The developers of these platforms provide no architecture and no props, all that the system gives is a barren plot of land upon which the incoming avatar is expected to place his or her own creations. However, and possibly even more importantly, is the fact that there are also no narratives, goals or quests that are system-defined.

It would thus appear that a very good reason to stay in the metaverse is to become creatively active in it, to participate in the building activity that one is surrounded by at all turns, indeed to turn building into a raison d'être for a 'second life.' In this sense the metaverse can, and should be understood first and foremost as a fascinating experiment in collaborative as well as individual creativity. Attractive as this proposition may initially sound, it may also be appropriate to heed Michael Cervieri who was one of the first to proclaim that the metaverse is *"a wildly provocative experiment in user generated content,"* but in the same breath also cautioned that *"unlike most 'upload your content and we'll share it in some sort of social media web-2-point-oh way,' content creation in Second Life is really, really, difficult."* (Cervieri 2007) These difficulties relate to content creation as the core of defining a purpose and an identity within, what is after all, a vastly

novel experience for humanity – extending one's existence through pixelated, three dimensionally embodied personas.

The model that brings this to the fore more so than any other is Second Life, which made its debut in 2003 as the first metaverse that allows its users to retain the intellectual property rights of the virtual objects that they create within the structure of an online economy, one that is complete with all instruments such as a competitive marketplace, a currency and an exchange system with which virtual funds can be transferred into Real Life currencies. Everything created in Second Life, from the formation of its very terrain to the architectural constructs placed thereupon, and down to the vast array of objects and wearables on sale and in usage is user-generated.

Although in its current embodiment the metaverse relies heavily upon its three dimensional attributes, the concept of a builders' world in which participants could create their personal artifacts goes back to the 1980s when 'Habitat,' a text based domain, was launched on Commodore; some years before Stephenson had coined the term 'metaverse.' Better known early versions of the genre however are 'Active Worlds' and 'There,' introduced in 1995 in 1998 respectively. Both of these three dimensional domains attempted to provide building tools for users so that they could create additional content to what was inherently provided by the game developers themselves.

Atomistic Construction: The Building Blocks of the Metaverse

Following this lineage Second Life, the first truly viable metaverse that was based upon a technological infrastructure robust enough to enable building activity to commence in the fullest sense of the term, was launched in 2003. One of the major reasons that Second Life succeeded where its forerunners had failed was the usage of a system of simple building blocks specifically designed for human-scale creation, bringing about a design principle that one of the creators of Second Life, Cory Ondrejka, calls 'atomistic construction.' These primitive objects constitute the atoms of Second Life which can be endlessly combined to build structures, and indeed behaviors through the scripts that can be embedded inside them. They are designed to support maximum creativity while still being simple enough for everyone to play with and use, in other words 'small pieces, loosely joined' that enable the creation of complex constructs of all descriptions, for a plethora purposes, indeed often carrying multiple purposes all at once. What is also significant is that all metaverse objects exist in a physically simulated world, therefore resulting in fairly predictable behaviors. Such simulation allows new residents to attain an intuitive understanding of how things operate within the virtual world in which they are now immersed by juxtaposing their real world experiences with the novel ones which they encounter upon entering the metaverse (Ondrejka, 2008, pp.229-252).

At its onset in 2003 Second Life only allowed for building through geometric primitives, such as cubes, spheres, cylinders and so forth that were created inside the virtual world itself through a compact, yet highly versatile editor palette which did not only create the primitives but allowed them to be linked to create remarkably complex shapes that could be further enhanced through the addition of textures. This continued to be the only means of creating 3D objects in the virtual world until 2008 when 3D mesh objects were first introduced in a simplified format called the 'sculpty.' While this early addition went quite a distance towards enriching creative output, the real breakthrough came in 2012 when detailed 3D mesh objects that could be created in external 3D editors and then imported into the metaverse made their first appearance.

One of the founding strategies behind Second Life was the notion that the virtual world would draw a cadre of elite content creators whose endeavor would be compelling enough to attract sizable numbers of players into joining the world to make usage of their output. (Castronova, 2007) This early vision appears to have been well founded as the state of the health of the Second Life economy will readily show. Although getting an approximate number of how many items are distributed for sale or as freebies in Second Life seems to be a somewhat futile effort due to the distribution of this merchandise across a very broad and rapidly changing virtual geography, an idea can still be obtained by conducting some broad searches on the website of the Second Life marketplace: A query for items that contain the keyword 'avatar' gives a result of 633557, while a search for the keyword 'dress' yields a result of 431645, and a search for 'hair' shows 166526 results, at the time of the writing of this text. What is also noteworthy is that the bulk of this proliferation is modifiable, meaning that the next owner will be able to manipulate, change and improve upon it, as well as be able to combine it with other items that could either be of his/her own creation or be obtained from yet another content creator.

While a relatively small percentage of content creators will work 'from scratch' (by creating all of their three dimensional building components and scripts, as well as importing each and every texture and animation that is needed for their work), a far greater number take advantage of the affordances of the metaverse's economy and acquire building components from elsewhere, thus utilizing the output of others to realize their own creative contributions – which in their turn may well be transferred onto others, thus bringing about a seemingly endless chain of creative collaboration in which the previous link in the chain acts as a passive collaborator, a state which comes about quite naturally through manipulations of the initial output by the new owner. In many instances, the new owner will proceed in the same manner as described above – by combining the original work with their own efforts or with the output of others. What comes about can potentially be interpreted as a novel implementation of the Surrealist 'cadavre exquis,' albeit one that is spread over time, and one in which the novel additions are built through one another, rather than as a continuation of one from the other.

Granted – many of the products generated through these creative chains result in fairly predictable everyday usage based products which more often than not closely mimic their Real Life counterparts. What is of special interest to the subject matter of this text however, is that the same strategy of building as part of a creative chain can also be often evidenced as an artistic strategy: What makes the world particularly attractive as a platform for creative expression is the largely unstructured, indeed sometimes emergent, nature of the artistic activity that the first-order user-generated content seems to breed quite spontaneously in its turn: Residents will combine output generated by others, sometimes with their own as well, to create extraordinary wearable collages and environments that have been assembled entirely or partially out of 'objets trouvés.' This conglomerated apparel, architecture and landscape, as well as a diverse range of objects will then be utilized as points of trajectories for the creation of involved play/rituals, photographic and video material, storytelling sessions, and props for fantasies which then become the incubators for the generation of personal artwork by their participants. Thus, far from being an activity held solely in the hands of an elite cadre, creative activity in the metaverse seems to have materialized as a mass pursuit, forging its own way and devising its own procedures for personal expression.

While a silent type of collaboration is already present in personal building through 'objets trouvés,' yet another form of creative expression that the metaverse seems to be particularly well suited for are collaborative projects between individuals which are embarked upon consciously, with a joint outcome in mind. In other words, while during personal building the awareness of working on something that may already be inherently collaborative due to its building blocks – some of which are more than likely to have originated

from others – might not be consciously perceived at all times; in projects involving many individuals working together the notion of collaboration is, of course, consciously acknowledged.

Produsage and Metaverse Creativity

There is an enhanced new examination of this process that comes to pass through building upon (and enriching) previously existent content; based upon telematically enabled creative collaboration, defined as 'produsage' by Axel Bruns in his book 'Blogs, Wikipedia, and Beyond.' While Bruns's main examples to this term are websites such as Wikipedia, which are fed as well as monitored by many individuals; he also takes a very close look at Second Life, finding a noteworthy correlation between content creation in Second Life and produsage, noting upon a "massively parallelized and decentralized creativity" (Bruns, 2008, p.1); which, for him, is one of the primary characteristics of the metaverse.

The terms 'produsage' and 'produser' bring together the words 'producer' and 'user' into novel hybrid configurations that describe the creative undertakings of collaborative, electronically based communities where the productive act takes place in a networked, participatory environment that breaks down the traditional boundaries between producers and consumers and instead enables all participants to be users as well as producers of information, artifacts and knowledge – frequently in the hybrid role of 'produser' where usage is necessarily also productive. In such building spaces the distinctions between producers and users of content have faded into comparative insignificance. Users are also producers of the shared knowledge base – they have therefore become produsers who do not engage in a traditional form of content production, but are instead involved in 'produsage' – the collaborative and continuous building and extending of existing content in the pursuit of further improvement.

Hence, the two most intrinsic properties of produsage can be described as follows: That the output is community-based and that within this community the roles of creator/user remain fluid and interchangeable at all times (Bruns, 2007).

The Unfinished Artifact

One of the most compelling points which Bruns raises is related to the notion of the 'unfinished artifact' as the output of produsage: Given that the work involved in produsage entails a constant back and forth between the participants, such output is bound in a continuous process of transformation and improvement. Bruns explicates upon this by quoting Brian Eno:

Think of cultural products, or art works, or the people who use them even, as being unfinished. Permanently unfinished. We come from a cultural heritage that says things have a 'nature,' and that this nature is fixed and describable. We find more and more that this idea is insupportable – the 'nature' of something is not by any means singular, and depends on where and when you find it, and what you want it for. The functional identity of things is a product of our interaction with them (Eno, 1995).

While the physical world which is comprised of atoms is not conducive to such extended manipulations of material objects; the electronic environment with its building blocks of bits provides fertile ground for the existence of creations whose inherent nature is to remain in a perpetual state of being worked upon: Unlike atoms, bits remain malleable throughout their lifespan; and even though the lifespan of the bits themselves may be finite, the lifespan of the artifact itself can be infinitely extended by making novel copies of it. The outcomes are creative systems that, unlike their physical counterparts, can be endlessly improvised upon, altered, reworked, played with and added onto by others; and as such they appear

to provide the constitutional material of all produsage. For Bruns the metaverse is a particularly compelling example to such perpetually evolving systems *"since the world remains permanently unfinished as participants move through it, [and] create content... the world of Second Life remains a process, not a product"* (Bruns, 2008, p.299).

DRESSED WITH PRIMS: FROM AVATAR-ART TO ART-ECOSYSTEM

The project 'Moving Islands [Rafts]' was instigated and curated in 2013-2014 by a Second Life avatar named Eupalinos Ugajin (Figure1), who decided to put a LEA (Linden Endowment for the Arts) simulator that had been awarded to him for half a year at the disposal of a group of artists whom he invited to build rafts that would be in the nature of outlandish floating constructs, or 'moving islands,' rather than materialize as sea vessels dedicated to transportation, as the term 'raft' usually implies.

Avatar-Art

The underlying concept of the project resides in a pervasive notion of Ugajin's, namely the creation of novel identities through novel appearances, which, within a virtual world context, manifests through avatar attire. The artist defines this process as *"becoming someone else by putting on someone else's prims."* (Ugajin, personal communication, 21-02-2014) Indeed, a large part of Ugajin's artistic practice revolves around investigating such personal transformations through prims in the metaverse: Ugajin's output brings together the 'ludic' and the 'ludicrous' into aggregations which can best be described as the carriers of 'ludicrum'; i.e., complex stage-plays, situating Eupalinos Ugajin as their protagonist, who is also the creator of the props through which an elaborate state of enactment is achieved.

Figure 1. Avatar-Art, as exemplified by the creator of the project 'Moving Islands [Rafts]' Eupalinos Ugajin. Second Life, 2014
Photograph by Elif Ayiter.

Many of these props are extensions of the avatar, attached to the avatar's body, bringing about bizarre, elaborate costumes that may also hold seemingly unrelated components. These extensions derive their inspirations from seemingly unrelated ideas, phrases, artworks and ephemera which the artist makes no effort to disown, indeed proudly proclaims possession of. Thus, it can be said that Ugajin does not only *"become someone else by putting on someone else's prims,"* but takes the whole notion of creating novel visual identities through associative processes beyond the tools of metaverse building by weaving together ideas and concepts that have been stored in a bewilderingly large mental repository. These ideas and concepts are represented by artifacts that come from the vernacular as well as the high end of technological devices, cultural items and art/design objects.

Noted should be that Ugajin's avatars do not necessarily always have body parts that can be associated with organic beings such as humans or animals. Neither are they easily identifiable as robots, extra-terrestrial beings, or other such creatures that online virtual world appearances are often related to. Instead, Ugajin creates his own amalgam, ending up with creatures that can display many attributes simultaneously – from the architectonic, to ordinary household objects such as radiators, fans and bicycles, many of which can also be placed away from the avatar at considerable distances. These extensions are assembled as visual manifestations of (possibly verbal) statements that may range from the nonsensical, to the humorous, to the somber ; oftentimes also incorporating a political stance that revolves around environmental issues, albeit always delivered enshrouded in a cloak of hilarity and hermetic undercurrents/subtexts that discourage the easy readings and clichés with which such proclamations are all too often associated with – all of which also seems to reflect upon Arthur Koestler's definition of creativity, that is one which involves a mental state that can bounce back and forth between jester and sage, bringing forth a creative end product which transcends the sum total of its disparate parts. (Koestler 1964, p.121, pp.145-148)

The 'Moving Islands [Rafts]' project can be seen as an extension of this concept from the mere body of the avatar to an entire virtual landmass that acquires an aggregated identity that reflects the participants of the project, coming into being through their combined prims. Put differently, it can be said that Ugajin enlisted the help of those he invited into his collaborative project in order to realize his primary tenet of *"become someone else by putting on someone else's prims,"* as an artistic strategy on a grandiose scale, by treating a virtual landmass as a composite and yet individuated entity that would acquire an ever-evolving, ever-changing identity through collective building – a strategy that despite its seeming contradiction nevertheless possesses an inherent logic in that the avatar and the land that it moves upon are made out of the same material – bits that can be infinitely manipulated and played with; while a further analogy to this mode of creative expression can also be potentially derived from our physical existence in which our homes can be seen to be extensions of our identities, populated with objects created by others whilst at the same time reflecting our innermost beings.

Moving Islands

The project opened its doors to metaverse residents in the late Fall of 2013, on a simulator dedicated to artistic activity provided by the Linden Endowment for the Arts (LEA). Recognizing the artistic potential that Second Life seemed to hold, and the needs of the many avatars who were creating artworks that required considerable more than what the small, privately owned exhibition spaces with which the gird is inundated with could provide;

starting from 2010, Linden Labs, the owners of Second Life, set aside over 30 full simulators that are awarded for a period of six months to artists and/or art events of outstanding merit which are selected by a committee.

The bi-annually renewed activity that occurs on these simulators constitutes the basis of operations of LEA, which describes itself as follows:

A collaborative venture between Linden Lab and the arts community. Guided by a dedicated board of renowned Second Life artists, the LEA is committed to providing access to engaging experiences in the arts for the Second Life community. Through its exhibitions, programs, and events, the LEA fosters awareness of artists' contributions to our virtual world and encourages others to get involved and be inspired.[2]

When awarded a LEA simulator for the second half of 2013, Ugajin decided to share the bounty with others and instigated a number of activities in which he would not be only active as an artist, but also work as a curator; and 'Moving Islands [Rafts]' was preceded during the first half of the grant period by a showing of the 'Bogon Flux,' an emergent metaverse art habitat that had been created in 2008 by avatars Cutea Benelli and Blotto Epsilon.

T.R.I.M: Temporary Rezz Inventory Mess Zone

A good way of understanding Ugajin's idea of giving a landmass an agglomerated persona through collective creativity may be to look at his own approach to metaverse building which is exemplified in T.R.I.M, (Figure 2) a collection of artifacts created by others arranged into an endemic habitat which he placed upon the simulator of moving islands.

It would of course be widely off the mark to proclaim that what Ugajin did in T.R.I.M., through the creative handling of found or purchased objects

Figure 2. 'Moving Islands [Rafts]' project: T.R.I.M. Second Life, 2013
Photograph by Eupalinos Ugajin.

is indigenous to the metaverse, is a form of creative expression that has not been encountered before. Appropriation to this end is common throughout 20th century art, and has become one of the tenets of post-modern art; to the extent where Olivia Gude placed the concept within her 8 principles of post-modernist art education (2004, pp.6-13).

In 'Art and Agency' Alfred Gell discusses the found object as part of a specific form of artistic activity, stating that in the idea of the 'found object' or the 'ready-made,' the artist does not so much 'make' as 'recognize' the particular cognitive index of the object. By this account, even the purportedly arbitrary ready-mades of the Dadaists, forced themselves on these artists *"who responded to the appeal of their arbitrariness and anonymity, just as the Buddhist landscape artists responded to their mutely speaking boulders"* (Gell, 1998, pp.30-31).

Looking at a related field however we find that western collage consists of reassembling preexisting images in such a way as to form a new image answering a poetic need. Max Ernst defined it as *"the chance encounter of two distant realities on an unsuitable level,"* (Carrouges, 1974, p.66) a formula that also finds resonance in Lautréamont's proposition: *"Beautiful as the encounter of a sewing machine and an umbrella on a dissecting table, it gives us a remarkable method of triangulation that does not provide measures, but brings to the surface unrevealed mental images"* (Carrouges, 1974, p.171). Louis Aragon is also remembered as having said that collage is more reminiscent of the operations of magic than those of painting since it hinges on the artist's success in persuading us to recognize the connection of visual elements on the plane of poetry. Asked, if his collages were visible poetry Jean Arp replied "Yes, this is poetry made through plastic means." (Arp, 1972)

What may differentiate metaverse appropriative art from its Real Life precursors such as Dadaist ready-mades or Surrealist collages could lie in the purpose that instigated the actual acquisition:

Personal experience and observation have revealed that many of these purchases are not initially made with an artistic end product in mind; instead they seem to be bought as toys first and foremost. These toys however, often become transformed, not only in their appearance but also, and more importantly, in their usage. In other words, it is the play state that brings on the creative mindset, much as it is also described by Brian Sutton-Smith in the chapter entitled 'Rhetorics of the Imaginary,' found in his book 'The Ambiguity of Play.' (Sutton-Smith, 1997, pp.127-150).

This playful stance also makes creative output in the metaverse become 'behavioral.' (Ascott: 2003: 109-123) Far from being work meant to be viewed and admired but not interfered with in any fundamental way, design output as well as art objects are manipulated, re-structured and combined with others as fits the needs of the present user; to suit specific needs - or as is the case in Ugajin's T.R.I.M may be an unexpected by-product of an entirely different activity: *"I was looking for chairs and ended up rezzing a few things, more will come maybe."*[3]

What may however be the most compelling difference is that T.R.I.M, and other such metaverse installations, are meant to be lived in, should be considered to be avatar habitats. Indeed, this distinction appears to be important enough for the following section to be given over to a further discussion of this manifestation.

The Art Habitat

When looking at artistic activity in virtual worlds it very soon becomes apparent that a considerable amount of creative output is created very much along the lines of its physical counterpart; with the objective of being viewed within a gallery/museum setting – albeit virtually. This accounts for the proliferation of virtual galleries and museums inside Second Life to which visitors are meant to come to with their avatars, very much as one would do so in Real Life with one's physical body; complete with openings and purchases of the displayed work – more often as limited editions but sometimes also as a unique original (in which case the buyer would inevitably have to rely upon the word of the creator that there is no further copy of the bought item). During such events the exhibited artworks consist of standalone virtual artifacts, such as sculptures that are created in-world or virtual photographs which are presented as framed paintings and more recently also video art which is played back on virtual screens inside the virtual gallery.

There is however a second type of creative undertaking to be found in the metaverse: These are all-inclusive art-habitats that come into being through a custom created geography and climate, usually stretching themselves out over an entire metaverse simulator which is used to create a continuously engaging experience, comprised of many interrelated artifacts that cannot be easily separated from one another and that provide a complex visual/sonic system to be perceived in its entirety. What is displayed grows out of its own artificial ecology, meant to be visited and experienced therein.

Such spaces may be thematic, indeed oftentimes follow tangible concepts and storylines that may also be defined as artistic Role Play environments in which visitors are meant to experience the artwork by following up on the presented concepts/storylines by taking on the roles that are made available to them through clues within the environment itself. However, in many cases these ecologies may also be based upon concepts and abstractions from which visitors are expected to derive their own meanings and experiences, out of which very often substantial virtual photography and machinima output comes forth, working as further links that constitute the chain of metaverse creativity, discussed earlier on in this text under the terms of 'produsage' and the 'unfinished artifact.'

As a general rule such virtual art ecologies do not have a specific duration or a statically defined appearance; more often than not they will be around for many months, whilst undergoing continuous changes during their lifespan. As is already implicit from this lack of predetermined timeframe, with this type of output the objective can be defined as an invitation for others to come and live inside the created space – to make it their own, and ultimately to become creatively active in it. The desire is that the piece slowly unfolds through many lengthy visits, some lasting for days or even weeks, and that the incomers proceed to utilize the landscape for their own ends – to play in it, and by extension to become creatively active through it on a personal level.

Thus it may be claimed that creativity in the metaverse acquires some very compelling attributes when it is made as a part of the world in which it is meant to come into effect; and the 'Moving Islands [Rafts]' project is indubitably one such art-ecosystem that unfolds within its own site-specifically generated artificial geography and climate, inviting others to come and live in it and to become creatively active in it.

The Virtual Eco-System

While the social aspects of the art-ecosystem, its ability to draw in others for extended stays and creative activity is certainly a very important consideration, what is equally important, and what can be evidenced very impressively on the 'Moving Islands [Rafts]' simulator also, is how geography and climate can become highly effective tools for developing visual strategies in these environments.

At its onset, and for many more years to follow, Second Life did not have a proper atmosphere or a climate to speak of, a sad circumstance which accounts for the many screenshots of those years, showing a cardboard-like world, devoid of all allure, mystery and harmony, displayed under a stark midday sun – an early visual stigma that the world has probably not managed to rid itself of completely even today, when, despite the vast improvements that have occurred in this regard

over the years, Second Life is still largely associated with bad graphics by those who have never joined the world, or those who have but found it lacking in visual sophistication and finesse.

Although Windlight, Second Life's atmospheric rendering system that enhances skies, lighting and other graphical aspects of the environment, was introduced in late 2007, in terms of building it continued to be ineffective for several years due to two reasons: The first of these was that until recently very few residents had sufficiently powerful graphics cards on their computers to allow for the atmospheric rendering setting to take effect; and the second was that setting windlight remained a personal choice that a builder could not override. In other words, while a builder could see his own build under the atmospheric and lighting conditions that he/she envisaged, sharing this setting with others was not much of an option. Over the past few years however, creating custom skies, atmosphere and light as an embedded setting for the virtual land itself has become possible and furthermore these settings are nowadays automatically shown by the visiting avatar's machine, provided that they have enabled that preference. That said, builders do still need to take on the fact that even today, with vastly improved conditions in this regard, not all visitors will have hardware or internet connections that are sufficient to the demands of atmospheric rendering and may therefore not be able to see the work under the lighting conditions that the builder envisioned. And further, even if they do have the requisite set-up they may still prefer to view the work under atmospheric conditions of their own choosing.

Following these developments, it was a foregone conclusion that many metaverse builders would bring custom, site-specifically created atmospheres and climates into their building strategies – that climate and atmosphere would constitute the visual framework against which art and architecture was placed.

What is an important consideration whilst implementing atmosphere and climate as building blocks is that the ambient lighting slider that is present in these settings will colorize all constructs placed within it to the extent that this slider is actuated. In the case of 'Moving Islands [Rafts]' Ugajin decided to use ambient lighting as a device of unification: Since the rafts, which will be discussed in the following section, had color schemes that differed to quite a considerable extent, there was a danger of their colors clashing with one another, especially given the circumstance that most of these vessels were in perpetual motion and therefore were likely to often come within very close proximity of one another. The usage of an ambient lighting scheme provided a very effective solution to this conundrum. What was as important however, was that the lighting scheme set a pervasive mood that helped pull things together conceptually as well: Ugajin chose an atmosphere that was made out of gold, ochre and burnt umber tones materializing under a green-gold sky which set the stage for a stormy, otherworldly, tarnished feel; creating a historic overtone that brought to mind things such as historic manuscripts, old engravings, and classical sea battle paintings.

Turning to the creation of a custom geography however, indeed a milieu reminiscent of sea paintings was very much in the offering since Ugajin decided upon a landscape that was in fact a seascape: All landmass was removed from the simulator, creating a flat water mass that stretched to the horizon. What made this sea quite remarkable however was that the windlight settings could also be used to create a sea-mirror in which all vessels were reflected, that they dipped into and floated out of in a perpetual dance of collisions.

An Idiosyncratic Armada

Visitors who arrived on the simulator landed inside a huge red building, created by the avatar Scottius Polke, called the 'Funhouse.' This edifice was actually a pier for departing pleasure boats, each of them manned by a crew of two, bowling pin-like, widely grinning figurines whose boats furiously flew down a ramp into the sea ahead, whilst impeding one's personal ingress – setting a scene for unexpectedness and play from the very onset of the visit (Figure 11). What also heightened this state of expectation for play were the numerous gifts that were placed inside the 'Funhouse.' Once outside the pier building however, this edifice transpired to be festooned with a clown-faced pediment; further strengthening the sense that one had landed in a place of impetuous, child-like, toy inspired encounters (Figure 3).

A *"Cosmogony of Rafts and other improbable floating beings,"*[4] was the way in which Ugajin himself described the parade of eccentricity that was displayed through some thirty constructs that floated, rose and dipped into a virtual sea through a special script that also utilized the z-axis for movement (Figure 6). While some of these were immediately recognizable as rafts – in a few cases even with a sculpted crews placed upon them (Figure 7) – yet many others were indeed highly improbable beings floating above sea level:

A fragile, antenna-like construct placed in the sky (Lolito Larkham, 2013) (Figure 8), a spheroid auditorium (Madcow Cosmos, 2013), a towering nautilus inspired object which was tethered to a platform floating on the sea's surface (Artistide Depres, 2013) (Figure 5), a massive abstract edifice created out semi-transparent colored planes that covered a plethora of boulder-like, black objects (Merlino Mayo, 2013) (Figure 3) were some of the big builds that the visitor was immediately accosted with upon entry into the seascape. Further large-scaled, immediately identifiable constructs were the two large, minimalistically flat platforms, one of which periodically spewed forth pink to purple colorized columns; while the other one was a hermetic surface of green concentric circles, populated with numerous windbags fastened to brittle tripods, to which its creator had given the mysterious name 'Charm Raft' (Figure 10). One

Figure 3. 'Moving Islands [Rafts]' project: Panorama shot. 'The Fun House,' the entry point to 'Moving Islands [Rafts]' by Scottius Polke is in the background (right), while Merlino Myoo's gigantic tower is in the foreground (left). Also visible are Pallina60 Loon's Nautilus raft (top-center-left), Haveit Neox's raft with its wooden crew (right) and Kake Broeck's gigantic pencil (back right)
Photograph by Elif Ayiter

Figure 4. 'Moving Islands [Rafts]' project: 'The Forest,' underwater installation by Meilo Minotaur. Second Life 2013
Photograph courtesy of the artist

Figure 5. 'Moving Islands [Rafts]' project: 'Radeau' by Artistide Depres. Second life 2013
Photograph by Elif Ayiter.

Figure 6. 'Moving Islands [Rafts]' project: One of Maya Paris's two octopi sinks into a submarine city placed by Haveit Neox. Second Life 2013
Photograph by Elif Ayiter.

Figure 7. 'Moving Islands [Rafts]' project: 'Mythic Raft' by Haveit Neox. Second Life 2013
Photograph by Eupalinos Ugajin.

Figure 8. 'Moving Islands [Rafts]' project: 'UFO' by Lollito Larkham. Second Life 2013
Photograph by Elif Ayiter.

of the most impressive of these big constructs however was placed on the simulator by Ugajin himself: A wildly distorted, three dimensionalized trapezoid building moored to a small boat, the title of which proclaimed it to 'Moor the Wind' (Figure 9).

Moving below sea level – the underwater of the metaverse holds a lot of fascination for many Second Life builders due to the beautifully diffuse, foggy lighting conditions that can be found down there. At the 'Moving Islands [Rafts]' simulator, two participants chose to build submarine water gardens 8 Meilo Minotaur and Cutea Benelli, 2013) (Figure 4), while a third added an entire underwater city (Haveit Neox, 2013) – again three builds that should be counted amongst the large and mostly stationary installations.

Floating amongst these big structures were the many smaller rafts. To describe just a few of these: A rustic raft manned by a wooden crew (Haveit Neox, 2013), a nut-shell boat pulled by a fish and topped by a classical chair facing a dressing table of sorts (Uan Ceriaptrix, 2013), a big, steampunk-like nautilus constructed out of sheet metal (Pallina60 Loon, 2013), and yet another raft, this one rusted into a deep dark hue, upon which an elephant and a parasol sat in a garden of flowers constructed out of gears. (Cica Ghost, 2013) And then – not exactly rafts – dipping in and out of the virtual waters were also two colorful octopus-like creatures which were attached to complex pulley systems, and that proclaimed to be upside down and asked the visitor to please turn them over. (Maya Paris, 2013)

Figure 9. 'Moving Islands [Rafts]' project: 'Moor the Wind' by Eupalinos Ugajin (back left) and 'Rusty Raft' by Cica Ghost (front right). Second Life 2013
Photograph by Elif Ayiter.

Figure 10. 'Moving Islands [Rafts]' project: 'Charm Raft' by Simotron Aquila. Second Life 2013
Photograph by Elif Ayiter.

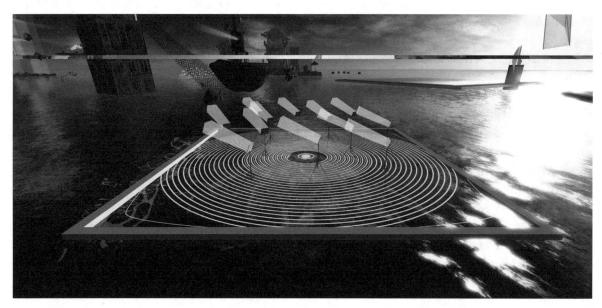

Figure 11. 'Moving Islands [Rafts]' project: Tucked in one corner of the simulator, 'My Dear' by Livio Korobase was a large static raft that incorporated shadow projections and audio. Second Life 2013
Photograph by Eupalinos Ugajin.

Metaverse Collaborations

We now come to the crux of the matter – the question of how this medley of eccentricity came about, the nature of the collaboration involved in the workings of the project. How did Ugajin manage to bring together such a motley cast of characters to build a conglomeration that transformed a virtual seascape into a cumulative, evolving visual identity, composed of unrelated parts which could nevertheless operate together in a closely knit choreography?

Second Life Friendships

A good way of approaching this question is by taking a look at how friendships between metaverse builders seem to usually come about, since the project started out with an invitation that Ugajin sent out to a number of his personal friends.

Although there are of course individuals who join Second Life through Real Life contacts who attract them to the metaverse for manifold purposes, it would be safe to say that for the most part avatars who enter Second Life do so out of a personal quest; in other words they come in 'cold' without the safeguard or infrastructure of pre-existent Real Life social networks that would enable them to meet others and form relationships in a similar manner to which these are established in Real Life. Consequently, for the most part, friendships in the metaverse have to be formed from scratch, as Tim Guest describes at the start of his book 'Second Lives.' (Guest, 2007, pp.35-49)

What has to be taken into account at this juncture is that all of the physical clues such as body language, personal affinity, physical rapport and attraction will be missing from the equation while avatars go about finding new friends. In addition, references provided through common acquaintances may also be missing – at least they may not be there when one encounters one's very first future friend. What seems to remain as a credible means for establishing friendships

therefore are common interest areas. While for many avatars this could mean encountering like-minded persons at social gatherings such as the meetings of Second Life groups who cater to joint interests (Boellstorff, 2008, pp.183-185); for creatively inclined avatars a very common way of befriending others appears to be through an appreciation of their creative output. Thus, it is not surprising that many Second Life artists' contact lists will hold other artists whose work they have recognized as noteworthy enough to have brought about the initial impetus of contact.

Ugajin tells us how he befriended Scottius Polke, the creator of the 'Funhouse' pier at 'Moving Islands' [Rafts]:

I once saw his 'Rusty Winged Totem' in a gallery, edited the object to see who was the creator and found an event where he had it on sale. I later wanted to use it as a backpack but it was 'no modify' so I contacted him to have a smaller version which he sent me. This is probably when I added him as a contact. I started checking what he had in SL and taking pictures of his work, such as the 'Wandering Giraffe,' and he came to visit my installations/builds. Nowadays you might see me in Real Life wearing a tee-shirt with a piece that he made.[5] (Ugajin, personal communication, 21-02-2014)

This tale can be considered to be quite typical of how metaverse friendships between artists are often formed, and it is indeed typical of how the friendships between most of the invitees to the project and Ugajin came about – he contacted them, or they contacted him – out of interest for the work that either party was displaying within the virtual world. Although, at first glance, this does seem to be very much a case of 'birds of a feather, flocking together' it should still not be read as a search for a similarity of output or artistic credos. If anything, Ugajin emphasizes the pleasures attained from the diversity of the metaverse when it comes to encountering creative personas of many different persuasions, working in many different styles and under different concepts, who may well end up becoming friends – not despite, but precisely through their very diversity.

Thus, when the time came to pick a team Ugajin decided to look at his own friends list which he felt would provide the diversity that the project, as he envisioned it, called for – not a conglomeration of tastefully assorted, harmonious objects that moved in synchrony, but instead a mutation through creative work that would lead to unexpected results since he was already familiar with what their building interests or strategies were, since he knew what these people had done before, knew that they had very few hang-ups, emphasized play and unexpectedness in their work, held the telling of bizarre tales through objects over the mere aesthetics that these objects might hold in themselves.

It should also be added that while the first phase was based upon invitations, as the project progressed, Ugajin opened the call to all metaverse artists through a poster in which a list of the names of ongoing participating artists was ended with a line that asked the question 'You?', rendered in a type style that emphasized the query through a lightened font color.

However, early planning went beyond a sole selection of participants, since it also involved the planning of the environment in which the armada would materialize. One important component of this – the movement of the rafts, as Ugajin anticipated it, would also reflect the aimed haphazardness since the vessels would not be moving along predetermined, gracefully choreographed paths; instead they would be taking random trajectories that would bring them into precarious, indeed oftentimes awkward seeming proximities.

Seeding the Project: Web-based Collaborations and the 'Sandbox'

The project kicked off with an invitation that Ugajin sent to his friends in early Fall 2013. Of

the twenty+ early invitees very few turned the call down, and those who did had compelling reasons to do so. The ones who did come on board however were indeed a motley crew and the first challenge was to create an environment of seeding where the participants would be able to form an understanding as to what exactly the curator was anticipating, what the – albeit very loosely held – parameters/expectations of the project were to be. Ugajin resolved this initial conundrum by inviting his crew to an online, internet based collaborative platform[6] where he felt that ideas could potentially be exchanged and developed.

One thing that may have helped to get the early ball rolling was what Ugajin placed on the board himself, namely images of a loose inspiration that he harbored for the project and that came from a Real Life precursor realized by American street artist Swoon who has created precarious-looking swimming mini cities, inhabited by bands of steampunk sailors, that are being periodically assembled since 2006.[7]

Around this initial seeding invitees began to assemble images and verbalizations of their own ideas and inspirations for the vessels that they proposed to build, as well as commenting on what others were placing. However, it should be emphasized that Ugajin's expectations for the board were not all-encompassing, or overly ambitious. Knowing the highly spontaneous nature of metaverse building, where decisions are almost always made on the fly and at the very last minute, he did not expect finalized products to come out of the board:

The board was just to start things. To think about improbable floating objects that could be considered to be rafts. I didn't expect too much from the board in the sense of a blueprint for the subsequent building. It was just a way to get the ball rolling, to start relationships maybe, to get a collective project going through exchanges. (Ugajin, personal communication, 21-02-2014)

The second phase of the project came about when a 'sandbox' materialized high in the sky of the simulator, at 4000 meters. Here, participants of the project were able to see what others were working upon. A critical question to ask at this juncture would be whether seeing what others were crafting changed individual output. Ugajin, does not think so, cannot recall a specific instance where a build underwent a drastic change in appearance or content after it was placed in the sandbox. One reason behind this may be that most, if not indeed all, of the artists that were invited to the project already had well established careers as content creators in Second Life, had been creatively active in the virtual world for quite some time, having had ample opportunity to develop individualized procedures and well established visual languages along the way.

Yet another reason may well be that Ugajin chose wisely, and that the invitees all shared his overall vision of diversity as a crucial component of the project – that the very point of the project was to get things that were intrinsically different to move together. That said, there is at least one instance of modification, which came about when the avatar Alpha Auer found her vessel to be lacking in narrative after she saw it in proximity to what the others had created. However, in this case also, the modification did not entail an all-out rebuilding, but instead unfolded as additions to her original raft that amplified its narrative potential without in any way changing the essence of the build itself.

CONCLUSION: A COSMOGONY OF RAFTS AND THE 'UNFINISHED ARTIFACT'

For close to a year the armada of improbable floating beings – some populated with silent sculpted crews constructed of prims and mesh objects, some evincing as fantastical creatures in and of themselves, some containing reflec-

tive spaces and some devised as playgrounds for avatars – floated, rose from and sank into the virtual waters of the metaverse; all manifesting under Ugajin's carefully orchestrated virtual sky and atmospheric conditions that greatly aided in bringing visual congruity to a highly variegated content through which the simulator took on *"the personalities of many others."* (Ugajin, personal communication, 21-02-2014)

The vessels did not materialize all in one day, more and more were added to the initial twenty or so, accumulating to a total of approximately thirty, as the project progressed over its almost one year life-span. What needs to be pointed out is that with each new addition the visual as well as the kinetic dynamics of the entire simulator changed since the rafts found less and less space to move in freely, were brought into ever-escalatingly precarious collisions, affecting the overall feeling and atmosphere that a seascape populated with an increasingly crowded flotilla gave out. In this sense, 'Moving Islands [Rafts]' would appear to be much in synch with Brian Eno's definition of the 'unfinished artifact' as an expected, indeed desirable (non)goal of virtual creativity.

Yet another way in which Eno's notion of the 'unfinished artifact' can be approached is by deeming the viewer/audience/participant of the artwork to be a crucial component that extends the circuit to further states of impermanence. Eno describes it through music:

What people are going to be selling more of in the future is not pieces of music, but systems by which people can customize listening experiences for themselves. Change some of the parameters and see what you get. So, in that sense, musicians would be offering unfinished pieces of music - pieces of raw material, but highly evolved raw material, that has a strong flavor to it already... []... I imagine a musical experience equivalent to playing SimEarth, for example, in which you are at once thrilled by the patterns [] and the metaphorical resonances of such a system. Such an experience falls in a nice new place - between art and science and playing. This is where I expect artists to be working more and more in the future. (Eno, 1995)

As has been discussed earlier on in this chapter, the metaverse can be seen to be a world in which art breeds art, a world where residents can in fact tweak the parameters of what is on offer and attain new, individual results. In that sense the metaverse is an open system that we feel is much in accord with Eno's vision of where art may be headed in the future. When it comes to the 'Moving Islands [Rafts]' project what may be relevant is the creative activity that has evolved out of the project, and that may bear testimony to the evolving, collaborative and ultimately unfinished nature of the entire venture:

While two of the original builders, Pallina60 Loon and Haveit Neox, took their input into the project even further by creating videos that were based upon the output on the simulator, what is probably as significant is the work generated by in-comers to the project, those who had not been a part of the building process itself. Thousands, indeed tens of thousands of avatars visited the seascape given that the project was listed in the Second Life Destination Guide, a portal for new residents maintained by Linden Labs. Since creative expression through virtual photography and video, especially through a usage of pre-existent artwork as the framework for such activity, are wide-spread occupations of most metaverse residents, it was only to be expected that much photographic/video output ended up being generated from the project; and indeed Ugajin has collected some of this work in a Flickr group[8].

What is especially noteworthy however are the various site-specific undertakings such as the 'Belly of the Whale' project instigated by Second life machinima artist Ole Etzel, jointly with Ugajin. The project invited visitors to create and submit their own whale stories using photography or machinima. The participating artworks were shown at a dedicated website[9] and were also screened at an in-world party. to which end Ole Etzel urged visitors of the simulator to explore Moving islands at LEA20:

Reflect on the topic 'In the Belly of the Whale'. Reflect harder! Now do us a film, a picture or a photo story at LEA20. Wear [your] own builds or use existing ones from the sim, create a short photo story or a 120 minute epic film, sing, shout or shoot a harpoon into the last whale! Perhaps you may decide to feel like being in any special kind of belly or to produce your work in that special Cadavre Exquis look? Special Russian dictator bellies floating through your mind? NOW you are ready to go! Give us the honor and donate a work to our interactive extravaganza![10]

Other remarkable ventures that came out of the 'Moving Islands [Rafts]' project were the various performances that were held on the simulator, such as many concerts and, most notably, a series of performances by metaverse artists Kikas Babenco and Marmaduke Arado. Aside from these scheduled performances, Arado also created a number of performative 'instant scenes' (Figure 12) that could be used by visitors to create further tales of hilarious absurdities.

One important distinction that should be emphasized is that what is being described here as a form of second-order creativity is not founded in 'interactivity' but instead relates to something that goes considerably beyond what this term has come to imply. To turn yet again to Eno:

In a blinding flash of inspiration, the other day I realized that "interactive" is the wrong word. The right word is 'unfinished.'... [] ... The "nature" of something is not by any means singular, and depends on where and when you find it, and what you want it for. The functional identity of things is a product of our interaction with them. And our own identities are products of our interaction with everything else. (1995)

Figure 12. 'Moving Islands [Rafts]' project: 'Rocket Science.' Eupalinos Ugajin is testing one of the many 'instant scenes' by Kikas Babenco and Marmaduke Arado. Second Life, 2014
Photograph by Eupalinos Ugajin.

Such engagement transforms visual art works into experiential, behavioral objects that become crucial components in creating the identities of our virtual extensions, our avatars and their domiciles. We no longer view art works as externalized objects, but rather we live inside and through our creations – we wear them, we reside in them, indeed we become them – and ultimately this is what the project discussed in this chapter has been all about.

Interestingly, the 'unfinished artifact' seems to also have been in the thoughts of John Dewey who, in as early as 1934, connects the concept with his understanding of art as an experiential process:

No amount of ecstatic eulogy of finished works can of itself assist the understanding or the generation of such works. [] The answers cannot be found, unless we are willing to find the germs and roots in matters of experience that we do not currently regard as aesthetic. Having discovered these active seeds, we may follow the course of their growth into the highest forms of finished and refined art. (Dewey, 1934, p.12)

John Dewey points at cultures where aesthetic appreciation is inextricably bound with day to day usage, saying that *"we do not have to travel to the ends of the earth nor return many millennia to find peoples for whom everything that intensifies the sense of immediate living is an object of intense admiration,"* taking us to a place that closely resonates with the art-habitat, to spaces such as Ugajin's T.R.I.M, to what was possibly his main motivation for instigating 'Moving Islands [Rafts],' to *"become someone else by putting on someone else's prims,"* and then to take this notion to an entirely different level by transforming the identity of an entire metaverse simulator through the prims of others.

The present task then, according to Dewey, *"is to restore continuity between the refined and intensified forms of experience that are works of art and the everyday events, doings, and sufferings that are universally recognized to constitute experience."* (Dewey 1934: 10) Thus what Dewey proposes is an elevation of artwork from its current state of being the provider of mere *"transient pleasurable excitations"* into once again becoming the powerful carriers of experience – a stance, we believe, is shared by many metaverse artists who dedicate their craft to the building of such all-encompassing experiences, as we hope has also been the case with the collaborative project presented in this chapter, 'Moving Islands [Rafts].'

ACKNOWLEDGMENT

We wish to put on record our huge appreciation for the work and enthusiasm which the following list of Second Life avatars put into the 'Moving Islands [Rafts]' project:

Alpha Auer, Artistide Despres, CapCat Ragu, Cica Ghost, Cutea Benelli, Derek Michelson (programming), Eupalinos Ugajin, Haveit Neox, Kake Broek, Kikas Babenco, Livio Korobase, Lollito Larkham, Marmaduke Arado, Madcow Cosmos, Maya Paris, Meilo Minotaur, Merlino Mayo, Misprint Thursday, Oberon Onmura, Ole Etzel, Pallina60 Loon, Scottius Polke, Simotron Aquila, Takio Ra, Uan Ceriaptrix, Trill Zapatero. Many more images of their contributions can be viewed on Eupalinos Ugajin's Flickr, collected in an album especially dedicated to the project: https://www.flickr.com/photos/eupalinos/sets/72157637216288526/.

REFERENCES

Arp, J. (1972). *Arp on Arp: poems, essays, memories*. The Viking Press.

Ascott, R., & Shanken. E. (ed.). (2003). Telematic Embrace: Visionary Theories of Art, Technology, and Consciousness. Berkeley: University of California Press.

Boellstorff, T. (2008). *Coming of Age in Second Life: An anthropologist explores the virtually human* (pp. 183–185). Princeton, NJ: Princeton University Press.

Bruns, A. (2007). *Produsage: A Working Definition.* Retrieved from http://produsage.org/node/9 Read 18/01/2012

Bruns, A. (2008). Blogs, Wikipedia, and Beyond (Digital Formations). New York: Peter Lang.

Carrouges, M. (1974). Andre Breton and the Basic Concepts of Surrealism. Tuscaloosa: University of Alabama Press.

Castronova, E. (2007). *Exodus to the Virtual World* New York, NY: Palgrave MacMillan.

Cervieri, M. (2007). *User Generated Content in Second Life with Cory Ondrejka.* Scribemedia.org, http://www.scribemedia.org/2007/03/20/2nd-life/

Dewey, J., (1980). *Art as Experience*. New York: Perigree Books.

Eno, B. (1995). *Gossip is Philosophy, Wired magazine interview with Kevin Kelly*. Wired. http://www.wired.com/wired/archive/3.05/eno.html?pg=4&topic=

Gell, A. (1998) Art and Agency. Oxford: Oxford University Press.

Gude, O. (2004). Postmodern Principles: In Search of a 21st Century Art Education. *Art Education*, *57*(1), 6–13.

Guest, T. (2007). *Second Lives*. New York: Random House Inc.

Koestler, A. (1964). *The act of creation*. London: Hutchinson & Co.

Ondrejka, C. (2008). Education Unleashed: Participatory Culture, Education, and Innovation in Second Life. In K. Salen (Ed.), *The Ecology of Games: Connecting Youth, Games, and Learning* (pp. 229–252). Cambridge: The MIT Press.

Sutton-Smith, B. (1997). *The Ambiguity of Play.* Cambridge: Harvard University Press.

KEY TERMS AND DEFINITIONS

Avatar: Originating from the Hindu concept of a descent of a deity to Earth, the word can be broadly be related to an appearance or a manifestation. Today, in a narrower sense, the term is associated with the 3D or 2D image based representation of the human behind the keyboard within online worlds.

Commodore: Commodore (C64) is an 8-bit home computer introduced in January 1982 by Commodore International. The C64 dominated the low-end computer market for most of the 1980s and retains its all-time record as the highest-selling single computer model of all time to this day.

Habitat: This is a term that defines an ecological or environmental area which is inhabited by a particular type of organism. In this text the term is used to define a space that would constitute a natural environment for virtual world avatars.

Objets Trouvés: A natural or discarded object found by chance and held to have aesthetic value.

Prim: A 'prim' is the name given to the basic building block of Second Life, out of the combinations of which almost all artifacts of the metaverse - be they buildings, vehicles/gadgets or clothing elements are created.

Rezz: In Second Life this means to create or to make an object appear. Rezzing an object/prim can be done by dragging it from a resident's inventory or by creating a new one via the edit window. The term "rezzing" can also be used for waiting for a texture or object to load, such as "Everything is still rezzing." or "Your shirt is still rezzing for me."

Sandbox: Experimental building locations inside virtual worlds are named sandboxes. These are sites in which buildings are placed only temporarily, whilst still being worked upon.

Second Life: Second Life is an online virtual world which was launched in 2003. According to Linden Labs, in 2014 Second Life had about 1 million regular users. Although in many ways, Second Life is similar to Massively Multiplayer Online Role Playing Games; the world is not a game but rather a builder's world in which users define their own goals and objectives - very much as is also the case in the physical world.

ENDNOTES

[1] The second author of this text is referred to by his avatar name (Eupalinos Ugajin) only. This is due to a sensitivity on behalf of the artist that relates to a separation between Real Life and Second Life personas, and an acknowledgement of the artistic activity generated under the virtual persona which is perceived to be quite distinct and separated from the productions of its Real Life counterpart.

[2] Linden Endowment for the Arts website: http://lea-sl.org/about

[3] https://www.flickr.com/photos/eupalinos/11859647023/in/set-72157637216288526

[4] Description of the project taken from the in-world invitation note that was sent out to participants of the project.

[5] View images of the works mentioned in this quote here: http://www.multiurl.com/l/kzY

6   http://mural.ly/

7   http://www.messynessychic.com/2013/07/26/the-real-life-waterworld-project/

8   https://www.flickr.com/groups/movingislands/

9   http://whale.boxfolio.com/

10   http://zikiquesti.blogspot.com/2014/01/in-belly-of-whale.html.

Chapter 9
Meta_Body:
Virtual Corporeality as a Shared Creative Process

Catarina Carneiro de Sousa
Polytechnic Institute of Viseu, Portugal

ABSTRACT

This chapter discusses the Meta_Body participatory art project. Initiated in a collaborative virtual environment and in a "real life" art exhibition, it now continues in the metaverse creative flux. Meta_Body focuses on two aspects: first, the avatar as body/language, open to experimentation and potency; second, avatar building as a shared creative process and as aesthetical experience. Through the practice of avatar creation, distribution, embodiment and transformation, the artists aim to understand the processes of virtual corporeality constitution: to question the role of the body in virtual environment, its importance in engaging with the world and in self-expression, and explore its metaphorical aspects. The method used to implement this project is a shared creative process, in which multiple subjects come to be authors along different phases of the project. Through the embodiment and transformation of avatars, the artwork's aesthetical experience becomes a creative process.

INTRODUCTION

Meta_Body is an ongoing project initiated in 2011 by the duo Meilo Minotaur (Sameiro Oliveira Martins)[1] and CapCat Ragu (Catarina Carneiro de Sousa) in the Second Life (SL) virtual environment platform, in the Delicatessen region[2][3]. Initially, this project consisted of a set of eighteen avatars[4], distributed in a virtual installation[5], which were free, copyable, transformable and sharable. SL residents who got them were invited to share

with us any derivative creation, which resulted from the manipulation of these avatars. These manipulations were first presented in the form of machinima[6] and virtual photography[7] and in a second phase of the project as derivative avatars.

As an art-based research project, *Meta_Body* can be considered both a practice based and practice oriented research, since its theoretical framework informs but is also informed by artistic practices carried out in the virtual world. This project is focused on two aspects — the avatar

DOI: 10.4018/978-1-4666-8384-6.ch009

as body/language, open to experimentation and potency, and avatar building as a shared creative process and aesthetical experience.

Through avatar creation, distribution, embodiment and transformation, the artists aimed to understand the processes of virtual corporeality constitution: to question the role of the body in virtual environment, its importance in engaging with the world and in self-expression.

The project is conducted mainly in SL's collaborative virtual environment, but has also been displayed in "real life" contemporary art exhibitions. The actualization of the project varies in each context, but it is never possible to cover all aspects of the project in an exhibition, since its interactive and participatory dimensions can only be experienced in a virtual environment. As an artwork, *Meta_Body* can be experienced in many different ways, as we will discuss later, but the embodiment and transformation of the avatars may turn the aesthetical experience of the work into a creative process. This is why the avatars were distributed not only for free, but also transformable, copyable and transferable, giving full freedom of use to the participants.

The method used to implement this project is therefore a shared creative process, in which multiple subjects can be regarded as authors along different phases of the project and where some of these individuals can switch between users and producers of materials distributed, making them produsers (Bruns, 2007), as we will describe later. We present three different approaches to the concept of shared creativity: the first, collective creation, is the process used by Meilo Minotaur and CapCat Ragu in the construction of avatars and virtual installations, a cell group acting as a single author, in a very intimate form of creative process; the second, distributed creation, is how derivative work was created using the first set of avatars to build new creations which, in turn, fueled a reserve of materials available for the realization of new creations; and the third, collaborative

creation, is a process in which each artist retains her personal mark in a creative dialogue with others — as was the case with Takio Ra (Luís Eustáquio), who contributed to the project by creating "soundscapes"[8] for the virtual installations, as we shall see ahead (Sousa, 2013, 2014).

BACKGROUND

The project began as a response to the invitation to participate in the contemporary art exhibition *All My Independent Women* (AMWI), an event curated by Carla Cruz, a contemporary Portuguese artist and curator, interested in gender and the democratization of art. AMIW takes place irregularly across the world, based on a network of artists who address gender issues through their work. Its 6th edition, subtitled *Or Rather, What Can Words Do?*, was held at Vienna in 2011.

Meilo Minotaur and CapCat Ragu had already participated in 2010's 5th edition with SL based work. That edition revolved around the *Novas Cartas Portuguesas/New Portuguese Letters* by Maria Isabel Barreno, Maria Teresa Horta and Maria Velho da Costa, an important Portuguese feminist book from 1972, banished by the dictatorship and consequently causing the political persecution of its authors. The 6th edition was an extension on this theme.

In its 1980 edition, *Novas Cartas Portuguesas/ New Portuguese Letters* was prefaced by Maria de Lourdes Pintasilgo, a Portuguese politician who was the only woman prime minister in Portugal, from 1979 to 1980. She stressed the way the body operated in the book: going beyond its representation and working as a metaphor for all forms of oppression hidden and not yet overcome. This notion of a metaphorical appropriation of the body was paramount to the *Meta_Body* project. The body has a semiotic aspect that impacts our everyday lives (Pollock, 1996), for when the body is stripped from its physical form, its symbolic dimension becomes prevalent in virtual worlds. The avatar thus becomes a body of language and expression, open to further symbolic investments.

This metaphorical approach to the body is more commonly found in a gender studies context. Working with avatars brought new perspectives to this concept, raising new questions about the body. What can we call "body" in virtual environment? Is the avatar really our virtual body? That prompted a new investigation in the form of the *Meta_Body* project. One main idea was crucial from the beginning: that the virtual experience of the body is not exactly an experience of the flesh. These sensations, albeit having a physical sensorial aspect, continue to be experienced in our bodies behind the screen, not in our avatar body. The virtual body is a metaphorical body, all language; therefore open to experimentation and possibility. These ideas were already in the call for artworks and have been central in several preliminary studies published (Sousa, 2012, 2013, 2014). These originated mainly from practice and direct experience of the world, building and embodying avatars. Most of the research in literature and secondary sources was parallel to practical development.

The research that has been developed can be defined as action research integrating an art-oriented and art-based project, as the theoretical approach informs, but is also informed by practice.

The following alignment of research themes tries to show, in an understandable way, an inquiry into the place of the body in virtual environments, starting with the sense of presence, crucial for embodiment. We follow by delving into what constitutes a virtual body, finally returning to our initial claim of the avatar as a metaphorical body.

PRESENCE

When referring to virtual worlds, one needs to address the problem of "presence" in those environments. There is a widely spread definition of presence as "the sense of being there". American experience designer Carrie Heeter refers to it as a "feeling like you exist" (Heeter, 1992, p. 2). Frank Biocca, director of the networked Media Interface and Network Design (M.I.N.D.) Lab, also describes it as a "compelling sense of being in a mediated space other than where [the] physical body is located" (Biocca 1997, p. 18). He highlights that presence is a basic state of consciousness (Biocca, 1997, p. 20), although he relates it mostly to distal attribution or externalization—the perceptual sense of a world around us, other than our selves. This notion is shared by the media researcher Jonathan Steuer who defines it as "the sense of being in an environment" (Steuer, 1993, p. 6). In his studies on telepresence, Steuer (1993) seems to focus mainly on "immersion". He divides it into "vividness" and "interactivity". The author defines vividness as "the ability of a technology to produce a sensorially rich mediated environment" (p. 10). Vividness depends on "breadth" (number of sensory channels stimulated) and "depth" (resolution of each of the channels). Although depth has been progressively increasing in the last few years, desktop virtual environments like SL are actually low on breadth; only the visual and auditory channels are stimulated.

The focus of presence studies on mediation, in psychology researchers Wijnand A. Ijsselsteijn and Giuseppe Riva's opinion, diverted the notion from its core—presence is not necessarilly conected to technology, it is "a product of the mind" (Ijsselsteijn & Riva, 2003, p. 5). This point was particularly stressed by Biocca's later studies, where he criticises the fact that research on presence tends to assume that "the primary causes of psychological presence are the immersive properties of technology" (Biocca, 2003, p. 3). He actually advances the possibility of a total internal sense of presence (in dream states, for instance). The main issue seems to be whether or not presence needs actual sensory input, or on the contrary, it can be achieved with little to no real sensory engagement.

This means that for this author, presence is not only the subject's "sense of being there", but also the social perception of the subject. For Ijsselsteijn and Riva (2003) one of the main problems in establishing a stable concept of presence could be the generalized misconception about the notions of immersion and presence. While the first is focused on environmental presence, the latter depends on social and cultural aspects. Thus distinguishing between the immersive and social components of presence is an important element for clarifying the concept.

The difference between presence and immersion is particularly important when addressing desktop virtual environments like SL. Virtual worlds anthropologist Tom Boellstorff (2010) even states, "this notion of immersion does not accurately characterize the dominant cultural logics at play in Second Life" (p. 112). Boellstorff advocates the possibility that in SL there could be a "presence without immersion", especially in "away from keyboard"(AFK) states, where the avatar is present in the virtual world but the user is absent (Boellstorff, 2010, p.112). This avatar can even be interacting with others, if it is being animated, e.g. it can continue to dance in a party or club while its user is away having dinner.

Social presence and co-presence, in fact, do not depend as much on this notion of immersion as they do on social and cultural aspects, considered central by Ijsselsteijn and Riva (2003). These authors understand that the first is focused on environmental presence, while in the other social and cultural aspects are crucial. For these authors there are three main elements that promote the sense of presence: the possibility of "action", a "cultural framework" and the "negotiation" of both action and its meaning (that links the previous ones). The possibility of action depends on the affordances of the medium and on what the user needs to do to explore them. The authors highlight that these affordances are not always self evident to users, requiring knowledge and the will to explore them. In a shared environment, this implies a common

ground of references and rules, a cultural framework. In collaborative activities it is also crucial that the actions of a user are perceived by other participants (as corroborated by Heeter (1992) in her description of "social presence"), only in this way can one have interaction between users, a kind of interaction that implies negotiation. SL residents have various possibilities of acting upon the world: they can chat in a window available to everyone in the same region, in specific groups, or in private windows with other avatars that can even be in different regions; they can speak, using voice input; they can build objects, and their actions will be perceived by others; and they can transform and animate their avatars in many different ways, as we shall see, that will also be perceived by others.

Sensory inputs may not be the primordial aspects in the enhancement of presence in virtual worlds such as SL (Pearce, 2009, p. 122). But if the social and cultural aspects are prevalent, is the body completely absent in these environments? How does the body connect to the avatar and what is its role in this feeling of presence?

Virtual Body

French philosopher Pierre Lévy states that the word "virtual" refers to "potential rather than actual existence" (Lévy, 1998, p. 23). Lévy draws on Gilles Deleuze and Félix Guattari's definition of virtual as the difference between actual and potential existence, corroborated by Brian Massumi (1992, p. 35) (see also key term "virtual"). Thus, for this author, the term virtual doesn't oppose the term real, but the term actual. While the real is the materialization of the possible, the actual is an answer to the virtual. This means that actualization implies a solution to a problem, "a solution not previously contained in its formulation" (Lévy, 1998, p. 25). The author then considers virtualization to be the reverse movement of actualization:

The virtualization of a given entity consists in determining the general question to which it responds, in mutating the entity in the direction of this question and redefining the initial actuality as the response to a specific question. (Lévy, 1998, p.26)

In this sense, a good part of art has long been about virtualization, as it tends to problematize concepts, conventions, and even ideologies.

Lévy sees the virtualization of the body not as disembodiment, but as a form of "re-creation" and "reincarnation" (Lévy, 1998, p. 44). This includes the impact of television on human perception, telepresence, the use of imaging technology (radiography, ultrasound, etc), transfusion, transplants, plastic surgery, bodybuilding and even extreme sports (Lévy, 1998, pp. 37-44). Here we will naturally focus on the digital virtualization of the body through the use of avatars in collaborative virtual environments. This virtual body does not oppose the real body but the actual body, it questions and problematizes it. It is not a possible body, but a potential and complex one.

Biocca tried to understand this complexity when he studied bodily presence in virtual environments. Biocca's research led him to believe that the always-unstable phenomenal body could be radically altered by the use of media:

The social role of the avatar body is partially determined, but not defined, by its geometry and kinematics. Implicit and explicit social norms that may be partially idiosyncratic to the virtual environment and imported from the user's social environment finalize the social-semiotic role and identity of the avatar. Issues of class, gender, occupational role, body type, etc. are raised when considering this aspect of embodiment. (Biocca, 1997, p. 23)

Communication researchers Nick Yee, and Jeremy N. Bailenson, with computer scientist

Nicola Ducheneaut (2009) developed a research about the embodiment of avatars and its effects beyond the virtual worlds. They called their findings the Proteus Effect, and it seems to corroborate this perspective. The authors demonstrated that a subject's behaviour could change according to the avatar's body constitution, e.g. taller avatars perform better in negotiating with shorter avatars, with this effect persisting in offline interactions.

Mike Molesworth and Janice Denegri-Knott, in their research about consumer imagination and digital play, argue that virtual worlds can be considered virtual world can be seen as "liminoid" spaces. They use Victor Turner's definition "of a liminoid as a place of inversion for the purpose of transformation" (Molesworth & Denegri-Knott, 2007, p. 116), and draw from Rob Shields perspective:

Like liminal zones and events, virtual spaces are 'liminoid' in that they are participated in on a temporary basis, and distinguished from some notion of commonplace 'everyday life'. [...] The greatest power of digital virtuality – and perhaps its most widely discussed feature – has been in providing a matrix in which new modes of being and practices of becoming could be experimented with. (Shields, 2003, p. 13)

Pre-modern societies used ritual performances and spaces to mark moments of transition, e.g. the beginning of adulthood or marriage. Turner called these spaces "liminal", as their function was to maintain social structure in moments of change (Molesworth & Denegri-Knott, 2007, p. 121). In post-modern society, on the other hand, liminal was replaced by the less structured liminoid:

The liminoid differs from the liminal in that it is freer: more an outcome of choice and participation. In pre-modern societies, the liminal was an obligation; in modern times, the liminoid is a matter of free will. The liminoid is observed

as moments of individual change or disorder, although the aggregate impact of many individual transformations may result in changes to society as new practices and ideas are generated [...] (Molesworth & Denegri-Knott, 2007, p. 121)

In liminal events social norms are suspended, opening a space for transformation of the social order and offering a breach for cultural metamorphosis (Shields, 2003, p. 12). The embodiment and transformation of avatars can be seen as an event of this kind, both socially and individually. When manipulating avatars, users can experience a shift from social, economical and physical constraints they might have in their everyday life. In many virtual environments, e.g. videogames, however, this embodiment can be restricted to the characters of a particular narrative or aesthetical model, but in the specific case of SL avatars, customization goes further. The platform offers a wide range of possibilities, the avatar shape can be greatly transformed by the use of the interface, through sliders that allow both macro and micro changes in the avatar's anatomy. In addition, SL allows the user to upload several kinds of content that can be used to build the avatar, e.g. image files for skin, eyes, hair and clothes, 3D models that can be attached to it or even replace it[9]. Transparency layers can be used to hide parts or the entire avatar's body, making invisible or fragmented bodies possible. Animations and sounds can also be uploaded and associated with the avatar, contributing to its expressiveness. Unlike the use of interface sliders, the creation of items outside the platform requires special skills to handle particular software. However, SL artists and designers often share or sell these items, allowing any other residents to extensively modify their avatars. The transformative potential of the SL avatar is enormous, making this platform ideal for liminoid experimentations with the virtual body. Users can experience gender swap, being animals, being younger or older, ethnical change or being a completely fantasy character. They can engage in

activities that they otherwise cannot, because of physical constraint, or will not, because of social constraint, in their everyday lives.

But can these experiences be considered body experiences in any way? Performance, media and communication researcher Maeva Veerapen studied the constitution of a phenomenal body in the collaborative virtual environment of Second Life. She refers to the co-existence of two bodies in these environments—the user's organic body and the avatar graphic body. Between these two, controlled by a single subject, a phenomenal body emerges. The author proposes four conceptions of the avatar: the avatar as an object, the avatar as prosthesis, the avatar as a phantom limb and the avatar as an equal.

The avatar as an object is the complete alterity of the avatar—it does not constitute a part of one's self. In this conception the avatar becomes instrumental in virtual worlds, it is an object manipulated by the user in the virtual environment. However, this is an object that allows the user to perform an identity, like a clothing item (Veerapen, 2011, p. 89).

As prosthesis, the avatar turns into more than an object, it acts as an augmentation of the potential of the phenomenal body; it extends the frontier of the user's body into the virtual world, which thus becomes accessible to the user (Veerapen, 2011, p. 90).

The conception of the avatar as a phantom limb adds an emotional dimension to the experience of the body in virtual environments, which goes beyond the prosthetic extension:

The phantom limb differs from the prosthesis because it does not extend the body schema but instead it is a quasi-present body part of the person who feels sensations through it as well as attempts to act in the world with it. (Veerapen, 2011, p. 91)

Phantom limb sensations have long been reported by amputees (Price, 2006), however the avatar never was an actual part of the user's physical body. Still, the use of avatars can trigger sensations that are not prompted by direct physical stimulation. Veerapen accounts that she almost smelled the bamboo when her avatar visited a virtual kabuki theatre. This is consistent with JesseFox, Jeremy N. Bailenson and Joseph Binney's findings of satiety in those who observe their avatar eating in virtual environments (Fox, Bailenson, & Binney, 2009).

During her experience in the virtual world, the user's organic body loses the ability to perform some of the tasks of a phenomenal body, because it does not directly access the world. It is the avatar's body that reaches into the virtual environment. On the other hand, the avatar's body is deprived of sensorial and perceptual abilities. Only between these two bodies is it possible to establish a phenomenal body. The conception of the avatar as equal requires the symbiosis of these two bodies (Veerapen, 2011, p. 92).

Embodiment in virtual worlds juxtaposes two bodies and two conceptions of materiality, co-dependent to form an entity.

Why does the physical body establish this link with the avatar? We will argue that this link can be enhanced by the avatar body's metaphorical nature.

Metaphorical Body

Our bodily experiences and metaphors seem to considerably affect the way we conceive not only the virtual world, but also the world in general. The linguist George Lakoff and the philosopher Mark Johnson argue that reason is not extra-corporeal, but rather born of the very nature of our brains, our bodies and our bodily experience. The mind is thus deeply embodied and reason, coming from the body, does not transcend it (Lakoff & Johnson, 1999, pp. 4-5). The authors not only question the mind/body dichotomy, but the conceptual/perceptual system dichotomy too, claiming "concepts are created as a result of the way the brain and body are structured and the way they function in interpersonal relations and in the

physical world" (Lakoff & Johnson, 1999, p. 37). Thus, they consider that complex thinking is only possible using the sensorimotor and perceptual domains metaphorically. The conceptual metaphors are common to thought and language—it becomes difficult or even impossible to describe complex concepts, such as love, without resorting to metaphor (Lakoff & Johnson, 1999, p. 45). For the authors, the ordinary conceptual system is fundamentally metaphorical—the way we think, what we experience and what we do every day is a matter of metaphor. A significant part of our concepts is organized in terms of spatial metaphors: up / down, in / out, forward / backward. "I feel down", "cheer up", "he is out of reach", "she is in love", "I look forward to meet you". These metaphors are rooted deeply in our physical and cultural experience of the body and became embedded in our language (Lakoff & Johnson, 1999).

Metaphors are also paramount to the way we handle computers—we "drag" items from one "window" to another or to our "desktop", we archive data in "folders" or send them to the "trash". In fact we are just providing commands to the computer, but we experience them through simulations. These are conceived in a metaphorical way that is fundamental in the design of digital interaction, states the interaction designer and digital narrative researcher Janet Murray (2012).

For these simulations to be effective and interaction to be intuitive, users need to understand these metaphors quickly. For that to occur Murray argues that the user needs to recognize "mental models", based on appearance and behaviour of objects they know and handle daily. "Mental models can derive from existing conventions and past experience. For example, we expect wall switches to turn on overhead lights" (Murray, 2012, p. 59). She draws from Donald A. Norman's idea of "conceptual models", but for this author the model doesn't form solely from convention and past experience. As a cognitive science, design and usability researcher Norman states that we find clues in objects' visible structure for how they work, because we understand how our bodies will interact with them. "A good conceptual model allows us to predict the effects of our actions" (Norman, 1998, p. 13). This means that even if we never used a pair of scissors before we will know how to use them. This happens because of the limited options our body has to interact with them (Norman, 1998, p. 12). Norman thinks of objects and Murray of digital medium in terms of "affordances", basically what objects and media are for and how we perceive those affordances and draw from them. But what about body/virtual body affordances? Are they similar? How do we perceive and draw from them?

Consider hands: they are primarily for manipulating objects, but we use them in a lot of different ways: for touching and petting, for sensing texture and temperature, to gesture and communicate, etc. Can we afford to do that with our digital hands on a virtual world? Depending on the platform our avatar hands will have different affordances, in a fighting video game they probably will afford punching, and in a car, driving. But are we actually driving and punching with our avatar hands in a video game? Motion sensing input devices can synchronize our body with our avatar's body and make its hands do what our hands are doing, but it is still our physical hands doing it, represented visually on screen by images of our avatar's hands. The same can happen without motion sensors when we make our avatar do things with computer commands. Just like when "dragging" an item to the "trash", it is metaphorical. We can move our avatar as a puppet through a motion sensor or with a joystick, or simply using the arrows on our computer's keyboard—in any case, the affordances of our virtual body will be determined by the program and dependant of our physical bodies. The way we manipulate what the program affords will be perceived by us, on screen, as a metaphor. That is the main affordance of the avatar, to make our actions in the program visible, and it does that by using metaphors. We command our avatar to walk by pressing a key, and its legs will move in a way probably similar to walking, but the avatar does not need its legs to move (Pacman did fine without them). It is the program's code that makes it look as if the avatar is walking, not the graphics of its legs. Usually in online virtual worlds, avatars can fly. There seems to be no need for stairs, yet we find them very often. Virtual stairs become a sign—they indicate that there is a floor above and a path to get there, and communicate visually by engaging with our bodily experience in a metaphorical way. We cannot perceive virtual worlds by reading them from code lines. We need these metaphors not only to engage a virtual environment but also to actually conceive it.

THE *META_BODY* PROJECT

Project Description

As stated, *Meta_Body* is an ongoing project initiated by Meilo Minotaur and CapCat Ragu in SL's collaborative virtual environment. It started in 2011, prompted by the AMIW exhibition, but its development extends far beyond the physical and temporal limits of the show.

Even though this is a fluid ongoing artwork, with processual participation, one can distinguish two different phases of the project. The first, we shall call it Phase I, was directly related with the AMIW exhibition and involved the distribution of 18 original avatars by Meilo and CapCat in SL, and the subsequent call for derivative artworks in the form of machinimas and virtual photography. Phase II, not directly connected with AMIW, happened entirely online and involved the call for derivative artworks in the form of new avatars; environmental installations were made by Meilo and CapCat for the distribution of these avatars.

Even though this project encompassed calls for artworks in different phases, it shouldn't be seen as a curatorial project, as the focus was not in selection or archival, but rather the triggering of a participatory and creative aesthetical experience.

Phase I

Meta_Body was initiated for the 6th edition of AMIW; this was largely a continuation of the previous edition, which engaged with the collective reading of the NPL, as stated earlier, under the subtitle *Or Rather What Words Can Do?*, a question quoted from the book.

This is a book written by three authors, which takes the form of letters, signed by fictional characters. The authorship of each text is never revealed.

Mariana Alcoforado appears as central subject, a seventeenth century character from another book—*Portuguese Letters*. A nun that writes letters to her lost lover, from a convent in Beja. She arises in this new book as an excuse to dissect a number of issues related to gender and womanhood during the dictatorship in Portugal. In NPL the individual branches and fragments itself. There is a multiplicity of voices in addition to the authors', whom often write on behalf of Mariana, her mother, her sister, her lover, and others.

The impact of this book in Portugal was such that it was immediately apprehended by the censorship and its authors faced charges of affront to public decency and pornography. This became known as the Three Marias process. Only after the April 25th revolution, in 1974, were the authors acquitted and the book made public (Macedo, 2010, p. 56).

In the 1980 edition preface of NPL, Pintasilgo notices an obsessive focus on the materiality of body as a first battlefield for women emancipation. But the body, as the place of denunciation of oppression of women, excels itself, goes beyond mere representation: it "Works as a metaphor for all forms of oppression hidden and not yet due" (Pintasilgo, 2010, p. 6).

It is precisely this idea of a metaphorical body that interested us in *Meta_Body*. We designed

eighteen avatars to distribute with full permissions, i.e. all parts that constituted each avatar (skin, shape and attachments) were open to be transformed, copied and redistributed by all SL residents.

The inspiration for the avatar design came from different places; there were some animalistic avatars, like *Meta-Birds*, two anthropomorphic male and female bird avatars; *Dragonfly*, half human, half insect; *Dinosaur*, with some Jurassic features; *Lizard*, an avatar slightly inspired by the sci-fi series V (1983); and *I see your inside,* not an animal avatar, but animalistic in its appearance, full of eyes all over the body.

There were also some "queen" avatars: *Ice*, the cold queen; *Fog*, the misty queen; *Godiva*, the fragile queen (see Figure 1); and *Silver7*, the queen of burlesque.

Our primary form of relationship with the SL platform was like 'playing with dolls', dressing and undressing, hairstyling and generally changing the avatar (Sousa, 2012, p.138), so some of these avatars were inspired by dolls. In some cases quite literally so, as with *Ragdoll*, that looked like a rag doll. There were also clown doll avatars—*You my inside*, a small doll, with another head in her open chest; and *Pipiua,* a harlequin with a big seventeenth century collar.

The aquatic environment was also an inspiration, with *Aqua* and *River Avatar*. Another two avatars were inspired by Hans Silvester's photography of the tribes of the Omo River in Ethiopia—*Indigo* and *Jungle*. Finally, the two most improbable avatars, with bodies entirely made of net—*Frame Girl* and *Chart Man*.

To distribute these avatars an installation was built in SL, where framed pictures of the avatars hover in the air. There are no walls, as there is no gravity or atmosphere in the virtual environment (Manovich, 1996). By touching each picture the residents receive the avatars, as well as a note inviting them to participate in the project with their derivative work by sharing it with us in *Meta_Body*'s Flickr and Koinup groups[10]. We

Figure 1. Godiva, one of the original Meta_Body avatars
Virtual photography by CapCat Ragu. ©2011, Catarina Carneiro de Sousa.

also informed that a selection of artworks would be made from these groups, to be displayed at the AMIW exhibition in Austria. 120 artworks were selected with 80 SL residents[11] integrating the *Meta_Body* project for AMIW's 6th edition[12].

Our selection tried to be as extensive as possible, and not based on personal taste criteria. We aimed to have a representative sample of different sensibilities and cultures in metaverse art, as well as different ways to approach the original avatars — e.g. in Harbor Galaxy's (Deborah Lombardo) virtual photography *Beneath the Stream* (see Fig-

ure 2), we can see the *River Avatar*, unmodified and maintaining the original avatar's narrative (given solely by its configuration and name). But in the case of *Fog of War,* we can see that Eupalinos Ugajin attached new elements to the *Fog* avatar (see Figure 3), changing its narrative and meaning.

These different approaches also happened in machinimas— e.g. the machinimas by Fuschia Nightfire (Nina Camplin), and SpyVspy Aeon (André Lopes). The first, *Meta_Body Dragonfly*[13], is a very short and simple, yet very poetic machin-

Figure 2. Beneath the Stream, virtual photograph by Harbor Galaxy (Deborah Lombardo)
©2011, Deborah Lombardo. Used with permission.

ima. The second, *Sound Of Colors - Meta_body Experience¹⁴*, is a complex creation, using several avatars and modifications.

In AMIW in Austria these virtual photographs and machinima were looped on two screens.

Phase II

We decided to promote a second phase of this project, *Meta_Body II*, in 2012.

This idea was born out of a chance meeting in the metaverse with Fitch Woodrunner. We recognized in Fitch's avatar *Meta_Body* modified avatar parts, an amazing recombination and transformation. In a private conversation, we congratulated Fitch and regretted that a picture of his avatar had not been submitted in time to be exhibited in

AMIW. Fitch asked us if we intended to make a new distribution of avatars made from the first set. We thought that this would be a great idea and so we started *Meta_Body II,* which featured, among others, Fitch Woodrunner's avatar, *Aquavariel* (see Figure 4).

We then made an open call, using social media networks like Delicatessen's Facebook page, our personal Flickr pages and the Delicatessen blog. We invited SL residents to share their derivative avatars that had the Meta_Body project avatars as a starting point. Any part of Meta_Body avatars could be used, as well as parts built by residents themselves and/or built by other creators, since those items were licensed for copy, redistribution and transformation. All avatars would be provided with full permissions — 22 creators built 26 new

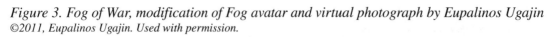

Figure 3. Fog of War, modification of Fog avatar and virtual photograph by Eupalinos Ugajin
©2011, Eupalinos Ugajin. Used with permission.

Figure 4. Aquavariel, avatar by Fitch Woodrunner
Virtual photography by CapCat Ragu. ©2011, Catarina Carneiro de Sousa.

avatars. The variety of participants ranged from renowned metaverse artists and designers to new residents, experiencing the SL platform and avatar building for the first time.

The approach taken by creators also varied. Kikas Babenco, a well known performance artist from SL, recombined and transformed parts of some of the first avatars (*Fog, Aqua, Dragonfly, You see my inside* and *Pipiua*) to build a new character—*Sophia*[15].

Many participants used this approach but also included parts from open avatars from another project where we were involved—the *Kromosomer*

project (Dahlsveen & Sousa, 2013). This was the case of Elia Magnolia (Melania Pereira Ribeiro), a new resident and first time avatar builder, who shared the avatars *Alma Blood* and *Shiverdoll,* and *Suppressed Red Riding Hood* by Mimesis Monday (Heidi Dahlsveen)[16]. The latter is a quite interesting case, first because Mimesis Monday was, in fact, the initiator of the *Kromosomer* project (she commissioned us to create the avatars), but also because the avatar she built was connected to yet another project entirely independent from Meta_Body and Kromosomer — the LRRH - The other side of the story, a new vision of the *Red Rid-*

ing Hood tale, also curated by Mimesis Monday. Fluid and open projects, like *Meta_Body*, invite this sort of rhizomatic connections (Deleuze and Guattari, 1987), heterogenic and non hierarchical relationships, as projects have completely different origins and do not have any dependency between them.

Many creators combined *Meta_Body* parts with their own creations. This was the case of Alpha Auer's (Elif Ayiter) avatar design brand, alpha.

tribe. *Alpha.Tribe*'s *Meta_Body Avatar* combined a skin by alpha.tribe with elements of *Meta_Body* avatars, however these items were so drastically modified that they became almost unrecognizable, revealing the distinct alpha.tribe style[17].

Ragdohcchio (see Figure 5) by Veleda Lorakeet (Christine Romeijn) was a very unique case. Before the submission period was finished, Veleda contacted us asking if we would consider an avatar a derivative, if only the concept of one

Figure 5. Ragdohcchio, avatar by Veleda Lorakeet (Christine Romeijn) and Ragdoll, avatar by Meilo Minotaur and CapCat Ragu. Virtual photography by CapCat Ragu
©2014, Catarina Carneiro de Sousa.

of the *Meta_Body* avatars was used. We were apprehensive but curious, so we decided to consider her avatar. *Ragdohcchio* was conceptually based on *Ragdoll*, but Veleda herself built all its components. *Ragdoll*, a rag doll, was turned into a wooden doll with similar features.

To distribute these avatars, four virtual installations were built in four separate levels, each designed as a tribute to the avatars it housed. For each level, Takio Ra created a particular soundscape, composed of environmental sounds. By varying and replicating sounds over space, Takio managed to circumvent the ten second limitation imposed by SL for sound files, modeling a soundscape that changes when moving the avatar in space, thus creating a more immersive aural experience. These levels we call "stages" are built vertically across the region, far enough from each other so we cannot see one from the other. They become isolated, self-contained, like four completely different regions. Each of them addresses different imaginary imagery, related to their native avatars.

Stage 1 is the level of origin or birth (see Figure 6). It is placed at the region's ground[18] level and is covered in dark water at ankle level. A huge central tree dominates the space, with large cocoons hanging from its naked branches. Wrapped around the trunk of the tree, the residents can follow a tubular transparent path, and a melodic sequence forms as one moves in space. Fallen cocoons become vessels to "travel" in, since it is possible to sit inside them and follow their erratic jumps by the flooded region.

This is the level for avatars with references to animals or plants—insect wings, animal legs, foliage hair, etc.. These are avatars that evoke nature, further away from urban or cultural connotations.

The interior of the cocoons recalls the comfort of a womb or nest. Inside we find the chrysalis of the avatars, a 3D model that represents a fetal shape, textured with the image of each avatar distributed. When touched they give the residents the avatar, in which they can immediately transform. Some of these cocoons, instead of the chrysalis,

Figure 6. Stage 1. Virtual photography by CapCat Ragu
©2014, Catarina Carneiro de Sousa.

are parasitized by strange insects, and therefore sterile. There are indeed several repulsive critters in the water too, whose bodies throb and sound like an internal organ.

Stage 2 is for "lace and frills", avatars inspired by Renaissance or Baroque apparel - puffed long skirts, big lacy collars, etc.; so we decided to use antique theater setting models as inspiration to create various types of illusion of motion or depth. The scenic structures and mechanisms of XVI and XVII centuries can be adapted to the operating logic of the three-dimensional virtual environments, giving the same visual effects. The manipulation of primitive objects[19], through freely available scripts[20], can be very similar to the traditional mechanical stage machines—e.g. using rotation scripts in several twisted cylinders, mimicking XVII century stage design by the architect Nicola Sabbatini's system to create the impression of ocean waves (Campbell, 2013, p.156). Another case is the use of the illusion of depth through the effect of trompe l'oeil, achieved with the accumu-

lation of plans depicting decreasing architectural arches, creating the illusion of perspective and extending the space, complemented by a ramp floor textured with an perspective image of tiles, reinforcing the illusion of depth, based on studies of the XVI century architect Sebastiano Serlio (Mullin, 1970, pp.14 - 15).

The other inspiration for this stage was the complexity of metaverse curatorial processes. The simulation of conventional museum and art galleries space, with pictures hanging on the wall, although the most common on SL art exhibitions, is a subject of constant controversy in the SL art world. Many question the relevance of this approach, which is accused of not exploring the specificity of the virtual environment medium.

This level intentionally and precisely simulates a conservative museum environment, where the whole range of rooms becomes overwhelming for its disproportionately large dimensions, in relation to the average avatar's size (see Figure 7). The "paintings hanging on the walls", however,

Figure 7. Stage 2. Virtual photography by CapCat Ragu
©2014, Catarina Carneiro de Sousa.

are not two-dimensional—three-dimensional constructions are framed, creating the illusion of a two-dimensional image, which breaks with the change in viewpoint of the avatar, that could at any moment reveal the illusion by a simple twist of the SL camera[21]. Each of these framed dioramas also had a specific sound scheme associated with them.

Stage 3 houses "steampunk" avatars, one of the most cultivated genres in SL. This is a "retrofuturistic" trend, i.e. a mix of elements from the past with futuristic technology, exploring the limits and tensions between rationality and alienation from the advances of technology (Pegoraro, 2012, p. 393).

This installation depicts a machine city that coexists with its idealized reflection—the same city but reversed and with some differences. The most important difference is the fact that the ideal city is freed from cage structures that trap houses in its pragmatic counterpart. It is the utopian part of the machine that keeps the city functioning, but not very effectively—it cannot keep the bird planes from crashing into buildings or robot monkeys from being trapped in them (see Figure 8).

The entire city was built as derivative work. Parts of Ggabriel Madruga's avatars, *Wind Girl* and *Steam Boy*, were used in modified scales to build the city's machines. Metallic textures de-

Figure 8. Stage 3. Virtual photography by CapCat Ragu
©2014, Catarina Carneiro de Sousa.

signed and marketed by Sextan Shepherd were also used, as well as Galatic Baroque's blue houses and Aley's glazed structures, both reinvented to build this floating city.

The sound for this stage had a more industrial connotation, evoking turning gears, pressured steam and creaking metal.

This level was invited to be a part of the exhibition *Intermundos @ Metaverse: Virtual Biennale*, curated by Celeste Cerqueira and Silvestre Pestana for the *17th Cerveira Biennial*, in 2013, Portugal. In this event, the mechanic bird and monkey that appear in the building were distributed as avatars.

Stage 4 was designed for the most disembodied and ethereal avatars. For these we wanted to build a more mystical level, however we are not religious or even particularly mystical persons. Thus, we turn to the only religion we could understand—Pastafarianism. According to its followers, the Church of the Flying Spaghetti Monster has existed in secret for hundreds of years, but only

became public when Bobby Henderson wrote an open letter to the Kansas School Board. In this document Henderson demanded that the theory of the Flying Spaghetti Monster were taught to the students along with the Theory of Intelligent Design and Evolution. He claimed that "a Flying Spaghetti Monster created the universe", and the "overwhelming scientific evidence pointing towards evolutionary processes is nothing but a coincidence, put in place by Him" (Henderson, 2005). This ironical religion became a cyberculture symbol of protest against the advancement of creationism in U.S.A. schools.

We built a dark starry level, in black and white only, presided by a gigantic Flying Spaghetti Monster, surrounded by glowing white trees and melancholic sounds (see Figure 9). Revolving around the divine creature one can find the Celestial Teapot, and even "catch" it and take a ride on it[22]. This is a direct reference to British philosopher Bertrand Russell's 1952 article *Is there a God?*,

Figure 9. Stage 4. Virtual photography by CapCat Ragu
©2014, Catarina Carneiro de Sousa.

commissioned but not published by *Illustrated Magazine*. The article highlighted that the burden of proof lies upon she who defends a particular idea. For that he gave an example:

Many orthodox people speak as though it were the business of skeptics to disprove received dogmas rather than of dogmatists to prove them. This is, of course, a mistake. If I were to suggest that between the Earth and Mars there is a china teapot revolving about the sun in an elliptical orbit, nobody would be able to disprove my assertion provided I were careful to add that the teapot is too small to be revealed even by our most powerful telescopes. But if I were to go on to say that, since my assertion cannot be disproved, it is intolerable presumption on the part of human reason to doubt it, I should rightly be thought to be talking nonsense. (Russell, 1997, pp. 547-548)

Russell's teapot became known as the Celestial Teapot, that now orbits the Flying Spaghetti Monster in our mystical Stage 4, whistling in Morse code: "I have been touched by His noodly appendage", citing Arne Niklas Jansson parody image *Touched by His Noodly Appendage,* a recreation of Michelangelo's *The Creation of Adam*, with the Flying Spaghetti Monster in the place of God.

SHARED CREATIVITY

This project is based on a creative process we call shared creativity, i.e. the creative input of Meta_Body, as an artwork, is distributed by several creators, integrating this process in different times, places and in different approaches, creating a fluid creative stream that escapes the control of the project initiators.

It is important, however, not to confuse creative process with group organization. Many of this project's participants are not organized as a group at all, and yet they contribute creatively to a project that would not exist without them. One can think

of *Meta_Body* as a typical cyberculture artwork that resists what Pierre LŸvy calls "totalization", i.e. "the closure of meaning", by "intention", i.e. a stable author or by "extention", i.e. a stable final fixed form (LŸvy, 2001). Meaning, form and authorship are always unstable throughout the several moments of actualization of the project, which can happen as the simple embodiment of the avatars or a stroll through the installations, but can also be a virtual photograph, a machinima, a performance, a new avatar, a narrative, a sound work, an installation, etc..

Bits shared through *Meta_Body* can, in fact, be used in entirely new projects, e.g. this happens with Takio's sounds, that were used by Eupalinos Ugajin in his project *Moving Islands,* or with some of the *Meta_Body* avatars, used by Ervare Farroretre (Reiner Schneeberger) in his project *The Volcano of Art.*

One can distinguish three different ways in which shared creativity may occur — "collective creation", "distributed creation", and "collaborative creation". Any of these processes can inevitably be defined as collaboration in the generic sense of the term, however there are different ways to create together.

In this sense, collective creation would be the creative process that is undertaken by more than one creator acting as a single author. Creative input happens collectively, synchronously or asynchronously. All participants are equal partners in credit and responsibility, and each contribution is largely indiscernible. This kind of creative process requires a high level of intimacy between co-creators and is very difficult to achieve in large and even medium size groups, as it usually requires a cellular structure in order to be successful (CAE, 2002). It depends on complete openness—to share goals, motivations, inspirations, but also uncertainties, fears, etc.. It is very important that each co-creator feels comfortable in stating whatever is on her mind without fearing for the future of the relationship. Not only a high level of mutual artistic respect is necessary but also, in fact, full trust.

This almost symbiotic process is very rewarding, but it is also very demanding and requires a very strong emotional bond between the co-creators. This was the preferred creative process used by the project initiators, Meilo Minotaur and CapCat Ragu. Being mother and daughter facilitates this kind of relation, dependent on unconditional trust.

The term distributed authorship was coined by British artist and theorist Roy Ascott in 1986 to describe the interactive and remote authoring project *La Plissure du Texte: A Planetary Fairytale* (LPDT), which had been created in 1983, long before the existence of virtual worlds (Ascott, 2005). Recently the term has been used by New Media and Creative Industries researcher Axel Bruns (2010) to refer to a creative process that has been intensified by the Internet's affordances. We are talking about projects in which a large number of participants contribute to a common pool of artistic material. These, however, do not act as a team, but as single contributors in each step of this creative process, which can be called distributed creation.

Bruns refers to these participants as "produsers", individuals who shift their position towards a project from users to producers and vice-versa, sometimes using the pool material, sometimes feeding the pool. The participatory aspect of *Meta_Body* required this kind of engagement from its participants, i.e. the use of the project avatars to make a new machinima, which would in turn integrate the project as well. This kind of creation leads to a metamorphic, fluid artwork, without a stable finished form.

Finally, parts of this project were built using what we can call a collaborative creation. The term collaboration has been used to describe all kinds of creative methods involving more than one person (Lind, 2007, p. 17). When we refer to collaborative creation we do not aim to address that vast term "collaboration", but to describe a shared creative process that differs from the previous ones. In this case each participant maintains her own authorial mark, but the limits or borders of each work are difficult to determine. This type of creation often happens as a dialogue between authors—each creation is a response to another creation. Meilo Minotaur and CapCat Ragu sometimes use this creative process, along with the collective creation (although always co-signing all works), but this process is especially useful to describe the way the duo worked with Takio Ra in building the virtual installations for *Meta_Body II*. As described, Takio Ra is the creator of these installations' soundscapes. Even if his work did not change any of the visual aspects of the work, which remained untouched, it radically altered the perception of space and became a key part of the project's design. The sounds used are also being distributed with full permissions, feeding the distributed creation branch.

Participatory Aesthetical Experience

Researchers and management consultants for arts and culture Jennifer L. Novak-Leonard and Alan S. Brown noticed that the term "arts participation" is too often interpreted as "art attendance"; however, there are multiple modes of engagement with art, that include but also go beyond attendance (Novak-Leonard & Brown, 2011, p. 26). They proposed a five mode framework to describe these several forms of participation: inventive participation, interpretative participation, curatorial participation, observational participation, and ambient participation. They depict a gradation of creative control—from total in inventive participation, to very little in ambient participation (Novak-Leonard & Brown, 2011, p. 32).

1. Inventive Participation engages the mind, body, and spirit in an act of artistic creation that is unique and idiosyncratic, regardless of skill level (e.g., composing music, writing original poetry, painting).
2. Interpretive Participation is a creative act of self-expression that brings alive and adds value to pre-existing works of art, either

individually or collaboratively, or engages one in arts learning (e.g., playing in a band, learning to dance).

3. Curatorial Participation is the creative act of purposefully selecting, organizing, and collecting art to the satisfaction of one's own artistic sensibility (e.g., collecting art, downloading music, and burning CDs).

4. Observational Participation occurs when you see or hear arts programs or works of art created, curated, or performed by other people (e.g., attending live performances, visiting art museums). We define two sub-types of observational participation: 1) participation in live events, and 2) electronic media-based participation.

5. Ambient Participation includes encounters with art that the participant does not select (e.g., seeing architecture and public art, hearing music in a store). (Novak-Leonard & Brown, 2011, p. 32)

The project *Meta_Body* can be said to prompt the all five modes of art participation. The simple unexpected visit to the region, or the encounter with photography or machinima in social media would be ambient participation, mode five. Observational participation for those who willing visit the region or exhibitions, type 2) in the first case, type 1) in the second. The curatorial participation could be understood in more in a formal way (e.g. Carla Cruz curatorial work for AMIW) or in an informal one (e.g. personal galleries made on Flickr, personal posts on social media, private collections of the avatars in the metaverse, etc.). Interpretative participation in the embodiment of the avatars. Finally, inventive participation in all the shared creative forms: collective, by Meilo Minotaur and CapCat Ragu; distributed, by all the produsers; and collaborative, by Meilo Minotaur, CapCat Ragu and Takio Ra.

This last mode is the one that makes it possible to refer to the *Meta_Body* project as participatory aesthetical experience.

Art historian and critic Claire Bishop (2012) connects participatory art to the desire to challenge the traditional status of art object, artist and audience; claiming that in this kind of artistic approach:

[T]he artist is conceived less as an individual producer of discrete objects than as a collaborator and producer of situations; the work of art as a finite, portable, commodifiable product is reconceived as an ongoing or long- term project with an unclear beginning and end; while the audience, previously conceived as a 'viewer' or 'beholder', is now repositioned as a co-producer or participant. (Bishop, 2012, p. 2)

Even though we can establish a beginning of a sort in the *Meta_Body* project—the moment when Meilo Minotaur and CapCat Ragu decided to make the avatars—we can also identify several "new beginnings": the two calls for artworks, or the opening of *Meta_Body II*. An end, however, is impossible to establish—even when the SL region closes or is rebuilt, the avatars will continue to exist and fuel new artworks.

Bishop (2006) also identified three major concerns in participatory art—"activation", "authorship" and "community".

Activation implies that aesthetical experiences contribute to the empowerment of an active subject (Bishop, 2006, p. 12). In the *Meta_Body* project we addressed this concern by using embodiment as a trigger for becoming, questioning the body through virtualization. Stressing the interlacement between flesh body and avatar body, we tried to open paths for rethinking the body and self-consciousness. The simple act of embodying an avatar, as demonstrated before, is problematic and asks for a resolution, which does not lie in pre-given answers by avatar designers, but in the users' creative appropriation of this new body. By providing all avatar parts with full permissions, we opened them to radical creative experimental transformation, empowering participants to take control of a metaphorical body, open to be invested with new meanings.

Authorship, or more specifically, relinquish of authorial control is the second concern referred by Bishop (2006, p. 12) with respect to participatory art. As demonstrated, this project questioned a stable individual authorship in several ways, but one picture can illustrate the way authorship is problematic in *Meta_Body*—Tim Deschanel's virtual photograph of Eupalinos Ugajin's avatar[23]. The picture depicts a transformation of one of the avatars, embodied and created by Eupalinos Ugajin and photographed by Tim Deschanel. This presents us with several questions about authorship, originality, creative process and even the concept of artwork. What is the artwork? The original avatar? The avatar rebuilt by Eupalinos Ugajin? The photograph by Tim Deschanel? The Meta_Body project with a distributed authorship? Or can we consider several creative/artistic moments that can be regarded either in isolation or integrated into the overall project?

The third concern is community, or the crisis of common responsibility (Bishop, 2006, p. 12). The artifacts distributed in the *Meta_Body* project were open, not only to transformation, but also to be copied and redistributed. These items can be considered a new kind of common property "different from private property or public (state) property" (Bauwens, 2006, p. 1). By creating common property and encouraging produsage, *Meta_Body* addressed the issue of common responsibility within the SL community.

This leads us to conclude that one can refer to the *Meta_Body* project as a participatory aesthetical experience. However, this project did not only rely on produsers' participation, in fact, it depended on their creative input and output. Participation exceeded mere interaction, it demanded creativity from produsers. This leads us to believe that, in this project, aesthetical experience and creative process may overlap.

CONCLUSION

In her doctoral dissertation, Portuguese anthropologist Paula Justiça referenced that it was her experience of the project Meta_Body that led her to change her hypothesis that virtual communication could annul the physical and real body. She concluded that it was not the body that was cancelled in SL, but it is only the flesh that can not go into the screen and is replaced, and we might add, complemented by the avatar (Justiça, 2013, pp. 270-271). The metaphorical nature of this digital body makes it an open space to invest with new meanings.

Project Meta_Body had two major concerns: on one hand the constitution of virtual corporeality in the metaverse; on the other, the participatory nature of this process.

Any creation and development of avatars in SL is a shared creative process. There is always a balance between what the platform (hence its creators) can provide and what the residents create with it. The possibility of customization of the avatar, by using only the SL interface and its affordances, is already quite vast. To this we can add the possibility of uploading materials developed using other software. The users become designers of themselves in this virtual world. But residents can also share what they create with other users, and this makes the constitution of corporeality in collaborative virtual worlds a shared creative process.

Residents are free to invent, reinvent and multiply themselves in any way they can imagine. Some choose to create a virtual representation of their flesh bodies, or an improved version of themselves, while others prefer an idealized body of youth and beauty. Some try to maintain a stable, fixed identity, while others are shape shifters, disassembling and reassembling their bodies constantly.

SL avatars are the result of a creative process that connects each resident to others. Even someone who does not master the creativity and technology required to build an avatar can create one using only materials designed by others. But even here a creative approach is needed, to choose and mix different materials in order to make a unique avatar. The embodiment of avatars requires a techne, an intentional way of making (Boellstorff, 2010, p. 129). The constitution of corporeality in collaborative virtual environments makes the avatar a form of distributed artistic expression, not just for professional artists, but for any user. By focusing on this creative aspect of the metaverse, engaging residents in cooperative tasks, this project can enhance a sense of co-presence. By distributing free and open material, it enhances the pool of available resources, further enabling users to experiment and express themselves through their avatar, actively inciting their transformation and the process of becoming in the liminoid space of the metaverse. In doing so, we also embrace the utopia of a new mode of production and ownership defended by the founder of the Foundation for Peer-to-Peer Alternatives, Michael Bauwens—a drift from an "exchange value for market" to a "use-value for a community of users", a common property that differs from private property and public (state) property (Bauwens, 2006, p. 33).

As an artwork, *Meta_Body* can be experienced on many levels, from contemplation to participation, but in the embodiment and transformation of the avatars, the aesthetical experience of the work can become a creative process. We feel privileged to play a part in this creative flux, turning our artwork into a constantly changing organism that we can observe as it grows and mutates.

ACKNOWLEDGMENT

The author would like to thank Sameiro Oliveira Martins, without whom this project would never be possible, Manuel Portela, Elif Ayiter and Luís Eustáquio for their brilliant insights, and all the produsers that made this project meaningful.

REFERENCES

Ascott, R. (2005). Distance Makes the Art Grow Further: Distributed Authorship and Telematic Textuality in LaPlissure du Texte. In A. Chandler & N. Neumark (Eds.), *At a distance: precursors to art and activism on the Internet* (pp. 282–296). Cambridge: The MIT Press.

Barreno, M. I., Horta, M. T., & Velho da Costa, M. (1998). *Novas Cartas Portuguesas*. Lisboa: Publicações Dom Quixote.

Bauwens, M. (2006). The Political Economy of Peer Production. *Post-autistic Economics Review* (37), 33-44.

Biocca, F. (2003, May 5-7). *Can we resolve the book, the physical reality, and the dream state problems? From the two-pole to a three-pole model of shifts in presence.* Retrieved from: http://www.mindlab.org/images/d/DOC705.pdf

Biocca, F. (1997, 9). *The Cyborg's Dilemma: Progressive Embodiment in Virtual Environments.* Retrieved from: http://jcmc.indiana.edu/vol3/issue2/biocca2.html

Bishop, C. (2006). Viewers as Producers. In C. Bishop (Ed.), *Participation* (pp. 10–17). London, Cambridge: The MIT Press.

Bishop, C. (2012). *Artificial hells: participatory art and the politics of spectatorship.* Londo: Verso.

Boellstorff, T. (2010). *Coming of Age in Second Life, An Anthropologist Explores the Virtually Human. Nova Jersey.* Princeton University Press.

Bruns, A. (2007). *Produsage, Generation C, and Their Effects on the Democratic Process. MiT 5 (Media in Transition).* Boston: MIT.

Bruns, A. (2010). Distributed Creativity: Filesharing and Produsage. In S. Sonvilla-Weiss, Mashup Cultures (pp. 24-37). Vienna: Springer.

CAE. (2002). Collective Cultural Action The Critical Art Ensemble. *Variant, 2*(15), 24–25.

Campbell, L. B. (1923). *Scenes and Machines on the English Stage During the Renaissance.* Cambridge: Cambridge University Press.

Coleman, B. (2011). *Hello Avatar: Rise of the Networked Generation.* Cambridge, MIT Press.

Dahlsveen, H., & Sousa, C. C. (2013). Kromosomer – an Experience in Shared Creative Work and Expression. *Journal of Virtual Worlds Research, 6*(2), 1–21.

Deleuze, G., & Guattari, F. (1987). *A thousand plateaus: capitalism and schizophrenia.* Minneapolis: University of Minnesota Press.

Fox, J., Bailenson, J., & Binney, J. (2009). Virtual Experiences, Physical Behaviors: The Effect of Presence on Imitation of an Eating Avatar. *Presence, 18*(4), 294–303. Cambridge. doi:10.1162/pres.18.4.294

Heeter, C. (1992). *Being There: The Subjective Experience of Presence.* Retrieved from: http://commtechlab.msu.edu/randd/research/beingthere.html

Henderson, B. (2005). *Open Letter To Kansas School Board.* Retrieved from: http://www.venganza.org/about/open-letter/

Ijsselsteijn, W., & Riva, G. (2003). Being There: The experience of presence in mediated environments. In G. Riva, F. Davide, & W. IJsselsteijn, Being There: Concepts, effects and measurement of user presence in synthetic environments (pp. 3-16). Amsterdam: Ios Press.

Justiça, P. (2013). *A ausência do Corpo na Comunicação Online – a descoberta da identidade no Second Life.* Lisboa: Universidade Aberta.

Lakoff, G., & Johnson, M. (1999). *Philosophy in the Flesh - The Embodied Mind and Its Challenge to Western Thought. Nova Iorque.* Basic Books.

Lévy, P. (1998). *Becoming Virtual, Reality in the Digital Age.* New York: Plenum Press.

Lévy, P. (2001). *Cyberculture.* Minneapolis: University of Minnesota Press.

Lind, M. (2007). The Collaborative Turn. In J. Billing, M. Lind, & L. Nilsson (ed.), Taking The Matter Into Common Hands: On Contemporary Art and Collaborative Practices (pp. 15-31). London: Black Dog Publishing.

Macedo, A. G. (2010). Uma Leitura das Novas Cartas Portuguesas em Vésperas de Abril. In C. Cruz, & V. Valente (ed.), All My Independent Women — Novas Cartas Portuguesas (pp. 53-56). Coimbra: Casa da esquina.

Manovich, L. (1996). The Aesthetics of Virtual Worlds: Report from Los Angeles. *CTheory* (ga103).

Massumi, B. (1992). *A user's guide to capitalism and schizophrenia: deviations from Deleuze and Guattari.* Cambridge: The MIT Press.

Molesworth, M., & Denegri-Knott, J. (2007). Digital Play and the Actualization of the Consumer Imagination. *Games and Culture, 2*(2), 114–133. doi:10.1177/1555412006298209

Mullin, D. C. (1970). *The Development of the Playhouse: A Survey of Theatre Architecture from the Renaissance to the Present.* Berkeley: University of California Press.

Murray, J. H. (2012). *Inventing the Medium: principles of interaction design as a cultural practice.* Cambridge: The Mit Press.

Norman, D. A. (1998). *The Design of Everyday Thins*. London: The MIT Press.

Novak-Leonard, J. L., & Brown, A. S. (2011). *Beyond attendance: A multi-modal understanding of arts participation*. Washington: National Endowment for the Arts.

Pearce, C. (2009). *Communities of play: emergent cultures in multiplayer games and virtual worlds*. Cambridge: MIT Press.

Pegoraro, É. (2012). Steampunk: As transgressões temporais negociadas de uma cultura retrofuturista. *Cadernos de Comunicação*, *16*(2), 389–400.

Pintasilgo, M. d. (2010). Prefácio (leitura breve por excesso de cuidado). In C. Cruz, & V. Valente, All My Independent Women — Novas Cartas Portuguesas (pp. 3-6). Coimbra: Casa da Esquina.

Pollock, G. (1996). The politics of theory: genarations and geographies in feminist theory and histories of art histories. In G. Pollock (ed.), Generations and Geographies in the Visual Arts: Feminist Readings (pp. 3-22). New York: Routlege.

Price, E. H. (2006). A critical review of congenital phantom limb cases and a developmental theory for the basis of body image. *Consciousness and Cognition*, *15*(2), 310–322. doi:10.1016/j.concog.2005.07.003 PMID:16182566

Russell, B. (1997). Is There a God? In B. Russel, The Collected Papers of Bertrand Russell, Volume 11: Last Philosophical Testament 1947-68 (pp. 542-821). London: Routledge.

Shields, R. (2003). *The virtual*. London, New York: Routledge.

Sousa, C. C. (2012). Mom and me through the looking glass. *Metaverse Creativity: Building, Performing, Learning and Authorship in Online 3D Worlds, 2* (2), 137-160.

Sousa, C. C. (2013). Meta_Body — A Project on Shared Avatar Creation. *International Conference in Illustration & Animation — CONFIA* (pp. 147-163). Porto: IPCA.

Sousa, C. C. (2014). Project Meta_Body. In J. P. Cravino, G. Christian, P. Martins, & J. Bernardino Lopes (Ed.), Procedia Technology — SLACTIONS 2013: Research conference on virtual worlds – Learning with simulations. 13, pp. 33 – 37. Vila Real: Elsevier.

Sousa, C. C., & Dahlsveen, H. (2012). The Kromosomer Project. *1st International Conference on Ilustration and Animation* (pp. 421-436).

Steuer, J. (1993, October 15). *Defining Virtual Reality: Dimensions Determining Telepresence*. Retrieved from: http://ww.cybertherapy.info/pages/telepresence.pdf

Veerapen, M. (2011). Encountering Oneself and the Other: A Case Study of Identity Formation in Second Life. In A. Peachey, & M. Childs (ed.), Reinventing Ourselves: Contemporary Concepts of Identity in Virtual Worlds (Springer Series in Immersive Environments) (pp. 81-100). London: Springer. doi:10.1007/978-0-85729-361-9_5

Yee, N., Bailenson, J. N., & Ducheneaut, N. (2009). Implications of Transformed Digital Self-Representation on Online and Offline Behavior. *Communication Research*, *36*(2), 285–312. doi:10.1177/0093650208330254

Yee, N., Bailenson, J. N., & Ducheneaut, N. (2009). The Proteus Effect: Implications of Transformed Digital Self-Representation on Online and Offline Behavior. *Communication Research*, *36*(2), 285–312. doi:10.1177/0093650208330254

KEY TERMS AND DEFINITIONS

Avatar: In Sanskrit, the word refers to the incarnation of a deity, the materialization of an intangible being. Apparently, in the digital era culture, its meaning is reversed and the avatar is the virtualization of the body. However, for digital media researcher Beth Coleman (2011) the avatar is not a virtualization but an actualization. She extended the concept of avatar to refer to all digital extensions of the subject that actualize it in real time in the telecommunications network, proposing a notion of co-presence and "reality-x" to account for this distributed mode of relocation of the subject. In the context of this chapter, however, avatar refers to the digital image that represents the user in collaborative virtual environments.

Metaphor: A stylistic figure of speech where a concept, object or subject is replaced by another in order to describe it. This, however, is not a simple substitution, but an interaction between two concepts, creating a new one (Sousa & Dahlsveen, 2012). Conceptual metaphor is a designation used by linguist George Lakoff and the philosopher Mark Johnson (1999) to refer to the linguistic use of a concept in terms of another, especially regarding abstract concepts treated as physical ones; the authors consider this a cognitive aspect of language that helps people conceive the world. As a cognitive strategy, the metaphor is paramount to digital interface design.

Metaverse: The writer Neal Stephenson coined this word in 1992 in the novel Snow Crash. In it, the metaverse was a fully immersive three-dimensional space where people interacted through avatars. Nowadays the term has been used to refer to the collective line space in general, but has been used particularly with regard to virtual worlds, i.e. distributed, digital spaces, capable of hosting collaborative activities—places, inhabited by people and made possible by online technologie (Boellestorff, 2010).

Produsage: Mode of collaborative content creation, led by users or involving them as producers. The user acts as a hybrid user/producer or produser, during the whole production process. This type of creation is community-based, i.e. a large group and not a team. With fluid roles, pro-

dusers can participate in different ways throughout the process, alternating between producers and users (Bruns, 2010).

Shared Creativity: Creative process that depends on multiple creators, either synchronously or asynchronously, whose participation is crucial to the creation of the object, regardless of the degree or mode of that involvement.

Virtual Corporeality: in this chapter, this term refers to the digital virtualization of the body through the use of avatars in collaborative virtual environments. In its creation, a virtual body does not oppose the real body but the actual body, it questions and problematizes it. It is not a possible body, but a potential and complex one. Its embodiment, the way it makes someone present in other, or even multiple locations, offers forms of distributed actualization of the subject. This is not, however, a simple materialization of a subjectivity, but rather a creative, yet transient, precarious, unstable, and fluid answer to several problems that the Internet era poses to the body and the self in its distributed relocation. The avatar's body or physicality is flexible, multiple, and metamorphic. One can be talking on the phone, and at same time posting something on a social network, while dancing in a club on a virtual environment. All without leaving one's desk chair.

Virtual: According to Rob Shields (2003) the word's origin is the latin term "virtus", that means power or strength. In the Middle Ages this word transformed into "virtualis" and gained a connotation of moral strength—a virtuous person would be someone whose "*actual* existence testified to a moral and ethical *ideal*" (Shields, 2003, p.3). Shields traces the contemporary philosophical use of the term to three French philosophers: Marcel Proust, to whom Henry Bergson attributes the origin of the term, who in his turn was paramount to Gilles Deleuze's definition (Shields, 2003, p.26). For the latter, virtual is the difference between "actual existence" and "potential existence"— both are considered "real" (Massumi, 1992, p. 35). Deleuze also distinguishes "potencial" from "possible", as "possibility" is only a "restricted range of potential"(Massumi, 1992, p. 38). To the better understanding of these notions, Shields proposed an ontological tetrology of the real and the possible in which he defined: the "virtual" as "real idealization", the "concrete" as "actual real", the "abstract" as "possible ideal", and the "probable" as "actual possibility"(Shields, 2003, pp. 28-29). It is also on Deleuze's definition that Pierre Lévy draws on. In this chapter, this author was of particular significance for two reasons: first, he relates this definition of virtual to digital virtualization; second, he relates it to art forms native to the digital medium.

ENDNOTES

[1]   Throughout this paper we will use the avatars' real names whenever possible on first mention, but we will prefer the in world avatar name for subsequent references, as this is usually the name used to sign artworks.

[2]   A region is a 65,536 m² parcel of a "sim", i.e. a simulator supported by the Second Life platform and servers, which can host several users (usually referred to as "residents"), digital artifacts and collaborative activities.

[3]   Delicatessen landmarks, i.e. hyperlinks to places in the region on Second Life: Phase I: http://maps.secondlife.com/secondlife/Porto/134/110/703; Phase II: Stage 1 http://maps.secondlife.com/secondlife/Porto/167/168/21; Stage 2 http://maps.secondlife.com/secondlife/Porto/178/125/1147; Stage 3 http://maps.secondlife.com/secondlife/Porto/143/144/3475; Stage 4 http://maps.secondlife.com/secondlife/Porto/156/112/2565

[4]   The initial set of avatars and the second set of derivative avatars can be seen in the following video: https://vimeo.com/79818095

[5]   A virtual installation in Second Life is a set, digitally built, that can be experienced by residents as a three-dimensional simulation. The initial installation for the original Meta_Body avatars distribution can be seen in a machinima by Ruth Latour: https://www.flickr.com/photos/ruthlatour/6216634834/

[6]   Machinimas are videos captured in virtual environments.

[7]   Virtual photography refers to screen captures from virtual worlds.

[8]   We refer to the audio work as a "soundscape", given the purposefully environmental nature of its relation with the virtual landscape.

[9]   It is now possible to upload meshes that are rigged to the avatar skeleton, i.e. 3D models specially suited for animation by the Second Life avatar structure.

[10]   *Meta_Body* Flickr Group: https://www.flickr.com/groups/meta_body/pool/; *Meta_Body* Koinup Group: http://www.koinup.com/group/meta_body/

[11]   Acacia Merlin, Aili Panthar, Alexandra Shepherd, Anna Anton, Annie Klavinham, Ashling ~ Alchemal Art, B. Bode, Biox Varonia, Bobby Yoshikawa, CapCat Ragu, Cat Shilova, Chic Aeon, Corinne J. Helendale, Dantelicia Ethaniel, PraxisField (Dave Searby Mason), Harbor Galaxy (Deborah Lombardo), Domitalia Jinx, Eirela Lane, Eupalinos Ugajin, Fae Varriale, Flora Clayflower, Fuschia Nightfire (Nina Camplin), Gabrielle Swindlehurst, GuinneV, Hans Petter Meirik, Mimesis Monday (Heidi Dahlsveen), HivaOa Insoo, Ilanit Orsini, Isabella Alphaville, Jasmine Ballinger, joaopedro Oh, Joe Balbozar, Kalyca McCaalen, Karro Lean, La Baroque, L_B, Leeleu Lemondrop, Lili Ivanova, Lillyane Inshan, LILY, Patricie Sapphire (Lucie Sinclair), Lyra Meili, Lookatmy Back, Looker Lumet, Luminis Kanto, Maagiha, Maloe Vansant, Meer Bluebird, Meilo Minotaur, Miguel Rotunno, Mila Tatham, Misscheevers Borkotron, Mitsuki Faith, nur_moo_, Paola Mills, Piedra Lubitsch, Phil Sidek,

Podenga, Riviera Medier, Roxie Davidov, Ruth Latour, Sanam Sewell, ṣαяε, SaveMe Oh, Scarlet Highfield, Senna, Siri Woodget, Solange Simondsen, spyvsspyAeon (André Lopes), Syene, Tary Allen, Tess Falworth, Thea Maiman, Tim Deschanel, Ursula Floresby, wise_Sandalwood, Yasmina, Zeeva Quintessa, Zuzu Pelous.

[12] Virtual Photography in the AMIW exhibition can be seen in the following slide show: https://vimeo.com/31369231

[13] https://www.flickr.com/photos/fuschia-nightfire/6226676260/

[14] http://vimeo.com/30534519

[15] The avatars *Amazonzia*, by Wanda Beamish, and *Aquavariel*, by Fitch Woodrunner were also built in the same way.

[16] Other avatars that combined *Kromosomer* parts with Meta_Body items were *Golden Brown,* by Cold Frog; *Metamorphosis*, by Piedra Lubitsch; *Smoke*, by Ursula Floresby; and *Suppressed Red Riding Hood* by Mimesis Monday (Heidi Dahlsveen).

[17] This was also the case of *Gorgonia*, by Moki Yuitza; *Green Lagoon Man* and *Erato Fractal*, both by Fuschia Night Fire; *Chess*, by Cherry Manga; *Christina*, by CapCat Ragu; *Darkdoll*, by Meilo Minoaur; *Blind Train*, by Eupalinos Ugajin; *Appointment in the garden*, by Simotron Aquila; *Wind Girl* and *Steam Boy*, both by *Ggabriel Madruga; Cica's Meta_Body Avatar*, by Cica Ghost; *Cosmic Radiance*, by Rhojen Resident; and *Vibrance Av*, by Serenvide (Dave Searby Mason). Some submissions also featured

third party creations, whose authors generously consented to be included. This was the case of Cherry Ravinelli's *Can't stop dancing*, which included parts by Cherry Manga; and *Hands Free Av*, by Serenvide, with hair by Fuschia Nightfire.

[18] In Second Life one can build on the "ground" or in the "air", therefore on different levels, as mentioned. The ground level is where virtual terrain and water is found. In air levels everything must be built from scratch, so a "natural" landscape is not as easy to simulate.

[19] Primitive objects, usually known as "prims", are basic 3D shapes that can be produced within the Second Life platform: cubes, spheres, cones and cylinders.

[20] In Second Life the behavior of objects and avatars can be changed by scripts. The Linden Scripting Language (LSL) is used for this purpose.

[21] By default, the avatar on Second Life is third-person observed, that is, the user views the avatar from up and behind. However the platform's interface enables the displacement of this simulated camera, allowing residents to change their viewpoint without moving the avatar.

[22] In Second Life, scripts attached to objects can allow avatars to sit on and have their movements controlled by them. This is what allows avatars to be linked with the teapot and travel with it.

[23] https://www.flickr.com/photos/timdeschanel/6276102377/in/photostream/

Section 4
Performance Practices in Virtual Worlds

The final section brings together both practitioners and theorists in the three chapters that consider firstly the issues surrounding digital embodiment and the status of the body in performance art, the practice of blended reality through the virtual and physical performer, and finally the ways in which SL-Bots can be explored for their aesthetic and creative potential.

Chapter 10
"Follow Me, Comrades in Flight, into the Depths!"
Body–Related Performance Art in Second Life

Maja Murnik
Independent Scholar, Slovenia

ABSTRACT

The chapter discusses the changes the body has been subjected to in the 21st century and especially when it enters the digital worlds. The starting point for the reflection of the body today is its floating position in contemporary mixed and augmented reality. By deploying the notions of 'body image' and 'body schema,' elaborated by French phenomenologist M. Merleau-Ponty, various features of digital embodiment are discussed. After discussing several forms of the techno-modelled body (also mentioning the issue of life addressed in it), the chapter turns to the examples of body-related performance art in the virtual world of Second Life that explicitly raise questions about the body in the digital world, and within Second Life in particular (the examples discussed are: Synthetic Performances and I know that it's all a state of mind by 0100101110101101.ORG, Come to Heaven by Gazira Babeli and ZeroG SkyDancers by DanCoyote, etc.).

INTRODUCTION

In 1977 the space probe Voyager 1 was launched into space and a decade later flew past the most distant planets in our solar system. In August 2012, Voyager 1 entered the interstellar space, the region between stars, filled with material ejected by the death of nearby stars millions of years ago. Being currently (in November 2014 when this chapter was finished) more than 130 AU (astronomical units, i.e. the distance between the Sun and the Earth) away, it is the farthest human-made object from Earth. It is still sending scientific information about its surroundings through the Deep Space Network, or DSN.[1] After exploring the giant planets of our outer solar system, their moons, and magnetic fields, the mission was extended into the outermost edge of the Sun's domain and beyond (Jet Propulsion Laboratory, 2014). Anyway, Voyager is slowly approaching one of its ends: in

DOI: 10.4018/978-1-4666-8384-6.ch010

2025–2030 it is expected that the space probe will no longer be able to power the instruments. But this does not mean that Voyager will disappear; it will wander further into the Milky Way, nobody knows for how long. For our understanding of time, it will travel forever. Being turned into a kind of "space debris," into a worn-out material, it will travel further, carrying aboard the message about the Earth and human civilization. In about 40,000 years, Voyager 1 will probably drift within the next star, i.e. AC+79 3888.

It maybe sounds quite odd that I have started the chapter about performance art in Second Life with the description of a space probe, lost somewhere in the outer space. However, I believe both spaces, the outer space as well as the virtual one of Second Life, share certain similarities. It's not just the fact that both spaces are hard to imagine and conceive within the confines of our fundamentally terrestrial thinking. In a certain sense, they are both abstract and infinite for our perception. They cannot be sensed and experienced directly by our senses and bodies, on the contrary, the experience of them is bound to be mediated. Though, this does not mean that we cannot reach into them by our physicality; we can make this, but our embodied presence in these places is quite different than here.

Broadly speaking, we approach and explore these spaces by a kind of probe that becomes the area of sensitivity, thus extending our human perception. When, for example, the space probe is travelling through the outer space, it can do this because it has been turned into a body equipped with sensors, helping it to sense, move, and navigate through the space. Although an artificial body, or a technological body, it has kept certain features human bodies possess. Even if we lose the direct grip or control of it, it does not cease to be the (extended) part of us, of our human bodies. It is still the probe in the literal sense – an exploratory device, designed to investigate and obtain information on a remote and unknown region. Besides, it is the probe in its symbolic

meaning – created to delve and explore the new, secret, unknown territories, either physical spaces or virtual, imaginary ones, being an extension of humanity in general.

Like avatars, created by men and inhabiting 3D virtual worlds, space probe Voyager 1 is an intelligent extension of our bodies, being itself a kind of virtual body, an avatar. Its autonomy can even proceed to such an extent that Voyager 1 can liberate itself from man's management and become an independent device, living on its own. However, it is not just a weird, utopian suggestion, this is truly going to happen. In the following years, NASA is planning to shut down Voyager 1 and cut off the communication with it as its energy resources will slowly decrease. Then, the space probe will turn into an emancipated techno-object, the technological form of life that will "breathe" and move on its own. It will lose its utilitarian, anthropocentric and control-oriented management and will turn into a life-like system. Such an anticipated destiny of Voyager 1 has also become of interest to artists; it is not the first time that outer space has gained their interest – the Russian avant-garde had already dreamt about outer space as an aesthetic space (*cf.* Malevich's exclamation "Follow me, comrades in flight, into the depths!" from the title of this chapter).[2] In 2013 Slovenian artists Miha Turšič and Špela Petrič presented the first part of the project on Voyager, entitled *Voyager/ 140 AU* that included the preparations for turning the Voyager into an independent, emancipated technological form of life (more about the project: Petrič, 2013). The project was produced by The Cultural Centre of European Space Technologies (abbreviated KSEVT), located in a small Slovenian town of Vitanje, and is a part of the broader initiative for "space culturalization" and post-gravity art, taken by KSEVT (KSEVT, 2014).[3]

One of the issues addressed by art project *Voyager/ 140 AU* is the problem of life. By creating protocellular patterns with emergent characteristics (Petrič wrote more about the creation of this algorithm of life in Petrič, 2013), a new form of life-like system was made. Here, I do not wish to immerse deeper into *Voyager/ 140 AU*, yet I find important to stress the recent turn of the paradigms occuring in contemporary theory and culture that is relevant when encountering both *Voyager/ 140 AU* and the virtual world of Second Life. This is the turn from the paradigm of mind, language, text, and culture, to the paradigm of body, materiality, life and living, life experience, and biopolitics (the representatives of the latter are Giorgio Agamben, Antonio Negri, Donna Haraway, Eugene Thacker, Brian Massumi, et al.). Alternative forms of life, semi-living and life-like, inorganic, anonymous, artificial, undefined, technological, etc. life – all this previously neglected and unknown, unspeakable, absent centre of life has begun to attract contemporary philosophers and theorists. As one of them, namely Eugene Thacker, argues, we should turn to the so-called biophilosophy, instead of thinking within the constraints of philosophy of biology. Whereas the latter is concerned with articulating the concept of 'life' that would describe the essence of life, i.e. universal characteristics for all life, biophilosophy focuses on "those modes of biological life that simultaneously escape their being exclusively biological life: microbes, epidemics, endosymbiosis, parasitism, swarms, packs, flocks, a-life, genetic algorithms, biopathways, smart dust, smartmobs, netwars – there is a whole bestiary that asks us to think the life-multiplicity relation" (Thacker, 2005, para. 8).

Alternative forms of living and life-like (phenomenologists would say "as-if-life") have been recognized in spaces where they were previously not expected to emerge. Artificial and technological life in outer space, as well as art and culture in outer space, artistic practices on the platform of commercial virtual worlds – these places provide totally new opportunities not only for life and art but, more broadly speaking, for creative practices in general. They emerge in a huge variety of different and multiple spaces and contexts.

PERFORMANCE AS ONE OF THE CENTRAL PARADIGMS IN CONTEMPORARY CULTURE

Related to the issues discussed above I should mention another important dimension we are witnessing today. Ever since life has been understood as a process (whose beginning or end has been always a discussable issue), where the durational features have been foregrounded. Durational and performative aspects are relevant also in the issue of art: since the 1960s, if not since the advent of the historic avant-gardes at the beginning of the 20th century, art has been conceived as time-based and performative, far from being made and understood as an accomplished object, as an artifact. Even more, durational and performative aspects are foregrounded today to such an extent that it is not an exaggeration to claim that performance has become one of the central paradigms in our culture over the last decades. Theatre theorists recognized the performative turn occuring within the performing arts since the 1960s, meaning that the shift in considering theatre as a static work of art has moved to the event (Fischer-Lichte, 2004), and addressed performance beyond its purely artistic bound connotations, broadening the scope of research also on the social, political, and religious events, like concerts, sporting events, performances of everyday life, rituals, etc. (Schechner, 1988; *cf.* also the notion of 'performance studies'). Other theorists, however, proposed to discuss the performative properties and dimensions in economic science framing markets and economies (Michel Callon), in sociology discussing daily behavior and gender development (Eve Kosofsky Sedgwick, Judith Butler, et al.), etc.

By stressing the performative modes in science, it is suggested that reality cannot be captured and described purely through the representation and with a critical, objective distance 'from above.' The performance as the method, technique, practice, and world-view, in contrast, suggests that "there is not a reality *pre-given* before one's experience of it but rather that the world is *enacted* or actively performed anew" (Salter, 2007, para. 9). The emphasis on the non-verbal, embodied and immanent act of *doing* research, argued by Christopher L. Salter, corresponds to the phenomenological point of view. Namely, in the abolishment of the demarcation between subject and object, self and world that Salter recognizes in contemporary science, the phenomenological modes of knowledge production are echoed. Our interactions with the world which is not filled with fixed entities just waiting to reveal in front of us, now come to the fore. Knowledge emerges over time, subjected and transformed due to our interactions with the world. The shift from the focus and faith into the human being as the top of the great chain to other, unstable, durational, ever-changing, performative aspects of life, knowledge production, and culture in general, echoes here. Here, the awareness of the interaction of non-human forces with the human ones also comes to the fore.

The shift to performance as one of the central contemporary paradigms is addressed also in today's transition from the economy of products to the economy of experiences and adventures.[4] More than the material, completed products such economy emphasizes performative aspects of consumption. This coincides with the more general turn from the industrial to the post-industrial society which, broadly speaking, has moved the focus from the material, completed products to the immaterial labor. Dematerialization and the general emphasis on durational, performative aspects are significant for the world of Second Life, too.

BACK TO THE BODY AND EMBODIMENT IN PHILOSOPHY AND SOCIAL SCIENCES

Over the last decade we are witnessing the increasing interest in the issues of body and embodiment which has resulted in recognition of these topics as key issues for the understanding of many phenomena of contemporary society, culture, and art. The issues of the body have been truly addressed at the beginning of the 20th century in philosophy by German and later by French phenomenologists (e.g. Max Scheler, Edmund Husserl, Gabriel Marcel, Maurice Merleau-Ponty) that called into question the key position represented in the extreme by Cartesianism dominating the last three centuries. According to Cartesianism, the body was understood as objectified and mechanical, as being wholly separate from the mind and consequently as inferior and less interesting part of human being. In contrast to Cartesian aversion to the issues of body, the above-mentioned phenomenologists addressed the body as a lived entity, emphasizing its motility and extremely changeable, protean nature (for instance, Husserl put the notion of body as flesh (Ger. *Leib*) in contrast to the notion of objectified body (Ger. *Körper*)). Through ceaseless interaction with the environment, the phenomenological lived body has become an active and original tool for perceiving, learning, and living in the world, conceived even as the *body-subject* (the term was coined by early Merleau-Ponty and elaborated in one of his key works *Phenomenology of Perception*, 1945).

Phenomenology was the first philosophical movement that has developed a consistent criticism of the Cartesian model of the body-as-object and has offered alternative models for thinking the body. The notions of lived body and body-subject as they were elaborated by Merleau-Ponty are to some extent very useful for today's phenomena, too. Merleau-Ponty's focus was primarily the sensing and moving body in its pre-reflective and unmediated interaction with the world, and he also elaborated the notion of body schema which he compared to the widely known notion of body image. Both of them can be useful in discussing various aspects of today's technologically modeled and extended body. I shall return to these topics later.

However, rather than theoretical approaches, foregrounded in phenomenological investigations, we are witnessing today socially oriented research of the body. Social sciences and cultural studies have emphasized the body as being fundamentally "constructed" by external mechanisms and its experience being thoroughly mediated and involved into the games of power. In sociology, for instance, the increasing interest in the issues of body and embodiment has been recognized since 1984 when Bryan Turner's agenda-setting work *The Body and Society: Explorations in Social Theory* was published in its first edition, renewing the attention to the body.[5] The turn to the body in social theory has been addressed by Turner as the rise of a "somatic society," by which he means "a society within which our major political and moral problems are expressed through the conduit of the human body" (Fraser & Greco, 2005, p. 2).

While the phenomenological tradition emphasized the body as a sensing, mobile, affective entity that fundamentally shapes the being-in-the-world, socially oriented philosophy and criticism (its postmodern, post-structuralist, post-colonial, feminist, and queer versions), prevailing today, believe that the bodies are multiple and are determined by society, race, gender, culture, etc. But – as we cannot escape living in today's mixed and augmented reality – how has the issue of body been conceived and discussed in the digital paradigm? Are the techno-bodies we have and *are* today different to previous ones, and more precisely, what does this mean when encountering with the virtual world of Second Life?

THE REDEFINITION OF THE BODY IN THE DIGITAL PARADIGM

In the cyber-culture of the 1980s and the 1990s the attitude to the issues of body was to some extent ambiguous. It seemed that cyber-culture was focused primarily on the questions of mind and artificial life, supported by computer networks, and thus remained in the domain of "cyber" mind, meaning that the issue of embodiment was left behind. Cyberpunk was a movement in science fiction from the early 1980s on, combining an urban punk sensibility with a highly technological and utopian future (for example, novel *Neuromancer* by William Gibson, 1984; movies *The Lawnmower Man*, 1992, directed by Brett Leonard, and *Terminator 2: Judgment Day* by James Cameron, 1991, etc.). In the majority of these cultural "texts," the flesh (in cyberpunk texts flesh is usually referred to as "meat") typically carries a negative connotation: it is conceived as something vulnerable and obsolete that should be upgraded by the technological. The central significance and value were given to the upgraded mind. In Gibson's novel *Neuromancer*, for instance, cyberspace is described as "a consensual hallucination experienced daily by billions of legitimate operators," and as "lines of light ranged in the nonspace of the mind, clusters and constellations of data" (Gibson, 1984, p. 69). In the comic book *Cyberpunk* the protagonist Topo mentally enters the 'Playing Field' – in fact it is cyberspace – wishing he could leave his meat behind and just live there as pure consciousness. He argues that here you are what you will, no restraints and no limits (except how good your software is). In theory this view was described in the following way: "Suspended in computer space, the cybernaut leaves the prison of the body and emerges in a world of digital sensation" (Heim, 1991, p. 64). Such attitude was fueled by the theory of information that viewed information as disembodied (Shannon-Weaver theory), and was strengthened in the debates among members of the early cybernetics movement in the Macy conferences held from 1943 to 1954.

The flesh, incapable of excellent performances of mind freely floating in the "nonspace" of cyberspace; the flesh, being full of physiological constraints and unable to compete with the power, speed, and range of developing technologies, is the mental starting point for Stelarc's performances from the late 1970s on. The human body is "obsolete," Stelarc announced at the outset of his career as an artist. Therefore it should be re-shaped by high-tech advances and continuously updated, like computer software, in order to follow the numerous changes and modifications taking place nowadays. The metaphor of the cyborg has been adopted by feminist and postmodern cultural theorists (e.g. Donna Haraway's "A Cyborg Manifesto," 1985) but in fact very vividly performed in Stelarc's performances. Stelarc explored such cyborg body and its voluntary and involuntary prostheses, probes, mods, interfaces, extensions, and amplifiers in numerous techno-performances (e.g. *Exoskeleton*, *Third Hand*, *Third Ear*, *Stomach Sculpture*, *Fractal Flesh*, *Ping Body*, etc.).

Not only Stelarc, others artists-performers as well showed numerous variants of techno-performance in the 1980s and 1990s, exploring versions of the cyborg body, i.e. a body combining the biological and cybernetic parts: Marcel-lí Antúnez Roca (e.g. *Epizoo*, 1994, and *Afasia*, 1998), Stahl Stenslie (*Cyber SM*, 1993), Eduardo Kac (*Time Capsule*, 1997), Chico MacMurtrie with anthropomorphic robots, as well as *Orlan* by a series of plastic surgeries (*The Reincarnation of Saint-Orlan*, 1990–1993).

Over the last decade corporeality has become the integrated part of the digital world in general. The mind/body duality, as well as matter/mind and real/virtual problems, inherited from Cartesian modes of thinking that in fact privileged the domination of one part of duality and the subjugation of the other, normally the physical by the mental, have been overcome today. They tend to be re-shaped and conceived in a different way: "The tension between embodiment/disembodiment can not be constructed as a choice of either/or but rather has to be understood as a reality of both/and" (Paul, 2003, p. 170). Today both parts of the afore-mentioned dualities are present all the time, emerging and vanishing in sudden, novel combinations. Rather than addressing the dualities and binary oppositions it has become more appropriate to talk about Deleuzian multiplicity: "So that we give up taxonomies of difference and celebrate in patterns, rhythms, multiplicities, vi-brations, pivots, joints, points of contact, crossings and energies of this new way of bodying forth" (Brown, 2011, p. 98).

That the corporeality has been admitted today as the integral part of the digital world, is obviously almost the fact; however, which aspects are addressed in such novel techno-body? I have briefly discussed the ambiguous position of the body in cyberpunk, as well as I have mentioned the cyborg body in techno-performance of the 1980s and 1990s, but what are the changes the body has been subdued in the 21st century?

We are the contemporaries of great changes in the domain of body modifications – artificial life, robotics, biotechnology, nanotechnology, regenerative medicine, neuroscience, virtual reality, etc. have contributed a lot to the openings and extensions of the body we have been used to. By the help of smart technologies we can observe, modify, and create life. The skin is no longer the boundary between the inside and the outside, between the self and the world; it has become a permeable membrane through which it is possible to insert modules which enable techno-extensions of the body; on the other hand, the body appropriates tools that expand its perception, action, and reflection into multiple times and spaces far beyond the place where its bones are currently located.

The position of the body today seems to be one of the key questions of contemporary thought in general. How to think and perceive such dispersed, decentralised and outward turned, chiasmatic body, in fact, new forms of techno-modelled body which significantly influence the contemporary organisation of life and are distinctly contextualised and immersed into current culture, is the question and challenge for contemporary theory as well as for art. Such techno-bodies – strengthened, intensified, accelerated, software- and wetware-supported, open to novel functions, extended by telepresence – have challenged humanities to search for new answers regarding the embodiment under the present conditions, and to redefine their views on traditional philosophical mind/body problem, actual/virtual problem, to-be-in-the-world issue, and the traditional ideas of perception and thinking.

The starting point for the reflection of the body today is its position. What and where is the "true" position of such dispersed and extended techno-bodies I have briefly described above? In order to better capture their ambiguous presence let me turn to the contributions of existential phenomenology, namely to Maurice Merleau-Ponty. Of course he was not able to think about digital technology at his time – i.e. in the 1940s and 1950s when he wrote most of his *oeuvre*. But many of his ideas still echo today.

As I have already mentioned, Merleau-Ponty elaborated two notions dealing with the position of the sensing and moving body – body image and body schema (Merleau-Ponty, 2007). The notion of body image consists of the representations of someone's body/bodies in the consciousness. Body image consists of perceptions, attitudes, and beliefs concerning one's body; it may involve a person's conscious perception of her own physical appearance or picturing herself in her mind. However, Merleau-Ponty was more interested in the concept of body schema. He defined body schema as the perception and internal experience of the moving body and its parts. For Merleau-Ponty, body schema therefore refers to the sensory-motor capacities that control movement and posture, and it mainly remains outside of the consciousness.

More than the historical concepts of body schema the interesting issues today are its possible extensions which are linked to the skilful use and the integration of different tools. The possibility of extensions of body schema was already conceived and described by Merleau-Ponty, too. One of his well-known examples of such an extension is a typewriter integrated into the body schema of a typist. A skilful typist knows very well where the letters on a keyboard are, and she can adjust without special effort to another, different keyboard, either bigger or smaller, however different, than the one she has been used to. The adjustment is done somehow non-consciously, at least outside explicit consciousness; the body adjusts to a new situation by itself. It does so as a whole, without any special, conscious reflection on the act of adjustment. Similarly (and this is another Merleau-Ponty's example), the blind man's stick which he has learnt to use through acquiring the habit and integrating it into his body schema, has ceased to be an auxiliary object for him and has become a legitimate part of the blind man as its point has become an area of sensitivity (Merleau-Ponty, 2007, pp. 165–66; here, the comparison between a tool integrated into body schema and the space probe from the beginning of the chapter can be made).

By the help of the notions of body schema and body image we can roughly distinguish between two main domains where the body in the digital paradigm has been redefined. The first domain is linked primarily to the issues of user and her manipulation of interfaces. The corporeal features of her experience in contemporary mixed and augmented reality, for instance its affective, proprioceptive, and tactile components, are emphasized now (*cf.* Hansen, 2004; Massumi, 2002; Strehovec, 2014). The awareness that the body is an important agent in the constitution of space, even in the digital realm, has emerged and spread in last decade. Besides, Anna Munster believes that Cartesian aesthetics aligned the digital with the disembodied and the placeless; therefore the digital culture has to be "materialized" (Munster, 2006). According to this opinion, she examines the roles of body and affect in their relations to the digital.

Importantly, these features are always addressed with the emphasis on their processuality. The body manipulating the interface is fundamentally the sensing and the moving body (for example, my hand-in-motion provides me with more information about environment as if it would just statically touching the object on one single spot). Contemporary cognitive science has proved that the body shapes the cognition through its motor abilities. As phenomenologist and cognitive scientist Shaun Gallagher argues, the shape and size of objects are not perceived simply in phenomenal terms (phenomenal size of an object depending on distance from the perceiver), but in pragmatic terms – as something I can grasp or manipulate (Gallagher, 2005, p. 8).

The questions of the user's body and her manipulation of the digital are challenging also for new media art, as well as for new media performances. Let me mention just one performance which I find interesting because it turns the issue discussed upside down. In the performance *Brainloop* (2006) by Slovenian new media artist Davide Grassi[6] motor activity in the performer's manipulation of interfaces has been avoided. So-called Brain Computer Interface (BCI) system is deployed here, enabling the performer to operate the devices merely by *imagining* motor commands. With the help of this interface the performer operates the machine and his avatar without hand activity, without touching the devices or eye moving, but only by mind activity while his body remains still, immobile. *Brainloop* is dealing with the imagination, more precisely, with the movements imagined – and this is totally different mode than movement itself or its motor preparations.

While the issues of the user's body and her manipulation of devices can be aligned with the phenomenological notion of body schema and the problem of its extensions, the issue of body image, on the contrary, can roughly correspond to the second domain of the digitally redefined body we are witnessing today. Digital extensions in virtual worlds such as avatars can be conceived as the modes of virtual representations. When talking about Second Life, the second domain of the digitally redefined body comes to the fore. The art projects discussed in the following section correspond to this domain, i.e. to the ways and modes of virtual representations of the bodies rather than to the questions of the user's manipulation and

handling with the devices, interfaces, and with the avatars as well. Namely, Second Life does not support the sensation of touch (force feedback).

When talking about Second Life and its avatars put in the 3D space we come across to the questions of identity. Playing with these issues is one of the main topics in SL and as such it raises questions about the position and features of the user's body image. What I find very important in this issue is the role of the user's inner world. It's not just that body image consists of perceptions, attitudes, and beliefs concerning one's body, more extensively, participating in the virtual world of Second Life awakes a very complex world of user's feelings, emotions, beliefs, affects, behavior, etc. that extend beyond their relation just to the user's body. To shed light on this a little bit more let me take a short trip to the issue of pain.

In the real world, the issue of pain was one of the key questions of performance art, and along with the sense of suffering it is one of the basic problems of the human being-in-the-world at all. But what happens with the pain in virtual environment? Is it still real and so heavy as in real life? The systems of virtual reality (VR) have an effect directly on the senses, they touch and stimulate them very intensely; a user's body plugged into VR is in fact sexualized in the extreme. On the contrary, the body in the avatar-based virtual world of Second Life is impoverished, it does not have a direct access to sensual pleasure. In fact, the body in SL is desexualized, it is no more than a shallow, nonproblematic visual representation. The body represented in an avatar is in a way full of constraints, due to the software, and user's manipulation of it depends on her skill and digital literacy. However, the pain within Second Life lies elsewhere. It can be the pain of not being involved, of not being able to successfully participate in the social rituals in SL. As an image is never just an image but is always embedded into the whole context of backgrounds and projections, of past, present, and future, of actual and virtual, similarly the avatar is embedded into the complex context of users' attitudes, social and technical skills, affects, packs of meanings, etc. Each gesture (in the virtual world) always has a meaning.

However, Second Life offers a specific point of view (POV) of the user. Set a little above the scene, a floating point of view reminds me to the camera travelling of a classic movie. Such a position suggests my body is weightless, without gravity and volume, as the avatar flies beyond the boundaries and restrictions and can also be teleported – i.e. transferred from one point to another in a moment. Flight is also one of the issues that several performances in SL address and explore (e.g. *Come to Heaven* by Gazira Babeli, *ZeroG SkyDancers* by DanCoyote).

BODY-RELATED PERFORMANCE ART IN SECOND LIFE

The examples discussed in the following section are chosen by their main theme: they explicitly raise questions about the body in the digital world, and in Second Life in particular. Although Second Life was not intended mostly to satisfy the artistic inclinations of its residents, there is also a place for the residents to express themselves creatively, for example through art exhibitions (also of classical artistic techniques and media) in virtual galleries. However, what is more interesting in the issue of art in SL, are the art forms that depend exactly on the new medium of Second Life, with all its limitations. One such art form is avatar-based performance art. In performances taking place on such specific platform, the issues of the body and corporeality are addressed anew – without the normal terrestrial constraints of the body that were at the center of classical performance art. The issues of the body emerging on the platform of code appear to be very interesting – namely, changing the code shapes the way in which the body performs within virtual worlds (*cf.* pieces by Gazira Babeli).

As the starting point I will discuss *Synthetic Performances* (2007–2010), prepared by net. art duo Eva and Franco Mattes, also known as 0100101110101101.ORG. These are a series of six reenactments of seminal historic performances of the 1960s and 1970s, staged by the artists' virtual alter-egos in the synthetic world of SL.[7] Instead of live bodies of the original performers we are here witnessing the virtual bodies (the avatars) of Eva and Franco Mattes. While the original performances were exploring the live body in real spaces in all its unpredictability and uncertainty, the Mattes' pieces are performed in the virtual space and by avatars.

Since its rise in the 1960s and 1970s when it was established as an individual art form, the essential focus of performance art has been on the performing body in its different modalities and manifestations. Several historians and theoreticians even argued that body art – i.e. a performance art genre where the exploration of the body is in the very centre of the event – is performance art *par excellence* (e.g. Goldberg, 1979, 2001; Carlson, 2004; Jones, 1998). The body of the performer became a new art medium, as well as the central theme and focus of artistic exploration. The physical presence of the performer was brought to the foreground by starting programmatically revealing mostly forgotten, ignored and overlooked moments – not only of the individual, single body, but also of the broader, social context inevitably imprinted into its flesh. Here the body was understood as a temporary nomadic intersection without a focal point, more appropriately said, a field across which society, politics, and culture cross in time and process, i.e. in an open, unterminated and unfinished modality. The tortured, mutilated, naked body, bodily attributes and functions as an ambiguous space of individual and socio-political research, the body as the only refuge of freedom in totalitarian regimes which escapes their control, the body which liberates itself from social, sexual, racial, beauty ideals – all these fields were put in the centre by performance art.

One of the Mattes' "synthetic" reenactments was made after Chris Burden's *Shoot* from 1971 that has been recognized as one of the first performative explorations of the body as the new artistic medium in the then counterculture. In the original performance, at 7:45 p.m. on November 19th 1971, performance artist Chris Burden was shot. His friend shot him into his left arm in an empty gallery space, surrounded by white walls. The scene was observed by ten people and documented by a black and white photograph (Donofrio, 2012).

In the interviews, Burden emphasized that such acts are much closer to reality than the illusory world of theatre: "It seems that bad art is theatre. Getting shot is for real ... there's no element of pretense or make-believe in it" (Carlson, 2004, p. 113). For Burden, such actions were the means to attain the more appropriate, more "real" reality. In the sixties and seventies, when performance art came into being as a contemporary art practice, it did not only test the limits of a new medium and call into question high modernism (according to Amelia Jones' theory – *cf.* Jones, 1998). An important endeavor of performance art was also its desire to reach the authentic, "real" life. This desire was a part of the broader context: the counterculture of the 1960s rejected conventional social norms of the 1950s and the 1940s. The liberation movements for civil rights, gender equality, gay's and women's liberation, sexual revolution, etc. spread. Revolt and the questioning of social norms reached also into the field of performance art; one of the most burning issues was the liberation, including the liberation of the body. Experimentation and new explorations in spirituality, as well as the search for new experience in general were in the air. The liberation movements appreciated individuality, and the search for truth, however, has gained a particular value – the search for personal, unique truth, even by the means of physical/sexual liberation and the drug culture.

However, what happens with these values in the age of ubiquitous mediatization and computing? In such mixed reality we live today the issues of authenticity, truth, copy, and repeatability are quite different. The Mattes' duo stated, "To me there's no distinction between reality and fiction, facts and fantasy, authentic and simulated. Nothing is real, everything is possible" (Mattes, 2007a).

The message of *Synthetic Performances* is therefore entirely different. The body there is not exposed any more in all its vulnerability and fragility, as it was in the original pieces, and as it was also one of the points of the original Burden's performance. 0100101110101101.ORG "mischievously invert the values of authenticity and vulnerability that were attributed to the original pieces in the 1960s and 1970s" (O'Reilly, 2009, p. 128). In Burden's *Shoot* the performer's body is exposed to pain; the shot is "real," the injury is authentic. It seems that the digital reenactment, conversely, escapes interfering with the live body; the action is accomplished in the seemingly safe virtual place. It is mediated and mediatized at the most, changing the focus and the message of the original performance from the value of the then authenticity to the today's mediatized and mixed reality and the problems of its authenticity.

Later the Mattes added some new, original pieces to the *Synthetical Performances*, exploring the avatar's body as well as the real bodies of the authors. In the durational performance *I know that it's all a state of mind* (2010) the nude bodies of the avatars of Eva and Franco Mattes keep falling over and over for hours in an ascetic virtual gallery space in Second Life. The performance was performed alive in Plymouth Art Centre, as well as in the virtual SL. So, there were several types of audience. Although the performance was not meant to be participatory, other avatars of the audience in SL joined the avatars of the performers. Here, the struggle of falling bodies in the virtual world was also the real struggle of the bodies of the artists: "... we accepted to perform for four days, four hours a day. At the end, we were almost throwing up on keyboards and for the first time, we felt the pain that our avatars usually don't feel in our performances" (Shindler, 2010).

The dialogue with western art historical tradition is foregrounded in a series of performances of *ZeroG SkyDancers*, created and directed by DC Spensley aka DanCoyote (the latter is the name of his avatar in Second Life). The performances were made for the audience in a form of avatars that attended the show, after paying the entrance ticket.

In these shows, Sky Dancers perform breathtaking choreographies using specific movement commands of flight, available in Second Life. They dance and fly in the architectural space with zero G, while the audience in the form of avatars remains seated and watching the spectacle. The avatars perform in the typical Second Life space and iconography which are augmented by abstract lines, forms, vivid colours, and shapes floating around. Subtle dances of avatars, of vivid colours and their shades define this spectacle, a real eye-catcher.

Spensley's work does not emerge from the internet-based or new media art but rather from the modernist tradition. The author itself defines his style as "hyperformalism." With software tools he generates abstract, spatial artworks that have no reference in physical reality, no recognizable elements except the play of colours and shapes that reminds me of modernist explorations of the medium. But here, the "paintings" move and fly, their layers are animated and flow through the SL space.

CODE PERFORMANCES OF GAZIRA BABELI

Gazira Babeli was born in Second Life in March 2006. She is the artist that exists and performs only in Second Life while the creator of her identity remains hidden. Gazira made herself famous with manipulating and subverting virtual world with her actions like invading Ars Virtua Gallery within SL and subverting the opening of the exhibition of Mattes' duo. In her performance, titled *Come to Heaven* (July 2006), she stages a simple question: what happens if she hurls her body from above, from millions of meters high, against the force of gravity and at a speed of 900 kilometers per hour?

In some cases the performing space shatters and disintegrates and her body is hard to recognize as the body. In other cases, on the other hand, the visual reference on Gazira's body remains but her limbs multiply in a weird way while her body is changing into a messy pulp of multiplied eyes and hair.

To subdue the body to extreme conditions of high speed (comparable to an airplane's one), testing the borders of the body's endurance, exploring its capabilities – this is all very close to the endeavors of body art in the 1970s. But this action is "real" only within Second Life. It cites the imaginary leap into the void by Yves Klein (*Le saut dans le vide*, 1960), about which only the photograph, in fact the photomontage, testifies. Within SL, the action is not performed by a live performer's body, however, here the avatar's body flies through the space, but the moments of unpredictability and uniqueness that were crucial for historical body art, still persist. The test of the endurance and "performance" of Gazira's body is in fact the test of the endurance and the performance of the graphics card installed on the computer being used and its reactions according to extreme conditions. The performance cannot be repeated in exactly the same way; its versions exist due to the fact that it is impossible to predict how the graphics card will behave, therefore an interface that has been gaining more and more importance in today's culture in general that is changing into interface, software, and algorithmic culture (*cf.* Johnson, 1997; Galloway, 2012; Strehovec, 2013). Interface shapes our perception, action, and thinking, therefore our way of being human.

This and other Gazira's performances show that the body is always embedded into a particular context; it is never the body in-itself. Domenico Quaranta writes that Gazira "knows that the body is a construct, and enjoys deforming it or rendering it interchangeable. She knows that space is an illusion and she plays around with these contradictions. She knows that 'reality depends on our graphic card'" (Quaranta, 2007). Gazira Babeli plays with the rules of the world she lives in, i.e. with those of which her existence depends on – the program code (she even calls herself a "code performer").

Gazira's corporeality, her existence, is thoroughly intertwined with the environment she lives in. That the body is fundamentally embedded in the world is also the belief of Merleau-Ponty. In *Phenomenology of Perception* he writes that we understand the world, things, others, and oneself through our body. I am aware of the world through my body, and I am aware of my body through the world, more precisely, through the kinaesthetic sensations and actions my body performs. Merleau-Ponty shows that the body is not merely "*in* space, or *in* time" but "*inhabits* [*habite*] space and time" (Merleau-Ponty, 2007, p. 139). It inhabits space by moving through it and thus carrying out meaningful projects. Therefore the body is at the very origin of any signification.

The comparison of two different things – of an example of software art, in which the body of an avatar is performing, and the philosophical notions of the representative of existential phenomenology from the mid-twentieth century who has not known anything yet about the digital worlds – seems to be a little bit out of joint. But some aspects are similar and comparable, especially when we think about corporeality as the fundamental expression of the being in the world, without taking into consideration what and of what kind this world is. Gazira's world is based on programming code which is also the basis for every social practice in it. Her performances manipulate and activate the code, intervening directly into the heart of Second Life, and by doing this, explore also her own existence as she knows very well she is also made from code.

CONCLUSION

We come to the recognition that avatars when awakened to life, always gain new meanings that exceed our manipulation and control of them. The question that emerges here is to a certain extent the same question we have when encountering "traditional" artworks: does the author of an artwork fully have control over his work, does he control everything he puts into it, everything he intends to be written, painted, filmed, etc.? The answer is no; the artwork always transcends its creator, not just because of the psychic features the author has put into it and he was not aware of them (this is of course the traditional theory of art creation) but also by the context into which the work is embedded.

Like an artwork, the virtual body, too, is to a certain extent immaterial, it is full of symbolic meanings, evoking them with its actions. An interesting piece, existing in the in-between spaces of Second Life and physical world, addresses this issue. This is the project *Objects of Virtual Desire* (2005) by G + S (Simon Goldin and Jakob Senneby) which explores how the objects in virtual worlds that are commonly seen as the representations of physical counterparts, gain new meanings in virtual environment and through virtual use. In their virtual use, they have special value to their owners, whereas in physical world, they "die" in a certain way. When they are exhibited as physical, materialized objects in "real life" gallery, they lose their aura of originality which they possess as the virtual objects.

Virtual spaces have become the places on their own. New forms of corporeality inhabit them and lead new forms of life there. In the last decade, these new forms cannot be found just in physical hybrids between humans and machines (as it was in the 1980s), but are as well extended and dispersed in digital worlds. Embodiment today is modeled by high technologies and software-shaped, and as such it influences back on our physical bodies and transforms them.

It seems that in the 21st century the issue of space has gained a high importance. New forms of human creativity colonize spaces in new, previously unknown ways. But while in the previous decades men desired to launch the human being into outer space, a man in the space today is no longer a challenge. Other questions and issues are more important now. Human presence in outer space tends to be much more sophisticated and indirect. The space has been already colonized by different threads and traces of the human. The huge grid of outer space corresponds to the virtual space. Imagination and creativity are those forces that forge new possibilities, forms, and paths for their colonization, or better, settlement. In the light of these endeavours, Second Life emerges as a new mental space where the rules of cause and effect, of gravity and weight cease to exist. Here, the place for new creativity appears. At the same time, this world is limited and defined by its code, and so are its bodies.

REFERENCES

Babeli, G. (2006). *Come To Heaven*. 2006. Retrieved from http://www.gazirababeli.com/cometoheaven.php

Brown, C. (2011). Learning to Dance with Angelfish: Choreographic Encounters Between Virtuality and Reality. In S. Broadhurst & J. Machon (Eds.), *Performance and Technology. Practices of Virtual Embodiment and Interactivity* (pp. 85–99). Hampshire, UK: Palgrave Macmillan.

Carlson, M. (2004). *Performance: a critical introduction*. London: Routledge.

Donofrio, A. (2012). Seeing Gray: The Power of Interpretation in Chris Burden's *Shoot. The Stoa Online*, 1(Fall). Retrieved October from http://icstoa.wordpress.com/fall-2012-volume-i/seeing-gray-the-power-of-interpretation-in-chris-burdens-shoot-by-amber-donofrio/

Fischer-Lichte, E. (2004). *Ästhetik der Performativen*. Frankfurt am Mein, Germany: Suhrkamp.

Fraser, M., & Greco, M. (2005). Introduction. In M. Fraser & M. Greco (Eds.), *The Body. A Reader* (pp. 1–42). London, New York: Routledge.

Gallagher, S. (2005). *How the Body Shapes the Mind*. Oxford: Clarendon Press. doi:10.1093/0199271941.001.0001

Galloway, A. R. (2012). *The Interface Effect*. Cambridge: Polity Press.

Gibson, W. (1984). *Neuromancer*. New York: Ace.

Goldberg, R. (1979). *Performance: live art 1909 to the present*. London: Thames & Hudson.

Goldberg, R. (2001). *Performance Art: From Futurism to the Present*. London: Thames & Hudson.

Grassi, D. (Janša, J.). (2006). *Brainloop*. Retrieved from http://vimeo.com/42691853

Hansen, M. B. N. (2004). *New Philosophy for New Media*. Cambridge, MA: MIT Press.

Heim, M. (1991). The Erotic Ontology of Cyberspace. In M. Benedikt (Ed.), Cyberspace: First Steps (pp. 59-80). Cambridge, MA, & London, UK: MIT Press.

Jet Propulsion Laboratory. NASA. (2014). Voyager. The Interstellar Mission. Retrieved from http://voyager.jpl.nasa.gov/

Johnson, S. (1997). *Interface Culture. How New Technology Transforms the Way We Create and Communicate*. San Francisco: Harper.

Jones, A. (1998). *Body Art/Performing the Subject.* Minneapolis: University of Minnesota Press.

KSEVT – The Cultural Centre of European Space Technologies. (2014). Retrieved from http://www.ksevt.eu/Site/ksevt_eng/

Massumi, B. (2002). *Parables for the Virtual. Movement, Affect, Sensation.* Durham, London: Duke University Press. doi:10.1215/9780822383574

Mattes, E. & F. (0100101110101101.ORG). (2007a). Nothing is Real, Everything is Possible [Excerpts from various interviews]. Retrieved from http://0100101110101101.org/press/2007-07_Nothing_is_real.html

Mattes, E. & F. (0100101110101101.ORG). (2007b). *Reenactment of Chris Burden's* Shoot. Retrieved from http://0100101110101101.org/home/reenactments/performance-burden.html

Mattes, E. & F. (0100101110101101.ORG). (2010). *I know that it's all a state of mind.* Retrieved from http://vimeo.com/21651866

Merleau-Ponty, M. (2007). *Phenomenology of Perception.* London, New York: Routledge.

Munster, A. (2006). *Materializing New Media. Embodiment in Information Aesthetics.* Lebanon: University Press of New England.

O'Reilly, S. (2009). *The Body in Contemporary Art.* London: Thames & Hudson.

Paul, C. (2003). *Digital Art.* London: Thames & Hudson.

Petrič, Š. (2013). Voyager/ 140 AU. Retrieved from http://www.spelapetric.org/home/projects/voyager140au/

Quaranta, D. (2007). Gaz', Queen of the Desert. Retrieved from http://www.gazirababeli.com/TEXTS.php?t=gazqueenofthedesert

Quaranta, D. (2014). RE:akt! Things that Happen Twice. In A. Caronia, J. Janša, D. Quaranta (Eds.), RE:akt! Reconstruction, Re-enactment, Re-reporting (pp. 43-52). Brescia, Italy: LINK Editions, & Ljubljana, Slovenia: Aksioma – Institute for Contemporary Art.

Rockwell, S. (1989). Cyberpunk (book one, Vol. 1, no. 1). Wheeling, West Virginia: Innovative Corporation.

Salter, C. L. (2007). *Unstable Events: Performative Science, Materiality and Machinic Practices.* Paper presented at Re:place: Second international Conference on the Histories of Media, Art, Science and Technology, House of World Cultures (HKW), Berlin, Germany. Retrieved from http://www.google.si/url?sa=t&rct=j&q=&esrc=s&frm=1&source=web&cd=19&ved=0CGQQFjAIOAo&url=http%3A%2F%2Fpl02.donau-uni.ac.at%2Fjspui%2Fbitstream%2F10002%2F447%2F1%2FSalter_Unstable%2520Events.docm&ei=u8GOUc75F6bw4QSH1YGQDw&usg=AFQjCNF9tOoXI4Bsce8336uzEM1lUMloyw&sig2=isSrQwQNKMuRpmnRS9ur_w

Schechner, R. (1988). *Performance Theory (revised and expanded edition, with a new preface by the author).* London, New York: Routledge.

Shindler, K. (2010, May 28). Life After Death: An Interview with Eva and Franco Mattes. *ART21 Magazine.* Retrieved from http://blog.art21.org/2010/05/28/life-after-death-an-interview-with-eva-and-franco-mattes/

Strehovec, J. (2013). Algorithmic Culture and E-Literary Text Semiotics. *Cultura. International Journal of Philosophy of Culture and Axiology, 10*(2), 141–156. doi:10.5840/cultura201310218

Strehovec, J. (2014, April 5). E-Literary Text in the Nomadic Cockpit. *Electronic Book Review.* Retrieved from http://www.electronicbookreview.com/thread/electropoetics/cockpit

Thacker, E. (2005, September 6). Biophilosophy for the 21st century. *CTHEORY*. Retrieved from www.ctheory.net/articles.aspx?id=472

KEY TERMS AND DEFINITIONS

Body Schema: The perception and internal experience of the moving body and its parts. The notion has become very interesting in today's techno-culture because of the possible (techno) extensions of body schema.

Cyberpunk: A movement in science fiction of the 1980s and the 1990s, combining urban punk sensibility with highly technological and utopian future (e.g. novel *Neuromancer* by William Gibson, 1984; movies *The Lawnmower Man*, 1992, *Terminator 2*, 1991, etc.).

Embodiment: The bodily aspects of human subjectivity. It is one of the key themes in phenomenology (esp. in Merleau-Ponty). The term refers also to the physical presence of our bodies that are a precondition for subjectivity, emotion, thinking, social activity, etc. Our bodies are the means with which we encounter the world.

Performance Art: A genre in art, emerged as far as in the beginning of the 20th century (in Futurism and Dadaism), in the 1960s and 1970s it was established as an individual art form. It is often defined as an antithesis to theatre and classical visual arts since the anti-representational tendencies are stressed; processuality, experimentation, the performing body in its different modalities and manifestations are often emphasized as well.

Phenomenology: A movement in the history of philosophy launched in the first half of the 20th century by Edmund Husserl, Martin Heidegger, Maurice Merleau-Ponty, Jean-Paul Sartre, et al. Basically, it studies the structure of various types of experience from perception, thought, imagination, to embodiment and emotion, which are traditionally experienced from the first-person point of view.

Reenactment: A repetition of an event that occurred at an earlier time. The number of the reenactments of artistic performances and events has increased around the beginning of the 21st century. No matter how precisely they imitate the original pieces the reenactments are always different from their original due to new contexts in which they appear.

ENDNOTES

[1] DSN is a world-wide network of large antennas and communication facilities, located in California, Spain, and Australia, that supports interplanetary spacecraft missions (Wikipedia).

[2] An exclamation by Kasimir Malevich (1878–1935), the Russian painter and the inventor of the *Black Square* (shown to the public in 1915). The author of Suprematism and his students made also some designs that were aesthetic visions that anticipated the conquest of outer space and the construction of satellites. He believed that true art is possible only in outer space. In many different positions in contemporary art Malevich's ideas continue to echo.

[3] The institution was established to facilitate the humanization and culturalization of outer space, an arena that has been up till now almost exclusively in the domain of the military, science, and technology. The process of space culturalization has the potential to radically change the accessibility to these exclusive technologies, thus enabling society to inscribe them with different meaning, purpose, and goal.

[4] In tourism, for instance, we are witnessing an increased offer of participations in various types of events, of being part of breathtaking adventures and experiences, be it sports, safari, gastronomy, theme parks, or

shopping. Such offer has become sometimes even more popular than classical sightseeing of "objects" from point to point.

[5]   An exponential growth of publications, body-oriented journals and undergraduate courses have fixed the theoretical focus of a novel discipline, the sociology of the body. The body is also a concern for a wide range of disciplines, including the sociology of health and illness, of the emotions, of sport, as well as social studies of science and technology.

[6]   In 2007, Davide Grassi changed his name into Janez Janša, the name of the then Slovenian right-wing prime minister.

[7]   Around the beginning of the 21st century, the practices of reenactment have enjoyed an increasing success in the artistic context. But the reenactments, no matter how precisely they imitate the original pieces, are always inevitably different from their original, since they have been brought to life in entirely new contexts. Italian theorist Domenico Quaranta believes that "the advent of reenactment in the artistic context appears to lie at the point where two parallel, only seemingly conflictual processes converge: the predominance of 'mediatized' (or mediated) experience over direct experience, and the resurfacing of performance art" (Quaranta, 2014, p. 45).

Chapter 11
Blended Reality Performance

Joff Chafer
Coventry University, UK

ABSTRACT

This chapter focuses on the integration of live performance that blends virtual (avatars animated live in Second Life) and physical performers. To start with the author will briefly look at some of the ways practitioners have integrated and played with new technologies in performance. Following this a number of case studies that have explored this blending of the physical and the virtual will be examined. This will then be followed by a discussion about the nature of this type of performance both from the point of view of physical performers and those performing with avatars.

INTRODUCTION

An avatar is a representation of a human operator in the online world, specifically in the sense I am using the word here, within a three-dimensional virtual world. The use of an avatar by an operator enables a person to move from being a detached observer of a space to become present within it, to participate and interact with objects and others within that space, and to be perceived by them. Using an avatar within these worlds enables the two realities, the physical and the virtual, to become mixed together, as the person operating the avatar can cross over the dividing line (i.e. the screen) between the two worlds. This space is sometimes referred to as liminal, in that it has the same dividing role as the limen, the edge of the stage that separates the performers and the audience in the theatre.

Maeva Veerapen describes how she relates to her avatar Ninoo Nansen in a number of different ways: "Ninoo is an object for me but also possesses subjective qualities when she functions as a prosthesis,[or] phantom limb ..." (Maeva Veerapen, 2011 p.98). After the initial acclimatisation to the virtual world her avatar has at times become akin to a physical extension, in the same way that a tennis player might use a tennis racket, or it might also make her physically feel or sense as I did with the kick. Writing about her experiences when performing in *Telematic Dreaming*(1992), Susan Kozel describes similar feelings "Great care and concentration was required to make intricate web patterns with the finger of a stranger, or to cause one fleshy finger to meet up with one video finger... The occasions when the movement worked well felt very much like good contact improvisation: a hypnotic feeling of not knowing what is com-

DOI: 10.4018/978-1-4666-8384-6.ch011

ing next but letting the strong flow of movement carry you onward. When the movement moved through us in this way, based on openness and trust, the distinction between which bodies were real and which were virtual became irrelevant." (Kozel,S 2007 p.93-4) She also describes how when somebody elbowed her in the stomach she instinctively doubled over and on another occasion felt "little electric shocks pass through my body" (p.97) in response to a caress. On the occasion however when she was deliberately and violently attacked by two men she was able to mentally step back in an act of "self-preservation-a primordial reaction in a sophisticated technological context."

The work I am discussing in this chapter is about the use of avatars in a virtual world for performance, simultaneously performing with physical people in the physical world. I will also look at the historical precedents for mixing realities in theatre and film, as it is these technological devices that I have particularly focused on in performances. I also cover how the liminal space between reality and fiction/ performer and audience is a constant theme in art and performance and one which constantly fascinates audiences and creators. As a practitioner I have been drawn to this area for exploration.

This blending of the real and the virtual could be seen as a form of telepresence, often, though not always, the performers animating the avatars could be completely remote, distance-wise from the physical action, but even when they are physically located in the same space the blended performance is mediated through a third combined space, usually a projection screen. Indeed, where there is a sense of connectedness or embodiment between a person and an avatar, any foray into a virtual world could be seen as telepresence.

"Telepresence as a term was first used by Marvin Minsky in 1980 to describe the experience of the operator of remotely located devices. ... the term telepresence has since been adopted (and continuously redefined) by many researchers concerned with the experience of interacting

remotely"(Kuksa and Childs, 2014). I use it as a term to describe the act of feeling present at a remote location via some form of technological mediation or feeling or sensing the presence of others by the same means. This could be as commonplace as a telephone or Skype conversation through to more complicated, bespoke, set ups in galleries or theatres.

Since 2006 I have been actively exploring the possibilities of performing with avatars both in virtual and mediated spaces. I am using the term "mediated" here to refer to spaces that rely on some form of technology, more often than not a video camera, as the intermediary between the performer and the audience. I was first drawn to this when watching my daughter playing an early version of 'The Sims' video game and wondering whether it would be possible to perform *Look Back in Anger (Osborne, 1956)* on it. I mentioned this to a colleague at work who suggested I look at Second Life as a potential platform for doing this.

I have spent a considerable amount of time exploring Second Life, learning not just the practicalities of controlling an avatar, but also building and scripting. I also came to feel part of a community or communities, whether that be as an actor with Metaverse Shakespeare Company, MSC, (formerly known as the Second Life Shakespeare Company, SLSC) and Avatar Repertory Theater, ART as an audience member at countless theatre, dance and cabaret performances or at art galleries or recreated historical sites through to online teaching at Danish Visions, (a group in Second Life that offers free classes on various building, scripting and design techniques). As both an actor and educator, both real and virtual, I feel it is vital to really know and understand your medium even if only a tiny percentage of that knowledge and understanding is visible in the work that is created.

The examples that I will be looking at ultimately aim to blend or mesh the two, with the technology being an enabler rather than the point of interest, though in this journey a number of the examples have been about exploring what the technology can do, where the performance itself could be seen as an excuse to play with the kit. This playing I see as a vital component of the exploration, getting to know and understand the different technical aspects, whether this be video projection or animating an avatar, so that eventually the technology can take a back seat. This was something that I was advised to do back in the early 1990s by Pete Brooks (a founder member of Impact Theatre Co-operative and Insomniac Productions and currently a regular collaborator with Imitating the Dog) when, as a director and performer with Trestle Theatre Company, we were looking to use video projection in a production. His advice was to get the kit and play with it and let that lead you in the way that it is integrated into the performance rather than deciding beforehand what you want it to do.

BACKGROUND

Theatre has exploited new technologies over the centuries from the Ancient Greeks' use of cranes and other mechanical devices, through to elaborate stage mechanics in the 19th century, the use of focused lighting once electricity took over from gas[1]. In the 19th century some of the mechanics used (particularly by Bruce 'Sensation' Smith at Drury Lane) tended to overshadow the actors, creating a theatre that was more about spectacle than narrative and acting ability. One piece of theatre technology that came to prominence in 19th century theatre is the Pepper's Ghost illusion. This is a theatrical illusion dating from the late 1800s which was used to allow ghosts or other apparitions to appear or vanish from scenes. It is managed by reflecting a person or image in a sheet of glass angled at 45% to the audience. The person is hidden from view, either by being below the stage level in a pit, or off to the side of the stage or behind flats, the area around them is black. When a light is shone on them their reflection appears and when the light is turned off the audience see straight through the glass. It is named after John Pepper who was first to modify the illusion for use in the theatre, though the effect can be traced back as far as the 16th century. This technique has been brought up to date by Musion with Musion Eyeliner, which replaces the glass with a patented film and uses video projection to create the image. This has been used to spectacular effect at various music concerts as well as corporate events. Looking at the videos, the meshing of the live performers with the recorded or computer generated image looks seamless but the effect relies on the framework supporting the film being hidden, the audience being as central as possible to the image and at a reasonable distance. Seen from close up and from the side the image may not line up with the floor or the physical performers, so for smaller scale performance it may not be that useful, and for a performer it is an odd feeling being on a stage with a large sheet of plastic between you and the audience.

From the dawn of the recorded image people have played with the possibilities of mixing realities or creating hybrid realities. In the early days this may have come about from accidental superimpositions, multiple exposures, camera shake and the like, but artists, both amateur and professional soon saw the possibilities of deliberate subversions of the media. Georges Méliès (1861–1938) was a master of this and, as a stage magician, quickly incorporated film projection into his act. Initially, the novelty of the moving image alone was enough but he was soon exploring the possibilities of multiple exposures and camera 'tricks' to entertain. He went on to make great strides in developing film narrative, taking a lot of his cues from the world of theatre, but for me it is his playing with the hardware, the kit, and the manipulation of the data, the raw footage, that intrigues me and is something that I have been exploring a century on.

Another early pioneer was Winsor McCay (1867-1934) the American cartoonist who created the animation *Gertie the Dinosaur* in 1914.

He first showed the cartoon as part of his live vaudeville stage show where he would talk to the character in the guise of a ringmaster and get it to perform tricks. For the finale of the act he would leave the stage and reappear in cartoon form on screen with the dinosaur, where she would pick him up in his mouth and lift him up to take their bows and finally walk off screen. Later he added filmed footage at the beginning and end of the cartoon so that it could be shown without him having to be present.

In the 20th and 21st centuries there are still instances where the balance between spectacle and narrative in theatre has been uneven with many productions promoting the use of 'real holograms' or other 'techno-geekery' over the story. Some practitioners and companies have deliberately fore fronted their use of technology, for example, 'Imitating the Dog' in their production *The Zero Hour* (2013).

On a formal level, The Zero Hour continues ITD's exploration of the relation between live action, computer generated animation and recorded material. In particular, the events of the stage are filmed and projected by a Chinese film crew, a device which helps to frame the audience's interrogation of the process of the writing of history and the production of fictions. (The Zero Hour, (n.d.) retrieved from http://www.imitatingthedog. co.uk/projects/the-zero-hour/)

Here cameras, and indeed a film crew are very visibly present and it is through their lens, both literally and figuratively, that the audience piece together a fragmented narrative. Less visible, though equally integral, is the use of back projection with backgrounds deliberately sourced from 3D computer games and seamlessly orchestrated by means of Isadora software. This software is still being developed by Mark Coniglio of Troika Ranch and has been used in many of their dance pieces for, as Coniglio says:

Tools like video, digital media software packages and tele-presence are important to us because art, to be relevant in contemporary society, must simultaneously embrace and examine contemporary culture and currency. Integrating emergent media keeps live theater vital in a world where the most widely experienced channel of aesthetic expression is broadcast media. But, most importantly, it imparts a real and necessary density that mirrors the media intense world in which we live." (Coniglio, (n.d.) retrieved from www.troikaranch. org/technology.html)

Dance practitioners have, over the years, been in the vanguard of those exploring the use of computer technology, from Merce Cunningham's use of choreographic software and motion capture (Mo-cap) technology, through to a number of companies (for example, Random Dance) currently using live and recorded video and bespoke software in their performances. Mo-cap is the process of recording the movement of people, tracking individual points of the body. This information can be used to animate avatars and animated characters for use in video games or films.

Though not technically a dance company, a lot of Igloo's work explores dance and movement in general, and they have been creating work since the mid-1990s meshing the physical and the virtual on stage and in galleries. Often their work draws influences from computer games, whether that be using game engines to design virtual environments, or having gallery visitors use joysticks and tracker balls or, most recently, Augmented Reality phone Apps and Oculus Rift headsets to access their work. Augmented Reality (often referred to as AR) refers to the overlaying of digital information onto a real space. In this instance by pointing a phone camera at an installation in a shop window the image of dancers, captured using Mo-cap, appear on the screen.

Contemporary theatre companies seem to be catching up with dance companies in their regular use of video manipulation software. The theatre company 1927's production of *The Children and Animals took to the Streets* (2012) made use of Qlab software. In this piece, the three performers worked in front of a white set containing a number of windows and doors onto which animation footage was projected. The animation not only allowed the performers to change locale and interact with other characters, but was also used as one of the main means of lighting them. By using a cartoon style for the animation they were able to highlight the unreality of this 'other world' whilst at the same time drawing the audience in to believe this mixed reality.

Another theatre piece exploiting the Qlab software was the Tigerlillies production of *Lulu – A Murder Ballad* (2014). This utilised front projection onto a false proscenium frame around the stage, which also lit a gauze screen in front of a raised platform, situated behind the band. Behind this platform there was a back projection screen, with the result that a performer could be in the middle of an entirely projected set. Again there was a choice to go with a stylised animated set of images, though these were more akin to video game aesthetic, even if there was still a hand drawn feel to some of the elements, as with 1927's production.

Stationhouse Opera have used recorded video in a number of their performances and more recently (since 2004 with their production of *Live from Paradise*) used live video to create telematic performances that link actors from different venues to create simultaneous performances for audiences in those locations. In their most recent production Dissolved (2014), rather than just projecting images from the different locales onto screens, they combine the images so that the actors appear to occupy the same physical space.

In *Telematic Dreaming* (Sermon, 1992), two beds were set up in separate spaces, one hidden where the performer lay on a bed and another space that had a white bed with the image of the performer, where gallery visitors could interact telematically. Susan Kozel, who performed in an iteration of the piece in 2004, described performing in the piece as "emotionally taxing as well as enriching."(Kozel, 2007) Whilst the gallery visitor could interact with her projected image on the bed her view was mediated through television screens around her bed.

A piece that particularly inspired me is Paul Sermon's *Liberate your Avatar (2007)*. The press release for the work explained that:

"In this new project, Paul Sermon will recreate the actual All Saints Gardens on Oxford Road in Second Life, allowing both members of the public and virtual inhabitants ('avatars') of Second Life to co-exist and share the same park bench in a live interactive installation." (Sermon, P, (n.d.) Press Release retrieved from http://creativetechnology.salford.ac.uk/paulsermon/liberate/press%20 release.pdf)

To enable this 'coexistence', avatars were filmed against a blue background in Second Life and then blended with the live image of the park via a Chromakey vision mixer and the resulting composite image was projected onto a screen in front of the bench. Chromakey is a technique for layering two video images together, an actor or object is filmed against a coloured background, usually blue or green, which can be processed out of the image. The resulting image without the coloured background is layered on top of another image. This may also be referred to as bluescreen or greenscreen. From the reactions of the audience, it was clear to see how quickly and effortlessly the park users adapted to this superimposed presence. The ease with which they interacted with the avatars and accepted them was heartening, as they could so easily have taken affront at this imposition on their space, or simply ignored them. This was helped by the playful nature of the avatar interactions; not demanding a response but offering the possibility of one. Also, the appearance of the avatars, which were more like cartoons than flesh and blood, may also have helped to emphasise their benign presence. In examining the affinity or unease that people may experience in relating to avatars the concept of "The Uncanny Valley" has sometimes been adopted. This is a term coined by Masahiro Mori who hypothesised "that a person's response to a humanlike robot would gradually shift from empathy to revulsion as it approached, but failed to attain, a lifelike appearance"(Mori,M,1970). A similar effect has been seen in relating to avatars and it may be that the *Liberate Your Avatar* avatars, with their more cartoon-like appearance, were a good step back from 'The Uncanny Valley', whereas a more realistic looking avatar would have triggered the revulsion that has been observed in other interactions. More recently the graphics used in public interactions of this kind have become more realistic as technology moves forward but the public's interest seems to be just as accepting, for example the 7D Show at Dubai Mall.

I had presumed that it must be possible to blend avatars and physical people and places, but it was not until I saw this, and the schematic of the performance, that I realised the 'relative' simplicity of the set up. (Sermon, P, (n.d.) Schematic retrieved from http://creativetechnology.salford. ac.uk/paulsermon/liberate/video%20flow%20 diagram.jpg) After meeting with Paul Sermon and having confirmation that I would need little more than a camera, a vision mixer and a computer I started work on my own exploration.

CASE STUDIES

In the following case studies I will give an overview of the physical and virtual set ups with schematics

and an outline of what took place followed by a short appraisal of the event as a whole and lessons learnt. Once all five have been described I will then discuss the nature of both the physical and virtual performers within these pieces of Blended Reality Performance in greater detail.

Issues that I will be looking at during these case studies include: the use of different techniques in creating 'Blended' performance spaces; creating 2D and 3D mediated spaces; how avatar size in relation to the physical performer changes the performance relationship, and how audiences engage with the work.

Summer Dancing (2008)

This took place in June 2008 at Coventry University where I worked with a group of dancers, and a computing student who operated one of the avatars (See Figure 1). The technical set up was similar to Sermon's *Liberate your Avatar*, but all performers, animators and audience were in the same physical space; a large 'black box' theatre studio at Coventry University. The composite image of physical performers and avatars was projected onto a screen so that everyone could see, in real time, the same image as the audience.

Artistically, I was inspired by an event in Second Life in which a group of actors from the Second Life Shakespeare Company (SLSC) were waiting backstage before a performance of *Hamlet* and sitting on chairs that had set animations scripted into them. On sitting on the chairs

Figure 1. Summer Dancing (2008)
© *Joff Chafer*

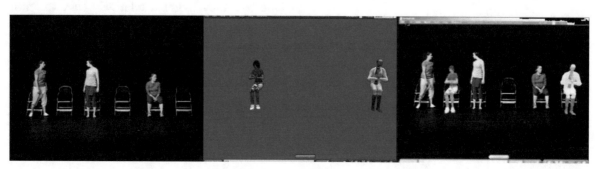

the avatars would go through a series of poses in a set order, in varying degrees of synchronisation with the others sitting next to them. I wanted to mix this with an improvisation game purloined from James Yarker of Stan's Café, a UK-based theatre company. In this game there are six chairs set out in a line. There are five performers waiting offstage who have each been individually briefed as to who they want to end up having sitting to their right and to their left. They enter one at a time and take a seat at random, once all are seated they then move in the same order and they can either move to the empty seat or sit back down in order to end up sitting next to the correct people. Stan's Café developed this into a performance piece *Simple Maths* (1997).

I was working with three dancers from the Dance and Professional Practice course at Coventry University, who would be performing in the real space, while Gemma McLean and myself were operating avatars in Second Life. In the space the chairs set up at one end of the room with the two computers off to one side. A camera caught the live action and an avatar, acting as a virtual camera, was set up in Second Life with similar orientation, but looking at a bluescreen. In the bluescreen space I had the same configuration of chairs but these were set to be invisible to the Second Life camera. The chairs each had three set animations:

1.   The SLSC set of poses,
2.   A neutral sitting pose over which other animations could be played
3.   An animation that I had recorded using a motion capture suit.

Both cameras were relayed to a vision mixer and the composite image was projected onto a screen in the physical space, and angled so that both performers and audience could see. (See Figure 2)

I recorded the animation using a wireless motion capture suit.[2] The sequence comprised a loop of sitting poses: leaning forward; leaning back; scratching head; looking around, etc that could either be played as a set, or split up into the individual moves. This was then edited in Qavimator[3] and imported into Second Life as a BVH file (Bio-Vision Hierarchy is the standard motion capture file format supported by Second Life), and the dancers learnt this set of moves from watching the avatars. In performance, the idea was that the dancers would introduce elements of this movement during the improvisation and pick up/copy the movements from each other. Then, in turn, the avatars would start to join in with the movement sequence, until they were all doing the full sequence in unison or in cannon, once all had found their correct seats. This conformity would then break down, with the dancers/avatars becoming out of sync with each other, and finally, one by one, they would leave.

Mixing live images is not new, but one of the real benefits of working in Second Life is the ability to create a perfect bluescreen space and also the relative ease of being able to line up the two camera positions. This was something that Sermon had mentioned to me before, but said that at times he had inadvertently moved the Second Life camera during his piece, leading to 'glitches' in the performance. I managed to secure the camera position by sitting the camera avatar on a box with a script to set the camera view. As I was relatively new to Second Life at this time, I was not yet aware of the range of camera scripts available. (See Figure 3)

Working with dancers on this piece, I discovered that they found it relatively easy to learn and play with the simple choreography that I had created, and by having the large projected composite image, they could quite quickly take note and adjust to the positioning and actions of the avatars. Operating the avatars themselves was

Figure 2. Summer Dancing schematic
© *Joff Chafer*

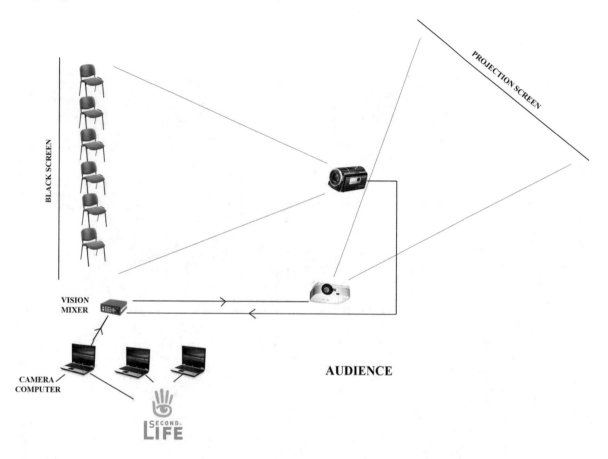

less fluid as their movements, particularly when walking, was quite jerky and they would often move further than planned. This could possibly be overcome by pre-recording more animations but, in this instance, I wanted there to be a strong element of improvisation about the piece, and for those operating the avatars to have an artistic input rather than just a technical one. Also for this first piece the choreography was kept deliberately simple to test the medium.

Second Life permits the operator of an avatar to choose between two views, a first person perspective, when one looks from the point of view of the avatar, and a third person perspective, where the view of the world is as if through a camera close to, but detached from, the avatar. The default third person view when moving an avatar in Second

Life is from a camera position a few feet behind and slightly above the avatar, which meant that when we first tried to move them, they would go out of sight as the camera went behind the back screen. This was relatively easy to overcome in the virtual space, by either moving the back wall farther back, or making it transparent. However, when performing on stage sets this can become an issue, particularly as one of the better ways of steering an avatar is by clicking on the middle of the back and guiding with the mouse whilst using the arrow key to move forward.

We opted for simple costumes throughout as the final rendering of the avatars was not as clear as it might have been. A higher specification computer could have rectified this issue, allowing the virtual camera to record at a higher resolution.

Figure 3. Screenshot from Second Life showing the bluescreen environment (2 10mx5m prims coloured blue and set to full bright). View is set to Highlight Transparent so that the seats are visible, and specific animations are set up on the screen, a basic sitting pose was preloaded into the seats so that when clicked the avatar would automatically sit and face the right direction.
© Joff Chafer

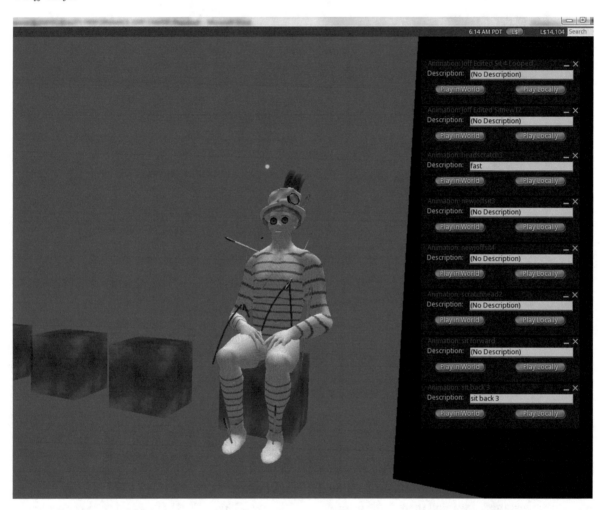

Similarly, we kept the physical space as clear as possible, having just the six chairs against a black background to make sure that the avatars stood out.

For this performance I deliberately worked with the dancers and computer operators in the same physical space, but the computers could have been situated remotely (as they were in *Liberate Your Avatar*) with a live video feed to see what was happening in the physical space. It is possible to stream within Second Life, but then one would need to work around the 5 to 10 second delay.

Furthermore, I wanted the audience to be aware of the mechanics of the piece, and be witness to the whole event: the live action; the computer operation; the composite projected image, and to be aware of it all as a 'live' performance.

After the performance we let the audience have a go at playing 'musical chairs' and, from the immediate responses we got back, there was a clear sense of the presence of the avatars, not just in the mediated space of the screen, but next to them in the chairs. Many participants invariably tried to touch the avatars as they moved about the space, and more than once they apologized for sitting on them! In these times of Oculus Rift and other fully immersive possibilities, it is interesting to note how something as simple as a superimposed image on a screen can have this effect.

Coincidentally, *Machinima Futurista* (2008) was a similar piece of work that was being undertaken by Jennifer Vandagriff working with Michael Nitsche at Georgia Tech, using a specially designed Second Life augmented reality viewer. They stated that the viewer, "allows us to combine real actors and virtual ones (avatars) on a shared visual plane." (Farley, Nitsche, Bolter, Lang, and MacIntyre, 2009 96-97. This viewer, (which unfortunately is no longer available), was a great improvement on the standard viewer as it enabled camera movement in Second Life rather than the static camera position that I had used.

Staging Second Life (2008)

In August 2008, I went to visit the University of Southern Australia in Adelaide to work with Russell Fewster (Programme director MBMA (Bachelor of Media Arts)) assisted by Nic Mollison (lighting designer) and Kyle Tripodi (computer programmer and Second Life expert) and a class of 21 students on the Electronic Arts: Visual Theatre course. As part of the course, the students were being introduced to Second Life and using it as a stimulus to create an intermedial performance; Intermedial in the sense that the project,

...played upon the liminal space between 'real' and digital and gave the students an opportunity to transpose a virtual world into a theatrical setting. The students actively played between these two media in turn becoming intermedialists. (Fewster, Wood & Chafer in Vincenti, Braman: 2011, p.217)

The educational aspects of this module are well covered in the above book, so I will focus on the practical and technical aspects of creating the piece (See Figure 4).

Fewster (co-director) took the lead on this project and, by the time I arrived, the students had already started work on their avatars and getting to grips with the orientation process of Second Life and the peculiarities of navigating this particular environment. They had also started work on a number of scenes reinterpreting their first virtual steps: walking; talking (instant messaging to be precise, with its associated typing animation); 'rezzing' objects; flying; dancing etc. Mollinson was working on the set up of the stage, with a large black gauze (or scrim) covering the front of the proscenium space, and a mixture of top, side and foot lights to illuminate the performers, whilst leaving the rest of the space as dark as possible. About half way back in the auditorium were a couple of computers and a projector, where Tripodi would project live and recorded images from Second Life.[4] (See Figure 5.)

In Second Life Tripodi built a similar 'black box' space and set the camera (using the Bijou camera set up)[5] to match the position of the projector. Fortunately, because of the rake in the auditorium, the projector was level with the middle of the screen, so he did not have to worry about the image distorting. By matching the 3D space, the effect of the projection on the gauze was to place the avatars within the stage space, and consequently avatars could 'enter' from the wings just as the actors. The limitation for this was that there was a 'sweet spot' directly behind the projector where everything matched up perfectly, and the further away from that spot that the audience member sat, the less accurate the positioning became. With this in mind we made sure that the actors kept enough lateral distance from the avatars as necessary.

Figure 4. Staging Second Life - Mollison (avatar), Chafer, Fewster, Tripodi (avatar)
© *Joff Chafer*

For a number of the scenes, we used Bunraku style puppetry and manipulation, where the puppeteer was entirely in black, including gloves and head. When unlit and against a black background they became, to all intents and purposes, invisible. In this way, the actors were able to mimic how in Second Life, it is possible to make objects 'float' through space.

Performing in a traditional theatre space was quite different from the 'black box' studio in that it was seen as piece of theatre that happened to have virtual world elements. To as great an extent as possible the technology was hidden and the focus within the piece was on the physical performers and their stories, allowing a more seamless meshing of the two. (See Figure 6).

SD2 (2009)

In June 2009, Fewster, Mollison and I collaborated on a piece at Coventry University blending elements of the two previous pieces and exploring scale. For this we used a bluescreen space in Second Life to superimpose avatars into the physical space; Luma Key in the physical space to superimpose actors into the virtual space, and a black gauze to explore the projection of virtual sets (See Figure 7). We also broadcast on Livestream for the first time, to an online audience, as well as those present in the physical space. Technically this was a more complicated set up, but taken separately, the different elements were relatively simple. (Figure 8)

Figure 5. Staging Second Life — 3D Side Elevation by Nic Mollison. Shows a cross section of the Hartley Theatre Space, and the projector and control system position in the auditorium. The performer is on-stage behind black translucent scrim on which the avatars were projected. Also shows steep lighting positions from above and floor lighting from below.

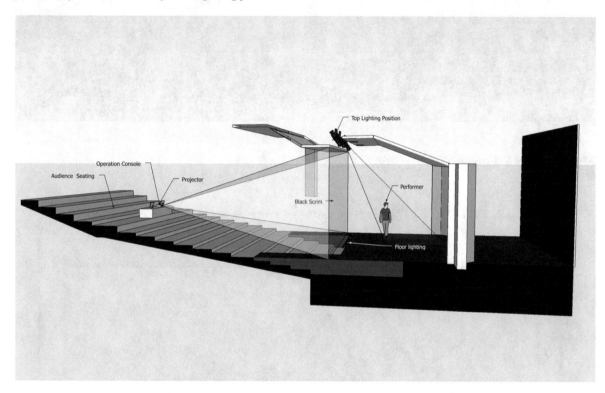

Figure 6. Staging Second Life: Student (Physical) calls his pet dinosaur (Avatar)

Figure 7. SD2

Figure 8. SD2 Schematic
© *Joff Chafer*

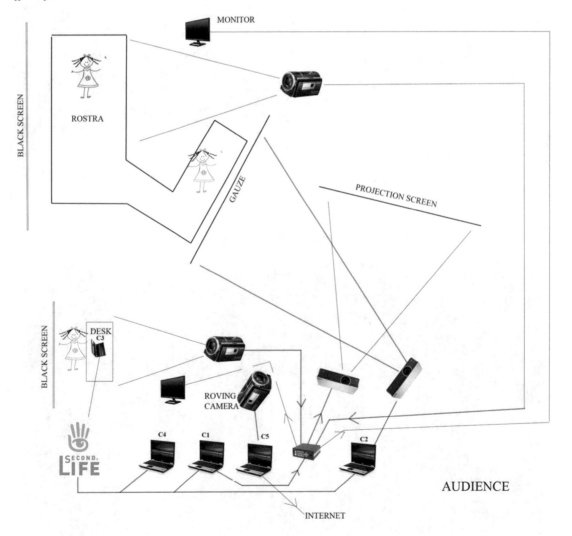

For the first part I was sat at a desk, in a similar position to the chairs in *Summer Dancing* and with a similar configuration of camera and computer capturing the Second Life blue screen space both inputting to a vision mixer with the result being projected onto a screen. There was one computer on the desk for me to operate my avatar as well as a couple of others out of shot for Fewster and Mollison to operate theirs. In Second Life a giant bluescreen table and laptop had been created, so that the avatars could appear small and also pass behind the laptop where their image was occluded.

For the second section we moved to a raised performance area where a different camera sent a feed to the vision mixer, which used Luma key to separate the lit performers from the black background and superimposed onto the Second Life background. Luma key is similar to Chroma key except that instead of an image being separated from a coloured background, on object or person that is lit will be separated from a black background. In Second Life, a model of the desk had been built with photographs of the desk and laptop used as textures. In this section we also used the puppetry technique from *Staging Second Life*, with an unseen puppeteer manipulating a beach ball attached to a stick.

For the third section, the performers stayed on the rostra and a Second Life image of arches was projected onto the gauze. The audience, in the physical space, were positioned to see all the elements, including the composite images on a projection screen, for the streamed version we had a roving camera that could switch angles to capture the different elements.

Playing with scale was an interesting development in this piece, at first with the diminutive avatars on the desk they could be seen as 'pawns' being manipulated. When moving to the second space, the avatars and physical performers are a similar scale and the avatars take on a more pro-active role and have a degree of equality. Finally, for the third part, the virtual environment itself comes to the fore with the physical performers having to respond and react to it. It could be said that seeing the avatars in their diminutive form in the first section heightened their theatricality giving them an other-wordly, magical quality.

ALICE IN WONDERSLAND AT THE SLCC (2010)

This exploration was the first time that avatar performers were remotely collaborating (See Figure 9). It physically took place at the Second Life Community Convention at the Oakland Marriot City Center in Boston in 2010. I was joined in person by Iain McCracken (Sodovan Torok SL)[6] and Michelle Fowler (Mickie Nickolaides SL) and

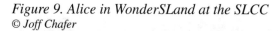

Figure 9. Alice in WonderSLand at the SLCC
© *Joff Chafer*

remotely by other members of Avatar Repertory Theater in the USA and Australia. Previously we had done an entirely in-world production of *Alice in WonderSLand,* but for this we were using luma key to superimpose the live performer (Fowler playing Alice) onto a Second Life background peopled by avatars. The physical set up of the equipment in the space was similar to the *Summer Dancing* configuration, with the addition of live sound streamed into and out of Second Life. This was accomplished (with the help of Thundergas Menges SL) by having a microphone aimed at the performance area, which was fed through a sound mixer into the computer, which acted as the Second Life camera, and a line-out went to the house P.A. system. There was also a second computer running Second Life, so that Instant Message (IM) cues and conversations could take place with the online actors, without the messages coming up on the projection screen. (See Figure 10).

By using Annabeth Robinson's (Angrybeth Shortbread SL) Machinima Multi-Camera Switcher (8Cam Version)[7] setup (see figure 11) in Second Life, we were able to have multiple virtual sets in one place and use keyboard controls

to switch between cameras that had previously been positioned. McCracken controlled the live editing, and I was in a black suit providing Bunraku style animation of props. Similar to *Summer Dancing* and *SD2,* the audience watched both the live performer in the physical space, as well as the composite image. This was simultaneously streamed via Ustream . To test this set up out I worked with Ruth Gibson (performer) and Polly Hudson (narrator) in the theatre studio in Coventry prior to travelling to Boston. The virtual sets were built on Coventry University Island in Second Life, using a mixture of pre-existing sets from the previous 'in-world' production (made by a team of designers led by Jubjub Forder SL) and new, purpose-built elements. (See Figure 11)

I wanted to play with scale again and to first encounter the characters from the story in diminutive form as they fell from the pages of her book, before encountering a human sized White Rabbit. To do this I made two identical sets of the tree and rabbit hole, which was relatively easy in Second Life as I just stretched the original set (including the camera position) so that when I cut from one to the other there was a seamless transition, simi-

Figure 10. Alice in WonderSLand - The set in Second Life
© *Joff Chafer*

Figure 11. Alice in WonderSLand schematic

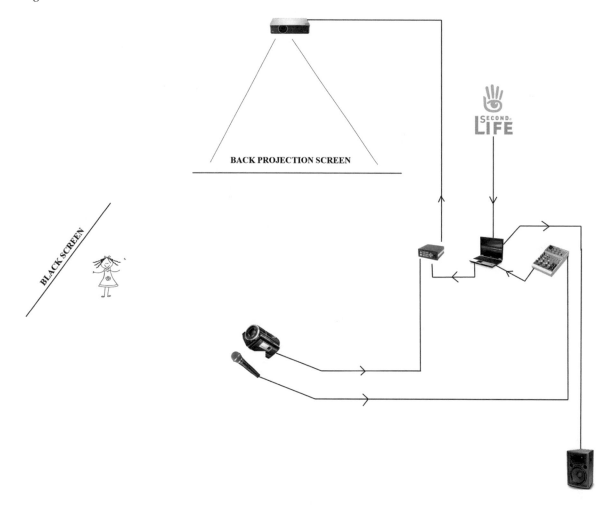

BACK PROJECTION SCREEN

BLACK SCREEN

SECOND LIFE

AUDIENCE

larly when Alice eats the cake and shrinks I used a script created by Ian Upton which changes the size of objects on the table object so that when it was touched it would stretch (normally this would not work on a multiple prim object but I was able to use one of Jubjub's single prim sculptie tables).[8] (See Figure 12)

This was the first time, in this blended reality work that I had worked with avatar performers working remotely, however, as a virtual theatre company we had all had plenty of experience with this for entirely in-world performances. Despite the event being streamed live, it was not possible for all of the performers to watch this as well as be in-world, running Second Life can make quite an intensive demand on bandwidth, so many were acting blind in relation to Alice and were reliant on her voice for cues. As with some of the physical performers in Staging Second Life, they just had to hit their marks and hope that the 'other' was there.

Figure 12. Alice in WonderSLand. Groundplan of the Second Life space showing camera positions
© *Joff Chafer*

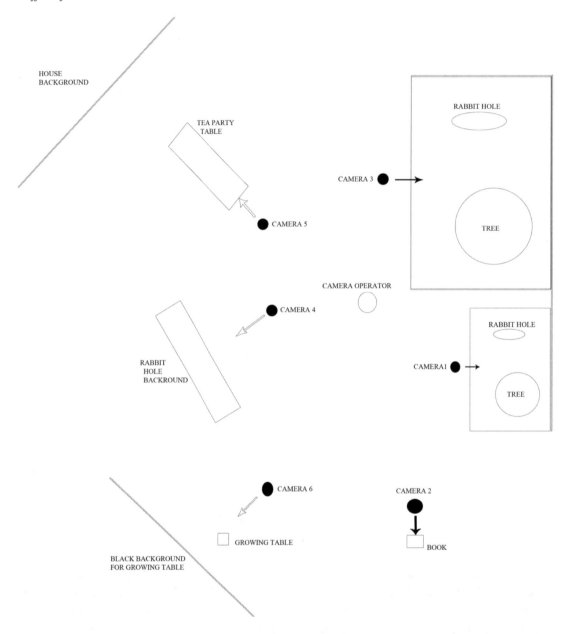

EXTRACT/INSERT (2012)

This installation was a collaboration between Stelarc, Ian Upton and myself, and ran for a month at the Herbert Art Gallery in Coventry. It had over 5000 visitors both online and in the live space. Unlike the previous projects the audience played a key performative role, in fact if they were not there either online or physically, nothing happened. In a sense this was the closest piece to Sermon's *Liberate Your Avatar* (See Figure 13).

On entering the installation visitors were given an introduction to the piece and a pair of 3D glasses, they then entered the room and were

Figure 13. – EXTRACT/INSERT
© *Joff Chafer*

confronted by a large projection screen showing a similar space in Second Life which contained two projection screens reflecting back images from the gallery space. Also in the Second Life space there were a number of avatars who, if they chose to move up to the screen, appeared to 'cross over' into the physical space because of the stereo projection. Technically the stereo projection was accomplished using More3D software and the standard Second Life viewer. During some of the research and development we used the anaglyph feature of the Kirstin's Viewer (which unfortunately is no longer available due to lack of funding).

There was a live microphone hanging above the gallery space through which the two audiences could communicate if they wished. To the right in the gallery space was a small, lit plinth, which if physical audience members chose to stand on, would insert their image, captured by an infra-red camera, onto a separate screen in the Second Life space visible on the screen. This insertion into the virtual space was heightened by the light on the plinth going out and the familiar teleport "whoosh" sound being played. When the person stepped off the pressure pad on the plinth the light came back on, the whoosh sound played and their image disappeared from the screen. This was mirrored in Second Life with an extraction unit that, when sat on by an avatar, would teleport their avatar away from the main space where their image was captured and projected onto a screen behind the gallery audience. The screen in Second Life was scripted so that if an avatar knocked it, it would shake. Behind this screen a separate speaker was mounted so that the avatars could communicate with the gallery audience from that position.

The cameras used to take images from the space automatically sent images to a website which then relayed them onto the Second Life screens. By capturing still images every couple of seconds and displaying them there was negligible latency, had it been a video stream this would have been quite noticeable (often between 5 and 10 seconds delay).

The Second Life construction and scripting was done by Ian Upton after a number of research and development weeks over the previous 18 months, and it was built on an island loaned to the project by The Linden Endowment for the Arts. This was situated amongst a group of islands containing artworks that meant the in-world audience, as well as those who were specifically invited, already had an interest in the arts in a similar way to those physical gallery viewers who were also self-selecting. (See Figure 14)

Because the gallery was open to all ages, and recognising that a lot of the visitors would be new to virtual worlds, in-world participants were given advice on behaviour and a suggested 'dress code' as well as the layout and practicalities of the space. After a few days, this side of things became self-policing as there were a core group of avatars who came repeatedly and inducted newcomers. There was one instance where one of the avatars was changing outfit and got stuck halfway, as is often the case in Second Life where new objects take time to fully 'rezz', and the others formed a wall in front of her to hide her embarrassment!

For the opening of the exhibition, Stelarc gave a durational performance, entitled *Involuntary, Improvised and Avatar Arms. (Stelarc, (2012))* He stood on a plinth in front of the screen and had electrodes to stimulate the flexor, extensor, biceps and deltoid muscles coupled up to a device that randomly triggered them, he also had bend and pressure sensors attached to his joints, so that as his arm contracted and flexed signals were sent

to a computer which triggered various sounds. He was accompanied by mezzo-soprano Lori Lixenberg (with whom he had previously collaborated with on a *Prosthetic Head* performance, (Stelarc, 2011)) providing an improvised vocal score. On the screen in-world, his naked yellow avatar was also performing a series of gestures mimicking him whilst a series of coloured cubes moved through the space and, on collision with the avatar, generated analogue signals and brainwave sounds, with Lori's live image projected behind him. (See Figure 15)

SOME REFLECTIONS (IAN UPTON, 2014)

'Lessons Learned'

EXTRACT / INSERT requires highly technological infrastructure. Many preconceived this would result in a technological experience. We worked hard to strip away all technological barriers. Participants were only required to wear plastic glasses to engage. There were no abstract interfaces or controls to negotiate. Virtual and physical participants could see each other and talk. We have learned it is possible to create a non-technological augmented experience that the general public can relate to.

We discovered that, once orientated, participants engaged. We were not sure that they would. That was a risk with our installation. Engagement was inter-generational, young, old and everyone in between. After a few minutes the space became very human and very normal - despite the 'sur-reality' of the virtual participants involved!

We discovered a normal visit would last between about 10 and 15 minutes. Many stayed a lot longer taking the time to explore and share with the virtual world. We had many repeat visitors. A surprise was the extent of our cross-generational reach. The gallery engaged family groups, groups

Figure 14. EXTRACT/INSERT SCHEMATIC - The black lines refer to the main set up, the blue lines the extraction part and the red lines the insertion part. See Extract/Insert 2012 set up for a video walk through of the set up. (Upton, I, (n.d.) Installation walkthrough, retrieved from http://vimeo.com/89687380 © Joff Chafer

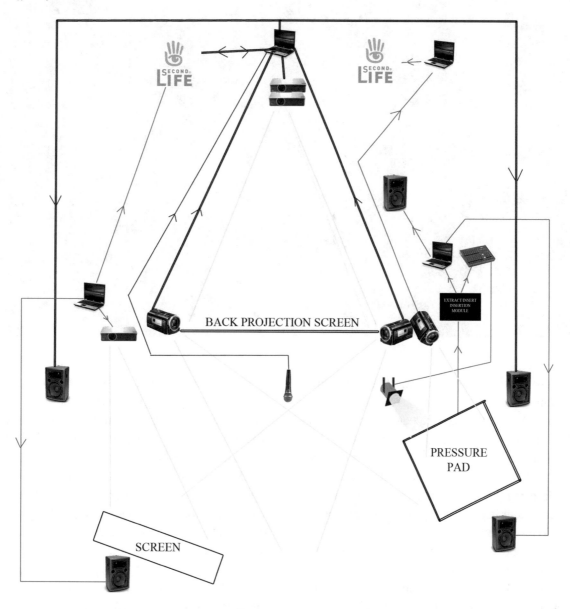

who participated in our exhibition. A typical encounter would see grandparents engaging first and providing permissions for the rest of the family group. Social skills came to the fore. The more socially adept (often older) participants were the more effective the experience. Stereotypical ideas

of only younger people engaging with technology were not observed. Fundamentally, our environment was social and a space within which people wanted to engage.

A major contributor to our exhibition was proactive invigilation. Participants (both physical and

Figure 15. Involuntary, Improvised and Avatar Arms- Body Installation by Stelarc for the opening of Extract/Insert
© Joff Chafer

virtual) needed explanation to understand what they had stepped into and be given permission to engage. We had always expected this would be the case, given the alien nature of what we had created, but the real importance of pro-active invigilation became absolutely clear as the exhibition progressed. If we were to host such an environment in the future pro-active invigilation would be essential.

The gallery network infrastructure was barely adequate for the installation. Despite special wiring and fabulous support, we struggled to host our technology. EXTRACT / INSERT could be seen to represent a new wave of media exhibition which requires serious network bandwidth. The idea that gallery bandwidth capable of supporting 'web page access' is 'enough' may be a little outdated.

It was clear the public wanted more. Many were surprised we were only running for a month and comments reflect the public would like to see similar exhibitions in the future. We had a number of requests asking if we could show the work elsewhere. Requests were from UK and abroad. There was real interest in the wider application of the immersive environment.

Our installation hosted an environment within which a unique community developed. Regular visitors (both virtual and physical) developed relationships. Email addresses were exchanged and photos together (avatar and human) were taken and shared. Many of the gallery staff spent breaks within the environment. There was a genuine feeling of loss when the installation closed.

Timezones and gallery opening hours were an unforeseen issue. Participation outside of Europe was difficult without engaging with unsocial hours. Although we had regular participation from around the globe (East Coast and West Coast America, Australia, New Zealand and Europe for example) we really needed 24 hour physical gallery opening for true international engagement. The virtual gallery was often occupied during gallery close hours. One would often open the physical gallery to discover a roomful of virtual participants already in place!

We proved that an augmented space is an appropriate space for creative endeavour. Technology, if transparent, can be used to create environment. People will engage quite normally with the fantastic if given the opportunity and permission to do so. (Ian Upton, 2014) (See Figure 16).

In an interview with Mark Childs,[9] Stelarc reiterates that "the idea is to mesh the actual space of the gallery with a virtual space... having an interface between the actual and the virtual and being able to interact seamlessly between the two and because this is 3D that more optically meshes the two worlds together." (Stelarc interview with Childs, M, 2012). He then goes on to say, "Of course what people take away from a work of art is open to interpretation, and it wouldn't be an artwork if there wasn't a certain amount of ambivalence and uncertainty. We are not doing journalism, we are not trying to be explicit, but what is implicit is this meshing of the virtual and the actual." (Stelarc quoted in Kuksa & Childs, 2014)

THE PHYSICAL PERFORMER IN BLENDED REALITY

In *Summer Dancing* and *SD2*, the performers had immediate feedback, in that they could see in real time the mediated composite of themselves and the avatars, and to various degrees improvise within the score of the piece. Indeed, for these two pieces it was vital that there was a degree of flexibility given that not all of the avatar moves were scripted or set animations. With this feedback it is interesting to note how quickly the performers became accustomed to, and comfortable with interacting with the avatars in the space. Perhaps this is a

product of our heavily mediated and technically manipulated age, (with augmented reality phone apps and regular use of CGI, not just in blockbuster films, but on TV and adverts), that we are able to process and accept this blended reality, or maybe it is just about being human and our need to make sense of what we see.

Working with a projected image on a gauze in *Staging Second Life* was more technically challenging for the actors. They had to 'hit their marks' for the composite image to work, and the further upstage they were, the less control they had. Also, with audience members sitting either side of the projector in the auditorium, they saw a different composite image. Taking this into account, the bulk of the scenes were played as close to the gauze as possible. This had an added disadvantage for the actors, as at times the projected avatars would only be in their peripheral vision, or not at all. For *SD2* the projection onto the gauze did not include avatars, just an architectural landscape of arches, which the performers explored and then played with the images being projected onto them.

Alice in WonderSLand was another case in which the actor had to be in the right place, as the cameras in both the physical space and in Second Life were all fixed, and where the actor would disappear behind a black screen, this had to match the Second Life object (for example, following the white rabbit into the rabbit hole). Also, because this was on a stage in a formal venue, with a fixed projection screen, it was not always possible to see the composite image.

For *Extract/Insert* there were no performers as such, just the attendees at the galleries, both physical and virtual, who took on this role to varying degrees willingly or unwillingly. Despite being given an explanation of the nature of the installation by the staff before they entered the space, it generally took a few minutes for people to adjust and become comfortable with the environment. Comments in the visitors' book ranged from "fantastic" and "amazing" through to "bor-

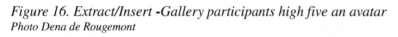

Figure 16. Extract/Insert -Gallery participants high five an avatar
Photo Dena de Rougemont

ing" and "pretentious" (the vast majority being positive, however). One response that summed it up well stated that:

"This was a new experience for me, and I never really felt comfortable communicating in a virtual world. I guess this was an experience that the first users of the telephone also felt. However it challenged my thinking of communication, reality, social interaction. I don't know if this is art... but it certainly caused us as a family (1x adult 2 x kids aged 9 and 6) to debate / discuss what we had experienced, so much so we intend to visit again next weekend and contribute more to the experience.

"In short...thanks for challenging the way my children and I interact with the world." (Unsolicited email sent to The Herbert Art Gallery 2012)

It is interesting to note in the above feedback that the writer, despite admitting the challenging nature of the event for them, sites themselves within the work - with the need for their 'contribution'. From the younger participants, the focus was generally on 'physical' interaction, with high fiving or dancing with an avatar being very popular. Older participants spent more time connecting through voice: often asking the online participants about their physical whereabouts and current events, (one person was located in New York and able to give an eyewitness account of the aftermath of Hurricane Sandy).

THE AVATAR OPERATOR/ PERFORMER IN BLENDED REALITY

Controlling, operating, puppeteering, performing with, or inhabiting an avatar is a subjective experience, just as the various terms used above may strike a chord with some and not others. One's relationship with one's avatar in Second Life can depend on many factors, from how old the avatar is (since it was first created), how long one spends 'in-world', through to what groups or communities one is involved with, and how and

if this relates to one's regular 'offline' life. For the most part, I have been working with people who have a real life connection to the arts and theatre. In response to my online question to ART members regarding their relationship to their avatar when performing, whilst all acknowledged a degree of connectedness (to a lesser or greater extent) to their avatar, some describe the process as 'technical' (given the amount of multi-tasking that takes place during a performance both on the physical desktop and in-world).

An interesting response was: "We have been using the term 'avateering' to refer to pushing an avatar around for filming machinima since we're only doing physical capture and recording audio separately to be punched into the film during the editing process." (Personal communication June 2014, An ART member's response to question about how to describe one's relationship to one's avatar when performing.) This term 'avateering' sounds, in this instance, quite technical as well, but in the way that puppeteering could be seen as just a technical operation of inanimate objects there are many puppeteers, myself included, who see it as an art form to be mastered.

Performing with an avatar in the same physical space as the actors/dancers for me is quite a different experience to working remotely. There is an automatic connectedness to the physical space, co-performers and the kit. Working remotely as I have done with ART on many occasions, it can be hard to cross over that threshold to the virtual space and feel totally 'present' but when it does happen, and the technology to make it happen becomes seamless, there are a lot of similarities with stage performance, the same connectedness with the other performers and place. There can be a lot of distractions working remotely, not just the practical set up on the desk and the vagaries of internet connections in Coventry, but 'in-world'. For example, when not in a scene, it is possible to swing one's camera out into the auditorium to watch the show or there may be comments from the audience or other actors on the screen. However, this recognises a connectedness to the place and event, these may be distractions from the art of acting, but not from being present in Second Life.

Performing in *SD2* whilst controlling an avatar, the operation became one of the practicalities of the performance, the avatar was initially a prop, but when the camera was not on me and the avatar was interacting with Fewster, I 'felt' it kick him. In *Summer Dancing*, being a relative newbie in Second Life, the avatar control felt quite technical, and was at times quite stilted, but there was still a feeling, not unlike working a puppet, where you have trained your hands or body to do one thing that then expresses something in something that would otherwise be an inanimate object. As well as manipulating you are mentally projecting yourself, in a sense inhabiting that object, or, in this case, avatar.

As described in the introduction, the experiences of Veerapen and Kozel both recount their senses of how avatars can be an extension of the physical self and enable a crossing from one space to another. The Extract/Insert installation expanded the liminal space so that it became more than a boundary, but a transitional space between the two worlds that could be inhabited by both avatars and physical bodies, enabling both types of participant to interact and explore what that space meant to their sense of self. This aspect felt, in some ways, as a culmination of the drive of the creators and artists, from Melies and McCay through to Simon and Kozel, to merge these two realities to an extent where they could almost touch.

In *Extract/Insert* it felt as if the avatars were most comfortable in the combined space. They had a similar briefing to those physically present but arrived with the understanding that if there was to be any interaction someone would have to make the first move, and they were not slow to do so. They were also quick to adapt to their audience, changing appearance, showing off gadgets engage in synchronised dance routines but also,

to a lesser or greater extent, saw themselves as ambassadors for virtual worlds keen to explain. One online visitor noted,

"Having 'real' people in the space made me feel my AV presence as much more real than usual. I'm not sure why this was — something about being in contrast or opposition or having to hold up my end — "my end" being the online "reality." It was like I had to convince "them" that I was real too — like being a participant in the Turing test and having to "sell" the idea of my authenticity." (Personal communication, June 2014, An ART member's response to question about how it felt being present as an avatar at the EXTRACT/INSERT installation.)

Similarly another noted that they got quite annoyed when some of the children in the gallery kept ordering them to do something as if they were characters in a video game, an example of how comfortable a younger generation are with avatars, but see them as purely technological phenomenon, and not as representing people. Others felt compelled to be there because of the unique nature of the event, often staying up all night to do so as they were located in the west coast USA.

CONCLUSION

As Brenda Laurel says, in the introduction to her book 'Computers as Theatre': "...these technologies offer new opportunities for creative, interactive experiences and, in particular, for new forms of drama."(Laurel, B, 1993) Here, she is talking in particular about computers, but artists in general and theatre practitioners in particular, have never been slow in subverting new technologies to their own ends. Given that theatre audiences implicitly buy in to the idea of a 'willing suspension of disbelief', it would seem that the use of virtual worlds either, as a site for performance in its own right, or as part of a blended reality, should not be such a huge leap of the imagination.

As Ian Upton wrote, above, "People will engage quite normally with the fantastic if given the opportunity and permission to do so." That said, as new examples of the fantastic arise, no doubt artists and performers will continue to subsume them into their work.

A FINAL WORLD ON TECHNOLOGY

In this chapter I have not mentioned specific pieces, or technological specifications, of equipment rather mentioned cameras or computers etc. in general. This is because both hard- and software is constantly evolving and just as new things are available to us so some older things become obsolete or incompatible. The case studies above may all be repeatable but there may be cases where there need to be different solutions to solve the same problems.

ACKNOWLEDGMENT

Summer Dancing Joff Chafer, 2008

Gemma McLean - avatar performer
Hannah Litherland, Gemma Collard-Stokes, Kerry Allsop, Dancers from Dance and Professional Practice course, Coventry University, UK
Technical support - Cath Cullinane
Coventry University, UK

Staging Second Life Russell Fewster, Joff Chafer, Nic Mollison 2008

Rusell Fewster – Co Director, physical performer
Joff Chafer – Co Director, physical performer
Nic Mollison - Lighting design
Kyle Tripodi - computer programmer, Second Life design and avatar performer
Students on the Electronic Arts: Visual Theatre Course
University of Southern Australia and Coventry University, UK

SD2 Joff Chafer, Russell Fewster, Nic Mollison 2009

Joff Chafer - physical performer, avatar performer
Russell Fewster - physical performer, avatar performer
Nic Mollison - technical support, avatar performer
Lou Lomas - puppeteer
Cath Cullinane - technical support
Coventry University, UK; University of Southern Australia

Alice in WonderSLand Avatar Repertory Theater 2010

Joff Chafer - director, puppeteer
Michelle Fowler - physical performer
Iain McCracken - technical support, live editing
Thundergas Menges SL - technical support sound
JubJub Forder - technical and building support in-world
Ian Upton - technical support, scripting
Members of Avatar Repertory Theater - avatar performers
Judith Adele (Ada Radius SL); Craig Allen (Corwyn Allen SL); Mary Linn Crouse (MadameThespian Underhill SL); Kayden OcConnell SL; Rowan Shamroy SL; Em Jannings SL; AvaJean Westland SL; Thundergas Menges SL; Elegia Underwood SL and JudyArx Scribe SL, (Australia, Canada, New Zealand, UK and USA)
Ruth Gibson – physical performer for test run
Polly Hudson – narrator for test run
Second Life Community Convention 2010, Boston; Coventry University, UK

Extract/Insert Stelarc, Upton, Chafer 2012

Stelarc - Concept. Design. Physical/Avatar performer (Involuntary, Improvised and Avatar Arms).
Ian Upton - Concept. Design. Augmented stereo space. Avatar performer.
Joff Chafer - Concept. Design. Physical space, effects and lighting design. Avatar performer.

Greg Millican - technical support, electronics and scripting

Cath Cullinane - technical support, lighting

Jessica Pinson - Herbert Art Gallery, Coventry, UK

Herbert Art Gallery staff and volunteers, physical build and invigilation

Dena de Rougemont - photography

More3D / Stepan J. Koch (3D Software Support)

Daniel Ploeger - Sound sensor hardware and software design (Involuntary, Improvised and Avatar Arms)

Daniel Mounsey - Performance assistance (Involuntary, Improvised and Avatar Arms)

Mark Childs - Documentation

The Linden Endowments for the Arts (and the Second Life Arts Community)

Coventry University, UK, Brunel University, UK

REFERENCES

Angrybeth Shortbread's Second Life Camera switcher. Retrieved from: http://slurl.com/Second Life/The%20Port/64/49/26

Avatar Repertory Theater. (2010). Alice test for SLCC. Retrieved from: http://www.ustream.tv/recorded/8439672

Avatar Repertory Theater. (2010). Alice in WonderSLand SLCC. Retrieved from: http://www.ustream.tv/recorded/8926639

Avatar Repertory Theater – Retrieved from: www.avatarrepertorytheater.org

Canemaker, J. (2005). *Winsor McCay his Life and Art*. New York: Harry N Abrams Inc.

Carver, G., & Beardon, C. (2004). *New Visions in Performance the Impact of Digital Technologies*. The Netherlands: Swets and Zeitlinger.

Chafer, J. (2008). Summer Dancing. Retrieved from: https://vimeo.com/92740424

Chafer, J. (2008). Summer Dancing 2008 (set up). Retrieved from: https://vimeo.com/92738793

Chafer, J. (2011). VWBPE. Retrieved from: http://business.treet.tv/shows/bpeducation/episodes/virtual-theatre

Chafer, J., Fewster, R., & Mollison, N. (2009). SD2 mixed reality 2009. Retrieved from: https://vimeo.com/92743286

Cunningham, M. (2014). Retrieved from: http://www.mercecunningham.org

Dordrecht, Heidelberg. *Worlds.London.*. New York: Springer

Farley, K., Nitsche, M., Bolter, J. D., Lang, T., & MacIntyre, B. (2009). Augmenting Creative Realities: Second Life Performance Project. In *Leonardo, 42, 1* (pp. 96–97). Cambridge: MIT Press. doi:10.1162/leon.2009.42.1.96

Giannachi, G. (2004). Virtual Theatres an Introduction. London, New York.: Routledge Igloo. Retrieved from: http://www.gibsonmartelli.com/

Imitating the Dog Theatre Company. (n.d.). Retrieved from: http://www.imitatingthedog.co.uk/

Kozel, S. (2007). Closer Performance, Technologies, Phenomenology. Cambridge: MIT Press

Kuksa, I., & Childs, M. (2014). *Making Sense of Space. The Design and Experiences of Virtual spaces as a Tool for Communication*. Oxford: Chandos Publishing.

Lang, T & MacIntyre, B. (2007). Avatar in Room. Second Life Augmented Reality. Retrieved from: http://www.youtube.com/watch?v=ODgZtriNYoc&feature=share&list=PLCBB13931C4E5AF60&index=2

Laurel, B. (1993). *Computers as Theatre*. USA: Addison Wesley.

McCay, W. (1914)Gertie The Dinosaur video. Retrieved from: http://www.youtube.com/watch?v=wyQlqd62l4o&list=PLue4rhsHxp6-IQi8Ad8gLWHnDldPXKok9

Mori, M. (1970). The Uncanny Valley in Energy, 7(4), pp. 33-35, *Japan Translated by Karl F. MacDorman & Takashi Minato.* Retrieved from: http://www.androidscience.com/theuncannyvalley/proceedings2005/uncannyvalley.html

Peachey, A., & Childs, M. (2011). *Reinventing Ourselves: Contemporary Concepts of Identity in Virtual Qavimator software.* Retrieved from: www.qavimator.org

Qlab software. Retrieved from: http://figure53.com/qlab/

Schrum, S. (1999). Theatre in Cyberspace Issues of Teaching, Acting, and Directing. Retrieved from: http://wiki.Second Life.com/wiki/

Sermon, P. (n.d.) Liberate your Avatar schematic. Retrieved from: http://creativetechnology.salford.ac.uk/paulsermon/liberate/video%20flow%20diagram.jpg

7D. Show at Dubai Mall. (n.d.). Retrieved from: http://www.youtube.com/watch?v=OjIPOKMTY5o

Stan's Cafe Theatre Company. Retrieved from: www.stanscafe.co.uk

Stelarc, U. I, Chafer, J, (2011). Extract/Insert time-lapse. Retrieved from: http://vimeo.com/32502129

Stelarc, U. I, Chafer, J (2012). Extract/Insert anaglyph. Retrieved from: http://vimeo.com/58571590

Stelarc, U. I, Chafer, J (2012). Extract/Insert clip. Retrieved from: http://www.youtube.com/watch?v=vKanHILj6X4

Stelarc (2011). Prosthetic Head Performance. Retrieved from: http://www.youtube.com/watch?v=dprvwAWfy9Q

Stelarc - Involuntary & Improvised Arm at the Herbert Art Galley & Museum. (n.d.). Retrieved from: http://www.youtube.com/watch?v=yhwIgLtsueA/

Stelarc, Upton, I, Chafer, J. (n.d.). Extract/Insert Galaxias Dance RAW filmed in SL. Retrieved from: http://www.youtube.com/watch?v=UNtHSS_gcrQ

Stelarc, Upton, I, Chafer, J. (n.d.). Extract/Insert set up. Retrieved from: http://vimeo.com/89687380

1927. Theatre Company. (n.d.). Retrieved from: http://www.19-27.co.uk/

Tigerlillies. (n.d.). Retrieved from: www.tigerlillies.com

Troika Ranch Dance Company and Isadora software. (n.d.). Retrieved from: http://www.troikaranch.org/

Vandagriff, J. (n.d.). Machinima Futurista. Retrieved from: http://www.youtube.com/watch?v=yDTYgsmcqqM&feature=share&list=PLCBB13931C4E5AF60&index=4

Veerapen, M. (2011). *Encountering Oneself and the Other: A Case Study of Identity Formation in Second Life. Chapter in Peachey, A, Childs, M (2011) Reinventing Ourselves: Contemporary Concepts of Identity in Virtual Worlds.* New York: Springer.

Vincenti, G., & Braman, J. (2011). *Teaching through Multi-User Virtual Environments.* Hershey, New York: IGI Global. doi:10.4018/978-1-60960-545-2

ADDITIONAL READING

Auslander, P. (1999). *Liveness: Performance in a mediated culture*. London: Routledge.

Biocca, F. & Levy, M.R., *Communication in the Age of Virtual Reality*, New Jersey: Lawrence Erlbaum Associates, 33 - 56

Blascovich, J., & Bailenson, J. (2011) Infinite Reality, HarperCollins, USA: New York

Boellstorff, T. (2008). *Coming of Age in Second Life: An Anthropologist Explores the Virtually Human*. Princeton: Princeton University Press.

Castronova, E. (2007). *Exodus to the Virtual World*. New York, USA: Palgrave Macmillan.

Childs, M., Baker, D., Beacham, R., Brownbill, R., Chafer, J., & Duffy-McGhie, G. et al. (2007). *Digital Performance a History of New Media in Theatre, Dance, Performance Art, and installation. Cambridge, Massachusettes*. London, England: MIT Press.

Childs, M., & Withnail, G. (Eds.). (2013) Experiential Learning in Virtual Worlds, UK, Oxford: Interdisplinary.Net doi:10.1007/978-1-4471-5370-2

Dibbelll, J. (1998) My Tiny Life: Crime and Passion in a Virtual World, UK:London: Fourth Estate, Goldberg, K. (ed.) The Robot in the Garden: Telerobotics and Telepistemology in the Age of the Internet, Cambridge, MA.: The MIT Press

Hammond, P. (1974). *Marvellous Melies*. London: Gordon Fraser.

Hayles, N. K. (1999). *How we became Post-Human: Virtual Bodies in Cybernetics, Literature and Informatics*. Chicago, USA: Chicago Press. doi:10.7208/chicago/9780226321394.001.0001

Meadows, M. S. (2008). *I, Avatar; The Culture and Consequences of Having a Second Life, US*. Berkeley: New Riders.

Molka-Danielsen, J., & Deutschmann, M. (2009). *Learning and Teaching in the Virtual World of Second Life, Sweden*. Trondheim: Tapir Academic Press.

Murray, J. H. (1997). *Hamlet on the Holodeck: The Future of Narrative in Cyberspace*. New York: The Free Press.

Nitsche, M. (2011, April). A Look Back at Machinima's Potential. *Journal of Visual Culture*, *10*(1), 13–18. doi:10.1177/1470412910391549

Peachey, A., & Childs, M. (Eds.). (2011). *Reinventing Ourselves: Contemporary Concepts of Identity in Virtual Worlds, UK*. London: Springer.

Rufer-Bach, K. (2009). *The Second Life Grid*. Indianapolis, USA: Wiley Publishing.

Savin-Baden, M., Tombs, C., White, D., Poulton, T., Kavia, S., & Woodham, L. (2009). *Getting Started with Second Life*. Bristol: JISC.

Schroeder, R. (2002). *The Social Life of Avatars*. London: Springer-Verlag.

Stanney, K. M. (Ed.), *Handbook of Virtual Environments; Design Implementation and Applications* (pp. 1065–1078). New Jersey: Lawrence Erlbaum Associates.

Turkle, S. (1995). *Life on the screen: Identity in the age of the Internet*. New York: Simon & Schuster; http://cms.cch.kcl.ac.uk/theatron/

Wankel, C., & Kingsley, J. (2009). *Higher Education in Virtual Worlds: Teaching and Learning in Second Life*. Bingley, UK: Emerald Publishing.

Williams, G. (2009). *Theatron Project Report Appendices, Eduserv/King's College London, Coleman, B (2011) Hello Avatar Rise of the Networked Generation. Cambridge, Massachusettes*. London, England: MIT Press.

Yee, N. (2014). *The Proteus Paradox New Haven*. London: Yale University Press.

KEY TERMS AND DEFINITIONS

Avatar: Figure in a virtual world that represents the operator.

Avateering: The act of manipulating an avatar in a virtual world.

In-World: Within a virtual world or online within a virtual world.

Kit: Equipment.

Prim: Primitive. A building block in Second Life, they start as simple 3D geometric shapes but can be manipulated or combined to make complex objects.

Rezz: verb. Refers to the resolving of objects in a virtual world. (example: I was rezzing an object. It took a long time to rezz. Eventually it was fully rezzed.).

Script: Computer code. In Second Life a script can be attached to an object to make it perform a specific function, for example a door opening when touched.

Sculptie: Sculpted Prim. A more complex geometric shape than an ordinary prim, often designed in an art package before being imported into Second Life.

ENDNOTES

[1] Even in the age of gas lighting lenses were being used and different qualities of light were being explored, the limelight being an example, where quicklime was used because of its ability to burn at a higher temperature and thus created a more intense light source.

[2] The Moven motion capture suit is an easy-to-use, cost efficient system for full-body human motion capture. Moven is based on unique, state-of-the-art miniature inertial sensors, biomechanical models and sensor fusion algorithms. Moven does not need external cameras, emitters or markers. It can thus be used outdoors as well as indoors, there are no restrictions for lighting, it does not suffer from problems of occlusion or missing markers. In addition, unique for inertial motion capture technology: the sensor-suit captures any type of movement, including running, jumping, crawling and cartwheels. Retrieved June 14, 2015 from http://www.motioncapture.at/index_en.php?nav=te&con=technologie_en

[3] Qavimator is a simple open-source tool for creating and editing avatar animations for Second Life. Retrieved June 14, 2015 from http://www.qavimator.org/

[4] When using a gauze it is vital to have very specific lighting to either allow actors or sets to be seen behind the screen or to make the screen become opaque. A common use is in British pantomime, where a painted gauze will be used to enable a scene change to happen behind the screen and then by switching the lighting to then reveal it. When lit from the front at an acute angle the screen becomes opaque but when the scene behind the gauze is lit it becomes transparent. When projecting onto a gauze, one must be aware that because it is an open weave only a percentage of the projected image will be caught and, coupled with the fact that the gauze itself is black, a higher lumens projector is needed compared to projecting onto a normal projection screen. There is also the possibility that light from the projector that passes through the gauze will leave a ghost image on anything behind the screen.

[5] The Bijou camera set up – this is currently unavailable in the Second Life marketplace but maybe available in-world

[6] Names with SL after them refer to avatar names used in Second Life. In some cases, due to the collaboration being remote, only SL names are known.

[7] Angrybeth Shortbread 8-camera setup Available at http://slurl.com/SecondLife/The%20 Port/64/49/26

[8] A Sculpted Prim, or *sculptie*, is a prim whose shape is determined by an array of x, y, z coordinates stored as RGB values in an image file (a Sculpt Texture or Sculpt Map). Sculpted prims can be used to create more complex, organic shapes that were not pre- viously possible with the Second Life prim system. Retrieved June 14, 2015 from http://wiki.Second Life.com/wiki/Sculpted_prim retrieved June 2014

[9] Mark Childs is a Senior Research Fellow at Coventry University, UK and a sessional lecturer in Learning and Teaching at Worcester University

Chapter 12
SL–Bots:
Automated and Autonomous Performance Art in Second Life

Jeremy Owen Turner
Simon Fraser University, Canada

Michael Nixon
Simon Fraser University, Canada

Jim Bizzocchi
Simon Fraser University – Surrey, Canada

ABSTRACT

This chapter explores the history, state-of-the art, and interactive aesthetic potential of "SL-Bots". SL-Bots are avatars (i.e. "agents") that are designed and controlled using Artificial Intelligence (AI) in Second Life. Many of these SL-Bots were originally created in Second Life for purposes such as: rudimentary chatinventory management and copying, asset curation, embodied customer service, generic responsive environments, scripted objects, or as proxy-audience members (aka "campers"). However, virtual performance and installation artists – including two of the chapter's authors [ca. 2011-present] - have created their own SL-Bots for aesthetic purposes. This chapter suggests ways in which SL-Bots are gradually being extended beyond their conventional applications as avatar-placeholders. This book chapter concludes with the speculation that future virtual agents (including next generation SL-Bots) might one day transcend their teleological aesthetic purpose as mere automated-objects by evolving into more complex autonomous aesthetic personas.

OVERVIEW

We will begin this book chapter by defining bots in the larger context of artificial agent research, and then specifically in the context of the virtual world Second Life as SL-Bots. We will situate SL-Bots in the context of Second Life's corporate and artistic history. This includes an explanation of the finite-state affordances of Second Life's proprietary programming language, Linden Scripting Language (LSL). Then, we will distinguish between automation and autonomy. In brief, automation involves the direct execution of programmed commands and occasionally supervision, while

DOI: 10.4018/978-1-4666-8384-6.ch012

autonomy implies unsupervised and self-directed/self-generated behavior. Then, we situate automation and autonomy within the context of SL-Bots. This history and conventional application of early SL-Bots will be analyzed through the utilitarian lens of automation and also the recent genre of "code performance". Mid-way through the chapter, we will summarize early artistic experiments in Second Life with SL-Bots. These experiments include implementations for automated story-telling and theatrical performance [2006-2008] (Unterman & Turner, 2014). Further, this history will acknowledge Gazira Babeli's treatment of SL-Bots as scripted objects [2006], Adam Nash's intelligent responsive environments [2007-2008] and Alan Sondheim's usage of a large number of customized SL-Bot swarms for environmental impact [ca. 2007-present]. We will also show examples of those state-of-the-art SL-Bots used for artistic purposes that were designed with some level of "autonomy", however rudimentary. These include exhibitions such as Ascott et al 2012, Stelarc 2012, Ellsmere/Mounsey 2012, Turner/Nixon 2011, Glasauer 2010, Ayiter/Glasauer/Moswitzer 2010, and Moswitzer 2009. Then, we will mention the state-of-the-art of SL-Bots outside of an explicitly artistic domain. To conclude, we will speculate on future implementations of autonomous SL-Bots based on a consideration of historical examples and the current state-of-the-art. The primary purpose of this chapter is to contextualize the perceived evolution from contemporary automated SL-Bots using more narrow Artificial Intelligence (AI) systems towards the next-generation of autonomous bots that employ a broader and less specialized Artificial General Intelligence (AGI).

BOTS IN THE ARTIFICIAL INTELLIGENCE (AI, AGI) CONTEXT

Artificial agents have been defined as computer systems capable of flexible autonomous action in some environment in order to meet their design objectives (Wooldridge, 2009). Their properties include the following (Wooldridge & Jennings, 1995a):

- *Autonomy*: agents operate without direct intervention,
- *Social ability*: agents interact with other agents (and possibly humans),
- *Reactivity*: agents perceive their environment and respond,
- *Pro-activeness*: agents follow goal-directed behavior.

While this "weak" definition of agency can apply to a variety of low-level system tools, agents are more usefully understood with a stronger definition that refers to systems that are conceptualized and implemented using anthropomorphic terms. Typically, this involves designing an agent around human mental notions such as knowledge, belief, intentions, obligations, and even emotions (Wooldridge & Jennings, 1995a). There is a spectrum of approaches to control structures for such agents, from reactive to cognitive strategies. These control systems provide the appropriate degree of reasoning required for the agent to perform tasks in a given environment. Agents that are intended for social and narrative contexts take on whole new kinds of behavior-related "tasks" to perform as an actor in those scenarios.

The most straightforward kind of system responds directly to sensed stimuli with an action, and is therefore called a reactive system. The most popular example of reactivity is the so-called subsumption approach. Brooks designed this approach, originally for autonomous mobile robots, based on the principle of embodiment and the importance of embodiment in the development of artificial intelligence (Brooks, 1991). A recent example of this approach is that of Isla et al. who propose a layered model for an artificial brain, where different layers communicate via a shared blackboard, allowing high-level functions to control lower ones (Isla, Burke, Downie, & Blumberg, 2001). Once percepts extract meaning from sensors, the agent's action selection mechanism is based on a function that looks for the highest expected reward among the possible actions. Another reactive approach uses Finite State Machines to control the behavior of a conversational agent by taking into account the user's perceived emotion along with the mental state of the agent (Egges, Kshirsagar, & Magnenat-Thalmann, 2004). To make the agent less predictable, probabilistic effects can be used in the decision-making process (Chittaro & Serra, 2004). These approaches are straightforward in nature, although they are correspondingly reductive. As we will see, agents in Second Life necessarily follow the Finite State Machine approach.

On the other end of the spectrum are systems that model human cognition in order to take advantage of – or at least portray – the kinds of deliberation we perform before acting. One of the most popular of these models is the Belief, Desires, & Intentions (BDI) model (Rao & Georgeff, 1997) that incorporates some of the practical constraints of being human. Another cognitive approach uses Dynamic Belief Networks to model the human mind and thereby enable a conversational agent (Rosis, Pelachaud, Poggi, Carofiglio, & Carolis, 2003). Agent architectures in this style have focused on the importance of simulating the effects of human characteristics e.g. emotions on the cognitive and decision-making processes of the agent.

Modeling agents after humans provides a useful high-level abstraction for systems that involve human engagement and interaction. In these cases, it is often desirable to render agents visually as a human character. Intelligent virtual agents (IVAs), also called virtual humans, are particular types of artificial agents embodied with a graphical front-end or even a physical robotic body, although the latter are outside of the scope of this chapter. These have been proven useful as a way to progress towards more natural human-computer interactions (Preece et al., 1994). Virtual humans are employed in interactive applications using 3D virtual environments, including simulations and digital games. To be convincing, the motion of such virtual humans should look realistic (or 'natural') and allow for interaction with the surroundings and other (virtual) humans. In this context, Badler (1997) distinguishes between an agent (a virtual human controlled computationally through an algorithmic process) and an avatar (a virtual human under the control of a live participant). It is worth noting for clarity that while some other definitions refer to a virtual body as an avatar regardless of whether it is under human control, we will adhere to Badler's clear convention.

More specifically, we now turn to virtual worlds, which are simulations that often have overt entertainment purposes. Virtual worlds such as *Second Life* [2003], *There.com* [2001], *Active Worlds* [1995], *Traveler* [2001], and *Habbo Hotel* [2000] provide users with customizable avatars in graphical environments with a range of communicative affordances including text and voice chat. These avatars will sometimes be given automated features to support the human inhabiting them, such as expressive body language or surrealistic clothing (as we will explore later in this chapter). However, these worlds must also be populated, and that is where artificial agents come in, albeit typically with fairly limited capabilities. In virtual worlds, these are often called "bots" - an etymological derivation of "robot" from *"Rosumovi Univerzální Roboti" (Rossum's Universal Robots)* by Karel Čapek in 1921. Bots refer to a software entity with its own automated or autonomous agency and with the capacity to act independently from a human being, following Badler's categorization.

Bots are semantically different from automated environmental processes and animated-objects. In contrast to automated "natural" phenomena, bots are often anthropomorphized as characters with personality (Leonard, 1997, p. 71). Prior to the modern definition of "bots" explicitly representing disembodied or avatar-embodied "software-robots"; bots have implicitly existed under different aliases throughout history. During times of antiquity (e.g. Socrates' "daemon" trial in 399 B.C.) and also during the 19th century (e.g. Maxwell's hypothetical "demon" in 1867), for example, entities acting independently of human agency were originally referred to as supernatural "daemons" (Leonard, 1997, pp. 15–21, 88–89, 123). Supernatural semantic associations with such agents as intermediaries between worlds continues through the eons into the hyper-rational history of Artificial Intelligence (Leonard, 1997, pp. 18–21). A darker version of this phenomenon can be seen in the history of hoaxes and scams, such as *"The Mechanical Turk"* (von Kempelen, 1769).

By 1950, the suggestion of a Turing Test (Turing, 1950) set the first benchmark for assessing human-level believability in an artificially intelligent agent. To pass the Turing Test, the agent had to convince – through a networked text-chat terminal – to more than 30% of human judges that was "human". Controversially in 2014, one chatterbot named "Eugene Goostman" (Veselov, Demchenko, Ulasen, 2001) technically passed a Turning Competition with 33% of human judges believing it to be human. However, otherwise optimistic advocates from the AGI community (i.e. Goetzel 2014, Kurzweil 2014) stated that Goostman only passed this test by relying on its pre-programmed "flaws" and human-communication "shortcomings" such as using English as a second language and claiming to be only 13 years old.

On mainframe terminals, early text-based chatterbots such as the simulated Rogerian psychotherapist, *"Eliza"* (Weizenbaum, 1964-66) already began to challenge the ontological boundaries of humanness by blurring the semantic distinctions between "automation" and "autonomy". Culminating with the commercialization and eventual domestication of the (home)-computer; ludically-driven "gamebots" (an early example is the *"Wumpus"* [Yob 1972-73]) or "mobiles" [mobs] (Bartle, 2003) also pervaded the social virtual space of solitary and networked human-users via text and/or graphical based Multi User Domains (MUDs/MOOs) as well as video-games (Leonard, 1997, pp. 29–58, 61–84). There, bots provided humans with automated adversaries. As the internet matured, web-based bots took additional roles such as: search-engine spiders (meta-crawlers), cartoon personalities, viruses, pets and office assistants known as Microsoft Agents (Leonard, 1997, pp. 6, 74, 78–84, 103–188). Today, bots also act as NPCs (Non-Player Characters) in video games including MMOGs (Massively Multi-Player Online Games) (Isbister, 2006).

State-of-the-Art in the Non-Artistic Domain

In the non-artistic and non-celebrity realm, Selmer Bringsjord's AGI-research team at the Rensselaer Polytechnic Institute has made as an academic demonstration, their own SL-bot personality "Eddie" (Bringsjord et al., 2008). In principle, Eddie extends Iaconesi's SL-chatter-bot conventions for the purpose of moving closer to genuine autonomous human-like: perceptions, beliefs, emotions and behavior. Simulating the logic of human-children, Eddie can possess false and true beliefs about the world with limited degrees of maturity. Eddie might be a pilot-project but has already demonstrated some cognitive ability to "[…] understand, predict and manipulate the behavior of other agents and human players" (Ayiter et al., 2013, p. 16). Eddie's complex affective thought processes attempt to accomplish near-human level capability through the assistance of arcane specialized AI-programming languages such as "Applescript" and "Common Lisp" as well as an automated theorem-prover from the Stanford Research Institute known as "Snark" (Bringsjord et al., 2008, p. 90). Despite Bringsjord's encouraging cognitive developments with SL-Bots, the cognitive level of the most state-of-the-art bot is barely approaching the cognitive abilities of a human child.

One way to simulate more age-generalized cognitive processes is through an SL-Bot implementation of the popular BDI architecture (Rao & Georgeff, 1997). A BDI-Agent (SL-Bot) can draw from pre-authored or stochastically learned internal cognitive processes (e.g. emotions, thoughts) and/or empirically perceive external virtual events to "continually pursue [...] multiple, possibly nested plans (intentions) to achieve goals (desires) in the context of up-to-date knowledge about the world (beliefs)" (Weitnauer et al., 2008, p. 3). Two established BDI-enabled SL-Bots are "Max" (Weitnauer et al., 2008) and a soccer player named "Jason" (Ranathunga et al., 2012). Going beyond Iaconesi's text-parsing chatterbot celebrities, Max is able to continually monitor his own emotional state at any given time. These emotional states are quantitatively weighted and are "[...] mapped to Max's facial expression" (Weitnauer et al., 2008, p. 4). Max also knows 2,000 plans that are derived from pairs of condition-action rules (Weitnauer et al., 2008, p. 4) Max can use these rules to dynamically update his knowledge about the world including: "[...] object and avatar positions, status updates, avatar appearances, avatar profiles, chat and instant messaging, as well as changes of friends and inventory status" (Weitnauer et al., 2008, p. 5).

Jason is named after the JASON BDI (Belief Desire Intention) interpreter that he uses to interact with LIBOMV libraries. Jason also can rationally distinguish between higher-level and lower-level Second Life information. Jason can then use this categorized semantic interpretation of this information in the service of its pre-programmed beliefs, desires and intentions. With his rational and belief structure, Jason can predict and prioritize the most actionable percept-sequences it receives from direct interactions with the Second Life environment. Jason can even simulate more complex cognitive behavior by having LSL and LIBOMV work in tandem to episodically produce a semantic "snapshot" of its immediate Second Life environment (Ranathunga et al., 2012, p.

6). Using LSL, Jason may react directly partially available sensory data (e.g. touch activation only). Or, Jason might choose to be more patient by logically contemplating the rate of change in a more autonomous manner by gradually receiving "contextual information" (Ranathunga et al., 2012, p. 10). This type of information includes ontological updates and context-dependent rules from LIBOMV and the JASON BDI Architecture about the status of virtual entities/objects/identifiers. Jason can also determine when its goal and belief structure is being subverted by stochastic events in the Second Life environment and modify its next action-sequences accordingly.

Despite their complex goal and emotion structures, Max and Jason still represent general templates of social humanoid SL-Bots. For more aesthetic or advanced applications, the customization of idiosyncratic personality characteristics and levels of reactivity are contingent on the creative authoring of each SL-Bot's particular beliefs, desires and intentions (Ranathunga et al., 2012, p. 3). Despite these significant advances in SL-Bot behavioral design, there still remains much growth in both chat-based virtual worlds and NPCs in video games where AI-capabilities can truly provide meaningful aesthetic interactive experiences.

WHAT IS *SECOND LIFE*?

"Your World. Your Imagination" – Second Life's Corporate Slogan.

Still in existence as of 2014, Second Life remains the most popular non-ludic graphical social virtual world for adults (Fominykh & Prasolova-Førland, 2011, p. 1559), and is produced by Linden Labs and founded by Philip Rosedale. Ludic experience often involves exploiting game-mechanics and playing for a quantitative score rather than necessarily for an emergent story-experience (see Huizinga 1951, Salen and Zimmerman 2004 etc.).

Non-ludic worlds such as Second Life allow the agents to act as social and/or ornamental characters in the service of a story-world setting. Such agents would not possess any explicitly game-oriented purpose or goals. An open-ended chat-based world that possesses no explicit rules or points as a prerequisite for playing such as Second Life can be considered "non-ludic".

Second Life is an open "desktop VR" world in that its: environment, virtual inhabitants, scripted automation, graphical poses & animations, and character accessories are entirely user-generated and user-organized. Desktop VR differs from the fully immersive virtual reality (VR) installations that were developed in earnest from the 1960s to roughly the mid-1990s (Krueger, 1969; Lanier, 1982 etc.). However, the recent inclusion of the Oculus Rift Head-Mounted Display has made immersive VR commercially available to desktop VR platforms such as Second Life.

Second Life has a proportionally high artist demographic (Corbett, 2009) due to the world's openness and emphasis on user-created content. As early as 2006, for example, users had already spent a total of sixty thousand hours creating content in Second Life (Ondrejka, 2008, p. 238). By 2007, artists, academics, philosophers, scientists and art-critics representing all online countries, ethnicities and genders rose to prominence during Second Life's peak marketing period (Quaranta, 2007). To date, most of the artists in Second Life exhibit representations of conventional art-gallery shows and art-works. Some Second Life artists have turned to avatar-performance art ("ZeroG SkyDancers," n.d.) and have used scripted objects as automated performance props. However, only a minority have created art-bots within Second Life.

What Are SL-Bots?

In contrast to avatars in Second Life that are controlled remotely by humans using access software called "viewers", SL-Bots employ varying degrees of artificial intelligence to control and mediate their virtual bodies without direct human intervention. Prior to their aesthetic utilization by artists, the majority of SL-Bots were originally created by Linden Labs for: rudimentary chat (Burden, 2009), inventory management and copying (e.g. the notorious CopyBot), asset curation, guided tours (Galanis, Karakatsiotis, Lampouras, & Androutsopoulos, 2009), and embodied customer service. Some SL-Bots also acted as scripted objects (e.g. animated virtual debris, particles, touch activated appliances). Mainstream usage of personified SL-Bots involved populating social spaces as proxy-audience members (aka "campers"). Second Life is still seen as an ideal venue for testing AI concepts (Ranathunga, Cranefield, & Purvis, 2012, p. 4), multi-agent systems, and even simulations of robot experiments as it is "more sophisticated than conventional 2D simulation tools, and is more convenient than cumbersome robots" (Ranathunga et al., 2012, p. 1). Installation and performance artists - including two of the chapter's authors [2011-present] - have created their own SL-Bots for aesthetic purposes. For example, some scripted objects were used as automated props for performance-art interventions Gazira Babeli, 2007] and responsive ambient environments that catered to the unique personality profiles of avatar visitors [Selavy Oh, 2010, Mosmax Hax, 2008, Adam Nash, 2007 etc.]. Helpfully, avatars can be identified via a UUID (Universally Unique Identifier, see http://wiki.secondlife.com/wiki/UUID) and then used in scripting.

What Is LSL?

To encourage user-generated content creation, Second Life also has its own proprietary scripting language to enable automated interactions. This language is known as the "Linden Scripting Language" (LSL) (Weber, Rufer-Bach, & Platel, 2007; Winters, 2008) and documented online (http://wiki.secondlife.com/wiki/LSL_Portal). LSL adds functionality to objects by allowing scripts to be directly embedded into atomic geometrical primitives ("prims"). Like any programming language, there is a learning curve for non-programmers. However, the population of Second Life has risen to the challenge in order to manipulate their environment. By 2008, an average of 15 percent of Second Life's residents reported experimenting with scripting "[…] every week" (Ondrejka, 2008, p. 239).

LSL is an event-driven "finite-state" programming language similar in vocabulary to Java or C. Fundamentally, scripts are on standby and their instructions are only executed when a discrete sensory event occurs in Second Life. Common examples of Second Life "events" include: an avatar's virtual touch, proximity, or specified text-chat commands. Integral to the event system is LSL's sensor function, which is also limited as a sensor can only detect "16 avatars and/or objects in one sensor function" at a time-step (Ranathunga et al., 2012, p. 5). Also, the "[…] maximum sensor range is 96 [virtual] metres" (Ranathunga et al., 2012, p. 5). The use of multiple sensors only compounds this problem as it consumes bandwidth and other computing resources, and causes the SL-Bot to experience performance "lag" (Ranathunga et al., 2012, p. 5). Despite the ability to include Boolean operations (Weber et al., 2007, p. 37) as well as looping control operations, the event-driven nature of scripted items in Second Life means that they are typically simple as they cannot easily deliberate while idle. Alternatives to LSL such as LIB-SecondLife ("Libsecondlife," n.d.) or LIBOMV ("OpenMetaVerse Foundation," n.d.) might allow for autonomous logical deliberation, more robust sensor-parsing capabilities and expedient performance speeds but are dependent on a persistent and deterministic placement of additional objects for dynamic position updating (Ranathunga et al., 2012, p. 5; Weitnauer, Thomas, Rabe, & Kopp, 2008, p. 5). Because of the finite-state design of LSL, as well as latency-based environmental limitations within Second Life, SL-bots are usually perceived as "automated" robots or scripted objects rather than as fully autonomous entities.

About the Automated Nature of SL-Bots

Many established AI designers and Second Life artists have stated their own expert advice – based on their respective discipline - on matters regarding their subjective perceptions of agent automation compared with autonomy. These expert opinions are gradually making ambitious next-generation virtual agents become a tractable reality. The functionality of such agents over time, will be objectively assessed directly through next-generation implementations, empirical observational and/or literary (e.g. code) analysis, behavioral tests and user-studies.

The Second Life artist Alan Sondheim feels confident in his subjective assessment of the semantic distinction between automatic and autonomous agents in Second Life. Of his own performances Sondheim says that he, "didn't have bots but had robotic followers of whatever was going on" (Personal communication with Jeremy O. Turner, March 15, 2014). For Sondheim, his followers were "[…] not independent" of the human-avatar controller and he explicitly saw all of his SL-bots as "automated" (Ibid.). With Sondheim's "Julu Twine" (2009) (shown in Figure 1) SL-Bot in particular, he felt that although its visual avatar design was diverse and could blend in with its architectural surroundings or function as a discrete figural presence; its actual interactions with other entities seemed "stiff and dying, […] as if nothing was alive but a control-system" (Ibid.). Without possessing true autonomy, these automated SL-Bots – and similar agents such as NPCs in video games – have been criticized for acting as puppet-automatons by being "cognitively empty" (Bringsjord et al., 2008, p. 89). Avatars and Agents (bots) alike are "spotted in digital environments as mere shells" representing genuine agency, emotion and intellect (Bringsjord et al., 2008, p. 89). However, these "mindless shells" can at least sometimes persuade an interacting human that they possess a convincing simula-

Figure 1. Various screenshots of "Julu Twine" in Second Life
(© 2009, Alan Sondheim. Used with permission.)

tion of autonomy, if only due to visual similarity. Otherwise, there is no strong cognitive indication that these bots might one day become genuinely human-like or at the very least, be contemplated as discrete beings with their own sense of teleological agency and autonomy.

Scripted Objects: The Personified Illusion of Autonomy

The creation of scripted objects led to a new genre of automated performance art in Second Life called "Code Performance". Code Performances "[…] use code rather than avatar action as the expressive form of the work. […]" and have been known to "on occasion, challenge the agency of other avatars within the virtual space" (Unterman & Turner, 2014, p. 214). With some occasions, the environment itself would be scripted and take over the unwitting avatar "participants" by forcing them to "dance, emit particles, etc." (Unterman & Turner, 2014, p. 214), as well as altering their avatar's visual appearance. In other instances, such as Adam Nash's scripted responsive environments (he is known as Adam Ramona in SL), objects collaborate with the avatar explorer to create harmonious aesthetic interactions. The most bot-like of these scripted objects for code performance was a tornado-bot designed by the Italian avatar performance artist, Gazira Babeli (avatar name). *"Don't Say"* (2008-2009)[1] is an automated semi-anthropomorphic scripted tornado that provides the illusion of acting as a personified force-of-nature suggestive of autonomy (shown in

Figure 2). When touched by an avatar, the tornado will persistently stalk and rattle that avatar until he/she apologizes for both touching the tornado and for every recorded text-string the avatar utters in the public chat-log (Baumgartel, 2007). This aggressive persistent willpower combined with the tornado's personified ability to provide chatterbot-style text-chat responses, compels the human interactor to create more conceivable interactive states in his/her imagination about the relative autonomy of this tornado-bot than actually exist within Second Life's finite-state architecture. While creating a larger world of possibilities is a powerful effect, Crawford's perspective on interactive systems is that "one way to judge the interactive quality of a design is to examine the ratio of accessible states to conceivable states (Crawford, 2003)." Ultimately, participants can become frustrated if easily conceivable states end up being inaccessible.

In modification (mod) culture[2], there is a consensus impression that most bots have similar characteristics to Gazira's tornado. There are many examples where scripted-entities seem to have an agency of their own, are out of our control, and seem alive as "pests". In the early days of mod-culture (see Leonard, 1997), these persistent pests (e.g. the Barney-bot and Cthulu-bot examples in Point MOOT, Leonard, 1997, pp. 3–8) were tolerated by moderators as embodied icons of a wild and lawless frontier mentality of cyberspace (Leonard, 1997, p. 92). Leonard provides plenty of evidence from text-based virtual communities to suggest that such bots are perceived by community members as inherently autonomous (Damer et al., 1997). This perceived ludic autonomy was initially at odds with this community's social norms within cyberspace – especially within video game communities (Morningstar & Farmer, 1991). Despite the initial ludic frustration caused

Figure 2. A tornado-bot forces Gazira Babeli to apologize in "Don't Say"
(© 2006, Gazira Babeli. Used with permission.)

by interaction with these "pests", the virtual community inadvertently fundamentally re-writes the interaction norms through their ludic and/or behavior that eluded the ludological constraints (Taylor 2003) set by the community designers (Leonard, 1997, p. 13).

About Autonomy

Unlike the illusory impressions of autonomy evoked by some SL artists, actual autonomy has been defined where "learning occurs both automatically, through exposure to sense data (unsupervised)" and must possess "bi-directional interaction with the environment, including exploration and [self-supervised] experimentation" (Voss, 2007, p. 132). This type of intelligent interaction would give these SL-Bots a semblance of teleological agency and situate them closer to the ideals of Strong-AI or Artificial General Intelligence (AGI). To meet the baseline for genuine human-level autonomy, a SL-Bot would at the very least need to be able to communicate through a language, have the capacity to reason about the world, and have some representation of will-power (Bringsjord et al., 2008, p. 31). The "will" is defined loosely as the ability to independently "make choices and decisions, set plans and projects" (Ibid.) with an intentional force towards action in a stochastic (non-deterministic) environment. Ideally, an SL-bot would need a human-like capacity for both 'consciousness' ("for experiencing pain and sorrow and happiness, and a thousand other emotions – love, passion, gratitude" (Bringsjord et al., 2008, p. 31)) and 'self-consciousness' ("for being aware of his/her states of mind, inclinations, preferences, etc., and for grasping the concept of him/herself" (Bringsjord et al., 2008, p. 31)) as well as a unique set of desires (towards objects, characters and the self), beliefs, intentions and goals. These base-line standards for autonomy in virtual worlds have been confirmed as the capabilities to perceive, act and reason, along with social skills (Weitnauer et al., 008, p. 2).

We will now explore examples of automated processes before discussing examples of SL-Bots with some detectable level of autonomy. Some bot-artists have re-purposed proprietary software created by scripters in the community as the "AI" (in contrast to "AGI") interface for automated performance art. For example, "Jo Ellsmere" (her Second Life moniker) and various collaborators have customized bot-animation sequences using an automated avatar-choreography ("dance machine") program called *"DanceMaster Pro"* (aka "DM Pro").[3] DM Pro can accommodate controlling the animation sequences of up to 36 automated "dancers". Ellsmere finds DM Pro to be a very robust and scalable tool for automated animation-sequences of virtual bodies. In fact, Ellsmere has technically designed her bot-performances around her gradual fluency with DM Pro's pre-designed interface, system affordances and proprietary programming sub-language, PCL. "Performance Control Language" is a proprietary sub-language created by Brynden Burton (SL avatar name), which sits on top of the code-base of LSL. It allows less code-literate choreographers to design interactive functionality. Catering to either discrete run-time and/or continuous real-time interaction scenarios, DM Pro gives the bot animation designer a finite amount of simultaneous bot formations[4] but otherwise, many choreographed options. These options can either be executed automatically without human supervision and/or improvised via the human-controlled avatar's step-wise manual control and supervision of the SL-Bot. For example, bot-designers in DM Pro can dynamically "create and assign [...] animation patterns to [...] formation positions"; and "create complete automated animation performances with timed and choreographed changes to animations, formations, music, and particle effects" (Burton, n.d.). Further, an SL Bot's automated performance-animation sequence can make a bot's virtual objects/props/accessories appear on command and also utilize event-based idling sequences by having finite-state animation loops that "contain repeating sections, [and] timed waits" (Burton, n.d.). DM Pro also goes beyond Second Life's generic chatter-bot functionality through the capability to automate the movement-synchronized presentation of text-chat string narrations (Burton, n.d.).

"The Mask: a synchronicity" (Ellsmere, 2011)[5] and *"ANIMAanimus"* (Ellsmere, 2012)[6] represents Ellsmere's first experiments with the automated choreography capabilities of DM Pro. These performances automate DM Pro sequence routines that showcase the visual merging of texture-mapped and texture-less bot-bodies (shown in Figure 3) with gender-ambiguous animations.[7] These bot-bodies seamlessly merge through each other due to an option in Second Life's physics engine to remove the collision detection that distinguishes between different virtual bodies. However, these SL-Bots are not at all interacting with the audience members. For Ellsmere, "there is the *appearance* of interaction, but that's all" as it is "[…] up to the choreographer to time things and choose animations that work well and smoothly together" (Personal communication with Jeremy O. Turner, April 29, 2014). In other words, Ellsmere and many other SL-bot-designers are not as concerned with the AI-functionality of the SL-Bots behind the scenes as they are with composing synchronized animation sequences and finite state-transitions with precision. Instead, they are more concerned at this historical stage with automating and conserving their authorial expression into a coded performance document

Figure 3. This screenshot shows the automated merging of 3 bot-bodies in "The Mask: a synchronicity" (© 2011, Ellsmere. Used with permission.)

(i.e. scripted "notecard") much in the way music composers and theatre directors have done prior to the authorless innovations of "indeterminacy" pioneered by John Cage (Cage, 1961).

Ellsmere has also created collaborative bot-works that utilize DM Pro's PCL language. For example, *"Homage to Meyerhold"*[8] (Ellsmere 2014) and *"Legs on Coppelia"* (Ellsmere/Kazyanenko 2013)[9] (shown in Figure 4) retrieved their scripted animations via what are known as multi-animation "poseballs".[10] In the latter performance, the leg-bots would have their animations synchronized to in-world streaming media such as videos and virtual shadow effects. This direct human/avatar authorial control over SL-Bots is most apparent in the dyadic bot-performance, *"Pardon our Zeitgeist"* (Ellsmere/Kazyanenko 2012) (shown in Figure 5).

Composed as a non-verbal dialog between two geometrically abstracted SL-Bots, this performance used DM and some LSL code to trigger an automated sequence of choreographed emoticons. With this performance especially, Ellsmere explicitly represented each trigger as a coded command within the performance document script. Ultimately, Ellsmere had total control over the durations and visibility of each animation trigger. Further, Ellsmere had the SL-Bots "listen" to conversation scripts and when a cue was triggered, react by generating a new emoticon "prim" speech-bubble (Personal communication, April 30, 2014). Ellsmere's mixed-reality performance collaboration with the Australian body-artist, STELARC, "OUT OF YOUR SKIN" (*Stelarc - Discussion on "Outside Your Skin" Performance*, 2014) also exploited the affordances of DM Pro. However, as mixed-reality input, STELARC included "[…] scripted movements and mapped sounds which […] also featured [his] brainwaves and heartbeat and other analog sounds […] including white noise" (*Stelarc - Discussion on "Outside Your Skin" Performance*, 2014, 06:02–06:24). Similar to Ellsmere's earliest experiments with DM Pro performances, STELARC created SL-Bots that were choreographed to merge with each other's bodies. In this case, the bot-bodies represented "automatons" or "clones" of STELARC's physical self (*Stelarc - Discussion on "Outside Your*

Figure 4. "Legs on Coppelia"
(© 2013, Ellsmere & Kazyanenko. Used with permission.)

Figure 5. "Pardon our Zeitgeist"
(© 2012, Ellsmere & Kazyanenko. Used with permission.)

Skin" Performance, 2014, 02:10–02:22). Inspired by autonomic biological system reactions, STE-LARC's involuntary muscle movements were mimicked by one of the virtual agents.

Selavy Oh's *"Identity Absent"* (Oh, 2010) is an immobile gender-ambiguous humanoid "script driven avatar […] that continuously switches its appearance between the 16 default appearances" available in Second Life. Oh's SL-bot also utilizes template humanoid body shapes and accessories. Coupled with Oh's "avatar", rests a kind of nearby webpage surface that approximates the form of a stage (shown in Figure 6). Correspondingly, this stage is also scripted but for a different yet related purpose. Essentially, the stage performs an automated Google search for the nametag of the nearest avatar/agent in closest proximity to this in-world web page. Oh's SL-bot can be subjectively perceived to possess varying degrees of ontological autonomy. In other words, Oh's agents are not actually autonomous. Rather, they invite the audience to perceive the agent's interactions as if they were acting autonomously mirroring the "Open Source" movement of the coding community, Oh wants the audience members to shape her agents' hybrid identity as an "open work" (Eco, 1962) whose ontological interpretation can be freely manipulated by human-controlled avatars.

In the near future, one could envision Oh revising this piece to allow for additional interaction features. In one instance, the relative proximity of the avatar audience member could feed his/her UUID to this SL-bot so it could shape-shift into a visual clone of that avatar. This functionality that we have previously identified helps artists as it makes uniquely identifying entities much simpler (Weitnauer et al., 2008, p. 2). Most of the issues of designing SL-Bots right now are due to determining the appropriate level of cognitive abstraction for which percepts from Second Life's environment should be logically parsed into a tractable semantic representation by the

Figure 6. An SL-bot with Google "stage" by Selavy Oh in "Identity Absent"
(© 2010, Selavy Oh. Used with permission.)

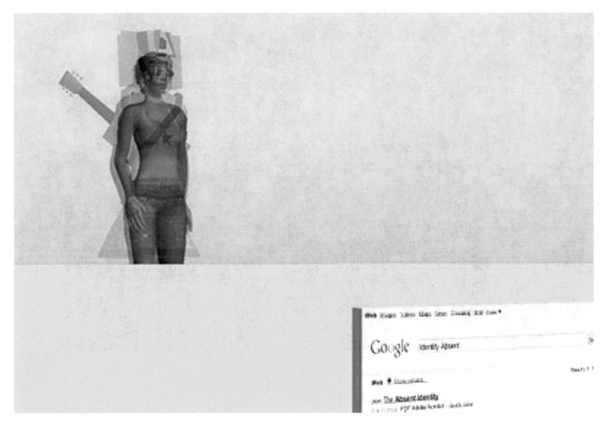

SL-Bot's "unreliable sensors" (Ranathunga et al., 2012, pp. 1–2). Otherwise, an SL-Bot might experience "cognitive overload" and confuse its reasoning processes if it is overwhelmed by too much lower-level information from Second Life (e.g. avatar position, avatar position, proxemic coordinate information etc., Ibid., p. 2). At present, it is difficult to determine how to interpret semantic meaning to sensory data in a direct enough way that an agent can teleologically interpret this data as being something useful, and with purpose. Generally, Oh's SL-bot could plausibly have access to a larger database of avatar designs – including non-human ones - that are tagged using keywords, proximity coordinates and UUIDs. Therefore, Oh's agent would not just exist without any distinct personality but would also provide a window of opportunity for the end-user to cogni-

tively converge with the agent as a proto-gestalt "pure expression of personality" (Ranathunga et al., 2012, p. 97). Oh's more conventional SL-bot performance was *"Last Exit"* (Oh/Turner, Ars Virtua Gallery, Second Life, shown in Figure 7) (Oh, 2010) – a collaborative endeavor with Jeremy O. Turner (shown posing together in Figure 8).[11] For this performance, a group of texture-less SL-chatterbots used persuasive text-string prompts and path finding coordinates with the goal of guiding avatar audience members through a gate to "the other side".

For his *"Whitenoise NPC"* series (Moswitzer, 2009, shown in Figure 9), Max Moswitzer has created a similar meta-avatar SL-bot-system to "Identity Absent". However in this case, his SL-bot literally wears "freebie" inventory items as part of its evolving body-schema. Whitenoise NPC

Figure 7. Selavy Oh posing with Qiezli's more abstract configuration that shows some of the early skinned and illuminated video textures – "Last Exit" - March, 2010

Figure 8. Qyxxql Merlin (i.e. Qiezli's "alt" avatar, on the right) poses alongside Qiezli's shifting abstract video configuration – "Last Exit" - March, 2010

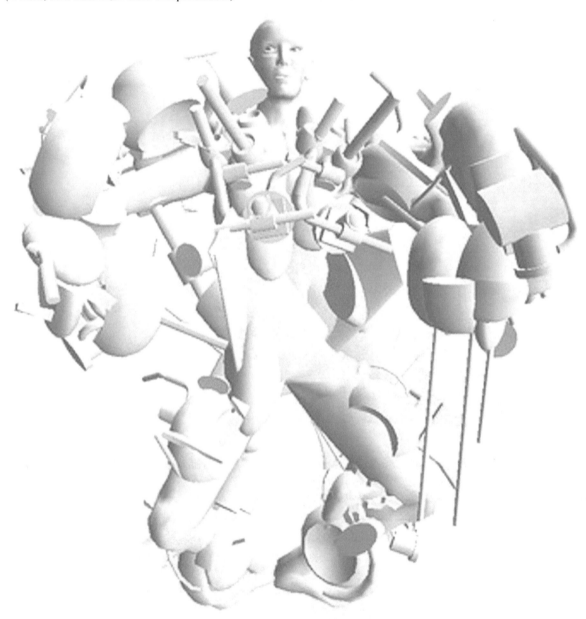

becomes the sum of its scavenged accessories. Whitenoise NPC is composed of modular mono-chromed (i.e. entirely white) bots that assemble into an over-accessorized generic and unadorned male humanoid form. Before being attached to the core-humanoid body, these inventory items are automatically whitewashed to match the de-personalized hue of Whitenoise NPC. In some instances, the bots accumulate so much "white trash" that their humanoid form becomes visually obscured by the objects it wears.

Whitenoise NPC differs in a subtle way from Oh's "Identity Absent" because of its more explicit autonomous tendencies towards autopoiesis.

However, this particular type of autopoiesis only simulates semi-autonomous procedures but does not genuinely achieve absolute autonomy. According to Ayiter (Alpha Auer in Second Life), autopoiesis (i.e. self-production) is "…the process by which a system recursively produces its own network of physical components, thus continuously regenerating its essential organization in the face of wear and tear" (Auer, 2009). The LSL-script that engineers Whitenoise NPC's "essential organization" is actually part of its gestalt body-schema and ontological identity. Moswitzer's inventory-collection algorithm literally shapes the modularity of its overall dynamic visual appearance. Furthermore, Moswitzer's systems-based entity conforms to the ideals of a "second order cybernetics" that "…emphasizes autonomy, self-organization, cognition, and the role of the observer/controller in modeling a system, recognizing the observed system as an agent in its own right, interacting with another agent, i.e. the observer" (Auer, 2009). The agents' uniform and minimalist visual appearance suggest a complete objectification and depersonalization from any sense of social uniqueness and agency that any one of these bots might one day possess. To compound the situation, Moswitzer's design choice insisted that these nude agents wear only template inventory objects – thus removing any sense of ontological autonomy from their pre-designed object-hood. Incidentally, Moswitzer seems to have also chosen to use templates as his agent-system's autopoietic body schema in order to emphasize the avatar/object selection-processes usually ubiquitous in other virtual worlds. In most virtual worlds, creativity is seen as a customization of modular template items and appearances that are configured and tweaked according to one's personal preferences (see Manovich, 1995, p. 5). Similarly, in Second Life, the use of templates is still a cultural norm as are compromises towards automation over autonomy.

One ambitious SL-bot project acted as an official sequel to Roy Ascott's canonical asynchronous teletype chat-room performance on the subject of distributed authorship, *"La Plissure De Texte"* (1983). *"LPDT2"* (Ayiter/Glasauer/Moswitzer, 2010) featured SL-Bots (Ayiter, Glasauer, & Moswitzer, 2013, p. 3)[12] whose algorithm (listed in detail on Ibid., p. 5) could dynamically parse text-strings – that were inputted by manually controlled avatars (Ibid., p. 203) - for both communication and aesthetic self-ornamentation (shown in Figure 10). These SL-Bots' primary role was to act as "communication nodes between the narrators" and automatically distribute the collective authorship from text-strings originating from multiple literary sources (Ayiter et al., 2013, p. 4). These partially generative text-strings were drawn and remixed from: a corpus of literature classics harvested from the Project Gutenberg website, human-controlled avatar text-string inputs, SMS text-chats and twitter feeds (Ayiter et al., 2013, p. 4). The artists chose Project Gutenberg because this "[…] repository holds over 30000 texts which have been authored by countless individuals throughout history" (Ibid.). These SL-bots acted effectively as literary facilitators but it was the installation portion showing the massed participatory text in the form of chat-responses, and dynamic floating block text-objects for ornamentation that were the real defining features of Ascott's virtual-world sequel. The randomization of sentences from the literary corpus provided a compelling illusion of intellectual/cerebral autonomy and the randomization of actions indicated a clever way to bypass the limitations of a finite-state architecture.

ARTISTIC ATTEMPTS TOWARDS SL-BOT AUTONOMY

We now discuss examples where there were some design-intentions towards autonomy – rather than

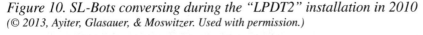

Figure 10. SL-Bots conversing during the "LPDT2" installation in 2010
(© 2013, Ayiter, Glasauer, & Moswitzer. Used with permission.)

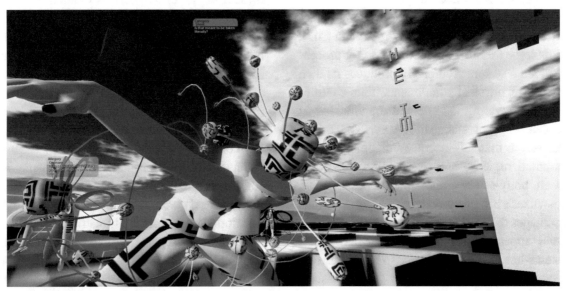

mere automatic processes. However, we concede that these attempts – although with genuine intent – produced at best, rudimentary results. These results do open the line of inquiry and praxis towards increased innovation in both AI and AGI fields.

Qiezli (Turner/Nixon, 2010) is a zoomorphic geometrically abstract and modular cloud-mass with the ability to transform the appearance and resolution of its limbs. Qiezli is a virtual being whose exposed skeletal-frame is composed from perpetually transforming illuminated textures (shown in Figure 11 and online (Turner, 2012)). Designed to function as a living discrete performance-art entity, Qiezli's teleological purpose is purely aesthetic rather than practical. Qiezli exists to "strongly express [...] a personality". Qiezli was not intended as an AGI-level implementation that intends to, as Mateas frames it, "fool the viewer into thinking [it is] human" (Mateas, 1997 cited in Anstey, Pape, & Sandin, 2000, p. 77). Qiezli's AI architecture, however, was designed to possess a rudimentary level of autonomy while its abstract body transformations employed combinatorial creativity (Boden, 1999). Qiezli demonstrates this crude interactive trajectory toward autonomy

through oscillating "mood" states, its ability to scan avatar UUIDs and via its emotional threshold function.

Qiezli randomly roams Second Life, scanning its environment and occasionally displaying a non-anthropomorphic animation (such as those reserved for animating vehicles in Second Life). It materializes ("rezzes") up to six large-scale textured prims as part of its inter-changeable body while roaming. While no interactors are detected by Qiezli's gaze, these large-scale prim-limbs are rezzed with bright colors but no animations. Once entities are sensed, Qiezli will change its mode of selection and presentation.

When encountering scripted objects (whether alone or in the possession of an avatar), Qiezli then scans that object's barcode and retrieves that object's owner's personal UUID in order to display the owner's profile page as an image texture for one of its "inspired" prims. In the meantime, Qiezli will also consult its inventory for similar UUID strings. Whenever such scripted objects are encountered, Qiezli can retrieve that object's UUID and use this encrypted string as "inspiration" for particular objects in its inventory. Such

Figure 11. Didactic panel presentation showing Qiezli in the "Systems of Existence" exhibition at the Turing Gallery on Extropia Island. Curated by Kristine Schomaker in December 2012
(© 2012, Turner & Nixon.)

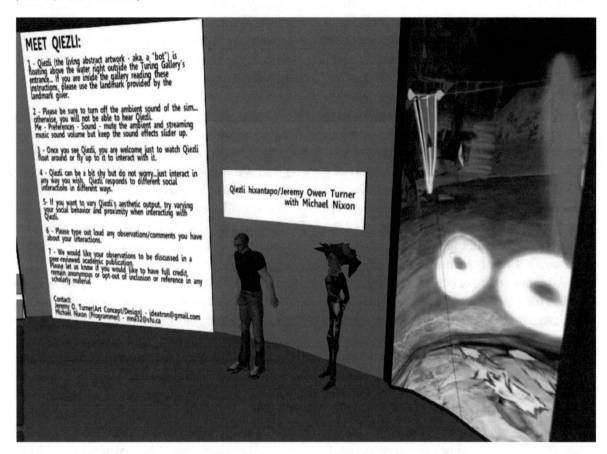

"inspired" video-prims (symbolically expressed using the more abstract purple-pink and green color spectra) reflect a switch from a purely self-reflective state.

Qiezli possesses a pair of cartoonish anthropomorphic eyes. These eyes utilize an embedded script that uses the llSensor() function to scan along their rotational axis. Qiezli uses its eyes to detect the presence, proximity, and velocity of other avatars and agents. When at least one entity has been detected, Qiezli switches its binary state from "solitary/daydreaming" to "social/presenting". When observing one avatar, Qiezli's body prims will display video-textures that depict close-up portraits of single avatars. However, when more than one virtual entities enter Qiezli's gaze, Qiezli

derives its video-texture content from videos of groups of avatars. When no virtual entities are within Qiezli's gaze range for a fixed duration of time, Qiezli switches back to its solitary/daydreaming state. Qiezli's portrait-assets are not reflecting back the interacting avatar's own self, as these assets have been pre-recorded. Therefore, these portraits are not directly correlated with Qiezli's real-time gaze as in the manner of functioning as a "transforming mirror". Rather, Qiezli is similar to a context machine only in that Qiezli does "not focus on [a particular] viewer but reflect[s] the whole visual context of the [art]work back onto itself" (Bogart & Pasquier, 2013, p. 116).

In terms of cognitive ability, Qiezli uses four "emotional" conditions during the social interaction process. Inspired by the SOAR (State Operator and Result) cognitive architecture (Laird, Rosenbloom, & Newell, 1986, p. 17) with its four types of impasse ("no-change, "tie", "conflict", "rejection"), and Anstey's four emotional categories ("praise", "encouragement", "criticism", "explanation") (Anstey et al., 2000, p. 75); Qiezli's social conditions are ambient, passive, conversational and hostile. If virtual entities have left Qiezli's gaze range for more than a minute, Qiezli will activate the random roaming animation as part of an ambient condition and depart at a slow velocity but will continue scanning for new avatars/agents while running its daydreaming loop. The passive condition is publicly expressed if the detected virtual entities are still within Qiezli's gaze range but have been idle for at least two minutes. After this period of lengthy idleness, Qiezli switches back to its solitary/daydreaming mode, re-activates the roaming animation, departs at a random velocity and delays any re-scanning for new avatars/agents for 5 minutes. This delay is intended to reinforce the interpretation that Qiezli has come to the conclusion that others are uninterested in its artistic presentation-performance. Therefore, Qiezli eventually lowers its saliency values (from the lead author's perspective, Qiezli appears "bored") and returns to its self-absorbed daydreaming state. The conversational condition is met if the detected virtual entities are not idle but move around at a very low velocity and with little or no visceral interaction (collision) with the video-prim limbs. Under this condition, Qiezli will present video-prims with the color scheme that matches the current level of interaction/collision. For example, the more each prim is touched, the redder it will get. Unless the other three conditions are met (ambient, passive, hostile), then Qiezli will engage in this presentation mode for a random duration of time. After which, it will re-activate its roaming animation and depart at a random velocity. If the agents/avatars cross this comfort threshold by making all of Qiezli's 6 video-prim limbs completely red, Qiezli's will

perceive this behavior as a hostile condition and initiates a contingency plan. Under this condition, Qiezli immediately switches to its roaming animation while intentionally avoiding those "hostile" avatars and escapes at a much faster velocity than in the passive mode. Then, Qiezli "sulks" and delays re-scanning new avatars/agents for at least 5 minutes.

Fundamentally, Qiezli's content-storage capacity, behavioral mechanism and cognitive architecture are scalable so this agent will likely be given eventually implement increasingly complex cognitive functionality and aesthetic possibilities. The scalability of content and behavioral/cognitive aptitude might one day correlate with an enhanced perception of creative agency by others. Virtual agents inspired by Qiezli's aesthetic and technical design could eventually be perceived as truly 'autonomous' and employ more explicit cognition models rather than simulations of autonomous behavior.

The Italian media-art hacker Salvatore Iaconesi (aka. "xDxD vs. xDxD") has created a species of culturally recognizable humanoid SL-chatter-bots with logic-enhanced AI capabilities and via an Artificial Intelligence Markup Language (AIML) database. AIML chatter-bots such as "Alice" have a relatively long history, as they have been around since 2001, and are still being improved as AIML 2.0 was released in 2013 by Stephen Wallace. However, AIM combined with Iaconesi's use of the XSB Prolog logic architectures suggests future autonomous interactive possibilities for SL-bots. This SL-bot performance-art series is called *"Dead on Second Life"* (Iaconesi, 2007) (shown in Figure 12). These SL-bots represent virtually embodied personality proxies of philosophical, literary and cultural celebrities such as Karl Marx, Franz Kafka, and Coco Chanel.

Just as we conceptualized Qiezli, Iaconesi considers the property of "autonomy" important to his SL-bots. For Iaconesi, "each character has been recreated as an autonomous agent in Second Life's virtual world. The agents travel autonomously

Figure 12. The SL-bot Karl Marx from "Dead on Second Life"
(© 2007, Iaconesi. Used with permission.)

through Second Life, walking and flying at [their] own will, seeking some company in the form of in-world avatars" (Iaconesi, 2007). Each celebrity chatter-bot randomly teleports and roams around virtual properties and when encountering an avatar, retrieves "his/her" text-chat responses off-grid from the entire corpus of each authors' collected writings. The logic component of the database is to ensure that the text-responses are produced from that particular personality's original literary or philosophical corpus and that these responses are semantically and linguistically appropriate to the questions asked by an avatar. Further, each SL-bot can rudimentarily reason about the semantic content of each text-chat thread. Therefore, Iaconesi is showcasing the concept that chatterbots in Second Life are meant to be "inhabited by unique human personalities" (De Angeli, Johnson, & Coventry, 2001, p. 3). To clarify, the uniqueness of each SL-Bots's personality is provided by the semantic and literary content of the text-responses provided by each character's personal corpus.

The SL-bot celebrities themselves would listen, record, archive and compile text-strings from the avatar audience interactions public channel. The purpose of this compiling process is to prepare a batch of new text-input in the markup database from which Iaconesi could manually formulate new responses lest the agent meets these same avatars in a future meeting.

CONCLUSION: TOWARDS INCREASED AESTHETIC AND SOCIAL SIGNIFICANCE FOR NEXT-GENERATION SL-BOTS

This historical research into the state-of-the-art for SL-Bots has heuristic utility for bot-creators and automated performance artists in Second Life. This chapter has articulated the limitations of finite-state machines in SL-Bot bot design so that avatar artists today can consider ways in which the technical functionality of LSL could be expanded. Ultimately, such suggestions could inspire and evolve the next versions of Second Life. Further, next-generation worlds independent of Second Life might also improve upon Second Life's limitations and allow a new species of bot – for aesthetic purposes - that has the capacity for Artificial General Intelligence (AGI).

Currently, SL-Bots's finite-state architecture implements a narrow or weak category of single-purpose Artificial Intelligence. At best, single purpose agents such as SL-Bots are only minimally "intelligent" within the context of predetermined roles that depend on persistent social interactions with external forces for its perceived personality-development and unique characterization. In other words, SL-bots have a strictly reactive personality and are directly shaped by an avatar, another bot or the environment. This is why SL-Bots are ideally suited for subordinate social roles such as a "greeter" or a "tour guide". This is also why SL-Bots are seen as automated rather than autonomous characters.

In contrast, AGI foregrounds principles of autonomy, autodidactic learning, and autopoeisis. The goal of next-generation agents is to fully simulate and implement human-level capabilities (Goertzel & Pennachin, 2007, p. VI). Such capabilities include at the very least, the ability to communicate fluently using natural language, to learn independently (Voss, 2007, p. 132) and to achieve some level of self-awareness and common-sense reasoning. Such capabilities could allow SL-Bots to achieve a social baseline for human-level believability and make Second Life (and equivalent next-generation worlds) "level the playing field" between avatar and agent (bot). With such a level playing field, social interactions between the automated and autonomous will become more emotionally and intellectually dynamic. Truly autonomous SL-Bots would evolve from being mere automated and limited social representations of roles, personalities and archetypes from "real life". The eventual implementation of these evolved synthetic beings would help fulfill

the Modernist aesthetic ontological imperative that art should be free from social representation and literally "be itself". Within such a formalist aesthetic framework (see Kant 1790, Greenberg 1940, Judd 1965), SL-Bots would exist for its own sake by functioning as "living art-work", instead of instrumentally acting as token personality simulations, postmodern references, service workers and personified props.

Second Life and other social virtual worlds can use AGI-enabled SL-Bots to help enhance their ontological distinctness from ludic-obsessed video games. Opportunistic artists making SL-Bots as believable as humans might possibly draw in more human audience-members and interactors to social based virtual worlds than video-games – unless next-generation video-games themselves also incorporate such AGI heuristics for their NPCs. Going back to at least the late 1990s, there has been a trend towards lifelike computer character behavior within simulated environments. The research agenda of the Oz Project at Carnegie Mellon University both exemplified and helped to define thus movement. Their 'broad agents' (Bates, Loyall, & Reilly, 1994) incorporate human-like behavioral and emotional components to portray believable characters. Badler, Allbeck, Zhao, and Byun (2002) call the "creation of effective real time autonomous embodied agents" one of the "last research frontiers in computer animation."

Loyall work (1997) provides a definition of believability that demonstrates the variety of disciplines that will need to come to bear on this new computational problem: believable agents must concurrently pursue parallel actions, be appropriately reactive and responsive, be situated, be resource bounded, exist in a social context, be broadly capable, and have well integrated modes of communication. To be broadly capable, he states that agents must portray a personality, display emotions, be self-motivated, change over time, experience social relationships, be consistent, and maintain the overall illusion of life. This requires providing agents with the attributes of autonomy, social ability, reactivity and pro-activity (Wooldridge & Jennings, 1995b). To do so reframes the traditional agent research agenda to include a variety of expressive communication modalities as well as efficient task-completion. We believe that this goal of believability is key to creating artificial agents that both think and act humanly. However, if this cognitive baseline is reached, we believe that virtual worlds such as *Second Life* provide an artistic context where SL-Bot creators might one day create aesthetically dynamic "unbelievable" characters that appear more than "merely" human.

REFERENCES

Anstey, J., Pape, D., & Sandin, D. (2000). The Thing Growing: Autonomous characters in virtual reality interactive fiction. In *Virtual Reality Conference, IEEE* (pp. 71–78). Retrieved from http://www.computer.org/csdl/proceedings/vr/2000/0478/00/04780071.pdf

Auer, A. (2009, May 10). Semiautonomous Puppet Architectonics: Second order cybernetics and MosMax Hax. Retrieved from http://npirl.blogspot.ca/2009/05/semiautonomous-puppet-architectonics.html

Ayiter, E., Glasauer, S., & Moswitzer, M. (2013). LPDT2: La plissure du texte 2. In D. Harrison (Ed.), Digital Media and Technologies for Virtual Artistic Spaces (pp. 75–90). Hershey, PA: IGI Global. Retrieved from http://research.sabanciuniv.edu/22148/ doi:10.4018/978-1-4666-2961-5.ch006

Babeli, G. (n.d.). *Don't Say*. Retrieved from http://www.gazirababeli.com/dontsay.php

Badler, N. (1997). Real-time virtual humans. In *Pacific Conference on Computer Graphics and Applications* (pp. 4–13). Seoul: IEEE Computer Society. doi:10.1109/PCCGA.1997.626166

Badler, N., Allbeck, J., Zhao, L., & Byun, M. (2002). Representing and Parameterizing Agent Behaviors. *Proceedings of Computer Animation, 2002*, 133–143.

Bartle, R. (2003). *Designing Virtual Worlds*. New Riders Publishing.

Bates, J., Loyall, A. B., & Reilly, W. S. N. (1994). An Architecture for Action, Emotion, and Social Behavior. In *Selected papers from the 4th European Workshop on Modelling Autonomous Agents in a Multi-Agent World, Artificial Social Systems* (Vol. 830, pp. 55–68). Springer-Verlag.

Baumgartel, T. (2007, March 23). *Interview with Gazira Babeli*. Retrieved from http://www.turbulence.org/blog/archives/003987.html

Boden, M. A. (1999). Computer Models of Creativity. In Handbook of Creativity (pp. 351–372). Cambridge University Press. Retrieved from http://books.google.com/books?hl=en&lr=&id=d1KTEQpQ6vsC&oi=fnd&pg=PA351&dq=Computer+Models+of+Creativity.+Handbook+of+Creativity&ots=FsX_Zfsjt-&sig=ZrqsZvjxDsHTOqd78T-IRoSZtyo

Bogart, B. D. R., & Pasquier, P. (2013). Context machines: A series of situated and self-organizing artworks. *Leonardo, 46*(2), 114–122. doi:10.1162/LEON_a_00525

Bringsjord, S., Shilliday, A., Taylor, J., Werner, D., Clark, M., Charpentier, E., & Bringsjord, A. (2008). Toward logic-based cognitively robust synthetic characters in digital environments. *Frontiers in Artificial Intelligence and Applications, 171*, 87–98.

Brooks, R. A. (1991). Integrated systems based on behaviors. *ACM Sigart Bulletin, 2*(4), 46–50. doi:10.1145/122344.122352

Burden, D. J. (2009). Deploying embodied AI into virtual worlds. *Knowledge-Based Systems, 22*(7), 540–544. doi:10.1016/j.knosys.2008.10.001

Burton, B. (n.d.). *Pro*. Retrieved from http://bryndynburton.wordpress.com/dancemaster/pro/

Cage, J. (1961). Indeterminacy. In *Silence: lectures and writings* (pp. 35–40). Middletown: Wesleyan University Press.

Chittaro, L., & Serra, M. (2004). Behavioral programming of autonomous characters based on probabilistic automata and personality. *Journal of Computer Animaion and Virtual Worlds*, *15*(3-4), 319–326. doi:10.1002/cav.35

Corbett, S. (2009). *Portrait of an Artist as an Avatar*. Retrieved from http://vhil.stanford.edu/news/2009/nyt-portrait.pdf

Crawford, C. (2003). *The Art of Interactive Design*. San Francisco: No Starch Press.

Damer, B., Judson, J., Dove, J., Illustrator-DiPaola, S., Illustrator-Ebtekar, A., & Illustrator-McGehee, S. … Produced By-Reber, K. (1997). *Avatars! Exploring and Building Virtual Worlds on the Internet*. Peachpit Press. Retrieved from http://dl.acm.org/citation.cfm?id=550319

De Angeli, A., Johnson, G. I., & Coventry, L. (2001). The unfriendly user: exploring social reactions to chatterbots. In Helander, Khalid, & Tham (Eds.), *Proceedings of The International Conference on Affective Human Factors Design, London* (pp. 467–474). London: Asean Academic Press. Retrieved from http://www.alicebot.org/articles/guest/The%20Unfriendly%20User.html

Eco, U. (1962). The open work (A. Cancogni, Trans.). Cambridge: Harvard University Press. Retrieved from http://philpapers.org/rec/ECOTOW

Egges, A., Kshirsagar, S., & Magnenat-Thalmann, N. (2004). Generic personality and emotion simulation for conversational agents. *Computer Animation and Virtual Worlds*, *15*(1), 1–13. doi:10.1002/cav.3

Ellsmere, Jo. (2012). *ANIMAanimus*. Retrieved from https://www.youtube.com/watch?v=DnlNed4EY8g&feature=youtube_gdata_player

Flimflam, W. (2007, January 24). *Gaza Stripped*. Retrieved from http://turbulence.org/blog/2007/01/24/performing-second-life/

Fominykh, M., & Prasolova-Førland, E. (2011). Virtual research arena: presenting research in 3D virtual environments. In *Global Learn* (Vol. 2011, pp. 1558–1567). Retrieved from http://www.editlib.org/p/37372/

Galanis, D., Karakatsiotis, G., Lampouras, G., & Androutsopoulos, I. (2009). NaturalOWL: Generating texts from OWL ontologies in Protégé and in Second Life. In *EACL '09 Proceedings of the 12th Conference of the European Chapter of the Association for Computational Linguistics: Demonstrations Session* (pp. 17–20). Retrieved from http://www.researchgate.net/publication/253371102_NaturalOWL_Generating_Texts_from_OWL_Ontologies_in_Prot_eg_e_and_in_Second_Life/file/60b7d52e787f79bf8b.pdf

Goertzel, B., & Pennachin, C. (Eds.). (2007). Artificial general intelligence. Springer. Retrieved from http://link.springer.com/content/pdf/10.1007/978-3-540-68677-4.pdf doi:10.1007/978-3-540-68677-4

Greenway, P. (2014). *Peter Greenaway: Golden Age of the Russian Avant-garde - 14.04.2014*. Retrieved from https://www.youtube.com/watch?v=eQeUf_Ua6EY&feature=youtube_gdata_player

HeZ. (n.d.). *Multi-Sit Script*. Retrieved from https://marketplace.secondlife.com/p/HeZ-Multi-Sit-Script-Multiple-poses-and-sit-targets-in-one-prim-without-poseballs/370403?id=370403&slug=HeZ-Multi-Sit-Script-Multiple-poses-and-sit-targets-in-one-prim-without-poseballs

Iaconesi, S. (2007). *dead on Second Life*. Retrieved from http://www.artisopensource.net/dosl/main.html

Isbister, K. (2006). *Better Game Characters by Design: A Psychological Approach*. San Francisco: Morgan Kaufmann.

Isla, D., Burke, R., Downie, M., & Blumberg, B. (2001). A layered brain architecture for synthetic creatures. In *International Joint Conference on Artificial Intelligence* (Vol. 17, pp. 1051–1058).

Laird, J. E., Rosenbloom, P. S., & Newell, A. (1986). Chunking in Soar: The anatomy of a general learning mechanism. *Machine Learning, 1*(1), 11–46. doi:10.1007/BF00116249

Leonard, A. (1997). *Bots: The Origin of the New Species*. San Francisco: Wired Books. Retrieved from http://dl.acm.org/citation.cfm?id=549684

Libsecondlife. (n.d.). Retrieved from http://secondlife.wikia.com/wiki/Libsecondlife

Loyall, A. B. (1997). *Believable agents: building interactive personalities* (Doctoral thesis). Carnegie Mellon University.

Manovich, L. (1995). *The aesthetics of virtual worlds*. C-Theory Online.

Morningstar. C., & Farmer, F. R. (1991). The Lessons of Lucasfilm's Habitat. In M. Benedikt (Ed.), Cyberspace: First Steps. Austin: MIT Press.

Oh, S. (2010, February 28). identity absent. Retrieved from http://ohselavy.blogspot.ca/2010/02/identity-absent.html

Ondrejka, C. (2008). Education unleashed: Participatory culture, education, and innovation in Second Life. In K. Salen (Ed.), The ecology of games: Connecting youth, games, and learning (pp. 229–252). Cambridge: The MIT Press. Retrieved from http://www.socialinformation.org/readings/MMORPG%20learning/Ondrejka_2008.pdf

OpenMetaVerse Foundation. (n.d.). Retrieved from http://libomv.sourceforge.net/

Preece, J., Rogers, Y., Sharp, H., Benyon, D., Holland, S., & Carey, T. (1994). *Human-Computer Interaction: Concepts And Design* (1st ed.). Addison Wesley.

Quaranta, D. (2007). Life and Its Double. In Fabio Paris Art Gallery catalogue. Brescia: Portraits. Retrieved from http://domenicoquaranta.com/public/CATALOGUES/2007_01_Mattes_LOL.pdf

Ranathunga, S., Cranefield, S., & Purvis, M. (2012). Interfacing a cognitive agent platform with Second Life. In M. Beer (Ed.), Agents for Educational Games and Simulations (pp. 1–21). Springer Berlin Heidelberg. Retrieved from http://link.springer.com/chapter/10.1007/978-3-642-32326-3_1 doi:10.1007/978-3-642-32326-3_1

Rao, A. S., & Georgeff, M. P. (1997). Modeling rational agents within a BDI-architecture. *Readings in Agents*, 317–328.

Rosis, F., Pelachaud, C., Poggi, I., Carofiglio, V., & Carolis, B. D. (2003). From Greta's mind to her face: Modelling the dynamics of affective states in a conversational embodied agent. *International Journal of Human-Computer Studies, 59*(1), 81–118. doi:10.1016/S1071-5819(03)00020-X

Stelarc - Discussion on "Outside Your Skin" Performance. (2014). Retrieved from https://www.youtube.com/watch?v=ikauPUYRbrk&feature=youtube_gdata_player

The Mask: a synchronicity. (n.d.). Retrieved from https://vimeo.com/41673225

Turing, A. M. (1950). Computing machinery and intelligence. *Mind, LIX*(236), 433–460. doi:10.1093/mind/LIX.236.433

Turner, J. O. (2012, December 1). Qiezli - A personified Art-Agent in Second Life. Retrieved from http://qiezli.blogspot.ca/

Unterman, B., & Turner, J. O. (2014). Loss of Agency as Expression in Avatar Performance. In J. Tanenbaum, M. Seif El-Nasr, & M. Nixon (Eds.), Nonverbal Communication in Virtual Worlds: Understanding and Designing Expressive Characters (pp. 205–217). ETC Press. Retrieved from http://repository.cmu.edu/etcpress/14/

Voss, P. (2007). Essentials of general intelligence: The direct path to artificial general intelligence. In Artificial general intelligence (pp. 131–157). Springer Berlin Heidelberg. Retrieved from http://link.springer.com/chapter/10.1007/978-3-540-68677-4_4 doi:10.1007/978-3-540-68677-4_4

Weber, A., Rufer-Bach, K., & Platel, R. (2007). Creating your world: the official guide to advanced content creation for second life. Indianapolis: John Wiley & Sons. Retrieved from http://books.google.com/books?hl=en&lr=&id=YjdkS8HNpGgC&oi=fnd&pg=PA2&dq=Creating+Your+World:+The+Official+Guide+to+Advanced+Content+Creation+for+Second+Life&ots=jofEk2XiU6&sig=6ikfQwh0M4hBcF1rbIGfKqeS_Q4

Weitnauer, E., Thomas, N. M., Rabe, F., & Kopp, S. (2008). Intelligent agents living in social virtual environments–bringing Max into Second Life. In Intelligent Virtual Agents (pp. 552–553). Springer. Retrieved from http://link.springer.com/chapter/10.1007/978-3-540-85483-8_85 doi:10.1007/978-3-540-85483-8_85

Winters, C. (2008). Using the Linden Scripting Language. In M. Rymaszweski (Ed.), *Second Life: The Official Guide*. Hoboken, N.J: Wiley Publishing.

Wooldridge, M. (2009). *An Introduction to MultiAgent Systems* (2nd ed.). John Wiley & Sons.

Wooldridge, M., & Jennings, N. R. (1995a). Intelligent Agents: Theory and Practice. *The Knowledge Engineering Review, 10*(2), 115–152. doi:10.1017/S0269888900008122

Wooldridge, M., & Jennings, N. R. (1995b). Intelligent Agents: Theory and Practice. *The Knowledge Engineering Review, 10*(2), 115–152. doi:10.1017/S0269888900008122

Zero G. SkyDancers. (n.d.). Retrieved April 3, 2015, from http://zerogskydancers.com/

KEY TERMS AND DEFINITIONS

Agent: In virtual worlds, an agent is an automated avatar controlled either in an automated and/or autonomous manner by a scripted program.

Artificial General Intelligence (AGI): AGI or "strong AI" is characterized by domain-generality. In other words, an AGI-agent can - in principle - learn and interact with various domains. An AGI-agent is not limited by any particular domain of expertise. In contrast, most contemporary AI is heavily specialized or "weak" AI (e.g. expert systems).

Automation: Automation involves the direct execution of programmed commands and occasionally supervision.

Autonomy: Autonomy implies unsupervised and self-directed/self-generated behavior.

Avatar: An Avatar are a user's self-representation in cyberspace. Unlike agents, NPCs and bots; avatars are manually controlled by the user.

Bot: A bot (aka. SL-Bot) is the colloquial name for agents in Second Life.

Second Life: Second Life (aka. SL) is a popular chat-based graphical virtual world inhabited by avatars and agents (bots).

ENDNOTES

[1] Babeli hosts screenshots, a video of the Second Life event, an a sample of the LSL code on her exhibit page (Babeli, n.d.). See also *"Gaza Stripped"* (Flimflam, 2007)-

an interview with Gazira Babeli by Wirxli Flimflam (Jeremy O. Turner).

2   Modification (Mod) culture is not to be confused with Modernism or the sub-culture in 1960s England. Mod culture is where creators modify video games to create artistic statements.

3   Developed by Bryndyn Burton (SL name). According to email correspondence, Burton considers DM Pro to be an "animation control system" and not an "AI-system". This might mean that he does not consider DM Pro, whose features he describes (Burton, n.d.), to be an AGI system.

4   "There are limits to the number of 'formations' that can be on any given internal notecard. It is possible, though, to use multiple formations notecards for a performance." (Jo Ellsmere, personal communication, April 29, 2014).

5   A collaboration with Pyewacket Kazyanenko (SL name) and Kai Steamer (SL name) to illustrate Carmen Auletta's (SL name) poem "'A Maschera" for Museo del Metaverso's "Art and Poetry" series took place in Second Life, September 2011 (*The Mask*, n.d.).

6   "Systems of Existence" (October 2012) exhibition uploaded to YouTube (*ANIMAanimus by Jo Ellsmere*, 2012). Extropia Core, Extropia Island, Second Life.
Aesthetic consultation provided by Philos Kidd (SL name).

7   Ellsmere and Kazyanenko explore the Jungian archetypal limitations of gender identity and are inspired by the extreme gender stereotyping of typical male-/female-specific animations available within Second Life (Personal correspondence, April 29, 2014). "*Mask [...]*" features 3 animated SL-Bots while "*ANIMAanimus*" showcases 6 textureless but mono-chromed bots of different colors.

8   Part of the Peter Greenaway/Saskie *Boddeke "The Golden Age of Russian Avant-garde"* project, exhibited live in Moscow, Russia, April/May 2014 with an overview on YouTube (*Peter Greenaway: Golden Age of the Russian Avant-garde - 14.04.2014*, 2014).

9   Exhibited for the opening ceremony of the "*Coppelia*" sim (virtual property). Image provided with permission by Jo Ellsmere, April 29, 2014.

10   The code for activating poseballs can be found in the SecondLife marketplace (HeZ, n.d.).

11   This was the first public collaborative performance for the lead author's SL-bot, "Qiezli". However, Qiezli at this time was manually controlled as an avatar, rather than possessing automated or autonomous AI capabilities.

12   These SL-Bots initially resided in Second Life but later were populated inside of an Opensim called the "*New Genres Grid*".

Compilation of References

1927 Theatre Company. (n.d.). Retrieved from: http://www.19-27.co.uk/

7D .Show at Dubai Mall. (n.d.). Retrieved from: http://www.youtube.com/watch?v=OjIPOKMTY5o

Abramović, A. & Ulay (1977) *Imponderabilia* [performance/installation]. Bologna, IT: Galleria Communale d'Arte Moderna.

Academy of Machinima Arts & Sciences (2002-2009). New York, NY: Paul Marino.

Acconci, V. (1972, January 15-29). *Seedbed* [performance]. New York, NY: Sonnabend Gallery.

Agamben, G. (2013). *Nymphs*. London: Seagull Books.

Albert, D. Z. (1992). *Quantum Mechanics and Experience*. Cambridge, MA: Harvard University Press.

Allen, H. (Producer). (2014, August 24). Hoodie Allen - "movie" (official video). Video retrieved from https://www.youtube.com/watch?v=SjDfh2Xz9CA

Allen, I. (Producer). (2009). *The story of Susa Bubble - Rose Borchovski artwork*. Paris, France: Iono Allen. Video retrieved from http://www.youtube.com/watch?v=aJdVCqG3bZs&list=UUau2uwcAq_piedjavtmqp9A

Allen, I. (Producer). (2010). *A question of honour*. Paris, France: Iono Allen. Video retrieved from http://www.youtube.com/watch?v=YftouEm3CT4&list=UUau2uwcAq_piedjavtmqp9A

Allen, I. (Producer). (2013). *The arrival*. Paris, France: Iona Allen. Video retrieved from http://www.youtube.com/watch?v=BHzGe5KwulY

Amsterdam, P. (2008, November 10). Why watch TV when you can star in your own cartoon movie every night. *Pooky Media* [Blog]. Retrieved from http://www.pookyamsterdam.com/2008_11_01_archive.html

Angrybeth Shortbread's Second Life Camera switcher. Retrieved from: http://slurl.com/Second Life/The%20 Port/64/49/26

Anstey, J., Pape, D., & Sandin, D. (2000). The Thing Growing: Autonomous characters in virtual reality interactive fiction. In *Virtual Reality Conference, IEEE* (pp. 71–78). Retrieved from http://www.computer.org/csdl/proceedings/vr/2000/0478/00/04780071.pdf

Anton, C. (2001). *Selfhood and Authenticity*. Albany: State University of New York.

Appiah, K. A. (2007). *The Ethics of Identity*. New Jersey: Princeton University Press.

Apter, E. (2008, January). Technics of the Subject: The Avatar-Drive. *Postmodern Culture*, *18*(2). doi:10.1353/pmc.0.0021

Arp, J. (1972). *Arp on Arp: poems, essays, memories*. The Viking Press.

Artaud, A. (1994). *The theater and its double* (M. C. Richards, Trans.). New York, NY: The Grove Press. (Original work published 1958)

Ascott, R., & Shanken. E. (ed.). (2003). Telematic Embrace: Visionary Theories of Art, Technology, and Consciousness. Berkeley: University of California Press.

Ascott, R. (2005). Distance Makes the ArtGrowFurther:Distributed Authorship andTelematic Textuality in LaPlissure du Texte. In A. Chandler & N. Neumark (Eds.), *At a distance: precursors to art and activism on the Internet* (pp. 282–296). Cambridge: The MIT Press.

Ascott, R. (2008). Cybernetic, Technoetic, Syncretic: The Prospect for Art. *Leonardo, 41*(3), 204. doi:10.1162/leon.2008.41.3.204

Ashe, G. (1968). *Gandhi: A study in revolution.* London: Heineman Ltd.

Attali, J. (2009). *Noise: The Political Economy of Music.* Minneapolis: University of Minnesota Press.

Au, W. J. (2007) *Remake the Stars.* New World Notes. Available at: http://nwn.blogs.com/nwn/2007/07/remake-the-star.html#more

Au, W. J. (2007a). Robbie Dingo, unmasked: Avatars and identity crystallized into four lovely minutes. *New World Notes* [Blog]. Retrieved from http://nwn.blogs.com/nwn/2007/11/robbie-dingo-un.html

Au, W. J. (2007b). This is truly China Tracy. *New World Notes* [Blog]. Retrieved from http://nwn.blogs.com/nwn/2007/07/this-is-truly-c.html

Au, W. J. (2009, July 11). My five favorite things from New World Notes: Weekend machinima: Lainy Voom plays with time in *Push. New World Notes* [Blog]. Retrieved from http://nwn.blogs.com/nwn/2009/07/weekend-machinima.html

Au, W. J. (2012, January 17). Peter Greenaway acclaims SL artist Bryn Oh, donates to crowdfunder to re-open Immersiva -- and so can you! *New World Notes* [Blog]. Retrieved from http://nwn.blogs.com/nwn/2012/01/peter-greenaway-acclaims-bryn-oh-second-life-artist.html

Auer, A. (2009, May 10). Semiautonomous Puppet Architectonics: Second order cybernetics and MosMax Hax. Retrieved from http://npirl.blogspot.ca/2009/05/semiautonomous-puppet-architectonics.html

Au, W. J. (2008). *The making of Second Life.* New York, NY: Harper Business.

Avatar Repertory Theater – Retrieved from: www.avatar-repertorytheater.org

Avatar Repertory Theater. (2010). Alice in Wonder-SLand SLCC. Retrieved from: http://www.ustream.tv/recorded/8926639

Avatar Repertory Theater. (2010). Alice test for SLCC. Retrieved from: http://www.ustream.tv/recorded/8439672

Ayiter, E., Glasauer, S., & Moswitzer, M. (2013). LPDT2: La plissure du texte 2. In D. Harrison (Ed.), Digital Media and Technologies for Virtual Artistic Spaces (pp. 75–90). Hershey, PA: IGI Global. Retrieved from http://research.sabanciuniv.edu/22148/ doi:10.4018/978-1-4666-2961-5.ch006

Babeli, G. (2006). *Come To Heaven.* 2006. Retrieved from http://www.gazirababeli.com/cometoheaven.php

Babeli, G. (n.d.). *Don't Say.* Retrieved from http://www.gazirababeli.com/dontsay.php

Bachelard, G. in Davies, C. (1997) Changing Space: Virtual Reality as an Arena of Embodied Being. In Packer, R. & Jordan, K. (ed.) *Multimedia: From Wagner to Virtual Reality.* New York, W.W. Norton & Company. [Online] Available at: http:///www.immersence.com

Badiou, A. (2004). Fifteen Theses on Contemporary Art. *Lacanian Ink.* (23).

Badiou, A. (2006). *Third Sketch of a Manifesto of Affirmationist Art. Polemics.* London: Verso.

Badler, N. (1997). Real-time virtual humans. In *Pacific Conference on Computer Graphics and Applications* (pp. 4–13). Seoul: IEEE Computer Society. doi:10.1109/PCCGA.1997.626166

Badler, N., Allbeck, J., Zhao, L., & Byun, M. (2002). Representing and Parameterizing Agent Behaviors. *Proceedings of Computer Animation, 2002*, 133–143.

Bard, A., & Söderqvist, J. (2012). *The Futurica Trilogy.* Stockholm: Stockholm Text.

Barreno, M. I., Horta, M. T., & Velho da Costa, M. (1998). *Novas Cartas Portuguesas.* Lisboa: Publicações Dom Quixote.

Bartle, R. (2003). *Designing Virtual Worlds.* New Riders Publishing.

Bates, J., Loyall, A. B., & Reilly, W. S. N. (1994). An Architecture for Action, Emotion, and Social Behavior. In *Selected papers from the 4th European Workshop on Modelling Autonomous Agents in a Multi-Agent World, Artificial Social Systems* (Vol. 830, pp. 55–68). Springer-Verlag.

Baumgartel, T. (2007, March 23). *Interview with Gazira Babeli*. Retrieved from http://www.turbulence.org/blog/archives/003987.html

Bauwens, M. (2006). The Political Economy of Peer Production. *Post-autistic Economics Review* (37), 33-44.

Bay, M. (1998). *Armageddon* [Motion Picture]. Burbank, CA: Touchstone Pictures.

Bay, M. (2001). *Pearl Harbor* [Motion Picture]. Burbank, CA: Touchstone Pictures.

Benjamin, W. (2002). Selected writings: Volume 3 1935-1938. (E. Jephcott, H. Eiland, and Others, Trans.) Cambridge, MA: Harvard University.

Bergson, H. (1910). Time and Free Will: An Essay on the Immediate Data of Consciousness (F.L. Pogson, M.A., Trans.). London: George Allen and Unwin.

Bergson, H. (2007). Mind-Energy (H. Wildon Carr, Trans.). 2007 England: Palgrave Macmillan.

Berkeley, L. (2006). Situating machinima in the new mediascape. *Australian Journal of Emerging Technologies and Society*, *4*(2), 65–80.

Biocca, F. (1997). The Cyborg's Dilemma: Progressive Embodiment in Virtual Environments. *Journal of Computer-Mediated Communication. 3(2)*. Retrieved from http://onlinelibrary.wiley.com. DOI: 10.1111/j.1083-6101.1997.tb00070

Biocca, F. (1997, 9). *The Cyborg's Dilemma: Progressive Embodiment in Virtual Environments*. Retrieved from: http://jcmc.indiana.edu/vol3/issue2/biocca2.html

Biocca, F. (2003, May 5-7). *Can we resolve the book, the physical reality, and the dream state problems? From the two-pole to a three-pole model of shifts in presence*. Retrieved from: http://www.mindlab.org/images/d/DOC705.pdf

Birch, A., & Iohe, T. (2011). *Wollstonecraft Live!* (Vol. 2). London: Fragments and Monuments.

Bishop, C. (2006). Viewers as Producers. In C. Bishop (Ed.), *Participation* (pp. 10–17). London, Cambridge: The MIT Press.

Bishop, C. (2012). *Artificial hells: participatory art and the politics of spectatorship*. Londo: Verso.

Blackman, C. (2010). Can avatars change the way we think and act? In *Stanford News* (2010, February 22). Retrieved from http://news.stanford.edu/news/2010/february22/avatar-behavior-study-022510.html

Bloustien, G. F., & Wood, D. (2013). Face, Authenticity, Transformations and Aesthetics in Second Life. *Body & Society*, *19*(1), 52–81. doi:10.1177/1357034X12462250

Boden, M. A. (1999). Computer Models of Creativity. In Handbook of Creativity (pp. 351–372). Cambridge University Press. Retrieved from http://books.google.com/books?hl=en&lr=&id=d1KTEQpQ6vsC&oi=fnd&pg=PA351&dq=Computer+Models+of+Creativity.+Handbook+of+Creativity&ots=FsX_Zfsjt-&sig=ZrqsZvjxDsHTOqd78T-IRoSZtyo

Boellstorff, T. (2006). A Ludicrous Discipline? Ethnography and Game Studies. *Games and Culture*, *1*(1), 29–35. doi:10.1177/1555412005281620

Boellstorff, T. (2008). *Coming of Age in Second Life: An anthropologist explores the virtually human* (pp. 183–185). Princeton, NJ: Princeton University Press.

Boellstorff, T. (2008). *Coming of Age in Second Life: An Anthropologist Explores the Virtually Human*. New Jersey: Princeton University Press.

Boellstorff, T. (2010). *Coming of Age in Second Life, An Anthropologist Explores the Virtually Human. Nova Jersey*. Princeton University Press.

Bogart, B. D. R., & Pasquier, P. (2013). Context machines: A series of situated and self-organizing artworks. *Leonardo*, *46*(2), 114–122. doi:10.1162/LEON_a_00525

Bohm, D. (1994). *Thought as a System*. London: Routledge.

Bohm, D. (2002). *Wholeness and the Implicate Order*. London: Routledge.

Bostrom, N., & Sandberg, A. (2009). Cognitive Enhancement: Methods, Ethics, Regulatory Challenges. *Science and Engineering Ethics*, *15*(3), 311–341. doi:10.1007/s11948-009-9142-5 PMID:19543814

Bourriaud, N. (2002). Relational Aesthetics. *Collection Documents sur l'art. Les Presses Du Reel*. Retrieved from http://www.lespressesdureel.com

Bradbury, R. (1953). *Fahrenheit 451*. New York, NY: Ballatine Books.

Braidotti, R. (2013). *The Posthuman*. Cambridge: Polity Press.

Brand, P. Z. (n.d.). Pastiche. *Encyclopedia of Aesthetics*. Retrieved from http://www.oxfordartonline.com.ezproxy-library.ocad.ca/subscriber/article/opr/t234/e0391?q=pastiche&search=quick&pos=2&_start=1#firsthit

Bringsjord, S., Shilliday, A., Taylor, J., Werner, D., Clark, M., Charpentier, E., & Bringsjord, A. (2008). Toward logic-based cognitively robust synthetic characters in digital environments. *Frontiers in Artificial Intelligence and Applications*, *171*, 87–98.

Brooks, R. (1960). *Elmer Gantry*. Beverly Hills, CA: United Artists.

Brooks, R. A. (1991). Integrated systems based on behaviors. *ACM Sigart Bulletin*, *2*(4), 46–50. doi:10.1145/122344.122352

Brophblog. (2007, November 28). Why machinima is good for Hollywood? [Blog]. Retrieved from http://brophinator.wordpress.com/2007/11/28/why- machinima-is-good-for-hollywood.

Brown, C. (2011). Learning to Dance with Angelfish: Choreographic Encounters Between Virtuality and Reality. In S. Broadhurst & J. Machon (Eds.), *Performance and Technology. Practices of Virtual Embodiment and Interactivity* (pp. 85–99). Hampshire, UK: Palgrave Macmillan.

Bruns, A. (2007). *Produsage: A Working Definition*. Retrieved from http://produsage.org/node/9 Read 18/01/2012

Bruns, A. (2008). Blogs, Wikipedia, and Beyond (Digital Formations). New York: Peter Lang.

Bruns, A. (2010). Distributed Creativity: Filesharing and Produsage. In S. Sonvilla-Weiss, Mashup Cultures (pp. 24-37). Vienna: Springer.

Bruns, A. (2007). *Produsage, Generation C, and Their Effects on the Democratic Process. MiT 5 (Media in Transition)*. Boston: MIT.

Bruns, A. (2008). *Blogs, Wikipedia, Second Life, and Beyond: From Production to Produsage*. New York: Peter Lang Publishing.

Burden, C. (1971, November 19). *Shoot* [performance art]. Santa Ana, CA: F Space Gallery.

Burden, D. J. (2009). Deploying embodied AI into virtual worlds. *Knowledge-Based Systems*, *22*(7), 540–544. doi:10.1016/j.knosys.2008.10.001

Burton, B. (n.d.). *Pro*. Retrieved from http://bryndynburton.wordpress.com/dancemaster/pro/

Cadava, E., Connor, P., & Nancy, J.-L. (1991). *Who comes after the subject?* New York: Routledge.

CAE. (2002). Collective Cultural Action The Critical Art Ensemble. *Variant*, *2*(15), 24–25.

Cage, J. (1961). Indeterminacy. In *Silence: lectures and writings* (pp. 35–40). Middletown: Wesleyan University Press.

Cameron, D., & Carroll, J. (2011). Encoding liveness: Performance and real-time rendering in machinima. In H. Lowood & M. Nitsche (Eds.), *The machinima reader* (pp. 127–142). Cambridge, MA: The MIT Press.

Campbell, L. B. (1923). *Scenes and Machines on the English Stage During the Renaissance*. Cambridge: Cambridge University Press.

Canemaker, J. (2005). *Winsor McCay his Life and Art*. New York: Harry N Abrams Inc.

Cardenas, M. (2009) Becoming Dragon, Mixed-Reality Performance. Available at: http://secondloop.wordpress.com/

Cardenas, M. (2010) *Becoming Dragon: A Transversal Technology Study*, Code Drift: Essays in Critical Digital Studies 009. Available at: http://ctheory.net/articles.aspx?id=639

Cárdenas, M., & Head, C. Margolis, & T., Greco, K. (2009). *Becoming Dragon: a mixed reality, durational performance in Second Life.* University of California, San Diego. Retrieved from http://transreal.org/wp-content/uploads/2009/08/becoming-dragon-micha-cardenas-edit1.pdf

Carlson, M. (2004). *Performance: a critical introduction.* London: Routledge.

Carrier, D. (2002). *The Aesthetics of Comics.* Pennsylvania State University Press.

Carrouges, M. (1974). Andre Breton and the Basic Concepts of Surrealism. Tuscaloosa: University of Alabama Press.

Carver, G., & Beardon, C. (2004). *New Visions in Performance the Impact of Digital Technologies.* The Netherlands: Swets and Zeitlinger.

Castronova, E. (2007). *Exodus to the Virtual World* New York, NY: Palgrave MacMillan.

Celeste Martins, M. (2013). *Research as *poiesis*? Interdisciplinary landscapes expanded by the art and methdologies.* São Paulo, Brazil. Retrieved from http://art2investigacion-en.weebly.com/uploads/2/1/1/7/21177240/celeste_miriam.pdf

Cervieri, M. (2007). *User Generated Content in Second Life with Cory Ondrejka.* Scribemedia.org, http://www.scribemedia.org/2007/03/20/2nd-life/

Chafer, J. (2008). Summer Dancing 2008 (set up). Retrieved from: https://vimeo.com/92738793

Chafer, J. (2008). Summer Dancing. Retrieved from: https://vimeo.com/92740424

Chafer, J. (2011). VWBPE. Retrieved from: http://business.treet.tv/shows/bpeducation/episodes/virtual-theatre

Chafer, J., Fewster, R., & Mollison, N. (2009). SD2 mixed reality 2009. Retrieved from: https://vimeo.com/92743286

Chaitin, G. (1998). *The Limits of Mathematics.* Singapore: Springer-Verlag.

Chaitin, G., da Costa, N. C. A., & Doria, F. A. (2012). *Gödel's Way: Adventures in an Undecidable Universe.* CRC Press.

Chittaro, L., & Serra, M. (2004). Behavioral programming of autonomous characters based on probabilistic automata and personality. *Journal of Computer Animaion and Virtual Worlds, 15*(3-4), 319–326. doi:10.1002/cav.35

Chun, W. (2011). *Programmed Visions: Software and Memory.* Cambridge: MIT Press. doi:10.7551/mitpress/9780262015424.001.0001

Clarke, E. G., & Justice, E. M. *Identity Development - Aspects of Identity.* Retrieved from http://social.jrank.org/pages/322/Identity-Development.html

Clarke, A., & Mitchell, G. (2007). Introduction. In A. Clarke & G. Mitchel (Eds.), *Videogames and art* (pp. 7–22). Bristol, Chicago: Intellect.

Cleland, K. (2008). *Avatars: Self-Other Encounters in a Mediated World.* Retrieved from http://www.kathycleland.com/

Clemens, J. (2008) Babelswarm: A real-time 3D art and audio project by Adam Nash, Christopher Dodds and Justin Clemens. Available at: http://babelswarm.blogspot.com/

Clemens, J. (2011). Virtually anywhere real-time new-old avatar-human entertainment art: Cao Fei online. *Australian and New Zealand Journal of Art, 11*(1), 113–131.

Clemens, J. (2014). The virtual extimacies of Cao Fei. In L. Hjorth, N. King, & M. Kataoka (Eds.), *Art in the Asia-Pacific: Intimate Publics* (pp. 191–203). New York, NY: Routledge.

Clemens, J., Dodds, C., & Nash, A. (2007). *Babelswarm. Mixed reality artwork, Photographic prints, single channel video and Second Life installation.* Australia: Lismore Regional Gallery.

Clemens, J., Dodds, C., & Nash, A. (2009). *Autoscopia. Mixed reality artwork, single channel video and Second Life installation.* National Portrait Gallery of Australia.

Colebrook, C. (2010). *Deleuze and the Meaning of Life.* London: Continuum.

Coleman, B. (2011). *Hello Avatar: Rise of the Networked Generation.* Cambridge, MIT Press.

Coleman, R. (2008). The becoming of bodies: Girls, media effects, and body image. *Feminist Media Studies, 8*(2), 163–179.

Collins English Dictionary. (2013). *Avatar.* Retrieved from CollinsDictionary.com

Combes, M. (2013). *Gilbert Simondon and the Philosophy of the Transindividual.* Cambridge: MIT Press.

Cooper, P. (n.d.). Assemblage. *Grove Art Online.* Oxford Music and Art Online. Retrieved from http://www.oxfordartonline.com.ezproxy-library.ocad.ca/subscriber/article_citations/grove/art/T004631?q=assemblage&search=quick&pos=1&_start=1

Cooper, M. C., & Schoedsack, E. B. (1933). *King Kong {Motion Picture}.* New York, NY: RKO Pictures.

Cooper, R. (2007). *Alter Ego- Avatars and their creators.* London: Thames and Hudson.

Corbett, S. (2009). *Portrait of an Artist as an Avatar.* Retrieved from http://vhil.stanford.edu/news/2009/nyt-portrait.pdf

Coronet, J. (2011). Immersiva. San Francisco, CA: Second Life. Video; retrieved from http://www.youtube.com/watch?v=4B5DJZVthqY

Crawford, C. (2003). *The Art of Interactive Design.* San Francisco: No Starch Press.

Crone, R. A. (1999). *A History of Color. Dordrect.* Kluwer Academic Publishers. doi:10.1007/978-94-007-0870-9

Cunningham, M. (2014). Retrieved from: http://www.mercecunningham.org

Dahlsveen, H., & Sousa, C. C. (2013). Kromosomer – an Experience in Shared Creative Work and Expression. *Journal of Virtual Worlds Research, 6*(2), 1–21.

Dalton, D. (2012). *Mahatma Gandhi: Nonviolent power in action.* New York: Columbia University Press.

Damer, B., Judson, J., Dove, J., Illustrator-DiPaola, S., Illustrator-Ebtekar, A., & Illustrator-McGehee, S. … Produced By-Reber, K. (1997). *Avatars! Exploring and Building Virtual Worlds on the Internet.* Peachpit Press. Retrieved from http://dl.acm.org/citation.cfm?id=550319

Davies, C. (1995) Osmose. Virtual Reality Environment. Available at: http://www.immersence.com/osmose/index.php

Davies, C. (1998) Ephémère. Virtual Reality Environment. Available at: http://www.immersence.com/

Davies, C. (2003). Landscape, Earth, Body, Being, Space, and Time in the Immersive Virtual Environments Osmose and Ephemere. In J. Malloy (Ed.), Women, Art and Technology. Cambridge, Massachusetts: MIT Press; Available at http://www.immersence.com

De Angeli, A., Johnson, G. I., & Coventry, L. (2001). The unfriendly user: exploring social reactions to chatterbots. In Helander, Khalid, & Tham (Eds.), *Proceedings of The International Conference on Affective Human Factors Design, London* (pp. 467–474). London: Asean Academic Press. Retrieved from http://www.alicebot.org/articles/guest/The%20Unfriendly%20User.html

De Certeau, M., & Rendall, S. (2011). *The Practice of Everyday Life.* University of California Press.

De Landa, M. (1993). *Non-organic Life. Incorporations.* New York: Zone Books.

De Landa, M. (2002). *Intensive Science and Virtual Philosophy.* London: Continuum.

de Mul, S. (2007). Travelling to the Colonial Past as Migratory Aesthetics: Aya Zikken's *Terug naar de atlasvilinder.* In S. Durrant & C. M. L. Lord (Eds.), *Essays in Migratory Aesthetics: Cultural Practices Between Migration and Art-Making* (Vol. 17, pp. 95–108). Rodopi.

Debord, G. (1997). *Theory of the Dérive. Internationale situationniste.* Paris: A. Fayard.

Debord, G., & Knabb, K. (2002). *The Society of the Spectacle.* Canberra: Treason Press.

DeLanda, M. (2006). *A New Philosophy of Society: assemblage theory and social complexity.* London: Continuum.

DeLappe, J. (2008) Re-enactment: The Salt Satyagraha Online. Available at: http://saltmarchsecondlife.wordpress.com/

DeLappe, J. (2008, April 2). Re: April 2nd, dragons, wolves, Nixon…. Retrieved from https://saltmarchsecondlife.wordpress.com/2008/04/02/april-2nd-dragons-wolves-nixon/

DeLappe, J. (2008, April 3). Re: April 3rd, trailer parks, performance art, cow.... Retrieved from https://saltmarchsecondlife.wordpress.com/2008/04/03/april-3rd-trailer-parks-performance-art-cow/

DeLappe, J. (2008, March 14). Re: March 14, 2008 starting location.... Retrieved from https://saltmarchsecondlife.wordpress.com/2008/03/13/march-14-2008-starting-location/

DeLappe, J. (2008, March 16). Re: Sunday, March 16th start point.... Retrieved from https://saltmarchsecondlife.wordpress.com/2008/03/16/sunday-march-16th-start-point/

DeLappe, J. (2008, March 20). Re: A conversation in SL about the walk.... Retrieved from https://saltmarchsecondlife.wordpress.com/2008/03/20/a-conversation-in-sl-about-the-walk/

DeLappe, J. (2008, March 20). Re: Starting location March 20, 2008.... Retrieved from https://saltmarchsecondlife.wordpress.com/2008/03/20/starting-location-march-20-2008/

DeLappe, J. (2008, March 24). Re: March 25th, later start time.... Retrieved from https://saltmarchsecondlife.wordpress.com/2008/03/24/march-25th-later-start-time/

DeLappe, J. (2008, March 24). Re: Monday, March 24, rest day #2. Retrieved from https://saltmarchsecondlife.wordpress.com/?s=march+24

DeLappe, J. (2008, March 26). Re: March 26th, 12 more miles and several friends.... Retrieved from http://saltmarchsecondlife.wordpress.com/2008/03/26/march-26th-12-more-miles-and-several-friends/

DeLappe, J. (2008, March 29). Re: March 29th, start – snapshots, shorefront properties.... Retrieved from https://saltmarchsecondlife.wordpress.com/2008/03/29/march-29th-start-snapshots-shorefront-properties/

DeLappe, J. (2008, March 30). Re: Sunday, March 30...8 days to Dandi.... Retrieved from https://saltmarchsecondlife.wordpress.com/2008/03/30/sunday-march-308-days-to-dandi/

DeLappe, J. (2008, March 31). Re: Monday, March 31st... rest day – steps towards the final miles.... Retrieved from https://saltmarchsecondlife.wordpress.com/2008/03/31/monday-march-31st-rest-day-steps-towards-the-final-miles/

DeLappe, J. (2008, May 27). Re: Cardboard Gandhi sculpture in progres.... Retrieved from https://saltmarchsecondlife.wordpress.com/2008/05/27/cardboard-gandhi-sculpture-in-progres/

DeLappe, J. (2008, May 6). Re: On joining a "real" march in NYC.... Retrieved from https://saltmarchsecondlife.wordpress.com/2008/05/

DeLappe, J. (2010, January 21) quoted by Glasser, A. Gandhi's Second Life continues in prison. *Network-World*. Retrieved from http://www.networkworld.com/news/2010/012110-gandhis-second-life-continues-in.html

DeLappe, J. (2011). The Gandhi Complex: The Mahatma in Second Life. In X. Burrough (Ed.), *Net Works: Case Studies in Web Art and Design*. New York: Routledge.

DeLappe, J. (2013). *Private correspondence with P. Wardle.*

Deleuze, G. (1988). *Bergsonism*. New York: Zone.

Deleuze, G. (1988). *Spinoza: Practical Philosophy*. San Francisco: City Lights Books.

Deleuze, G. (1989). *Cinema 2: The time-image* (H. Tomlinson & R. Galeton, Trans.). Minneapolis, MN: University of Minnesota.

Deleuze, G. (1990). *Spinoza: Expressionism in Philosophy*. New York: Zone Books.

Deleuze, G. (1990). *The logic of sense. C. V. Boundas* (M. Lester & C. Stivale Trans. & Eds.). New York, NY: Columbia University Press.

Deleuze, G. (2004a). *Difference and Repetition*. London: Continuum.

Deleuze, G. (2004b). *The Logic of Sense*. London: Continuum.

Deleuze, G., & Guattari, F. (1987). *A thousand plateaus: capitalism and schizophrenia.* Minneapolis: University of Minnesota Press.

Deleuze, G., & Guittari, F. (2004). *A Thousand Plateaus: Capitalism and Schizophrenia.* England: Continuum. (Original work published 1988)

Demos, T. J. (2009). The Ends of Exile: Toward a Coming Universality. In N. Bourriaud (Ed.), *Altermodern, Tate Triennial.* London: Tate Publishing.

Derrida, J. (1982). *Différance. Margins of Philosophy.* Brighton: Harvester Press.

Derrida, J. (1994). *Specters of Marx: The State of the Debt, the Work of Mourning, and the New International.* Routledge.

Derrida, J. (1997). *On grammatology* (G. Chakravorty Spivak, Trans.). Baltimore: Johns Hopkins University Press.

Derrida, J. (2013). *Derrida and Joyce: Texts and contexts* (A. J. Mitchell & S. Slote, Eds.). Albany: State University of New York.

Derrida, J., & Bass, A. (2004). Positions. *Continuum.*

Derrida, J., & Spivak, G. C. (1976). *Of Grammatology.* Baltimore, London: Johns Hopkins University Press.

Despres, D. (2013-2014). *The Drax Files: World makers.* Los Angeles, CA: Draxtor. Video retrieved from http://www.youtube.com/user/draxtordespres

Dewey, J., (1980). *Art as Experience.* New York: Perigree Books.

Dick, P. K. (1996). How to Build a Universe that Doesn't Fall Apart Two Days Later. In P. K. Dick & L. Sutin (Eds.), *The Shifting Realities of Philip K. Dick: Selected Literary and Philosophical Writings* (259–280). New York: Vintage.

Dingo, R. (2007) Watch the World. Machinima. Available at: http://digitaldouble.blogspot.com/2007/07/watch-worlds.html

Dingo, R. (2007, July 16). Watch the world(s). *My Digital Double* [Blog]. Retrieved from http://digitaldouble.blogspot.com/2007/07/watch-worlds.html

Dinnen, Z. (2012). *Pictures of Self-Portraits: Eva and Franco Mattes' Avatar Portraits.* Retrieved from http://mediacommons.futureofthebook.org/imr/2012/05/01/pictures-self-portraits-eva-and-franco-mattes-avatar-portraits

Donofrio, A. (2012). Seeing Gray: The Power of Interpretation in Chris Burden's *Shoot. The Stoa Online,* 1(Fall). Retrieved October from http://icstoa.wordpress.com/fall-2012-volume-i/seeing-gray-the-power-of-interpretation-in-chris-burdens-shoot-by-amber-donofrio/

Dordrecht, Heidelberg. *Worlds.London..* New York: Springer

Dove, T., & Mackenzie, M. (1993). Archaeology of the Mother Tongue. Virtual Reality Installation. Alberta, Canada: Banff Centre for the Arts; Available at http://www.banffcentre.ca/bnmi/coproduction/archives/a.asp

Doyle, D. (2010). *Art And the Emergent Imagination In Avatar-Mediated Online Space.* Unpublished thesis (Doctor of Philosophy), University of East London, London.

Doyle, D. (2008). Art and the Avatar: The Kritical Works in SL project. *International Journal of Performance Arts and Digital Media,* 4(2&3), 137–153. doi:10.1386/padm.4.2_3.137_1

Doyle, D. (2013). Living between worlds: Imagination, liminality, and avatar-mediated presence. In D. Harrison (Ed.), *Digital Media and Technologies for Virtual Artistic Practices* (pp. 59–74). Hershey: IGI Global. doi:10.4018/978-1-4666-2961-5.ch005

Doyle, D., & Harrison, D. (2010). Kritical art works in Second Life. In G. Mura (Ed.), *Meta-plasticity in Virtual Worlds: Aesthetics and Semantics Concepts.* Hershey: IGI Global.

Dyson, T., & Harvey, C. (2014). The Bobbekins. San Francisco, CA: Scissores. [Second Life], Retrieved from http://bobbekinworld.com

Earle, N. (2001). *Designing a Visual Component of Communication within 3D Avatar Virtual Worlds.* (Doctoral Thesis). University of Plymouth.

Eco, U. (1962). The open work (A. Cancogni, Trans.). Cambridge: Harvard University Press. Retrieved from http://philpapers.org/rec/ECOTOW

Edwards, C. (2009). *Women's home-crafted objects as collections of culture and comfort, 1750-1900. Material Cultures, 1740-1920: The Meanings and Pleasures of Collecting* (pp. 37–52). Farnham, England; Burlington, VT: Ashgate.

Egan, G. (2010). *Permutation City*. London: Gollancz.

Egges, A., Kshirsagar, S., & Magnenat-Thalmann, N. (2004). Generic personality and emotion simulation for conversational agents. *Computer Animation and Virtual Worlds*, *15*(1), 1–13. doi:10.1002/cav.3

Eladhari, M. (2010). *Characterising Action Potential in Virtual Game Worlds Applied with the Mind Module*. (Doctoral Thesis). Teeside University.

Ellsmere, Jo. (2012). *ANIMAanimus*. Retrieved from https://www.youtube.com/watch?v=DnlNed4EY8g&feature=youtube_gdata_player

Eno, B. (1995). *Gossip is Philosophy, Wired magazine interview with Kevin Kelly*. Wired. http://www.wired.com/wired/archive/3.05/eno.html?pg=4&topic=

Eno, B. (2007) 77 Million Paintings. Exhibition. Available at: http://www.longnow.org/events/02007/jun/29/77-million-paintings-brian-eno/

Expo, M. (2012). Web site. Retrieved from http://www.MachinimaExpo.com

Fall, R. (2009). Strange Fruit: Billie Holiday tribute. MMIF - MaMachinima International Festival 2009. San Francisco, CA: Second Life. Video; retrieved from http://www.youtube.com/watch?v=3rCAraAD92U

Fall, R. (2010). *Across the universe - Craig Lyons*. San Francisco, CA: *Second Life*. Video retrieved June 23, 2014, from http://www.youtube.com/watch?v=zw5iwrEOBRg

Fall, R. (2014). *FallFilms*. Video retrieved from http://www.youtube.com/user/FallFilms

Fang, H. (2008). *Cao Fei Journey. Monograph*. Paris, France: Vitamin Creative Space.

Farley, K., Nitsche, M., Bolter, J. D., Lang, T., & MacIntyre, B. (2009). Augmenting Creative Realities: Second Life Performance Project. In *Leonardo, 42, 1* (pp. 96–97). Cambridge: MIT Press. doi:10.1162/leon.2009.42.1.96

Fei, C. (2007) *iMirror*. Multimedia Installation. [Available at: http://blogs.walkerart.org/offcenter/2007/07/16/cao-feis-imirror/

Fei, C. (2008- ongoing) *RMB City. Second Life* Sim. Available at: http://www.serpentinegallery.org/2008/05/cao_fei_rmb_city.html and http://rmbcity.com/

Fischer-Lichte, E. (2004). *Ästhetik der Performativen*. Frankfurt am Mein, Germany: Suhrkamp.

Fitzroy, S. (2012, July). The magical man behind Star Wars R2-D2 and the Bobbekins: An interview with Tony Dyson and Chantal Harvey. *Best of SL Magazine* (pp. 166-187). Second Life: BOSL Inc.

Fitzroy, S. (2013). *Magnum: The Machinima Review* [Blog]. Retrieved from http://magnummachinima.blogspot.com

Fitzroy, S. (2013, October). The blackened mirror: Prim perfect machinima. *Best of SL Magazine* (pp. 138-149). Second Life: BOSL Inc.

Fitzroy, S. (2014). Gangnam furry style *Second Life*. Chicago, IL: A Ring My Bel - So Nice Production. Video retrieved from http://www.youtube.com/watch?v=0kWYId5-NIw

Fitzroy, S. (2014). Video channel. Chicago, IL: A Ring My Bel - So Nice Production. Retrieved from http://www.youtube.com/channel/UCBUFGaaIh61Bd2lfMtR9jZA

Flanagan, M. (2011). Play, participation, and art: Blurring the edges. In M. Lovejoy, C. Paul, & V. Vesna (Eds.), *Context providers: Conditions of meaning in media arts* (pp. 89–100). Bristol, Chicago: Intellect.

Flimflam, W. (2007, January 24). *Gaza Stripped*. Retrieved from http://turbulence.org/blog/2007/01/24/performing-second-life/

Floridi, L. (2011). *The Philosophy of Information*. New York: Oxford University Press. doi:10.1093/acprof:oso/9780199232383.001.0001

Floridi, L. (2014). *The 4th Revolution: How the Infosphere is Reshaping Human Reality*. Oxford: Oxford University Press.

Fominykh, M., & Prasolova-Førland, E. (2011). Virtual research arena: presenting research in 3D virtual environments. In *Global Learn* (Vol. 2011, pp. 1558–1567). Retrieved from http://www.editlib.org/p/37372/

Fox, J., Bailenson, J., & Binney, J. (2009). Virtual Experiences, Physical Behaviors: The Effect of Presence on Imitation of an Eating Avatar. *Presence*, *18*(4), 294–303. Cambridge. doi:10.1162/pres.18.4.294

Fraser, M., & Greco, M. (2005). Introduction. In M. Fraser & M. Greco (Eds.), *The Body. A Reader* (pp. 1–42). London, New York: Routledge.

Fredkin, E. (2003). An Introduction to Digital Philosophy. *International Journal of Theoretical Physics*, 42(2). p. 189–247). Retrieved from: http://64.78.31.152/wp-content/uploads/2012/08/intro-to-DP.pdf

Freenote, F. (2010). String me up (Lance Rembrandt). San Francisco, CA: Second Life. Video; retrieved from http://www.youtube.com/watch?v=wuAtHaLkvHY

Frieling, R. (2008). *The Art of Participation: 1950 to Now*. San Francisco: Thames & Hudson.

Gabriel, Y., & Lang, T. (2006). *The Unmanageable Consumer*. United Kingdom: SAGE Publications Ltd. Retrieved from http://knowledge.sagepub.com.ezproxy-library.ocad.ca/view/the-unmanageable-consumer-2e/SAGE.xml

Gadamer, H. (1987). *Philosophical apprenticeship* (R. R. Sullivan, Trans.). Cambridge: MIT.

Galanis, D., Karakatsiotis, G., Lampouras, G., & Androutsopoulos, I. (2009). NaturalOWL: Generating texts from OWL ontologies in Protégé and in Second Life. In *EACL '09 Proceedings of the 12th Conference of the European Chapter of the Association for Computational Linguistics: Demonstrations Session* (pp. 17–20). Retrieved from http://www.researchgate.net/publication/253371102_NaturalOWL_Generating_Texts_from_OWL_Ontologies_in_Prot_eg_e_and_in_Second_Life/file/60b7d52e787f79bf8b.pdf

Gallagher, S. (2005). *How the Body Shapes the Mind*. Oxford: Clarendon Press. doi:10.1093/0199271941.001.0001

Galloway, A. R. (2012). *The Interface Effect*. Cambridge: Polity Press.

Gayeton, D. (2007). *Molotov Alva and his search for the creator: A Second Life odyssey*. Submarine Channel. Video retrieved from http://molotovalva.submarinechannel.com

Gell, A. (1998) Art and Agency. Oxford: Oxford University Press.

Gestalt. (2000, June 10). Hugh Hancock of Strange Company [Interview]. Eurogamer,net. Retrieved from http://www.eurogamer.net/articles/i_strangecompany

Giannachi, G. (2004). Virtual Theatres an Introduction. London, New York.: Routledge Igloo. Retrieved from: http://www.gibsonmartelli.com/

Gibson, W. (1984). *Neuromancer*. New York: Ace.

Gilbert & George. (1970). *The Singing Sculpture* [performance/sculpture]. Chelsea, UK: Nigel Greenwood Gallery.

Global. Retrieved from http://www.igi-global.com/chapter/the-gamification-experience/87045

Goertzel, B., & Pennachin, C. (Eds.). (2007). Artificial general intelligence. Springer. Retrieved from http://link.springer.com/content/pdf/10.1007/978-3-540-68677-4.pdf doi:10.1007/978-3-540-68677-4

Goffman, I. (1956). *Self in Everyday Life*. Edinburgh: University of Edinburgh Social Sciences Research Centre.

Goldberg, R. (1979). *Performance: live art 1909 to the present*. London: Thames & Hudson.

Goldberg, R. (2001). *Performance Art: From Futurism to the Present*. London: Thames & Hudson.

Gould, C., & Sermon, P. (2012) Mirror on the Screen. Available at: http://creativetechnology.salford.ac.uk/paulsermon/mirror/

Grassi, D. (Janša, J.). (2006). *Brainloop*. Retrieved from http://vimeo.com/42691853

Greenway, P. (2014). *Peter Greenaway: Golden Age of the Russian Avant-garde - 14.04.2014*. Retrieved from https://www.youtube.com/watch?v=eQeUf_Ua6EY&feature=youtube_gdata_player

Griefer - Second Life Wiki. (n.d.). Retrieved from http://wiki.secondlife.com/wiki/Griefer

Gromola, D., & Sharir, Y. (1994). Dancing with the Virtual Dervish: Virtual Bodies. Virtual Reality Installation. Alberta, Canada: Banff Centre for the Arts; Available at http://www.banffcentre.ca/bnmi/coproduction/archives/d.asp#dancing

Grosz, E. (2001). *Architecture From the Outside: Essays on Virtual and Real Space*. Cambridge, Massachusetts: MIT Press.

Grosz, E. (2012). *Identity and Individuation: Some Feminist Reflections. Gilbert Simondon: Technology and Being*. Edinburgh: Edinburgh University Press.

Grosz, E. A. (2001a). *Architecture from the Outside: Essays on Virtual and Real Space*. Cambridge, Massachusetts and London: MIT Press.

Grosz, E. A. (2001b). *'Lived Spatiality (the Spaces of Corporeal Desire)'. Architecture from the Outside: Essays on Virtual and Real Space* (pp. 31–47). Cambridge, Massachusetts and London: MIT Press.

Grosz, E. A. (2008). *Chaos, Territory, Art: Deleuze and the Framing of the Earth*. New York: Columbia University Press.

Groys, B. (2008). *Art Power*. Cambridge: MIT Press.

Grunenberg, C., & Hollein, M., Schirn Kunsthalle Frankfurt and Tate Gallery Liverpool. (2002). *Shopping: a century of art and consumer culture*. Ostfildern-Ruit: Hatje Cantz.

Gržinić, M. (2011). Identity operated in new mode: Context and body/space/time. In M. Lovejoy, C. Paul, & V. Vesna (Eds.), *Context providers: Conditions of meaning in media arts* (pp. 151–174). Bristol, Chicago: Intellect.

Guattari, F. (1995). *Chaosmosis: an ethico-aesthetic paradigm*. Bloomington: Indiana University Press.

Gude, O. (2004). Postmodern Principles: In Search of a 21st Century Art Education. *Art Education, 57*(1), 6–13.

Guest, T. (2007). *Second Lives*. New York: Random House Inc.

Gunkel, D. J. (2010). The Real Problem: Avatars, Metaphysics and Online Social Interaction. *New Media & Society, 12*(1), 127–141. doi:10.1177/1461444809341443

Hall, S. (1995). The Question of Cultural Identity. In *Modernity: An Introduction to Modern Societies*. Cambridge, UK: Polity.

Halo. (2001). Video game. Seattle, WA: Bungie.

Hancock, H. (1999). Eschaton. Edinburgh, Scotland: Strange Company. Video; retrieved from http://www.strangecompany.org

Hancock, H. (2006). Blood spell. Edinburgh, Scotland: Strange Company. Video; retrieved from http://www.strangecompany.org

Hancock, H. (2010; 2014). *Death knight love story*. Edinburgh, Scotland: Strange Company. Video retrieved from http://www.strangecompany.org

Hancock, H., & Ingram, J. (2007b). Women who have changed machinima. *Machinima for Dummies: Blogging the book*. Retrieved from http://machfordu.wpengine.com/articles/2009/03/24/women-who-have-changed-machinima

Hancock, H., & Ingram, J. (2007a). *Machinima for dummies*. Hoboken, NJ: Wiley/For Dummies.

Hansen, M. (2004). *New Philosophy for New Media*. Cambridge, MA: MIT Press.

Hansen, M. (2006). *Bodies in Code: Interfaces with digital media*. New York, Abingdon: Routledge.

Hansen, M. B. N. (2006). *Bodies in Code: Interfaces with Digital Media*. London: Routledge.

Hanson, A. R. (2012). *What is Colour. Colour Design: Theories and Applications*. Oxford: Woodhead Publishing.

Hare, A. (2013). Bridging divides: Transference in the work of Lynne Heller. *Scene, 1*(2), 165–178. doi:10.1386/scene.1.2.165_1

Harrower, D. ([c1958]). *Decoupage: a limitless world in decoration*. New York. Retrieved from http://hdl.handle.net/2027/coo.31924014500676

Harvey, C. (2010, September 24). Peter Greenaway speaks at 48hour film project machinima 2010. Keynote. Retrieved from http://vimeo.com/15253336

Harwood, T. (2012). Emergence of gamified commerce: Turning virtual to real. *Journal of Electronic Commerce in Organizations, 10*(2), 16–39. Retrieved from http://www.igi-global.com/article/emergence-gamified-commerce/70212

Harz, C. (2006, January 31). *The holy grail of previs: Gaming technology. Animation World Network* (AWN).

Hayles, K. (1999). *How we became posthuman, Chicago: University of Chicago Press. Quoted by Zizek, S. (2001). On Belief (Thinking in Action).* London: Routledge. doi:10.7208/chicago/9780226321394.001.0001

Hayles, N. K. (1996). Embodied Virtuality: or how to put bodies back into the picture. In M. A. Moser (Ed.), *Immersed in Technology: art and virtual environments* (1–28). Cambridge, MA: MIT Press.

Hayles, N. K. (2012). *How We Think: Digital Media and Contemporary Technogenesis.* Chicago: University of Chicago Press. doi:10.7208/chicago/9780226321370.001.0001

Heads-up displays (HUDs) - Second Life. (n.d.). Retrieved from http://community.secondlife.com/t5/English-Knowledge-Base/Heads-up-displays-HUDs/ta-p/700083

Heeter, C. (1992). *Being There: The Subjective Experience of Presence.* Retrieved from: http://commtechlab.msu.edu/randd/research/beingthere.html

Heim, M. (1991). The Erotic Ontology of Cyberspace. In M. Benedikt (Ed.), Cyberspace: First Steps (pp. 59-80). Cambridge, MA, & London, UK: MIT Press.

Heisenberg, W. (1949). *The Physical Principles of the Quantum Theory.* New York: Dover.

Heisenberg, W. (1965). Nobel Lecture: The Development of Quantum Mechanics (1933). In *Nobel Lectures, Physics 1922-1941* (290–301). Amsterdam: Elsevier.

Heisenberg, W. (2000). *Physics and Philosophy: The Revolution in Modern Science.* London: Penguin.

Heller, L., & Stuckey, C. (2014, June 9). Duchamps shopping habits... email.

Henderson, B. (2005). *Open Letter To Kansas School Board.* Retrieved from: http://www.venganza.org/about/open-letter/

Hershman Leeson, L. (2012). *Excerpt from the Artist Talk with Lynn Hershman Leeson.* Karlsruhe. Retrieved from https://www.youtube.com/watch?v=vC69xR4smAI

Hershman Leeson, L. (2014). private correspondence with P. Wardle.

Hershman, L. (2007-ongoing) Life to the Second Power (L2). Available at: http://presence.stanford.edu:3455/LynnHershman/261

HeZ. (n.d.). *Multi-Sit Script.* Retrieved from https://marketplace.secondlife.com/p/HeZ-Multi-Sit-Script-Multiple-poses-and-sit-targets-in-one-prim-without-poseballs/370403?id=370403&slug=HeZ-Multi-Sit-Script-Multiple-poses-and-sit-targets-in-one-prim-without-poseballs

Higley, S. (2013). Dangerous sim crossings: Framing the *Second Life* art machinima. In J. Ng (Ed.), *Understanding machinima: Essays on filmmaking in virtual world* (pp. 109–126). London: Bloomsbury Academic.

Hill, D. (2011). *The Ethical Dimensions of a New Media Age: A Study in Contemporary Responsibility.* (Doctoral Thesis). University of York.

Hoesterey, I. (2001). *Pastiche: Cultural Memory in Art, Film, Literature.* Bloomington: Indiana University Press.

Horvath, S. (2011a). Reanimated: The 15 best videos of all time - Diary of a Camper. *Complex Gaming.* Retrieved from http://www.complex.com/video-games/2011/04/15-best-machinima-videos/camper

Horvath, S. (2011b). Reanimated: The 15 best videos of all time - Red vs.Blue. *Complex Gaming.* Retrieved from http://www.complex.com/video-games/2011/04/15-best-machinima-videos/red-vs.-blue

Husserl, E. (2005). *Cartesian Meditations; An Introduction to Phenomenology* (D. Cairns, Trans.). London: Martinus Nijhoff Publishers. (Original work published 1950)

Iaconesi, S. (2007). *dead on Second Life.* Retrieved from http://www.artisopensource.net/dosl/main.html

iClone (2013). 3D animation software. San Francisco, CA: Reallusion. ILL Clan. (2014). Web site. Retrieved from http://www.illclan.com/tiny-nation

Ihde, D. (2002). *Bodies in Technology*. Minneapolis: University of Minnesota Press.

Ijsselsteijn, W., & Riva, G. (2003). Being There: The experience of presence in mediated environments. In G. Riva, F. Davide, & W. IJsselsteijn, Being There: Concepts, effects and measurement of user presence in synthetic environments (pp. 3-16). Amsterdam: Ios Press.

Iliadis, A. (2013a). A New Individuation:Deleuze's Simondon Connection. *MediaTropes eJournal*, IV(1), 83–100.

Iliadis, A. (2013b). Informational Ontology: The Meaning of Gilbert Simondon's Concept of Individuation. *Communication+1*, 2(5). Retrieved from http://scholarworks.edu/cpo/vol2/iss1/5

Imitating the Dog Theatre Company. (n.d.). Retrieved from: http://www.imitatingthedog.co.uk/

Isbister, K. (2006). *Better Game Characters by Design: A Psychological Approach*. San Francisco: Morgan Kaufmann.

Isla, D., Burke, R., Downie, M., & Blumberg, B. (2001). A layered brain architecture for synthetic creatures. In *International Joint Conference on Artificial Intelligence* (Vol. 17, pp. 1051–1058).

Jack, H. A. (1956). *The Gandhi Reader: A Source Book of His Life and Writings*. Bloomington: Indiana University Press.

Jackson, P. (Director) (2005). *King Kong* [Motion Picture]. Universal City, CA: Universal Pictures.

Jackson, P. (Director/Producer). *The lord of the rings* [Motion Picture]. Los Angeles, CA: New Line Cinema.

James, W. (1890). *The Principles of Psychology*. Retrieved from http://psychclassics.asu.edu/James/Principles/prin10.htm

Jameson, F. (2003). The End of Temporality. *Critical Inquiry*, 29(4), 695–718. doi:10.1086/377726

Jenkins, H. (1992). *Textual poachers: Television fans and participant culture*. New York, NY: Routledge.

Jenkins, H. (2003). *From Barbie to Mortal Kombat; Further reflection* (A. Everett & J. T. Caldwell, Eds.).

Jenkins, H. (2006). *Convergence culture: Where old and new media collide*. New York, NY: New York University Press.

Jet Propulsion Laboratory. NASA. (2014). Voyager. The Interstellar Mission. Retrieved from http://voyager.jpl.nasa.gov/

Johnson, P. (2010). *Second Life, Media and the Other Society (First printing.)*. New York: Peter Lang Publishing.

Johnson, P. (2010). *Second Life, media and the other society*. New York, NY: Peter Lang.

Johnson, P., & Pettit, D. (2012). *Machinima: The art & practice of virtual filmmaking*. Jefferson, NC: McFarland.

Johnson, P., & Pettit, D. (2014). The machinima expo 6: A snapshot of the state of machinima. Machinima Review. *Journal of Gaming and Virtual Worlds*, 6(1), 89–96.

Johnson, S. (1997). *Interface Culture. How New Technology Transforms the Way We Create and Communicate*. San Francisco: Harper.

Jones, D. E. (2006) I, Avatar: Constructions of Self and Place in Second Life and the Technological Imagination. *Gnovis, Journal of Communication, Culture and Technology*. Available at: http://gnovis.georgetown.edu

Jones, A. (1998). *Body Art/Performing the Subject*. Minneapolis: University of Minnesota Press.

Jones, A. (2008). This Life. In S. Broadhurst & J. Machon (Eds.), *Frieze (117, Sept 2008). Quoted by Mock, R. (2012). Lynn Hershman: The Creation of Multiple Robertas. In Identity, Performance and Technology: Practices of Empowerment, Embodiment and Technicity*. Hampshire, England: Palgrave MacMillan.

Jones, R. (2011). Pink vs. blue: The emergence of women in machinima. In H. Lowood & M. Nitsche (Eds.), *The machinima reader* (pp. 277–300). Cambridge, MA: The MIT Press.

Jung, C. G. (1968). *The Archetypes and the Collective Unconscious*. Princeton: Princeton University Press.

Justiça, P. (2013). *A ausência do Corpo na Comunicação Online – a descoberta da identidade no Second Life*. Lisboa: Universidade Aberta.

Juul, J. (2005). *Half-real: Video games between real rules and fictional worlds*. Cambridge: MIT.

Kachur, L. (n.d.). Collage. *Grove Art Online*. Retrieved from http://www.oxfordartonline.com.ezproxy-library.ocad.ca/subscriber/article/grove/art/T018573?q=collage&search=quick&pos=1&_start=1#firsthit

Kahney, L. (2003, July 9). Games invade Hollywood's turf. *Wired*. Retrieved from http://archive.wired.com/science/discoveries/news/2003/07/59566

Kang, K. A. (2006). *Anna*. Video retrieved from http://www.youtube.com/watch?v=1oDHUESNHgI

Kant, I. (1787). *Critique of Pure Reason*. (J. M. D. Meiklejohn, Trans.). Retrieved from www2.hn.psu.edu/faculty/jmanis/kant/Critique-Pure-Reason.pdf

Kant, I. (1987). *Critique of judgment* (W. S. Pluhar, Trans.). Indianapolis: Hackett.

Kildall, S. (2008). Scott Kildall | KILDALL.COM | Artwork: No Matter. Retrieved from http://www.kildall.com/artwork/2008/no_matter/index.html

Kim, S-H. (2004) I Want to Hijack an Airplane: Selected Poems of Kim Seung-Hee.

Kim, E. (2008). Questioning the Modernity of Rha Hye-Seok&Quot;S Idea of "Newness" in Colonial/Modem Chosun. *Journal of Korean Women's. Studies*, *24*, 147–186.

King, B. (2002, July 23). Machinima: Games act like films. *Wired*. Retrieved from http://archive.wired.com/gaming/gamingreviews/news/2002/07/53929

Kitchin, R., & Dodge, M. (2011). *Code/Space*. Cambridge: MIT Press. doi:10.7551/mitpress/9780262042482.001.0001

Kittler, F. (1999). *Gramophone, Film, Typewriter*. Stanford: Stanford University Press.

Kittler, F. A. (1999). *Gramophone, film, typewriter* (G. W. Young & M. Wutz, Trans.). Stanford: Stanford University.

Klein, Y. (1992). *Sorbonne Lecture. Art in Theory 1900-1990*. Oxford: Blackwell Publishers.

Klevjer, R. (2007). What *is the Avatar? Fiction and Embodiment in Avatar-Based Singleplayer Computer Games*. University of Bergen. Retrieved from http://runeklevjer.wordpress.com/

Koestler, A. (1964). *The act of creation*. London: Hutchinson & Co.

Korolov, M. (2010, October 14). Machinima pioneers launch Pixel Valley Studio. *Hyper grid Business*. Retrieved from http://www.hypergridbusiness.com/2010/10/machinima-pioneers-launch-pixel-valley-studio

Kozel, S. (2007). Closer Performance, Technologies, Phenomenology. Cambridge: MIT Press

KSEVT – The Cultural Centre of European Space Technologies. (2014). Retrieved from http://www.ksevt.eu/Site/ksevt_eng/

Kuksa, I., & Childs, M. (2014). *Making Sense of Space. The Design and Experiences of Virtual spaces as a Tool for Communication*. Oxford: Chandos Publishing.

Lacan, J. (1977). *The Four Fundamental Concepts of Psycho-Analysis*. London: The Hogarth Press.

Lacan, J. (2001). *Ecrits; A selection* (A. Sheridan, Trans.). London: Routledge Classics

Laird, J. E., Rosenbloom, P. S., & Newell, A. (1986). Chunking in Soar: The anatomy of a general learning mechanism. *Machine Learning*, *1*(1), 11–46. doi:10.1007/BF00116249

Lakoff, G., & Johnson, M. (1998). *Philosophy in the Flesh: The Embodied Mind and Its Challenge to Western Thought*. New York: HarperCollins Canada / Basic Books.

Lakoff, G., & Johnson, M. (1999). *Philosophy in the Flesh - The Embodied Mind and Its Challenge to Western Thought. Nova Iorque*. Basic Books.

LaMarre, T. (2013). Afterword: Humans and Machines. In M. Combes (Ed.), *Gilbert Simondon and the Philosophy of the Transindividual*. Cambridge: MIT Press.

Lang, T & MacIntyre, B. (2007). Avatar in Room. Second Life Augmented Reality. Retrieved from: http://www.youtube.com/watch?v=ODgZtriNYoc&feature=share&list=PLCBB13931C4E5AF60&index=2

Lastowka, F. G., & Hunter, D. (2006). Virtual Worlds: A Primer. In J. M. Balkin (Ed.), *State of Play: Law, Games, and Virtual Worlds*. New York: New York University Press.

Laurel, B., & Strickland, R. (1993). Placeholder. Virtual Reality Installation. Alberta, Canada: Banff Centre for the Arts; Available at http://www.banffcentre.ca/bnmi/coproduction/archives/p.asp#placeholder

Laurel, B. (1993). *Computers as Theatre*. USA: Addison Wesley.

Leonard, A. (1997). *Bots: The Origin of the New Species*. San Francisco: Wired Books. Retrieved from http://dl.acm.org/citation.cfm?id=549684

Lévy, P. (1998). *Becoming Virtual, Reality in the Digital Age*. New York: Plenum Press.

Lévy, P. (1998). *Becoming Virtual: Reality in the Digital Age*. New York: Plenum Press.

Lévy, P. (2001). *Cyberculture*. Minneapolis: University of Minnesota Press.

Libsecondlife. (n.d.). Retrieved from http://secondlife.wikia.com/wiki/Libsecondlife

Lichty, P. (2008) Why Art in Virtual Worlds? E-Happenings, Relational Milieux & "Second Sculpture". *CIAC Electronic Magazine*. Available at: www.voyd.com/texts/LichtySLCIACWhyVirtualArt.pdf

Lichty, P. (2009). The Translation of Art in Virtual Worlds. In *Leonardo Electronic Almanac* (Vol 16 Issue 4–5). Retrieved from http://www.leoalmanac.org/wp-content/uploads/2012/09/11_lichty.pdf

Lichty, P. (2011). *Phantom Limbs: Affect and Identification in Virtual Performance, Panel Paper, ISEA2011*. Istanbul: Sabanci University.

Liman, D. (Director). (2014). *Edge of tomorrow* [Motion Picture]. Los Angeles, CA: Warner Bros.

Lind, M. (2007). The Collaborative Turn. In J. Billing, M. Lind, & L. Nilsson (ed.), Taking The Matter Into Common Hands: On Contemporary Art and Collaborative Practices (pp. 15-31). London: Black Dog Publishing.

Locke, J. (2007). *An Essay Concerning Human Understanding* (Book 2). J. Bennett (Annotations). Retrieved from http://www.earlymoderntexts.com

Lovejoy, M. (2008). *Digital currents: Art in the electronic age*. New York: Routledge.

Lowood, H. (2011). Video capture: Machinima, documentation, and the history of virtual worlds. In H. Lowood & M. Nitsche (Eds.), *The machinima reader* (pp. 3–22). Cambridge, MA: The MIT Press.

Lowood, H., & Nitsche, M. (2011). *The machinima reader*. Cambridge, MA: The MIT Press.

Loyall, A. B. (1997). *Believable agents: building interactive personalities* (Doctoral thesis). Carnegie Mellon University.

Lucas, G. (Director). (1977). *Star Wars* [Motion Picture]. Los Angeles, CA: 20th Century Fox.

Macedo, A. G. (2010). Uma Leitura das Novas Cartas Portuguesas em Vésperas de Abril. In C. Cruz, & V. Valente (ed.), All My Independent Women — Novas Cartas Portuguesas (pp. 53-56). Coimbra: Casa da esquina.

Machinima Artist Guild (MAG). (2014). Membership site. Tampa, FL: Lowe Runo Productions. Retrieved from http://slmachinimaarts.ning.com

Machinima Open Studio Project. (2014). Blog. Eugene, OR: Chic Aeon. Retrieved from http://machinimasl.blogspot.com

Machinima, Inc. (2014). Machinima.com. Retrieved from http://www.machinima.com

Mackenzie, A. (2002). *Transductions: Bodies and Machines at Speed*. London: Continuum.

Macleod, D. (1996). Preface. In M. A. Moser (Ed.), *Immersed in Technology: Art and Virtual Environments*. Cambridge, Massachusetts: MIT Press.

Mahovlich, P. (2009, August). Retrieved from http://blog.koinup.com/2009/08/lainy-vroom-and-art-of-machinima.html

MaMachinima. (2014). MaMachinima International Festival.(MMIF). Amsterdam: Chantal Harvey. Retrieved from http://mmif.wordpress.com

Mann, A. (1947). *T-Men*. Los Angeles, CA: Edward Small Productions.

Manovich, L. (1996). The Aesthetics of Virtual Worlds: Report from Los Angeles. *CTheory* (ga103).

Manovich, L. (1995). *The aesthetics of virtual worlds.* C-Theory Online.

Manovich, L. (2002). *Language of new media.* Cambridge, MA: The MIT Press.

Manovich, L. (2011). Image future. In H. Lowood & M. Nitsche (Eds.), *The machinima reader.*

Manovich, L. (2013). *Software takes command (International Texts in Critical Media Aesthetics).* London, UK: Bloomsbury Academic.

Manovich, L., & Kratky, A. (2005). *Soft cinema: Navigating the database.* Cambridge, MA: MIT.

Marache-Francisco, C., & Brangier, E. (2013). The gamification experience: UXD with a Gamification Background. In K. Blashki & P. Isaias (Eds.), *Emerging research and trends in interactivity and the human-computer interface* (pp. 205–223). Hershey, PA: IGI.

Marino, P. (2004). *3D Game-based filmmaking: The Art of Machinima.* Scottsdale, AZ: Paraglyph Press.

Massey, D. B. (2010) Spatial Justice Introduction in the Spaces of Democracy/Democracy of Space Network.

Massey, D. B. (1994). *A Global Sense of Place. Space, Place and Gender.* Minneapolis: University of Minnesota Press.

Massey, D. B. (2005). *For Space.* London: SAGE.

Massumi, B. (2011) Hair-Trigger Action Replaced Deliberation in the Bush Era. *The Guardian.* Video retrieved from: http://gu.com/p/3xgp4/tw

Massumi, B. (1992). *A user's guide to capitalism and schizophrenia: deviations from Deleuze and Guattari.* Cambridge: The MIT Press.

Massumi, B. (2002a). *Introduction: Concrete Is as Concrete Doesn't. Parables for the Virtual: Movement, Affect, Sensation.* Durham: Duke University Press. doi:10.1215/9780822383574

Mattes, E. & F. (0100101110101101.ORG). (2007a). Nothing is Real, Everything is Possible [Excerpts from various interviews]. Retrieved from http://0100101110101101.org/press/2007-07_Nothing_is_real.html

Mattes, E. & F. (0100101110101101.ORG). (2007b). *Reenactment of Chris Burden's* Shoot. Retrieved from http://0100101110101101.org/home/reenactments/performance-burden.html

Mattes, E. & F. (0100101110101101.ORG). (2010). *I know that it's all a state of mind.* Retrieved from http://vimeo.com/21651866

Mattes, E. & F. (2006) Thirteen Most Beautiful Avatars. Photography Exhibition. Available at: http://www.0100101110101101.org/home/portraits/thirteen.html

Mattes, E. & F. (2007-). *Synthetic Performances.* Retrieved from http://0100101110101101.org/synthetic-performances/

Mattes, F. (2007). *Nothing is real, everything is possible.* Retrieved from http://0100101110101101.org/press/2007-07_Nothing_is_real.html

Maturana, H. R., & Varela, F. J. (1980). *Autopoiesis: The Organization of the Living. Autopoiesis and Cognition: The Realization of the Living.* Dordrecht: D. Reidel Publishing.

McCarthy, T. (1995). Through a lens darkly: The life and films of John Alton. In J. Alton (Ed.), *Painting with light* (pp. ix–xxxiv). Berkeley, Los Angeles: University of California Press.

McCay, W. (1914)Gertie The Dinosaur video. Retrieved from: http://www.youtube.com/watch?v=wyQlqd62l4o&list=PLue4rhsHxp6-IQi8Ad8gLWHnDldPXKok9

McCormick, J. & Nash, A. (2010 - 2012). *Reproduction.* Artists' Residency, Neutral Ground Gallery, Regina Saskatchewan, Canada. 2011; Screen Space Gallery, Melbourne, Australia. Hine, 2012.

McCormick, J., & Nash, A. (2008). *Ways To Wave. Mixed reality artwork, arduino circuit board, wood, acrylic and Second Life installation. 01SJ Festival.* California: San Jose Museum of Art.

McLuhan, M. (1994). *Understanding media.* Cambridge, MA: The MIT Press.

McLuhan, M. (2001). *Understanding Media.* New York: Routledge Classics.

McLuhan, M., & Fiore, Q. (2001). *The Medium is the Massage. Corte Madera.* Gingko Press.

Mead, G. H. (1934). *Mind, Self, and Society.* Retrieved from http://www.brocku.ca/MeadProject/Mead/pubs2/mindself/Mead_1934_toc.html

Meadows, M. S. (2007). *I, Avatar: The Culture and Consequences of Having a Second Life.* Berkley: New Riders.

Menges, T. (2010). *Little Red Riding Hood.* San Francisco, CA: *Second Life.* Video retrieved from http://www.youtube.com/watch?v=p5zZ6_RPYIg

Merleau-Ponty, M. (2002). *Phenomenology of Perception* (C. Smith, Trans.). London, New York: Routledge.

Miellassoux, Q. (2008). *After Finitude: An Essay on The Necessity of Contingency.* London: Continuum.

Mills, S. (2011). FCJ-127 Concrete Software: Simondon's mechanology and the techno-social. *Fibreculture Journal* 18. Retrieved from http://eighteen.fibreculturejournal.org/2011/10/09/fcj-127-concrete-software-simondon's-mechanology-and-the-techno-social/print/

Minecraft (2014). Video game. Stockholm, Sweden: Mojang.

Minnelli, V. (1951). *An American in Paris.* Beverly Hills, CA: Metro-Goldwyn-Mayer Studios Inc.

Min, P. G. (2003). Korean "Comfort Women": The Intersection of Colonial Power, Gender, and Class. *Gender & Society, 17*(6), 938–957. doi:10.1177/0891243203257584

Mitchell, W. J. T. (2005, August01). There Are No Visual Media. *Journal of Visual Culture, 4*(2), 257–266. doi:10.1177/1470412905054673

MMIF - MaMachinima International Festival. (2009). Video Archive. Retrieved from http://www.youtube.com/user/firstAMF2009/videos

Mock, R. (2012). Lynn Hershman: The Creation of Multiple Robertas. In S. Broadhurst & J. Machon (Eds.), *Identity, Performance and Technology: Practices of Empowerment, Embodiment and Technicity.* Hampshire, England: Palgrave MacMillan. doi:10.1057/9781137284440.0016

Molesworth, M., & Denegri-Knott, J. (2007). Digital Play and the Actualization of the Consumer Imagination. *Games and Culture, 2*(2), 114–133. doi:10.1177/1555412006298209

montage. (n.d.).*The Concise Oxford Dictionary of Art Terms.* Oxford Music and Art Online. Retrieved from http://www.oxfordartonline.com.ezproxy-library.ocad.ca/subscriber/article/opr/t4/e1110?q=montage&search=quick&pos=3&_start=1#firsthit

Mori, M. (1970). The Uncanny Valley in Energy, 7(4), pp. 33-35, *Japan Translated by Karl F. MacDorman & Takashi Minato.* Retrieved from: http://www.androidscience.com/theuncannyvalley/proceedings2005/uncannyvalley.html

Morie, J. (2010). A (virtual) world without limits: Aesthetic expression in *Second Life. Journal of Gaming and Virtual Worlds, 2*(2), 157–177. doi:10.1386/jgvw.2.2.157_1

Morie, J. F. (2007). Performing in (virtual) spaces: Embodiment and being in virtual environments. *International Journal of Performance Arts and Digital Media, 3*(2-3), 123–138. doi:10.1386/padm.3.2-3.123_1

Morningstar. C., & Farmer, F. R. (1991). The Lessons of Lucasfilm's Habitat. In M. Benedikt (Ed.), Cyberspace: First Steps. Austin: MIT Press.

Moser, M. A. (Ed.). (1996). *Immersed in Technology: art and virtual environments.* Cambridge, MA: MIT Press.

Moviestorm. (2010). 3D animation software. Cambridge, UK: Moviestorm Inc.

Mullin, D. C. (1970). *The Development of the Playhouse: A Survey of Theatre Architecture from the Renaissance to the Present.* Berkeley: University of California Press.

Mumford, L. (1963). *Technics and Civilization.* Orlando: Harcourt Brace & Company.

Munster, A. (2006). *Materializing New Media. Embodiment in Information Aesthetics.* Lebanon: University Press of New England.

Munster, A. (2006). *Materializing New Media: Embodiment in Information Aesthetics.* Hanover: Dartmouth College Press.

Munster, A. (2013). *An Aesthesia of Networks.* Cambridge: MIT Press.

Murray, J. H. (2012). *Inventing the Medium: principles of interaction design as a cultural practice.* Cambridge: The Mit Press.

Nash, A. (2007) A Rose Heard at Dusk. Available at: http://yamanakanash.net/secondlife/rose_heard_at_dusk.html

Nash, A. (2008) Babelswarm. Available at: http://yamanakanash.net/secondlife/babelswarm.html

Nash, A. (2012). Affect and the Medium of Digital Data. *Fibreculture Journal* 21. Retrieved from http://twentyone.fibreculturejournal.org/fcj-148-affect-and-the-medium-of-digital-data/

Naumova, K. (2009). *Kisa Naumova: Artist Statement.* Retrieved from http://wiki.secondlife.com/wiki/User:Kisa_Naumova

Navarathna, T. (2011). Journey into the metaverse. San Francisco, CA: Second Life. Video; retrieved from http://www.youtube.com/watch?v=iw5md8RpfWs

Navarathna, T. (2011). Welcome to the other side. San Francisco, CA: Second Life. Video; retrieved from http://www.youtube.com/watch?v=dm4XY49gdzc

Navarathna, T. (2012). MetaSex. San Francisco, CA: Second Life. Video; retrieved from http://www.youtube.com/watch?v=s0VA0IH1-SA

Navarathna, T. (2013). Narcissus. San Francisco, CA: Second Life. Video; retrieved from http://www.youtube.com/watch?v=-XEaJASA2Fs

Navarathna, T. (2013). The last syllable of recorded time. San Francisco, CA: Second Life. Video; retrieved from http://www.youtube.com/watch?v=SQq6OYx1m1c

Navarathna, T. (2014, June). *Homeless.* San Francisco, CA: Second Life. Retrieved from http://www.youtube.com/watch?v=gsEJW4VmkgQ&list=UUbfOwWpYoWo5l0Tz-q29Tbg

Negroponte, N. (1996). *Being Digital.* New York: Vintage.

Ng, J. (2013). *Understanding machinima: Essays on filmmaking in virtual worlds.* London, UK: Bloomsbury Academic.

Nichols, B. (1988). The work of culture in the age of cybernetic systems.[Winter.]. *Screen, 21*(1), 22–46. doi:10.1093/screen/29.1.22

Nitsche, M. (2007). Claiming its space: Machinima. *A Journal of Art and Culture in Digital Media.* Video retrieved from http://www.dichtung-digital.de/2007/Nitsche/nitsche.htm

Nitsche, M. (2013). Moving digital puppets. In J. Ng (Ed.), *Understanding machinima: Essays on filmmaking in virtual worlds* (pp. 63–83). London, UK: Bloomsbury Academic.

Nitsche, M., Mazalek, A., & Clifton, P. (2013). Moving digital puppets. In J. Ng (Ed.), *Understanding machinima: Essays on filmmaking in virtual world* (pp. 63–83). London: Bloomsbury Academic.

Norman, D. A. (1998). *The Design of Everyday Thins.* London: The MIT Press.

Novak-Leonard, J. L., & Brown, A. S. (2011). *Beyond attendance: A multi-modal understanding of arts participation.* Washington: National Endowment for the Arts.

Nusselder, A. (2009). *Interface Fantasy: a Lacanian cyborg ontology.* Cambridge: MIT Press.

O'Reilly, S. (2009). *The Body in Contemporary Art.* London: Thames & Hudson.

objet trouvé, [found object]. (1994). *The Thames & Hudson Dictionary Of Art and artists.* Retrieved from http://search.credoreference.com.ezproxy-library.ocad.ca/content/entry/thaa/found_object_french_objet_trouv%c3%a9/0

Oh, B. (2010). *The Rabbicorn story part one – The Daughter of Gears*. Retrieved from http://brynoh.blogspot.co.uk/2010/09/rabbicorn-story-part-one-daughter-of.html

Oh, B. (2011). Rusted gears. San Francisco, CA: Second Life; Retrieved from http://www.youtube.com/watch?v=3t2FQpNY0ck

Oh, B. (2013) Imogen and the Pigeons – Closing. Available at: http://brynoh.blogspot.co.uk/2013/10/imogen-and-pigeons-closing.html

Oh, B. (2013) Imogen and the Pigeons. Available at: http://brynoh.blogspot.co.uk/2013/04/imogen-and-pigeons-part-one.html

Oh, B. (2013a). *Imogen and the Paintings*. Retrieved from http://brynoh.blogspot.co.uk/2013/01/imogen-and-paintings.html

Oh, B. (2013a, November 13). *Dance of death*. San Francisco, CA: *Second Life*. Video retrieved from https://www.youtube.com/watch?v=Coo6P-uzQWI&feature=c4overview&list=UUI7NrJQ5vpg2PmVQKpwXSbw

Oh, B. (2013b, October 28). The dance of death with Peter Greenaway. *Bryn Oh*. Blogspot.Retrieved from http://brynoh.blogspot.com/2013/10/the-dance-of-death-with-peter-greenaway.html

Oh, B. (2014b, January 30). *The singularity of Kumiko*. San Francisco, CA: *Second Life*. Video retrieved from http://www.youtube.com/watch?v=JONF4tgTh34

Oh, S. (2010, February 28). identity absent. Retrieved from http://ohselavy.blogspot.ca/2010/02/identity-absent.html

Oh, B. (2014a). *Immersiva*. San Francisco, CA: Second Life.

Olson, E. T. (2010). Personal Identity. (E. N. Zalta, Ed.) *The Stanford Encyclopedia of Philosophy*. Retrieved from http://plato.stanford.edu/archives/win2010/entries/identity-personal/

Ondrejka, C. (2008). Education unleashed: Participatory culture, education, and innovation in Second Life. In K. Salen (Ed.), The ecology of games: Connecting youth, games, and learning (pp. 229–252). Cambridge: The MIT Press. Retrieved from http://www.socialinformation.org/readings/MMORPG%20learning/Ondrejka_2008.pdf

Ondrejka, C. (2008). Education Unleashed: Participatory Culture, Education, and Innovation in Second Life. In K. Salen (Ed.), *The Ecology of Games: Connecting Youth, Games, and Learning* (pp. 229–252). Cambridge: The MIT Press.

Online Etymology Dictionary. (2001). Retrieved June 16, 2014, from http://www.etymonline.com/index.php?allowed_in_frame=0&search=avatar&searchmode=none

OpenMetaVerse Foundation. (n.d.). Retrieved from http://libomv.sourceforge.net/

Palmer, H. (2014). *Deleuze and futurism: A manifesto for nonsense*. New York, NY: Bloomsbury Academic.

Papows, J. (2011). *Glitch: The hidden impact of faulty software*. Boston: Pearson Education.

Parisi, L. (2004). *Abstract Sex: Philosophy, Bio-technology and the Mutations of Desire*. London: Continuum.

Parisi, L. (2013). *Contagious Architecture: Computation, Aesthetics, and Space*. Cambridge: MIT Press.

Paul, C. (2003). *Digital Art*. London: Thames & Hudson.

Paul, C. (2008). *Digital art* (2nd ed.). London: Thames and Hudson.

Paul, C. (2011). Contextual networks: Data, identity, and collective production. In M. Lovejoy, C. Paul, & V. Vesna (Eds.), *Context providers: Conditions of meaning in media arts* (pp. 103–121). Bristol, Chicago: Intellect.

Pea, M. (2014). *Mad Pea Productions*: Mari Mitchell. Retrieved from http://www.madpeagames.com

Peachey, A., & Childs, M. (2011). *Reinventing Ourselves: Contemporary Concepts of Identity in Virtual Qavimator software*. Retrieved from: www.qavimator.org

Pearce, C. (2009). *Communities of play: emergent cultures in multiplayer games and virtual worlds*. Cambridge: MIT Press.

Pegoraro, É. (2012). Steampunk: As transgress ões temporais negociadas de uma cultura retrofuturista. *Cadernos de Comunicação*, *16*(2), 389–400.

Penny, S. (Ed.). (2011). *After Media: Embodiment and Context*. Irvine, Calif.: Digital Arts and Culture / Arts and Comp.

Penzin, A. (2012) Rex Exsomnis: Sleep and Subjectivity in Capitalist Modernity. *100 Notes - 100 Thoughts*. (13).

Petrič, Š. (2013). Voyager/ 140 AU. Retrieved from http://www.spelapetric.org/home/projects/voyager140au/

Pickens, H. (2010). Dancing with art. Rochester, NY: Textcavation Productions; Retrieved from http://www.youtube.com/watch?v=VBTvQoX5sV8

Pickens, H. (2012a). Instructions from the dead on how to recall the source code. Rochester, NY: Textcavation Productions. Video; retrieved from http://www.youtube.com/watch?v=-cGqC6eOqrE

Pickens, H. (2012b). The four gods of folly. Rochester, NY: Textcavation Productions; Retrieved from http://www.youtube.com/watch?v=-nUM19N9iYc

Pickens, H. (2012c). Wulf and Eadwacer. Rochester, NY: Textcavation Productions. Video; retrieved from http://www.youtube.com/watch?v=SbwbuDc-oT8

Pickens, H. (2014). The travelers and the angel. Rochester, NY: Textcavation Productions. Video; retrieved from http://www.youtube.com/watch?v=toYnxNgL4S0

Pigott, M. (2011). How do you solve a problem like machinima. In H. Lowood & M. Nitsche, (Eds.), *The machinima reader* (pp. 177-194). Cambridge, MA: The MIT Press. Put yourself in the director's chair. (2006, October 22). *The London Sunday Times* Retrieved from http://roosterteeth.com/info/?id=15. [Archived]

Pintasilgo, M. d. (2010). Prefácio (leitura breve por excesso de cuidado). In C. Cruz, & V. Valente, All My Independent Women — Novas Cartas Portuguesas (pp. 3-6). Coimbra: Casa da Esquina.

Plant, S. (1992). *The Most Radical Gesture: The Situationist International in a Postmodern Age* (1st ed.). London: New York, NY: Routledge.

Pollock, G. (1996). The politics of theory: genarations and geographies in feminist theory and histories of art histories. In G. Pollock (ed.), *Generations and Geographies in the Visual Arts: Feminist Readings* (pp. 3-22). New York: Routlege.

Popat, S., & Preece, K. (2012). Where am 'I' present? In S. Broadhurst & J. Machon (Eds.), *Identity, Performance and Technology: Practices of Empowerment, Embodiment and Technicity*. Hampshire, England: Palgrave MacMillan.

Potvin, J., & Myzelev, A. (Eds.). (2009). *Material Cultures, 1740-1920: The Meanings and Pleasures of Collecting*. Farnham, England; Burlington, VT: Ashgate.

Preece, J., Rogers, Y., Sharp, H., Benyon, D., Holland, S., & Carey, T. (1994). *Human-Computer Interaction: Concepts And Design* (1st ed.). Addison Wesley.

Press.

Price, E. H. (2006). A critical review of congenital phantom limb cases and a developmental theory for the basis of body image. *Consciousness and Cognition*, *15*(2), 310–322. doi:10.1016/j.concog.2005.07.003 PMID:16182566

Qlab software. Retrieved from: http://figure53.com/qlab/

Quake (1996). Video game. Richardson, TX: Id Software.

Quaranta, D. (2007). Gaz', Queen of the Desert. Retrieved from http://www.gazirababeli.com/TEXTS.php?t=gazqueenofthedesert

Quaranta, D. (2007). Life and Its Double, Portraits. EVA E FRANCO MATTES (0100101110101101.ORG) LOL Exhibition Catalogue. Brescia: Fabio Paris Art Gallery. Retrieved from http://domenicoquaranta.com/

Quaranta, D. (2007). Life and Its Double. In Fabio Paris Art Gallery catalogue. Brescia: Portraits. Retrieved from http://domenicoquaranta.com/public/CATALOGUES/2007_01_Mattes_LOL.pdf

Quaranta, D. (2014). RE:akt! Things that Happen Twice. In A. Caronia, J. Janša, D. Quaranta (Eds.), RE:akt! Reconstruction, Re-enactment, Re-reporting (pp. 43-52). Brescia, Italy: LINK Editions, & Ljubljana, Slovenia: Aksioma – Institute for Contemporary Art.

Ramirez, F. G. T. (2012). *Because I am not Here. Selected Second Life-Based Art Case Studies: Subjectivity, Autoempathy and Virtual World Aesthetics*. (Doctoral Thesis). University of Western Ontario.

Ranathunga, S., Cranefield, S., & Purvis, M. (2012). Interfacing a cognitive agent platform with Second Life. In M. Beer (Ed.), Agents for Educational Games and Simulations (pp. 1–21). Springer Berlin Heidelberg. Retrieved from http://link.springer.com/chapter/10.1007/978-3-642-32326-3_1 doi:10.1007/978-3-642-32326-3_1

Rao, A. S., & Georgeff, M. P. (1997). Modeling rational agents within a BDI-architecture. *Readings in Agents*, 317–328.

Rehak, B. (2003). Playing at Being. In M. J. P. Wolf & B. Perron (Eds.), *The Video Game Theory Reader*. New York: Routledge.

Reinhard, C. D., & Amsterdam, P. (2013).. . *Journal of Virtual Worlds Research*, 6(2), 1–19.

Rockwell, S. (1989). Cyberpunk (book one, Vol. 1, no. 1). Wheeling, West Virginia: Innovative Corporation.

Roffe, J. (2012). Time and Ground. *Angelaki: Journal of the Theoretical Humanities*, 17(1), 57–67.

Ronell, A. (1996). A Disappearance of Community. In M. A. Moser (Ed.), *Immersed in Technology: art and virtual environments* (119–128). Cambridge, MA: MIT Press.

Rosis, F., Pelachaud, C., Poggi, I., Carofiglio, V., & Carolis, B. D. (2003). From Greta's mind to her face: Modelling the dynamics of affective states in a conversational embodied agent. *International Journal of Human-Computer Studies*, 59(1), 81–118. doi:10.1016/S1071-5819(03)00020-X

Rothenberg, S. (2008) Invisible Threads. Available at: http://www.pan-o-matic.com/projects/invisible-threads

Rottner, N. (2011, June 2). Relational aesthetics. Grove Art Online. Retrieved from http://www.oxfordartonline.com.ezproxy-library.ocad.ca/subscriber/article/grove/art/T2093934

Russell, B. (1997). Is There a God? In B. Russel, The Collected Papers of Bertrand Russell, Volume 11: Last Philosophical Testament 1947-68 (pp. 542-821). London: Routledge.

Rymaszewski, M., Au, W. J., Wallace, M., Winters, C., Ondrejka, C., & Batstone-Cunningham, B. (2006). *Second Life: The Official Guide*. Chichester; Hoboken, N.J.: John Wiley & Sons.

Ryu, J-A. (2010) Na Hye-Seok as a Feminist: Accomplishments of Feminism through Writing 여성연구논집, 21, 133-176.

Salen, K., & Zimmerman, E. (2004). *Rules of play: Game design fundamentals*. Cambridge: MIT.

Salter, C. L. (2007). *Unstable Events: Performative Science, Materiality and Machinic Practices*. Paper presented at Re:place: Second international Conference on the Histories of Media, Art, Science and Technology, House of World Cultures (HKW), Berlin, Germany. Retrieved from http://www.google.si/url?sa=t&rct=j&q=&esrc=s&frm=1&source=web&cd=19&ved=0CGQQFjAIOAo&url=http%3A%2F%2Fpl02.donau-uni.ac.at%2Fjspui%2Fbitstream%2F10002%2F447%2F1%2FSalter_Unstable%2520Events.docm&ei=u8GOUc75F6bw4QSH1YGQDw&usg=AFQjCNF9tOoXI4Bsce8336uzEM1lUMloyw&sig2=isSrQwQNKMuRpmnRS9ur_w

Saorsa, J. (2011). *Narrating the Catastrophe: An Artist's Dialogue with Deleuze and Ricoeur*. Bristol: Intellect.

Sarup, M. (2005). *Identity, Culture and the Postmodern World*. Edinburgh: Edinburgh University Press.

Schaeffer, P. (2004). *Acousmatics. Audio Culture: Readings in Modern Music*. New York: Continuum.

Schechner, R. (1988). *Performance Theory (revised and expanded edition, with a new preface by the author)*. London, New York: Routledge.

Schmidt, E., & Cohen, J. (2013). *The New Digital Age: Reshaping the Future of People, Nations and Business*. New York: Alfred A. Knopf.

Schomaker, K. (2010). *My Life as an Avatar*. Retrieved from http://graciekendal.wordpress.com/

Schrum, S. (1999). Theatre in Cyberspace Issues of Teaching, Acting, and Directing. Retrieved from: http://wiki.SecondLife.com/wiki/

Second Life Grid Survey. (2008). Retrieved on October 14, 2014, from http://www.gridsurvey.com

Second Life. (2003-2014). Virtual world. San Francisco, CA: Linden Lab.

Selvaggio, L. (2013). *You Are Me: Overview of my so called (2nd) Life*. Retrieved from http://www.youareme.net/search/label/2nd%20Life

Sermon, P. (2007) Liberate your Avatar. Public Performance Installation. Available at: http://creativetechnology.salford.ac.uk/paulsermon/liberate/

Sermon, P. (n.d.) Liberate your Avatar schematic. Retrieved from: http://creativetechnology.salford.ac.uk/paulsermon/liberate/video%20flow%20diagram.jpg

ShareFestival. (2008). *Watch the world(s)*. San Francisco, CA: Second Life. Video retrieved from http://www.youtube.com/watch?v=vV1YbWBSXS8

Shields, M. (2012, April 3). Machinima! Adventures of a digital content company. Millions are watching. When will they cash in? *AdWeek*. Retrieved from http://www.adweek.com/news/technology/machinima-adventures-digital-content-company-139319?page=2

Shields, R. (2003). *The virtual*. London, New York: Routledge.

Shindler, K. (2010, May 28). Life After Death: An Interview with Eva and Franco Mattes. *ART21 Magazine*. Retrieved from http://blog.art21.org/2010/05/28/life-after-death-an-interview-with-eva-and-franco-mattes/

Shoemaker, S. (2003). Consciousness and co-consciousness. In A. Clearmans (Ed.), *The Unity of Consciousness: Binding, Integration and Dissociation*. Oxford: Oxford University Press. doi:10.1093/acprof:oso/9780198508571.003.0003

Shortbread, A. (2006a). *Avatar DNA: notecard*. Retrieved from http://maps.secondlife.com/secondlife/The%20Port/28/87/26

Shortbread, A. (2006b). *You Demand Too Much of Me…: notecard*. Retrieved from http://maps.secondlife.com/secondlife/The%20Port/14/75/34

Shostakovich, D. (2010). *Bryn Oh's Identity Discovered!* Retrieved from http://dividni.blogspot.co.uk/2010/08/bryn-ohs-identity-discovered.html

Sim, O. (2014). Open Source Simulator. Rehoboth, MA: Avacon; Retrieved from http://conference.opensimulator.org

Simondon, G. (1993). *The Genesis of the Individual. Incorporations*. New York: Zone Books.

Simondon, G. (2009). The Position of the Problem of Ontogenesis. *Parrhesia*, 7, 4–16.

Simondon, G. (2010). The Limits of Human Progress: A Critical Study. *Cultural Politics*, 6(2), 229–236. doi:10.2752/175174310X12672016548405

Simondon, G. (2012). Technical Mentality. In *Gilbert Simondon: Technology and Being*. Edinburgh: Edinburgh University Press.

Slazar, M. (2009). Immersiva - moments, art & love (Second Life). San Francisco, CA: Second Life. Video; retrieved from http://www.youtube.com/watch?v=VmkJ9iIby8k

Smith, G. R. (2011). *Art 2.0: identity, role play and performance in virtual worlds*. Masters Research thesis, VCA School of Art, The University of Melbourne. DOI. 10187/14591 Retrieved from http://repository.unimelb.edu.au/10187/14591

Smith, G. R. (2013, March 24). Georgie Roxby Smith's Playful Performances. Interview with M. Jansson, *GameScenes*. Retrieved from http://www.gamescenes.org/2013/03/interview-georgie-roxby-smiths-playful-performances.html

Smith, R. (2007, March 9). Art in Review; Eva and Franco Mattes. *The New York Times*.

Soleil, C. (Rockerfaerie) (2009). *My Friends are robots*. San Francisco, CA: Second Life. Video retrieved from http://www.youtube.com/watch?v=8h0sOIREUEo

Sousa, C. C. (2012). Mom and me through the looking glass. *Metaverse Creativity: Building, Performing, Learning and Authorship in Online 3D Worlds*, 2 (2), 137-160.

Sousa, C. C. (2014). Project Meta_Body. In J. P. Cravino, G. Christian, P. Martins, & J. Bernardino Lopes (Ed.), Procedia Technology — SLACTIONS 2013: Research conference on virtual worlds – Learning with simulations. 13, pp. 33 – 37. Vila Real: Elsevier.

Sousa, C. C. (2013). Meta_Body — A Project on Shared Avatar Creation. *International Conference in Illustration & Animation — CONFIA* (pp. 147-163). Porto: IPCA.

Sousa, C. C., & Dahlsveen, H. (2012). The Kromosomer Project. *1st International Conference on Ilustration and Animation* (pp. 421-436).

Spensley, D. C. (2008) ZeroG Skydancers III. Online Performance. Available at: http://zerogskydancers.com/

Spielberg, S. (Director) (1975) *Jaws* [Motion Picture]. Los Angeles, CA: Universal Pictures.

Stan's Cafe Theatre Company. Retrieved from: www.stanscafe.co.uk

Steinmetz, L. & Green away, P. (1995). *The world of Peter Greenaway*. Boston, MA: Journey Editions.

Stelarc - Discussion on "Outside Your Skin" Performance. (2014). Retrieved from https://www.youtube.com/watch?v=ikauPUYRbrk&feature=youtube_gdata_player

Stelarc - Involuntary & Improvised Arm at the Herbert Art Galley & Museum. (n.d.). Retrieved from: http://www.youtube.com/watch?v=yhwIgLtsueA /

Stelarc (2011). Prosthetic Head Performance. Retrieved from: http://www.youtube.com/watch?v=dprvwAWfy9Q

Stelarc, U. I, Chafer, J (2012). Extract/Insert anaglyph. Retrieved from: http://vimeo.com/58571590

Stelarc, U. I, Chafer, J (2012). Extract/Insert clip. Retrieved from: http://www.youtube.com/watch?v=vKanHILj6X4

Stelarc, U. I, Chafer, J, (2011). Extract/Insert time-lapse. Retrieved from: http://vimeo.com/32502129

Stelarc, Upton, I, Chafer, J. (n.d.). Extract/Insert Galaxias Dance RAW filmed in SL. Retrieved from: http://www.youtube.com/watch?v=UNtHSS_gcrQ

Stelarc, Upton, I, Chafer, J. (n.d.). Extract/Insert set up. Retrieved from: http://vimeo.com/89687380

Stephenson, N. (1992). *Snow crash*. New York: Bantam.

Stets, J. E., & Burke, P. J. (2005). A Sociological Approach to Self and Identity. In M. R. Leary & J. P. Tangney (Eds.), *The Handbook of Self and Identity*. United States: Guilford Press.

Steuer, J. (1993, October 15). *Defining Virtual Reality: Dimensions Determining Telepresence*. Retrieved from: http://ww.cybertherapy.info/pages/telepresence.pdf

Stewart, S. (1993). *On Longing (New edition.)*. Durham, N.C.: Duke University Press.

Steyerl, H. (2006) The Language of Things. Retrieved from http://eipcp.net/transversal/0606/steyerl/en

Steyerl, H. (2010a) Aesthetics of Resistance? Artistic Research as Discipline and Conflict, *Mahkuzine*. 8, Winter, Retrieved from: http://eipcp.net/transversal/0311/steyerl/en

Steyerl, H. (2010b) *In Free Fall: A Thought Experiment*. BAK.

Steyerl, H. (2011) Hito Steyerl Discusses in Free Wall. *Picture This*. Retrieved from: http://goo.gl/Wb9An

Steyerl, H. (2012). *Hito Steyerl: The Wretched of the Screen*. Sternberg Press.

Stiegler, B. (1998). *Technics and Time* (Vol. 1). Stanford: Stanford University Press.

Stiles, K. (1998). Uncorrupted Joy: International Art Actions. *Out of Actions: between performance and the object, 1949–1979*, Paul Schimmel (ed.), New York: MoCA Los Angeles. Cited in http://www.medienkunstnetz.de/works/cut-piece/

Strehovec, J. (2014, April 5). E-Literary Text in the Nomadic Cockpit. *Electronic Book Review*. Retrieved from http://www.electronicbookreview.com/thread/electropoetics/cockpit

Strehovec, J. (2013). Algorithmic Culture and E-Literary Text Semiotics. *Cultura. International Journal of Philosophy of Culture and Axiology*, *10*(2), 141–156. doi:10.5840/cultura201310218

Sutton-Smith, B. (1997). *The Ambiguity of Play*. Cambridge: Harvard University Press.

Taylor, C. (1989). *Sources of the Self*. Cambridge, England: Cambridge University Press.

Teeth, R. (2003). *Red vs. Blue* [Machinima]. Austin, TX: Rooster Teeth Productions.

Tenhaaf, N. (1996). Mysteries of the Bioapparatus. In M. A. Moser (Ed.), *Immersed in Technology: art and virtual environments* (51–72). Cambridge, MA: MIT Press.

Thacker, E. (2005, September 6). Biophilosophy for the 21st century. *CTHEORY*. Retrieved from www.ctheory. net/articles.aspx?id=472

The Korean Council. (2012). *Objectives & Activities*. The Korean Council for the Women Drafted for Millitary Sexual Slavery by Japan.

The Mask: a synchronicity. (n.d.). Retrieved from https:// vimeo.com/41673225

The Sims. (2000). *Video game*. Redwood City, CA: Electronic Arts.

The Sims2 (2004). Video game. Redwood City, CA: Electronic Arts.

Tigerlillies. (n.d.). Retrieved from: www.tigerlillies.com

Tittle, P. (2005). *What If... Collected Thought Experiments in Philosophy*. United States: Pearson Education.

Tracy, C. (2007a). *i.Mirror Part2*. San Francisco, CA: Second Life. Retrieved from https://www.youtube.com/ watch?v=jD8yZhMWkw0

Tracy, C. (2007b). RMB CITY-A Secondlife city planning. San Francisco, CA: Second Life; Retrieved from https:// www.youtube.com/watch?v=9MhfATPZA0g

Trapdoor, K. (2010). *The Gracie Kendal Project-My Life as an Avatar*. Retrieved from http://karasecondlife. blogspot.co.uk/2010/08/gracie-kendal-project-my-life-as-avatar.html

Trapdoor, K. (2014). The station. *Kara's korner: Second Life adventures*. Retrieved from http://karasecondlife. blogspot.com

TrapdoorK. (2014, February13). http://karasecondlife. blogspot.com/search/label/The%20Singularity%20of%20 Kumiko

Troika Ranch Dance Company and Isadora software. (n.d.). Retrieved from: http://www.troikaranch.org/

Turing, A. M. (1950). Computing machinery and intelligence. *Mind*, *LIX*(236), 433–460. doi:10.1093/mind/ LIX.236.433

Turkle, S. (1984). *The second self: Computers and the human spirit*. New York: Simon & Schuster.

Turkle, S. (1995). *Life on the screen: Identity in the age of the Internet*. New York: Simon & Schuster.

Turkle, S. (1997). *Life on the Screen: Identity in the Age of the Internet*. UK: Touchstone, Simon & Schuster Inc.

Turner, J. O. (2012, December 1). Qiezli - A personified Art-Agent in Second Life. Retrieved from http://qiezli. blogspot.ca/

Unterman, B., & Turner, J. O. (2014). Loss of Agency as Expression in Avatar Performance. In J. Tanenbaum, M. Seif El-Nasr, & M. Nixon (Eds.), Nonverbal Communication in Virtual Worlds: Understanding and Designing Expressive Characters (pp. 205–217). ETC Press. Retrieved from http://repository.cmu.edu/etcpress/14/

Upton, I., & Wilkes, S. (2007). A Passing Moment 1st May to 30th June 2007, Charlotte Gallery, Eduserve Island, Second Life.

Van Sickler, M. (1996). *Diary of a camper*. United States: United Ranger Films.

Vandagriff, J. (n.d.). Machinima Futurista. Retrieved from: http://www.youtube.com/watch?v=yDTYgsmcqqM&fe ature=share&list=PLCBB13931C4E5AF60&index=4

Vandagriff, J., & Nitsche, M. (2009). Women creating machinima. *Digital Creativity*, *20*(4), 277–290. doi:10.1080/14626260903290224

Vaneigem, R. (1994). The revolution of everyday life. Seattle: Rebel Press; Left Bank Books.

Varela, F. (1992). *The Reenchantment of the Concrete*. *Incorporations*. New York: Zone Books.

Veerapen, M. (2011). *Encountering Oneself and the Other: A Case Study of Identity Formation in Second Life. Chapter in Peachey, A, Childs, M (2011) Reinventing Ourselves: Contemporary Concepts of Identity in Virtual Worlds*. New York: Springer.

Veerapen, M. (2011). Encountering Oneself and the Other: A Case Study of Identity Formation in Second Life. In A. Peachey & M. Childs (Eds.), *Reinventing Ourselves: Exploring Identity in Virtual Worlds*. A. US: Springer. doi:10.1007/978-0-85729-361-9_5

Vincenti, G., & Braman, J. (2011). *Teaching through Multi-User Virtual Environments*. Hershey, New York: IGI Global. doi:10.4018/978-1-60960-545-2

Voom, L. (2006). Zombie mummies from outer space. Redwood City, CA: Electronic Arts. Video; retrieved from http://www.youtube.com/watch?v=zBZ_4x_Fr2U&list=UUZJaGJLbwBOUiXtYYygQqHg|

Voom, L. (2008). The dumb man - Sherwood Anderson. San Francisco, CA: Second Life. Video; retrieved from http://www.youtube.com/watch?v=fvxyzPnI9mU&list=UUZJaGJLbwBOUiXtYYygQqHg

Voom, L. (2009). Fall. San Francisco, CA: Second Life. Video; retrieved from http://www.youtube.com/watch?v=k4MmiaBcHAA&list=UUZJaGJLbwBOUiXtYYygQqHg

Voom, L. (2009). Push. San Francisco, CA: Second Life. Video; retrieved from http://www.youtube.com/watch?v=hLeK9Lanh94&list=UUZJaGJLbwBOUiXtYYygQqHg

Voom, L. (2009). *The stolen child - W. B. Yeats*. San Francisco, CA: Second Life. Video retrieved from http://www.youtube.com/watch?v=g9hnUYV06t4&list=UUZJaGJLbwBOUiXtYYygQqHgVoom, L. (2007). *Tale from midnight city*. San Francisco, CA: Second Life. Video retrieved from http://www.youtube.com/watch?v=PCSknY0Sa6I&list= UUZJaGJLbwBOUiXtYYygQqHg

Voom, L. (2010). *Dagon - H. P. Lovecraft*. San Francisco, CA: Second Life. Video retrieved from http://www.youtube.com/watch?v=CMOHpuxFbm0&list=UUZJaGJLbwBOUiXtYYygQqHg

Voss, P. (2007). Essentials of general intelligence: The direct path to artificial general intelligence. In Artificial general intelligence (pp. 131–157). Springer Berlin Heidelberg. Retrieved from http://link.springer.com/chapter/10.1007/978-3-540-68677-4_4 doi:10.1007/978-3-540-68677-4_4

Wainwright, L. (2010). Lynne Heller Chelsea Girls. Toronto: G44

Walser, R. (1990). *Elements of a cyberspace playhouse*. Paper presented at the National Computer Graphics Association, Anaheim. Quoted by Cleland, K. (2008). *Avatars: Self-Other Encounters in a Mediated World*. Retrieved from http://www.kathycleland.com/

Weber, A., Rufer-Bach, K., & Platel, R. (2007). Creating your world: the official guide to advanced content creation for second life. Indianapolis: John Wiley & Sons. Retrieved from http://books.google.com/books?hl=en&lr=&id=YjdkS8HNpGgC&oi=fnd&pg=PA2&dq=Creating+Your+World:+The+Official+Guide+to+Advanced+Content+Creation+for+Second+Life&ots=jofEk2XiU6&sig=6ikfQwh0M4hBcF1rbIGfKqeS_Q4

Weir, P. (1995). *The Truman show*. Los Angeles, LA: Paramount Pictures.

Weitnauer, E., Thomas, N. M., Rabe, F., & Kopp, S. (2008). Intelligent agents living in social virtual environments–bringing Max into Second Life. In Intelligent Virtual Agents (pp. 552–553). Springer. Retrieved from http://link.springer.com/chapter/10.1007/978-3-540-85483-8_85 doi:10.1007/978-3-540-85483-8_85

White, B. A. (2007). *Second Life: A Guide to Your Virtual World*. Indianapolis, Ind.: Que Publishing.

Whitehead, D. H. (2003). Poiesis and Art-Making: A Way of Letting-Be. *Contemporary Aesthetics, 1*. Retrieved from http://hdl.handle.net/2027/spo.7523862.0001.005

Widdershins, S. (2012). The blackened mirror episode 1: The quest begins. San Francisco, CA: Second Life. Video; retrieved from http://www.youtube.com/watch?v=9yhBAniwYVc

Winters, C. (2008). Using the Linden Scripting Language. In M. Rymaszweski (Ed.), *Second Life: The Official Guide*. Hoboken, N.J: Wiley Publishing.

Wolfram, S. (2002). *A New Kind of Science*. Champaign: Wolfram Media, Inc.

Wooldridge, M. (2009). *An Introduction to MultiAgent Systems* (2nd ed.). John Wiley & Sons.

Wooldridge, M., & Jennings, N. R. (1995a). Intelligent Agents: Theory and Practice. *The Knowledge Engineering Review*, *10*(2), 115–152. doi:10.1017/S0269888900008122

Works, A. (2009). Cao Fei: Love your avatar. Art Magazine. Deutsche, Germany: Deutsche Bank; Retrieved from http://www.db-artmag.com/en/58/feature/cao-fei-love-your-avatar

World of Warcraft . (2004). Video game. Irvine, CA: Blizzard Entertainment.

Yee, N. (2008). Avatar and Identity. In *The Daedalus Gateway: The Psychology of MMORPGs*. Retrieved from http://www.nickyee.com/daedalus/gateway_identity.html

Yee, N., Bailenson, J. N., Urbanek, M., Chang, F., & Merget, D. (2007). *The Unbearable Likeness of Being Digital: The Persistence of Nonverbal Social Norms in Online Virtual Environments*. Retrieved from http://www.nickyee.com/

Yee, N., Bailenson, J. N., & Ducheneaut, N. (2009). Implications of Transformed Digital Self-Representation on Online and Offline Behavior. *Communication Research*, *36*(2), 285–312. doi:10.1177/0093650208330254

Zero G. SkyDancers . (n.d.). Retrieved April 3, 2015, from http://zerogskydancers.com/

Zizek, S. (1997). *The Plague of Fantasies, Cyberspace, Or, The Unbearable Closure of Being*. London: Verso.

Zizek, S. (2001). *On Belief (Thinking in Action)*. London: Routledge.

Žižek, S. (2006). *Interrogating the Real*. London: Continuum.

Žižek, S. (2007). *The Indivisible Remainder: on Schelling and related matters*. London: Verso.

Žižek, S. (2009). *The Parallax View*. Cambridge, MA: MIT Press.

Žižek, S. (2012). *Organs Without Bodies: on Deleuze and consequences*. London: Routledge.

About the Contributors

Denise Doyle has a background in Fine Art Painting and Digital Media. She is an Artist-Researcher, Senior Lecturer in Digital Media at the University of Wolverhampton, and Adjunct Professor in Virtual Worlds and Digital Practice, Ontario College of Art and Design University (OCAD U), Toronto, Canada. Denise has published widely on the subject of the virtual and the imaginary, the experience of the avatar body in virtual worlds and game spaces, and the use of virtual worlds for creative practice. She sits on two international editorial boards: *International Journal of Performance Arts and Digital Media* (Routledge) and *Journal of Gaming and Virtual Worlds* (Intellect). Her research interests include: virtual worlds, art-sci dialogues, interactive film, philosophies of the imagination, practice-based research methods and digital narratives. She is currently developing a series of projects exploring digital embodiment in art and technology.

***

Elif Ayiter, aka. Alpha Auer, is a designer, educator and researcher whose creative interests are based in three dimensional online virtual worlds and their avatars, as well as in developing and implementing hybrid educational methodologies between art & design and computer science, teaching full time at Sabanci University, Istanbul. Her texts have been published at academic journals such as the Leonardo Electronic Almanac, the Journal of Consciousness Studies, and Technoetic Arts and she has authored several book chapters in edited academic anthologies. She has presented creative as well as research output at venues including ISEA2011, Siggraph, Creativity and Cognition, and Computational Aesthetics and Cyberworlds; and is the chief editor of the academic journal Metaverse Creativity with Intellect Journals, UK. http://www.citrinitas.com/.

Garfield Benjamin is a digital artist and cultural theorist working with new conceptions of the relation between consciousness and technology. Having previously studied electroacoustic composition and mixed media digital art with BEAST at the University of Birmingham, Garfield Benjamin undertook a doctoral studentship in the Centre for Art, Design, Research and Experimentation at the University of Wolverhampton, where he has recently completed his thesis entitled 'The Cyborg Subject: Parallax Realities, Functions of Consciousness and the Void of Subjectivity'. His digital art practice involves interactive works, avatar-mediated spaces and computer animation, incorporating a remediation of cultural artefacts from both the arcane and the ultramodern, fusing alchemy with 'geek' culture and an often harsh, fractal, digital aesthetic. Research interests include the work of Žižek and Deleuze, the philosophy of quantum physics, science fiction, computer games and digital art theory.

Jim Bizzocchi is an Associate Professor in the School of Interactive Arts and Technology at Simon Fraser University. Jim's research interests include the design of interactive narrative, the emergent aesthetics of digital video experience, and the development of generative media sequencing and presentation systems. He has presented and published widely in a variety of academic conferences, journals and books. Jim teaches courses in Interactive Narrative and New Media Aesthetics. He is a recipient of the Simon Fraser University Teaching Award. Jim is also a practicing video artist, producing both linear and computationally generative video art works that complement his scholarly writing.

Joff Chafer is a Senior Lecturer in Theatre and Professional Practice at Coventry University, UK. His current area of research is Virtual Performance and has performed in Second Life with both the Second Life Shakespeare Company and the Avatar Repertory Theater as well as working on mixed live real/virtual interactive performances. From 1981 – 2000 Joff worked with Trestle Theatre Company as an actor, mask maker, co-writer and joint Artistic Director. Since moving into Higher Education he still occasionally finds time to work on a number of projects with various UK theatre companies.

Natasha Chuk is a scholar and independent curator based in New York City. She received her PhD in Media and Communication Philosophy from the European Graduate School in Saas-Fee, Switzerland. She teaches courses in film studies, digital culture, visual culture, and art history. Her research focuses on the intersections between technology, interface, and perceptions enabled by and within media objects, particularly the ways invisibility is created, controlled, and negotiated. Her first book (Intellect Books) is called Vanishing Points: Articulations of Death, Fragmentation, and the Unexperienced Experience of Created Objects.

Lynne Heller is a post-disciplinary artist/educator. Her interests encompass material culture, new media performative interaction, graphic novels and sculptural installation. Heller completed her MFA at the School of the Art Institute of Chicago in 2004 and is currently undertaking a doctoral program at University College Dublin, Ireland. She is a cross-appointed Assistant Professor at OCAD University in the Faculties of Design, Liberal Arts & Sciences and School of Interdisciplinary Studies, as well as being an Interim Director of the Data Materialization Lab. Heller has exhibited internationally and is the recipient of grants from the Ontario Arts Council, the Canada Council for the Arts and the Department of Foreign Affairs, Canada. Recent exhibitions include Slippage at the Robert Langen Art Gallery, University at Waterloo, Waterloo, ON, Chelsea Girls, Gallery 44, Toronto, ON, Homeostasis Lab, The Wrong – New Digital Art Biennale, made and exhibited worldwide, Another Season: An International Exchange Project, Gallery 44, Toronto, ON (the exhibition travelled to the Three Shadows Photography Art Centre, Beijing, the Detroit Centre for Contemporary Photography, and the Hippolyte Photographic Gallery, Helsinki) and Hysteria: Past, Present, Future curated by Anonda Bell, Paul Robeson Galleries, Rutgers University, Newark, New Jersey, USA.

Taey Iohe is an artist-researcher working in the areas of visual art, memory studies, creative industries and visual culture. Her artworks are widely shown internationally. She is particularly interested in the status of women in technology and society, seeing the cultural spaces occupied by women as physical and philosophical environments. She was nominated for the award of Best Creative Player at the Blackberry Women & Technology Awards in 2008 in the UK. Her original theoretical concept is of the *Translating Space*, which stems from her doctoral thesis (School of English, Drama and Film, University College

Dublin, 2014). She has received a scholarship in *Writing on Borders* from the John Hume Institute of Irish Global Studies in 2013. She has taught on the programmes in MA Poetic Practice (Royal Holloway), MA Film Video and New Screen Media (UEL), and MA Expanded Media (Kansas) as a visiting lecturer.

Phylis Johnson, Ph.D., is a full professor of sound and new media at the Department of Radio, Television & Digital Media at Southern Illinois University, Carbondale, IL, USA. She is author/co-author of four books, the editor of two international journals, and has extensively presented and published internationally. She works on machinima and transmedia projects for her university within Second Life, as well as teaches on sound, virtual communities, and machinima there. She has served as a judge for many international machinima competitions. Sonicity Fitzroy is her *Second Life* pseudonym and avatar's name.

Maja Murnik holds a PhD in Philosophy and Theory of Visual Culture (at the Faculty of Humanities Koper, Slovenia). She graduated in comparative literature and in theatre studies in Ljubljana. She has worked as an Assistant at the Faculty of Humanities Koper, as an art critic, and as editor-in-chief of the journal of performing arts "Maska" and its book editions. Currently she is an independent scholar and a freelancer in culture. She frequently presents papers at conferences (in France, China, Turkey, Mexico, Slovenia, etc.). Her research interests include philosophy of embodiment, performance art and new media art.

Adam Nash is widely recognized as one of the most innovative artists working in Multi-User Virtual Environmnets. He is a new media artist, composer, programmer, performer and writer. His sound/composition and performance background strongly informs his approach to creating works for virtual environments, embracing sound, time and the user as elements equal in importance to vision. Adam's work has been presented in galleries, festivals and online in Australia, Europe, Asia and the Americas, including SIGGRAPH, ISEA, the Venice Biennale and ZERO1SJ. He was the recipient of the inaugural Australia Council Second Life Artist in Residency grant, as well as an Inter-Arts Connections Residency and Ars Electronica FutureLab residency in 2009. He was shortlisted for the National Art Award in New Media in 2008. He founded SquareTangle with John McCormick to develop immersive mixed reality performances. He founded the Australian Centre of Virtual Art with Christopher Dodds. He has worked as composer and sound artist with Company in Space (AU) and Igloo (UK), exploring the integration of motion capture into real-time 3D audiovisual spaces. He has a PhD from the Centre for Animation and Interactive Media at RMIT University, Melbourne, researching multi-user 3D cyberspace as an audiovisual performance medium; and he ís Program Manager of the Bachelor of Design (Digital Media) in the School of Media and Communication at RMIT University, Melbourne, Australia.

Michael Nixon is a PhD Candidate at the School of Interactive Arts & Technology at Simon Fraser University. He researches how to make characters in digital environments more believable through the use of better cognitive models and non-verbal behavior within social contexts. Michael's M.Sc. thesis describes an investigation of the suitability of Delsarte's system of movement as a framework for believable characters. His dissertation research focuses on the use of social signals as cues in the creation of unique identities.

Catarina Carneiro de Sousa is a Portuguese artist and researcher born in 1975 at Oporto, Portugal. She is a professor at Polytechnic Institute of Viseu — School of Education, in the Communication and Art Department, since 2007. She has devoted her artistic activity to Collaborative Virtual Environments since 2008, working individually and collaboratively, holding several solo exhibitions and collaborating with artists from different fields and nationalities. She has dedicated herself to the development of avatars and the conception of virtual environments. Together with Sameiro Oliveira Martins she is the builder of the Second Life Sim Delicatessen, that held projects like "de Maria, de Mariana, de Madalena" in 2010, "Petrified" in 2011 and the ongoing project "Meta_Body". She explores the metaphorical nature of the art language and the problematization of gender, but she is also interested in the possibility of a new kind of shared creativity opened up by new media art.

Jeremy Owen Turner is a PhD Candidate at the School of Interactive Arts & Technology at Simon Fraser University. Since 1996, Turner has developed an international portfolio as a performance artist, music composer, media-arts historian and art-critic within virtual worlds and video games. As the avatar Wirxli Flimflam, Turner co-founded Second Front – a performance-art group in Second Life (ca. 2006-2008) and composed for the Avatar Orchestra Metaverse (ca. 2007-2008). Turner's academic history includes an MA about avatar-design in Second Life and an interdisciplinary BA that focused on both Art-History and Music Composition. Turner's current PhD research explores developing audio-visual and behavioral design heuristics for virtual agents (automated characters/NPCs/bots) in virtual worlds and video games.

Eupalinos Ugajin, the avatar came into being on May 17th 2008 in Second Life where he quickly proceeded to make his mark upon the virtual world through art works that often also manifest as highly eccentric avatars of all shapes, appearances and combinations bringing together humanoid, biological, mechanical components. Ugajin is also known for numerous large scaled art installations, including "Taxy! To the Zircus" (Fall 2014), "There is no ground" (2013) in collaboration with Susanne Graves, "Catapult" (2012), and "Kou: A Simulation" (2011). Beyond these personal projects however, Ugajin has also participated in numerous collaborative art projects that brought together some of the best content creators of the virtual world. Some of these are "Moving Islands [Rafts]" (Winter/Spring 2013-2014) of which he was also the curator, "The Golden Age of Russian Avant Garde" (2014), "Tophonia: 4 Realizations in Sound" (2012) and "Further Along the Path" (2012).

Pete Wardle graduated in 2009 with a Distinction grade in the MA in Creative Technology at the University of Salford, Manchester. During this time he worked on a project 'Experiments in Embodiment' in Second Life with Alan Hook which led to a collaboration on the SL/RL interactive installation 'Human/Avatar' for the Tech Museum in San Jose. His final MA project was 'Second Life Storyteller' an installation held in Manchester, and he has been invited twice to present at the Prospectives conference at the University of Nevada, Reno, organized by Professor Joseph DeLappe. He is employed full time as a college lecturer and is currently studying for his PhD investigating the development and perception of identity within Second Life at the University of Salford, Manchester under the supervision of Professor Paul Sermon and has recently undertaken an installation 'Second Selves' in Media City, Salford, to collect research data for his PhD.

Index

Information Resources Management Association

Become an IRMA Member

Members of the **Information Resources Management Association (IRMA)** understand the importance of community within their field of study. The Information Resources Management Association is an ideal venue through which professionals, students, and academicians can convene and share the latest industry innovations and scholarly research that is changing the field of information science and technology. Become a member today and enjoy the benefits of membership as well as the opportunity to collaborate and network with fellow experts in the field.

IRMA Membership Benefits:

- **One FREE Journal Subscription**

- **30% Off Additional Journal Subscriptions**

- **20% Off Book Purchases**

- Updates on the latest events and research on Information Resources Management through the IRMA-L listserv.

- Updates on new open access and downloadable content added to Research IRM.

- A copy of the Information Technology Management Newsletter twice a year.

- A certificate of membership.

IRMA Membership $195

Scan code to visit irma-international.org and begin by selecting your free journal subscription.

Membership is good for one full year.

Printed in the United States
By Bookmasters